The History of Prime Time Television

Revised First Edition

Written by George Lee Marshall, WGA

San Diego State University
Chapman University

cognella™
San Diego, CA

Bassim Hamadeh, CEO and Publisher
Michael Simpson, Vice President of Acquisitions
Jamie Giganti, Managing Editor
Jess Busch, Senior Graphic Designer
Seidy Cruz, Acquisitions Editor
Sarah Wheeler, Senior Project Editor
Stephanie Sandler, Licensing Associate

Copyright © 2014 by Cognella, Inc. All rights reserved. No part of this publication may be reprinted, reproduced, transmitted, or utilized in any form or by any electronic, mechanical, or other means, now known or hereafter invented, including photocopying, microfilming, and recording, or in any information retrieval system without the written permission of Cognella, Inc.

First published in the United States of America in 2012 by Cognella, Inc.

Trademark Notice: Product or corporate names may be trademarks or registered trademarks, and are used only for identification and explanation without intent to infringe.

16 15 14 13 12 1 2 3 4 5

Printed in the United States of America

ISBN: 978-1-62661-208-2 (pbk) / 978-1-62131-076-1 (binder)

cognella™

www.cognella.com 800.200.3908

Contents

Section Three
Niche TV: A New Century of Television

Appendices

Acknowledgments

Writing has always proven to be a process with me and so it was with the evolution of this text as well. I want to begin by thanking *Dr. Joyce Gattas*, Dean of the College of Professional Studies and Fine Arts at San Diego State University, for greeting me at the onset of this process, in 2000, and inviting me back to my alma mater to teach. And to *Professor Jack Ofield*, my mentor, friend and former SDSU Department Chair, who allowed me the freedom to develop new classes, including one in television history, I give my heartfelt thanks as well. It must be noted that *Dr. Nick Reid*, formerly the Director of SDSU's School of Theatre, Television & Film, shepherded my TV History class through the course validation process, twelve months ahead of schedule; and that *Dr. Randy Reinholz*, Nick's successor, was instrumental in helping me grow the class over the next five years. Thanks to both directors for their leadership and friendship. A very special thank you must be passed along as well to *Janell Shearer-Bassett*, Chairman of the Media Arts Division at the Dodge College of Film and Media Arts at Chapman University, who first suggested I write this book, and then assigned me a TV History class in which to use it.

Highest accolades go out as well to my long-time friend and colleague *Andy Hill*, a best-selling author and the former President of both CBS In-House Productions and the Channel One Network, with over a hundred TV production credits to his name. Andy's purview of television knowledge over the past

25 years and his willingness to share it with me and with my film-school students on two university campuses has provided me with an opportunity to gain accurate, first-hand information on the inner-workings of network television. Moreover, with deference to Chapter 12, herein, Andy's expertise was instrumental in bringing to light the UCLA-Houston "Game of the Century." As one of only 13 college athletes to ever play on three NCAA D-1 National Championship Basketball teams (UCLA 1970–72), Andy wanted to make sure "the game," with its historic corollary, was duly noted in the text.

Likewise, my heartfelt appreciation runs to writer-producer-executive-producer, series creator and network executive, *Gerry Sanoff*, for a quarter-century's worth of friendship and insight as well. "Mr. *Matlock*," as was Gerry's unofficial handle during the 1980s and '90s (having penned over 60 hours of the *Matlock* series' 194 episodes), provided a wealth of information for the book (specifically for Chapters 13 and 14), just as he has the past four years for my students at Chapman University.

To my entertainment attorney and good friend, *Gordon Firemark*, I tender my deepest recognition for a job well done; and for a dozen years of loyal support, both in Hollywood as well as in my classrooms at two university film schools. Thanks, too, to the editors, designers and marketing professionals at Cognella Publishing, who were all wonderful to work with. Editing contributions made by educators *Geri Louise Ogle* and *Mardell Nash*, relating to the book's structure, text, and bibliography must be singled out as well. Their knowledge and patience and willingness to read and re-read the text proved invaluable to the book's evolution. My grateful thanks and sincere appreciation go out to each for their efforts.

Finally, to my daughters, *Hailey Lorraine* and *Tory Brooke*, I bequeath thanks to both for their encouragement, patience, collegiate perspective and love—and for first introducing me to Big Bird, Lil' Elmo and the Cookie Monster on *Sesame Street*, all those years ago.

Author's Note

As the spring 2004 term came to an end at San Diego State University, I received a call from Nick Reid, then the Director of SDSU's School of Theater, Television and Film, asking me what I thought about the idea of creating a survey class that would span the history of prime time television and tell its story. I told him that a course like the one he was describing was certainly needed and that I was very interested in the subject, but wondered why he was calling on me in particular. Dr. Reid paused for a long moment. "Because you're the one in our film school who's written for prime time television," he answered. Indeed, my pedigree did run through series television in the '80's and '90's as well as through feature films and documentaries. As a Lifetime Member of the Writers Guild of America, I'd written for both television and film in the 20th century and throughout the first decade of this new century as well. After a moment or two of reflective contemplation, the thought of creating a course on the subject of television history seemed an exciting opportunity and one I suddenly found myself very interested in tackling.

The course came to be titled: *History of Prime Time Television in the 20th Century* and took about a semester to build, though a second semester was needed to create the 800 Power Point slides that were used to supplement the lectures. That first semester, only eight people signed up, but by the third semester, spring 2006, the number of students taking the course reached one hundred-fifty. In subsequent semesters, there were close to, and sometimes over, two hundred students walking through the door. In 2007, the course was declared the "Most Popular Class" on the SDSU campus and was covered in a 60-second blurb by the local NBC affiliate in San Diego during its Nightly News. The University followed up and made it one of their SDSU e-cover-stories for the year. More than 3500 students have taken the course since 2005 and most of those giving feedback say the same thing. "Engaging lectures." "Class project rocks." "Wish we had a different textbook." The feedback was appreciated and got me to thinking about how to remedy the situation surrounding the textbook.

At the end of the spring semester 2010, just before the class was to take their final exam, a single question was asked of each student. If there was one thing they could change about the class, what would it be? All but a handful of the 152 students in class that afternoon wrote down, in some form or fashion, that they would exchange the text for another if they could. Too dense, some said. Too cluttered. Too convoluted. Too much ink spilled on the first half of the century and not enough on TV programming and its relationship to the ongoing cultural changes in America. They were right, of course. But exchange the book for what?

While there *are* books that cover large chunks of television's fabled history, most of them are coffee table books, not textbooks. All of the broadcast networks, for example, have books out on the subject of television, but each of them covers only the history of that one network and reads more like a midnight infomercial than an unfettered work of history. There are books on quiz shows, game shows, news shows, late-night TV and the entire cable industry. Television almanacs cover thousands of shows that aired during the second half of the 20th century and a surprising number of books deal with the business of television as well. TV Documentaries have been made on civil rights, space exploration, world wars and political scandal. Series creators have put together retrospective films and books of their shows and series, but like the coffee table books and the documentaries, their historical coverage is also limited in its scope.

Of the academic works that purport to cover television's romp through the 20th century, few of them cover all of it. Even the latest editions of most of the books still exclude the last decade of the second millennium and the first decade of the third. And while all of these texts cover many of the historical milestones of television, the emphasis seems to lie with the beginning of the 20th century rather than the end. That is to say, around the invention and promotion of television before 1950, rather than with its programming and the influence that programming has had on American culture. Today's college-age students, born in the last decade of the 20th century, have every reason to feel slighted that three-quarters of their text book illuminates events that happened before their parents were even born.

Thus, in 2011, I set out with the editors at Cognella Academic Publishing to write a user-friendly textbook on the subject of prime time television history that was not only engaging to read, but would also help students in retaining what they learned in class. By streamlining television's early "technology" story and shifting the emphasis of TV's journey to include its impact on the six decades of programming since

1950, the content seemed more proportional to the way television history in the 20th century actually played out, and thus more relevant to the students looking back from the future.

There is an unwritten adage that permeates the television business: Less is more. If not a mantra repeated daily by producers, network executives and the CEO's of the world's entertainment conglomerates, it's at least an industry by-phrase. In writing the book, I kept that by-phrase close at hand. Television's unique history is all here in these pages, though its early journey from the drawing board to the living room has been judiciously pruned. Each decade's import to history as well as all of the nuance and chronological markers connected to television's colorful story are illuminated from cover to cover, as seen through the prism of prime time viewing. Same with the stories of the moguls and visionaries, the inventors and investors and the bevy of onscreen and off-screen talent that drove the medium through its first hundred years. Iconic names that grew a business. Lucile Ball. Desi Arnaz. Rod Serling. David Sarnoff. Philo Farnsworth. William Paley. Mary Tyler Moore. Fred Silverman. Bill Cosby. Pat Weaver. Norman Leer. Roone Arledge. Milton Berle. Guglielmo Marconi. Rupert Murdoch. Lorne Michaels. Newton Minow. Steven Bochco. David E. Kelley. Vladimir Zworykin. Tom and Dick Smothers. Simon Cowell. Mark Burnett. And so many more.

The prime-time series featured in the book are among best of their respective decades and iconic to both the 20th and 21st centuries as a whole. Some lasted only a season. Two of them spanned parts of five decades. One series franchise did the same. Some had Nielsen ratings up in the stratosphere. Others helped change the culture of television for its time. A treasured few managed to do both, landing huge syndication deals in the process. From *Streets of New York*, the first TV series of any kind to air in 1940, to the airing of *Survivor* in 2000, *Breaking Bad* in 2008, and webisodes on YouTube by 2010, this text covers scores of shows in between. Sitcoms and dramas and the birth of reality programming. Quiz shows and game shows that played in prime time. Variety shows and movies-of-the-week. Mini-series that blew us away—and one that crossed the racial divide to draw us all together like no other series before or since.

Peppered throughout the text are many of the historical milestones that knocked at television's door. The Red Scare of the 1950's and the Cold War that fueled the dogma. The Kennedy-Nixon Debate in 1960 and the Cuban Missile Crisis two years later. All of it covered right along with Civil Rights, the Vietnam War and the assassinations that shocked a generation. TV turned its lens on the 1968 Democratic National Convention and the Moon Landing, a year later. The space race had begun in earnest in 1959, when the Soviet Union launched a chimp into outer space in a ship the Russians named *Sputnik*. Yet it was the first manned-launch from Cape Canaveral in 1961 that caught the world's imagination. Not only because of the success of American astronaut John Glenn's first manned-orbits around the Earth, but equally as important, because television had officially been invited to watch. Television became the *E-ticket*[1] ride that brought the world to our front door.

---

1 Yesterland.com—"The Birth of the "E" Ticket at Disneyland

The 1970's saw the Watergate Break-in and President Nixon's subsequent resignation from office two years later. Television brought the story into our home as it did the Fall of Vietnam, and the Iranian Hostage Crisis that saw 52 American Embassy workers held for 444 days until returned to American soil only minutes after Ronald Reagan's Presidential Inauguration. Television covered the fall of the Berlin Wall, the birth of the home computer and that terrible day in September 2001, when international terrorism breached our shores.

Truthfully, television didn't miss much as it spanned the globe, and somewhere on its journey it found the *Wide World of Sports*. As our fascination with athletic events grew steadily over the last half of the 20th century, pay-TV of the 1950s turned into cable-TV of the 1980's and '90's. ABC's coverage of the 1980 Winter Olympics will always be remembered for the U.S. Hockey Team's "Miracle on Ice." Sports helped grow the broadcast television business. As late as 1985, the original three broadcast networks—NBC, CBS and ABC—still owned roughly ninety per cent of the television market, but not anymore. Those same networks today own less than half of the TV market and could lose even more ground with the emergence of a giant even bigger than cable looming up on the horizon—the Internet. Oddly, the growth of the Internet as a delivery medium for televised images resembles what television itself must've looked like a hundred years ago—the tidal wave of the future. Welcome to 21st century TV. Like the Yankee sage, Yogi Berra, was fond of repeating: "It's like déjà vu all over again."[2]

2 *Publisher's Weekly*—"When You Come to a Fork in the Road, Take It!" May 21, 2001

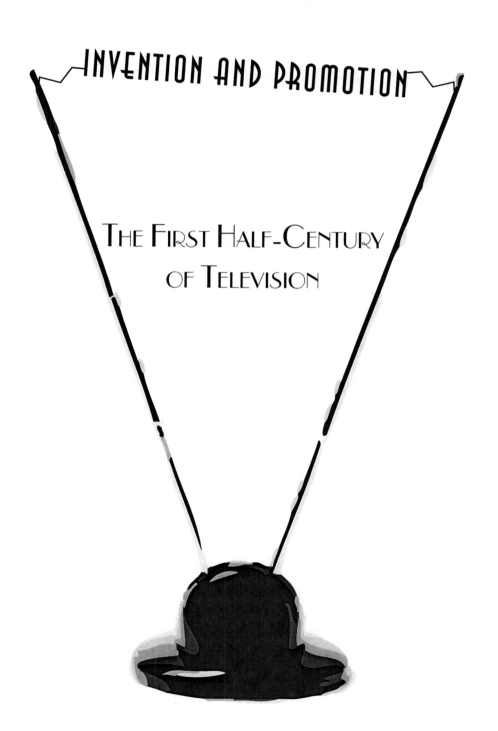

INVENTION AND PROMOTION

The First Half-Century of Television

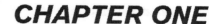

CHAPTER ONE

The Age of Invention

1840–1910

Perspective

Historical perspective is a relative term and one that almost always involves the passage of time. But how much time? How much distance is allowed to pass before revisiting a journey that defined an entire century and captured our attention like no other invention in the last hundred years? Television. Its presence in our lives has been both the bane of our existence and our saving grace. In its infancy, television was often cynically referred to as "the tube" or that "black box with wires"—but no longer. Whether "the box" has morphed itself into an app on our cell phone or a razor-thin, chrome-plated, wall-mounted flatscreen TV at home, the medium of television now provides every iPhone, BlackBerry, and household it serves with its very own window to the world.

Reflecting on any journey, while still in its grasp, often brings with it an emotional bent that can cloud one's objectivity. Wait too long and we chance to forget more facts than we remember. Imagine waking up in a car traveling past a given point—a town, perhaps; some small city. As we drive through the middle of it we see only the buildings around us. Our perspective is skewed. We have no idea how the setting we're looking at fits into the bigger picture. But as we move out of town, our rear view mirror begins to define where that town sits relative to the geography around it. As our journey continues, the town in the mirror becomes smaller and smaller. The distance between us and the buildings that once passed right outside our car becomes too great to even keep them in sight. Before we know it, the town too begins to fade away and eventually disappears from view.

So it is then with our survey of television history. The trick is to get the *distance* right so that our perspective is enhanced. More than a decade has passed since the second millennium gave way to the third. Time enough to look back with growing clarity on the extraordinary events that helped shape this past century, yet not so long that we've forgotten the passion and fervor that surrounded them. The advent of television was among the most important of these events. The invention was not only a part of the 20th century, it was the tool used to record the 20th century, and now this new one as well. Television has been the prism through which we viewed our world for the last sixty years and the medium that crossed a millennium to deliver the turbulent events, comedic entertainment and poignant drama of two adjoining centuries into two billion living rooms a day.

Historical Importance

Looking back at that last decade, in the final century of the second millennium, a phenomenon was taking place in America. Millennium hoopla had us in its grip and made for noisy celebrations, unprecedented fanfare, and count-downs aplenty. A century change only happens every hundred years, after all; a millennium change, every thousand. No one drawing breath at the time wanted to miss out on either. Certainly not the editors of magazines and newspapers across the land. From coast to coast and border to border, publications had taken it upon themselves to pick from the century's very *best*. They made lists of practically everything and published them in the months and weeks leading up to the century's end. The best films of the century. The best books. The best albums (like compact discs, only larger). Anything that could be measured in a poll was fair game. The greatest bands. The greatest athletes. The best TV series ever. No category, it seemed, was off limits.

Over at *Life Magazine*, the editors were burning the midnight oil like everyone else. Unlike most other publications, however—those that relied on employee input for their "Best Of..." lists—*Life Magazine* had spent months putting together a team of educated professionals. Men and women who would select from the very *best* that the last thousand years had to offer. The panel chosen by *Life* included doctors, jurists, teachers, poets, athletes and artists, architects and astronauts, lawyers, authors, historians, and scientists of all disciplines, each one chosen from the pinnacle of their professions. All were tasked with one goal: To pick the "Top 100 Events" during the last one *thousand* years. Not just inventions, mind you, but the people, places, things, and ideas that changed the way humankind lived on planet Earth during the second millennium. That was the challenge. To put these one hundred events and people together, not by year and date, but by order of each one's importance to history.[1]

The Number One event, according to *Life Magazine*, proved to be no surprise. The accolade fell to the printing press and for good reason. By the 15th century, a literate middle class had begun to emerge in Europe—ordinary folk with a thirst for knowledge. Up until then, the ability to read and write had been confined to tiny pockets of clergy and scribes and the very, very rich. This new thirst led inventors to seek a way to mass-produce the written word. In 1455, German goldsmith Johann Gutenberg did just that. He succeeded in creating a run of 200 typeset Bibles on the world's first printing press and jump-started an information epidemic that rages to this day.[2]

How about *Life Magazine's* second-most significant event in the last thousand years? Here's a hint. The man responsible for it was the most magnificent failure of his day. Four times he sailed in vain to find a western route to Asia, and four times he returned disappointed—the last one in chains. That aside, colonizers, African slaves, and immigrants by the millions followed Christopher Columbus to his discovery: The New World.[3]

In 1517, a German clergyman named Martin Luther nailed his "Ninety-Five Theses" to the door of the All Saints Church in Wittenberg, Germany, and so began the Reformation of Europe. *Life's* third-most significant event of the last millennium. No longer would political authority be subject to the dictates of a distant clergy, but rather to the nationalism inside its borders. Countries over empires—an event that still dominates world politics today.[4]

So what then follows Luther? How about the Industrial Revolution of 1769 and how it altered the face of Europe from rural agrarian to urban manufacturing in less than a century? There was Galileo's telescope in 1610, and gunpowder in China as early as the eleventh century. And a declaration to the world in 1776 that championed the notion that *all* people had been endowed by their creator with certain *unalienable rights*—an assertion of enlightened principle that helped end colonial rule. There was the seagoing compass in China in 1117, and Thomas Edison's light bulb in 1879, invented in part so that night baseball games could be played and watched. There was the birth of the slave trade in 1509; and the smallpox vaccine in 1796. The vaccine gave birth to the science of immunology and the millennium's thirteenth-most important event.[5]

---

1 The *Life* Millennium, p 8

2 The *Life* Millennium, p 166

3 The *Life* Millennium, p 165

4 The *Life* Millennium, p 162

5 The *Life* Millennium, p 145—161

Which brings us finally to television, *Life Magazine's* 14th-most important event[6] of the last thousand years and one that occurred quite late in the millennium. One of the most complicated inventions ever created by man, the art of television combines particle physics with chemistry and engineering to create the sights and sounds that visit a global population twenty times greater than it was in Gutenberg's day. This statistic alone beckons a pensive pause. If the printing press was created to mass-produce the written word for a global population and ends up Numero Uno on the millennium's event calendar, why is television Number 14? What is television, after all, if not *the* window to our world? A medium that mass-produces billions of global images every day then disseminates them to an estimated daily audience of over two billion people—nine times greater than the estimated world-population of the 15th century.

No one less than Walter Cronkite, the iconic face of CBS News for over 30 years and an anchor journalist who, in 1970, was declared the "Most Trusted Man in America," had this to say: *"Aside from the printing press, the invention of television was the single most important event in human history. Television has totally homogenized our culture; the corollary being that the medium has brought people together so that we understand each other much better than we ever have before."*[7] High praise for an invention that didn't come easily and wouldn't be cheap. And, truthfully, one that didn't really begin in the 20th century at all. It began with a *spark* of genius in December, 1887, during a period historians have come to call The Golden Age of Invention—a 70-year window, more or less, that churned out more practical innovation than any other comparative time to that point in history.

The Electronic Frontier

Less than a hundred years ago, the concept of sending televised images through the ether was the stuff of science fiction. In the end, however, it was men of science, not science fiction, who explored an uncharted course through the electronic frontier and led the world to *Edith and Archie* and *Lucy and Ricky* and a bar called *Cheers* where everybody knew your name. Television's journey from the drawing board to the living room was better than fiction and, in the end, took as much ambition and tenacity to complete it as it did sheer genius.

In 1874, inventor Thomas Alva Edison sold Western Union the rights to his Quadruplex Telegraph for $10,000 (205,000 USD 2012). The telegraph improved on Samuel Morse's version and allowed for four separate signals to be sent on a single wire at the same time. Edison used the money from this first invention to construct a research laboratory in Menlo Park, New Jersey. There, he built the phonograph, the electric light bulb, and tinkered with Alexander Graham Bell's telephone technology.[8]

6 The *Life* Millennium, p 144

7 History Channel Modern Marvels—"Television: Window to the World"

8 Time—"The Electrifying Edison" July 5, 2010

Yet Edison and Bell were far from alone with their practical innovations. In 1834, Clarence Birdseye chilled the world with the discovery of refrigeration. Five years later it was Charles Goodyear and his vulcanized rubber. In the 1840's and 50's, there was George Westinghouse and his railroad braking systems. Henry Bessemer's steel. Samuel Morse and the telegraph. Isaac Singer and his foot-powered sewing machine. In 1868, the typewriter was finally perfected. By 1880, George Eastman had invented photographic film; mechanic Elisha Otis, the elevator that bears his name. There was Charles Land and polarized photography. Willis Carrier and air-conditioning. And King Camp Gillette and the safety razor.

As the century turned, the Wright Brothers were flying over Kitty Hawk, North Carolina. Henry Ford was driving around Detroit. And Albert Einstein was out in the cosmos exploring special relativity. And all of this mind-boggling, world-shaking, life-changing, scientific wonder came to be within a 70-year window of time.

The Wireless

Yet the story of television really begins with another advance born during this Age of Invention: a precursor to both television and radio called the Wireless. Using simple Morse code, Italian inventor Guglielmo Marconi developed the first wireless telegraph in 1895. Marconi reasoned that just as wire could carry electrical charges, so could Hertzian waves, later referred to as radio waves.

Eight years earlier, German physicist Heinrich Hertz had been the first to satisfactorily demonstrate the existence of electromagnetic waves by building an apparatus (transmitter) to produce and detect radio waves. Hertz demonstrated that an electromagnetic wave could be transmitted and made to travel through space in a straight line. A millisecond later, it could then be received by an experimental apparatus (receiver) at the other end of the transmission. This transmission *straightened* the oscillating electromagnetic waves into what came to be known as Hertzian waves, and what we today refer to as radio waves. During his experiments, Hertz had shown how to actuate such waves by getting a coil-driven spark to leap across a gap.[9] In scientific circles of the day there was speculation that Hertzian waves might somehow be used to communicate across large distances, but no one until Marconi had figured out how.

Up until Marconi, the telegraph, limited to where wires could take a message, sat at the forefront of communication. Messages could be sent only by wire using Morse code and to only one location at a time. History varies some in its facts as to when exactly Marconi rang his first doorbell. But sometime during 1895 or 1896, Marconi perfected his wireless telegraph and began sending electric impulses without wires, through thin air. At first he took to ringing doorbells around his own house, but was soon

9 The Electrician—"Research in Wireless Telegraphy," vol. 43, p 41

Guglielmo Marconi, 1901

ringing others in his neighborhood as well. Dignitaries from his hometown wrote to the Italian Minister of Post and Telegraph about the young man's invention. When the Italian government failed to show interest, Marconi, with his mother's help, took his experiment to England.

For the British Empire, held together as it was at the time by threads of ocean cable, Marconi's new means of communication attracted immediate interest. The British Post Office ran tests of their own on Marconi's wireless and, in 1897, capitalized the invention to the tune of 100,000 pounds (4.5M USD 2012).[10]

It was in that moment that the wireless (telegraph) was truly born. Though the invention would one day lead to infrared and ultrasonic remote control devices, traffic control systems, two-way radio, cordless and cellular phones, GPS devices, computer appliances, and satellite television feeds, few people at the time imagined that these Hertzian waves could travel distances great enough to matter. Marconi disagreed and sent out the first long-distant message to prove it. The "message"—a single "S"—sent in 1901 from Cornwall, England, to a receiving station in St John's, Newfoundland, traveled 2,100 miles. Marconi heard the sound of three faint clicks—and with that sound the communications industry was hatched.[11] Before Marconi, we were landlocked by wires. Now, completely wireless messages could be sent to anyone with a receiver, in any direction, and to all those receiving the message at the same time.[12]

It wasn't so much that Marconi discovered some new and revolutionary principle in his wireless-telegraph system. Classically trained scientists like Heinrich Hertz and George Ohm had already done that. Rather, it was Marconi who assembled and improved an array of facts and then unified and adapted them to his innovative radiotelegraphy system.[13] By 1899, Marconi had set up shop on both sides of the Atlantic. As the 19th century turned, The Marconi Wireless Company of America, better known as "American Marconi," had set up shop in Massachusetts and was incorporated under the laws of New Jersey. In 1905, Marconi built a second sending/receiving station in New York City to complement his original U.S. station in Massachusetts. These stations were the heart and soul of American Marconi and dedicated to the development and advancement of a radiotelegraph system[14] that would one day become the core of what we now call ... television.

10 *Tube of Plenty*, pp 8–9

11 The *Life* Millennium, p 126

12 History Channel Modern Marvels—"Television: Window to the World"

13 *Nobel Lectures*—"Wireless Telegraphic Communication, Nobel Lecture: 11 December 1909," p 198

14 Encyclopedia Britannica ('93 ed.)—"Guglielmo Marconi"

The Nipkow Disc

In 1877, an artist at the *New York Daily Graphic* depicted what he called the "Terrors of the Telephone," showing a disheveled Svengali standing before a microphone in a studio haranguing groups of *terrified* people around the world.[15] Before the decade ended, speculation swirled around sight as well as sound. Alexander Graham Bell himself described the telephone as an apparatus for transmitting sound *telegraphically*. If people could talk and hear through a telephone over Hertzian waves, why couldn't they *see* things that way as well? To this end, French artist Albert Robida drew a series of pictures depicting an array of startling predictions including televised news, televised classroom learning, and televised entertainment—and all of these predictions made 75 years before prime time television ever came to be.[16]

Not surprisingly, laboratory inventions leading toward just such *prime time* predictions followed soon after. The first of those inventions came in 1884, when German engineering student Paul Nipkow proposed and patented the world's first mechanical television *system* (not television itself). Nipkow was the first person to discover television's scanning principle, in which the light intensities of small portions of an image are successively analyzed and transmitted.

To accomplish this, Nipkow designed a rotating disc camera called the "Nipkow Disc." The rotating disc had perforations arranged in a spiral pattern. The device consisted of a rapidly rotating disc placed between a scene and a light-sensitive selenium element. A beam of light shining through the spiral perforations as the disc revolved caused pinpoints of light to perform a rapid scanning movement over the object in front of it, something like the movement of eyes back and forth across a printed page. The device was at once seen as a way of transmitting pictures by wire—dots, as it were, of varying intensity—to relay stations around the world.

This early "disc image" had but 18 scan lines of resolution as compared to the 525 scan lines the FCC's National Television System Committee required from 1950's through 2009. Nevertheless, early inventors would use the Nipkow Disc as the basis for experiments in the transmission of images for electromechanical television for the next forty years.[17]

Voices in the Air

By the spring of 1902, less than six months after Marconi's first long-distance transmission from England to Newfoundland, Marconi's wireless telegraphy system had become the rage. Other countries in Europe

---

15 *Tube of Plenty*, p 3

16 *Tube of Plenty*, pp 4–5

17 History Channel Modern Marvels—"Television: Window to the World"

were copying Marconi's design, in part because of the Second Boer War between the British and the Dutch Afrikaners and their mutual need for advanced communication between the continents. Sending code out into the ether on the *wireless* was on everybody's mind. As excitement grew, so did the number of wireless operators or "hams" (amateur operators), and all of them putting more and more code through the air.

In America, competitors were emerging to challenge American Marconi. One of them was a Canadian named Aubrey Fessenden who had once taught electrical engineering in Pittsburgh while working for Westinghouse. As early as 1900, Fessenden had begun wireless experiments in voice transmission while supervising a research project for the U.S. Department of Agriculture. Fessenden's early success soon led backers to help him start his own company, the National Electric Signaling Company, and it was there that Fessenden concentrated on the communication boom's next big challenge—sending a voice over the airwaves.

Fessenden's work was designated by terms like "wireless telephone," "radiophone," and finally just "radio"—and all of it geared to one-up Marconi. Instead of sending a series of interrupted wave bursts (Morse code), Fessenden's idea was to send a continuous wave on which voice would be superimposed as variations of modulation. This idea, at first seen as heresy, became fundamental to radio. Limited success with early testing had, by 1906, reached a climax of sorts. On Christmas Eve of that year, ship wireless operators over a wide area of the Atlantic, sitting at their earphones, alert to the crackling of distant dots and dashes, were startled to hear a woman singing; then a violin playing; then a man reading passages from the Book of Luke.[18]

In a very real sense, Fessenden was conducting a series of scientific experiments and his audience was growing. One of those listening was the United Fruit Company, whose banana boats travelled to remote locations, some as far away as the West Indies. The company needed to communicate with their boats and found wireless a useful tool, indeed. Within months, United Fruit along with the U.S. Navy found themselves purchasing Fessenden's equipment.

Fessenden, as it turned out, was an irascible character and often unreasonable. After learning that United Fruit had formed its own equipment subsidiary and acquired a number of patents, the navy dumped Fessenden for U.F.C. leading, in time, to the collapse of NESCO, Fessenden's company.[19]

Like Fessenden, Lee de Forest was also dedicated to voice transmission and brought it to a new stage of development with his patented invention of the Audion Tube, in 1908. This glass-bulb detector (or receiver) of radio waves was also capable of amplifying and even generating radio waves. A Pandora's tube of endless ramifications, the Audion became nothing less than the foundation of the electronics

---

18 *Tube of Plenty*, p 12

19 *Tube of Plenty*, pp 12–13

industry. That said, it's now believed that de Forest stumbled onto the invention while *tinkering* and did not completely understand how it even worked. De Forest had initially claimed that the operation was based on ions created within a gas-filled tube when, in fact, it was later shown to operate best within a vacuum, or rather, a tube completely void of any gas at all.

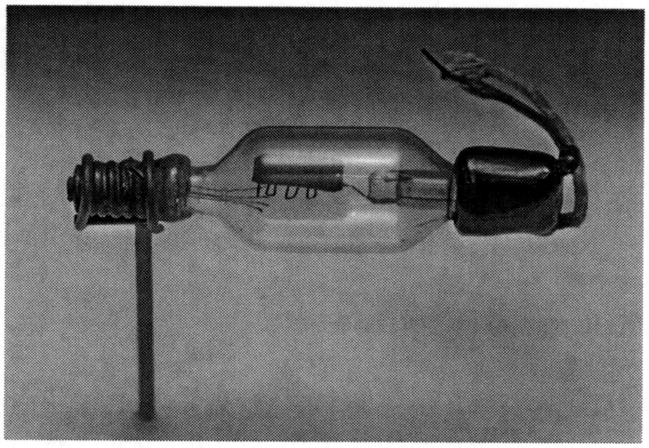

De Forest Audion from 1908.

To demonstrate and refine his Audion, de Forest began "broadcasting" in New York using phonograph records and inviting singers into his laboratory for tests.[20] Always a showman, de Forest picked Paris, in the summer of 1908, to perform similar demonstrations of his new amplified microphone. Standing high atop the Eiffel Tower, de Forest broadcast a human voice through his delicate invention. By capturing electrons in his Audion Tube, the tube would then convert them to electrical impulses and send them out as amplified sound waves to be received all over the world.

De Forest, like Fessenden, made sales to the navy and appeared to be holding his own. In the end, however, de Forest too ended up underfinanced and a constant prey to promoters wanting spectacular displays to sell their companies' stock. These "stock manipulations" kept de Forest in legal as well as financial hot water and routinely away from his work. In April 1923, the De Forest Radio Telephone & Telegraph Company, which had been manufacturing de Forest's Audion tubes for commercial use since 1910, was sold to a coalition of auto makers who were expanding the company's factory to cope with rising demand for car radios.[21] The sale also brought with it the services of Lee de Forest himself, who was now turning his sights toward producing innovations for automobiles.

A whole bunch of genius in a very short time. From lantern light to electric light. From the pony express to advent of radio. Morse to Bell and Edison. Nipkow, Hertz, and Marconi. Fessenden and de Forest. And all of this genius was pointing toward a 15-year-old Mormon schoolboy from Utah who would one day come along to take de Forest's work a giant step forward capturing sight as well as sound.

---

20 *Tube of Plenty*, p 15

21 *New York Times*—"Auto Interests Buy de Forest Radio Co." April 6, 1923

Discussion Questions

A. Perspective 1840–1910

- What advantages/disadvantages does *your* age and experience bring to finding the right perspective distance when looking at the origins and development of television?

B. Historical importance

- You read part of Life Magazine's "Top 100 Events" in the last 1000 years. What kinds of specialists were asked to ponder this question? Do you feel any specialist was left off the list that would have contributed to this brainstorming process? Would you pick the printing press as the number one event? Why or why not?

E. The Nipkow Disc

- How did Nipkow's Disc allow advances in the transmission of images for electromechanical television?

F. Voices in the Air

- If genius builds on genius, what was the technological path leading to capturing sound, starting with Morse and ending with de Forest?

CHAPTER TWO

Radio Comes of Age

1910–1920

Chaos

By 1912, the scent of a world war hung in the air and that *scent* was hardly alone. The sky above was nothing less than a cauldron of crackling codes and chattering voices all converging in a cacophony of overlapping frequencies. Then on April 15th of that year, just past midnight, the *RMS Titanic* sent out a distress call over its wireless telegraph that was initially received by only one ship in the area, a sister ship, the *RMS Olympic*, over a thousand miles away. The *Titanic* had struck an iceberg and was dropping by the bow. The ship that couldn't sink did just that. The liner went down in less than three hours, claiming over 1,500 lives. The tragedy became one of the deadliest peacetime maritime disasters in history.[1] Not wanting another misfortune like the *Titanic*, and not wanting the ether turned into a quagmire of overlapping "squawk talk," the government used the *Titanic's* sinking as impetus for the creation of The Radio Act of 1912—the first piece of regulatory communication legislation in American history. The law established, among other things, that in order to operate a radio frequency—that is

1 The Sinking of the Titanic, p 143

to say, in order to broadcast—you had to obtain a license from the government.[2] This way, the theory went, there would be order to the skies.

The problem with the government's theory wasn't in the law, but with the people who failed to follow it. While the 1912 Act required a license to transmit over the airwaves, the law was widely ignored by the irrepressible amateurs who were numbering in the thousands. If that weren't enough, there was Army–Navy communication relating to training maneuvers to contend with as well. Adding to the mayhem was the fact that these "ham" operators were said to be interfering with military communication.[3] The military wanted it stopped and therein lay the problem—it was 1912. Transportation being what it was at the time, automobiles were needed to track down amateurs using crystal sets in their barns or basements.

Moreover, the amateurs weren't the only ones interfering with military transmissions. Universities, government agencies, and private corporations were also experimenting in the ether—and not just with sound. The transmission of *images* was now being bandied about under handles like "visual wireless," "visual radio," and even "television." This latter term was actually used for the first time in a June 1907 issue of *Scientific American*. The "television" experiments taking place at the time were all linked to the Nipkow Disc—that rotating disc camera with the perforated holes. It was the key ingredient to the transmission of still pictures.[4]

Prominent among these experimenting corporations was the American Telephone and Telegraph Company. Alarmed by the rise of American Marconi, AT&T bought various patents of de Forest when the one-time world-shaking inventor was on the verge of bankruptcy.[5] Even so, American Marconi forged ahead undaunted. The sinking of the *Titanic* actually sparked a rise in the company's cachet. On that fated night, American Marconi won worldwide attention when David Sarnoff, Marconi's 21-year-old wireless operator, picked up the first faint signals of the *S.S. Titanic's* mayday call. A seven-year veteran at the company's New York office, Sarnoff alerted other ships in the north Atlantic as well the press. It was later learned that a second ship, much closer to the *Titanic* than the rescuing ship, did not receive Marconi's distress call because its sole wireless operator was not on duty. Accounts of how Sarnoff remained on the air for 72 consecutive hours relaying news of survivors to relatives abounded. Some in the press questioned the authenticity of the story but it didn't seem to matter. Truth or fiction, it was now the heroic stuff of wireless lore and seemed to fit in well with the young man's cocky demeanor and a rags-to-riches story that was already beginning to unfold.

2 Radio and Television Regulation: Broadcast Technology in the United States 1920–1960, pp 6–8

3 *Tube of Plenty*, p 18

4 The Edison Motion Picture Myth, p 23

5 *Tube of Plenty*, p 17

American Marconi

In 1905, at the age of fourteen, David Sarnoff, a Russian emigrant and eighth-grade drop-out, wanting to escape the grinding poverty of New York's Lower East Side, answered an ad at a Hearst newspaper company in need of a delivery boy. Sarnoff's father was dying of tuberculosis and support of the family had fallen to him. A wrong turn on the way to the delivery job landed him in the New York Herald Building. When he went to inquire about the delivery boy position for the newspaper, Sarnoff discovered that he was in the wrong building and had ended up at the offices of the Commercial Cable Company instead. Commercial Cable was a telegraph company that had also taken out an ad for a delivery boy and, as fate would dictate, Sarnoff got the job. Four months later, Sarnoff was fired by a superior who refused him unpaid leave for Rosh Hashanah.

Soon after, Sarnoff ended up at the door of the Wall Street offices of American Marconi with his telegraph key in hand. As it turned out, Guglielmo Marconi, the company's owner, was in town at the time and in need of a personal messenger. Sarnoff talked himself into that job as well. Quickly, Sarnoff discovered that he had a penchant for promotion—most notably his own. Sarnoff's notoriety, however, always seemed to work in Marconi's favor and Sarnoff was rewarded with a series of company promotions. Over the next 13 years, Sarnoff rose from office boy to commercial manager of the company, learning about the technology and the business of electronic communications while on the job.[6]

By July of 1914, the *scent* of a world war had become reality. World War I had been declared. Wartime rules were immediately instated in America and many of those regulations impacted communication. It was now declared illegal for anyone other than the government or military (or their designee) to operate a radio device. The government's reasoning here was sound. These early crystal radio sets weren't just receivers, they were transmitters, too. The U.S. government didn't want secret messages sent to the enemy during wartime. Thus, the airwaves in the public sector went dormant for the next four years.

Within the military, radio technology grew far more robust, though several civilian corporations helped make that happen. Before WWI, the glass tubes necessary to make a radio had been hand-blown, one at a time. Now, the military suddenly needed huge quantities of radio equipment to coordinate battlefield operations and ordered 80,000 units at once. Two corporations were unusually well suited to filling this order—GE and Westinghouse, two names that still resonate big in broadcasting today. As it turned out, both corporations had assembly lines already in place—lines that had been turning out light bulbs for homes across the country for years. Quickly, both companies were modified to the extent that they now turned out glass radio tubes instead.

By 1916, with America moving into its third year of World War I, David Sarnoff was moving up the ladder at American Marconi. Early that year, Sarnoff was appointed chief inspector and contracts manager for

6 Museum of Broadcast Communications website—"David Sarnoff"

the company.[7] Following passage of the Radio Act of 1912, four years earlier, Marconi's revenues had swelled to record levels. The 1912 law not only required that "broadcasters" have a license to transmit, it also mandated continuous staffing of commercial shipboard radio stations. In an effort to ensure that the *Titanic* tragedy was never repeated, every American ship that sailed had to now "man the key" around the clock. American Marconi was in business with the majority of these U.S. shipping magnates and their operators, and with twice as much wireless service now being used, profits at Marconi rose proportionately. Though the start of WWI had curtailed most commercial transmission, many of the larger shipping lines had been accorded permission by the U.S. military to transmit over the airwaves and were thus exempt from the wartime rules.

Shortly after taking over the chief inspector position, Sarnoff demonstrated the first use of radio on a railroad line (another wartime *designee* entitled to transmit)—and American Marconi grew larger still.[8] It didn't take a prophet to see that Sarnoff was a cut above. As the year wound down, Sarnoff outlined his idea of "home-radio" to the brass at American Marconi in a document that would later come to be known as the "Radio Box Memo." The memo talked of a "radio music box" in every house, where the listener could receive music, news, and sports. In short, an organized list of regular programming five years before it would actually happen.[9] Unlike many involved with early radio communications who viewed radio as a "point-to-point product," Sarnoff saw the potential of radio as "point-to-mass product," where one person (say a broadcaster) could speak to millions of listeners at the same time. Reception to this idea by Guglielmo Marconi himself was surprisingly cool. In the end, Sarnoff later confided, it was simply a case of technology needing to catch up with promotion.

RCA

By the time WWI ended in 1918, radio technology and the ability to mass produce transmitters and receivers had improved dramatically. The navy, which had been a key player in these advances, proposed that there be a monopoly in radio and that the navy be in charge of licensing all radio broadcasting. While the U.S. State Department endorsed this idea, Americans making and using little crystal radios in their basements did not. Many of these "hams" or amateurs had actually fought in the war and helped develop the new radio technology. The last thing they wanted was to be shut out by virtue of a government monopoly.

It took a year, but by 1919, Congress agreed with them and fought the notion of a governmental radio monopoly, creating instead a gigantic private monopoly called the Radio Corporation of America—RCA. Then Secretary of the Navy Franklin D. Roosevelt gathered all the transmitting stations that had a stake

7 Last Lone Inventor, p 37

8 Museum of Broadcast Communications—"David Sarnoff"

9 History Channel Modern Marvels—"Television: Window to the World"

in this new development and consolidated them under this one banner. The navy's attitude was that British Marconi, American Marconi's parent company, would not be a participant in RCA—only American Marconi. Moreover, government-sponsored RCA could expect to be a government favorite. To individual stockholders, this would become extremely important.[10] RCA's first job was to buy out American Marconi—and with that buy-out came David Sarnoff.

David Sarnoff, RCA, 1919

With Sarnoff in place, the first order of business for RCA was to expand their hold on current patents. In particular, RCA wanted the rights to the Audion Tube, a cornerstone invention that enabled modern radios to receive signals from great distances. De Forest, inventor of the Audion, had sold his rights to AT&T during his bankruptcy. Sarnoff urged RCA Chairman Owen Young to obtain the rights to the Audion in return for a percentage of RCA stock. A similar agreement was arranged with Westinghouse, which was rapidly expanding into broadcasting. In short order, a partnership of sorts was born between GE, Westinghouse, AT&T, American Marconi, and United Fruit, as RCA filled its patent pool.[11] While ordinary Americans could still operate their little shed-based crystal sets, radio was about to become big business—a business in which RCA and the other sub-companies would be the dominant players, though none more influential than David Sarnoff.

RCA PREFERRED STOCKHOLDERS[12]

COMPANY	COMMON	PREFERRED	TOTAL	PERCENT
GE	2,364,826	620,800	2,985,626	30.1%
WESTINGHOUSE	1,000,000	1,000,000	2,000,000	20.6%
AT&T	500,000	500,000	1,000,000	10.3%
UNITED FRUIT	200,000	200,000	400,000	4.1%

By 1920, radio had officially come of age. In Pittsburgh, a Westinghouse engineer named Frank Conrad had been experimenting with voice and music for several months as a hobby after work. Conrad's superior at Westinghouse, Harry Davis, knew of Conrad's hobby. After learning of a 20-minute "concert" Conrad had played over the airwaves by placing a Victrola (record player) beside a wireless phone transmitter in his home, Davis had a kind of epiphany. If Conrad could broadcast concerts like this on a regular basis, Davis reasoned his division at Westinghouse could sell receivers.[13] This vision put the idea of broadcasting in

10 History Channel Modern Marvels—"Television: Window to the World"

11 Last Lone Inventor, p 45

12 *Tube of Plenty*, p 22

13 *Tube of Plenty*, p 31

an entirely new light. A merchandising element had been added, turning a hobby into a sound business concept. Westinghouse would build and sell receivers to enthusiasts interested in listening to music.

In October of that year, Westinghouse secured the required broadcasting license from the Department of Commerce and assigned the call letters KDKA to the license. Davis gave Conrad permission to build a transmitting "shack" atop the Westinghouse rooftop and instructed Conrad to assemble a 100-watt transmitter inside. An antenna was run from a steel pole on the roof to one of the smokestacks rising up from a part of the Westinghouse plant across the street. On Election Day, November 2, 1920, Conrad broadcast from his rooftop shack and the first radio station in America, KDKA, went on the air. KDKA made history by broadcasting live returns of a presidential election, telling listeners that Warren Harding had defeated Democrat James Cox and his running mate, Franklin Roosevelt.

By the following January, KDKA was setting up remote pick-ups from a variety of locations around Pittsburgh. Conrad quickly determined the station would soon need a bigger transmitter and replaced the original 100-watt unit with one five times more powerful. A month later, Westinghouse was shipping these 500-watt transmitters to other "rooftop venues" in the hope of increasing their broadcast audience and upping demand for their "radio receivers."[14]

Broadcast fever was quick to follow. RCA wanted Sarnoff to turn their wireless business into a radio business and the race for the family living room was on.[15] Truthfully, radio was, by this time, more than a business. It had become a fad. Getting into broadcasting seemed much too cheap and easy for one corporation to control an entire industry. Transmitters were affordable to buy and operating them was pretty simple. An early cover of Hugo Gernsback's *Radio News* magazine captured the fanfare perfectly when it depicted a cartoon of a monkey wearing headphones while operating a giant transmitter.[16] The U.S. Department of Commerce, meanwhile, had approved licenses for dozens of new stations. Audiences in New York City, Schenectady, Pittsburgh, Boston, Chicago, and Los Angeles were exploding. Program schedules were appearing in local newspapers across the country.

By 1921, licenses had been granted for 28 commercial radio stations. Six months later that number grew to 430 stations. Soon, radio *networks* were formed and this was significant. It signaled for the first time the commercial value of a point-to-mass product and the promise of an untapped global market. And there was the practical side. It made more sense, economically, for a network hub to produce programming centrally in New York and broadcast it to an affiliated group of stations across the country than for each station, in each city, to produce every single show by themselves. It also meant advertisers could now reach radio customers nationally like they did in the magazines of the day.

---

14 *Tube of Plenty*, pp 31–34

15 History Channel Modern Marvels—"Television: Window to the World"

16 Last Lone Inventor, p 47

Yet, not everyone was happy. A group of independent radio makers formed an association to lobby Washington into taking action against RCA's patent pool. Eugene McDonald, president of Zenith, spearheaded the effort. His criticism of RCA as a monopolistic predator often veered to personal attacks on Sarnoff himself. This led Sarnoff to spend more and more time cultivating his image, granting interviews, and speaking at important functions.[17] He told everyone who would listen about his heroic role in the *Titanic* episode and how he'd come up with the Radio Box Memo five years earlier, outlining back then everything that was now coming true. The only thing Sarnoff had misjudged, he confessed, was that radio was catching on even faster than he'd predicted it would.

The message to Sarnoff's enemies and potential rivals couldn't be clearer. Here was a man who could not only see the future, but also mold it to his will. In short order, David Sarnoff became the personification of radio and steamrolled over anyone and everyone who got in his way. Everyone, that is, but the 10th-grade schoolboy from Beaver, Utah, who would challenge David Sarnoff on an even bigger stage with an invention he called television.

Discussion Questions

A. Chaos

- The term "television," first coined in 1907, actually referred to what technology?
- How did the tragedy of the Titanic contribute to the unfolding of the possibilities of global communication and a future key player?

B. American Marconi

- How was American Marconi able to expand under the Radio Act of 1912? What role did WWI play in the expansion of wireless technology?
- Why was David Sarnoff's idea of point-to-mass product considered so revolutionary over the current point-to-point product?

C. R.C.A.

- What was the sequence of events that led R.C.A., formed in 1919, to begin its ascent as a private American monopoly of radio transmission?

---

17 Last Lone Inventor, p 49

CHAPTER THREE

Sarnoff v. Farnsworth: Round One

1920–1930

The Sketch

About the time David Sarnoff was walking through the front door of American Marconi, Philo Taylor Farnsworth was coming into the world. Born on August 19, 1906 to Lewis and Serena Farnsworth, Philo spent his early years with his Mormon parents living in a log cabin built by his grandfather in a place called Indian Creek, near Beaver, Utah. At age eleven, the boy from Beaver was already poring over scientific journals by candlelight. Working far into the evening, night after night, young Farnsworth's aim was to try to decode the complex phenomena of particle physics in an effort to create a tube like de Forest's that carried picture as well as sound. It was into this exciting world of invention that Farnsworth, having no formal training in science of any kind, immersed himself.[1]

By 1918, Lewis Farnsworth had moved the family up to a farm in Rigby, Idaho, where he planned to supplement his farming income by hauling freight with his horse-drawn wagon. During the journey from Beaver to Rigby, the family passed through Salt Lake City and drank in the marvels of modern

1 History Channel Modern Marvels—"Television: Window to the World"

life.[2] Electric street lamps, endless power lines, bustling automobile traffic, and the telephone—all of it a wonder to young Philo Farnsworth's eyes.

Upon arriving in Rigby, Philo was excited to find that his new home was wired for electricity. A Delco generator provided power for both farm machinery and indoor lighting. Farnsworth found himself a quick study in electro-mechanical technology and discovered that he could repair the troublesome generator when it broke down. A few weeks after moving in, Philo retrieved a burned-out electric motor among some items discarded by the previous tenants and proceeded to convert his mother's hand-powered washing machine into an electrically powered one. Philo had been helped in his task by his first telephone conversation with an out-of-state relative who seemed to know "a little kitchen chemistry and a thing or two about electric motors"; and by the discovery of a large reserve of technology magazines and Sears Roebuck catalogues in the attic of the family's new home.[3]

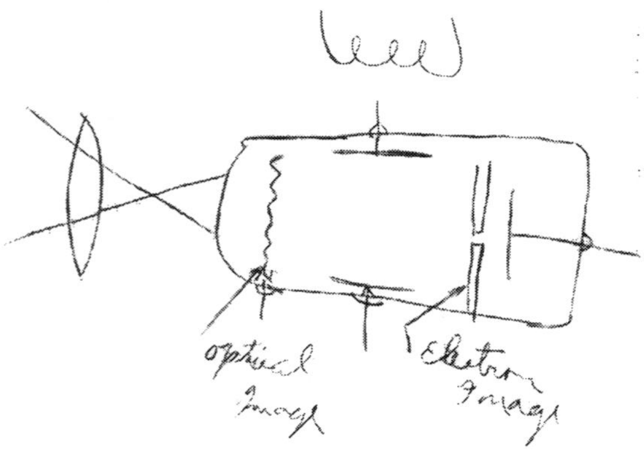

Farnsworth's Blackboard Sketch, Image Dissector Tube, 1922

Philo Farnsworth excelled in chemistry and physics at Rigby High School and was always producing sketches and prototypes of electron tubes. As soon as Farnsworth enrolled in high school, he asked permission to sit in on chemistry teacher Justin Tolman's lectures, and would periodically go to Tolman for advice about an electronic television system he was contemplating building. The science teacher found merit in the diagrams Farnsworth would draw on Tolman's blackboards and encouraged Farnsworth to continue his exploration. In the spring of 1922, though just 15 years old and a second-semester high school sophomore, Farnsworth took to the blackboard in Tolman's class with what was to become the centerpiece of a system he called "television." Now an official student in Tolman's class, Farnsworth astounded Tolman as well as his classmates with a sketch showing how mechanical television might be accomplished *electronically*.[4] In effect, Farnsworth's sketch gave birth to the electronic television camera, even though it would be another five years before one was built.

One of the more important things to note from Farnsworth's sketch is that all the elements in the working Image Dissector (camera tube) are there. The magnetic deflection, the electrostatic deflection, the aperture of analysis, the anode, photocathode, and a lens are all depicted here in one manner or another. The notations "optical image" and "electron image" are key descriptions of the internal changes

2 Last Lone Inventor, p14

3 Distant Vision: Romance and Discovery of an Invisible Frontier, p 21

4 History Channel Modern Marvels—"Television: Window to the World"

necessary to transform a regular picture made of light into a picture made of electrical charges.[5] Even more amazing was that there was nothing extraneous in the sketch. Everything that was needed for an electronic television picture tube was in the drawing and nothing more. "The sketch," as it would come to be referred to, became the blueprint for the television camera tube and the cornerstone of electronic television. Uncertain whether Farnsworth was a genius or just plain crazy, Tolman paid for the train ride that sent Philo down to Provo, Utah to see the "brains" over at Brigham Young University.[6]

Young Farnsworth explained his ideas to these astute professors of science like he was one of them,[7] though he was scarcely old enough to drive. Farnsworth's theory was that an image could be read by a lens and captured on a plate and then scanned by a beam of lightning-fast electrons emanating from a cathode ray tube like the one featured in his "sketch." [Note: The cathode ray tube, invented by German

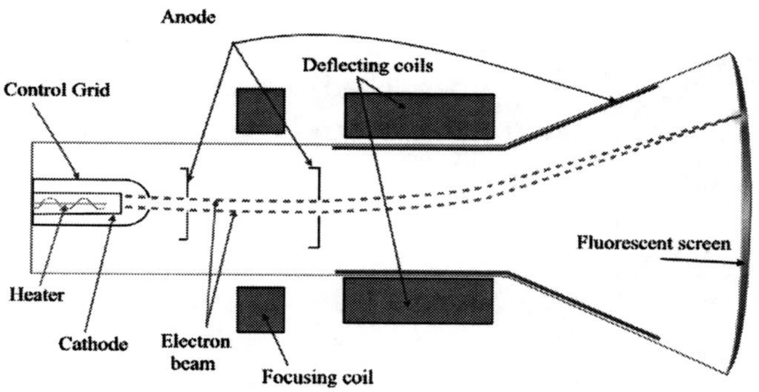

Cathode Ray Tube Invented by Karl Braun, 1897

scientist Karl Braun in 1897, is a vacuum tube that produces images when its phosphorescent surface is struck by electron beams.] The electrons would bounce back from the plate to the tube reflecting light and dark areas of the image just scanned. These electrons would then be converted into electrical energy and transmitted like radio through the ether.

The professors that day were staggered and wired Tolman to tell him of Farnsworth's genius.[8] The science teacher, having a hunch the drawings left behind on the school blackboard were important, had already committed them to paper. Ten years later, Tolman reproduced Farnsworth's drawings for the patent court from a pencil-drawn copy he'd made of his classroom's blackboard the day Farnsworth chalked his image. This act would be pivotal in the "interference case" between Farnsworth and the Radio Corporation of America (RCA)—a case that netted millions of dollars to Farnsworth down the road.

---

5 The Philo Farnsworth Archives—"The Sketch"

6 History Channel Modern Marvels—"Television: Window to the World"

7 History Channel Modern Marvels—"Television: Window to the World"

8 History Channel Modern Marvels—"Television: Window to the World"

In the fall of 1922, the Farnsworth's moved to Provo, Utah. Philo, however, stayed behind in Idaho to finish high school, and took a job working for the railroad in his spare time to earn money for college. Philo hoped to save enough money to begin classes at BYU when he rejoined his family in Utah in the fall of 1923. In January of that year, however, Lewis Farnsworth, Philo's father, died of pneumonia, leaving sixteen-year-old Philo in charge of the Farnsworth family.

Philanthropic Support

Philo Taylor Farnsworth, Inventor of Television

Instead of completing high school, Farnsworth found himself working in a hardware store near his home in Provo, Utah. Philo worked while older sister Agnes took charge of the house. The Farnsworth's later moved into half of a Provo duplex, and Philo quickly developed a friendship with his neighbor, Cliff Gardner, who lived in the other half of the building. Gardner shared an interest in electronics and the two soon moved to Salt Lake City to start a radio repair business.[9]

The business failed and Gardner returned to Provo. Farnsworth, however, remained in Salt Lake City. It was there, while enrolling in a job-placement service connected to the University of Utah, that Farnsworth found work at the regional headquarters of a national charity organization, the Community Chest. Soon after arriving, he introduced himself to a pair of San Francisco philanthropists, George Everson and Leslie Gorrell, who were conducting the Salt Lake City fundraising campaign for their charity.[10] After hearing Farnsworth's television pitch one day at lunch, Everson thought it a pipe dream, but not Gorrell. He'd taken some engineering courses in college and the more he thought about Farnsworth's ideas, the more he liked the young man's concept. Gorrell went to Everson to revisit the television concept, extolling its virtues. In due time, the two men agreed to fund Farnsworth's early research.

The three men entered into a 50-50 partnership in which Everson and Gorrell would set Farnsworth up in a laboratory in Los Angeles to begin experiments and split half of any profits that came of their venture. Thus, by May 1926, while David Sarnoff was collecting all the patents and properties required to complete the fierce industrial monopoly that was American Radio, Philo T. Farnsworth was giving up his day job at the Community Chest.[11]

9 Last Lone Inventor, p 53

10 Distant Vision: Romance & Discovery on an Invisible Frontier, p 6

11 Last Lone Inventor, p 53

Rising Son

As early as 1916, David Sarnoff, the Bill Gates of his day, had urged American Marconi to manufacture Radio Music Boxes, but the idea had fallen on deaf ears. In 1920, he pitched his idea again to the brass at RCA. Sarnoff estimated that the music boxes would sell for $75 and that in RCA's first year of production they could expect to see sales of close to eight million dollars. Sarnoff thought that figure would triple in year two and increase sevenfold by year three. Though his predictions would prove to be surprisingly accurate, his boss, Edward Nally, then president of RCA, was not yet ready to believe. But by the end of the year, with the success of Westinghouse's radio station, KDKA, it was painfully obvious to Owen Young, RCA's CEO, that the Radio Corporation of America had missed the proverbial boat. Young soon promoted 30-year-old David Sarnoff to General Manager of the company and encouraged Nally, who had dismissed Sarnoff's music box idea, to retire.[12]

In a mad scramble to reach this new audience, stores all over America were selling factory-made receivers. Manufacturers had produced 100,000 radios in 1922, and over half a million by the following year. By 1926, more than two million had been sold. Everyone was starting stations. Hospitals and colleges took to the airwaves; clothing retailers and pharmacies, too. Banks and poultry farms and ice cream parlors followed suit. Companies saw radio as an efficient new way to communicate with their customers.

At RCA, David Sarnoff wanted to show the world that one company towered above them all and approved a new logo for the company that featured a line-drawing of planet Earth. At the top of the world was the distinct shape of North America. At the bottom were the words: "World Wide Wireless."[13] The logo was plastered on RCA buildings, tacked onto transmission towers, and displayed in magazine and newspaper advertisements of the day. Sometimes abbreviated as "WWW," the logo went right to the heart of David Sarnoff's vision of RCA as a leader of the global communication revolution. Yet despite all the hoopla and RCA's incredible growth, RCA was still public enemy number one as far as the rest of the industry was concerned. The competition branded RCA a monopoly. Hearing the rumors, the Federal Trade Commission (FTC) began investigating the complaints and it found merit to them. The FTC noted in its 1923 report to Congress: *"The Radio Corporation of America apparently has the power to stifle competition in the manufacture and sale of receiving sets."* The press was no ally either, comparing Big Radio to the reviled trusts in oil, the railroads, and steel.

Sarnoff needed a way to pull RCA back from the limelight and out of what he saw as an absurd situation. Here the government and the press were proclaiming RCA a monopoly when 75% of the radio market was owned by other companies. The way Sarnoff viewed it, RCA was the one being mugged. Then, late one night at his office, Sarnoff was struck with an idea he felt should have been obvious to him all along. Instead of trying to put the competition out of business, why not just license RCA's patents to anyone

---

12 *Tube of Plenty*, p 36

13 Last Lone Inventor, p 68

who wanted them. The new business model was simple. RCA would provide its entire pool of patents in return for a percentage of sales from the companies purchasing the patents. If a radio in a competitor's store cost $100, then say $7.50 of that rival's sale would flow into the coffers of RCA.[14] The plan was nothing short of brilliant and had the potential to turn RCA's most contentious foes into its friendliest customers. Within a short time, ninety percent of the existing radio makers, including Philco and Zenith, RCA's biggest rivals, were under license to the Radio Corporation of America. The plan worked so well that within a very short time, Sarnoff reduced the 7.5% licensing fee to 5% in an effort to spur the sales of even more officially licensed radio makers.

Sarnoff's patent-licensing scheme created revenues for RCA that no one could have predicted, making the company far more profitable than if they had been selling radios alone.[15] Its chief business had been selling boxes of tubes and wires, but now RCA was selling intellectual property (patents). And it wasn't really even doing that. It was merely *licensing* its patent pool and could thus receive a return on its original investment hundreds and hundreds of times over, without expensing a minute of assembly-line overhead.

For Sarnoff, the biggest challenge to his plan for a greater RCA wouldn't come from other corporations. How could it? Virtually everyone else in the radio business was already paying royalties to RCA. By making these payments, rival radio makers were essentially acquiescing to Sarnoff, relying on RCA for their innovation. More and more companies had less and less incentive to invest in their own research and development. Thus, what worried Sarnoff wasn't rival companies. What worried David Sarnoff were upstart inventors working in obscurity on patents RCA did not control. After all, such an inventor had already come along.

Edwin Armstrong, an independent inventor, was already well-off from the so-called regeneration patents he had sold to Westinghouse, patents that later became part of the RCA pool. Armstrong would, in 1933, go on to invent FM radio, the greatest discovery of his life, as a way to eliminate the ever-present static from radio broadcasts. Ten years earlier, while still working in his lab at Columbia University, Armstrong came up with something he termed "super-regeneration." He'd developed a new set of tubes that could amplify a radio signal five times greater than had previously been possible. When Armstrong began testing it publicly, the press decided to cover it and Sarnoff began to get nervous. Fearful that Armstrong would get the patent and undermine the RCA patent monopoly, Sarnoff made Armstrong an offer he couldn't refuse. Armstrong was given $200,000 (2.3M USD 2012) cash plus 60,000 shares of RCA stock.[16] By the time the two got around to signing the document, the stock had doubled and was worth more than the cash. David Sarnoff was annoyed by the fact that he'd been caught with his technological pants down, and how much he'd paid for the privilege. He would see to it that nothing like that ever happened again.

---

14 Last Lone Inventor, p 69

15 Last Lone Inventor, p 70

16 Last Lone Inventor, pp 72–73

Going Hollywood

Elma "Pem" Gardner had been the first person Philo Farnsworth told of his new partnership with George Everson and Leslie Gorrell, only hours after giving notice at the Community Chest. Pem was Cliff Gardner's sister—Philo's good friend and former partner—and a best friend to Philo's sister, Agnes. Days later, though they'd hardly dated, Philo asked Pem to marry him and accompany him to Los Angeles where he and Everson and Gorrell were about to set up shop. The two teenagers were married in the hours preceding their departure for Los Angeles by train; the marriage was consummated while riding the Union Pacific.[17]

Within days after arriving in Los Angeles, Farnsworth immersed himself in books about electronics and the motion picture sciences at the downtown library. Farnsworth had to learn about the workings of the human eye; specifically, how many frames per second needed to flash before the eye in order to fool it into seeing fluid motion. Everson and Gorrell arrived shortly after the newlyweds and volunteered to help their inventor any way they could. The two were sent out around town to find, among other things, tubes and hoses and other equipment that typically was used by bootleggers making moonshine in their basements. The investors came home with lamps, crystals, prisms, lenses, and different types of wires, a barrel of shellac, a hand-cranked coil winder, and all sorts of tools.[18]

Farnsworth drew up a sketch of a custom-made tube that was to have a closed, flat bulb shape on one end, and a round, open mouth shape on the other. With the exception of its shape, this sketch was identical to the one Farnsworth had created for his science teacher five years earlier. A glassblower from Cal Tech who made scientific tubes for the eggheads at the university was called in to blow this one. Gorrell and Everson both helped assemble the tube. Everson was saddled with winding the coils and attaching them near the open mouth of the custom-built tube using globs of pungent shellac. These coils would serve to guide the electron beam through the vacuum tube. When the proper signal was applied to the coils, they would develop a magnetic field that would deflect the beam to a positively charged anode or metallic finger.[19]

Farnsworth was creating an electromagnet but using it in a far different way. What he was planning to do can be better understood by comparing it to a somewhat similar invention built years later—the laser. A glass tube is filled with a mixture of gases, such that when a stream of electricity is shot into the compound, the molecules vibrate and bump into one another, inciting a highly concentrated beam of electromagnetic radiation. Farnsworth wanted to shoot electricity into a tube as well, but one whose interior was a vacuum, void of any gas at all.[20] Philo would rely on the electromagnet that Everson helped put together to manipulate his electron beams, or cathode rays. This first tube was the prototype of what

---

17 Distant Vision: Romance & Discovery on an Invisible Frontier, p 108

18 Last Lone Inventor, p 80

19 Last Lone Inventor, p 82

20 Last Lone Inventor, p 82

would one day become the television camera tube and be turned out by the millions for the rest of the century.

Shortly after arriving in California, Farnsworth needed to find a patent attorney who was nationally recognized as an authority on electro-physics, with whom he could share his models and drawings. Only then, Farnsworth felt, would he gain credibility to attract investors. Television systems in use at the time used image scanning devices employing rotating "Nipkow discs"—lenses arranged in spiral patterns such that they swept across an image in a succession of short arcs while focusing the light they captured on photosensitive elements. An electrical signal was produced that corresponded to the variations in light intensity. Farnsworth saw the limitations of these mechanical systems and the need for an all-electronic scanning system that could produce a superior transmission.

The trial-and-error process of research and development, however, proved to be a costly one, and by the fall of 1926, it was clear the partnership needed to raise another $25,000 to continue their research. The task was destined to take months. When Everson and Gorrell failed to find financial support in Los Angeles, Everson took the train to San Francisco to ask the advice of an old colleague who happened to be vice president of the Crocker First National Bank. Problem was, the friend was out of town and Everson was forced to see J.J. Fagan, an executive vice president of the bank with a reputation for saying "no" to entrepreneurs looking for funding. As Everson talked, Fagan listened. The more the conservative banker listened, the more Fagan liked what Everson had to say. Fagan arranged a lunch later in the week that Farnsworth would attend. That luncheon turned out to be a watershed event in the annals of television history.

On the bank's side of the table were Fagan alongside the bank's president and principal owner, William H. Crocker, and his son, William Jr. Both men had helped Leland Stanford finance the construction of the transcontinental railroad and had a reputation for taking big but carefully calculated risks. Crocker Bank would invest $25,000 in Farnsworth's invention but would take a 60% ownership stake in the company. Obviously, the original "partnership pie" would have to be resized.[21] The meaning of this new division wasn't lost on Farnsworth. Instead of owning 50% of his invention, he would now own 20% and would no longer have control over his own fate. Philo Farnsworth was now working for the bankers and the first thing the bankers wanted in place was a patent. Farnsworth complied and filed the application for his all-electric television system on January 7, 1927.

As a part of this new partnership with Crocker Bank, the bankers agreed to make available free laboratory space at 202 Green Street in San Francisco that another one of their ventures had recently vacated.[22] On September 7, 1927, working at the Green Street Lab, Farnsworth's Image Dissector (camera tube) transmitted its first image, a straight line. Within a year, Farnsworth had sufficiently developed the system to

21 Last Lone Inventor, p 82

22 The Virtual Museum of the City of San Francisco—"Philo Taylor Farnsworth (1906-1971)"

hold a demonstration at the lab for the press. His backers at Crocker Bank had demanded to know when they would see dollars from the invention, so the first image Farnsworth decided to show the world was, appropriately, a dollar sign. In addition to the press, Farnsworth decided that a bit of promotion couldn't hurt and invited Hollywood stars Douglas Fairbanks and Mary Pickford up to San Francisco to promote this revolutionary product called television.

The demonstration, after working perfectly in practice, failed miserably when shown to the press and the Hollywood elite. The iconic actors from Hollywood who'd helped form United Artists Studios left dismayed and Farnsworth's backers began to get nervous. Maybe *mechanical* television was the way to go.[23]

Mechanical Television

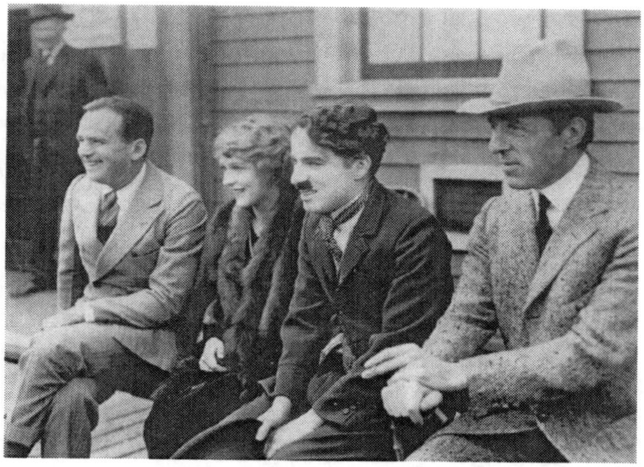

Pickford and Fairbanks, seen here with Charlie Chaplin and Director DW Griffith, Visit Farnsworth's Green Street Lab—1928

The competitor to electronic television was mechanical television, a system relying on a small disc dotted with perforated holes, through which light beamed creating television scan lines. Simply put, mechanical television transmitted images electro-mechanically, while electronic television moved them at the speed of light. While mechanical television was less complex, it was, in truth, not much more advanced than Paul Nipkow's disc of forty years earlier. For that reason, they were easier to build and easier to use. The critical *mechanical* component in mechanical television was the Nipkow Disc, or a disc similar to Nipkow's. The disc, as mentioned in Chapter One, was perforated with a series of holes designed in a spiral pattern. The premise was simple. Each hole takes a "slice" of the image as it passes. That slice is in turn picked up as light patterns—light and dark areas—by a sensor. This sensor—or more aptly put, a photoelectrical cell—then converts the light's energy directly into electricity.[24] Essentially, as each hole flies by the image, it produces an electric scan line that is then carried by radio waves to the TV receiver.

---

23 History Channel Modern Marvels—"Television: Window to the World"

24 Users.swing.be—"The Nipkow disk"

Inventor Charles Jenkins, a native of Ohio with over 400 patents to his name, was mechanical television's biggest proponent. But then that would figure. Seventy-five of his patents were devoted to mechanical television alone. The inventor of such conveniences as the self-starting engine and the 35mm motion picture projector, Jenkins was as much a promotional genius as David Sarnoff and a bigger showman than Lee de Forest. Jenkins had begun developing mechanical television systems in the early 1920's, and by 1923 he had transmitted the first moving silhouette images. In 1925, Jenkins publicly demonstrated the synchronized transmission of images and sound. Two years after that, Jenkins, while still working for AT&T, sent a crude 48-line image of then-Secretary of Commerce, Herbert Hoover, from Washington to New York making it the first long-distance telecast in history.[25] Mechanical television had indeed struck the first blow.

Farnsworth was frustrated. Here, electronic television, relying on charged electrons to first scan an image and then amplify it, created a much better picture, yet it was mechanical television that was getting all the attention. And the worst part was Farnsworth knew that their version of television could never work. After all, each Nipkow Disc allowed for only a limited number of holes. If you doubled the disc size and produced twice as many holes, the unit became impractical to use. And that wasn't even its biggest drawback. Whether your disc was big or small, you could never spin it fast enough to produce a crystal-clear image. Resolution on mechanical television broadcasts was relatively low, ranging from about 30 scan lines up to 120, but nothing close to the 400–600 lines you would need to draw more than a carnival audience to your product. Scanning, transmitting, and recreating a sharp moving picture on a screen requires speeds so fantastic that only by manipulating electrons in vacuum tubes can you achieve them.[26] Electronic television, heralded Farnsworth, was the only way the invention would ever grow a business.

U.S. Secretary of Commerce, Herbert Hoover—1927 Mechanical TV Broadcast

Charles Jenkins disagreed and in 1928 the Jenkins Television Corporation opened W3XK, the first television broadcasting station in America. On July 2 of that year, Jenkins sent out his initial broadcast from his labs in Washington, D.C. At first, the station could send only silhouette images because of its narrow bandwidth, but soon enough real black-and-white images were transmitted.[27]

In London at this time, Scottish inventor John Baird, an engineer by trade and the inventor given credit for being the first to produce a live moving grayscale television image, was working on an electro-mechanical television system of his own. Baird called it a

25 History Channel Modern Marvels—"Television: Window to the World"

26 Last Lone Inventor, p 85

27 History Channel Modern Marvels—"Television: Window to the World"

"Televisor" and in October, 1925, he successfully used it to transmit a television picture of a static gray-scale image, using the head of a ventriloquist's doll as the image to be transmitted.

The following January, 1926, Baird demonstrated his Televisor for the British press. Baird's system combined mechanical picture scanning with electronic amplification at the transmitter and at the receiver.[28] The "electronic amplification" component was where Baird's electro-mechanical system differed from Jenkins' mechanical system and from Farnsworth's electronic system, too. Unlike Farnsworth's electronic television system with several hundred lines of resolution, Baird's vertically scanned image, using a Nipkow-like disc embedded with a double spiral of lenses, and had only 30 lines—barely enough to reproduce a recognizable human face. Below is the first known photograph of a moving image.

For the purposes of the 1926 demonstration, the doll's head was done away with and a human face was reproduced, instead—a 20-year-old office mate named William Edward Taynton (image below).[29]

In 1927, employing 438 miles of telephone line between London and Glasgow, Baird transmitted the world's first long-distance television pictures to the Central Hotel at Glasgow Central Station. This transmission was Baird's response to a 225-mile long-distance telecast earlier that April between the AT&T station in New York and the Bell Labs station in Washington, D.C., the day Jenkins photographed Herbert Hoover.[30] Soon after Baird's demonstration, he formed the Baird Television Development Company Ltd, near London, and it was from there that Baird made the first transatlantic television transmission to Hartsdale, New York.

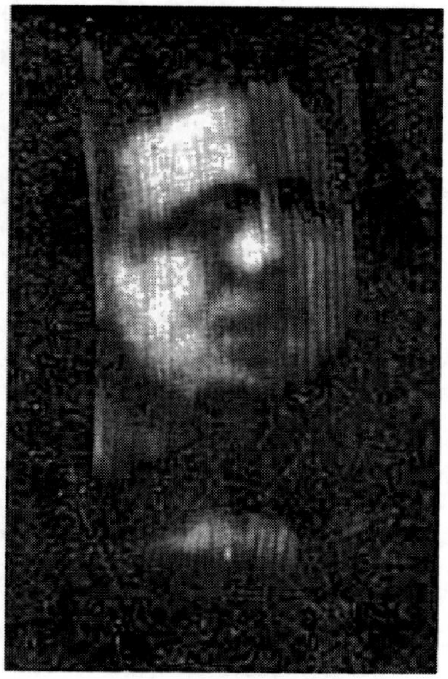

First Live Moving Image. Produced by Baird's Televisor, 1926

In 1929, Baird's design was further improved by elimination of a motor-generator, so the television system now had no mechanical parts.[31] That year, too, Farnsworth transmitted the first live human images using his electronic television system. Many inventors had built electro-mechanical television systems prior to Farnsworth's seminal contribution, but Farnsworth designed and built the world's first working all-electronic television system, employing electronic scanning in both the transmitting and receiving devices.

28 The History of Television, 1880 to 1941, p 15
29 The History of Television, 1880 to 1941, p 99
30 The History of Television, 1880 to 1941, p 101
31 John Logie Baird: A Life, p 286

Farnsworth first demonstrated his system to the press on September 3, 1928.[32] Later in London, the BBC wanted to set the standard for British television, but only after viewing both electronic and mechanical systems together. The competitors were Philo Farnsworth and John Baird. The two men had been afforded adjacent banquet rooms to display their two television systems side by side. Baird had gone first, but some in his audience had already departed for the other banquet room where Farnsworth was setting up. Baird caught sight of what they were all looking at and literally walked away from his audience in the middle of his pitch to view the images Farnsworth was screening on his side of the curtain. According to accounts of those who were there, Baird's mouth dropped open when he saw how much better the images were on Farnsworth's system than on his. It was in that moment, Baird later admitted, that he came to realize that he and Jenkins would soon be little more than footnotes to television history.[33]

By 1932, the world of mechanical television was coming to an end. In March of that year, the Jenkins Television Corporation was liquidated and its assets were acquired by Lee de Forest Radio Corporation. Within a few short months, the de Forest company also went bankrupt, leaving its assets from the bankruptcy to be bought up by RCA. Within days of the purchase, David Sarnoff, now president of RCA, decreed that all work on electro-mechanical television would hereby come to a grinding halt, never to surface again in the 20th century. While Baird's Crystal Palace laboratories outside London would continue to compete in the television market through much of the 1930's, the fire that burned Crystal Palace to the ground in 1937[34] further hampered the Baird company's bottom line and finally put mechanical television to rest later that year.

The Birth of NBC

In 1924, AT&T, one of the original four pillars of the RCA combine (along with Westinghouse, United Fruit, and GE) began behaving strangely. It sold its RCA stock and resigned its position from the RCA Board of Directors. As RCA's General Manager, David Sarnoff had been sitting in on the board meetings and had the gnawing feeling that AT&T was moving to compete with RCA. As it turned out, Sarnoff's concerns were warranted. AT&T was leaving RCA for the broadcasting business and had strung together twelve other stations to follow its lead. Until that moment, broadcasting had mainly been a local affair with programming among the different stations that was never synchronized. Since the technology of relaying programs through the airwaves from one station to another was still on the drawing board, AT&T was going to get the jump on the market. It would simply send the programming and the commercials over its own phone lines, where sister stations in the network would pick up the signals and broadcast them from radio towers to their local audiences.

---

32 History Channel Modern Marvels—"Television: Window to the World"

33 History Channel Modern Marvels—"Television: Window to the World"

34 John Logie Baird: A Life, pp 288–289

Sarnoff was furious. "Networking," after all, was an idea he alone had first brought to the boardroom. Gifford and AT&T were not only stealing it, but also bypassing the wireless delivery system everyone else would need to get started. AT&T didn't need one. They owned the phone lines and could, for the moment, bypass the "wireless" part of the equation. AT&T looked to have the upper hand and David Sarnoff was not about to let that happen. What came to pass proved to be one of the most consequential power struggles in the history of business—*any* business. The great irony was that because all of it took place behind the scenes in offices and boardrooms, the press failed to report a single word. Here we had a bitter clash between two monopolies (AT&T and RCA), and few beyond the principals at either company were aware it was even happening. When the dust settled, nothing less than the American broadcasting business emerged and began taking the shape it would maintain for the remainder of the 20th century.

The entire episode was centered on a personal feud between David Sarnoff, RCA's General Manager, and Walter Gifford, then AT&T's Harvard-educated CFO and soon-to-be-president that had a seat on the RCA Board of Directors. AT&T was already the world's largest public utility—an industrial behemoth with over 350,000 employees and an uninterrupted record of paying dividends to its shareholders for more than two decades. What few knew and no one talked about was that *Ma Bell*, as AT&T was affectionately referred to because of its phone monopoly, was also a bastion of discreet anti-Semitism.

As the only Jewish executive in all of the communication industry, David Sarnoff was acutely aware of AT&T's anti-Semitism. Yet, he was also mindful his own peculiarity. Sarnoff hadn't ended up in the garment trade or the movie business like most of his ilk. Sarnoff, a Jew, was a rising star in a tradition-rich industry and had worked twice as hard as anyone else to get there.

Sarnoff had recalled one dramatic story involving Harry Warner, of Warner Brothers Studios, who was outraged over a dispute with a Bell System executive stemming from the licensing agreement for the talking-pictures technology (the same technology used in *The Jazz Singer* several years later). Warner sensed the executive was anti-Semitic and demanded the executive name one Jewish employee working for his company. When he couldn't, Warner vowed to take his business elsewhere and let the public know why. The discomfited executive, worried about the negative publicity Warner could stir up, ordered his lawyers to settle the dispute at all costs.

Sarnoff took a page out of Harry Warner's play book. He began bad-mouthing Gifford and AT&T privately for their anti-Semitic hiring practices, but never leaked a word to the press. Word did manage to reach Gifford through back channels, however, and he sat down with Owen Young, RCA's CEO, to quell the talk. Gifford agreed to try to work out a fair deal with RCA just as soon as Young fired "that Jew Sarnoff." Gifford had misjudged Owen Young, who then dismissed Gifford unceremoniously as Sarnoff knew he would. Young vowed to back his 33-year-old general manager with everything in RCA's legal arsenal. What's more, they'd let Sarnoff lead the charge.

Sarnoff had anticipated all of this and was ready with a plan. He was pretty sure that what AT&T was doing—using one monopoly to gain another—was illegal under U.S. anti-trust laws. This left him two options. One, Sarnoff could launch an unseemly lawsuit in court against AT&T for breaching its 1921 patent-sharing agreement with RCA, and challenge Ma Bell's homespun image in the newspapers. Or two, RCA could goad AT&T into submitting to a private arbitration over the same patent-sharing issue in an effort to keep their tarnished image out of the public eye. In choosing private arbitration, both sides knew that the arbitrator's decision was final. There would be no appeal of any kind and that's exactly how Sarnoff wanted it. Sarnoff knew something the Harvard-bred Gifford had forgotten—that most of the arbitrators were retired lawyers, and that most of the lawyers in New York were Jewish. Moreover, these lawyers knew all about AT&T's anti-Semitic hiring practices. The AT&T–RCA hearing lasted several months, but in the end, the arbitrator ruled in RCA's favor on every count.

The final settlement turned out to be a windfall for Sarnoff and RCA. The arbitrator found that AT&T had breached its 1921 patent-sharing contract with RCA and would be immediately exiting the broadcasting business by signing the agreement now in front of them. AT&T would sell RCA its flagship station WEAF and its "network" for one million dollars and grant RCA the rights to transmit on their phone lines for a nominal licensing fee. RCA's new acquisition became known as the National Broadcasting Company and initially consisted of the AT&T chain of stations.

Beloved Logo that put RCA in the Music Business—1929

Soon a second network containing the RCA-owned flagship stations in New York and Washington as well as General Electric's state-of-the-art center in Schenectady; the Westinghouse stations in Pittsburgh, Chicago, Boston, and Springfield, Massachusetts were added to the company.[35] Sarnoff was on top of the world. Among the stations he had amassed under the NBC subsidiary were AT&T's New York flagship WEAF as well as its sister station in Washington, WCAP. RCA quickly shut down this latter station and merged its facilities with the Washington affiliate RCA already owned there, WRC.[36] The new broadcast division at RCA was divided in ownership among the principals: RCA (50%), General Electric (30%), and Westinghouse (20%). The network was officially launched on November 15, 1926.[37]

The *windfall* that had spilled over David Sarnoff and RCA was almost too good to be true. Here you had AT&T's former New York affiliate, WEAF … and RCA's very own New York station, WJZ—both flagships of

35 Last Lone Inventor, pp 96–102

36 United States Early Radio History—"Announcing the National Broadcasting company, Inc."

37 *New York Times*—"Red and Blue Networks of NBC To Be Split; WJZ May Be Sold" 1942 January

the two earlier networks—operating side by side in the Big Apple for seven months as part of the *new* NBC. By the summer of 1927, however, with the two NBC stations seriously competing with one another, RCA made the decision to formally divide its programming.

NBC would be sliced into halves: the *Red Network* carrying commercially sponsored entertainment and music programming; and the *Blue Network* that carried non-sponsored broadcasts composed of news and cultural series. The denotation of the names (Red and Blue) assigned to each network actually hailed from the grease pencils and stick pins that were used to chart that network's growth and territory.

RCA Victor

NBC, now a subsidiary of RCA, threw itself a coming-out party and brought together the entire pantheon of movers and shakers in New York. Over the next few years, Sarnoff seemed to court them all. By the summer of 1928, with RCA's dominance over radio apparently secure, RCA president General James Harbord stepped down to help his old friend Herbert Hoover run for President.[38] While CEO Owen Young would wait two years to officially promote Sarnoff to president, he immediately shuttled him into Harbord's office before the vacating general had even cleared it out. Young let Sarnoff know that while he didn't yet have the official title of RCA President, he could act as if he did. With Sarnoff now able to wield the full power of the radio monopoly to initiate deals with anyone he wanted, the new interim-president of RCA entered three transactions in rapid order that transformed his company into the media kingdom it was destined to become.

The first of these transactions was with the automobile makers in Detroit—specifically the General Motors Corporation. For Sarnoff, the thought of becoming the exclusive provider of radio technology for the mammoth automaker was irresistible. Before that summer was over, Sarnoff had negotiated the formation of a new company, the General Motors Radio Corporation, of which, RCA would own 49% of GMRC's profit. A second, far more complex deal involved the phonograph. For almost a decade, America had debated which invention was superior, the radio or the phonograph. In 1926, Thomas Edison had unveiled his latest creation, a phonograph record that held an unprecedented forty minutes of music on its vinyl surface. Now, two years later, Sarnoff saw that vinyl surface as commerce and wanted to unify the two technologies by going into business with the Victor Talking Machines Company—the best loved and most recognizable name in phonographs of its day.

Sarnoff's real fear was that the Victor Company would start making radios and add programming from their music labels as a value-added inducement for their customers to buy their radios. The transaction

38 Last Lone Inventor, p 104

between RCA and Victor took months of tangling with the various interests and thousands of shareholders of both companies, but the deal was finally completed by the spring of 1929.[39]

With the General Motors and Victor deals in progress, Sarnoff turned his attention to the acquisition of the Film Booking Office (FBO), a minor film production and distribution company owned by a fast-rising financial whiz named Joseph P. Kennedy. In October of 1928, Joe Kennedy met with Sarnoff in New York to outline how RCA would invest $400,000 to help finance FBO's expansion into producing feature films.[40] In return, Kennedy would merge FBO with Keith-Albee-Orpheum, a company that was converting its chain of vaudeville theaters into movie houses that would soon be equipped with RCA sound systems. This new company would be called Radio-Keith-Orpheum, or RKO. Joe Kennedy netted eight million dollars from this merger—one that transformed him from a successful entrepreneur into one of the richest men in American industry.

For David Sarnoff, money ran a distant second to his business legacy. After building RCA into the first electronic media conglomerate in the world, Sarnoff wanted the one patent that still eluded RCA and one that was now beginning to get considerable press. It was a leap in technology that had been on his radar for years, now, and looked to Sarnoff like it might one day supplant radio as the ultimate step in mass communication—electronic television.

Discussion Questions

A. The Sketch

- What was the significance of "The Sketch" made by a 15 year old Philo Farnsworth?

B. Philanthropic Support

- On what basis did San Francisco based philanthropists Everson and Gorrell fund the research of Philo Farnsworth in 1926? The first year of research in San Francisco yielded what results?

C. Rising Son

- What bright idea of RCA's David Sarnoff turned a hostile competitive industry into friendly customers with the added perk of making RCA much richer?

---

39 Last Lone Inventor, p 106

40 Last Lone Inventor, p 107

E. Mechanical Television

- In the technological tug-of-war between mechanical and electronic TV, what was the most significant advantage that landed Farnsworth's electronic system the victory?

F. The Birth of NBC

- When AT&T left the RCA combine in 1924, how did Sarnoff use AT&T's anti-Semitism against them to resolve their patent sharing issues which ultimately led to the acquisition of the National Broadcasting Company (NBC)?

G. RCA Victor

- Under the leadership of Sarnoff, what were the three business deals in the late 1920's that cemented RCA as the "media king" it was destined to become?

CHAPTER FOUR

Sarnoff v. Farnsworth: Round Two

1930–1940

Patently Brilliant

In the fall of 1926, with Farnsworth working around the clock in Los Angeles on his Image Dissector, and Everson looking for money up in San Francisco, other scientists were getting into the television invention game. Farnsworth was no longer alone in his quest to birth electronic TV. Classically trained scientists like Russian immigrant Vladimir Zworykin, then working for Westinghouse, were figuring out the television puzzle at precisely the same time. Farnsworth knew that all of his theorizing and experimentation wouldn't be worth a dime if he didn't have a patent. The Crockers knew that, too, and upon investing in Farnsworth's invention insisted that he file a patent application for his television system as soon as possible. It had been regaled at an earlier meeting how Alexander Graham Bell filed his patent application for the telephone with the patent office two hours before Elisha Gray filed his for the same invention. Crocker's meaning wasn't lost on Farnsworth. Had Bell been delayed just 120 minutes that day, the telephone industry would have been owned and operated by Gray.[1] "We don't want to be *him*," Farnsworth confessed to his young wife, Pem, who recounted the admission years later. This confession reflected the sentiment of all of his backers as well.

---

1 Last Lone Inventor, p 121

In December of 1926, Farnsworth took the train down to the law offices of Lyon & Lyon in Los Angeles. The two brothers practiced, among other things, patent law and there under their guidance, Farnsworth formatted his drawings, descriptions, and claims into a formal patent disclosure of an all-electronic television system. The official filing date turned out to be January 7, 1927, but after an initial review by a patent examiner in Washington, D.C., Farnsworth was notified that there were too many claims for one application. He would have to parse them out into several smaller documents.

By then, Farnsworth had retained a patent law firm in San Francisco. An associate at that firm, Donald Lippincott, an engineer who had once worked in the legal department at the Magnavox Corporation, was the man who helped shepherd Farnsworth through the process. The original application was split into three separate applications from the original one, which now focused exclusively on the television's scanning system or Image Dissector, later to be known as the television camera. Farnsworth claimed that his camera would scan a moving image and break it down into 500 horizontal lines, completing this chore 500 times every second. Joining as co-pending applications were an "Electric Oscillator System," for modulating light in accordance with the strength of the available current, and a "Television Receiving System," which was essentially the Image Dissector in reverse. The receiving system employed the Cathode Ray (or picture) tube in place of the Image Dissector (or camera) tube.[2] The description given in the original patent application for the receiving system was a virtual schematic for what came to be referred to as a television set.

While Farnsworth was hard at work developing his television system in San Francisco, Vladimir Zworykin, a 39-year-old Westinghouse engineer, was trying to get the powers that be at Westinghouse to view a demonstration of an electronic television system he'd been working on since 1923. Zworykin had tried giving the same demonstration a year earlier (1926) to his superiors, but the experimental tube that he hoped would produce a televised image had blown up at the Westinghouse plant just before the brass arrived on the scene.[3] This demonstration in 1927, like the half-dozen others before, was far from the success Zworykin had hoped it would be. While his efforts glimmered with possibilities inherent in a system based on the cathode ray tube Zworykin was using to push around his electrons, he was nevertheless told by management to "*devote his time to more practical endeavors.*"[4] In Westinghouse's defense, there were still two types of television; two ways to capture and reproduce an image—mechanical and electronic—and the government had yet to choose the working system. They simply felt that Zworykin's efforts could well prove futile and expensive. Truth be told, they were mostly right. At the time Farnsworth was granted his patent in 1930, Zworykin's patent application for the "Iconoscope" image scanner (akin to Farnsworth's "Image Dissector") was *still* pending. It would be almost another decade before Zworykin's patent was finally issued to him in 1938, and then only after numerous revisions.

---

2 Last Lone Inventor, p 123

3 History Channel Modern Marvels—"Television: Window to the World"

4 The Boy Who Invented Television, p 111

By 1928, it was obvious that Westinghouse had little faith in the idea of electronic television and Zworykin was looking to find someone who did. Frustration, he would later say, pushed him to New York and to RCA, right into the office of David Sarnoff himself. There, Zworykin pitched the idea of television at a meeting that would change the course of broadcast history. Sarnoff had an intuitive understanding of television's vast potential, but would find, over time, in Zworykin a technological soul mate capable of bringing Sarnoff's dream to life.[5] At the time of the meeting, Zworykin was developing an all-electronic television system at Westinghouse that he was sure could be realized in two years with a mere $100,000 investment. Sarnoff finally opted to fund Zworykin's research and put him in charge of television development for RCA at their newly established laboratories in Camden, New Jersey. While Sarnoff liked Zworykin's enthusiasm from the beginning, he was also well aware that Zworykin had probably underestimated the development costs of his television system by $50 million and several years in duration.[6]

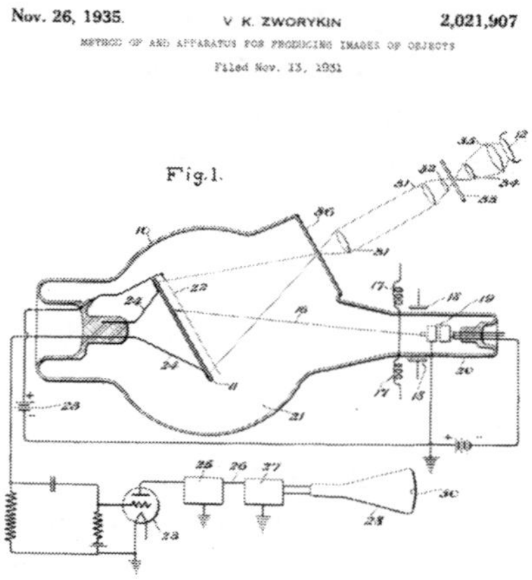

Vladimir Zworykin's "Iconoscope" patent, 1935

Upon coming to work for Sarnoff, Zworykin passed along information of what he had seen at Farnsworth's lab in San Francisco. He informed Sarnoff that he was so impressed with the young man's work that he'd given his former employers at Westinghouse sketches of Farnsworth's Image Dissector to study. Sarnoff determined that he would have to travel see "the device" for himself, so in the spring of 1931, he headed across the country to Farnsworth's Green Street lab in San Francisco. After witnessing a demonstration of Farnsworth's electronic television system, Sarnoff left unimpressed, noting that RCA already had Zworykin and his technology and would start their own brand of television on the east coast without having to infringe on Farnsworth's patents to make it work.

As soon as Sarnoff returned to RCA in New York, Farnsworth received an offer from Sarnoff and RCA to buy out Farnsworth's company (in total) for the paltry sum of $100,000 (1.4M USD 2012), with the stipulation that Farnsworth become an employee of RCA.[7] Farnsworth refused, of course, but even if he had wanted to take the job, on a purely financial level, Sarnoff's offer was hard to understand. As anxious as his partners at Crocker Bank were to see a return on their money, they'd never okay the low-ball figure Sarnoff was offering. That being obvious, the insulting offer seemed more an act of arrogance than a purchase price—and in fact it was. Remembering how much money he had paid another unknown inventor, Edwin Armstrong, ten years earlier still made Sarnoff furious. Armstrong had held RCA up for almost a quarter-million dollars and 60,000 shares of RCA stock—stock Armstrong still owned and

---

5 History Channel Modern Marvels—"Television: Window to the World"

6 Last Lone Inventor, p 180

7 Last Lone Inventor, p 181

which, by now, had made him a millionaire. And that wasn't even the worst part. Armstrong had gotten *all* the credit for the radio-amplification system for which RCA had paid him. Sarnoff had waited ten long years for another upstart inventor to take a shot at him and he was ready. Sarnoff would teach Philo Farnsworth the economic lesson of his young life.

Commercializing Television

The Philco Radio Company had demonstrated a keen ability to make radios more quickly, more cheaply, and with greater style than RCA, and the company was rewarded with a greater market share. Yet profit margins were still thin, especially in the second full year of the Great Depression, 1931—for everyone but RCA. Whatever RCA gave up in market share, it more than made up in patent licensing fees. What Philco needed from Farnsworth was a way around RCA. They might be saddled with RCA's radio patents, but Philco didn't want RCA spreading its control over television too. Thus, to Farnsworth's great delight, when Philco came knocking at his door it wasn't to buy his company. Instead, Philco wanted to take out a broad, non-exclusive license on all of Farnsworth's patents. The entire arrangement was to be kept entirely confidential. Under the terms of the secret pact, Philco would fund all of the expenses of Farnsworth's company, Television Laboratories (the company he'd formed with Crocker Bank), and pay for the relocation of Farnsworth, his family, plus five of his best engineers and their families, from San Francisco to Philadelphia.[8]

For the next two years, Farnsworth and the good folks at Philco tried to commercialize Farnsworth's television system, endeavoring to create a television set that people would actually want to buy. Meanwhile, directly across the Delaware River in Camden, New Jersey, Vladimir Zworykin and the RCA Laboratories team were making steady strides and lighting on occasional breakthroughs as they also attempted to bring commercial television to fruition. Since the distance between the two plants—RCA's in Camden, New Jersey and Philco's in Philadelphia—was less than two miles, both companies could easily pick up television signals from the other's camp.

The broadcasts were sophomoric to be sure, but Farnsworth was able to see clarity in the pictures RCA was producing; and that the quality of their image scanning was now much improved. Back across the river in Philadelphia, Philco had also won approval to open an experimental television station of its own and installed a broadcasting tower atop its Camden plant. When Farnsworth used the tower to transmit his own pictures, the RCA team on the other side of the Delaware picked up those images the same way he had first picked up theirs.[9]

---

8 Last Lone Inventor, p 184

9 Last Lone Inventor, pp 187–188

It was obvious to RCA that Philco was now poised to enter the business of commercial television, and that Farnsworth had to be behind their plan. Philco's "end run" to try to position itself in the television game was quickly squashed. It was rumored years later that when Sarnoff learned of the Farnsworth-Philco plan to commercialize television, he threatened to rescind Philco's license to produce radios under RCA's patents, which for all intents and purposes would have put Philco out of business during the grayest days of the Great Depression. While no paper trail could ever connect Sarnoff to the ultimatum given to Philco, the Philadelphia radio giant immediately severed its ties with Farnsworth.[10]

With his plan to circumvent RCA and commercialize television with another legitimate manufacturer having been stopped in its tracks, Philo Farnsworth took the only path left to him and went after RCA head-on. He'd had enough. By this time it was clear to Farnsworth that Sarnoff was behind all of this sabotage, to the detriment of Philo's hopes and dreams. Farnsworth also sensed something else. Sarnoff, a press hound, hadn't given an interview in almost a year. Farnsworth inferred from this that Sarnoff had gone into hiding to give Zworykin time to complete his experiments and produce a working television system. When that was in place, Sarnoff, having already eliminated the competition, would use Zworykin's system to corner the market on television like he had on radio.

Farnsworth wasn't going to let that happen without a fight. He would attack their patent applications and force Sarnoff and Zworykin out of hiding. With the help of Donald Lippincott, his trusted patent attorney, Farnsworth filed his 1934 suit against RCA, whom he felt sure was infringing on his work. This legal action became known as Patent Interference Number 64.027.[11] At issue was nothing less than "Who?" had invented electronic television. The Patent Office would be forced to clarify. It was quite a gamble on Farnsworth's part. After all, two-thirds of his young life had been wrapped up in his invention.

The night before the patent interference arbitration was to begin, Lippincott had an epiphany. When he awoke the following morning, he knew how to beat RCA. It would take him 14 months to accomplish the task, but Lippincott was sure he and Farnsworth would prevail. Lippincott began his opening statement by admitting that while Farnsworth's claim was incredibly broad, "all of the terms used in the count against RCA, with the single exception of the term 'electrical image' had meaning that was well understood at the time."[12] This one new term then would form the crux of the case. In a clever stroke, Lippincott submitted Zworykin's own words to help derail RCA's whole case. During one of Zworykin's earlier depositions, he'd described the term "electrical image" in the very same manner Farnsworth had.

Before RCA even knew what had happened, the case had been reduced to a simple matter of who had first come up with the term "electrical image," and who had been the first to demonstrate such an image.[13] On both counts, Farnsworth's team prevailed. While Zworykin maintained that he'd come up

10 Last Lone Inventor, p 196

11 Last Lone Inventor, p 200

12 Last Lone Inventor, p 201

13 Last Lone Inventor, p 202

with the idea in Russia, in 1917, only one witness came forward to corroborate Zworykin's findings and he was declared patently unreliable. In Farnsworth's corner, there was his tenth-grade chemistry teacher, Justin Tolman, who produced a sketch of the "television" drawings Farnsworth had left behind on the teacher's blackboard back at Rigby High School, in 1922. Additionally, Farnsworth had demonstrated his camera successfully in the fall of 1927, while Zworykin wouldn't have a working camera until 1931. While the gritty details of the case were highly technical and would keep the arbitration rolling on for months, in the end, the court held that television's "Priority of the Invention" would be awarded to Philo T. Farnsworth. The court had officially affirmed his controlling patent. At age twenty-nine, Farnsworth was now held to be the undisputed inventor of television.

Though Farnsworth's victory was immediately appealed by RCA, their appeal was ultimately turned down, but not before taking another three years off Farnsworth's 17-year patent life. In March of 1939, after another 18 months of red tape and delays related to the RCA patent appeal, the Securities and Exchange Commission (SEC) granted Farnsworth and his new company, The Farnsworth Television & Radio Corporation, its initial public offering. The offering of 600,000 shares at six dollars per share required nine brokerage houses to manage the surge of investors who gobbled up the television stock in under three hours.[14] The enthusiasm of the investors and the timing of the stock offering turned out to be serendipitous. The day following the stock sale, Hitler's Army marched into Poland and seized Czechoslovakia. Stock exchanges and brokers alike all agreed that the Farnsworth stock offering would have been canceled had they waited even one more day. After commissions and legal fees were paid to those who had earned them, FTRC received three million dollars—enough capital for Farnsworth's newly energized company to move ahead with its manufacturing plan and land itself an experienced executive to lead its way.

New York World's Fair

Edwin Nicholas officially signed on to lead FTRC in the early spring of 1939. Though Nicholas had defected from the executive ranks at RCA, he returned in short order as president of the Farnsworth Television & Radio Company to negotiate all of the past royalties RCA now owed to Farnsworth, after skating through an entire decade without paying him a dime. RCA was determined to control the television market like it did the radio market and told Nicholas that RCA owned patents and collected royalties. It never paid them. But Nicholas remained undeterred. After all, not only had RCA lost to Farnsworth in the 1934 patent suit, but it had also lost to Farnsworth on another interference case, in 1938, over RCA's Image Orthicon camera tube, which surpassed Zworykin's Iconoscope in quality. RCA had trademarked both names, but the Patent Office had ruled that the television camera was really a Farnsworth invention,

14 Last Lone Inventor, p 259

too. Nicholas recognized that RCA needed to pay Farnsworth for a license if it wanted to go on into the commercial television world and presented them with a deal.

RCA promised to look it over, but again Sarnoff was stalling. Only five years remained on the patent application Farnsworth had filed in 1927, and with the World's Fair coming to New York in late April, Sarnoff would stall a little longer. In truth, Sarnoff's motives were far more sinister than they sounded. Sarnoff knew that if RCA *paid* to Farnsworth what RCA *owed* to Farnsworth in unpaid royalties, Farnsworth would have the money needed to put up a pavilion of his own at the Fair and undercut the television market Sarnoff hoped to launch in earnest from the world exhibition. After all, 25 million visitors were expected to attend the Fair. The theme of the 1939 World's Fair was "Building the World of Tomorrow"[15] and Sarnoff intended to do just that without any interference from Farnsworth. The extravagant production was dedicated to future technology; to the things people of the future would need and use. In an odd irony, that year's Fair had positioned itself between the two darkest events of the young century: The Great Depression that was winding down, and the beginning of World War II, which was heating up. At the press conference Sarnoff held on April 20, ten days prior to the start of the Fair, he mentioned neither event, but instead shamelessly proclaimed himself the "Father of Television." At 48 years of age, Sarnoff was in command of his global enterprise and the most prestigious broadcasting network in the world. As he faced reporters, Sarnoff announced with rhetorical flourish:

> It is with a feeling of humbleness that I come to this moment announcing the birth in this country of a new art so important in its implications that it is bound to affect all society. Television is an art which shines like a torch of hope to a troubled world. It is a creative force which we must learn to utilize for the benefit of mankind. Now, ladies and gentlemen, we add sight to sound![16]

Farnsworth was also in New York during April of 1939. He'd invented the world's first incubator and his new invention was displayed by a manufacturer at one of the Fair's pavilions further down the walkway from RCA's. Farnsworth didn't know where it had been placed since he wasn't attending the Fair itself. He, of course, knew all about the RCA television pavilion and figured that seeing it would only serve to depress him, so he stayed away. Farnsworth had wanted to demonstrate his brand of television, too, but such a promotion would clearly have been too expensive for his fledgling company.

In New York City, Farnsworth was heading back to his hotel room from an FTRC board meeting he'd just attended, when he chanced to spot a row of RCA televisions in a department store window. Each held the same image on its screen—David Sarnoff speaking from the RCA pavilion at the New York World's Fair. Sarnoff was clearly taking credit for the invention of television in a way that Farnsworth knew he could never match. Worse yet, it was only through the power of television that Sarnoff was able to do

---

15 History Channel Modern Marvels—"Television: Window to the World"

16 You Tube (Retro Clip)—"Birth of TV at World's Fair"

it. Farnsworth couldn't believe what he was seeing. For Farnsworth, television was simply a tool used to bring real pictures to people; not an invention designed to subvert the truth.

In September 1939, after a decade-long legal battle, RCA finally conceded to pay a multi-year licensing agreement on Farnsworth's 1927 patent for television totaling one million dollars (16.1M USD 2012).[17] RCA, now equipped with Zworykin's television system, was free to sell electronic television sets to the public. After showcasing RCA's electronic television at the New York World's Fair, earlier in April, Sarnoff had promoted more than the RCA brand. He'd sold the world on *television* itself. Standing in front of that store window watching Sarnoff take credit for the birth of his (Farnsworth's) own invention, Farnsworth, it was said, grew quite morose. "The baby's been born with a beard," he was heard to mutter.[18] The verdict was in. Who in the country would want to buy a TV set from anyone other than RCA?

Addendum

The Farnsworth Television and Radio Corporation was purchased by International Telephone and Telegraph (ITT) in 1951. During his time at ITT, Farnsworth worked in a basement lab known as "the cave" on Pontiac Street in Fort Wayne, Indiana. From here, he introduced a number of breakthrough concepts including a defense early-warning signal, submarine detection devices, radar calibration equipment, and an infrared telescope. One of Farnsworth's most significant contributions at ITT, however, was the development of the PPI Projector, an enhancement on the iconic "circular sweep" radar display, which allowed safe control of air traffic from the ground. This system developed in the 1950's was the forerunner of today's air traffic control systems, safely guiding tens of millions of travelers to their destinations around the world.[19]

In December 1965, ITT came under pressure from its board of directors to terminate the nuclear fusion project Farnsworth had been heading and sell the Farnsworth subsidiary. A year later Farnsworth was terminated and eventually allowed medical retirement. Brigham Young University awarded Philo Farnsworth an honorary doctorate and allowed him space at the university to pursue his experiments in fusion power. For most of the last decade of his life, Philo Farnsworth would not allow the word "television" to be mentioned in his house. But on July 20, 1969, Farnsworth relented. As it came to pass, Farnsworth's Image Dissector was the camera used by Neil Armstrong and Buzz Aldrin to send shots of their moon landing from the surface of the moon back to Earth.

---

17 The History of Television, 1880 to 1941, p 209

18 History Channel Modern Marvels—"Television: Window to the World"

19 University of Utah Marriott Library Special Collections—"Biography of Philo Taylor Farnsworth"

"We were watching it," Pem Farnsworth later told a reporter. "And when Neil Armstrong landed on the moon, Phil turned to me and said, 'Pem, this has made it all worthwhile.'"[20] The final years, unfortunately, were not good ones for Philo Farnsworth. After running into money problems with the bank and tax problems with the IRS, Farnsworth took to drinking. In late February, 1971, as a consequence of his alcoholism, Philo Farnsworth became seriously ill with pneumonia and died in bed in his Utah home on March 11, 1971. Philo's wife, Pem, at his side until the end, outlived the century that her husband had forever bettered, passing from this Earth in 2006 at the age of 98.

Discussion Questions

A. Patently Brilliant

- Farnsworth's patent application was divided into three applications which covered what inventions?

- What was Sarnoff's response to witnessing first hand Farnsworth's *image dissector*?

B. Commercializing Television

- To become branded "The Inventor of Television," what legal action took place to determine the title?

C. New York World's Fair

- What did RCA's participation in the 1939 World's Fair do for the reputation of David Sarnoff?

D. Addendum

- Farnsworth's company, the Farnsworth Television and Radio Corporation, was bought by what huge conglomerate?

- What role did Farnsworth have after the acquisition?

- What 1969 milestone in human history helped to restore Farnsworth's attitude about his invention that married sight to sound?

---

20 The Last Lone Inventor, p 297

CHAPTER FIVE

Serious Programming Begins With Comedy

1925–1940

The Columbia Phonographic Broadcasting System

Just as Farnsworth had challenged Sarnoff with the invention of television for nearly twenty years, so, too, would a brash, young programming genius challenge him in television programming for the rest of David Sarnoff's life. William S. Paley, the legendary chairman of the Columbia Broadcasting System, used the sounds and images carried by radio and television waves to literally build an empire out of thin air. Bold and conservative, regal and ruthless, Bill Paley embodied the very contradictions of America itself as the country came of age in the 20th century. Paley had a nose for popular taste, an ambition that knew no bounds, and a force of personality that helped turn his ambition into reality and transform an entire era.[1]

William Paley's father, Samuel Paley, a Ukrainian Jewish immigrant, and his wife, Goldie, immigrated to Chicago in the late 1800's. By the time Bill was born in 1901, Samuel was already a successful entrepreneur in a small cigar manufacturing business he'd started with two hundred dollars.[2] All the while that Bill

1 Biography Channel—"William Paley: The Eye of CBS"
2 Once a Cigar Maker, p 308

was growing up, the Paley's lived a comfortable middle-class life. At school, Bill's appetite for attention was insatiable and rarely suppressed by family, friend, or teacher. At school, his ill-mannered demeanor became a distraction in class; and then later at home as well. Bill Paley was his father's pride and joy, but even so, Samuel wasted no time in sending his son away to military school to learn discipline before heading off to college.

While Bill Paley was a freshman at the University of Chicago, his father moved the family's cigar business to Philadelphia to avoid the cost of dealing with the labor unions in Illinois. There, Samuel Paley opened the Congress Cigar Company in 1919, hiring young women to wrap the company's high-end cigars in an effort to cut overhead. Women, after all, were paid far less at the time than men. The Cigar Workers Union called a strike in defiance of the practice, but Samuel Paley had an ace up his sleeve. Bill Paley, home from college on summer break, was tasked by his father to "charm the company women" who were out on strike into coming back to work.[3] William Paley, a man of classic style and movie-star looks, rallied the female workers at the Congress Cigar Company to return to the production line. That fall, Paley decided not to go back to the University of Chicago, but to enroll closer to home at the University of Pennsylvania's prestigious Wharton School of Finance, where he earned his degree in 1922.

The prodigal son returned home again after graduation to take an increasingly more active role in the family's growing cigar business by promoting the company's brand-name cigar, *La Palina*. In 1926, fortune struck as the Congress Cigar Company went public, selling 70,000 shares of stock at $40 per share. The Paley family suddenly went from comfortable to rich. Bill Paley's end of the public offering was one million dollars, money he would initially use to help grow the family's cigar business.

William S. Paley, CBS Founder-in-Chief, 1939

Sponsoring a local radio program with ads for his family's *La Palina* cigars, Bill Paley's career took a fateful turn. He discovered broadcasting and became enamored with the medium of radio. At the time, the only network in Philadelphia was NBC. In 1927, however, Samuel Paley was approached by a group of local businessmen looking for a deep pocket to help finance their start-up company, United Independent Broadcasters (UIB). It was the intention of the group to challenge NBC and its pit bull David Sarnoff in the Philadelphia area ... and well beyond.[4] Samuel Paley wasn't interested, and directed them instead to his son, William. Bill Paley had a sense of radio's potential and threw in with the businessmen, investing half of the $1 million he'd earned from the stock offering into UIB.[5]

3 Biography Channel—"William Paley: The Eye of CBS"
4 Biography Channel—"William Paley: The Eye of CBS"
5 Biography Channel—"William Paley: The Eye of CBS"

Paley's investment helped the UIB merge with a struggling Philadelphia-based radio network composed of sixteen small radio stations called the Columbia Phonographic Broadcasting System—one that had teetered on the verge of bankruptcy for years. Bill Paley's intention had initially been to use his broadcast acquisition as an advertising tool for promoting the family's cigar business and its prized *La Palina* brand. Soon, however, Paley discovered that "programming" was in his blood. Within a year, under Paley's leadership, cigar sales had more than doubled.

In 1928, Bill Paley used the family's cigar profits to secure a majority ownership in the CPBS network, and with the stroke of a pen he became its president. Over the next few months, Paley traveled to New York City in an attempt to contract other radio stations to his lowly network, signing 40 affiliates along the way. Over the next decade, Paley would go on to expand his network to 114 affiliate stations, changing the name of his upstart broadcast network from the Columbia Phonographic Broadcasting System to the Columbia Broadcasting System (CBS), in 1928.[6]

Black Tuesday

STAGE BROADWAY SCREEN

VARIETY

PRICE 25¢

WALL ST. LAYS AN EGG

Going Dumb Is Deadly to Hostess In Her Serious Dance Hall Profesh

DROP IN STOCKS ROPES SHOWMEN

Kidding Kissers in Talkers Burns Up Fans of Screen's Best Lovers

Hollywood Reports on Stock Market Crash, October, 1929

Between October 24, 1929 ("Black Thursday") and October 29th ("Black Tuesday"), stocks on the New York Stock Exchange lost 30% of their value and much of the country's growth and territorial gain made during an entire decade came to an abrupt and sudden halt. The stock market crash took the wind out of America's sails throwing the country into a worldwide depression for the next 15 years, and signaling the end of the "Roaring Twenties" in resounding fashion.

In May of 1930, the news worsened for RCA as the U.S. Department of Justice filed suit against the communication giant as well as against GE, AT&T, and Westinghouse.[7] The government demanded termination of the 1921 patent agreements and interlocking ownerships that existed between the broadcasting oligarchy—and the Justice Department was serious. This renewed anti-trust zeal was an obvious byproduct of the Wall Street crash six months earlier, and had come about because of the collapse of the American economy. It was because of economic

6 A Tower in Babel: A History of Broadcasting in the United States to 1933, p 68

7 *Tube of Plenty*, p 70

depression that many business scandals around the country suddenly came to light—and RCA now had one of their own. Needless to say, the four conglomerates named in the Justice Department's lawsuit were incredibly dismayed. For the past five years this complex but closely knit group had established a certain way of life, and here the Justice Department was stepping in to overturn the *monopolistic* barrel.

The Justice Department would not be deterred. They ordered that the four companies replace their 1921 patent agreements with an open patent pool and untangle their corporate liaisons, or face going to trial for as long as it took the government to do this for them. A year went by with no end in sight. Then, in the midst of the crisis, David Sarnoff, who'd been named president of RCA only weeks before the Justice Department launched its suit, emerged as the oligarchy's skilled negotiator and hammered home his favorite theme: unification.[8] The radio manufacturing facilities of GE and Westinghouse should be unified under the RCA banner. GE and Westinghouse, Sarnoff contended, would be reimbursed with RCA debentures and real estate. With AT&T no longer owning stock in RCA, its deal with the Justice Department came quickly, and was settled apart from the other three.

By the end of October, 1932, GE and Westinghouse had agreed to withdraw from the RCA and NBC boards, leaving NBC a wholly owned subsidiary of RCA. On November 21, 1932, a consent decree was signed. No longer owned by other corporations, RCA now had its own destiny in hand, owning two networks, dozens of broadcast stations, manufacturing facilities, international and ship-to-shore communication facilities, and research laboratories around the country. And at its helm was David Sarnoff, the man with the Midas touch, watching over the world of radio while preparing RCA for the tidal wave to come—television.

Golden Age of Radio

Meanwhile, over at CBS, William Paley moved quickly to solidify his network's financial footing. In the fall of 1928, Paley entered into talks with Adolph Zucor, head of Paramount Pictures, who had planned to move into radio in response to RCA's forays into motion pictures with the advent of "talkies." The deal came to fruition in September, 1929. Paramount would get 49 percent of CBS in return for a block of its stock worth $3,800,000 at the time. The agreement specified that Paramount would buy that same stock back by March 1, 1932 for a flat five million dollars provided CBS could earn two million dollars over the next 30 months.[9] For a brief time there was talk that Paley's network might be renamed "Paramount Radio," but the thought was short-lived. Three weeks later, the stock market crashed and all stock values tumbled. Yet for CBS, there was a silver lining. The market crashing like it did also served to galvanize Bill Paley and his troops into earning the two million dollars in the time allotted. Their trial-by-fire victory,

8 *Tube of Plenty*, p 69

9 A Tower in Babel: A History of Broadcasting in the United States to 1933, p 224

tempered as it was by this chaotic economic atmosphere, gave the CBS network an undeniable swagger that William Paley would soon employ to help launch the Golden Age of Radio.

To say Bill Paley fought the good fight in radio broadcasting was an understatement. He had to just to stay in business. From 1930 to 1940, it was NBC that stood at the pinnacle of American radio. A network that already had or would soon become home to many of the most popular performers and programs on the air. Al Jolson, Fred Allen, Jack Benny, Bob Hope, Edgar Bergen, and Burns and Allen all called NBC home. Same with Arturo Toscanini and his NBC Symphony Orchestra—an orchestra the network helped create. Other programs included *Fibber McGee and Molly*, *The Great Gildersleeve*, (arguably broadcasting's first spin-off program, from *Fibber McGee*), *Ma Perkins*, and *Death Valley Days*. NBC stations were often the most powerful, wattage-wise, and some even occupied unique clear-channel frequencies reaching out thousands of miles at night.[10]

Jim and Marian Jordan as Fibber McGee & Molly

Yet the radio series that started it all for NBC was one brought to the NBC Blue Network in the summer of 1929 by the sponsors of Pepsodent Toothpaste.[11] The series *Amos 'n' Andy* had already been running for over a year in Chicago on a CBS station, WMAQ, owned by the Chicago Daily News. Pepsodent found that consumers who used their toothpaste liked the Chicago-based program and decided to bring it into the national spotlight. *Amos 'n' Andy* was created and written by Freeman Gosden (as Amos) and Charles Correll (as Andy). Gosden and Correll portrayed all the male roles, performing over 170 distinct voice characterizations in the show's first decade.[12]

With the episodic suspense heightened by cliffhanger endings, *Amos 'n' Andy* reached an ever-expanding radio audience. The appeal of the two struggling title characters landed a broad audience, especially during the Great Depression. The fact that the title characters were black and that 70% of the audience tuning in to listen was white mattered not at all to the show's success. Ironically, both writers, Gosden and Correll, were white but sounded black. The writing, while racially slanderous by today's standards, is still considered by black and white critics alike to be some of the funniest work ever to appear on radio or television.

10 *New York Times*—"Red and Blue Networks of NBC To Be Split; WJZ May Be Sold" 1942 January

11 *The Pittsburgh Press*—"Amos 'n' Andy To Start New Radio Series"

12 Amos 'n' Andy—In Person, p 93

Set in Harlem, the series revolved around the Fresh Air Taxicab Company, *Incorpulated.* Word-distortion humor was a prominent element in the series.[13] The show set a standard for nearly all serialized programming in the original radio era, comedies and soap operas alike. It was the first radio program to be distributed by syndication in the United States, and by the end of its syndicated run, in August 1929, over 70 stations carried the program.

At the time Pepsodent brought the series to the NBC Blue Network, *that* NBC network was not heard on stations west of Kansas City. Western listeners, however, were complaining to NBC that they also wanted to hear the show. Thus, under special arrangements *Amos 'n' Andy* debuted coast to coast November 28, 1929, on both NBC's Blue and "Pacific Orange" networks, the latter handling everything west of the Rockies.[14] The comedy series would go on to become the first blockbuster hit of any kind in the annals of broadcast history. It was said in New York that when *Amos 'n' Andy* aired, water usage dropped dramatically as the eight o'clock hour approached, then promptly resumed at the show's conclusion.[15] Paley, whose Chicago station (WMAQ) owned the show through its first syndication run and had a chance to go national with it before NBC, admitted years later that it was one of the few mistakes in programming he could ever remember making.

Need for Legislation

By 1926, the technology and growth of radio had outpaced the existing Congressional regulation written in 1912. Back then, the term "radio" referred to ship-to-shore broadcasting. The 1912 Act had required that anyone transmitting had to first secure a license from the U.S. Commerce Department. Though it took time for this to happen, everyone finally did. After all, it was so simple. By mailing a postcard to Secretary of Commerce Herbert Hoover, anyone with a radio transmitter could get a license on a frequency chosen for them by Hoover. But therein lay the problem. In 1926, in *United States v. Zenith (Radio)*, the U.S. District Court for Illinois held for Zenith and declared that the Secretary of Commerce, in his efforts to bring order to the ether, had exceeded his authority. Hoover had been using the Radio Act of 1912 to justify his doling out transmission licenses. The District Court held that the 1912 Law conferred on Hoover no such powers.

Loosely regulated though it may have been through the early 1920's, radio's "open forum" had, by 1927, become just as chaotic as it was before 1912. With the recent District Court decision, stations were no longer beholden to the Commerce Department and began moving their radio channels to better wavelengths, increasing their power and extending their schedules. Chaos had rejoined the skies. Radio in the United States, at the time, included 15,111 amateur stations, 1,902 ship stations, 553 land stations

---

13 *Tube of Plenty*, p 56

14 United States Early Radio History—"Announcing the National Broadcasting company, Inc."

15 History Channel Modern Marvels—"Television: Window to the World"

for maritime use, and 536 broadcasting stations. For those 536 broadcasting stations, the government allocated only eighty-nine wavelengths. Geographical separation and power restrictions would make it possible to place six stations per broadcasting channel for a total of 534 stations.[16]

Congress, to its credit, finally saw the situation for what it was and passed the Radio Act of 1927. The new law transferred most of the responsibility for radio from the Department of Commerce to a newly created radio overlord named the Federal Radio Commission. The two key provisions in the act pointed first to the new government commission itself, and second to establish the Commission's mandate that radio be regulated in the "*public interest, convenience, and necessity.*"

Modeled after the Interstate Commerce Commission and the Federal Trade Commission, the Federal Radio Commission (renamed Federal Communications Commission in 1934), was to be composed of five *disinterested* commissioners nominated by the president and subject to Senate approval, to serve staggered five-year terms.[17] Each Commissioner was to represent one of the five geographical zones set up by the 1927 Act; each zone was to have equal allocations of licenses, time of operation, station power, and wavelength. Furthermore, the Commission was to regulate and control radio within the scope of their mandate so long as the Commission did not deny "free speech" to broadcasters. Having said that, however, Congress chose to limit free speech in its very next sentence by stating: "*No person within the jurisdiction of the United States shall utter any obscene, indecent, or profane language by means of radio communication.*"[18] Moreover, it was the FRC alone that would determine what language was considered objectionable.

Some saw this as an infringement of the First Amendment to the U.S. Constitution, which stated in part that the government was not to abridge the freedom of speech in the media. The FRC cared not and cracked down on "vulgar language and profanity-filled rants."[19] Then, in 1934, with the advent of television poised to enter the communication business, a recommendation was made for the establishment of a new agency that would regulate all interstate and foreign communication. On February 26, 1934, President Roosevelt sent a special message to Congress urging the creation of the Federal Communications Commission (FCC). Congress passed the Communications Act of 1934, which abolished the Federal Radio Commission and transferred jurisdiction over radio licensing to the newly created FCC. Much like the FRC, the FCC was also composed of five commissioners appointed by the President and approved by the Senate for staggered five-year terms. The 1934 Communications Act contained provisions similar to those found in the Radio Act of 1927 but went further in its scope. This change in power was needed to develop a better way of determining who got to use what radio bands and for what

---

16 Web Article: "The Radio Act of 1927 as a Product of Progressivism"

17 *Tube of Plenty*, p 58

18 Fairness Doctrine and the Media, p 33

19 Fairness Doctrine and the Media, p 35

purposes. The 1934 Act covered not only domestic radio communication, but all interstate and foreign communication by radio, telephone, and television now as well.[20]

Picture Perfect Programming

Being that NBC was the broadcast arm of radio set manufacturer RCA, David Sarnoff as its president had to make decisions both as a broadcaster and as a hardware executive, and sometimes what was good for the retail end of the business hurt the broadcast affiliates on the other. NBC's affiliates, for example, had the latest RCA equipment and were often the best-established stations with clear-channel frequencies. Yet they were still mistrustful of Sarnoff's business acumen. After all, the network-affiliate paradigm saw to it that networks charge affiliates for programming. Spikes in programming charges often accompanied pronouncements of new and better technology. It didn't take a rocket scientist to see that RCA was paying for hardware technology with broadcast dollars.

William Paley, on the other hand, had no such split loyalties. His success and that of his affiliates rose and fell with the quality of CBS programming. Programming, mind you, that only got better as CBS radio (and soon television) moved through the 1930's and 40's. It was noted by accomplished author David Halberstam that Bill Paley had a "pitch-perfect sense" of entertainment. "*A gift of the gods, an ear totally pure*," wrote Halberstam. "*He knew what was good and would sell, what was bad and would sell, and what was good and would not sell, and he never confused one with another*."[21] As the 1930's loomed ahead, Paley set about building the CBS talent stable. He was helped by the fact that in those early radio years, stars and programs commonly hopped between networks when their short-term contracts expired. Thus just as NBC had controlled much of the talent through the first ten years of radio, CBS had now begun to yank the talent reins from its hands.

If there was one thing Bill Paley had come to understand, it was that serious programming began with comedy. His network became home to many popular musical and comedy stars, among them Jack Benny in *Your Canada Dry Humorist*. Canada Dry was the beverage company sponsoring the show and Benny's humor was as dry as it got. Paley brought the two entities together for a perfect fit. Al Jolson and Burns & Allen also jumped the NBC ship for CBS, both managing to capture an even greater following at the rival network. And there was national sensation Kate Smith whom Paley personally selected for his family's *La Palina Hour*.[22] Paley loved her voice and thought it wonderful for families. But he was also savvy enough to know that marketing a face to go with the voice would be important. Paley knew that Kate Smith's wholesome, cherub-faced likeness was not a presence that would provoke jealousy in American wives. On the contrary, thousands of families invited her into their homes every Sunday on radio for the next

---

20 Encyclopedia of Television News

21 *The Powers That Be*, p 24

22 A Tower in Babel: A History of Broadcasting in the United States to 1933, p 241

ten years. Paley himself described his singer as "unthreatening to home and hearth."[23]

Wholesome Kate Smith, Paley's Choice for La Palina Hour—*Circa 1930's*

Truthfully, it didn't matter where Paley was, he never seemed to miss a thing. He programmed popular musicians, soap operas, and comedians to garner a wider audience. While in the middle of an ocean voyage, Paley heard a phonograph record of an unknown crooner and wired CBS to have young Bing Crosby signed to a network contract before Paley returned home.[24] Later he would sign Lucille Ball and Frank Sinatra to contracts. It was said of Bill Paley that he was the best "talent scout" CBS had, even though CBS was paying a dozen people to do that job. Paley could spot real talent from a raft in the middle of the ocean on a moonless night, and gave George Burns and Gracie Allen their first national radio show just to prove it.

By the late 1930's, the CBS *prime time* lineup on radio featured music, comedy, and variety shows, and continued to gain in audience share as the decade rolled on. Bill Paley had a knack for spotting talent, all right, but NBC had the resources to pay them. Thus, it became common practice for much of the talent collected by Paley to migrate over to NBC after their CBS contracts expired. For that reason, it was the smaller CBS *daytime* schedule that became critical to the company's bottom line. Bill Paley was the first to see daytime programming as a direct conduit into American homes—and thus into the hearts and minds of American women. After all, for many women in the 1930's, radio composed the bulk of their adult human contact during much of the day. Husbands and men in general were off at work or trying to find it. To their credit, CBS salesmen quickly realized that this intimate connection between women (apart from men) and female-related products could be a bonanza for advertisers, and their observations sparked in Bill Paley an epiphany.

The way the broadcast paradigm had worked through the 1920's and much of the 1930's was that affiliates paid for network programming, collected a small percentage of the national advertising revenue that helped differ their costs, then went out and found their own local advertising dollars in order to make a profit. Paley changed broadcastings business model in a couple of ways. First, of course, CBS began providing a better inventory of shows. This was paramount. But also, from a tactical standpoint, CBS began viewing advertisers as the most significant element of the broadcast equation and *not* the affiliates.[25] CBS thus began providing programming to affiliates at a break-even costs, hoping to make up lost revenue with more advertising dollars derived from better programming. The plan exceeded expectations. Stations eager for a "discount" began leaving NBC for CBS. Advertisers needing an audience

---

23 Look Now, Pay Later: The Rise of Network Broadcasting, p 69

24 *The Powers That Be*, p 26

25 Look Now, Pay Later: The Rise of Network Broadcasting, p 63

followed the CBS migration. Truly, NBC became an unwitting accomplice in the CBS plan. NBC was always raising the price of its affiliate programming, but never the percentage of advertising revenue it paid for the airwaves. Affiliates had become discouraged with NBC, and the Columbia Broadcasting System began to grow.

The growth in audience share for CBS was immediate and exponential and sent the upstart network nipping at the heels of perennial favorite NBC. As the 1940's arrived, advertisers—not affiliates—had become the CBS network's primary clientele. As CBS affiliate strength grew, so did its area of distribution for both programming and advertising. Because of the wider distribution brought on by the growing network, Paley was able to charge more for the ad time. Reciprocally speaking, CBS affiliates were required to carry programming offered by the CBS network for only *part* of the broadcast day, receiving a portion of the network's fees from advertising revenue. At other times in the broadcast day, CBS affiliates were free to offer local programming and sell local advertising, keeping all of the revenue collected in local sales.

The network–affiliate relationship between the networks and local television stations was (and still is) based upon compatible needs. No one in broadcasting saw this more clearly than William Paley. Paley realized early on that successful broadcasting, in its simplest terms, needed to get the *best* programming into as *many* households as possible—a feat best accomplished through affiliated stations in *every* television market. These local stations, in turn, needed programming to fill their schedules, which the networks could supply without any direct cash payment. In short, the network receives airtime from the affiliate, and the affiliate receives shows from the network.

Under Bill Paley's astute management, CBS saw a twentyfold increase in gross income in his first decade of his broadcasting business. Paley's recognition of how to harness broadcasting's potential reach was the key to his growing CBS from a tiny chain of regional radio stations into what would eventually become one of the world's dominant communication empires.

Early Television Broadcasts

On the third floor of the RCA Building, better known in its day as Radio City, Studio 3-H was converted for television. Though other industry leaders at the time may have thought him crazy, David Sarnoff was simply anxious to begin TV broadcasting. On July 7, 1936, using the call letters W2XBS, a highly experimental television broadcast was attempted.[26] Members of the press and ad agency executives sat in front of a bank of televisions set up in the music hall on the building's ground floor. On screen these executives saw dancers, singers, and people giving speeches, while pictures of marching troops covered

26 History Channel Modern Marvels—"Television: Window to the World"

the set changes. Performers had to wear green and purple make-up for the camera to capture their faces. Because the lights used in the broadcast were so hot, Sarnoff, who had positioned himself on the set, was forced to change his shirt three times.[27]

By late December, 1938, however, the fanfare created by the experimental television demonstrations was growing thin. Worse yet, NBC Radio was at last beginning to feel the CBS surge in popularity, and found itself trying to emulate CBS achievements in radio news and drama. RCA had been working night and day on getting television up and running and that priority had cost them dearly. The fact that Sarnoff might soon find himself in second place in a radio industry he'd helped found irritated him to no end.

And then came the brainstorm. Sarnoff would launch television's official maiden broadcast from the RCA Exhibit at the 1939 New York World's Fair. Millions of consumers would attend from all parts of America and the world and then return home to tell family and friends about what they'd seen at the World's Fair: television. Though fewer than 200 sets existed in all of New York at the time of the broadcast, Sarnoff had no doubt that number would quickly mutate into millions. RCA was not only poised to sell the medium of television, but the sets the public would need to enjoy it, as well.

Through the fall of 1939, in New York, Manhattanites could tune into regular NBC broadcasts for two full hours every week.[28] Progress, however, was slow in coming and the problems network television still faced with technology, patents, and programming were formidable. Even so, television was gradually emerging as a potent social force and Washington was taking notice. The Federal Communications Commission had been formed in 1934 to help shape radio and television. By the spring of 1940, FCC Chairman James Fly, wanting to keep a strong hand over the world of television, felt that Sarnoff and RCA had become too monopolistic. After nearly six years of careful observation, Fly took a strong stand, pushing tough, new anti-trust legislation through Congress in an effort to weaken RCA's stranglehold on the broadcast industry.

Sarnoff, who'd expected television to be in homes by the 1930's, was furious. After all, he'd spent millions in his effort to get television off the ground and now the government was again trying to hamstring him and RCA. Making matters worse, this was all coming at a time when RCA, now armed with Zworykin's television system, was ready to usher in the television era. Yet, even without government interference, the obstacles to getting television on its feet were greater than anyone knew, Sarnoff included. Television signals, for example, could be sent by coaxial cable but there was no reliable way to send the signal by broadcast. Moreover, pictures received on the few sets in existence were not sharp. Sending a consistent signal was still difficult. Engineers had to figure out how to direct TV signals through trees, around buildings, and over hills. Interference was everywhere. Even the automatic spark from an automobile engine

27 History Channel Modern Marvels—"Television: Window to the World"

28 History Channel Modern Marvels—"Television: Window to the World"

could play havoc with television signals. Worse yet, there was almost no public demand for the medium. Who needed pictures, went the cry, when you had radio?[29]

In no time at all, Congress passed the anti-trust legislation and the Federal Communications Commission moved in on NBC. The FCC found that National Broadcasting Company, its two networks, and three owned-and-operated TV stations "dominated audiences, affiliates and advertising in American radio."[30] In 1939, the FCC ordered RCA to divest itself of one of the two networks. RCA fought the divestiture order, but after losing its final appeal before the United States Supreme Court in May of 1943, RCA sold Blue Network Company, Inc., (formerly NBC Blue) to Life Savers magnate, Edward J. Noble, for eight million dollars. The sale was completed on October 12, 1943, and included the network's name, its New York studios, two-and-a half wholly owned stations and about 60 affiliates.[31] Noble, the new owner, wanted a better name for the network and acquired the rights to the "American Broadcasting Company" in late 1944. On June 15, 1945, the Blue Network Company, Inc., once composed of the original RCA radio stations, officially became known as the American Broadcasting Company (ABC).

Discussion Questions

A. The Columbia Phonographic Broadcasting System

- Bill Paley was pursuing what end when he stumbled onto the business of programming, a passion that led to the formation of CBS?

B. Black Tuesday

- What was the end result of the U.S. Justice Department's insistence in 1930 on untangling the ties between RCA, GE, AT&T and Westinghouse?

C. Golden Age of Radio

- In the '30's decade, the radio show, *Amos 'n' Andy* topped NBC's strong list of stars and shows. How was this series pivotal in the expansion of the NBC Blue network west of Kansas City, making the show a national sensation.

---

29 History Channel Modern Marvels—"Television: Window to the World"

30 *New York Times*—"Red and Blue Networks of NBC To Be Split; WJZ May Be Sold" 1942 January

31 *New York Times*—"Approves Buying of Blue Network" 1943 October

D. Need for Legislation

- With the creation of the FCC in 1934, what changes were made in radio licensing?

E. Picture Perfect Programming

- Bill Paley's knack for talent and assessment for growth included his awareness of women as a "target audience." What insights did he observe that parlayed into advertising dollars?

- As CBS gained a foothold into strong programming, what kinds of shows were appealing to radio audiences in the '40's?

F. Early Television Broadcasts

- Why wasn't early 1930's television an instant success?

- What did the 1939 anti-trust legislation do to shake up the broadcasting industry, thus causing the advent of another future giant, ABC?

CHAPTER SIX

The World at War

1935–1950

"War of the Worlds"

As war loomed over Europe in the late 1930's, Bill Paley and CBS seized on Americans' desire for news coverage of the coming conflict and strived to build a news division that would match the success of the network's entertainment division. Unlike Marconi, Farnsworth, or Sarnoff, William Paley had little interest in the technology behind either radio or television. His genius lay in programming and he quickly went about gathering up the best newsmen and dramatists available for his radio broadcasts. Reporters like Edward R. Murrow and dramatists like Orson Welles were the reason that CBS Radio was quickly gaining ground on David Sarnoff and NBC Radio. Promotion and technology had meant everything in the birth of both radio and television, but programming was how networks would come to be defined.[1]

Comedy in the 1930's and 40's was the staple of NBC, though CBS had carved out a healthy piece of that market as well. Where CBS excelled was in drama—there the network was in a league of its own. Celebrity writers of their day like Norman Corwin, Archibald MacLeish, and Orson Welles had found their

---

1 History Channel Modern Marvels—"Television: Window to the World"

stride as themes from their radio dramas seemed relevant to the times. "They Fly Through the Air," a scathing verse play on fascism, won Corwin a worldwide following. MacLeish found the same kind of success with his play "The Fall of the City," in which the author foreshadowed with startling accuracy the Nazi takeover of Vienna.[2] And then there was the Orson Welles radio production of the H.G. Wells classic "War of the Worlds" that pointed audiences and advertisers alike to the potential of radio drama.

Sunday, October 30, 1938
Orson Welles takes "War of the Worlds" Radio Drama Too Far

The show had aptly been dubbed the "Halloween Episode" in the advertising leading up the evening's performance. Welles began his Mercury Theater radio drama that October 1938 evening as he always did with an introduction to the material that would be performed. Welles finished up his dramatic soliloquy with a warning about aliens observing Earth from outer space. An announcer cut in just then from the Meridian Room in New York City's Park Plaza Hotel introducing the music of Ramón Raquello and his orchestra. In short order, the audience had forgotten that they were listening to Orson Welles and actually thought they were listening to the orchestra. It was then that the music was unexpectedly interrupted by the first in a series of simulated news bulletins about Martian landing parties destroying parts of Grover's Mill, New Jersey.

Radio listeners tuning into the program late were transformed by the event into thinking that an actual alien invasion from Mars had occurred in the New York area.[3] Compounding the issue was the fact that Welles' radio series, *Mercury Theatre on the Air*, was a "sustaining show" that the network paid for and ran without commercial breaks. This fact only added to the program's realism.

The reaction to Welles' recreation of the H.G. Wells story was simply unprecedented. The CBS telephone switchboard was immediately flooded with calls from frightened listeners and those calls continued for days. One could easily argue that Welles' simulated "radio war" sparked the reaction it did because of the national edginess over the *real* world war that was threatening to erupt in Europe.[4] A possibility to be sure. What no one could argue away was the fact that the "War of the Worlds" broadcast had confirmed the competitive standing over at CBS, serving notice to David Sarnoff and NBC that Paley was moving his network into the 1940's with class, savoir-faire, and an unbridled bravado.

2 *Tube of Plenty*, p 86

3 *New York Times*—"Radio Listeners in Panic. Taking War Drama as Fact" October 31, 1938

4 The Unfinished Nation, p 615

Birth of The Nightly News

As good as the drama was at CBS Radio, their news division would grow to be even better. The extraordinary potential of radio news had reared its head as early as 1930, when CBS suddenly found itself, quite by accident, with a live telephone feed to an Ohio State Penitentiary prisoner. The man was describing an ongoing riot as it was happening, from inside the prison.[5] For CBS, it was a journalistic coup, though no one knew enough about on-air journalism at the time to follow it up. As late as 1934, in fact, there was still no regularly scheduled newscast on network radio. The reason, early on, was twofold. First, most sponsors did not want the network news as a part of its programming. This kind of non-fiction material simply wasn't attractive enough to listeners. Those few sponsors who wanted the news included in their programming also wanted veto rights over the copy being reported. Secondly, there was the shaky détente that existed between radio and the newspapers. Newspapers saw the upstart radio business as competition on two fronts—advertising dollars and news coverage.

By 1933, many newspapers stopped publishing radio schedules in their papers. Radio, in turn, pushed back when urban department stores, most of them among the newspapers' largest advertisers and some of them owners of radio stations, themselves, threatened to withhold *their* ads from the newspapers. An 18-month truce was broken again when newspapers began editorializing on their own pages that radio should be forbidden from running news *before* 9:30 am, and only *after* 9:00 pm. Furthermore, newspapers proposed that no news story could air until it was at least twelve hours old.[6] As preposterous as these ideas may sound today, they might very well have flown in 1935, at least for a while, had not the German army begun rolling through Eastern Europe—and with it the beginning of World War II.

An early 1935 hire at CBS, Edward R. Murrow quickly became the network's Director of Talks (radio interviews), though he didn't have the job for long. The war in Europe was heating up and Murrow was dispatched to London in 1937. By 1938, CBS Radio News aired what would become the longest-lasting continuous program of any kind on radio or television in the annals of broadcast history, the *CBS World News Roundup*. The show celebrated its 70th anniversary in 2008, and still airs each morning and evening for 15 minutes on radio. But in 1938, the nightly news report was *big stuff*. The radio news hour at CBS became nothing less than the national conduit bringing Ed Murrow's gripping stories back from the War and into living rooms across America.

Once arriving in Europe, Murrow became the European News Director for CBS at a time when the growing Nazi menace underscored the need for a tough, vigorous European bureau. Murrow began assembling the staff of broadcast journalists that included Charles Collingwood and Eric Sevareid among others. These journalists would come to be known as "Murrow's Boys" because they were molded in Murrow's own image—sartorial, literate, and prima donnas, one and all.[7]

---

5 Look Now, Pay Later: The Rise of Network Broadcasting, p 105

6 The Golden Web: A History of Broadcasting in the United States, 1933–1953, p 57

7 Look Now, Pay Later: The Rise of Network Broadcasting, p 110

Edward R. Murrow Reporting from London—1943

Murrow's nightly reports from the rooftops during the dark days of the "London Blitz" galvanized American listeners. With his "manly, tormented voice," Murrow contained and mastered the panic and danger he felt, thereby communicating it all the more effectively to his audience. Using his trademark self-reference "This reporter," Murrow did not so much report news as interpret it, combining simplicity of expression with subtlety of nuance. Murrow himself said that he tried "to describe things in terms that make sense to the truck driver without insulting the intelligence of the professor."[8]

World War II also signaled Bill Paley's own coming of age. Paley wanted to help the war effort and enlisted in the army under the honorary rank of colonel. He was stationed in Algiers as a consultant to the Psychological Warfare Branch in the Office of War Information. There, he put together an Italian radio network designed to deliver Allied propaganda.

Paley's rival, David Sarnoff, joined the Allied Headquarters in London just after Paley himself had returned there from Algiers to help the OSS with what they termed *black propaganda* (what some might call *psychological warfare* or *disinformation*).[9] It didn't really matter what you called it since Paley and Sarnoff rarely met. Sarnoff had been commissioned as a general in the army (to Paley's title of colonel) and this annoyed Bill Paley to no end. Both men were put up by the military in luxury hotels (as was the custom with officers of their rank) and worked separately from one another. In time, Sarnoff, now with the Army Signal Corps, was reassigned to Paris.[10] With room to breathe away from Sarnoff, Paley found himself more and more in the company of reporter Ed Murrow. The two attended dinners and social events, and formed a close friendship, though it was easy to see that Paley needed Murrow more than Murrow needed him. After all, Edward Roscoe Murrow was revered around the world as a pillar of courage and strength and had given CBS a legitimacy it had never before had. It was easy to see that Bill Paley liked rubbing elbows with his network's first international star.

The Middle Class

By 1945, with the victorious troops coming home from the war, America was poised to enter an era of prosperity and growth unparalleled in history. Millions of Americans were eligible for the G.I. Bill allowing them to purchase homes, something no other generation, in mass, had previously had the opportunity to do. Home ownership, after all, had been a product of the rich or the nouveau riche. The timeless adage,

8 Look Now, Pay Later: The Rise of Network Broadcasting, pp 112–114

9 Biography Channel—"William Paley: The Eye of CBS"

10 Biography Channel—"William Paley: The Eye of CBS"

"a man's home is his castle" was born out of truth. And now every soldier back from the war was in line to get one. With that purchase (and the millions more that followed over the next five years) came the birth of something America had never seen before—a true Middle Class. These working stiffs may not have been wealthy enough to buy a home, but thanks to Uncle Sam, they were now entitled to finance one.

That thought alone must have brought a smile to David Sarnoff's face. Just as every G.I. returning to the states needed a home, so too was every homeowner going to need a television set to put in it. RCA would see to that.

Americans had always worked hard, but in post-war America they were playing harder too. And why not? With the middle class came another novelty—leisure time. Sarnoff felt certain that television could become one of America's favorite pastimes. After all, TV technology was progressing steadily. At RCA, Vladimir Zworykin had invented a better camera tube requiring 50% less light to capture an image. Television signals were also being improved, in part due to research generated in battlefield communications during WWII.[11]

Of course, these innovations cost plenty of money. As David Sarnoff and Bill Paley had already discovered, the invention of television hadn't come cheaply. Up through the end of 1946, television had been nothing less than a *black hole* sucking in 200 million dollars in research, development and promotion, and the dollars going out didn't look to be slowing down any time soon. Adding to the problem was the fact that by the end of 1946, only a few TV stations were on the air, and broadcasting hours were very limited. The worst part was only 44,000 American homes had a TV set, generating just under $5M dollars in TV sales.[12] This unsettling fact pointed back at the lack of programming, and the fundamental question: What were consumers really getting for their money?

NBC Televises the Excitement of VJ Day in Times Square, August 14, 1945

If you'd purchased a TV set when they first went on sale at the 1939 New York World's Fair, you'd have spent $400 on the set itself. Not so bad, you say, until one stops to remember that the mean annual income in America in 1939 was just over $1,400. Putting that dollar figure in 2012 terms where the median household income was around $50,000, you would have spent $15,000 on your television set. And that's not the worst part. What you'd have gotten for your hard-earned money would have been downright depressing—a ten-inch, black-and-white television set that was lucky to pull

11 History Channel Modern Marvels—"Television: Window to the World"

12 History Channel Modern Marvels—"Television: Window to the World"

in all three networks clearly, and only for a few hours a day. That's what the average household could expect for one-third of their annual salary. Moreover, the only way you'd know what was scheduled for that day was if you sent a postcard to RCA (or CBS or DuMont) to let them know you now had a set. RCA would send back a weekly postcard to their customers listing the network's programming schedule on their experimental TV station, W2XBS—not that there was much to watch.

Try to imagine. It's *any* Wednesday in the fall of 1939 and the programming is positively Spartan. Throughout the morning on the 200 or so 10-inch screens in existence, there's not much to see. A test pattern glowing back at you from your tiny monitor is all you'd see until 3:30 that afternoon, when NBC aired the C-movie shorts obtained from minor Hollywood studios. The test pattern returned for another three hours until the evening news with Lowell Mather at 7:00 that night—a one-camera simulcast of Lowell Thomas' 15-minute radio news broadcast. The very same newscast that one hundred million other people had paid hundreds of dollars less to *hear.* It should be noted that along with NBC, both DuMont and CBS also had experimental TV stations in New York that could be picked up on RCA TV sets. Even so, the big event that Wednesday at 8:00 pm was intercollegiate basketball telecast from Madison Square Garden on NBC.[13]

As the decade turned there were still only 2,500 viewers for RCA's station, and this at a time when the population of New York City was over seven million. To make matters worse, viewers were now divided between all *three* networks—NBC, CBS, and the DuMont Television Network owned by inventor Alan B. DuMont. DuMont's television tubes boasted 600 scan lines for added picture clarity—better than any television on the market. The same could be said about his mobile television units. So good were they that Sarnoff decided to team up with DuMont toward the end of the decade to produce the 1947 World Series.[14]

With the 1940's upon him, Sarnoff pulled in every kind of talent to grace his television cameras—entertainers, sports celebrities, and any electrifying news event he could find. The nation needed programming and Sarnoff was going to give Americans what they wanted to see. Sets were rickety. The acting was exaggerated. And the lights were so hot that the talent often sweated profusely. In NBC's *The Streets of New York* (1940), the first drama to ever air on television, the lights were so hot on the actors that bits of paper made to look like falling snow stuck to the effusively sweating actors.[15] At one point, Sarnoff brought in The Rockettes to grace his cameras, but the dancers had to be turned away because only a few could fit on the set at one time.

In general, programming was amateurish at both NBC and CBS, and included cooking shows, B-movies, and watch-the-artist-paint kinds of programs. Finding talent wasn't easy. Actors felt there was a stigma that went with television acting and that any future in it would be limited. Even the commercials that

13 Chapman University Lecture (10) – "The Business of Sports on TV," pp 4–6

14 History Channel Modern Marvels—"Television: Window to the World"

15 History Channel Modern Marvels—"Television: Window to the World"

were cut into the programs were fraught with difficulties. In one Ford ad, for example, the agency making the arty car commercial killed a bowl full of fish when the set lighting brought the water in the fish bowl to a boil. For a while it looked like television might not catch on. Programming was intermittent. Sets were expensive. Signals were weak. And as the 1940's took root, more so than anything else, radio was still the preferred choice of the masses.

In its search for that one show that would transform the television industry, NBC attempted an early excursion to the world of sports, teaming up with Gillette razor blades in 1946 to televise prize fights at Madison Square Garden for veterans in hospitals home from the war. Then, in October, 1947, NBC combined efforts with Alan DuMont to present the first-ever network telecast of the World Series. It was a classic match-up between Joltin' Joe DiMaggio's New York Yankees, and those cross-town bums from Brooklyn, the Dodgers, toasting their rookie sensation, Jackie Robinson.

Baseball player Jackie Robinson

All over New York, bars and department store windows were filled with transfixed viewers. Each game of the World Series was more dramatic than the last. Sarnoff felt certain that consumers crowded outside appliance stores watching the games on RCA television sets would surely buy one. Bill Paley happened to be one of those driving through Manhattan during the '47 Series when he spotted the gaggle of people packed in around one of the aforementioned store windows. When Paley asked his driver if he knew what it was that had captured the crowd's attention, the driver replied without fanfare: Television.

By 1948, it was obvious that what the networks needed and both networks wanted was a hit show that would make television irresistible. It should be noted at this point that the DuMont Television Network, faced with the formidable problem of how to make a profit without the benefit of an already established radio network as a base, was faltering. DuMont struggled to produce black-and-white television sets in the 1940's and 50's, even though they were generally regarded as offering the highest quality and durability. Its stellar reputation became its biggest problem. DuMont's TV's were expensive. Many of them included a built-in AM/FM radio and record player. In short, DuMont had priced himself right out of the market. In 1956, after ten years of arduous struggle, DuMont shut down his network and sold what remained of his stock and television operations to John Kluge, a wealthy philanthropist who quickly renamed his new purchase *Metromedia*.[16]

16 Look Now, Pay Later: The Rise of Network Broadcasting, pp 112–114

Paley's Talent Raids

William Paley did not have any of the top advertisers in 1947 because he didn't have any of the top-ten shows.[17] No *Fibber McGee and Molly*, no *Ma Perkins*, no *Amos 'n' Andy*. Yet no one would ever argue that Paley wasn't still the "head talent scout" of CBS. To that end, Paley led a much-publicized "talent raid" on NBC. One day, while Freeman Gosden and Charles Correll ("Amos" and "Andy" respectively) were hard at work at NBC writing their venerable show, *Amos 'n' Andy*, a knock sounded at their office door. There stood William S. Paley, himself, with an astonishing offer: Whatever the two performers were getting now from NBC, Paley would double it.[18] Gosden and Correll made the leap from NBC to CBS before Paley left the room.

Capturing NBC's cornerstone show was *coup* enough, but Paley repeated the process in 1948 with long-time NBCers Edgar Bergen and Charlie McCarthy and Red Skelton, as well as former CBS defectors Jack Benny, radio's top-rated comedian, and Burns and Allen. Paley achieved this rout with a legal agreement reminiscent of his 1928 contract that had caused some NBC station affiliates to jump ship back then and join CBS. CBS would buy the stars' names as a property in exchange for a large lump sum and a salary. The plan relied on the vastly different tax rates between income and capital gains, which meant the stars could enjoy more than twice their income after taxes.[19]

Additionally, Paley allowed his stars to use their own production companies to produce their shows—something Sarnoff over at NBC would never sanction. Sarnoff wanted NBC to produce shows for its stars because that way he would own the show and not the star. By the time Paley had completed his raid, he'd given something to David Sarnoff that had taken him twenty years to deliver: For the first time since network radio began, CBS Radio had beaten NBC Radio in the annual audience ratings game. It was a new day, indeed. The two networks licked their wounds, sharpened their swords, and again headed into contention, this time for the biggest prize of all—the television market looming dead ahead.

Earl "Madman" Muntz

After the war, monochrome television production began in earnest, but there was already a problem. Television sets were really expensive. This fact frustrated most everyone but intrigued Los Angeles used car dealer Earl "Madman" Muntz. Muntz had earned his stripes as the first lunatic car salesman to grace the airwaves over L.A., and the thought of pushing electrons instead of tin got his salesman's blood rushing. By stripping the sets of RCA and others, and then mixing their parts and tubes, Muntz had found a way to cut the cost of the RCA or Dumont or Zenith television set by 70%, bringing the price of

---

17 Biography Channel—"William Paley: The Eye of CBS"

18 Look Now, Pay Later: The Rise of Network Broadcasting, p 181

19 *Tube of Plenty*, p 84

Gracie Allen and George Burns of Burns & Allen—*From 1938*

Jack Benny Leaving NBC for CBS—1948

Lucille Ball of the CBS Radio Show, My Favorite Husband—*1948*

the average set down from $700 to less than $200.[20] Turning his spiel from cars to TV sets, Muntz had the public in a frenzy to buy. In no time, sales took off forcing RCA and the rest to cut their prices in order to compete with the Muntz TV. By the end of 1949, just 20 months after Muntz had gotten into the TV selling game, the retail television world had sold FOUR MILLION more televisions—a 900% jump in what the TV industry had done in the last twenty years combined.[21]

At the end of the day, what the networks needed was a hit show that would make television absolutely irresistible. NBC struck first. In June of 1948, NBC launched *The Texaco Star Theater* and soon hired Milton Berle as its permanent host. Earlier that spring, Berle had been a guest host on the show's freshly revived radio version and was the obvious choice for television. Berle jumped on stage in drag wearing outlandish costumes, making his face a target for pies and powder puffs, all thrown at it in the name of comedy. Early TV audiences had never seen anything like the frantic infectious energy this comic genius brought to the screen. He was a perfect fit for this maiden voyage—highly visual and way, way over the top. Polling data in 1948 indicated that virtually every TV set in America that was operating at eight o'clock on Saturday night was tuned in to Milton Berle—a ratings phenomenon never to be repeated again in the 20th century.[22] TV set ownership exploded. Berle not only sold TV sets, but he, like Sarnoff, also helped sell the medium of television to a waiting audience—a love affair with *staying power* that was destined to outlast the millennium.

---

20 History Channel Modern Marvels—"Television: Window to the World"

21 History Channel Modern Marvels—"Television: Window to the World"

22 History Channel Modern Marvels—"Television: Window to the World"

Discussion Questions

A. War of the Worlds

- Why did the CBS broadcast of Orson Welles' *War of the Worlds* cause such a panic? What did this unprecedented show illustrate to the radio programming world?

B. Birth of the Nightly News

- How did WWII affect the dissemination of news on the radio? Trace the introduction of newsman Edward R. Murrow to the early days of broadcast news.

C. The Middle Class

- Post WW II brought home GI's and gave them what opportunities to thrive?
- What televised event in 1947 stirred mounting interest in the medium of television among Americans?

D. Paley's Talent Raids

- Bill Paley at CBS raided top talent from NBC in the late forties by using what tactics?
- Who were some of the stars of this era that jumped from the NBC ship?

E. Earl 'Madman' Muntz

- What did Earl "Madman" Muntz and Milton Berle have in common in 1948 and 1949 that helped propel television into American households?

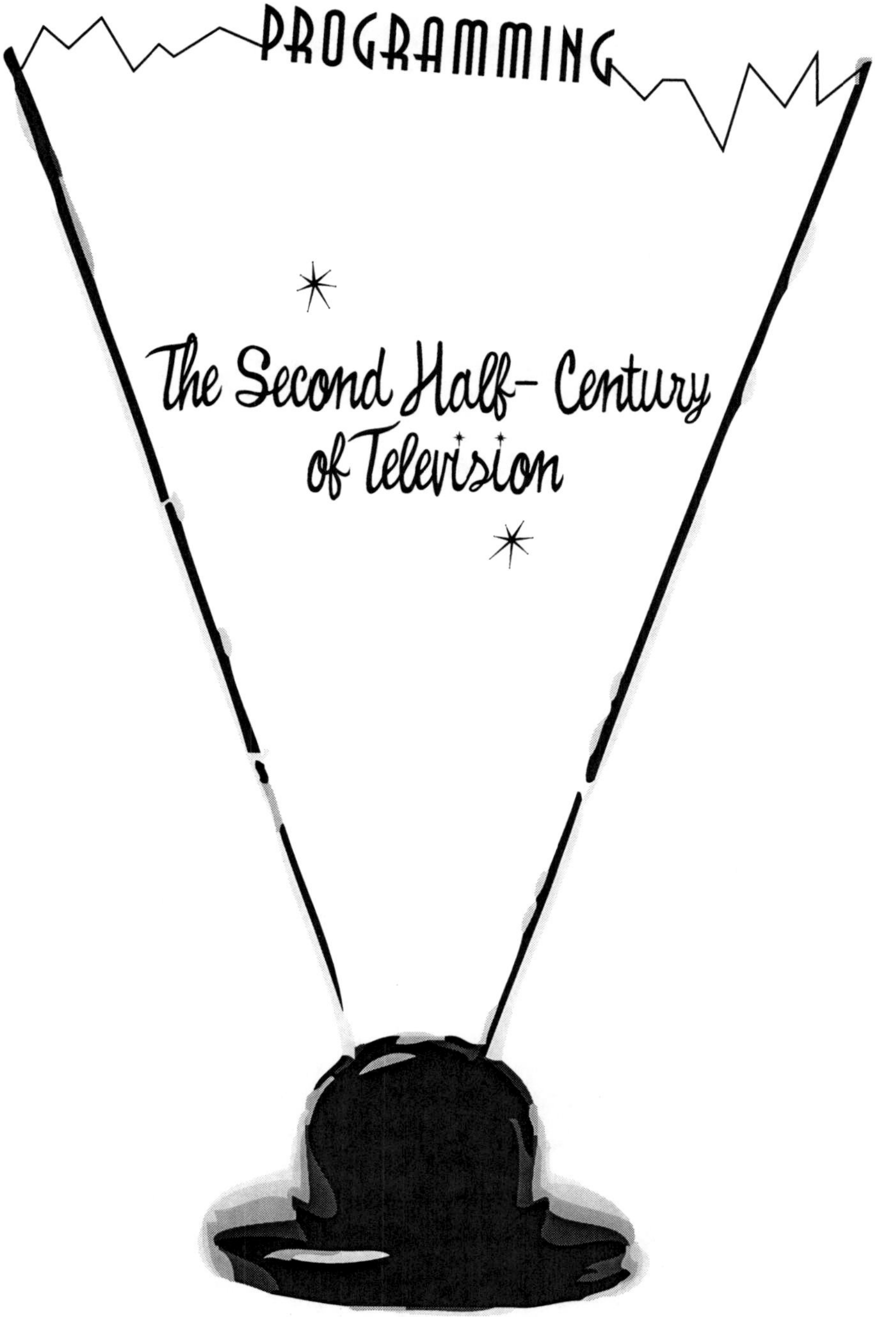

PROGRAMMING

The Second Half-Century of Television

CHAPTER SEVEN

Television's Golden Age

1948–1960

Red Scare

Television's "Golden Age" of programming certainly gave no indication it was coming anytime soon. In March of 1947, President Harry S. Truman signed into law Executive Order 9835, creating the Federal Employees Loyalty Program.[1] The Order established political-loyalty review boards whose job it was to determine the "Americanism" of federal government employees. The recommended *termination* by the review boards of those who had confessed to spying for the Soviet Union was easily understood and much appreciated. After all, we'd just fought a war beside an ally that was now turning out to be as ruthless as the enemy the Allied Armies had waged battle with and defeated. Rather, it was the review boards' treatment of those *suspected* of being "un-American" that began sparking protests.

Congress quickly entered the picture. The five-man House Un-American Activities Committee (HUAC), which had been around in various incarnations since the early 1930's, and officially sanctioned as a House Committee in May, 1938, was on the job. By 1947, the Committee, chaired now by Representative J. Parnell

1 *Tube of Plenty*, p 107

THE HOLLYWOOD TEN

Alvah Bessie
Herbert Biberman
Lester Cole
Edward Dmytryk
Ring Lardner, Jr.
John Howard Lawson
Albert Maltz
Samuel Ornitz
Adrian Scott
Dalton Trumbo

Thomas of New Jersey and featuring among its members Richard M. Nixon (R-CA),[2] was busy conducting character investigations of "American communists." These investigations, prompted by rumor, innuendo, and precious little fact, destroyed innocent lives and rattled First and Fourth Amendment rights for almost a decade.

In the fall of that year, Chairman Parnell opened public hearings on "Communism" in the Hollywood film industry—and the "witch hunt" was in full bloom. Witnesses were called before the Congressional Committee at their own expense to testify against their friends and colleagues and in some cases their own family, for fear they'd be labeled a communist sympathizer if they didn't cooperate. NBC, CBS, and ABC all had television cameras and microphones trained on and set up inside the caucus room at the House of Representatives building in Washington, D.C. Television was on the scene. America was now privy to events and people they had only heard about on radio or read about in the newspaper. TV set owners could see them live, in their living room while eating dinner. The invention was an absolute miracle. It was said that early viewers would have stared at a test pattern if that's all they had on their screen—and often enough in those first days of broadcast television they did.

Chairman Parnell was comfortable in front of the TV and newsreel cameras as was Committee member, Richard Nixon of California, soon to become the Republican Party's vice presidential nominee on the Eisenhower ticket. Committee Chairman Parnell spoke of the propaganda power of film and the need to study infiltration by those "whose loyalty is pledged in word and deed to the interests of a foreign power."[3] Ten writers from Hollywood decided not to cooperate with the Committee and became "unfriendly" witnesses. There, in front of the television cameras, under crystal chandeliers and surrounded by the press and scores of celebrities, all ten Hollywood screenwriters refused to discuss memberships of any kind, including their own affiliation with the Screen Writers Guild (later becoming the WGA). All were accused of being members of the Communist Party and thereby traitors to America. The Committee's charges amounted to little more than unsubstantiated hearsay, but they stuck none the less. "The Hollywood Ten" stood on the Constitution only to watch it buckle under the weight of those wrongly accused.

Initial reaction favored the writers. Actors, writers, directors, and many producers closed ranks, denouncing HUAC with both pen and soapbox. Speeches and written declarations abounded. Then, on November 24, 1947, a group of top film executives met at the Waldorf-Astoria Hotel in New York and decided that for the safety of the entire film industry, the *unfriendly* writers—The Hollywood Ten as it

2 *Tube of Plenty*, p 108
3 *Tube of Plenty*, p 108

were—would have to go.[4] Because of legal barriers, these writers couldn't be fired, so instead they were "suspended indefinitely." All were charged with contempt of Congress and all went to jail. The message spread quickly—radio would see to that, and now television as well. Speeches favoring the writers dropped off over night. A *blacklist* surfaced soon after alerting studios to writers, directors, and actors who might be "commie sympathizers." A few of those blacklisted found work writing under pseudonyms abroad, or ghost writing for other writers "still loyal to America." Dalton Trumbo, one of The Hollywood Ten, won two Academy Awards while blacklisted—one as a *ghost* for another *front* writer; and one was awarded to Robert Rich, Trumbo's pseudonym.

With the Hollywood Film Industry now safely in tow, HUAC was ready to take on the broadcasting business. As early as December 1947, executives and sponsors in New York City began receiving copies of a publication called *Counterattack: The Newsletter of Facts on Communism*. The weekly newsletter warned businessmen to be wary of company infiltration by "commies," "subversives" and "fifth columnists"—all three were interchangeable.[5] By the summer of 1948, while President Harry Truman was becoming the first sitting president to watch his opponent's party convention on television in the White House, the witch hunt for going on outside the White House gates was growing out of control.

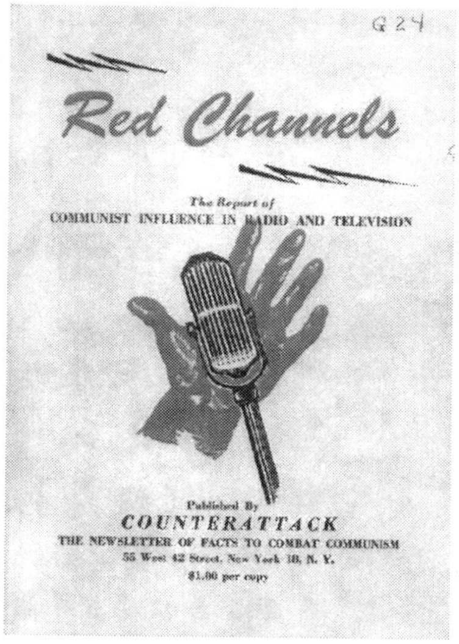

Publication produced at the height of the "Red Scare" 1950

<u>*Red Channels: The Report of Communist Influence in Radio and Television*</u> was an anti-communist treatise published in the United States at the height of the Red Scare. Issued by the right-wing journal *Counterattack* on June 22, 1950, the pamphlet-style book named 151 actors, writers, musicians, and broadcast journalists, purported to have communist manipulation of the entertainment industry. Some of those named were already being denied employment because of their political beliefs, history, or mere association with suspected subversives. *Red Channels* effectively placed the rest of the 151 names on the industry blacklist as well.[6]

4 *Tube of Plenty*, p 109
5 *Tube of Plenty*, p 122
6 Museum of Broadcast Communications website—"Blacklist"

The Goldbergs

One of the unlucky souls about to be placed on the blacklist was Philip Loeb, an actor in a leading role on the 1949 hit television show *The Goldbergs*. Defenders of the Golden Age of Television point proudly to the medium's ethnic diversity in its early years and *The Goldbergs* was certainly a part of that mosaic. As the decade turned and the 1950's arrived, there were Norwegians on CBS's *Mama*; a Lebanese father on ABC's *Make Room For Daddy*; Italians on CBS's *Life With Luigi*; a Cuban co-star on CBS's *I Love Lucy*; blacks on CBS's *Amos 'n' Andy*; and Jews on DuMont's *The Goldbergs*.[7]

Like many early TV series, *The Goldbergs* began on radio. Gertrude Berg sold her radio show to NBC in 1929 and kept it running as a 15-minute serial for the next twenty years. During that time, the radio show had made its way from NBC to CBS where it found a home on television in 1949, along with the radio show's original protagonist, Gertrude Berg. On TV, as with radio, Berg portrayed the affectionate mother and unrepentant gossip, Molly Goldberg. Early on television, everything was subject to experimentation. For the first four seasons, *The Goldbergs* was only 15 minutes long and carried three times a week. It wasn't until moving to the DuMont Network in 1954 that the series became a half-hour comedy.[8] A force to be reckoned with whether behind the camera or in front of it, Gertrude Berg won the TV Emmy Award for Best Actress in 1950. Later that year, while still at CBS, Berg was asked to sign a "loyalty oath," as was everyone else working on the series, including Philip Loeb.

Creator, writer, leading actress Gertrude Berg as Molly Goldberg on CBS's The Goldbergs*—1950*

Just before the start of the 1951 season, *The Goldbergs* became entangled in the Commie witch hunt on Capitol Hill, now in its third year, with no sign of letting up. Actor Philip Loeb, who had played Molly's husband Jake from 1949 to 1951, was accused of being a Communist sympathizer—this after signing the CBS loyalty oath. Loeb swore that he was not a member of the Communist Party and the allegations against him were never proven.[9] Even so, pressure was placed on Berg (who owned the series on television as she had on radio) to fire Loeb. When she refused, General Foods canceled their sponsorship and CBS dropped the show from its schedule. Eight months later, NBC, the show's original broadcasting home on radio, revived the series for the '52 and '53 seasons with one proviso—that Philip Loeb leave the show. Berg relented and terminated Loeb, but continued to secretly pay him his salary[10], though Loeb would never again find work as an actor.

---

7 *Hollywood Reporter*—"TV Milestones" 2004 September, p 22

8 *The Palm Beach Post*—"Have I got news for you about Molly" June 18, 1994

9 *New York Times*—"Actor Is Dropped From Video Cast" January 8, 1952

10 *The Palm Beach Post*—"Have I got news for you about Molly" June 18, 1994

RED CHANNELS' "BLACKLIST"
A ROLL OF HONOR

Larry Adler, Luther Adler, Stella Adler, Edith Atwater, Howard Bay, Ralph Bell, Leonard Bernstein, Walter Bernstein, Michael Blankfort, Marc Blitzstein, True Boardman, Millen Brand, Oscar Brand, J. Edward Bromberg, Himan Brown, John Brown, Abe Burrows, Morris Carnovsky, Vera Caspary, Edward Chodorov, Jerome Chodorov, Mady Christians, Lee J. Cobb, Marc Connelly, Aaron Copland, Norman Corwin, Howard Da Silva, Roger De Koven, Dean Dixon, Olin Downes, Alfred Drake, Paul Draper, Howard Duff, Clifford J. Durr, Richard Dyer-Bennett, Jose Ferrer, Louise Fitch, Martin Gabel, Arthur Gaeth, William S. Gailmor, John Garfield, Will Geer, Jack Gilford, Tom Glazer, Ruth Gordon, Lloyd Gough, Morton Gould, Shirley Graham, Ben Grauer, Mitchell Grayson, Horace Grenell, Uta Hagen, Dashiell Hammett, E.Y. Harburg, Robert P. Heller, Lillian Hellman, Nat Hiken, Rose Hobart, Judy Holliday, Roderick B. Holmgren, Lena Horne, Langston Hughes, Marsha Hunt, Leo Hurwitz, Charles Irving, Burl Ives, Sam Jaffe, Leon Janney, Joe Julian, Garson Kanin, George Keane, Donna Keath, Pert Kelton, Alexander Kendrick, Adelaide Klein, Felix Knight, Howard Koch, Tony Kraber, Millard Lampell, John Latouche, Arthur Laurents, Gypsy Rose Lee, Madeline Lee, Ray Lev, Philip Loeb, Ella Logan, Alan Lomax, Avon Long, Joseph Losey, Peter Lyon, Aline MacMahon, Paul Mann, Margo Myron McCormick, Paul McGrath, Burgess Meredith, Arthur Miller, Meg Mundy, Lynn Murray, Ben Myers, Dorothy Parker, Arnold Perl, Minerva Pious, Samson Raphaelson, Bernard Reis, Anne Revere, Kenneth Roberts, Earl Robinson, Edward G. Robinson, William N. Robeson, Harold Rome, Norman Rosten, Selena Royle, Coby Ruskin, Robert St. John, Hazel Scott, Pete Seeger, Lisa Sergio, Artie Shaw, Irwin Shaw, Robert Lewis Shayon, Ann Shepherd, William L. Shirer, Allan Stander, Johannes Steel, Paul Stewart, Elliot Sullivan, William Sweets, Helen Tamiris, Betty Todd, Louis Untermeyer, Hilda Vaughn, J. Raymond Walsh, Sam Wanamaker, Theodore Ward, Fredi Washington, Margaret Webster, Orson Welles, Josh White, Ireene Wicker, Betty Winkler, Martin Wolfson, Lesley Woods, Richard Yaffe.

The Goldbergs aired on NBC through those two seasons, and then on the DuMont network in 1954. The show was to run from April to October, but due to financial difficulties at DuMont, the network was unable to fulfill its five-million-dollar contract with the show, despite Nielsen ratings estimated at ten million viewers. Following the show's early cancellation in September 1955, Philip Loeb, beset by depression, signed himself into New York City's Taft Hotel, where he overdosed on sleeping pills and died alone in his room.[11]

11 *New York Times*—"Loeb Dead; Prominent Actor; Body Found in Midtown Hotel" September 2 1955

Change of Habit

By the end of 1950 there were eleven million television sets in America—up another 300% from the previous year—and all of them monochromatic.[12] It didn't matter. Nor did it matter that the reception was terrible. Or that every network was under-programmed. Americans didn't care. It was the world in their living room and that alone was mind-boggling.

The portent of America's need for television was quickly felt. Retailers like "Madman" Muntz were leaving bread-n-butter businesses to sell television sets. Lipstick maker Hazel Bishop, grossing $50,000 annually in her cosmetic business, saw her net worth soar to $4.5 million, just twelve months after selling her first TV set.[13] Yet with the yin, there was the yang. Cities receiving full television broadcasts from all four networks (including DuMont) reported waves of theater closures across the country. Live sporting events saw a sharp decline in business, too, especially boxing and baseball, since matches and games could now be seen at home.

A TV variety series starring comedy sensations Sid Caesar and Imogene Coca entitled *Your Show of Shows* became a Saturday night terror for restaurants and nightclubs in 1950. Patrons rushed home early or stayed away altogether to see the TV show. The irony was sublime. The same televisions that taverns had been using since 1946 to draw in crowds were now being used at home by the very patrons they'd hoped to attract. Television was becoming affordable and businesses outside of television were paying the price. Cities saw a drop in cab and jukebox receipts on Saturday nights in 1950. Public libraries were reporting sharp drops in book circulation as well. And then came the biggest news yet: Bob Hope's Saturday night *radio* show—a staple of every household in the 1940's—dropped from a rating of 23.8 in 1949 to 12.7 in 1951.[14] Television was rapidly encroaching on the world of radio—that was obvious. But what would it do the world of film?

That question was on the mind of every studio boss in Hollywood. Added to the terrifying statistics surrounding TV's arrival and the subsequent closure of movie houses in cities everywhere was the staggering blow delivered by the United States Supreme Court in the 1948 decision *United States v. Paramount et al.* The defendants were eight companies that had controlled the film industry: Paramount, Universal, MGM, 20th Century-Fox, RKO, Warner Brothers, United Artists, and Columbia Pictures. The Supreme Court held with the lower courts that the eight studios had kept out foreign products and prevented domestic competition by control over theaters. The high court now ordered studios that produced and distributed films must immediately divest themselves of their exhibition arms—their theater chains. The day of the studios watching the movies they produced in their own theaters was officially over. The monopoly had been broken.

---

12 History Channel Modern Marvels—"Television: Window to the World"

13 *Tube of Plenty*, p 114

14 *Tube of Plenty*, p 114

Studios, fearing they could not unload four to five hundred films per year on theaters they no longer controlled, began slashing production schedules. They canceled long-term contracts with actors, producers, writers, directors, and technicians, and looked to fire anyone who even remotely resembled a subversive. HUAC had been targeting the film business and a new wave of fear spilled over the studio lots. Artists set adrift by Hollywood began to eye television as a safer industry in which to make a living.

Spice of Life

By the fall of 1950, while "Mr. Television" (as TV star Milton Berle would come to be known) was hosting the *Texaco Star Theater* on NBC, dominating TV ratings and virtually *owning* Tuesday nights, other variety shows were finding their way into network schedules. While Tuesday belonged to Berle, Wednesday night belonged to NBC and vaudevillians Jimmy Durante, Danny Thomas, Jack Carson, and Ed Wynn performing in the *NBC All Star Revue*.

Jimmy Durante, a regular on NBC All Star Review *1950*

On Sunday night it was the *Colgate Comedy Hour* again on NBC, with Eddie Cantor, Abbott & Costello, and Dean Martin & Jerry Lewis.

And then there was Saturday night—what network programmers call "TV Night"—that one night of the week every decade where audiences can be counted on to watch TV. From 1950 through 1956, that night was Saturday and pretty much belonged to NBC and Sid Caesar and his hit comedy-variety series, *Your Show of Shows*.

Bud Abbott and Lou Costello Colgate Comedy Hour *1950*

When *Your Show of Shows* premiered February 25, 1950, its lead, Sid Caesar, was a 27-year-old rising star. He and Imogene Coca, Sid's co-star, returned to NBC to reprise comedy sketches they'd rehearsed while working on *The Admiral Broadway Revue*, another NBC show, the previous year. Carl Reiner and Howard Morris were soon added to the cast of *Your Show of Shows*, along with comedy guru Mel Brooks as one of the show's writers. In no time at all, Caesar's 90-minute variety show headlined the coveted 9 pm Saturday night time slot and soon became a network sensation. But then it should have

Sid Caesar and Imogene Coca's Sketch Comedy on NBC's Your Show of Shows*—1950–'54*

been. Look who Sid had writing for him—Mel Brooks (*The Producers*); Tony Award–winning writer from Broadway, Danny Simon and his Academy Award–winning older brother Neil Simon (*The Goodbye Girl*); and Selma Diamond and Mel Tolken, arguably the two best "unknown" television writers of their day.[15]

By the time its final show aired June 5, 1954, Sid Caesar was television's King of Saturday Night. In 1952, *Your Show of Shows* won three of the six Emmys presented, including Best Variety Show and Best Actor for Caesar. The next season, 1953, it was again named Best Variety Show. While *Your Show of Shows* wrapped up production in March of 1954, Sid Caesar didn't miss a beat. *The Caesar Hour* debuted in September of '54, again on NBC, and added Broadway star Nanette Fabray to a cast that already included Reiner and Morris. *The Caesar Hour* ran for three seasons, only to be replaced in stride by *Sid Caesar's Chevy Show*, which aired from 1958 to 1967, with writers Woody Allen and Larry Gelbart manning the scripts. Even into the 1990's, Caesar was still at the top of his game—and proved it in 1995 when he was Emmy-nominated for the twelfth and thirteenth times in his illustrious career for his guest appearances on another NBC comedy, *Mad About You.*[16]

The DuMont Network countered NBC in 1950 with its own variety series, *Cavalcade of Stars*, featuring Jackie Gleason and Art Carney. The show was broadcast live in front of a theater audience, and offered the same kind of vaudevillian entertainment common to early-TV revues. Production values were decent but not spectacular, owing to DuMont's humble facilities and a thrifty sponsor. By 1952, CBS president William Paley offered Gleason a heftier salary, one which DuMont could not hope to match. The series was re-titled *The Jackie Gleason Show* and premiered on CBS on September 20, 1952. The show typically opened with a monologue from Gleason, followed by sketch comedy involving Gleason and a number of regular performers, including Art Carney. By far the most memorable and popular of Gleason's characters was the Brooklyn blowhard, Ralph Kramden, a bus driver featured originally in a series of *Cavalcade* ... skits known as "The Honeymooners." The skits were so popular that in 1955 Gleason suspended the variety format and filmed *The Honeymooners* as a regular half-hour sitcom—and television's first spin-off.[17]

The CBS series revolved around two blue-collar workers and their wives—Ralph and Alice Kramden, and Ed and Trixie Norton. Kramden was a bombastic bus driver who lived inside a cold-water flat in

---

15 Encyclopedia Britannica ('93 ed.)—"Television in the United States"

16 Caesar's Hours: My Life in Comedy, with Love and Laughter, appendix

17 The Honeymooners' Companion—The Kramdens and the Nortons Revisited

a rundown Brooklyn duplex. Most of the shows were set in Kramden's dreary kitchen with his long-suffering but sharp-tongued wife, Alice, just a floor beneath Ed, a sewer worker, and his supportive wife Trixie.

Joyce Randolph and Art Carney star with Audrey Meadows and Jackie Gleason in CBS's The Honeymooners—*1955*

The two couples were not newlyweds as the title of the series suggested, but rather couples approaching middle age, making the show's title tongue-in-cheek.[18] Ralph was a portly loud-mouth—a colorful loser who was always looking to get rich quick. Alice, his pragmatic wife, was constantly bringing Ralph back to reality. Audrey Meadows did a masterful job as the stone-faced Alice, while Joyce Randolph played Trixie, and Art Carney played Ed Norton, the sanitation worker, who was always getting caught up in one of Ralph's schemes.

Red Skeleton as Freddie the Freeloader, right. Host of The Red Skelton Show, *1951–1970 on NBC and CBS*

Although initially a ratings success and the number-two show in America during its first season (1955), *The Honeymooners* faced stiff competition from *The Perry Como Show* and eventually dropped to nineteenth the following year, ending its production after only 39 episodes—now referred to as the "Classic 39." These "classic" episodes were subsequently rerun constantly in syndication, often five nights a week, with the cycle repeating every two months for decades. The 39 shows are probably the most familiar body of work from 1950's television, with the possible exception of episodes from *I Love Lucy*.[19]

Toast of the Town

As television settled into the 1950's, it might have appeared that NBC was in the catbird seat when it came to variety shows, but that was far from true. CBS had two hit variety shows that pitched their unique brand of comedy skits and musical numbers for parts of four continuous decades. Devoted fans made both series a Top Ten show,

---

18 Encyclopedia of 20th Century American Television, p 161
19 The Encyclopedia of 20th Century American Television, p 161

Kingmaker Ed Sullivan, host of The Ed Sullivan Show *on CBS 1949–1971*

year after year after year. One was *The Red Skelton Show*, hosted by the first entertainment star to have a weekly series on television, Red Skelton.

A visual comic, Skelton was perfectly suited for television, though many of the characters had long since been developed for radio, where Skelton debuted in 1937.[20] From 1941 to 1953, Skelton had his own radio show and was already a leading film comedian when he began his TV career on NBC in 1951. For the next 20 years, Skelton etched his gift for pantomime and his many memorable characterizations into the public mind with characters like Freddie the Freeloader and Clem Kadiddlehopper, Sheriff Deadeye and Cauliflower McPugg on the long-running variety series *The Red Skelton Show*. The series aired first on NBC from 1951 to 1953, then on CBS from 1953 to 1970.[21]

Across the country in New York, CBS clung to a second gem in the variety arsenal even more tightly than it did the first. From 1949 until its cancellation in 1971, *Toast of the Town* (known to most as *The Ed Sullivan Show*, which became the show's official title in 1955) ran on CBS every Sunday night from 8 to 9 pm, and is one of the very few prime time shows to have been run in the same weekly time slot, on the same day and at the same network, for more than two decades. Gathering around the television set to watch Ed Sullivan became an American family pastime. Sullivan was regarded as a kingmaker and an appearance on his program was practically a guarantee of stardom.[22]

Yet Ed Sullivan, himself a mega-television star, almost never happened. Critics to this day argue that Ed Sullivan's even making it to the airwaves spoke to the infancy of TV; the fact that audiences and producers alike just didn't know better. Ed Sullivan looked like the runner-up in a Humphrey Bogart-imitates-Richard Nixon contest. But that wasn't the worst part. It wasn't that he just looked stiff on stage, Sullivan really had a difficult time introducing his acts. He once heralded Massachusetts-born singer Robert Goulet as a Canadian. He turned clarinetist Benny Goodman into a trumpeter, then mistakenly introduced nationally syndicated columnist Walter Winchell as a sports star.[23] Yet what Sullivan may have lacked in on-air persona, he more than made up for with his reporter's instincts to jump on timely subjects, and a willingness to fly anywhere in the world to shag down an act. Elvis Presley, the Rolling Stones, and the Beatles were just a few of the world-class acts that illuminated his stage.

---

20 A Critical History of Television's The Red Skelton Show, 1951–1971, p 190

21 The News-Dispatch—"TV in Review" February 20, 1970

22 *Tube of Plenty*, p118

23 *Fifty Years of Television*, p 53

The variety show formula was a perfect fit for Sullivan. As the series prospered, even Sullivan's performing deficiencies became assets. Because he was a New York theater columnist whose columns were carried in the *New York Daily News*, Sullivan could give away "column items" in the form of favorable print to his guests—perks, as it were—in order to get the acts on his TV show.

The Beatles perform "A Hard Day's Night" on The Ed Sullivan Show, *1965*

One night in 1949, however, the powerful TV locomotive that would one day become *The Ed Sullivan Show* almost derailed before it ever left the station. Sullivan had booked a dancer named Paul Draper for a *Toast of the Town* performance. The Ford Motor Company sponsored Sullivan's show and word had come to them that Draper was a communist sympathizer. Draper, like so many others, denied any affiliation whatsoever with the Communist Party. After first checking with Ford and its ad agency, Sullivan decided to take Draper at his word and have him on the program.

While the incident speaks to Sullivan's courage, it also proved how intrusive HUAC was becoming to American workforce. The backlash to Paul Draper being allowed to come on the show was unanticipated. Sullivan was forced to hire a public relations firm to handle the fallout. To CBS's great relief, Ford, the show's sponsor, was staying put. Nevertheless, Sullivan was spooked. If Ford had run, the show would've died right then and there. Heeding a suggestion from William Paley himself, Sullivan turned to Theodore Kirkpatrick, publisher of *Counterattack*, for guidance as to which acts were safe for the show. Quickly, Sullivan and *Counterattack* melded themselves into an unholy alliance. *Counterattack* kept the wolves away from the show, and Sullivan asserted in his newspaper column that *Counterattack* was doing a magnificent job and that a publication exposing the "commie conspiracy" would be out soon. *The Red Channels Report* came out with "the blacklist" the very next day.[24]

See It Now

By the 1952 presidential election, the House Committee on Un-American Activities (HUAC) had become pervasively omnipotent in American society. So too had the junior senator from Wisconsin, Joseph McCarthy. McCarthy experienced a meteoric rise in national profile following a 1950 speech (*The Wheeling Speech*) he'd given to the Republican Woman's Club of Wheeling, West Virginia. There he produced a piece of paper that McCarthy claimed contained a list of known communists working

24 *Tube of Plenty*, p 122

for the State Department.[25] At the time of McCarthy's 1950's West Virginia speech, communism had become a growing concern in the United States. This concern was exacerbated by the fall of China to the Communists in 1948, the civil war in Korea in 1950, and the Soviets' development of the atomic bomb. Yet, as good as his original intentions might have been, Senator McCarthy's zeal over the next three years to uncover subversion led to disturbing excesses. The means he used fell woefully short of justifying any of his ends. His interrogation tactics destroyed careers and ruined families—and other senators began hearing about it from their constituents.

By 1953, beginning with McCarthy's second term as senator, Republican leaders were growing wary of his witch hunt tactics and gave him chairmanship of the Senate Committee on Government Operations, hoping to quiet him down by tying him to a dull committee that got little fanfare and could do no harm. However, the Committee on Government Operations included the Senate Permanent Subcommittee on Investigations—something the Republican Senate leaders had overlooked. This subcommittee's mandate was sufficiently flexible to allow McCarthy to use it for his own investigations of in government. Given the sensational nature of McCarthy's charges against the State Department, the Wheeling Speech soon attracted a flood of press interest in McCarthy. From 1950 until his death in 1957, Joe McCarthy exploited the fear of communism. His accusations received wide publicity, increased his approval rating, and gained him a powerful national following. McCarthy's methods also brought on the disapproval and opposition of many. Barely a month after McCarthy's Wheeling speech, the term "McCarthyism" was coined.[26] The word became a synonym for demagoguery, defamation, and mudslinging.

Censured by Congress
Senator Joseph McCarthy (R-WI)
circa 1954

Over at CBS News, Ed Murrow had seen and heard enough. *See It Now* was the first of the prime time news shows to focus on the growing number of controversial issues in the 1950's. At CBS, the news division was revered, and that sentiment filtered down from Bill Paley himself. That said, the relationship between Paley and his news staff was not always smooth. His friendship with Ed Murrow, by then a vice president of CBS, suffered during the 1950's. Paley respected Murrow as a journalist, but bristled over the hard-hitting tone of the Murrow-hosted *See It Now* series.

The show best remembered from the series was the show that criticized the Red Scare and contributed to the political downfall of Senator Joseph McCarthy. Murrow produced a number of episodes of the

25 The Great Fear: The Anti-Communist Purge Under Truman and Eisenhower, pp 311–314

26 The Politics of Fear: Joseph R. McCarthy and the Senate, p 49

Ed Murrow's Eloquent Close to His See It Now Show on Joe McCarthy, March 9, 1954

No one familiar with the history of this country can deny that congressional committees are useful. It is necessary to investigate before legislating, but the line between investigating and persecuting is a very fine one and the junior Senator from Wisconsin has stepped over it repeatedly. His primary achievement has been in confusing the public mind, as between the internal and the external threats of Communism. We must not confuse dissent with disloyalty. We must remember always that accusation is not proof and that conviction depends upon evidence and due process of law. We will not walk in fear, nor will not be driven by fear into an age of unreason, if we dig deep in our history and remember that we are not descended from fearful men—not from men who feared to write, to speak, to associate and to defend causes that were, for the moment, unpopular.

This is no time for men who oppose Senator McCarthy's methods to keep silent, or for those who approve. We can deny our heritage and our history, but we cannot escape responsibility for the result. As a nation we have come into our full inheritance at a tender age. We proclaim ourselves the defenders of freedom, wherever it continues to exist in the world, but we cannot defend freedom abroad by deserting it at home. The actions of the junior Senator from Wisconsin have caused alarm and dismay amongst our allies abroad, and given considerable comfort to our enemies. And whose fault is that? Not really his. He didn't create this situation of fear; he merely exploited it—and rather successfully. Cassius was right. "The fault, dear Brutus, is not in our stars, but in ourselves."

Good night, and good luck.

show that dealt with the "Communist Witch Hunts." On March 9, 1954, however, Murrow gave to the American people what has been referred to as television's finest hour. By using recordings of McCarthy interrogating witnesses and stumping speeches, Murrow displayed what he felt was the key danger to democracy—not suspected communists, but McCarthy's actions themselves. As Murrow said in his tailpiece:

> No one familiar with the history of his country can deny that Congressional committees are useful. It is necessary to investigate before legislating. But the line between investigating and persecuting is a very fine one, and the junior senator from Wisconsin has stepped over it repeatedly ...[27]

The broadcast provoked tens of thousands of letters, telegrams, and phone calls to CBS headquarters running 15 to 1 in favor of Murrow. McCarthy had risen into national prominence on the back of a list

27 See it Now—Transcript: March 9, 1954 Show

of names he had said belonged to a spy ring employed in the State Department—an allegation he was never able to prove.[28]

In succeeding months, McCarthy made additional accusations of Communist infiltration into the State Department, the administration of President Harry S. Truman, and the United States Army. He also used charges of communism, communist sympathies, or disloyalty to attack rival politicians and other individuals inside and outside of government. With the highly publicized Army–McCarthy hearings of 1954, however, McCarthy's support and popularity began to fade. On December 2, 1954, the Senate voted to censure Senator McCarthy, making him one of the few senators ever to be disciplined in this fashion.

Even so, network sponsors were uneasy about Murrow's March 9 airing of *See It Now*, as well as with other controversial topics of the series, leading Paley to worry about lost revenue. Unwelcome scrutiny during the era of *McCarthyism* was to be avoided at all costs. When Alcoa withdrew its sponsorship of *See It Now* in 1955, Paley used the event to drop the program's Tuesday night broadcast, though the show would continue as a series of special reports for the next few years. The move ultimately cost Paley his relationship with Murrow, tearing the fabric of the 20-year friendship that he and the journalist had forged during WWII.

Boon

Truthfully, even if CBS had not canceled Murrow's series, the quiz-show phenomenon that took the world of television by storm in the mid-1950's, would have eventually sunk the show. Murrow knew that the days of *See It Now* as a Tuesday-night fixture on CBS were numbered. Frightened by the Cold War being waged between the United States and the Soviet Union outside the insulated walls of network television, audiences turned more and more to television shows produced inside those walls to distract them from the concerns of the day. Audiences wanted to be entertained—it was as simple as that.

Television heard the call and rallied with more than just the quiz shows. Familiar faces from the silver screen brought in audiences and vested them in an array of westerns, crime dramas, and absurd comedies—all seen in no-frills black and white. There was *The Bob Cummings Show* starring (Who else?) Bob Cummings. Phil Silvers, Eve Arden, and Donna Reed had their own series. Same with Bob Hope, Ann Sothern, Danny Thomas, and Robert Young. Jack Webb had *Dragnet. Perry Mason* had Raymond Burr. *The Real McCoys* had Walter Brennan. And *Lassie* had … well, Lassie. A run of family sitcoms gave suburbanites a picture of how idyllic households *should* look; how parents could get along with their kids no matter what.

28 Reds: McCarthyism in Twentieth-Century America, p 489

The Adventures of Ozzie & Harriet; 435 episodes in 14 seasons on ABC

One of those situation-comedies, however, that was not entirely of this ilk was *The Adventures of Ozzie & Harriet.* The series ran from 1952 through 1966, for a whopping 435 episodes (a sitcom record lasting 42 years until broken by *The Simpsons*).[29] In truth, it might also stand as America's first *voyeuristic* reality series of all time (the G-rated version of *Keeping Up With the Kardashians*). Rather than feature actors playing the role of parents and kids, Ozzie and Harriet and David and Ricky Nelson were actually a family. Unlike *the Kardashians*, however, *Ozzie & Harriet* was scripted. Like many shows of the day, this comedy also began on radio, in 1944, with real actors playing the boys (David and Ricky) until the real Nelson kids were added to the show in 1949.

When *Ozzie & Harriet* moved to television, Ozzie received an unprecedented 10-year contract from ABC to write, direct, produce, and star in the series. The show's concept wasn't all that different from the aforementioned family comedies. There was still the utopian vision of the American family; Ozzie's cardigan sweaters and Harriet's ankle-length dresses all wrapped up in some simple moral lesson. The difference with the Nelsons, however, was that the family presenting these notions was real—and that reality added another layer to the mix that helped make the series' weekly morality play seem more relatable to viewers.

The 1950's, in a word, was a *boon* for television and the medium proved to be a powerful influence on American society. While the beginning of the decade saw only 9% of U.S. households owning a television, over half of American homes had purchased one by 1954; and 86% of U.S. households owned one by the end of the decade.[30] During this time, as a consequence of the Cold War (1945–1991), the United States was heavily engaged in a technology race with the Soviet Union. The Cold War referred to a continuing state of political and military tension between the powers of the Western world, led by the United States and its NATO allies, and the communist world, led by the Soviet Union and its satellite states. American military and political dominance was bolstered by our nation's ability to harness atomic power.[31] This focus on technological superiority contributed to more than just national security. College students plastered posters of Einstein on their dorm room walls. Every school kid wanted to be an astronaut. A national reverence for intelligence and knowledge was permeating the land and TV was picking up on the trend.

---

29 *Hollywood Reporter*—"TV Milestones" 2004 September, p 27

30 Fifties Television: The Industry and Its Critics, p 67

31 Fifties Television: The Industry and Its Critics, p 94

Scandal

Groucho Marx from NBC's You Bet Your Life 1950–'61

It was against this backdrop that quiz shows in the 1950's became popular. Each was 30 minutes long and all were relatively cheap to produce. Questions asked of contestants required substantial knowledge across a broad range of topics. The spectacle of people achieving huge financial success through the exercise of brain power was riveting to a nation that still revered intellectualism as much as wealth.

Oddly, one of the first quiz shows to successfully take to the airwaves wasn't much of a quiz show at all—not in the traditional sense, anyway. The NBC game show *You Bet Your Life* featured Groucho Marx as the show's Master of Ceremonies and ran for eleven seasons, beginning in 1950. *You Bet Your Life* was more of an iconic Groucho Marx performance with a few questions tacked on. Very little money was doled out on the show, but no one seemed to care—even the contestants. It was Groucho's razor-sharp wit and comic bantering that viewers tuned in every week to see and did so until 1961.

The $64,000 Question (475,000 USD 2012), debuting June 7, 1955, was a different story. Its pedigree was tied to a successful radio quiz show of the 1930's and 40's, *Take It or Leave It*, later to be re-titled (on radio): *The $64 Question*. With the top prize now ONE THOUSAND times its predecessor, the radio show's leap into television was no gradual escalation. Today, of course, many quiz and game shows hand out million-dollar prizes to winners, but that wasn't the case in 1955. No other game show came close to the prize money CBS was awarding to contestants on *The $64,000 Question*. So popular was the show that its title became a national catchphrase: "That's the $64,000 question ..." was a common quip of the day. *I've Got A Secret, What's My Line, Queen For A Day, To Tell The Truth, The Price is Right*—all of these quiz shows gave out lowbrow gifts like refrigerators, toasters, and cash prizes in the hundreds of dollars, not thousands.

On *What's My Line*, contestants received just $5 for each question that stumped a panelist, for a total of $50 should the contestant completely baffle the stars.[32] If that were the case, today (where the average haul for winners is well into five figures leading up to a million-dollar payday), try for a moment to imagine a game show like ABC's *Who Wants to Be a Millionaire?* suddenly offering their contestants millions of dollars against a BILLION dollar payday. What show would you rather be a contestant on? What series would you want to watch?

In September, 1956, two guys asked those same questions and decided they'd up the ante. Conceived by the quiz show's host Jack Barry and his producing partner Dan Enright, *Twenty-One* was a 30-minute

32 The Encyclopedia of 20th Century American Television, p 388

series they were certain would steal viewers away from CBS and *The $64,000 Question*. The two men had designed the game so that there was no prize-winning ceiling. The more rounds you won, the more money you won. The sky was virtually the limit.

Relative to the general stodginess that embraced the 1950's, *Twenty-One* had a more modern feel to it. Two contestants—a champion and an opponent—were both placed in separate but stylish isolation booths wearing headphones, arranged so they could neither see nor hear each other or the audience. The studio lighting had been designed to hit the booths' glass in such a way that made it impossible to see out. The host then revealed the category for that round of questions and asked the challenger to pick a point value to play for, ranging from one to eleven. The higher the point value, the tougher the question. A correct answer added those points to the contestant's score, while an incorrect one deducted them. The object of the game was to be the first contestant to get to twenty-one points.

Enright, the show's producer, had primed the executives from Geritol, the show's sponsor, with promises of high Nielsen ratings on opening night, but those ratings failed to materialize. The initial broadcast of *Twenty-One* was played fairly, with no manipulation of the game by the producers. The result proved to be (in Dan Enright's own words) "a dismal failure."[33] The only thing the first two contestants succeeded in doing was making a mockery of the show's format by how little the two really knew. Show sponsor Geritol, witnessing first-hand this opening-night catastrophe, reportedly became furious with the results and threatened to pull their sponsorship of the show if it happened again.

Enright and Barry got the message. Enright would rig the show. Although Barry claimed he was never privy to this knowledge, he certainly played a part in the overall fraud. The result found that *Twenty-One* was not merely "fixed," it was practically choreographed. Contestants became willing partners in the deception and were given instruction as to how to dress, what to say, when to say it, what questions to answer, what questions to miss, even when to mop their brows in their isolation booths. The show's numbers immediately improved, but on December 5 1956, they skyrocketed.

Lawyer Vivienne Nearing "defeats" reigning champion Charles Van Doren as Jack Berry moderates on NBC's Twenty-One, *1957*

Charles Van Doren, a polite, telegenic professor from Columbia University arrived on the show to challenge and defeat their reigning *Twenty-One* champion, Herb Stempel. Stempel, a dominant contestant, though somewhat unpopular with viewers, was getting on the sponsor's nerves. Worse, the show's ratings were dipping and Geritol wanted Stempel gone. Stempel's

33 *Fifty Years of Television*, p 111

exit was as scripted as all of the previous episodes he'd been on, and he was promised "a future in television" to bow out gracefully. Van Doren, still an innocent at this point, knew nothing of the ruse.

By January, 1957, that had all changed. Van Doren was well into a 14-week winning streak that ultimately earned him more than $129,000 (1,000,000 USD 2012) on a quiz show he was secretly helping to rig. His winning ways made him famous. On February 11, 1957, Van Doren's face graced the cover of *Time* magazine. By the time his run came to an end one month later, Van Doren had almost doubled the previous prize-winning record set by Herb Stempel. Van Doren's loss to Vivienne Nearing, a lawyer whose husband Van Doren had previously beaten, was "unscripted" and took the sponsors at Geritol by complete surprise. Van Doren would later admit that the cheating had weighed heavily on his conscience and that he simply wanted out. NBC, oblivious to the cheating going on right under their noses, signed Van Doren to a three-year contract.

The *Time* cover, the money and fame, and now a three-year contract—this was too much for Herb Stempel to take. He was jealous. Within weeks of Van Doren's "retirement" from the show, Stempel began making accusations that he had been coached by the show's producer, Dan Enright, to intentionally lose to Van Doren. Initially, Stempel was dismissed as a sore loser. It wasn't until the fall of 1958 when another *Twenty-One* contestant, James Snodgrass, emerged to bolster Stempel's claim. Snodgrass had also received the answers prior to each contest, but unlike the others, he had thought to send registered letters to himself, each one containing the answers-in-advance for that week's show. The unopened, time-stamped letters presented to prosecutors served as irrefutable evidence.

By October 1958, the story was everywhere. Nielsen ratings attached to quiz shows were plummeting. Networks found themselves apologizing for a scandal they maintained they knew nothing about. NBC's *Twenty-One* was immediately canceled. Same with the CBS quiz show *Dotto*—and for the same reason: It was rigged. Congress soon saw the political opportunity the scandal offered, and in the fall of 1959, the House Committee on Legislative Oversight began to hold hearings as they investigated the Quiz Show Scandal. Stempel, Snodgrass, and child actress Patty Duke who'd been a contestant on another game show, all testified that they'd been coached by the producers to ensure they knew the answers in advance.[34]

On November 2nd of that year, Van Doren took the stand before the Congressional Committee and admitted that he, too, had been deeply involved in the quiz show deception. While Congress would quickly pass legislation prohibiting the fixing of quiz shows of any kind, no one involved in the scandals served a day in prison. The actions of Enright and Barry, while disreputable, were not illegal at the time. Truth of the matter was, neither man could understand the uproar. To them it was a win-win-win-win situation. Geritol profits doubled while Van Doren was on the show, and where was the harm in that? NBC's Nielsen rating for the half hour rose right along with profits. The audience tuning in was thoroughly

34 The New Yorker—"All the Answers: The quiz-show scandals--and the aftermath" July 28, 2008

entertained and the contestants left the show wealthier than when they arrived.[35] Or so went their argument.

Truly, the biggest change resulting from the Quiz Show Scandal was the change in the paradigm that had existed between networks and sponsors in the 1950's. Throughout the decade it was the sponsor who pitched shows to the network and financed the series, much like any studio would do today. But if something went bad with the series—and in the case of the quiz shows, something did—it was the network's license that was at stake, not the sponsor's. The sponsor simply moved to another network while the old network paid the price. The quiz show scandals exhibited the necessity for stronger network control over programming and production; and over television advertising as it impacted licensing, scheduling, and sponsorship of programs.[36] By the mid-1960's, the networks were producing all of their own shows. Sponsors, who once pitched and owned the shows, found themselves on the sidelines forced to buy their advertising like they did in magazines, a little (30-second TV spots) at a time.

The Anthologies

Considered one of the finest programs ever presented to television, *Playhouse 90* was a dramatic anthology series that offered its CBS audience 90 minutes of outstanding drama each week, from 1956 through 1961. The class of the airwaves for the last half of the decade, *Playhouse 90* helped raise the bar on programming across the TV spectrum and helped brand CBS as the network of class and taste—"The Tiffany Network"—a handle it proudly acknowledged for the duration of the twentieth century.

Anthology shows had been around for years on radio with suspense thrillers in the vein of *Lights Out* and *The Whistler*. The anthology genre, though, was an expensive one, in that it presented a different genre of story and a different set of characters every week. While most anthologies used an entirely different cast for every show, there were a select few like the CBS anthology *Four Star Playhouse* that employed a permanent troupe of character actors who would appear in different roles and different dramas every week.

In 1957, *Playhouse 90* producer, Martin Manulis, told *TV Guide* that his only goals for the anthology show were "*to bring the greatest variety possible to the series and to strive for excellence … I feel that* Playhouse 90 *should entertain the grown-ups*." In just its second installment, the show did just that and its reputation was forever forged. Jack Palance's performance as a broken-down boxer in "Requiem for a Heavyweight"—the first 90-minute drama written specifically for a television show—won five Emmy Awards. As for variety, *Playhouse 90* presented a head-spinning assortment of productions: "Judgment at Nuremberg," "Days

35 Hollywood Pictures—"Quiz Show," 1994

36 Fifties Television: The Industry and Its Critics, p 169

of Wine and Roses," and "For Whom the Bell Tolls," just to name a few. An all-star roster of performers included Errol Flynn, Jack Lemmon, Carol Channing, Mickey Rooney, and Paul Newman, and the leading directors of the day, John Frankenheimer, Sidney Lumet, and George Roy Hill.[37]

Alfred Hitchcock: Acclaimed director tackles CBS television—1955–1965

For the next five years, the show was regarded as the paragon of the 1950's television era—an era that had started eight years before this landmark series reached the air. An *audience* was what the come-lately show needed and that would prove hard to find in numbers that mattered to television. During that time, other anthology series had already grabbed a share of the available audience making it tough, even for a great series, to get a foothold. *The Kraft Television Theater* and *Westinghouse Studio One* were anthology shows that had been around since 1947. *The Philco Television Hour*, since 1948. *The Lux Video Theater*, *Alcoa Presents*, and *The G.E. Theater*, hosted by Ronald Reagan, all had roots tied to the early 1950's. *The Kraft Television Theater*, alone, had presented over 500 plays by the time *Playhouse 90* burst on the scene.[38]

In addition to the 60-minute and 90-minute anthology series that were on the air, networks were trying 30-minute anthology series as well. CBS was trying two of them—competition to their own *Playhouse 90*. The first series belonged to the iconic twentieth century British director Alfred Hitchcock, titled *Alfred Hitchcock Presents*. The half-hour show was a testament to irony. The spooky plotlines of the 361 episodes provided viewers with shivers and thrills and lots of dark humor. The title sequence of the show set the tone: a simple line-drawing of Hitchcock's rotund profile filled the screen, while Charles Gounod's "Funeral March of a Marionette" played behind it.[39] Hitchcock appears in silhouette from the right edge of the screen, walks to center screen to eclipse the caricature, then turns to the audience and drolly says, "Good evening."

The Twilight Zone

As good as *Alfred Hitchcock Presents* might have been, it was a walk-on role when compared to the second of the two 30-minute dramatic anthologies to take to the airwaves. Rodman Edward Serling, the most decorated television writer of his day, had come up with a series like nothing anyone had ever seen. The series became a euphemism for the bizarre and the biggest dramatic hit of its day, *The Twilight Zone*.

---

37 *Fifty Years of Television*, p 133

38 *Encyclopedia of 20th Century American Television*, pp 281–282

39 Radio interview on KUSC's "The Evening Program with Jim Svejda" June 22, 2012

Twilight Zone *Opening Narration*

There is a fifth dimension beyond that which is known to man. It is a dimension as vast as space and as timeless as infinity. It is the middle ground between light and shadow, between science and superstition, and it lies between the pit of man's fears and the summit of his knowledge. This is the dimension of imagination. It is an area which we call *The Twilight Zone.*

— Rod Serling

Rod Serling "Submitted for Your Consideration..." The Twilight Zone *on CBS 1959–1964*

In 1955, Serling had made the leap to national prominence with "Patterns," an episode of the *Kraft Television Theater* that dealt with the cutthroat world of corporate business. The script won Serling his first of six Emmys and was made into a feature film. Other Emmy-winning scripts for *Playhouse 90* followed: *Requiem for a Heavyweight* in 1956 and *The Comedian* in 1957.[40]

By 1959, Serling was television's most esteemed and popular writer, but was finding himself increasingly constrained by sponsors censoring his material. To navigate around this problem, Serling decided to create a fantasy series, reasoning correctly that sponsors would dismiss the stories as fanciful and not notice that Serling was *actually* commenting on issues of the day.

During and after *The Twilight Zone*, Serling would continue to craft memorable work, including the TV series *Night Gallery* and two landmark features—*Seven Days in May* ... and *Planet of the Apes*. But it was *The Twilight Zone*, unveiled on October 2, 1959,[41] that has proven itself an enduring classic—and the first great fantasy series in the history of television. *TZ* was there before *Star Trek*, before *Outer Limits*, before *X-Files*—and in a very real sense made them all possible. The 156 episodes that comprised *The Twilight Zone* series was part psychological thriller, part science fiction, part fantasy, and part horror—and always with a macabre twist ending.

Rod Serling, the top writer of TV's *Golden Age*, was already a multiple Emmy winner when he created *The Twilight Zone* at the age of 34. With *TZ's* opening narration titillating viewers into watching, it was safe to say there was nothing else like it on television. Moreover, the series drew upon the hottest actors, directors, and writers to ever work in TV. Robert Redford, Robert Duvall, Lee Marvin, Jack Klugman, William Shatner. The same was true of directors, including Richard Donner who would guide the gremlin

---

40 *Fifty Years of Television*, p 133

41 *TV Guide*—"Special Collector's Issue: 100 Greatest Episodes of All Time" June 28, 1997

in "Nightmare at 20,000 Feet" before moving on to *Superman* and *Lethal Weapon*. Bernard Hermann, who had composed music for *Citizen Kane*, scored both the initial theme and a number of the *Twilight Zone* episodes before continuing on to *Psycho* and *Taxi Driver.*

What attracted these great talents was the writing. Serling knew how to create stories of astonishing variety at dizzying speed. Sitting by the swimming pool in the back yard of his Pacific Palisades mansion, he would dictate into a tape recorder, have a secretary transcribe it, then make the line changes by hand—and all in one afternoon.

For years, Serling had been storing up ideas for such a series and the stories literally poured out of him. In that first 1959 season, *TZ* produced 36 episodes and the quality was amazing. This maiden year contained such classics as "Time Enough at Last" and "Monsters Are Due on Maple Street." At the end of the year, Serling won his fourth Writing Emmy. More importantly, the stories had gotten past the sponsors. They hadn't seen the messages Serling was sending out to millions of viewers each week. "Time Enough to Last" wasn't a show about a henpecked man who'd lost his reading glasses; it was an editorial about the futility of waging a nuclear war. And "Monsters Are Due on Maple Street" wasn't a story about little green men from outer space terrorizing a sleepy suburban neighborhood; it was a morality play about the evils of "Red Scare" vigilantism.

The next two seasons saw 58 more Serling-penned scripts and garnered the author his second Emmy for *TZ* and fifth overall.[42] During *TZ's* fourth season ('63), CBS sought to attract a larger audience by expanding the 30-minute show to an hour, a strategy they had tried recently with *Alfred Hitchcock Presents* and *Gunsmoke*. The era of the half-hour dramas was ending. Although Serling had initially conceived of *The Twilight Zone* as 60-minute show, it felt padded at an hour; Serling admitted to being tired of often having to recycle his own clichés.[43] Still, though the episodes might've been weaker than in previous years, there was always a classic in every season. Serling saved his best for the last giving us "Nightmare at 20,000 Feet" during *TZ's* final 1964 season. Rod Serling died June 28, 1975 of complications from open-heart surgery.[44] The man who'd won six Emmy's for dramatic writing was only 50 years old when he left us—but true to his vision, *The Twilight Zone* will live on in syndication forever.

---

42 *TV Guide*—"Special Collector's Issue: 100 Greatest Episodes of All Time" June 28, 1997

43 *TV Guide*—"Special Collector's Issue: 100 Greatest Episodes of All Time" June 28, 1997

44 American Masters—"Rod Serling: Submitted For Your Approval"

Discussion Questions

A. Red Scare

- What was the "Red Scare" and how did it affect the motion picture, radio and television industry?
- Can you think of any parallel in your television memory to the "Hollywood Ten"? Why or why not?

B. The Goldbergs

- The radio-to-TV transition of the 1949 series, *The Goldbergs*, soon started to be affected by the political climate of the early fifties in what way?

C. Change of Habit

- How did the growing popularity of television affect other entertainment mediums in the early 1950's?

D. Spice of Life

- What did the *Show of Shows* have going for it that made it so popular in 1954?
- What other variety shows made their mark in the 1950's, one of which inspiring the first 'spin-off' series?

E. Toast of the Town

- Red Skelton and Ed Sullivan grabbed great ratings for CBS in the variety show arena. What did each series bring to the small screen that was such a hit in American living rooms?

F. See it Now

- What was the danger of "McCarthyism" and how did Edward R Murrow's CBS show, *See it Now*, begin to expose this threat?

G. Boon

- *The Adventures of Ozzie and Harriet* brought what kind of entertainment to television during its 13 seasons on ABC?

H. Scandal

- Do you think audiences today would be as shocked at the rigging of quiz shows as the 1958 audience was incensed at the producers of *Twenty One*? How did this scandal reshape the relationship between programs and their sponsors?

I. The Anthologies

- Although not the earliest anthology show on the scene, *Playhouse 90* 's popularity appealed to audiences on what levels?

J. The Twilight Zone

- *Twilight Zone* creator Rod Serling was driven to write this innovative, award- winning series because of what restrictions placed on him as a writer?

CHAPTER EIGHT

Escaping Black & White

1948–1960

Double Entendre

The battle for color television took RCA and CBS back to the drawing board in the early 1940's, and the entertainment giants spent the decade experimenting with the medium. The complex notion of breaking down the spectrum of color into manageable rays of electrons was a technological summit—David Sarnoff, now chairman of the RCA board, knew that. Whoever could solve the problem would reign supreme in the TV business. The fight for color would determine not only the battle for color televisions, but the future of computers, satellites, medical equipment, and space exploration as well.[1]

Yet even as scientists at CBS, RCA (parent to NBC), and DuMont were rolling up their sleeves in an effort to deliver "color television" to American homes, there was another battle for color supremacy being waged in America as well. A battle being fought on *this* side of the atomic nucleus that would outlast, by a decade, the trenchant technological infighting being waged by the TV networks. *This* battle for color

---

1 History Channel Modern Marvels—"Television: Window to the World"

outside the living room was recorded in stringent black and white, thus providing a nation of television viewers with the unspoken irony of the time.

The core to prime time television has always been the selling of the American Dream—that's what advertisers really do. At the center of that dream stands the mythic American family. Television, in the 1950's, gave us what it thought that quintessential family looked like. *The Donna Reed Show*, *Leave It to Beaver*, and *Father Knows Best* were three attempts at bringing the "perfect" American Family into every American home. In twenty-first century America, black families and all families of color are now a part of this dream; part of the mythic American TV Family. This was not the case in 1950.

As African American soldiers returned home from World War II, they were more determined than ever to attain the freedoms they had risked their lives for abroad. After all, black soldiers had fought a war to give "freedom" back to the people of Europe, when most African Americans fighting and dying on foreign soil had never savored that kind of freedom for themselves. In the end, the military had been integrated to win the war against Hitler and tyranny. Many black servicemen were hoping this process of integration would continue on at home.

Separate But Equal

Not only was there a great deal of anticipation about integration on the part of the returning soldiers, but also on the part of black women at home as well. Many African American women who'd worked as domestics *before* the war found themselves trading in their mops and brooms *during* the war for a riveting gun and soldering irons, and quickly became fixtures on the assembly lines of industrial America. These black women, like their fighting counterparts, had gotten a taste of what integrated life in America might be like and were anxious to savor more. "Thus, as the war ended," says Harvard Professor Henry Louis Gates, Jr., director of the university's W.E.B DuBois Institute for African and African American Research, "America found itself with a highly trained ex-military class of black men, together with a well-trained industrial class of black women, whose collective cultural histories had been transformed by World War II."[2] Most were now poised for a fully integrated life, in America, in the second half of the twentieth century.

Black optimism after the war was understandably high and coincided with the excitement surrounding the fresh technology arriving on the scene—television. Race relations in the new medium would be a critical link in the integration equation as television moved from the laboratory to the American living room. Yet as black servicemen returned home to resume their lives, ready for the process of integration to begin, the first black television show to reach the airwaves immediately dashed their hopes.

2 California Newsreel Production—"Color Adjustment"

Amos 'n' Andy had been a part of NBC Radio since 1929, until "raided" by Bill Paley, in 1949, for the CBS radio network. Two years later, CBS put the series on television. Set in Harlem, the series presented images of a completely autonomous, segregated black community where Amos and Andy thrived.[3] While the series on radio and television was enormously popular and wildly funny, it was also indescribably primitive in its use of stereotypes and clichés. The black ensemble of male characters was portrayed as shiftless, opportunistic, or lazy—a depiction that the television series inherited from radio where the characters had been forged into racial stereotypes for the past twenty years.[4] On radio, of course, series creators Freeman Gosden (as Amos) and Charles Correll (as Andy) were white. But now on television, white men in "black face" were not going to cut it, and black actors had to be found.

When *Amos 'n' Andy* went to television in 1951, African American actors graced the small screen as leads for the first time. This early display of "black" programming turned out to be little more than a blip on the radar screen of racial *equality* in television, not to be seen again with any regularity for over a decade. The first prime time television series to feature an all-black cast, *Amos 'n' Andy* played on a familiar theme: Black people might aspire to dream of success, but they were comically ill-equipped to achieve it.[5] Even before its premier, the show was sued by the NAACP to block its CBS broadcast. The suit charged that every character on the show was either "a clown or a crook."[6] The implication was that millions of white viewers would watch this series and think it an accurate portrait of an entire race.

In CBS's defense, the medium of television was struggling to find itself back in those early days. The networks were there to entertain the public and *Amos 'n' Andy* was certainly doing that. Despite the pending lawsuit, the series got off to an astonishing start, racing up the Nielsen ratings by its second show. Racially flawed as the show was, the series was laugh-out-loud funny. Black and white critics, alike, agreed on that. The series starred Alvin Childress as *Amos* and Spencer Williams, Jr. as *Andy*. The part of *George "Kingfish" Stevens* was played by Tim Moore. It should be noted that regardless of the show's title, the series, both on radio and television, revolved around the *Kingfish*, a rather crafty con man who would use his gift of gab (though colorfully cluttered with mispronunciations) to induce people to do things that would somehow benefit him and his wife, *Sapphire*, played by Ernestine Wade. Wade was the only voice from the radio show to be reprised on the television show, and thus she became the first black actress of import to "star" in a television series.

With millions of black and white viewers tuning in every Thursday evening to watch the show, *Amos 'n' Andy* was in the throngs of a legendary 30-year success story when the NAACP finally confronted the series. The National Association for the Advancement of Colored People cited that the *interests* of the black community of the 1950's were diametrically opposed to the *images* of blacks that *Amos 'n'*

3 California Newsreel Production—"Color Adjustment"

4 African American Viewers and the Black Situation Comedy: Situating Racial Humor (Studies in African American History and Culture), p 384

5 California Newsreel Production—"Color Adjustment"

6 California Newsreel Production—"Color Adjustment"

Andy was feeding to the nation at large.[7] Something had to give. Two seasons after its debut, something did—*Amos 'n' Andy* (the TV series)—was grudgingly canceled. The CBS radio show, however, featuring Gosden and Correll as the series' radio voices, would run until 1960, spanning parts of five decades of continuous programming.

Brown v. Board of Education

Early in 1951, great turmoil was felt among black students enrolled in Virginia's state educational system. At the time, Prince Edward County, Virginia, was segregated and students had decided to take matters into their own hands. Their protests centered on the overpopulated school premises and the unsuitable conditions in their school.[8] This particular kind of behavior coming from black people in the South was unexpected. The white expectation had always been for blacks to act in a subordinate manner. When the NAACP could not get the students to back off their demands, the NAACP promptly joined them in their battle against school segregation. This action became one of the five cases that comprised what is known today as *Brown v. Board of Education*. On May 17, 1954, the U.S. Supreme Court handed down its decision regarding the case, fully titled, *Brown v. Board of Education of Topeka, Kansas*, in which the plaintiffs charged that the education of black children in separate public schools from their white counterparts was unconstitutional. The opinion of the court held simply that the "segregation of white and colored children in public schools has a detrimental effect upon the colored children."[9]

Contrary to public opinion, *Brown v. Board* did not overturn *Plessy v. Ferguson* (1896). *Plessy v. Ferguson* had handed down the "separate but equal" clause that had led to rigid segregation in public transportation. "Separate but equal" became the call of Southern culture. Separate bathrooms, separate diners, and separate schools. Separate sections of the bus. *Brown v. Board* had to do with the desegregation of education, only, and not public transportation. Yet, while the landmark case did not directly overturn *Plessy v. Ferguson*, its influence in leading the nation to eventually do away with "separate but equal" cannot be denied.

The following year, in Montgomery, Alabama, while riding home from work on a municipal bus, a black woman refused to give up her seat to another white commuter ... and the winds of real change were starting to swirl. Few television cameras outside the South chose to cover the events unfolding in Montgomery, fixing their lens instead on the ongoing "commie witch hunts" being waged well to the north.

---

7 California Newsreel Production—"Color Adjustment"

8 "Little Rock Central High 40th Anniversary" website

9 Supreme Court Decision—"Brown v. Topeka Board of Education"

Birth of the Civil Rights Movement

On December 1, 1955, following a long day of work at a Montgomery department store where the 42-year-old black woman was currently employed, Rosa Louise Parks paid the ten-cent fare for the bus ride home and found a seat on the near-empty bus. Eventually, however, as the bus traveled along its regular route, all of the white-only seats in the bus began filling up. The bus driver noted that the front of the bus was filled with white passengers and two or three white men were still standing.[10] Following the prevailing practice, the driver moved the "colored section" sign behind Parks and demanded that she and three other black people give up their seats in the middle section so that the white passengers could sit.

Rosa Parks, a healthy, middle-aged housewife, would've gladly given up her seat to an elderly or disabled person needing to sit, regardless of color.[11] But this "back-of-the-bus" thing had to go. The bus driver, attempting to threaten and intimidate Parks to no avail, flagged down the cop who arrested the violator on the spot.

Rev. Martin Luther King, Jr. leads Montgomery bus boycott—1956

Bailed out by the African American community in Montgomery on Friday evening, Parks awaited her trial on Monday with great angst. Meanwhile, knowing that the Montgomery city bus system depended heavily on the black community, black leaders in Montgomery agreed to call a boycott of all city buses commencing that Monday. The voice announcing the boycott belonged to a new and popular minister in the Montgomery area, Martin Luther King, Jr. King was quickly chosen by African American leaders to lead the boycott that followed as well.

By Saturday morning, news of the upcoming boycott had already spread through the city. Radio was still a fixture in the South and every household in Montgomery with a Philco, a Zenith, or an RCA radio knew what was coming. On Monday morning, King and the other leaders waited nervously at a bus stop to see if their plan would work. To their surprise and great relief, bus after bus rolled by with no black riders aboard. United in protest, boycotters had chosen instead to walk, take carpools, pedal bicycles, and even ride mules to get to work rather than boarding buses.

Later that morning, Rosa Parks went to court with her lawyer. The judge, finding her guilty of breaking a city segregation law, levied a $14 fine.[12] Declaring the law unjust, Rosa Parks' attorney announced that they would appeal the case to the U.S. Supreme Court. With the support of most of Montgomery's 50,000 African Americans, the bus boycott lasted for 381 days until the local ordinance segregating blacks and whites on public buses was lifted. Ninety percent of African Americans in Montgomery partook in the

---

10 The Unfinished Journey, p 241

11 The Unfinished Journey, p 243

12 Daybreak of Freedom: The Montgomery Bus Boycott, p 9

boycotts, which reduced bus revenue by 80%.[13] It was not until a federal court ordered Montgomery's buses desegregated in November of 1956 that the boycott officially ended.

Ironically, even as television covered desegregation in both the transportation industry as well as in public education, its own industry was one of the most segregated in the country. One of the first prime-time series to bring racial integration into the white, white world of television was the CBS anthology series, *Westinghouse Studio One,* which was just as prestigious as CBS's own *Playhouse 90* or NBC's *The Kraft Television Theater.* In 1954, acclaimed screenwriter Reginald Rose wrote and produced a teleplay appropriately titled *Thunder on Sycamore Street*. The story was derived from an actual incident that took place in suburban Cicero, Illinois. A group of white residents living there, disturbed to find a Negro family moving into their neighborhood, organized to get the family out. The resulting events received national television and newsreel coverage.

In his teleplay, Rose envisioned three small, but virtually identical, suburban houses built side by side in the studio. Action would move from one house to another, showing the evolution of vigilante activity against the new family in the third house—the Negro family. In the end, a mild-mannered man in the second house turns against his white neighbor and makes his stand with the new family.[14]

Thunder on Sycamore Street was approved for production with one proviso. The Negro family had to be "something else." The network and sponsors would never hear the end of it if the Negro was some kind of beleaguered protagonist. They wanted something non-confrontational. Rose was furious. Weren't fear and vigilantism the essential themes here? The network was adamant and Rose finally agreed to make the Negro an ex-convict. The sponsors seemed satisfied—at least until the airing. To minimize the damage done by the changing of the Negro's character, Rose had come up with an ingenious strategy. The audience would not be allowed to know, throughout the teleplay, why the new neighbor was unwanted. It would only be aware of the resolve to get rid of him.

The evasive strategy turned the play into an extraordinary social Rorschach test.[15] Comments taken from the studio audience at every half-hour indicated that the viewers had filled in the missing information according to their own predilections. Some at once assumed the person living in the third house was a communist, an atheist, a Jew, a Catholic, a Russian, or an Oriental. The information that he was an ex-convict mentioned with utmost brevity in the final act was accepted as logical supplementary detail to their own assumption. Needless to say, the production caused quite a stir and presented the sponsors with precisely the kind of controversy they were trying to avoid.

---

13 The Unfinished Journey, p 245

14 *Tube of Plenty*, p 164

15 *Tube of Plenty*, p 165

One of those tuning in that night in 1954 was a black graduate student at UCLA named Estelle Edmerson, who was completing a graduate study of the Negro in Broadcasting.[16] The next day, Edmerson phoned the CBS personnel department in Los Angeles to address a series of questions. The woman in Personnel at CBS whom Edmerson spoke with had freely answered all her questions regarding the screening of *Thunder on Sycamore Street*, when Edmerson asked if CBS was devoid of racial discrimination. The CBS employee answered that jobs were open to all qualified workers ... but did add that *certain* positions required common sense. Receptionists and script girls, for example, sat in with sponsors when screening shows, the woman had indicated. The implication being that clients would never take to Negroes sitting and working directly with them. "However," she added with a note of enlightenment: "Except where our company must be diplomatic in its hiring, all jobs are open to Negroes."[17]

Discrimination at the networks was easy to spot—Estelle Edmerson concluded as much in her graduate thesis. Truthfully, you only had to turn on a television to spot the problem. It was not just that African Americans had but a single series on television during the remainder of the decade, no blacks or people of any color could hardly be *found* on network TV. To demonstrate how bad racial inequality really was in television, the roster of the great and famous visited CBS's *Person to Person* in 1956—the *60 Minutes* of its day—hosted by the journalist of the century, Edward R. Murrow. Everyone who was anyone was there: Liberace, Pat Weaver, Eddie Fisher and Debbie Reynolds, Jane Russell, Billy Graham, George Gallup, Jayne Mansfield, Admiral Richard Byrd, Rocky Marciano, and the Duke and Duchess of Windsor. Yet conspicuously absent was Martin Luther King, Jr. In truth, of the ninety-six guests who graced this hallowed ground between 1954 and 1956, only two, Dizzy Gillespie and Cab Calloway, were black. And this at a time when a second emancipation was beginning to spill over every corridor of life in our nation ... except television.

Nightly Ritual

Throughout the 1950's, television viewing became a family ritual. Not surprisingly, the nuclear family became the centerpiece in this prime time, seven-to-ten-pm time slot. There, on 10-inch screens, baby boom families found neatly packaged images of what the ideal American family should be, and what every household should have. Yet through the late 1940's and much of the 1950's, in the cultural landscape of prime time America, Negros remained "in their place," apart from those images. On television in the 1950's it was almost as if black people did not exist. Night after night, show after show, the only "color" on television was white. Occasionally, a black entertainer would make a guest appearance on a TV variety program, but between 1953 and 1965 only *one* of them got a show on television—singing sensation Nat King Cole.

16 A Descriptive Study of the American Negro in United States Professional Radio, 1922–1953

17 A Descriptive Study of the American Negro in United States Professional Radio, 1922–1953

Nat King Cole hosts NBC series The Nat King Cole Show *1957*

On November 5, 1956, *The Nat King Cole Show* debuted on NBC-TV. The Cole program was the first of its kind to be hosted by an African American and was immediately greeted with controversy. At first blush, this acrimony was hard to figure. National sponsors were initially willing to back the show, which featured one of the best singing voices of the day and a black man whom producers felt would be embraced by white audiences. Cole was a graceful, talented performer who was respected around the world as a "gentleman." If any one black entertainer held the key to prime time acceptance and inclusion into the American Dream, it was Nat King Cole, the model of assimilation.[18] The question was, would reputation and talent be enough to open the door to white America?

By July 1957, the answer seemed to be yes. *The Nat King Cole Show* had expanded from a 15-minute pops show on Monday nights to a regular half-hour variety show,[19] though it still needed a national sponsor if the series was to be renewed for a second season. Everyone at NBC was confident it would be. During that spring and summer, however, the new integration laws for education—the same ones that had been enacted with *Brown v. Board* in 1954—were finally being implemented in schools across the South. That included Little Rock, Arkansas, which, for a Southern state, was relatively progressive at the time. That was all about to change.

Nine black students had been chosen to attend classes at all-white Little Rock Central High School that September because of their excellent grades.[20] On the first day of school, only one of the nine showed up. The young girl had not gotten the message that white protestors outside the school were making trouble. Police had to take her away in a patrol car to protect her. The following day, Arkansas Governor Orval Faubus called out the National Guard to prevent the nine African Americans from entering high school and, in so doing, defied the high court order. President Dwight Eisenhower stepped in immediately and ordered the National Guard sent home, replacing them with troops from the Army's 101st Airborne Division, who escorted the "Little Rock Nine" to and from school and their classes for the remainder of the school year.[21]

The television images of the racial protest going on in the streets of Little Rock were beginning to trickle into American homes on the Nightly News. In the end, it proved to be enough of a deterrent that

18 California Newsreel Production—"Color Adjustment"
19 How Sweet It Was. Television: A Pictorial Commentary
20 "Little Rock Central High 40th Anniversary" website
21 Civil Rights Movement Veteran's Section website, 1957—"Little Rock Nine"

"The Little Rock Nine": Southern Desegregation begins in Arkansas 1957

national sponsors, deciding on whether or not to back *The Nat King Cole Show*, decided against it. The object of series television was to get high ratings and no national sponsor could achieve those ratings if they alienated their Southern constituency. Despite the efforts of NBC as well as Cole's black and white industry colleagues—many of whom worked on the show for industry scale (and even for free)—*The Nat King Cole Show* was canceled after only a year.[22]

RGB

Beginning in the late 1940's and running well through the 1950's, the world of American television was really two worlds in one. There was the world outside the atomic nucleus, the day-to-day world all Americans called home—the same one that was undergoing a seismic shift in racial assimilation. The social tremors were undeniable. The African American's historic dream of freedom was continuing to clash with the stark reality of early race relations in television. While TV was uniquely poised to make a dramatic difference in bringing races together, it chose instead, in those early years, to turn a blind eye to the inclusion of *color* in its weekly series.

Yet, while the issue of "color in television" *outside* the nucleus was being carefully sidestepped, the issue of "color" *inside* that nucleus was commanding the attention of three of the four networks. NBC (via RCA), CBS, and DuMont all put small armies of engineers on the challenge, banking on future returns. It was a good bet. By 1951 there were 11 million television sets in the United States, up another 300% over the last 24 months. And this number represented only 12% of the country. For Sarnoff, Paley, and Alan DuMont, color was the next big money-maker. Whoever could solve the "electron arrangement" puzzle first would have a real leg up in the business of television. Not only could that network interest new buyers with a color medium, but both Paley and Sarnoff felt certain that network could get all eleven

22 California Newsreel Production—"Color Adjustment"

million people who'd purchased black-and-white televisions to buy a second set in color. Branding a color television system that the FCC approved would mean hundreds of millions of dollars to the one network that was first able to decipher the riddle—and CBS was positioning itself to be first.

CBS had begun experimental color field tests using film as early as the summer of 1940, and with live cameras by November of that same year. NBC (owned by RCA) made its first field test of color television three months later, in February of 1941.[23] NBC, under Sarnoff's direction, wanted electronic color television. Paley at CBS was settling for electro-mechanical color television. The cost savings in research and development to Paley and CBS was huge. Paley was spending a fraction of what Sarnoff was spending for electronic color television over at RCA. Moreover, CBS was running ahead of schedule. Simplicity was the name of Paley's game.

In its most basic form, a color transmission can be created by broadcasting three separate monochrome images, one each in the colors red, green, and blue—what's known in television as an RGB image. The RGB color model is an additive color model where red, green, and blue light is added together in various ways to reproduce a broad array of colors.[24] When displayed together or in rapid succession, the three separate RBG images blend together to trick the human eye into seeing the full color spectrum.[25]

The electro-*mechanical* version of this process combined a conventional monochrome picture tube with a colored disc or mirror located somewhere in front of the lens. In these mechanical systems, of which there were several variations, the three colored images were then transmitted as successive images that relied on the human vision system to fuse these images into a full color picture. The CBS electro-mechanical color system was one of the "variations," and used a disc made of red, blue, and green filters spinning inside the electronic monochromatic television camera at 1,200 rpm. A similar disc spinning in synchronization in front of the cathode ray tube inside the receiver completed the transmission. In short, by January 1942, while RCA was plodding away trying to achieve *electronically* what CBS had already achieved electro-*mechanically*, CBS was primed to manufacturer color televisions using their "mechanical" color system.

By January 1942, however, the world was once again at war and the manufacture of television and radio equipment for civilian use was quickly shelved. Any opportunity to introduce color television to the general public would have to wait another four years—and that was very good for RCA. In late 1945, shortly after WWII had ended, the Federal Communications Commission (FCC) was inundated with requests to set up new television stations. By 1948, the FCC was beginning to worry again about the limited number of channels available and the congestion that even more new licenses would bring to the ether. The FCC acted quickly and sounded a moratorium on all new licenses while they considered

---

23 RCA Press Release—"RCA-NBC Firsts in Color Television, a Chronological List of Significant Firsts by the Radio Corporation of America" 1955

24 Digital Video and HDTV: Algorithms and Interfaces

25 Popular Science—"New Television System Transmits Images in Full Color" 1940 December

the problem. Toward that end, the FCC called for technical demonstrations of all color systems over the next several months and formed the Joint Technical Advisory Committee (JTAC) to study them.[26]

The Battle for Color

At the onset of television, in conventional black and white (B&W) TV sets, the cathode ray tube had an inside-facing screen that was uniformly coated with phosphor. This phosphor, when struck by a beam of electrons, emitted white light. Generated from a single electron gun at the back of the tube, the beam was deflected (most commonly) by the varying fields from magnetic coils so it could then be directed at any point on the phosphor-coated screen.

A color CRT (cathode ray tube) works on the same principle, but that's where the similarity ends. The electronic color picture tube was far more complicated to invent. The inside face of the color CRT, for example, had to be patterned with *three* phosphors—one for each of the primary colors (RBG). THREE electron guns were then needed to separately excite each phosphor by firing the appropriate electron burst (color signal) at its corresponding phosphor.[27] In those early days, the three-gun approach was still a theory with one very big problem. Seeing to it that the beam from the red gun struck only the red phosphor on the inside face of the CRT was akin to *Star Wars'* character Luke Skywalker firing a four-inch proton grenade into the Death Star's six-inch exhaust vent while flying his Jedi fighter at four times the speed of sound. Some kind of technical arrangement was needed to assure that the beam from the red gun struck only the red phosphor; the green gun, the green phosphor; and the blue, the blue.[28] And for RCA, that would take time.

CBS, meanwhile, had gotten off to a head start during WWII by perfecting its electro-mechanical system. By 1948, CBS had improved versions of its original design and was now using 405 lines of resolution. That summer, the FCC's Joint Technical Advisory Committee (JTAC) called for a demonstration of all color television systems so that the Federal Communications Commission could approve one for use. Color Television Inc (CTI) demonstrated its line-sequential system, while Philco demonstrated a dot-sequential system.[29] Both were electronic systems that still needed a lot of work. RCA sat out this first round of hearings waiting to see how CBS faired in the demonstration. Of the entrants judged, the CBS electro-mechanical color system was by far the best-developed and won head-to-head testing against all comers—all but RCA.

---

26 *Tube of Plenty*, p 112

27 *New York Times*—"Color Television Success in Test" August 30, 1940

28 *Wall Street Journal*—"CBS Demonstrates Full Color Television" September 5, 1940

29 *Wall Street Journal*—"CBS Demonstrates Full Color Television" Sept. 5, 1940

While those first demonstrations were taking place, it was widely known within the industry that RCA was working on a dot-sequential system of its own—but one compatible with existing black-and-white broadcasts. Just before the JTAC presented its findings in late August, 1949, RCA broke its silence and introduced its system as well. It didn't matter. The JTAC recommended the CBS system, anyway, feeling that the RCA system was still fraught with technical problems, inaccurate color reproduction, and expensive equipment.

The FCC formally approved the CBS color television system and licensed it as the U.S. color broadcasting standard on October 11, 1950. CBS was poised to sell millions of color television sets and beat Sarnoff to the punch. Sarnoff countered by filing a lawsuit against the FCC to suspend the ruling. RCA argued that the CBS mechanical television system was incompatible with the millions of electronic televisions already in homes across the country. The courts were not impressed. The RCA suit failed in the U.S. District Court as did RCA's appeal to the U.S. Supreme Court. The unsuccessful action served only to delay the first commercial network broadcast in color until June 14, 1951, when CBS aired a musical variety special titled *Premiere*. The initial broadcast reached only five of CBS's East Coast affiliates.[30]

While the CBS color broadcasting schedule gradually expanded to twelve hours per week (but never into prime time), and the color network expanded to eleven affiliates as far west as Chicago, its commercial success was doomed from the beginning. The refusal of television manufacturers to create adapter mechanisms for their existing black-and-white sets, the lack of color receivers necessary to watch the programs, and the unwillingness of advertisers to sponsor broadcasts seen by almost no one did not bode well for the CBS color system. If things weren't bad enough, color television production was suspended in October 1951, at the request of the DOD, for the duration of the Korean War.

When the Korean War ended in 1953, monochromatic television sales took off again, making it more and more unlikely that CBS could achieve any success with its incompatible color system. CBS had bought a television manufacturer in April of 1951 and by that October, only 200 sets had been shipped. In the end, lacking a manufacturing capability and saddled with a color set that was triple the cost of most monochromatic sets, CBS was unable to take advantage of the color market.

Determined to win the "color war," Sarnoff had organized his engineers and physicists into a battle-weary platoon and pushed them to perfect an all-electronic color television system that used a signal compatible with all existing monochrome sets.[31] It was this engineering feat of uncommon valor that finally won the day. David Sarnoff had been in many battles, but none fiercer than the one for color television. "Competition," said Sarnoff, "brings out the best in product and the worst in men." For him, the battle for color had been the worst slugfest he would ever encounter.[32]

---

30 *Wall Street Journal*—"RCA to Test Color TV System On Three Shows Daily Beginning Today" July 9, 1951

31 History Channel Modern Marvels—"Television: Window to the World"

32 History Channel Modern Marvels—"Television: Window to the World"

Prior to the Korean War, the National Television System Committee (NTSC) had been instrumental in leading the JTAC into giving CBS the early license on a color television system. But during the war, the NTSC was re-formed. New personnel had come on board and most of them felt that David Sarnoff had been right all along. Introducing mechanical television to an electronic medium was such an obvious oil-and-water scenario. When CBS testified before Congress in March 1953 that it had no further plans for its own electro-mechanical color system, the FCC's National Production Authority dropped its ban on the manufacture of electronic color television receivers (TV sets), and awarded RCA the license for its color television system on December 17, 1953. The RCA electronic color system would serve as the new standard for color broadcast through the remainder of the twentieth century.

Although the first national colorcast (the 1954 Tournament of Roses on NBC) occurred on January 1, 1954, it was not until the late 1960's that color sets started selling in numbers large enough to matter. The reason for the upturn in color TV sales was due in part to the color transition of 1965, in which over half of all network prime time programming would be broadcast in color that fall. In the 1950's, however, there was still the matter of high TV pricing and the lack of broadcast material. Both obstacles greatly slowed color's acceptance in the marketplace, though one felt certain that acceptance would one day come.

"Hi-Yo, Silver ... Away!"

Shot outside under blue skies using characters wearing a myriad of colorful costumes, it was the western, more than any other TV franchise, that brought what NBC would later call "living color" into our living rooms—though not until the end of the decade. So popular were westerns in the 1950's and '60's that at one stage between 1958 and 1961, the triumvirate atop the prime time ratings game for three consecutive years was *Gunsmoke*, *Wagon Train*, and *Have Gun, Will Travel*—in that order.[33]

All three series were initially shot in black and white, as was every other western in the 1950's. There was Hugh O'Brien in Wyatt Earp; *Tales of Wells Fargo* with B-feature actor Dale Robertson; *Wanted: Dead or Alive* with future movie star Steve McQueen; and *Cheyenne*, starring accomplished feature actor Clint Walker. *The Rifleman* cast a minor-league baseball star named Chuck Connors in the title role. There was *Bat Masterson*, starring heartthrob Gene Berry; and *Maverick*, starring feature film legend James Garner. *Laramie* and *Rawhide* were also hit series of their day—this latter show being responsible for giving actor-director-producer Clint Eastwood his 1959 starring role as Rowdy Yates.

When the popularity of television exploded in the late 1940's and 1950's, westerns quickly became a staple of small-screen entertainment. The first to be aired on June 24, 1949, was the *Hopalong Cassidy* show,

---

33 *Fifty Years of Television*, p 48

edited from the 66 B-movies made by William Boyd, the star of *Hopalong Cassidy*.[34] Many B-movie westerns were aired on TV as programming "filler" for networks that were still woefully under-programmed at this early juncture. While "Hoppy" never made the prime time schedule, he and his contemporary, Roy Rogers ("King of the Cowboys"), spent their Saturday afternoons for much of the 1950's in households across America hunting down "sidewinders" that had broken the law.

The peak year for television westerns was 1959, with 26 such shows from the genre airing in prime time. During one week, in March 1959, seven of the top ten shows were westerns.[35]

1959 *TOP-TEN* RATED SHOWS[36]

RANK	TITLE	NETWORK
1	**Gunsmoke**	CBS
2	**Wagon Train**	NBC
3	**Have Gun, Will Travel**	CBS
4	**The Rifleman**	ABC
5	The Danny Thomas Show	CBS
6	**Maverick**	ABC
7	**Tales of Wells Fargo**	NBC
8	The Real McCoys	ABC
9	I've Got a Secret	CBS
10	**Wyatt Earp**	ABC

Yet in the name of fairness, all of these western series owe a debt of gratitude to the birthmother of all TV westerns, *The Lone Ranger*. First of the westerns to air on prime time television, *The Lone Ranger*, airing in September of 1949, on ABC, filled living rooms with culture, class, and the William Tell Overture—the first exposure to classical music most baby boomers ever had. That said, however, this birthmother series was tragically flawed. White men on horseback—that's what critics would later call it, going on to say that the series was mired in such blatant stereotypes that any executive in power after 1970 would've dismissed it on grounds of unbridled chauvinism, racism, and condescension alone.

The Lone Ranger series had its beginnings as a local radio show in 1933 and had quickly become a nationwide smash on the Mutual Radio Network. In 1949, it was brought to ABC-TV as a series of half-hour films made in Hollywood especially for the new medium of television that was sweeping the nation. The series quickly became ABC's first ratings hit and TV's most popular series.

34 *Time*—"Westerns: The Six-Gun Galahad" March 30, 1959

35 *Time*—"Westerns: The Six-Gun Galahad" March 30, 1959

36 Screen Source presents: 20 Most Popular TV Shows Each Year in the 1950's

The premise of the series finds six Texas Rangers ambushed by a band of outlaws led by "Butch" Cavendish, a fiendish character with no moral backbone or wartime etiquette. Later, a Native American named Tonto stumbles on the scene and recognizes the lone survivor, John Francis Reid, as the man who had saved his life sometime in the past. Tonto nurses Reid back to health and helps him fashion a black Domino mask using material from another Ranger's vest to conceal his identity.[37] After the Cavendish gang is brought to justice, Reid continues to fight evil under the guise of "The Lone Ranger" who, with Tonto at his side, rides on for the next eight seasons bringing justice to the untamed West. The smash hit ran from 1949 to 1957 and helped fledgling ABC surmount the 1950's, while serving as a picture-perfect reflection of the decade at the same time. In both worlds, it seemed, there was only good and bad; black and white. Nothing was ambivalent or complex—a cold war mentality to be sure.

Clayton Moore as "The Lone Ranger" and Ranger's horse "Silver" 1950

And why not? Americans had just won the war against Hitler's tyranny and found solace in seeing villains get their just desserts. The TV western hero, like our country, followed a strict moral code making the Lone Ranger more like a knight in the wild West.[38] Yet, as was true of our country, with white men now firmly in charge of the West, African Americans and Native Americans got the short end of the stick. Tonto and all people of color on television served as faithful companions and dutiful serfs but could never dream of equal billing. In all fairness, however, it should not be forgotten that most women and virtually every person of color was all but completely out of *every* series in the 1950's, not just westerns, and that when they were depicted, it was always in subservient roles. But then again, wasn't television but a mirror of what America as a nation was all about then anyway? It was '50's Americana. A decade filled with a clear sense of right and wrong; black and white; and a "Me Tarzan, you Jane" chauvinistic mentality that was widely embraced by many of the westerns that followed *The Lone Ranger's* lead—but not all of them.

37 *Fifty Years of Television*, p 53

38 *Hollywood Reporter*—"TV Milestones" 2004 September, p 21

Gunsmoke

Cast of Gunsmoke *Ken Curtis (Festus), Amanda Blake (Kitty), James Arness (Marshal Dillon), Milburn Stone (Doc Adams) 1955–1975*

In 1955, one western came along to set itself apart from the conventions of the genre—*Gunsmoke*. Its premier on September 10, 1955, was no small deal. Legendary actor and Hollywood icon, John Wayne, strolled onto a CBS set and pitched the new series viewers were about to see. "I've been kicking around Hollywood for a long time," Wayne said. "I've made a lot of pictures out here, many of them westerns. That's why I'm here tonight, to tell you about a new western; a new television show called *Gunsmoke*. No, I'm not in it. I wish I were though because I think it's the best of its kind to come along. It's honest, it's adult, and it's realistic."[39] John Wayne was right. And because of its realism it was different and enduring.

That September night became historic—the start of a 20-year continuous run—the longest by a prime time live-action series featuring continuous characters in the annals of television history. Six-hundred and thirty-five prime time dramatic episodes[40]—a benchmark that will likely stand forever. The character that led the prime time march was Sheriff Matt Dillon (played by James Arness). Arness added to the show's realism and its ultimate success. Audiences accustomed to the impossibly courageous leading men on kid-oriented westerns, like ... *Ranger*, loved the bracing stories of a hero who wasn't particularly popular with anyone but his immediate friends. Moreover, those friends weren't liked by everyone either. Kitty, the saloon owner and prostitute, was Dillon's closest confidante. Cantankerous Doc Adams (played by Milburn Stone) was another. And Chester Goode, the crippled deputy (played by Dennis Weaver) was hardly what the traditional warrior was supposed to look like.

When interviewed by *TV Guide* in the late 1980's, some 13 years after the last show had aired, Arness told the interviewer: "What made the difference was that they didn't try to glorify the West—the writers, I mean. They really tried like hell to make it hot and dry and edgy, and the people were ready for it."[41] As it turned out, viewers in the late 1950's were ready for something else as well—color programming.

---

39 *Fifty Years of Television*, p 49

40 *Los Angeles Times*—"Gunsmoke" 1975 September

41 *Fifty Years of Television*, p 49

Bonanza

The Cartwrights: Hoss, Ben, Adam, and Little Joe on NBC's ratings champ Bonanza *1959–1972*

In an era that was still mostly black and white, there came a western like no other before it—literally. In 1959, NBC began airing its regular weekly color dramas commencing with the western series *Bonanza*. NBC was at the forefront of color programming, in part because its parent company RCA manufactured the most successful line of color sets in the 1950's. By 1959, RCA was the only remaining major manufacturer of color TV sets. CBS and ABC, which were not affiliated with set manufacturers, were not eager to promote their competitor's product and dragged their feet getting into color. With DuMont having gone under in 1955, there was, by the end of the decade, a relatively small amount of network color programming. The lack of color programming combined with the high cost of color television sets meant that as late as 1964, only 3.1 percent of television households in the U.S. had a color set.[42] NBC provided the catalyst for rapid color expansion by announcing that its prime time schedule for the fall of 1965 would be almost entirely in color. At the forefront of that charge for color programming was the network's signature series *Bonanza*.

Like the flaming title that burned across the screen during the opening credits, *Bonanza* left its brand on television history. The series occupies such a familiar face in TV lore that it's easy to overlook how atypical it seemed when it first began airing.

In an era of Shane-inspired heroes who were rootless loners, here was a TV western—the first broadcast in living color—that centered on a family, while still featuring gunplay and pounding hooves. And it wasn't just *any* family either. There the series broke new ground as well. The Cartwrights were a union composed of four grown men—thrice-married Ben Cartwright, played by Lorne Green, and his three grown sons who presided over 600,000 acres of the Ponderosa cattle ranch on the outskirts of Virginia City, Nevada.[43] Oldest of the sons was sensible Adam, played by Pernell Roberts; then big, lovable, 300-pound lummox Hoss, played by Dan Blocker; and finally, hot-headed Little Joe, played by teen heartthrob Michael Landon.

The series began in a lowly Saturday night time slot in October, 1959. But as it moved to Sunday nights, in early 1961, it soared into the ranks of the top five shows and stayed there for the rest of the decade.

---

42 The World Book Encyclopedia ('03 ed.)—"Television"

43 Bonanza—Episode One/Scene One 1959

From 1964 to 1967, *Bonanza* was the top-rated TV show in the country and remained on the air until 1973, spanning parts of three decades like CBS competitor *Gunsmoke*. As the series wore on, flashback episodes were aired to explain how each of the Cartwright sons had been born to a different mother. When Pernell Roberts left the show because of wage disputes in 1965, the series was considered doomed, yet held on to the number-one rating for the next two seasons, regardless of Roberts' departure. Truly, the series didn't lose a beat—not until Dan Blocker's death in 1972. A subsequent time-slot move by NBC from Sundays to Tuesdays finally delivered the series to a canyon too wide to cross.[44]

Joe Friday

Two series—one a drama, one a comedy—became synonymous with the 1950's, both ending up as icons from a Golden Age. The drama was titled *Dragnet* and in December, 1951, like *Burns & Allen*, *Amos 'n' Andy*, and *I Love Lucy* before it, *Dragnet* took its radio show to television. Perhaps the most famous and influential police procedural drama in television history, *Dragnet* gave millions of viewers a feel for the boredom and drudgery as well as the danger and heroism of real-life police work.[45] Actor, creator, and producer Jack Webb aimed for realism and unpretentious acting and gave us both, unrepentantly.

Jack Webb (left) reprises radio role as Sgt. Joe Friday with Harry Morgan as Officer Bill Gannon on NBC's long-running hit Dragnet circa 1967

The show's cultural impact was so potent that even after five decades since its last first-run episode aired, *elements* of *Dragnet* are known to those who have never seen or heard the program. The ominous, four-note introduction ("Dum De Dum Dum ...") to the base and tympani theme music (titled "Danger Ahead") is instantly recognizable, even today, sixty-five years after the original tracks were laid down. From Joe Friday's documentary style narration ... to the real cases drawn from the Los Angeles police files ... to the catch phrases it produced that made the series a hit through most of two decades and into a third, it's all easily remembered. Phrases like: "*This is the city, Los Angeles California*." "*My Name's Friday. I carry a badge*." And "*Just the facts, Ma'am*" became national by-phrases. And then there was the voice: "*Ladies and gentlemen—The story you're about to see is true. Only the names have been changed to protect the innocent.*"[46]

With those words began one of the most successful detective show in the history of series television. *NYPD Blue*, *Hill Street Blues*, *The Shield*, *Law & Order*, *Homicide: Life on the Street*, and especially the *CSI* franchise, all have *Dragnet* to thank. The show began inauspiciously as a radio program in

44 *Fifty Years of Television*, p 50
45 *Fifty Years of Television*, p 127
46 *Dragnet*—Episode One/Overtrue 1951December

1949. Jack Webb starred as Detective Joe Friday, a policeman with a serious dedication problem, and carried the role over to television two years later. The TV show ran on the NBC television network from December 1951 to August 1959 and then again from January 1967 to April 1970.[47]

Webb insisted on realism in every aspect of the show. The dialogue was clipped, understated, and terse, influenced by the hardboiled *noir* school of crime fiction. Scripts were fast paced but didn't seem rushed. Every aspect of police work was chronicled. From patrols and paperwork, to crime scene investigation, lab work, and suspect interrogations—viewers were treated to all of it. Scripts tackled a number of topics ranging from thrilling murders and armed robbery tales to the more mundane check-fraud and shoplifting beefs. Yet *Dragnet* made them all interesting with fast-moving plots and behind-the-scenes realism. The tone was usually serious, but there were moments of comic relief. Detective Frank Smith (played by Ben Alexander for most of the 1950's) was all the time complaining about his brother-in-law. When the show returned in 1967, following an eight-year hiatus, Jack Webb reprised his role as Friday, but with a new partner—actor Harry Morgan as Officer Bill Gannon. Ben Alexander's light-comedy lines now fell to Morgan who played the humor far more broadly.[48]

After four years of high TV ratings, NBC knew a hit when it saw one and wanted to make *Dragnet* part of the color broadcasts it was planning as early as 1955 (but wouldn't materialize until 1959). Webb, however, put his foot down. He wanted the stark realism that only black and white TV could give to every story and convinced the brass at NBC to go along. Webb was a stickler for detail, and believing viewers were enamored with the show's realism, he gave it to them in gritty, no frills black and white. It worked. *Dragnet* became the number-four show on television in its second season, and the second-rated show in its third. The only show left for it to catch and topple was that elusive number one.[49]

Number One with a Bullet

In July of 1948, actress Lucille Ball agreed to star with actor Richard Denning in a new radio show for the CBS network called *My Favorite Husband*, adapted from the book, Mr. & Mrs. Cugat, by Isobel Scott Rorick. The radio series centered on the travails of a ditzy housewife and her long-suffering banker husband. Lucy's character on the radio show was portrayed as a naïve but ambitious housewife with an overactive imagination and a knack for getting herself into trouble. This set-up would follow her to television and prove to be a recipe for sublime comedy that would outlast the rest of the century in syndication.[50]

---

47 *Encyclopedia of 20th Century American Television*, p 94

48 Encyclopedia of 20th Century American Television, p 95

49 Screen Source presents (website): 20 Most Popular TV Shows Each Year in the 1950's

50 Encyclopedia of 20th Century American Television, p 169

Lucille Ball had first come to Hollywood in 1933, following a successful stint as a New York model. The hardworking Ball had been able to secure film work briefly at Goldwyn Studios and Columbia Pictures, but it was the acting opportunities that opened up for her at RKO Radio Pictures that kick-started her career. Working at first as an extra and a bit player, Ball eventually worked her way up to co-starring roles in feature films and starring roles in second-rate B-movies, earning herself the nickname "Queen of the B's". In 1940, Lucy met Desi Arnaz, a Cuban bandleader who had just come off a successful run in the 1939 Broadway show "Too Many Girls." RKO purchased the film rights to the show and cast Ball as Arnaz's love interest in the picture. The duo began a whirlwind courtship leading to their elopement in November, 1940.[51] Yet as the decade progressed, Desi was always on tour while Lucy was stuck in Los Angeles making B-movies for RKO and later for MGM. Then came the hit radio show in 1948 and CBS's decision a year later to turn it into a television series.

Vivian Vance, Lucille Ball, Desi Arnaz, and William Frawley star in I Love Lucy

CBS's decision caused Lucy to make one of her own. The only way she'd do the TV show, she told CBS, was if her real-life husband played the role Richard Denning had played so successfully on radio. The network, wary of audience reaction to a *mixed marriage* on prime time television, feared the couple wouldn't be accepted. To prove CBS wrong, Lucy and Desi developed a vaudeville act and took it on the road with Arnaz's orchestra. The act was a hit and convinced CBS executives that a Ball-Arnaz pairing would be a worthwhile venture. A pilot was ordered and kinescoped in Hollywood in March 1951, which coincided with Lucy's first pregnancy and the ending of her radio show, *My Favorite Husband.*[52]

Ball and Arnaz used the same radio team to create the show for television, renaming the series *I Love Lucy*. After showing the pilot to several advertising agencies, cigarette giant Philip Morris agreed to sponsor the show. Lucy had stood her ground; the show that CBS feared would never see the light of day has never left the airwaves, becoming the longest running, most successful syndicated television show in history.

I Love Lucy featured Arnaz as Ricky Ricardo, a heavily accented Cuban bandleader; and Lucille Ball as Lucy Ricardo, Ricky's zany, scatterbrained wife who was always turning ordinary household chores into utter disasters. Also featured in the 181 episodes that comprised the show were William Frawley and Vivian

51 Desilu: The Story of Lucille Ball and Desi Arnaz, p 13

52 Desilu: The Story of Lucille Ball and Desi Arnaz, p 56

Vance, consummate stage artists in their own right, who played the Ricardo's neighbors, Fred and Ethel Mertz, former vaudeville stars.

Lucy and Desi had originally decided that the series would air on a biweekly basis much like *The Burns and Allen Show*, but Philip Morris was insistent that *I Love Lucy* air weekly, thus diminishing the possibility of Lucy continuing her film career alongside the television show. Another problem, however, loomed larger still. Both Philip Morris and Desilu (Desi & Lucy) wanted the show shot in front of a live audience—that was a given. Lucy thrived on the live audience energy and the good folks at Philip Morris knew it.[53] Her radio show had been recorded in front of a live audience and ended up a ratings bonanza for CBS.

Lucy and Ethel

Philip Morris wanted that bonanza to continue and thought it best if the series originated from New York rather than Hollywood. At the time, most television shows broadcasting live were produced in New York and aired "live" only for audiences east of the Mississippi River, where most of the population of the country then resided. Since the coaxial cable that carried the broadcast of every show up and down the Atlantic seaboard and through the Midwest did not yet reach the West Coast, audiences in Hollywood were not able to view the broadcasts live.

With videotape still five years off, the only affordable way in 1951 to provide a "delayed broadcast" for West Coast viewing was to have a kinescope made in New York on the night of the live broadcast. A kinescope was a primordial technology that included the use of a 35mm film camera to record the televised image off a monitor as it was being broadcast. The quality of the kinescope copy was grainy and substandard, even by early television standards, yet it was the only way for Hollywood to view a live image produced in New York.

The process was reversed, of course, for the few programs that originated live in Hollywood, such as *Burns and Allen*. And therein lay the rub. It was one thing to make blurry kinescopes for the relatively small television audience in L.A., and quite another to reverse the process for the vast majority of the network's national audience in the east. Most sponsors and audiences alike found kinescope viewing dreadful—Philip Morris, included. Yet with Lucy pregnant with the couple's first child, both she and Desi insisted on staying in Hollywood.[54] A creative solution was sorely needed—and fast.

---

53 Chapman University Lecture (6)—"Late Night and Daytime," p 12

54 Desilu: The Story of Lucille Ball and Desi Arnaz, pp 69–70

Lucy swims with dolphins

Desi got together with Karl Freund, a noted German cinematographer, and developed a way to use three film cameras on dollies shooting simultaneously, similar to the way TV cameras were used for live audience shows. Arnaz suggested to Philip Morris that they record the show on film in Hollywood in front of a live studio audience, thereby eliminating the issue of visual quality while avoiding a move to New York during Lucy's pregnancy. It was an intriguing idea. No one had ever tried this before—*filming* a show before a *live* audience. *Amos 'n' Andy* had begun recording in film, three months earlier, but theirs was a one-camera set-up supported by a laugh-track.[55]

Both CBS and Philip Morris initially balked at the idea—the cost, they felt, was too high. Film cameras would have to be used on TV pedestals requiring three operators per pedestal instead of one. Desi and Lucy countered by agreeing to take a one-thousand-dollar weekly pay cut in order to cover the additional expense connected with shooting the show on film, provided they were given ownership of the *I Love Lucy* films. Not really understanding what the "after-market" (syndication) of television really was, at this early juncture, CBS quickly acquiesced and allowed them to film (and own) their show in Hollywood.

I Love Lucy's pioneering use of three cameras led to its becoming the standard technique for the production of most sitcoms filmed in front of an audience. The process resulted in a much sharper picture quality, in contrast to blurry kinescopes. This led to an unexpected benefit for Desilu. During the series' second season, with Lucy well into her pregnancy, Desi realized that they would not be able to fulfill the show's 39-episode commitment. Thinking on his feet, Desilu decided to *rebroadcast* popular episodes of the series' first season to help give Lucy the necessary rest she needed after giving birth. This effectively allowed for fewer episodes to be filmed in season two.

The rebroadcasts proved to be ratings winners, giving birth to the *rerun*, which would later lead to the very profitable *rerun syndication market*[56]—one Desilu had bought its way into for a paltry $39,000 (one thousand per week) during the show's first season on TV. Before the series left the air in 1957, Desilu sold back the *I Love Lucy* films to CBS for four million dollars (32M USD 2012). The money allowed them to expand their company (Desilu) into a major supplier and syndicator of network TV shows. Ball bought Arnaz out after their divorce, in 1960, and ran the company by herself for several years. In 1967, Lucy sold her company to Gulf+Western, a manufacturing conglomerate looking to diversify into

55 Encyclopedia of 20th Century American Television, pp14–15

56 Desilu: The Story of Lucille Ball and Desi Arnaz, p 296

the communications business, for $67M (280M USD 2012).[57] Gulf+Western soon changed its name to Paramount Television, the core, of which, sprang from Desilu. Today, Paramount Television is referred to as CBS Television Studios.

After the *I Love Lucy* series ended in 1957, a modified version of the show continued for three more seasons with 13 one-hour specials running from 1957 to 1960. The specials first aired under the title *The Lucille Ball-Desi Arnaz Show* and later in reruns (original shows broadcast for a second time) as *The Lucy-Desi Comedy Hour*. *I Love Lucy* was the most-watched show in the United States in four of its six seasons, and was the first to end its run at the top of the Nielsen ratings—an accomplishment later matched by only *The Andy Griffith Show* and *Seinfeld*. In 2002, *I Love Lucy*, the show that had won five Emmy Awards and numerous nominations, ranked second on *TV Guide*'s all-time list of TV's greatest shows, behind only *Seinfeld* and ahead of *The Honeymooners*.[58]

Discussion Questions

A. Double Entendre

- To what does the heading, "Double Entendre," refer?

B. Separate but Equal

- What were the opposing perspectives on the value of *Amos 'n' Andy* as a racial breakthrough in television?

C. Brown v Board of Education

- Why do you think the events around the 1954 landmark *Brown V Board of Education* received so little media attention even while the witch hunts of McCarthyism were still front page news?

D. Birth of the Civil Rights Movement

- Our American history books all mention Rosa Parks and the 1955 bus incident in Montgomery, Alabama. What was it about this strike for civil rights that was so memorable?

---

57 Desilu: The Story of Lucille Ball and Desi Arnaz, pp 308–309

58 Encyclopedia of 20th Century American Television, p 102

- *Thunder on Sycamore Street*, the 1954 CBS teleplay aired on *Westinghouse Studio One*, had to be changed for the sponsors. What transpired and how was its affect on viewers as powerful a social statement as was the original script?

E. The Nightly Ritual

- *The Nat King Cole* Show had all the 'right' ingredients to be a 'crossover' black to white success but was ultimately unplugged by what southern social upheaval?

F. RGB

- The first national colorcast (the 1954 Tournament of Roses on NBC) occurred on January 1, 1954. This event was a long time coming. What was the drama behind the race to perfect the technology?

G. Hi-Yo, Silver … Away

- What were the flaws of the prototype western, *The Lone Ranger*, that were overlooked amid the postwar success of this trailblazing hit?

H. Gunsmoke

- *Gunsmoke*, the 1955 CBS western, was endorsed by what legendary star based on what unique characteristics that proved to be a winning combination for the enduring show?

I. Bonanza

- What did *Bonanza* bring to westerns that was different from typical western programming up to that point?

J. Joe Friday

- The NBC series, *Dragnet*, was written with a winning formula that kept it on the screen for years. What was its secret for success?

K. Number One with a Bullet

- The beloved *I Love Lucy* show was a game changer in more than one way for programming. What were these innovations that created a new TV language still in use today?

CHAPTER NINE

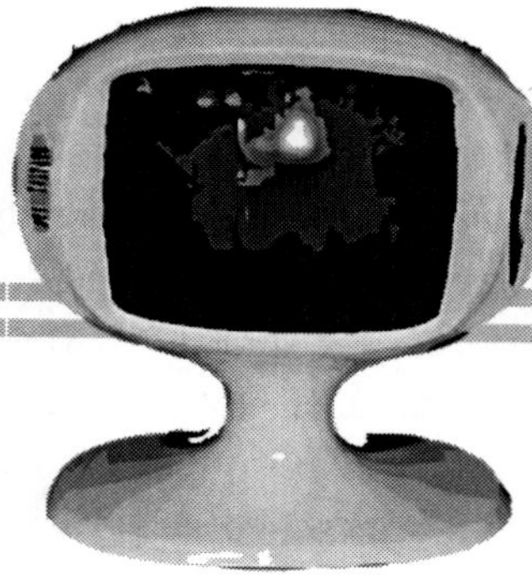

The New Global Audience

1960–1965

Prime Time Diplomacy

In the fall of 1959, emerging from a decade in which the Soviet leadership had been reclusive to a fault, Soviet Premier Nikita Khrushchev stepped from a Russian plane onto American soil and exposed himself to two weeks of prime time television. He was making this magnanimous effort to help Americans better understand their enemy in a cold war that had grown positively frigid. This was, of course, a huge gamble and one that would mean his job if he failed. Khrushchev would have to take questions he could not censor, while risking answers he could neither edit nor retract, in a land regarded by the most of the Soviet leadership as its mortal enemy.[1] Khrushchev was undeterred; the risk, he felt, was worth it. If successful, his visit could puncture American *misconceptions* of the Soviet Union and help ease the arms race that was fueling the cold war.

Khrushchev gave a bravura performance. He joked and cajoled, he argued and clowned, and denounced American capitalism through the warmest smile. Television caught it all. Khrushchev's trove of maxims was inexhaustible. *"Two mountains never meet,"* he told reporters while visiting Disneyland late in his visit.

1 *Tube of Plenty*, p 249

"But two people can."[2] Television loved Nikita Khrushchev. Ratings for the national six o'clock network newscast soared during his two-week stay in America. Regular prime time programming was interrupted several times during his visit so that networks could use the time usually saved for westerns and sitcoms to run specials on Khrushchev and the Soviet Union.

Nikita Khrushchev speaking in Washington during 1959 American visit

TV critics and political pendants alike thought him "bombastic," but the American public couldn't get enough of Nikita Khrushchev. By the time he left for home, the Soviet Premier was practically a household word in America and television was the reason. Clearly, Khrushchev's visit set changes in motion, both in the U.S. as well as the Soviet Union. Soon after Khrushchev's departure, the White House announced that Americans and Soviets would join French and British leaders at a Paris diplomatic summit meeting scheduled for the following May, 1960. President Eisenhower pledged to make a goodwill tour of the Soviet Union during the summer that followed.[3] The super powers were letting up on the reigns of world dominion, but how long would this uneasy détente really last?

Not long at all, as it turned out. On May 1, 1960, an American U-2 spy plane was shot down inside Russia's borders by a Soviet SA-2 Guideline surface-to-air missile.[4] At first denying knowledge of its high-altitude surveillance aircraft, the United States government was finally forced to admit to the spy plane and the mission when the Soviet government produced its surviving pilot, Francis Gary Powers, as well as photos of military bases in Russia taken by Powers. Thinking Powers had died in the crash, the United States had feigned ignorance while the world was watching. Television had seen to that. Newsreels and now videotape, though often delayed by as much as a week before broadcast, carried the message to the world via television. The incident, coming as it did roughly two weeks before the scheduled opening of an East–West summit in Paris, was of great embarrassment to the United States and prompted a marked deterioration in its relations with the Soviet Union that would span the 1960's and well beyond.

---

2 *Tube of Plenty*, p 249

3 *Tube of Plenty*, p 253

4 The U-2 Spyplane; Toward the Unknown website

The Great Debates

On the morning of September 26, 1960, John F. Kennedy was a relatively unknown senator from Massachusetts who just happened to be the Democratic presidential nominee for the 1960 presidential election, now six weeks away. Kennedy was young and he was Catholic and because no one of Catholic faith had ever been elected president of the United States, it was universally agreed that he was bound to lose. It didn't help that he was facing off that very evening, in the first televised presidential debate in American history, against ostensibly the toughest and craftiest political foe of the twentieth century, Richard M. Nixon.

Nixon had been on television before. Almost eight years to the day, as it turned out. On September 23, 1952, while running for vice president on the Republican presidential ticket, Senator Nixon had been accused of improprieties relating to a fund established by his backers to reimburse him for political expenses. With his place on the Republican ticket suddenly in doubt, Nixon flew home to his family in Los Angeles and delivered a half-hour, prime time television address in which he defended himself, attacked his opponents, and urged the audience to contact the Republican National Committee (RNC) as to whether or not Nixon should remain on the Republican ticket. During the speech, Nixon stated emphatically that regardless of what anyone said, he intended to keep one gift, a black-and-white dog the Nixon children had named Checkers.[5] The dog's name became forever attached to the address, thus giving it its popular handle: The Checkers Speech.

Thanks to television, Nixon not only survived the 1952 accusation, but his stock also rose. Critics to this day say the junior senator from California shamelessly used his wife, his two young daughters, and a dog to save his career, but what he really used was the American voter. A picture was truly worth a thousand words. Richard Nixon, while stiff looking on camera, came across the tube that night as a man of truth defending his children. Radio audiences, when later polled, were still uncertain of Nixon's complicity. Those who viewed the speech on prime time television, however, were 90% certain he'd done nothing wrong.[6] Television, it seemed, could convey instantly in pictures what radio could no longer cover adequately in words. With the advent of television and its success in postwar society, more and more *listeners* were now becoming *viewers* instead.

In the summer of 1959, Nixon again found himself on prime time television as the reciprocal piece of the Nixon-visits-Russia–Khrushchev-visits-America quid pro quo. On July 24, 1959, Vice President Nixon became President Dwight D. Eisenhower's emissary of goodwill, meeting with Soviet Premier Nikita Khrushchev on Russian soil at the American National Exhibition at Sokolniki Park, near Moscow. For the exhibition, an entire house had been built by American exhibitors who claimed anyone in America could afford it. The house was filled with labor-saving devices representing the fruits of consumer capitalism.

---

5 Richard Nixon: Rhetorical Strategist, p 43

6 Stay Tuned, p 63

The debate that followed Nixon and Khrushchev around the house ended up in the kitchen and was recorded on color videotape, a new technology pioneered in the U.S.—something Nixon made mention of, causing quite a political stir. *The Kitchen Debate*, as it would later be termed, was really a series of impromptu exchanges (through interpreters) between Nixon and Khrushchev. Both men argued for their country's industrial accomplishments, with Khrushchev stressing the Soviets' focus on "things that matter" rather than luxury.[7]

Soviet Premier Nikita Khrushchev and United States Vice President Richard Nixon debate the merits of Communism versus Capitalism in a model American kitchen at the American National Exhibition in Moscow July 1959

In the United States, all three major television networks intended to broadcast The Kitchen Debate during prime time on July 25, one day after the debate had taken place. The Soviets protested—the two countries had agreed to broadcast the debate simultaneously on the 27th of June. The Soviets threatened to hang onto the videotape until then if they had to. The American networks argued that waiting to broadcast the debate would cause the news to lose its immediacy. Russia finally acquiesced to American television and the videotaped show was finally released. U.S. reaction was mixed. Some saw the debate as a picture of how far apart the east and west really were, while others praised the way Nixon managed to convey pride in his nation's peaceful accomplishments while still confident of its power under threat.[8]

By the fall of 1960, however, Nixon's confidence, while still there, was withered by fatigue. Nixon had really been on the campaign trail since The Kitchen Debate in Moscow, 15 months earlier, and now came the first night of what newscasters were calling *The Great Debates*. The four debates took place in different cities, but the first was in Chicago at the CBS affiliate WBBM-TV.

What happened after the two candidates took the stage is a familiar tale. Nixon, pale and underweight from a recent hospitalization, and fatigued by the campaign trail, appeared sickly and sweaty, while Kennedy appeared calm and confident and tan. Nixon declined CBS's offer of makeup, though one of his own staff did manage to dab the vice president's face with something called *Lazy Shave* that Nixon often used to hide his *five o'clock shadow*.[9] Earlier that same day, Kennedy's aide and speech writer, Ted Sorensen, remembered prepping *his* candidate for the big night in quite a different light. He and Kennedy were on the roof of their Chicago hotel, running through a pile of note cards, with Sorenson

7 *New York Times*—"The Cold War's Hot Kitchen" July 24, 1959

8 *New York Times*—"Moscow Debate Stirs U.S Public" July 27, 1959

9 CNN Politics website—"Kennedy-Nixon debate changed politics for good" September 26, 2005

"The Great Debates"
Senator John Kennedy (left) and Vice President Richard Nixon (right) meet at center stage, September 26, 1960, in the first of four televised prime time Presidential Debates

quizzing Kennedy on likely debate topics as the presidential candidate sipped lemonade while working on his tan.[10]

As the story goes, those who listened to the debate on the radio thought Nixon had won. But those listeners were in the minority. By 1960, 88% of American households had televisions—up from only 11% the decade before.[11] The number of viewers who tuned in to the debate has been estimated anywhere from 60 to 80 million (*Broadcast Magazine* had it at 74 million out of a population of 179 million).[12] Suffice it to say it was the largest audience up until that time to view a TV show of any kind and gives a fair indication of the impact these debates had on one of the closest elections in presidential history. Those who watched the debate on TV thought Kennedy was the clear winner. Many pundits tuning in to the TV broadcast felt that Kennedy actually won the election that very night.

It's now routinely acknowledged that without the nation's first televised debate, John Fitzgerald Kennedy would likely never have been president. Yet beyond securing his presidential career, the 60-minute duel between the handsome Irish American senator (Kennedy) and the strident and perspiring vice president (Nixon) fundamentally altered political campaigns, television media, and America's political history. Up to that point, politics had not really been played out on television. "It was very much an entertainment medium," says Alan Schroeder, a media historian and associate professor at Northeastern University, when referring to television. "It wasn't a place for serious discourse."[13] The presidential debate that night

10 *Time*—"How the Nixon-Kennedy Debate Changed the World" September 23, 2010
11 TV Feeds My Family website—"50 Years Later: the Kennedy-Nixon Debates" September 28, 2010
12 *Time*—"How the Nixon-Kennedy Debate Changed the World" September 23, 2010
13 *Time*—"How the Nixon-Kennedy Debate Changed the World" September 23, 2010

punctured that myth forever. So *serious* a place had television become that it would be another 16 years before presidential candidates would dare to chance debating again.

While Nixon performed much better in the three subsequent debates, the damage had already been done. The *Lazy Shave* had failed to work its magic. Voters couldn't wipe away Nixon's sweaty, five o'clock shadow from their memory. Moreover, Kennedy spoke to the camera during the telecast while Nixon spoke to the reporters seated in the live audience. Nixon seemed uncomfortable looking into the camera and often enough (in the first Great Debate) didn't know which camera to look at. Kennedy's speech writer, Ted Sorensen, speculated years later that beyond what the debate did to vault Jack Kennedy into the White House, it fundamentally altered the world as we knew it then and as we know it now. In 1962, President Kennedy refused the recommendation by the Joint Chiefs of Staff to respond, militarily, to the Soviet Union's placing of nuclear missiles in Cuba. *President* Richard Nixon, Sorenson feared, would have taken the Joint Chiefs' advice and in so doing plunged America and the Soviet Union into World War III.[14]

Space Race

In 1961, President Kennedy accepted an invitation to address the annual meeting of the National Association of Broadcasters (NAB), many of whom speculated he would have censorship proposals to dole out—the same kind of censorship Senator Tom Dodd attempted pushing through three years later in an effort to stem the increased use of violence as entertainment on prime time TV. As it turned out, the reverse was true. Kennedy's speech surprised them as he took the lectern:

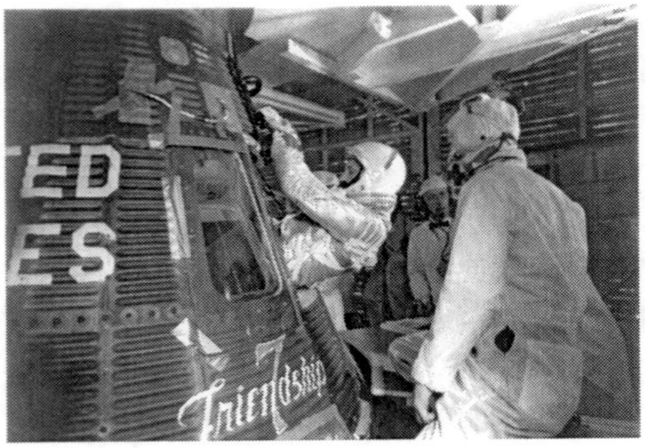

Mercury astronaut John Glenn climbs into Freedom 7. Glenn was the first American launched into orbit around the Earth, February 20, 1962

"The essence of free communication," he said, "must be that our failures as well as our successes will be broadcast around the world. The flow of ideas, the capacity to make informed choices, the ability to criticize—all assumptions on which political democracy rests—depend largely upon communication. And you [the broadcasters] are the guardians of it. Guardians of the most powerful and effective means of communication ever designed."[15]

The President was right. Television *was* the most effective means of communication ever designed and its reach was starting to have an impact on world order. On February 20, 1962, that world seemed to get a whole lot smaller as Lt.

14 *Time*—"How the Nixon-Kennedy Debate Changed the World" September 23, 2010

15 *Tube of Plenty*, p 299

President John F. Kennedy
Rice University
September 12, 1962

"We choose to go to the moon in this decade and do the other things, not because they are easy, but because they are hard, because that goal will serve to organize and measure the best of our energies and skills, because that challenge is one that we are willing to accept, one we are unwilling to postpone, and one which we intend to win, and the others, too.

It is for these reasons that I regard the decision last year to shift our efforts in space from low to high gear as among the most important decisions that will be made during my incumbency in the office of the Presidency."

President Kennedy ramps up the Space Race, delivering "Man on the Moon Speech" to Rice University, 1962

Col. John Glenn became the first American to be shot into orbit around the Earth. Though Glenn would scarcely be gone 90 minutes, no TV movie could have ever provided us with more suspense. His Mercury-Atlas 6 mission completed three orbits in the *Friendship 7* spacecraft, and splashed down safely in the Atlantic Ocean—but only after a nail-biting reentry due to false telemetry data pointing to a loose heat-shield.[16] You'd have almost thought the telecast was scripted. Yet, as momentous as the launch from Cape Canaveral was that February morning, equally important was the fact that television had been *invited* to watch. Within months, Lt. Commander Scott Carpenter repeated Glenn's achievement. And again, television was on the scene.

Viewers now had front-row seats for all blast-off and recovery operations for space flights that would take us from Earth's orbit to moon-walking before the decade was out. Kennedy had publicly announced his support for the Apollo Space Program that would take us to the moon, before a special joint session of Congress, not a year earlier. Said Kennedy in 1961: *"I believe that this nation should commit itself to achieving the goal, before this decade is out, of landing a man on the moon and returning him safely to the earth."*[17]

Kennedy's justification for the Moon Race seemed legitimate. It was both vital to national security and it would focus the nation's energies in other scientific fields. In September, 1962, Kennedy reaffirmed his commitment to space in a speech he gave to Rice University (see insert). Focused on the President's commitment to deliver a moon landing by decade's end, the National

16 The Race: The uncensored story of how America beat Russia to the Moon, pp 156–164

17 "Special Message to the Congress on Urgent National Needs," p 4

Aeronautics and Space Association (NASA) introduced Project Gemini in 1962 to supersede its Mercury Program. Gemini featured a two-crew-member spacecraft that would support the ultimate Apollo Moon Program by developing the key spaceflight technologies—space rendezvous and docking of two craft; flight durations of sufficient length to simulate going to the Moon and back; and accomplishing "useful work" rather than just "walking in space."[18]

America was hooked on the Space Race and so was television. The two fed each other's insatiable appetite for *anything lunar*. Between 1962 and 1972, network television devoted hundreds of hours of prime time programming to America's Space Program. Through six manned Mercury launches, the ten manned Gemini flights, the seventeen manned and unmanned Apollo launches, and the nearly 200 Earth and moon orbits,[19] the nation watched in awe as all of these surreal events happened in real time in living rooms across America. What had been the stuff of science fiction was now very much a reality. As the space flights were always launched from Cape Canaveral, Florida (later re-named Cape Kennedy), those Americans living on the west coast would have to brave the dead of night to watch the launches live, but millions of Americans did just that.

But now to broadcast to all the world, live and simultaneously, just as we in America were receiving them—that was the next challenge. No more delayed videotape or kinescopes or newsreel footage showing up two weeks after the fact. It was positively revolutionary. Sporting events. News events. Nasty wars and royal weddings brought right into our living rooms as they happened, from anywhere on the globe. In 1961, this revolutionary concept was almost beyond belief. In fact, technically speaking, it was beyond belief. An annoying problem kept getting in the way.

Line of Sight

Since the beginnings of TV broadcasting, the relaying of programs from station to station in America had been the province of AT&T.[20] AT&T, having made many advancements in the transmission of signals had nevertheless been hampered with the persistent problem that radio signals travel linearly, not circularly—that is to say, they can't bend around objects on Earth or around the Earth itself. If only that were possible, AT&T would not only be relaying the message from station to station, but also from continent to continent; from millions of people to billions of people, overnight.

The Kennedy Administration was all for finding a way to do just that. President Kennedy reasoned correctly that satellite communication would be an essential key to international prestige and power. After all, hadn't Kennedy used television to win the 1960 presidential election? Hadn't Nixon used it to

18 Gemini Program, p 1

19 The Race: The uncensored story of how America beat Russia to the Moon, pp 156–164

20 *Tube of Plenty*, p 310

sustain his political career eight years earlier? Hadn't NASA used it to excite the American people into supporting the Space Race? The medium, as sociologist Marshall McLuhan had said, is the message. And the medium was television.

Thus in July of 1962, within weeks for the second manned launch from Cape Canaveral, Telstar I, the first communication satellite ever shot into space, was launched by NASA and boosted into orbit around the Earth, while AT&T picked up the tab. Actually, there were many in Congress who felt that statement a misnomer. Sure, AT&T paid for *this* launch, but that this particular launch even happened at all was due to the two previous, astronaut-driven launches from Cape Canaveral, not to mention the twenty unmanned test flights that came first. In short, the Telstar launching had cost the American taxpayer billions of dollars in public funds. So what was a private company like AT&T doing owning the public trust (aka the Telstar satellite)?

July 10, 1962, Telstar 1 becomes First Communications Satellite launched into orbit around the Earth

AT&T argued that they had sunk billions into the development of the satellite technology needed to relay all forms of communication, not just television. Suffice it to say the launching of Telstar 1 was right there beside the laying of the first Atlantic cable, or Marconi ringing his first doorbell. No one less than NBC news anchor David Brinkley, honoring the event and ushering in the new communications era with a memorable broadcast from Paris, said simply (via Telstar) ... there *was* no more important news than that revolving around the fact that *live* events could now be transmitted to and from all parts of the globe.[21]

Just one month after the Telstar launch, the Communications Satellite Act of 1962 was signed into law. The law called for privatizing the communications satellite and did so by creating COMSAT (Communications Satellite Corporation) composed of a fifteen-man board of directors—three to be chosen by the President; six to be selected by public stockholders; and six chosen by communications companies investing in COMSAT.[22] The only proviso was that no one company (RCA, for example) could have more than two representatives on the board. By February 1963, AT&T was joined by RCA, Western Union, and ITT as the principal corporate investors.

COMSAT stock doubled in value overnight. Yet as AT&T, RCA, and the others were soon to discover, nothing much had really changed. Why? Again: Line of sight. Telstar 1 could link only areas that were, at any given moment, within its own line of sight. Sure, the line was now longer (after all, Telstar was

21 *Tube of Plenty*, p 309

22 *Tube of Plenty*, p 310

up there orbiting 200 miles above the Earth), but it still had the Earth itself to contend with. As cutting-edge as Telstar was, it was already obsolete when Howard Hughes entered the picture only weeks later. Hughes was well acquainted with the *line of sight* problem from an article he'd read by British science fiction writer Arthur C. Clarke, in *Wireless World*, as early as 1945.[23] In that article, Clarke postulated an answer to the ongoing line-of-sight problem. Clarke envisioned a different kind of satellite or rather, a series of satellites all moving in an orbit so synchronized with the Earth's rotation as to seemingly hover in a fixed spot in the night sky.

In early 1963, as Telstar was just beginning its orbits, Hughes Aircraft Corporation launched its own satellite and put the first synchronous satellite into space. The first attempt met with failure, but the second satellite sent up by Hughes functioned perfectly. Quickly realizing what Hughes was on to, COMSAT saw the bigger picture. Rather than one orbiting satellite, it would take several fixed or synchronous satellites working in concert with participating ground stations located in various countries and on various continents to transmit anywhere on Earth *from* anywhere on Earth without any delay whatsoever.

A standard ground station would cost between three and seven million dollars and consist of a dish some 100 feet in diameter.[24] Because America and the Kennedy Administration couldn't force every country to spend this kind of money, it sought instead to entice them, offering economic and military aid to every country purchasing a dish and linking up to the synchronous satellite system.

Spotlight

The cheers following President Kennedy's 1961 speech at the National Association of Broadcasters' annual meeting soon faded as the second speaker of the morning approached the microphone. Newton Minow, an attorney appointed by Kennedy to chair the FCC, was an unknown quantity to the convention delegates, but his clerkish appearance and opening words of admiration for television quickly put the crowded room at ease. Minow was happy to find that the health of the TV industry was good. Television's 1960 gross revenue of $1.3B had earned broadcasters a profit of almost $244M—a return of 19%. Hoping to bring a smile, Minow played off the hit game show *The Price is Right* and joked: "For your investors, the price has indeed been right."[25]

Minow went on to laud several programs for meritorious achievement, specifically naming *CBS Reports*, the Army–McCarthy hearings, convention and campaign broadcasts, *See It Now*, *The Great Debates*, *Playhouse 90*, *Kraft Television Theater*, and *Studio One*, among others. Only two of his choices, however, were from the fantasy/entertainment side of television: *Peter Pan* and *Twilight Zone*. "When television

23 *Tube of Plenty*, p 311

24 *Tube of Plenty*, p 313

25 *Tube of Plenty*, p 299

> ### Newton Minow's 1961 Address to the National Association of Broadcasters
>
> "When television is good, nothing can match it. But ... when television is bad, nothing is worse. I invite you to sit down in front of your television set when your station goes on the air and stay there without a book, magazine, newspaper, profit and loss sheet or rating book to distract you and keep your eyes glued to that set until the station signs off. I can assure you that you will observe a vast wasteland. You will see a procession of game shows, violence, audience participation shows, formula comedies about totally unbelievable families, blood and thunder, mayhem, violence, sadism, murder, private eyes, gangsters, more violence and cartoons ... all of it tied together with an endless array of commercials—most screaming, cajoling and offending. I therefore ask is there one person in this room who claims that broadcasting can't do better? Gentlemen, your trust accounting with your beneficiaries is overdue. Never have so few owed so much, to so many."

was good," he added, "nothing was better. But when television was bad, nothing was worse."[26] Minow, aware that U.S. television was on the verge of reaching a global audience, thought networks owed it to their country to put their best foot forward. Newton Minow realized that the small flickering screen that graced some 90% of America's living rooms, by then, could influence the American population in ways previously unheard of—and so, too, the world. At its core, Minow worried that the now-established medium of television was in danger of becoming a "wasteland" and thus began his rant. Said Minow regarding prime time TV's sorry state of programming: "*You will see a procession of game shows, violence, audience participation shows, formula comedies about totally unbelievable families, blood and thunder, mayhem, violence, sadism, murder, private eyes, gangsters, more violence and cartoons ... all of it tied together with an endless array of commercials—most screaming, cajoling and offending.*"[27] The NAB could do better than that, Minow scolded—then intimated that he would be yanking broadcasting licenses if the television bar wasn't raised soon.

One of the worst "offenders" of this time was the hit show from Desilu Productions, *The Untouchables*—an American crime drama that ran from 1959 to 1963 on ABC. The series revolved around a fictionalized character based on the crime-fighting experiences of Eliot Ness, a federal prohibition agent working to clean up Chicago in the 1930's. As the story goes, Ness put together a special team of agents handpicked for their courage and incorruptibility, thus earning the team its nickname: The Untouchables. The show's gritty use of graphic violence drew harsh criticism. TV viewers used to watching villains die bloodless and at a distance were suddenly inundated with bloody machine gun deaths, up close and personal, where bullet holes could be seen in the victims' bodies.

---

26 *Tube of Plenty*, p 300

27 *Tube of Plenty*, p 300

Elliot Ness (starring Robert Stack, standing) in a scene from The Untouchables, *a series deemed "too violent" for early 60's viewing*

And that wasn't the popular series' only problem. The show drew harsh criticism from Italian Americans, including Frank Sinatra, who felt the show promoted negative stereotypes of Italians as mobsters and gangsters. Viewers of Italian American descent expressed displeasure with the program, which to them vilified Italian Americans, stereotyping them as *the* singular criminal element.[28] Boycotts against the show were so well organized that one of the series' two sponsors dropped the show. The show's executive producer, Desi Arnaz, managed to quell the firestorm, but not before *The Untouchables* came to the attention of Senator Thomas J. Dodd of Connecticut.

One of the public figures seizing the spotlight, in 1961, Dodd had begun his career in the Senate, two years earlier, with feisty cold-war rhetoric, but leaped into national prominence when, as chairman of the Senate Subcommittee on Juvenile Delinquency, the Democratic senator took on television violence.[29] Subpoenaing files from networks and production auspices, Dodd discovered a plethora of written notes spelling out "obsessions with violence" pertaining specifically to *The Untouchables,* though the Committee named other series (westerns mostly) as well. Dodd's subcommittee held hearings, calling witnesses from the television industry. Here, the committee learned that "violence" was more than a prime time problem. It was being syndicated now as well.[30] Independent stations throughout the country were scheduling programs filled with visceral scenes and dispensing violence to younger audiences, earlier in the day, when that demographic could be more easily reached by advertisers.

The 55-year-old, silver-haired, charismatic senator began getting his picture in the newspaper—Tom Dodd was becoming a national figure. There was even talk about Kennedy taking on a new vice presidential running mate in 1964. Yet for all the uproar, no report on TV violence was ever published by Dodd's subcommittee. In an ironic twist of politics, Dodd's newfound celebrity earned him campaign contributions and political gifts from the executives of companies wanting to be in the senator's favor. Metromedia Television was one of them. Metromedia had risen to power due to the valuable frequencies it had acquired when it bought out the DuMont Television Company in 1956. Metromedia's courtship with Dodd altered the senator's focus. Subtly, Dodd began to *distance* himself from the fray of TV violence, calling for fewer hearings and handing out more benign treatment of witnesses when they were called before his committee. Influence-peddling in politics had begun in earnest. The press branded Dodd a

28 *Esquire*—"Frank Sinatra Has a Cold," p 27

29 *Tube of Plenty*, pp 303–304

30 *Tube of Plenty*, p 304

"reluctant dragon," but members of Dodd's own staff, who knew the sordid story, deplored it as a complete "sell out." Historically, it was part of a series of campaign ethics violations that would lead to Dodd's 1967 Senatorial Censure—one of only six senators officially reprimanded in the twentieth century.

Escapism

Suffice it to say that as the fall of 1962 approached, the broadcasting industry was feeling easier about the Dodd threat—it appeared he was backing off. FCC head, Newton Minow, however, was another story. Minow still caused worry at the networks—after all, the FCC controlled all licenses to broadcast. The television industry countered with defensive measures in the form of more varied programming hoping to secure FCC blessings. Some of the programming played out during the day and included informational children's series like *Exploring* and *Discovery*, but most of the changes occurred in prime time.[31]

Fearing that they might lose their licenses, networks came up with shows that reached to raise the bar. The 1961–'62 arrivals included a rash of new television comedies as well as more meaty dramas. Notable was *The Defenders,* a series built on a legal franchise created by Reginald Rose who'd penned the critically acclaimed film script, *Twelve Angry Men*. In creating *The Defenders,* Rose reached out for more relevant stories. His efforts gave his series a prestige that evoked comparisons to the superb anthology dramas that had been broadcast a decade earlier. There were also impressive series with medical franchises like *Ben Casey* and *Dr. Kildare* and *The Nurses.* A social worker was featured in *East Side–West Side*; and a teacher in *Mr. Novak*. Both series made for exemplary viewing. To the surprise of network officialdom, the two medical series that network executives thought too boring were anything but. The success of *Ben Casey* and *Dr. Kildare* threatened a television stampede to the operating table every Monday and Thursday night, respectively.[32]

Among the comedy series, the deft and genial *Dick Van Dyke Show* exhibited exceptional talents, on screen and off. When the series aired in 1961, it was already three years old—at least on paper. In 1958, Carl Reiner, already a successful writer/actor on *Your Show of Shows*, created a new television program he titled *Head of the Family*—a sitcom depicting the life of a comedy writer named Rob Petrie.[33]

Dick Van Dyke and Mary Tyler Moore star as Rob and Laura Petrie in the CBS comedy smash The Dick Van Dyke Show *1961–1966*

31 *Tube of Plenty*, p 306

32 *Tube of Plenty*, p 306

33 Stay Tuned, p 12

Reiner wanted to star in the show, but the network thought the casting wrong. Reiner was funny, true, but acerbic by nature. Rob Petrie had to appeal to a less sophisticated demographic that loved pratfalls over sarcasm. The actor they chose for the role was the male version of Lucille Ball: Dick Van Dyke. Van Dyke proved to be one of the most versatile performers to ever grace a network set. His perfectly cast costars included luminous newcomer Mary Tyler Moore and veteran comic actors Morey Amsterdam and Rose Marie.

The Dick Van Dyke Show was tabbed by *TV Guide* in 2002 as the thirteenth greatest television series of the twentieth century, but only six prime time live-action comedies rode above it in their survey (*I Love Lucy* and *The Honeymooners*—'50's/*The Andy Griffith Show*—'60's/*All in the Family* and *The Mary Tyler Moore Show*—'70's/*Seinfeld*—'90's).[34] The "family" aspect of the CBS series was far more real and less stereotypical of what came before and after it and at the same time, always funny. Laura Petrie often wore Capris in the series, not dresses—nearly scandalous for the times. And Richie, their son, was a brat—nothing like the well-behaved Beaver Cleaver on ABC's *Leave It to Beaver* (or, for that matter, any other TV children of the time). And Rob (played to perfection by Van Dyke) is a pretty hip father who doesn't leave the parenting to Laura alone. This was the highbrow comedy Newton Minow had been looking for, but genius like this didn't grow on trees. As it turned out, there were those who would have argued that it bubbled up out of the ground.

CBS's The Beverly Hillbillies *come a clatterin' in from the Ozarks! Granny (Irene Ryan) and Jed (Buddy Ebsen) pictured here*

The Beverly Hillbillies clattered onto television in September of 1962 and soared to the top of the network ratings charts before the end of the year. It may have not been the highbrow comedy Minow was looking for, but it did help divert public indignation from the subject of violence. The series revolved around a mountain clan from the Ozarks who had struck oil in their back yard and moved to Beverly Hills in a flatbed truck loaded down with jugs of corn liquor and $25,000,000 (188M USD 2012) in cash.[35] The family remained unchanged by the new environment and this was the source of the show's laugh-out-loud humor and broad appeal.

The series was created by Filmways, a company that made a fortune in the advertising game and used it to move into television production. With their added success from ... *Hillbillies*, Filmways began

34 *Fifty Years of Television*, p 212

35 The Beverly Hillbillies stage play adapted from TV Series Pilot

shamelessly passing around a second series that was really *The Beverly Hillbillies* in reverse—a jet-set beauty and her lawyer husband trade in the bright lights of Manhattan for a farm in Hooterville.[36] The show reached the air in 1965 as the Eva Gabor–Eddie Albert series *Green Acres*. And just like hicks in Beverly Hills, the jet setters in Hooterville found an immediate audience.

While the era of the anthology series was disappearing, the rural sitcom and a whole collection of new genres that would come to define escapist-style television in the post-Golden Age era were being introduced. Replacing the older-skewing westerns of the 1950's were gimmicky sitcoms that appealed to a younger audience—stylish, visually jolting shows with high production values. An assortment of new series born in the first half of the decade reflect this transformation: ABC's *Gidget*, a beach comedy about an energetic 15-year-old playing in the California sun; *F Troop*, another ABC contribution, offered up an assortment of Native American stereotypes in a comedy set at a military fort in the post-Civil War West; and NBC's *I Dream of Jeannie*, a comedy about the relationship between an astronaut and a voluptuous 2,000-year-old genie. There was *My Mother the Car* from NBC, which delivered just what its title promised. Yet of all the new shows airing in the early 1960's, *Hogan's Heroes*, from CBS, best exemplified the bizarre direction TV entertainment was taking. Debuting in Nielsen's Top 10 (TV ratings) for the 1965 season, *Hogan's Heroes* was a sitcom set in a Nazi prison camp during World War II.[37]

Cast from CBS's Hogan's Heroes *(left to right) American POW Colonel Hogan (Bob Crane); German Colonel Klink (Werner Klemperer)*

Shameless as the era's programming was, it was precisely this kind of fantasy fare that flourished in the 1960 sitcom world. The sillier the sitcom, the better audiences liked it. And why not? With a cold war oppressing the homeland and the Vietnam War raging overseas, escapism television ruled the airwaves offering a welcome respite from the somber body counts reporting in from Vietnam across the nightly news.

A horse could converse in CBS's *Mister Ed*. A witch became a suburban housewife in ABC's *Bewitched*. A Martian took up housekeeping in suburbia in NBC's *My Favorite Martian*. There were *The Flintstones*, the prehistoric, animated equivalent of *The Honeymooners*; *McHale's Navy* with Academy Award–winner Ernest Borgnine; *The Farmer's Daughter* with silver screen star Inger Stevens; and the baby booming cult classic of the 1960's, *Batman*. No locale seemed too farfetched, be it a German POW camp or a deserted island run amok by an unlikely group of castaways led by a big-hearted sea-fearing buffoon named ... Gilligan. The storms that tossed the S.S. Minnow were nothing compared to the critical tsunami that

36 *The TV Guide TV Book: 40 Years of the All-Time Greatest Television Facts, Fads, Hits, and History*, p 174

37 *Encyclopedia Britannica*—Television in the United States

greeted this improbable comedy about a charter-boat crew and its passengers marooned on what looked more like the site of a Burbank luau than a tropical isle. Yet viewers to this day continue to make *Gilligan's Island* the long-running syndication champ that it has remained.

Lost on Gilligan's Island*: the Skipper, co-star Alan Hale Jr.*

The bizarre juxtapositions presented by American television in the early 1960's were more or less a reflection of what daily life in America was at that time. Here we were living in a world dominated by the Cold War and the potential for nuclear annihilation, yet all the while we pretended there was no angst at home, no pressure at the office, and no illness in the world. And there to back us up were *The Beverly Hillbillies* and *Mr. Ed* and the other Nielsen ratings gods to validate our denial. Escapist fantasy on the one hand; news specials filled with global reality on the other. Both worlds often seemed incompatible and yet both had somehow fused together inside our sets—interdependent but antagonistic. There was, of course, no doubt which world commanded viewer loyalty. Series like *Bonanza, The Andy Griffith Show*, and *Gunsmoke* hovered near the top of the ratings heap with a loyal following of between 13 and 18 million weekly viewers—no one would contest that they were the fanfare of television. Yet, every now and then that other world broke in and collided with our fantasies and gripped us by the throat like there was no tomorrow.[38]

The first consignment of Soviet-made R-12 missiles arrived in Cuba on the night of September 8, 1962, followed by a second shipment on September 16. The R-12 silo sites housed the first operational Intermediate-Range Ballistic Missile—the first missile ever mass-produced and the first Soviet missile deployed with a thermonuclear warhead

Missiles of October

One of those "collisions" materialized in October of 1962. It was 7 pm on a Monday night and America was where it always was—right in front of the television. On ABC, republicans and democrats alike were watching the hit western *Cheyenne*. On CBS it was *To Tell the Truth* and *The Lucy Show*. On NBC, viewers had tuned in to cheer on contestants on *The Price Is Right*. And then it came—the most sensational interruption in television history, preempting all network programming across the board. An international ultimatum was delivered without warning by President Kennedy to the Soviet Union concerning newly found missile silos in Cuba.

38 *Tube of Plenty*, p 315

A U.S. Navy Lockheed P-2H Neptune maritime patrol plane was flown over a Soviet cargo ship with crated Ilyushin 11–28 jet bomber on its deck during Cuban Missile Crisis

The CIA had presented the president with photographic evidence that missile sites were being built in Cuba to be used in the launching of long-range preemptive attacks on the United States. Worse, the nuclear warheads for the missiles were on their way from Russia. During feverish, behind-the-scenes debate, alternative plans and various scenarios had been played out in the War Room at the Pentagon. But now on October 22, 1962, the course of action had been charted. We'd quarantine Cuba by way of a blockade and force the Soviet ships carrying the deadly cargo to retreat or face thermonuclear war.

For those tuning in that Monday night to watch *I've Got a Secret, The Danny Thomas Show*, or the detective thriller, *Peter Gunn*, what America got instead was President John Fitzgerald Kennedy using television—with help from Telstar—to prepare a worldwide audience for the prospect of atomic war. Using the word "nuclear" eleven times during his speech,[39] Kennedy warned of a nuclear devastation enveloping the whole northern hemisphere. Said Kennedy:

> I call on Chairman Khrushchev to halt and eliminate this clandestine, reckless and provocative threat to world peace and to stable relations between our two nations. I call upon him further to abandon this course of world domination and to join in an historic effort to end the perilous arms race and transform the history of man. He has an opportunity now to move the world back from the abyss of destruction ...[40]

President Kennedy delivers prime time ultimatum to Soviet Union, October 22, 1962

As it came to pass, although Kennedy was prepared to make concessions with our own bases in Turkey and Italy, he chose not to mention them in his ultimatum to the Soviets. Kennedy's speech, in conjunction with numerous diplomatic and military efforts that were simultaneously being waged, proved so powerful that the crisis ebbed quickly. Soviet ships en route to Cuba halted in the Atlantic. A series of top-secret Soviet messages to the United States offered a basis for settlement. The Russians pledged to dismantle the missile sites in Cuba and America pledged never to invade the island.

39 *Tube of Plenty*, p 317

40 *Tube of Plenty*, p 317

By the end of the ordeal, television audiences were left with the misleading picture of a good-guy–bad-guy crisis. A villain had been caught in a fiendish plan and was vanquished by the hero. The whole good-guy–bad-guy scenario was an oversimplification to be sure—a defect not uncommon to television. What *was* "uncommon" was the timing of Telstar and its global reach allowing President Kennedy's speech that Monday night to be received by much of Europe *live*, without delays. With British and French diplomats using the extra time to weigh in publicly on the side of the United States, the deployment of Telstar just three months earlier could not have been better timed.

Discussion Questions

A. Prime Time Diplomacy

- Televised events such as Nikita Khrushchev's 1959 visit to the United States brought home to Americans in a positive way the personality of this leader of our nemesis, the Soviet Union. How did that same outreach of televised events, three months earlier, prove to be an embarrassment to the United States?

B. The Great Debates

- What presidential campaign was the first to be televised on radio and television?
- Why was the radio audience more impressed with one candidate while the TV audience had a better reaction to the other?

C. Space Race

- Watching the launching of the first American to orbit the earth rocketed the space race into living rooms. Apart from the launch itself, what else was important about that event?

D. Line of Sight

- How did advancing space technology also advance broadcasting capabilities?

E. Spotlight

- Censorship was alive and well in 1961, as demonstrated by what attitudes of Senator Thomas J. Dodd connected to his chairmanship of the Senate Subcommittee on Juvenile Delinquency? What diminished the spotlight on Dodd?

F. Escapism

- Escapist fantasy filled the airwaves in the '60's sitcom programming world. What were some of these series and why did the '60's viewing audience enjoy these programs so much?

G. Missiles of October

- What role did television play in the 1962 decision of President John F. Kennedy to confront Russia's building of missile sites in Cuba?

CHAPTER TEN

Tale of Two Decades

1963–1970

Status Quo

The sexy, free-love, hippie-living, peace-sign-giving, tie-dye-wearing, pot-smoking sixties didn't start out that way. In fact, the first half of the decade was anything but sexy. Truly, the sixties were a tale of two decades—'60's-One and '60's-Two—and the shows that graced our airwaves during those two halves of the same decade were a reflection of the social, political, and sexual beliefs of their respective eras.

You'll recall as the decade opened how the FCC interceded, in 1961, to ensure that the *Tube of Wonder* wasn't a picture tube devoid of values—specifically *family* values. Beginning with its attacks on the prohibition gangster series, *The Untouchables,* the FCC made it their lot in life to go about taking violence off the air. So good were they at their job that the first half of the 1960's looked just as homogenized as TV in the fifties, but without the bite, producing simple stories, void of controversy, as if every series had been written for a ten-year-old.

Critics called this monochromatic view of life in America *escapism*. It became the new industry buzzword and the name of the TV game during the early sixties that bolstered the rise of new television franchises,

Raymond Burr (right) as the unflappable defense attorney Perry Mason on the CBS Series Perry Mason 1957–1966

including both the spy series and the favorite franchise for the next 30 years, the P.I. series. Investigators—private and otherwise—wore out shoe leather on every network and came to us via shows like ABC's *The FBI*; NBC's *Adam 12*; and CBS's *Hawaii Five-0* as well as its long-running hit, *Perry Mason*.

This latter offering was drawn from mystery writer Erle Stanley Gardner's renowned defense attorney, Perry Mason. Every week for nine intriguing seasons, audiences were treated to the commanding presence of actor Raymond Burr, a broad-shouldered man with a sturdy appearance and confident manner that had viewers believing he might never lose a case. As defense attorney Perry Mason, Burr lost only one. The success of *Perry Mason* was the elixir that stirred two genres. True, the show was technically a legal series, but often enough there was detective work going on between Mason and his private investigator Paul Drake (played by William Hopper) and secretary Della Street (played by Barbara Hale), such that the show spilled into that genre as well.

While these P.I. shows might not seem to reflect escapism in the same way *Mr. Ed* or *The Flying Nun* did, they still took TV audiences away from the reality of their day. Every dramatic series during the early 1960's was self-contained—that is to say, a story began and ended in a single hour. No one had to remember what took place in the previous episode because it didn't matter. Next week's show would have a new set of guest stars playing roles relevant to that hour only. Aside from tracking the show's running cast of three or four regular characters, the audience didn't have to think. The euphemism "vegging out" wouldn't enter the lexicon for another 15 years, but that's exactly what viewers were hoping to accomplish in the early 1960's. These were tenuous times, after all—the Cuban Missile Crisis had clearly made that point. Viewers didn't want to have to think when they plopped down in front of the "boob tube." They wanted to "veg out" and be entertained. As it turned out, in September 1963, one of the best detective series to ever fill the airwaves arrived to do just that.

The Fugitive was not a detective series in its traditional sense, but rather a detective yarn featuring an escaped convict believed to have murdered his wife, who spent his Tuesday evenings with ten million American viewers searching for the one-armed killer who actually had.

Every week for four seasons, devotees of the show tuned in faithfully to watch Dr. Richard Kimble (played by David Janssen) search for the one-armed man responsible for his wife's death, while Lt. Philip Gerard relentlessly pursued Kimble. Each episode was filled with gripping suspense and breathless escapes until that fateful night, in 1967, when Kimble finally snags the one-armed man. Lt. Gerard, now realizing he'd been wrong about Kimble all along, grudgingly grants him his freedom. The odd note here is that while *The Fugitive* did have ten million weekly fans, no one was prepared for the audience share it received on August 29, 1967—the night the final episode aired. When the smoke cleared, a series that hadn't broken the Nielsen Top 30 in three of its four years on television, was watched that evening by 72% of the viewing public (61 million households)—a rating not topped for 13 years, until 1980, when the CBS series *Dallas* aired its famous opening episode, "Who Shot JR?"[1]

David Janssen Stars as Dr. Richard Kimble in ABC's The Fugitive, *1963–1967*

Walking in the internationally famous footsteps of James Bond, NBC also capitalized on the escapism era with a glut of spy series winners like *Man from U.N.C.L.E.* and *The Saint.* CBS gave us the long-running *Mission Impossible* and ABC followed with their own secret agents in the off-beat but popular, *The Avengers.* Across the television dial, the shows were filled with loads of action and unbelievable stunts for their time. These shows were fun to watch and most required that no intellectual ammo be spent while doing it.

One from this genre, however, was different. Up until September 1965, television's nightly prime time message was to protect the status quo. Families were white and paternal—virtually every show that aired during the fifties and sixties said so. Moreover, they always got along. There was no angst, no failure, and no concerns, save whether or not Mom would burn the dinner or crash the car the night Dad's boss dropped by for dinner.[2] More importantly, there was no sickness. Everyone looked and felt great all the time. And there to keep us that way were cops and docs who never ever failed. In short, the world on television was white, protestant, healthy, and upwardly mobile—and NBC was about to alter that dynamic.

Color Adjustment

The NBC adventure series of 1965, *I Spy,* put the first of many dents in the aforementioned mystique. The show that starred Bill Cosby and Robert Culp will not only be remembered as the first spy series on television, but the first series of any kind to integrate black and white stars on prime time TV. Originally, the role of Alexander Scott was to be a white, fatherly mentor to Culp's "Kelly Robinson," but after seeing Bill Cosby performing stand-up comedy on a talk-show, producer/showrunner Sheldon Leonard decided

1 Encyclopedia of 20th Century American Television, p 126

2 WGA Writer Speaks Series—"Norman Lear"

*Bill Cosby (left) and Robert Culp (right) stars in the hippest hour drama on television—*I Spy *1965–1968*

to take a chance on hiring him to play opposite Culp.[3] The concept was changed from a mentor–protégé relationship to same-age partners who were equals. It was also notable that Cosby's race was never an issue in any of the stories. Nor was his character in any way subservient to Culp's, with the exception that Culp's Kelly Robinson was a more experienced agent. As the straight-laced Rhodes scholar, fluent in many languages, Cosby's "Alexander Scott" was really the brains of the team. His partner (Culp) was the tennis star (his cover) and playboy who lived by his wits.

The success of the show was attributed to the chemistry between Culp and Cosby. Twelve million households each week tuned in more for their hip banter than for the espionage stories, making *I Spy* a leader in the buddy genre as well.[4] *I Spy* finished among the twenty most-watched shows that first year and Cosby would be honored with three consecutive Emmy Awards for Outstanding Lead Actor in a Drama Series in the seasons that followed. Cosby's acceptance by a national audience was immediate and overwhelming and this encouraged the medium to recognize the fact that "black leads" could draw good box office.[5]

It's important to remember, too, that no black actor, save for Nat King Cole, in an abbreviated one-year stint on prime time television, had starred on a prime time show of any kind since the days of *Amos 'n' Andy*, twelve years earlier—and that was a totally segregated show. *I Spy* was an integrated show and that fact had NBC executives understandably concerned that some affiliates might be unwilling to carry it—and some were. At the beginning of the 1965 season, NBC affiliates in Georgia, Florida, and Alabama declined the show, but the rest of the country was taken with the series' exotic locales as well as with the authentic chemistry between the stars.

In 1968, actress/singer Diahann Carroll became the first black woman to star in *her* own series since Ernestine Wade played Sapphire Stevens, wife to George "Kingfish" Stevens in the all-black series *Amos 'n' Andy* from 1951–'53. Carroll's short-lived NBC series, *Julia*, was about a widowed nurse whose husband had died in Vietnam, leaving her and her son to fend for themselves. Though *Julia* was only to last the

---

3 *Billboard*—"Cosby To Exit WB in August To Join Own Record Firm," p 1

4 Encyclopedia of 20th Century American Television, p 170

5 California Newsreel Production—"Color Adjustment"

better part of two seasons, the show was incredibly popular with females everywhere. When this series first went on, network executives were afraid that the public wouldn't accept a series that had a wholly integrated cast, with a black woman as lead and one that treated all series characters as equals. Their fears were unfounded and *Julia* helped lead the way for woman into the '70's—right alongside Mary Tyler Moore.

Diahann Carroll stars as Julia and Mark Copage co-stars as her son Corey in the groundbreaking series Julia, *1968–1971*

Where Carroll drew criticism was from black viewers, who painted her as an "Oreo cookie"—Carroll's own words describing what some had been saying. It was a crude accusation and nowhere near the truth. Carroll's portrayal of Julia, the character, was neither overly grateful nor overly subservient. Perhaps actress Esther Rolle, star of *Good Times* for five seasons and co-star on *Maude* for the show's first two, playing the same character in both series (African American housekeeper Florida Evans), put *Julia* in its proper perspective. Said Rolle: "It felt like a step above the grinning domestic, who had to be very stout, very dark, preferably with large eyes and a wide grin; and I guess we were so tired of being inundated with that imagery that we accepted *Julia* as a breath of fresh air."[6]

The political climate of the 1960's forbade liberal-thinking producers from breaching the stodgy, slow-moving status quo. Thus, part of their mission was to over-endow all black characters on the screen with white attributes, such that white, middle-class sensibilities would be appeased while watching the show. Both Alexander Scott from *I Spy* and Julia from *Julia* were *these* characters and both were designed to overcome the perceived images of black people from all forms of entertainment, vaudeville to television. These two African American characters could completely assimilate into any white neighborhood and not disturb a soul. Such were the early demands on television because such was the state of our nation in the slow-brewing turbulence of the 1960's.

Thus, when the controversy surrounding *Julia* began to surface, it came from black critics, not white. Many black critics felt the series, while noble in its effort to put people of color on the airwaves, had stripped Julia's character of its black ancestry and culture. It was a criticism typical of what lay ahead for black shows and reflective of what had come before. Because prime time images of black people were so rare to see on television, each one bore the burden of representing the entire race.[7] The problem inherent in that concept and in the paradigm of television, itself, was that such images were usually one-dimensional. Thus, despite high ratings, black shows came under attack not for what they brought to the

6 California Newsreel Production—"Color Adjustment"

7 California Newsreel Production—"Color Adjustment"

screen, but for what they *failed* to reflect. While *Amos 'n' Andy* had been faulted for depicting bumbling black men in a segregated society, *Julia* was rebuked for much the opposite—an integrated world with a successful black family, minus a black father who'd been *conveniently* killed in the Vietnam War.[8] Many blacks felt at the time that by depriving the show of a black father, the series was sending out the wrong message.

To that point, Herman Gray, Professor of Sociology at the University of California, Santa Cruz, had this to say in the 1992 documentary film, *Color Adjustment*: "The entertainment quotient of television is predicated on the notion that the world is a comforting place where we all aspire to be. That's where television's ideological function ... really starts to show up, though hidden [as it usually is] behind the more obvious notion that television is only there to entertain. In its entertainment, however, what it's doing is reinforcing, legitimating and normalizing that particular universe."[9]

By the late 1960's, *that* particular universe had little in common with the one Americans were actually living in; and audiences, by the mid-1960's, were coming to understand that. The myth of America as one big happy family was under a concerted assault, regardless of what prime time television was telling us. The *universe* we saw on television was one of sensible, reasonable folk working in a state of unilateral cooperation. But the one outside "the box" was anything but harmonious; and much of that acrimony came by way of the drive for a Civil Rights Amendment. The question ultimately became whether or not prime time television could address black life in America and still sell the American dream.

Winds of Change

The answer to that question arrived in Washington with Reverend Martin Luther King, Jr. as he delivered his 1963 *I Have a Dream* address in front of the Lincoln Memorial—an address that would turn out to be the catalyst that sent Bill Cosby into the limelight two years later on *I Spy*.

The search for an Equal Rights amendment began in earnest, in Birmingham, Alabama, earlier that summer, where a sequence of violence led the charismatic Reverend King to organize a mammoth march on Washington in search of Civil Rights. The incredibly well-disciplined migration had its climax on August 28, 1963, at the Lincoln Memorial where King told 200,000 people at the Washington gathering and millions more via television and radio:

> I have a dream. It is a dream deeply rooted in the American Dream. I have a dream that one day this nation will rise up and live out the true meaning of its creed: "We hold these truths to be

---

8 California Newsreel Production—"Color Adjustment"

9 California Newsreel Production—"Color Adjustment"

Day of Change
Dr. Martin Luther King, Jr.'s "I Have a Dream Speech," delivered August 28, 1963
Lincoln Memorial in Washington, D.C.

> self-evident, that all men are created equal ..." I have a dream that one day on the red hills of Georgia, sons of former slaves and sons of former slave owners will be able to sit down together at the table of brotherhood. I have a dream that even the state of Mississippi, a state sweltering with the heat of injustice, sweltering with the heat of oppression, will be transformed into an oasis of freedom and justice for all ...[10]

Reverend King's Dream became the dream of the youth of a nation. In defiance of their parents' pleas and threats, Freedom Marchers took off to help blacks everywhere, including Meridian, Mississippi. No one knew it at the time, but King's powerful speech and march that officially launched the struggle for an Equal Rights amendment was the tipping point for integration into television as well. While entertainment divisions at all three networks would avoid the issue for another two years, the prime time arena of public affairs was beginning to bring the real world into American households by way of Special News Bulletins.

Race riots in Miami, Chicago, and South-Central Los Angeles were stealing prime time away from escapist fare like *Peyton Place*, *Petticoat Junction*, and *The Patty Duke Show*. But it was the death of three Freedom Riders in 1964, in Meridian, Mississippi (two of whom were white), that found a national audience. Twenty-four-year-old Michael Schwerner and 20-year-old Andrew Goodman from New York had driven down to Mississippi to team up with a local black youth, James Chaney (21), to help rebuild churches and homes belonging to local Negroes and to serve in "freedom schools" where backwater kids, unaccustomed to school, could find an education. Mostly, however, the three were there to help with black voter registration and the Ku Klux Klan was afraid they might be successful.

---

10 U.S. Constitution Online—"The I Have A Dream Speech" August 28, 1963

When the bullet-ridden bodies of the three Freedom Marchers were finally found and the Ku Klux Klansmen indicted for their murder, the case won worldwide attention. Television carried this story and the Civil Rights Movement with it. Seth Cagin and Philip Dray's illuminating nonfiction account of the Mississippi murders in their book We Are Not Afraid looks at the mindset permeating the South at this time in American history. They write:

> Outsiders had never been welcome in Neshoba County [Mississippi], whether they were Yankee cavalry, carpetbaggers, or federal revenuers. The civil rights movement—the threat of invasion by "outside agitators"—had powerfully stirred up ancient hatreds. Race mixers, "nigger-lovers" and their FBI hand-holders were the biggest threats to "the southern way of life" since the Civil War.[11]

Late on the evening of June 21, 1964, the Civil Rights Movement took a lonely ride down a murderous road, but to its credit, television chose to follow up on the story. In a very real sense, television changed itself when, by covering hot-topic events surrounding the struggle for civil rights, they increased awareness of civil injustices—many of which were landing at the feet of television itself. Covering the tragic events of the fallen freedom riders, television reported that while Negroes represented 45% of the viewing areas in nearly all of the South and most urban metropolitan centers (inner-cities) around the country, their numbers were all but ignored by networks and affiliates alike.[12]

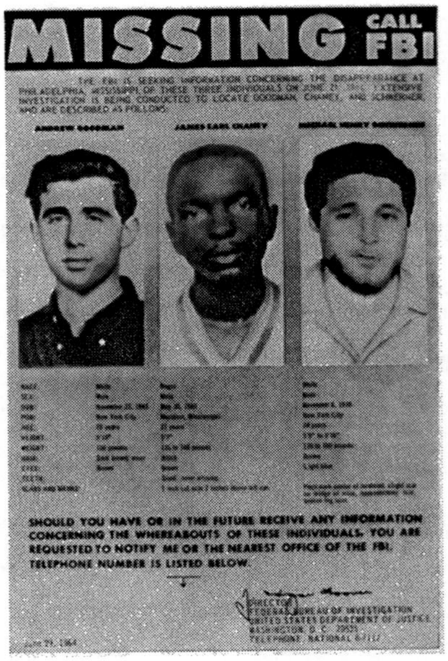

Freedom Marchers *Andrew Goodman, James Chaney, and Michael Schwerner are gunned down by the Ku Klux Klan on the first day of summer, 1964*

Slowly, whites were becoming sympathetic to this fact, as they witnessed via television not only the brutality put upon blacks in the South, but also the deep resistance offered up to black enfranchisement at the voting booth. Not only was the question of black disenfranchisement now being raised by white audiences, but also being discussed was what responsibility television had in "waking up" the American society.[13] In New York, the young wife of Michael Schwerner, one of the Freedom Riders murdered that summer in Mississippi, remarked on television how tragic it was that it took the murder of two white boys to fasten national attention on what Negroes had so long endured. Things had to change and would, eventually, though not nearly soon enough. Seven months before the murders in Mississippi, there had been another one in Dallas—and that one had left America reeling.

---

11 We Are Not Afraid, pp 8–9

12 *Tube of Plenty*, p 344

13 California Newsreel Production—"Color Adjustment"

Four Days in November

President John F. Kennedy used television to bolster his presidency much as Franklin Roosevelt had used radio to empower his. Throughout his time in office, JFK used the small screen to call attention to the social ills of the times, most notably the Civil Rights struggles, and the perils of global thermo-nuclear war; and to illuminate the importance of landing an astronaut on the moon as well. Yet, for all of his TV triumphs during those first 1000 days in office, it was the final day and the weekend that followed that forever tied the Kennedy Presidency to television.

President John F. Kennedy and First Lady Jacqueline Kennedy riding in the backseat of their open-air limousine moments before tragedy strikes

The Kennedy's had flown to Texas during a brief campaign swing to the South. Friday morning, November 22, 1963, began innocently enough. The president had given a breakfast speech in San Antonio then flown to Dallas where he planned to give a luncheon speech at the Trade Center Building just beyond Dealey Plaza, downtown. The president and First Lady Jacqueline Kennedy were in route to the prearranged gathering when their open-air limousine was ambushed as it passed the Texas School Book Depository building in the center of the plaza.

The triumphant spectacle turned suddenly tragic as gunfire echoed between the buildings. The President was shot twice before the limousine sped off for Parkland Memorial Hospital. Initially, news of what had happened was sketchy at best. United Press International (UPI) senior White House correspondent traveling at the rear of the motorcade hastily filed his first report: "DALLAS, NOV. 22 (UPI) THREE SHOTS WERE FIRED AT PRESIDENT KENNEDY'S MOTORCADE IN DOWNTOWN DALLAS."

Within minutes, ABC radio's Don Gardiner was on the network with the announcement. On CBS, the popular soap opera *As the World Turns* was suddenly interrupted by the voice-over bulletin from news anchor Walter Cronkite repeating the UPI report. For most of the next hour, the nation nervously awaited news of the President's condition. Then at 2:38 pm (EST), a teary-eyed Walter Cronkite, his baritone cracking, went on the air to deliver the news that would leave an indelible image in the mind of everyone who watched it: "From Dallas, Texas, a flash, apparently official. President Kennedy died at one pm, central standard time, two o'clock eastern standard time, some thirty-eight minutes ago."

For the next 70 hours, television provided uninterrupted, noncommercial coverage of the unfolding events. Heartbreak and disbelief ripped through the nation as television tracked two interconnected stories. The first involved the actual crime. Almost immediately, Dallas police sought a suspect, Lee

Cecil Stoughton's lone photograph of incoming President Lyndon Baines Johnson taking the oath of office inside the cabin of Air Force One, while former First Lady Jacqueline Kennedy looks on in shock and First Lady-to-be Lady Bird Johnson observes from behind her husband

Detective George Butler looks on as nightclub owner Jack Ruby shoots and kills accused presidential assassin Lee Harvey Oswald in the basement of the Dallas Police Department while on national television

Harvey Oswald, who worked at the book depository near where the President had been shot. Suspicions heightened, Friday afternoon, when a police officer was killed, shortly after the President, and Oswald subsequently tracked to a movie theater where he was subdued and arrested. Meanwhile, the networks followed a second, equally significant story—preparations for JFK's funeral to be held on Monday. President Kennedy's body was flown to Washington and then taken by ambulance to Bethesda Naval Hospital in nearby Maryland. During the flight, television showed that the transfer of power to the incoming President, Lyndon B. Johnson, had been peacefully achieved. The oath of office was administered by Dallas Federal District Judge Sarah T. Hughes, while in the cabin of Air Force One, moments before departing Dallas for Washington D.C.

On Sunday just after noon (EST), Kennedy's coffin was moved from the White House to the Capitol Rotunda on a horse-drawn caisson so that the public could view the casket and pay their last respects. ABC and CBS both covered the solemn ceremony, but NBC stayed in Dallas. They were there to watch as Oswald emerged from the basement of the jail, handcuffed and flanked by detectives for the short walk to a waiting armored truck. NBC had elected to cover the transfer of Oswald from the county jail to a federal lockup, ensuring that all events were being televised. As Oswald took his first steps down the hallway filled with reporters, millions watched in horror as Dallas nightclub owner Jack Ruby stepped forward and shot Oswald in the stomach on national television.

Jack Ruby was immediately arrested and Lee Oswald rushed to Parkland Hospital, as the President had been, where he died an hour later. The following day, President Kennedy was laid to rest at Arlington National Cemetery, where it would take the combined efforts of the three television networks for the country to view the funeral and mourn their fallen President. Combining efforts, the networks used over forty camera positions to provide unprecedented coverage.

America mourns its fallen leader as President Kennedy's caisson makes its way from the White House to the Capitol Rotunda

According to the A.C. Nielsen Company's audience research, the average home in America that weekend watched 31.6 hours of the 70 total hours of coverage. The President's funeral on Monday drew the largest audience, capturing 93% of the television market. Additionally, the funeral was telecast to 21 countries around the world and viewed by more than 600 million people. With their wall-to-wall coverage, the networks lost $10M (75M USD 2012) over the four-day weekend, but in doing so, television entered adulthood. No less than Don Hewett, creator of *60 Minutes* (the 44-year, Sunday night, prime time TV institution), speaking on the Kennedy Assassination had this to say: "It was the event that legitimized television in the eyes of the public. Never again in the twentieth century would print challenge television as the public's primary source of information and authority." From the assassinations of Rev. Dr. Martin Luther King Jr. and Senator Robert Kennedy in 1968, to the Challenger explosion in 1986, to the destruction of the World Trade Center towers on September 11, 2001, American now turned first to television for both information and solace.[14]

Relevant Programming

In the fall of 1967, the political beliefs, social mores, and sexual customs were, like the times, *a-changing*—and had been since 1965. The Vietnam War saw to that as television brought that war and the mayhem surrounding it into American homes on a twice-nightly basis. A cultural and political revolution was afoot in America and escapism was giving ground to relevancy. On campuses across the country, students were "just saying no to war." Parents and their children were finding themselves increasingly polarized on the numerous issues of the day. Leaders were being assassinated. Social movements became causes and the establishment was feeling the pinch. Those movements and causes turned into riots and anarchy. Cities became battlegrounds. Colleges became centers for debates and moratoriums. And television was there to watch.

Women, too, were coming into their own for the first time since the suffrage movement, fifty years before. To its credit, ABC television responded to this trend, offering up *That Girl* to the delight of female viewers

14 Stay Tuned, pp 68–73

Marlo Thomas (second from right) stars in first-of-its-kind series about the life of a single girl in ABC's That Girl *1966–1971*

everywhere. The series was the first one on TV about the life of a single girl. The American sitcom, running on ABC from 1966 to 1971, starred Marlo Thomas as the title character, Ann Marie, an aspiring (if sporadically employed) actress, who moved from her hometown in upstate New York to try to "make it big" in New York City. Ann had to take a number of offbeat temp jobs to support herself in between her various auditions and bit parts. Her relationship with nerdy magazine exec Donald Hollinger (played by actor Ted Bessel) never cramped her style. Thomas' character didn't want to sacrifice her career for marriage and pounded the point home through comic sarcasm that women didn't need to be married to be fulfilled.[15]

While the show itself didn't keep you on the edge of your seat, the series was novel and Marlo Thomas always upbeat. Though the show aired for only five seasons, it left a far-reaching vapor trail that women on television have been following ever since. *That Girl's* success paved the way for other independent women comedies that would follow a decade later and continue on through the end of the millennium. *The Mary Tyler Moore Show*, *Rhoda*, *Kate and Allie*, *Murphy Brown*, and even Elaine on *Seinfeld* and Rachel on *Friends* were single women on male-dominated shows. Yet it all started in 1966 with a show about a confident working woman whom audiences simply knew as *That Girl.*

It was because of *That Girl*, an ABC show, and because of something that CBS was trying with a couple of comedian banjo-playing folksingers named Tom and Dick Smothers that NBC decided the times were indeed changing, and that their network needed to change along with them. One of those changes included revamping the format and tone of the "garden variety" *variety* show into a sketch comedy show like nothing TV had seen before. The series was the creation of George Schlatter called *Laugh-In* and starred Dan Rowan and Dick Martin, consummate Las Vegas entertainers, who were destined to write a new chapter on TV comedy. This game-changing show broke down the traditional separation of comedy, musical performance, and dramatic interludes that marked most earlier variety shows and set the stage for future shows like *Saturday Night Live*, *In Living Color*, *The Daily Show*, and *The Colbert Report*.

Dan Rowan and Dick Martin host the #1 rated show of 1968, Laugh-In

15 *Fifty Years of Television*, p 201

Rowan and Martin didn't so much host the show as stay out of its way. The more they tried to orchestrate the weekly proceedings, the more they were assaulted by the gaggle of sight gags and eccentric performances surrounding them. From 1968 until 1973, *Laugh-In* was often seen by as many as 50 million weekly viewers, capturing the zeitgeist of the era with its unbridled energy and pop aesthetic.[16]

Appearing on the revolutionary show were a slew of comic regulars doing wonderful shtick: Goldie Hawn's graffiti-painted go-go dancer; Judy Carne's "Sock-It-To-Me" girl; Lily Tomlin's snorting telephone operator; JoAnne Worley's cackling vibrato resonating in her every laugh; Gary Owens' over-modulated announcer; Ruth Buzzi's perpetually frustrated spinster; Henry Gibson's soft-spoken banal poet; and Arte Johnson's lecherous old man. Many of these comic actors moved from total unknowns to household names, almost overnight. Others became important stars in the subsequent decades. Moreover, everyone wanted to appear on *Laugh-In*. So popular was the series that it soon had scores of celebrities and politicians clamoring to get on the show. One memorable episode in 1968 included John Wayne, Jack Lemmon, Sammy Davis Jr., Kirk Douglas, the Reverend Billy Graham, and presidential candidate Richard Nixon—the same Richard Nixon who personally saw to it that *The Smothers Brothers Comedy Hour* was canceled just two months after taking office.

Combining the blackout comedy of vaudeville with a 1960's-style "happening," a plethora of psychedelic costumes, paisley graphics, witty graffiti, outrageous characters, and a new political awareness, *Laugh-In* became one of the most popular shows in American history.[17] Arriving at NBC in 1968 to a schedule dominated by unthreatening fare like *Gomer Pyle, USMC* and perennial favorite *Bonanza*, *Laugh-In* brought an irreverent, machine-gun-like comedy to the small screen that captured both the frenetic social changes going on in America as well as the number-one Nielsen rating in each of its first two seasons.

Stylistically, the show was clearly in tune with the pop sensibilities of the time, but managed to keep its political antiestablishment messages safely wrapped in silliness, avoiding the in-your-face sarcasm that killed *The Smothers Brothers Comedy Hour* in less than three seasons.[18] Whereas *The Smothers Brothers* sketches on the Vietnam War and voter registration, on the Democratic Convention in Chicago and the assassination of Robert Kennedy were played to the ire of powerful politicians, *Laugh-In* made irreverence more about aesthetics than politics.[19]

The show's writers combined silly with meaningful, or sexy with political, but always there was a balance between those elements. If you took out the political pieces, the show became too silly. If you took out the silliness, it suddenly became too angry. In the end, few television shows have captured the spirit of their times so completely, while at the same time wielding so much influence.

---

16 PBS Programming website—"The Best of Laugh-In"

17 PBS Programming website—"The Best of Laugh-In"

18 Brought To You in Living Color, p 105

19 Brought To You in Living Color, p 105

Joan Ganz Cooney, one of the founders of morning programming for kids on the Public Broadcasting System (PBS), said about their long-running series *Sesame Street* that it owed much of its inspiration to *Laugh-In.*[20] Same with Lorne Michaels and his juggernaut, *Saturday Night Live*, a series nearing its fortieth season. Michaels had been a writer on *Laugh-In* and that show's influence on *SNL* cannot be denied. *SNL's* Weekend Update sketch is a case in point. If it was not a direct lift from *Laugh-In's* News of the Week—Past, Present & Future sketch, it has certainly been a very lengthy homage.

Comedy series and variety shows weren't the only changes to the late-1960's TV bill of fare. Dramas with a bite were coming back to the fold as well. *The Bold Ones*, a 60-minute dramatic series on NBC, was actually made up of three *different* sub-series that took turns airing in *The Bold Ones* time slot every third week. During the 1969–1970 season, three of these sub-series aired: *The Lawyers*, *The New Doctors*, and *The Protectors*. A year later, this latter offering was replaced with a new sub-series, *The Senator*. There was CBS's *Medical Center*, a drama about life and business at a university hospital near Los Angeles. Episodes explored stories involving both the treatment of patients *and* the teaching of student doctors. NBC's *Run For Your Life* and *Then Came Bronson* were two more. The former series featured a lawyer whose doctor had told him he had but two years to live, while the latter show told the saga of a guy escaping the doldrums of life to travel the open road on his motorcycle.

And there was *Love American Style*—a clever anthology comedy series offered up by ABC that explored up to five short stories per episode about the irony of love and emotional relationships and how people dealt with both. Relationship gaffes were never so funny. Each of these series had a common thread running through them, in that each was heavily grounded in reality—that unstable and acrimonious universe outside "the box" that was television (ergo our daily lives). And as 1968 approached, the universe outside the box was looking to explode.

The Televised War

In 1968, veteran newsman Walter Cronkite, "the most trusted man in America," anchored the *CBS Evening News*. Granted, the news division was not officially a part of the prime time network schedule, but often enough Vietnam War footage was seen there. The regularly scheduled, twice-nightly newscasts, in addition to a nightly array of "Special Bulletins" made the Vietnam conflict seem as if it was being fought on television. While Cronkite remained neutral on the air, it was now clear that he had originally supported the Vietnam War, believing that if the Communists overran Vietnam, all of Asia would later fall. [21]

---

20 *Tube of Plenty*, pp 436–437

21 Stay Tuned, p 74

U.S. President Dwight D. Eisenhower and Secretary of State John Foster Dulles greet President Ngo Dinh Diem of South Vietnam in Washington, May, 1957

That supposition was based in the reality of its day. Since the end of WWII, Americans had been inundated with anti-communist propaganda and the domino theory was the newest wrinkle in Western thinking. Thus, inheriting the Cold War foreign policy from the Truman and Eisenhower administrations, the Kennedy Administration inherited the theory as well. Kennedy intended to stay the course, but found himself in a credibility crisis on the subject of Communism. Here we were, as a nation, decrying Communism, while failing to surmount it at nearly every juncture. As Kennedy took over the presidency in 1961, the U.S. found itself with 50,000 troops still based in Korea, signaling a stalemate at best in the fight to turn back Communism abroad. On top of that there was the failure of the Bay of Pigs Invasion (the failed CIA attempt, earlier that same year, to invade Cuba and kill revolutionary leader, Fidel Castro); and the construction of the Berlin Wall separating East and West Germany.[22] These "failures" led Kennedy to believe that another miscue on the part of the United States to stop communist expansion would fatally damage U.S. credibility with its allies.

Vietnam was to be Kennedy's line in the sand and that had him worried. Kennedy's policy toward South Vietnam rested on the assumption that its President, Ngo Dinh Diem, and his South Vietnamese forces would ultimately defeat the Ho Chi Minh-backed communist guerrillas in the North on their own. Kennedy was against the deployment of American combat troops in Vietnam and sought to refocus U.S. efforts on pacification and "winning over the hearts and minds" of the population, while leaving military operations to the South Vietnamese. Yet therein lay a problem. The quality of the South Vietnamese Army remained poor. Bad leadership, corruption, and political promotions all played a part in emasculating the ARVN (South Vietnamese Army). So bad was it that even with the increased frequency of communist guerrilla attacks and the enemy's growing numbers, many still felt that the ARVN's *incompetence* was at the core of the current crisis.

By 1963, because of the ARVN's ineffectiveness, there were now 16,000 American military personnel in South Vietnam, up from Eisenhower's 900 advisors. With the assassination of South Vietnamese President Diem and the coup that followed that September, President Kennedy began to see that his concerns were well founded and began preparing a document that would extricate America from Vietnam over the next 18 months as well as bring a thousand troops home by Christmas, 1963.[23] It was not to be. By

---

22 Vietnam: A History ('91 ed.), p 264

23 Swathmore College Peace Collection—"Vietnam War"

U.S. Military Forces attack North Vietnam stronghold by ground and air, circa 1965

Thanksgiving, both Presidents Diem and Kennedy had been assassinated. The day following President Kennedy's internment at Arlington National Cemetery, incoming President Lyndon Baines Johnson signed Presidential Directive NSAM 273 geared to expand the war in Vietnam. "The battle against Communism," said Johnson, "must be joined ... with strength and determination."[24]

By the following August, 1964, the American destroyer *USS Maddox* claimed that while on an intelligence mission in the Gulf of Tonkin along North Vietnam's coast, the ship had been fired upon. A second attack in the gulf was reported two days later by the destroyer *USS Turner Joy*, though the circumstances surrounding the second attack were murky at best. Nevertheless, the second attack led to retaliatory U.S. air strikes and prompted Congress to approve the Gulf of Tonkin Resolution on August 5, 1964. Signed by President Johnson, the Resolution gave the President power to conduct military operations in Southeast Asia without declaring war. That same month, President Johnson pledged that even though he now had the power to wage war, he was not about to "... commit American boys to fighting a war that I think ought to be fought by the boys of Asia to help protect their own land."

As often happens, however, history proves us wrong. Between August 5, 1964—the day President Johnson signed the Gulf of Tonkin Resolution—and April 30, 1975—the day the last U.S. helicopter left the rooftop of the American Embassy in Saigon[25]—over nine million military personnel had served on active duty during the Vietnam Era. The war had escalated from 900 U.S. advisors under Eisenhower to 16,000 U.S. advisors and military support under Kennedy to 536,000 rotating U.S. combat troops under Presidents Johnson and Nixon, at a total cost of $125B (857B USD 2012).[26] The Vietnam War became the third most expensive war America had ever fought and the longest military conflict in American history.

In 1965, however, critics of the war were just beginning to ask the obvious question. If America was winning the war as Americans were being told via the nightly network news, why were troop counts still rising? Shouldn't we have begun sending our soldiers home by now? CBS anchor Walter Cronkite was listening to America and had pondered those same provocative thoughts himself. He had begun to doubt the military's resolve and the war's likely outcome.

This concern deepened when CBS began airing reports that same year that were critical of the military's operational conduct. CBS newsman Morley Safer, who would later become a prime time star himself

24 Vietnam: A History ('83 ed.), p 339

25 Pat Clark Productions—"The Last To Leave"

26 Sgt. Hacks Vietnam Wartime Facts website

U.S. paratroopers drop into Vietnam, 1963 (left); U.S. paratroopers are airlifted during a mission in south Vietnam, 1966.

on Sunday's mainstay *60 Minutes*, had filmed Marines razing a village and reported it to America via the *CBS Evening News*. "The [military] action," said Safer, "wounded three women, killed one baby, wounded one U.S. Marine and netted four old men as prisoners." The report so angered President Johnson that he ordered that Safer be investigated by the Justice Department. With the airing of Safer's report, Cronkite saw a big red flag. He was growing wary of Johnson's handling of the war and returned to Vietnam, in 1968, to ferret out the truth for himself—and the 30 million middle-American households that hung on his every word.

The 1968 Tet Offensive waged by the North Vietnamese (Vietcong) turned many Americans against the war. It was a definitive victory for the Vietcong and influenced incoming President-Elect Richard M. Nixon, in 1969, to advocate what he termed "Vietnamization."[27] According to this new strategy, the gradual withdrawal of American troops would occur at the same time that the South Vietnamese were given greater military responsibility. Cronkite, however, saw the Tet Offensive for what it really was—the beginning of the end to any notion that Americans could actually *win* the civil war in Vietnam.

CBS News anchor Walter Cronkite revisits Vietnam and declares: "It seems now more certain than ever that the bloody experience of Vietnam is to end in a stalemate," began Cronkite's famous criticism of the Vietnam War, February 27, 1968.

On February 27, 1968, Walter Cronkite aired a half-hour prime time news special on the Tet Offensive but closed the broadcast with an editorial. While he clearly saw military victory in Vietnam as an unrealistic goal, Cronkite remained even in tone and relatively balanced, giving him that much more

27 Vietnam: A History ('91 ed.), p 556

Anti-war rally in Washington, 45,000 Americans march on the Capital to protest Vietnam War, November 15, 1969

credibility. He began by commenting on the loss of "American lives and dignity" during recent battles as being the "tragedy of our stubbornness." At one point he clearly yet delicately blamed the government and the military for misleading the public. Said Cronkite: "We have been too often disappointed by the optimism of American leaders both in Vietnam and in Washington and the silver linings they find in the darkest clouds." The CBS network was surprised by the fact that they hadn't been deluged with complaints. It was either a true indication of public opinion or an endorsement of viewer trust in their anchorman. President Johnson, who respected Cronkite as he did no other journalist, certainly saw it that way. Reports have it that Johnson flipped off his television set and turned to an entourage of his inner sanctum: "If I've lost Cronkite, I've lost middle America."

A month later, President Johnson declared on prime time television that he would not run for reelection. It is uncertain whether Johnson actually shared Cronkite's assessment of the Vietnam quagmire or Cronkite's comments simply became the final straw in Johnson's appraisal of his chance for reelection. What is certain is that Vietnam showed what an emotionally explosive combination television and war could be. As David Halberstam wrote in his book The Powers That Be: "It was the first time in history that an anchor had declared a war over."

Richard Nixon would take over in 1969 and attempt, in 1970, to slow the flow of North Vietnamese soldiers and supplies into South Vietnam by sending American forces to destroy Communist supply bases in Cambodia. This action was in violation of Cambodian neutrality, provoking antiwar protests on the nation's college campuses.[28] But truly, those protests had already started in earnest, two years earlier, during the explosive summer of 1968.

28 Stay Tuned, pp 75–77

"The World Is Watching!"

By early 1968, Richard Nixon seemed certain to win the Republican presidential nomination and this, like much of television, seemed implausible. Six years earlier he'd been declared politically dead. And why not? In 1962, two years after his defeat by John Kennedy, he'd tried to reactivate his political career by running for governor in California, where he was defeated as well by the Democratic incumbent, Pat Brown, a man Nixon had publicly berated. When the outcome became clear, Nixon's press aide read a concession statement reporting that the candidate would be unavailable for questions. Then, without warning, Nixon pushed through venting his anger on the onslaught of reporters: "As I leave you," said Nixon, "I want you to know: Just think how much you'll all be missing. You won't have Nixon to kick around anymore."[29] The tirade was considered at the time to be Nixon's farewell to politics. Nothing could have been further from the truth.

These were, after all, the 1960's. Change was the watchword. The next six years were to tear this country apart like nothing short of our own Civil War. Fifty-nine thousand Americans would die in an undeclared war, in a jungle, half a world away. And with them, four American tours de force—Dr. Martin Luther King Jr., John and Robert Kennedy, and Malcolm X—all assassinated. There were the four students killed at Kent State by National Guardsmen two years later and the little girls killed in a Birmingham church bombing three years earlier. But the centerpiece of American tragedy was 1968—a year when discord and dissension spilled utterly and completely into politics. Half the Democrats wanted President Johnson (a Democrat) out. Half the Republicans wanted to see to it Republican Senator Barry Goldwater never surfaced again. Suffice it to say, political parties were split. Fathers and sons stopped talking. Some men of draft age fled to Canada. Others went to jail. Many, however, were sent to Vietnam to fight an undeclared war that half the country opposed and the French had already lost.

And then it came with a vengeance—the 1968 Democratic National Convention (DNC) in Chicago. Anticipating trouble weeks in advance, city officials had prepared for it. Police received special riot-control drills and equipment. Fences and barbed wire were erected around the convention area. Television engineers preparing their installations felt as if they were in an armed encampment. But more to the point, television was there. Like it had been there in 1954 for Joe McCarthy and the "Big Red Scare." And for the Nixon–Kennedy Presidential Debates in 1960. And for the televised ultimatum given by President Kennedy to the Soviets during the 1962 Cuban Missile Crisis. Television covered that cold day in November, 1963, when an American president was cut down in his prime, and again two days later when the president's accused assassin was slain as well. Television was there earlier that same year to witness Reverend King's March on Washington D.C. and record his "I Have a Dream" speech; as it was in Los Angeles, five years later, to cover Robert Kennedy's assassination, minutes after winning the California Primary.

---

29 Nixon: A Life, pp 304–305

As the 1968 DNC was setting up in Chicago, there was already a feeling of gloom in the air. After all, Martin Luther King and Bobby Kennedy had been gunned down in cold blood earlier that spring leaving the Democratic Party in a state of flux. Enter television—hundreds of people arriving with tons of equipment only to face an extraordinary problem. Chicago's Mayor Daley had rigged the convention so that the only *live* television would come from inside the Hall itself.[30] The 10,000 hippies and yippies who had come to aggressively protest the Vietnam War were relegated to remote areas, far from the Convention Hall, where television couldn't easily reach them. Mayor Richard Daley, an avid Hubert Humphrey supporter, was determined to move Humphrey into the Oval Office and pulled out all the stops to do it. Police armed with riot sticks were told to use them on *anyone* misbehaving.

It should be noted that not everyone wanted their pound of flesh. A delegation of the Poor People's March, led now by King understudy Ralph Abernathy, came to stage a nonviolent protest.[31] So did Democratic Senator Eugene McCarthy and his supporters who'd hoped the massive demonstrations outside the Convention Hall would stop VP Hubert Humphrey from winning the Democratic nomination. Unknown to Mayor Richard Daley, the networks, wanting to cover these more relevant protests, sent video mobile units and foot cameramen to find the yippies. Television arrived just as marchers and cops converged. Police clearly considered the television cameras an unwelcome presence, while the protestors cheered their arrival. The yippies were resolved to make their protest march to the Convention Hall and started forward. Cops armed with nightsticks, guns, tear gas, and mace were resolved to stop them.

The film arriving at the TV control rooms shortly after the melee began looked like carnage in the making. Networks threw it on the air as fast as possible. Viewers saw a dizzying blitzkrieg of nominating speeches, head-cracking, more speeches, tear gas, shouting crowds, cops wielding billy clubs, wounded bodies, convention balloting, anarchy in the streets[32]—and then it happened. Delegates inside the hall got wind of what was going on outside the hall. In the months to follow, the government's Walker Report, after amassing a great many eyewitness accounts, would brand the melee outside the Convention Hall in Chicago that summer a "Police Riot." Back inside the hall, the scene was much the same. The edgy relationship that had existed between broadcasters and convention management from the get-go suddenly deteriorated into a riotous brawl.

Fights and ad lib speeches began to erupt inside the hall. Cameras pushed in on the face of a furious Mayor Daley. Prime time television was treated to a white-collar rumble. Among the hundreds injured in the melees were twenty-one reporters and photographers clubbed by police while trying to cover the events.[33] CBS newsman Dan Rather was one of those injured by security police while speaking to anchorman Walter Cronkite *on the air*. "I think we've got a bunch of thugs here, Dan," said Cronkite to Rather. "The world is watching. Do they know that?" The polarization between generations that had

30 *Tube of Plenty*, p 418
31 *Tube of Plenty*, p 417
32 *Tube of Plenty*, p 419
33 *Tube of Plenty*, p 419

been seen in nightly bits and pieces was now being seen in one fell swoop by millions and millions of prime time viewers around the world. Mayor Richard Daley didn't care—not so long as Humphrey won the nomination. In the end, viewers saw Hubert Humphrey nominated in what appeared to be a fortified stockade and guessed that he had very little chance of winning the election.[34]

Commander Neil Armstrong becomes the first human being to step onto the surface of the moon, July 20, 1969. His historic words still resonate: "That's one small step for a man, one giant leap for mankind..."

Richard Nixon had been watching television as well that August, commenting to aides just how important the medium could be if used judiciously—and this from the man who lost to Kennedy because of bad make-up. The old political dog had learned a new trick. Yet, what television had really shown us that summer was how faith in our government process had been dangerously eroded. Forty percent of the eligible voters had stayed away from the polls the following November for just that reason. The result found Richard Nixon being elected president by a scant 27% of the eligible electorate.

Once in office, Nixon used television shrewdly. He had seen the Nielsen ratings from the Democratic Convention and they were impressive. "People," said Nixon, "will watch a train wreck if there's a camera lying around. It's up to us to properly promote it." And Richard Nixon did just that. As it came to be, all cameras that year and the next were aimed at the moon. The Apollo Missions, though born under Kennedy, had become Nixon's television bonanza. From the on-the-air tests of the Apollo spacecraft to the first manned launch and subsequent 163 Earth orbits to the first orbits of the moon itself to lunar touchdown on July 20, 1969, the world watched in awe. [35]

What had been the stuff of science fiction was now a reality and Richard Milhous Nixon got the credit. As badly as the Vietnam War was going, Americans (at least during his first term) didn't see it as Nixon's war. And besides, hadn't the President just put a man on the moon? Nixon, it seemed, couldn't lose—not for another five years, anyway. To make that point he flexed his muscles. In the spring of 1969, two months after taking office, President Nixon gave television a bird's-eye view of what presidential power was all about.

---

34 *Tube of Plenty*, p 421

35 *Tube of Plenty*, p 423

Censorship

Most of the issues relevant to the content of television programming are private rights that are exercised or waived by the persons involved in the issues. Lawsuits, as it were, between individuals, involving copyright, privacy, and publicity. There are, however, certain restrictions that are imposed and enforced by the government as a matter of criminal and civil law on the theory that these restrictions protect society at large. In keeping with the principles of the First Amendment, these restrictions—what some might call "censorship laws"—are neither numerous nor broad in their applicability. Nonetheless, when exercised properly (or improperly, for that matter) they can have powerful repercussions. The First Amendment to the American Constitution says that:

> Congress shall make no law respecting an establishment of religion, or prohibiting the free exercise thereof; or abridging the freedom of speech, or of the press; or the right of the people peaceably to assemble, and to petition the government for a redress of grievances.

Terrific stuff, the First Amendment. Yet, even though this amendment is the backbone of our Constitution's Bill of Rights, notice that it does not say: "All citizens living in the United States have the right to say whatever they want whenever they want to say it." It says only that Congress shall make no law abridging freedom of speech or of the press or religion. Yet, what we have today are numerous laws that now control or restrict various aspects of speech when it's used over the public airwaves. The use of *f-bombs* on commercial TV, for example, is not allowed. Neither can one legally use the airwaves to make threats or view pornography. All represent forms of expression that are restricted from airing on commercial television.

In seeking to protect American society, some of the perennial government concerns include sex, drugs, and violence—concerns that have been around since the early days of the medium. Societal jitters on these subjects have led to periodic attempts by the government to increase the level of censorship past suitable limits. Of course, that statement begs an even bigger one. What one person calls "suitable limits," another calls "censorship." The Supreme Court, as the final arbiter on the matter, over the years has wrestled with the definition of obscenity, and has produced a series of pronouncements. Perhaps the most forthright, if the least specific, was the statement by one Supreme Court justice who said only that he'd know pornography when he saw it.

Currently, the applicable test of obscenity resides with *Miller v. California, 1973*. Under this test, for material to be obscene, all three of the following factors must be proven:

- That the average person, applying contemporary community standards, would find that the work as a whole appeals to prurient interests;

- That the work as measured by contemporary community standards depicts or describes sexual conduct in a patently offensive way, specifically defined by the applicable state law;

- That the work taken as a whole lacks serious literary, artistic, political or scientific value.[36]

Not only is this a lot to prove in court, but more importantly, after digesting all these factors, how much different are they really from ... "I'll know pornography when I see it"? In effect, the government seems to be saying if the material in question contains explicit sexual depictions that are (in the opinion of a judge or jury) likely to arouse and offend a sufficiently broad segment of the population, the material will be deemed obscene.

On television, the dissemination of overtly sexual material is generally limited to home video, satellite delivery, or late-night cablecast. In each of these cases, because the subscriber is paying for the telecast, adults are making a personal choice to view it. To this point, the Supreme Court has held that the private possession and perusal of what might be described as obscene material in public is not punishable when viewed in the privacy of one's home. That said, the "consenting-adults argument" is, however, no defense for the *transaction* of obscene material.[37] The private sale of any explicit videotape or DVD from one adult to another could still be deemed illegal given the county and state one resides in at the time.

While most states have anti-pornography statutes of one kind or another on their books, some states are more willing to prosecute than others and some carry more stringent criminal penalties. The enforcement—or lack thereof—oftentimes indicates the level of community concern in that area. The more conservative the community, the more likely they are to prosecute cases involving obscene material. In truth, FCC regulations governing the appearance of obscene and indecent material on broadcast television had their origin in the Communications Act of 1934—the same act that gave birth to the Federal Communications Commission itself. In that 1934 provision, the FCC had the right to exercise any and all censorship over the content of all broadcasts. This FCC right has since been moved out of the Communications Act and into the courts, but the definitions used by the courts as to what is considered "obscene" and what is considered "indecent" have their roots tied to the 1934 Act.[38]

Indecency includes the use of offensive words, even in contexts where no graphic sexual description is involved. The late comedian George Carlin ran head-first into these "indecency" laws when he spoke the "seven dirty words you can't say on television" during a thoughtful comedy routine about language that he performed on stage in Milwaukee, in 1972. "There are no bad words," Carlin told the audience. "Bad thoughts, bad intentions, maybe" he smirked. "Yet, out of 400,000 words in the English language, there are seven that will infect your soul, curve your spine and keep the country from winning the war."[39] Someone

---

36 Justia.com—US Supreme Court Center—"Miller v. California" 413 U.S. 15" 1973

37 Museum of Broadcast Communications website—"Censorship"

38 Communications Act of 1934—Public Law No. 416

39 George Carlin website—"Filthy Words" (Seven Dirty Words You Can't Say on TV)

in his audience that night was thoroughly offended by the language (the seven unspeakable words). Following his performance, Carlin was taken from the stage and arrested on a charge of disturbing the peace. A Wisconsin judge ruled that though the monologue was indecent, there is a right to free speech in America and the prosecution had failed to produce any evidence that the "peace" in Milwaukee was actually disturbed.

Sometime the following year, a New York radio station replayed the same "routine" off Carlin's 1973 album, *Occupation: Foole*. John Douglas, an active member of Morality in Media in the Wisconsin area, claimed that he heard the broadcast while driving with his 15-year-old son during the daylight hours and complained to the FCC.[40] The case went all the way to the Supreme Court, which ruled that the government had a right to set a "watershed mark," before which obscenities could not be broadcast (in case children were listening). No specific sanctions were included in the court's order, which was tantamount to the high court's giving Carlin a do-over and the FCC the right to handle subsequent violations any way they saw fit.[41]

Today, Congress has mandated a late-night "safe harbor" of 10 pm to 6 am, where edgy language (profanity to some), nudity, and even marshmallow porn can be seen and heard on the airwaves.[42] Carlin reworked the material many times over the years in his stand-up routine, but following the advent of cable television, he turned to HBO as a forum from which to perform the material for a national audience. HBO waited until 10 pm to air the show—a time and place where adults elected to be and who were paying for the privilege to be there.

The FCC's "safe harbor" mandate is enforced, in part, to protect children's programming for obvious reasons. After many years of false starts, canceled proceedings, and vetoed legislation, Congress finally enacted a law regulating children's television. The Children's Television Act of 1990 restricted the amount of advertising that could run in children's programming on both broadcast and cable television. Children's programming is defined by the FCC as programming aimed at children 12 years old and under. The degree to which a broadcast station or network of stations has met this standard is considered annually when reviewing network license renewals. Additionally, this specifically designed children's programming was to air between 7 am and 10 pm and had to be a regularly scheduled weekly episode of at least 30 minutes in length.[43]

Most television censorship, as destructive as it might be to an episodic script, has logic to it. One could make an argument for either side of the question. Censorship is bad but ... children *do* have to be protected because they're too young to protect themselves. National security issues *are* delicate and it's reasonable to assume that in some instances censoring information that could incite riots or give away

40 The Story of FCC v. Pacifica Foundation (and Its Second Life), p 10

41 Law School at U of C—"The Story of FCC v. Pacifica Foundation (and Its Second Life)," p 24

42 United States Reports—"FCC v. Pacifica Foundation," 438 U.S. 726" 1978

43 *New York Times*—"U.S. Mandates Educational TV for Children," p 16

national secrets is pardonable. And obscenity and indecency, while subjective and sometimes arbitrary, *do* need to be monitored to at least some extent.

But what of censorship that exists for the sake of a difference in political opinion? Censorship that might, for example, lead to the cancellation of a prime time show at the height of its popularity, simply because that show's humor and satire failed to mesh with what the sitting president considered funny. Could the White House actually coerce a network into canceling its own hit show? Could a network's censors conform in such a way as to inhibit the humor of a variety series and effectively take the pen out of the show's creative hands? The answer that came in the spring of 1969 was yes to both.

Tom Smothers (on guitar) and Dick Smothers (on bass), host of the CBS hit The Smothers Brothers Comedy Hour, *took on perennial Sunday night ratings champ "*Bonanza*" and won! 1967–1969*

Smothered

The Smothers Brothers Comedy Hour, broadcast on CBS from 1967–'69, featured two beloved hosts and real-life brothers, Tom and Dick Smothers, who pioneered a turning point in American television history. Using friendly folk music and wholesome charm, the brothers brought a new brand of political commentary to the American public. In an era marked by caricature, not character, featuring predictable, plot-driven shows like *Bewitched*, *Bonanza*, and *The Beverly Hillbillies*, *The Smothers Brothers Comedy Hour* broke all the rules and captured the nation's attention by sneaking the rough-and-tumble universe *outside* "the box" into our living rooms on the well-plucked strings of a banjo and a bass guitar.

In doing that, however, the Smothers Brothers ran into that division lurking inside each and every network known as Standards & Practices. In general, this department issues and administers in-house guidelines on a variety of issues. Many of its concerns reflect the need to conform to the FCC regulations and restrictions. Other Standards & Practices recommendations reflect twin goals, serving both the good of society while preserving the image of the network and by association its advertisers at the same time. All of this more or less makes sense. The areas of concern to both the network and the FCC include alcohol, cigarettes, race, religion, criminal activities, drugs, human relationships, obscenity, physical infirmities, color, age, national origin, sex and sexuality, and, of course, violence. The list reads like a program guide for some of the more popular daytime talk shows—in short, all of society's hot-button topics.

Applying rules and regulations to creative material can be a dicey affair. One must balance the need to *creatively* attract a big audience against the *legal* consequences of offending some of the very viewers you are trying to win. It should be noted that outside the realm of broadcast networks, institutionalized hand wringing over program content is much less common.[44] A cable network, for example, would never have pulled their own hit show from the air because it offended a sitting president. Likely as not, they'd have given it a better time slot. But even within the *broadcast* networks' inner sanctums, where concerns for the above-mentioned topics run rampant, "politics" was *never* one of those topics. Not until 1967 when *The Smothers Brothers Comedy Hour* became the number-one show on Sunday night, knocking former number one *Bonanza* off a pedestal it had occupied for six consecutive years.

The Smothers Brothers Comedy Hour started out as a slightly "hip" version of the typical comedy-variety show of its era, but rapidly evolved into an incredibly hip show that extended the boundaries of television satire. While the Smothers Brothers themselves were at the forefront of these efforts, credit also goes to the roster of writers and performers they brought to the show. Included among those were Mason Williams, Steve Martin, Rob Reiner, Pat Paulsen, Don Novello, Leigh French, and David Steinberg. The series also showcased musical artists that other comedy-variety shows had mostly ignored because of the nature of their music or their political affiliations. Artists like Janis Ian, Joan Baez, Buffalo Springfield, Cass Elliot, Harry Belafonte, Donovan, The Doors, Jefferson Airplane, The Who, Simon and Garfunkel, and even Pete Seeger were showcased on the series despite the advertiser-sensitive nature of their music.[45]

The first sign of real censorship came nine weeks into the first show. Tom Smothers and writer Elaine May were "playing" television censors in a skit and were commenting on something in front of them that only they could see and we, the television audience, could only hear.[46] Whether it was that censors couldn't laugh at themselves, or whether they didn't want to let the audience behind the proverbial curtain, Standards & Practices cut the performance in its entirety. S&P was a powerful arm of the network and one that had William Paley's ear. The Smothers Brothers soon found themselves in regular conflicts with the CBS network censors, such that at the start of the 1968–'69 season, the network ordered the brothers to deliver their shows finished and ready to air ten days before airdate so that the censors could edit the shows as necessary. In the season-two premiere, CBS deleted the entire segment of Harry Belafonte singing *Lord, Don't Stop the Carnival* against a backdrop of the havoc during the 1968 Democratic National Convention. As the year progressed, battles over content continued, including a David Steinberg sermon about Moses and The Burning Bush.[47] Something had to give.

Pete Seeger's scheduled appearance was for that September as well—his first on network television since being blacklisted in the 1950's. His visit became controversial because of the song choice, *Waist Deep in the Big Muddy*. Seeger's song ran into conflict with CBS brass who objected to its political tone and censored the song prior to airing. Following support from the show's hosts, CBS relented and allowed Seeger to come back and sing the song in February, 1968.[48] The Johnson White House was appalled by the anti-war song and considered it an insult to both the President and his Vietnam War policy.

---

44 Dangerously Funny: The Uncensored Story of the Smothers Brothers Comedy Hour, pp 256–269

45 You Can't Air That: Four Cases of Controversy and Censorship in American Television Programming

46 Time-Life Productions—"Smothered"

47 Time-Life Productions—"Smothered"

48 Time-Life Productions—"Smothered"

Frank Stanton, CBS network president during the Johnson years, would routinely watch the show with the President on Sunday night. The relationship between Stanton and President Johnson did not seem altogether proper given their respective positions, but their friendship that evening did help to bridge the public relations gaffe presented by Seeger's song.[49] Coincidently, Johnson and Stanton left office at about the same time and the new regimes at both CBS and in Washington were far less tolerant of the nation's counter-culture. Moreover, the Nixon White House was substantially more hostile to television, in general, than was Lyndon Johnson. Nixon knew also that CBS was vulnerable to the federal government through its broadcasting license and let that fact be known through "reminders" delivered by his Vice President, Spiro T. Agnew.[50] Despite these significant hurdles, *The Smothers Brothers Comedy Hour* was picked up for the 1969–'70 season, ending the debate over the show's status. Then, on April 4, 1969, after meeting with his new network president Robert Wood, network CEO William Paley left the room and the show was abruptly canceled.[51]

The reason given by CBS was based on the Smothers Brothers' refusal to meet the pre-air delivery dates as specified by contract, in order to accommodate the network's censors. Truly, the "charge" could have been "insubordination." Speculation swirled around the fact that with the network Upfronts just over a month away, Bill Paley had heard from the White House. He'd gotten the message from Wood, who'd heard from someone in the Vice President's office. CBS would either cancel the show or lose its license to air it—or so it was whispered. What could a desperate network do?

Despite the series' popularity, the brothers' penchant for finding material that was critical of the political mainstream and sympathetic to the emerging counterculture ultimately led to the show's demise. The Smothers Brothers sued CBS and won a third year's salary as they were contractually guaranteed. Sadly, with the show's departure from the airwaves, so went an original piece of Americana, a bit of the First Amendment, and the last few months of the most turbulent, schizophrenic and culturally significant decade of the twentieth century.

Discussion Questions

B. Color Adjustment

- NBC's *I Spy* differed from all previous programs in what way? What significance can be applied to *I Spy* and *Julia* with regard to TV programming?

C. Winds of Change

- What do you know about Martin Luther King, Jr.'s *I Have a Dream* speech?

---

49 Time-Life Productions—"Smothered"

50 *Tube of Plenty*, pp 444–445

51 Museum of Broadcast Communications website—"The Smothers Brothers Comedy Hour"

- Among the many inspired youth, three young Freedom Marchers caught in the dream lost their lives due to the prejudices of 1964 Mississippi. How did this event manifest itself into one of TV reporting's finest hours?

D. Four Days in November

- Although not the first U.S. President assassinated, Kennedy was the first to die on national television. What was the American experience with the 70 hours of unprecedented coverage?

- What other national events received extraordinary coverage that glued Americans to their TV's?

E. Relevant Programming

- Why was the light hearted role of Marlo Thomas' *That Girl* in 1966 considered a landmark in television programming?

- How did NBC's *Laugh-In* sustain its popularity while poking fun at the status quo from 1968–1973, when other comedy shows with political overtones, such as *The Smothers Brothers* series, were short-lived in comparison.

F. The Televised War

- How did Walter Cronkite get credit in some quarters for helping to end the Vietnam Conflict?

G. The World is Watching

- Televising the 1968 Democratic National Convention curtailed voter turnout that year rather than increasing participation. What happened to turn away so many voters, thus altering the course of American history?

H. Censorship

- Each generation struggles with the balance of freedom of speech and the best interests of specific groups, such as children, or national security. Do you think there can be a balance or should the scales tip in favor of one or the other?

I. Smothered

- The very popular, edgy comedic variety show, *The Smothers Brothers Comedy Hour* was a casualty to censorship and "the powers that be." What were the "powers" and issues that led to this landmark series' cancellation?

CHAPTER ELEVEN

Emancipation

1970–1980

Shape-Shifting

The violence that erupted in Chicago in the summer of 1968 left its imprint on the broadcast industry as a whole. Even before the Democrats had launched their Presidential Convention that summer, network executives and studio producers alike felt that TV programming had become irrelevant to the times. The call now as the 1970's commenced was for relevant programming—a call that led to the cancellation of many long-standing series.[1] The cultural revolution of the 1960's had seen to that. The universe outside "the box" had signaled to all how different the TV world was from the tangible world around them and viewers were starting to listen. People didn't really marry genies or witches. Father didn't always know best. And the Nelson's, Cleaver's, and the Brady's of their world didn't always get along. The result was an ever-widening gap separating the silly sitcom from such issues of the time as civil rights, political corruption, and inflation. The proof was quick to follow. The "top ten" series of 1973–74 failed to include a single holdover from the 1968–69 list of leaders.

1 *Tube of Plenty*, p 430

CULTURAL SHIFT TO RELEVANT PROGRAMS[2]

1968–69	%TV	1973–74	%TV
Laugh-In (NBC)	31.1	All in the Family (CBS)	31.2
Gomer Pyle (CBS)	27.1	The Waltons (CBS)	27.9
Bonanza (NBC)	27.0	Sanford & Son (NBC)	27.6
Mayberry RFD (CBS)	25.8	M*A*S*H* (CBS)	25.8
Family Affair (CBS)	25.2	Hawaii Five-O (CBS)	23.7
Julia (NBC)	25.1	Sonny & Cher (CBS)	23.4
Gunsmoke (CBS)	24.8	Maude (CBS)	23.3
Dean Martin (NBC)	24.1	Kojak (CBS)	23.3
Here's Lucy (CBS)	23.7	Mary Tyler Moore Show (CBS)	23.2
Red Skelton (CBS)	23.6	Cannon (CBS)	23.0

The changes between TV eras involved a wider ethnic distribution, increased permissiveness in language and plot, and a trend that leaned toward more relevant subjects.[3] Instead of offering an escape from the real world, television programming took a page out of FCC Chairman Newton Minow's playbook and began tackling issues of the day head-on. Viewers embraced Mary Tyler Moore's independent, liberated working woman and Bob Newhart's befuddled psychiatrist. Beloved as well were the hapless working-class heroes of CBS's *Alice*, ABC's *Barney Miller* and *Taxi*, and NBC's *Sanford and Son*. People of color were beginning to be seen on television, and with the richer ethnic mixtures came sweeping changes in clothing and hairstyles. In 1968, a young man with long hair, no tie, and a rumpled look was at once known by the audience to be a "hippie," probably a protester, and was immediately thought to be living on welfare. Not five years later, such a person, whether in drama, news, or round-table discussions on PBS, might be found to be a distinguished attorney, legislator, or professor. He might—as in *The Mod Squad* or *The Rookies*—be a policeman. Even advertising agency personnel began to visit the studios looking like "hippies." They wanted to be in touch with the "youth culture"—a demographic that would rule the advertising roost for the remainder of the century.

Styles and roles were crossing race and gender lines. Men appearing on celebrity shows might wear ornamental shirts and necklaces. Women, who were suddenly prominent as newscaster correspondents, were no longer confined to reporting on fashion and household items. They reported now from courtrooms, factories, slums, and the halls of Congress as well. Moreover, programs *sounded* different. The tumultuous final years of the 1960's brought with them a new tolerance for bawdier language that startled older viewers, right along with most industry professionals[4]—but not all of them.

One of those forward-thinking professionals was Fred Silverman, a network television executive who between 1971 and 1981 not only presided over all three original broadcast networks—CBS, ABC, and NBC—but also led two of those networks from last place to first in the ratings. Silverman had earned

2 *Tube of Plenty*, p 432

3 *Tube of Plenty*, p 432

4 *Tube of Plenty*, pp 431–432

a Master's degree from Ohio State University and soon after went to work for CBS affiliate WGN-TV in Chicago, overseeing development of children's programming. Silverman's Master's thesis analyzed ten years of ABC programming and led to his first network job. In 1963, at the age of 25, Silverman became the youngest executive at CBS. There, he took over responsibility for all daytime programming and later, took charge of all entertainment programming, day *and* night.

By 1970, Fred Silverman had been promoted from vice president of program planning and development to the head of programming at CBS and was the chief architect of what has been labeled by TV critics as the "rural purge" of 1971.[5] The term refers to the systematic elimination of many popular country-oriented shows. By the late 1960's, many viewers—especially young ones—were rejecting rural-themed shows as irrelevant to current times. The series *Mayberry, R.F.D.*, for example, was really a continuation of *The Andy Griffith Show*, a beloved series (one of only three to leave episodic television as the number-one show), yet totally isolated from contemporary problems. This was part of its appeal, true, but after more than a decade of media coverage of the Civil Rights Movement and no mention of it on the show, the popular image of the small Southern town was losing its *youthful* following. *Gomer Pyle, U.S.M.C.* was another hit show that suffered from the same malaise. Set on a fictitious U.S. Marine base from 1964 to 1969, neither Gomer nor any other soldier on the show ever mentioned the Vietnam War. CBS executives, afraid of losing the lucrative youth demographic, purged their schedule of *hit* shows that were drawing huge but *older-skewing* audiences.[6]

Silverman wasn't acting capriciously; rather his cancellations were well calculated. As the new head of programming at the *Tiffany Network* (a handle CBS had earned from its cache of classic series from the Golden Age of Television), Silverman began slowly, if methodically, by first canceling *Petticoat Junction*, in the summer of 1970. In September of that year, *The Mary Tyler Moore Show* premiered on CBS. Four months later, *All in the Family* would follow. Both series provided the urban demographic and cutting-edge social relevance CBS sought, but above all else, it brought high ratings. These ratings successes prompted Silverman to make further cancellations—and thus the "rural purge" was on. Gone by the end of the 1970–'71 season were *Hee Haw*, *Lassie*, *Green Acres*, *Mayberry, R.F.D.*, and *The Jim Nabors Hour*. A year later *The Glen Campbell Goodtime Hour* had departed as well.[7]

In their place came a new wave of classics championed by Silverman and aimed at the upscale baby boomer generation. In addition to *All in the Family* and *The Mary Tyler Moore Show*, CBS, under Silverman, gave us *M*A*S*H*, *The Waltons*, *Cannon*, *Barnaby Jones*, *Kojak*, and *The Sonny & Cher Comedy Hour*. Newer variety shows like *The Flip Wilson Show* and *The Carol Burnett Show*, though not brought in by Silverman, fell under his regime and were now supplanting *The Red Skelton Show*, despite the fact that Skelton's series had finished the previous season as a top-ten show. A call like that could only have come from

5 My Life in "Toons": From Flatbush to Bedrock in Under a Century, pp 163–173

6 *The Blade* –"Jim Nabors finished with Gomer" January 31, 1969

7 Hillbilly: A Cultural History of an American Icon, p 203

William Paley.[8] He and Silverman were intent on capturing a younger, more urban market and many felt that's why Silverman had been made head of CBS programming in the first place. The youth market could just as easily have been called the baby boom market. "Boomers," as they were known, were the pig in the proverbial python. Their numbers alone would make them relevant through the rest of the century, so that today, in 2012, with just two years left before the last baby boomer hits 50, the 18–49 demographic measured by the A.C. Nielsen Company is still the most sought after by advertisers.

Fred Silverman had an uncanny ability to spot burgeoning hit material, especially in the form of *spinoffs*—that is to say, a new TV series developed with characters that had first appeared on an existing series. Silverman spun off *Rhoda* and *Phyllis* from *The Mary Tyler Moore Show* and *The Bob Newhart Show* from the MTM writers. But his greatest spinoffs were to come from his greatest series—*All in the Family*. *Maude* and *The Jeffersons* were spun off the original hit show and *Good Times* was then spun off *Maude*.

In a management style that well suited him, Silverman didn't do this on his own but worked his magic instead through the best creative producers each of the networks had to offer—and at CBS that creative producer was Norman Lear. More than any other show creator, Lear paved the way, in January 1971, for the thinking person's sitcom with his landmark series *All in the Family*—a series (to tweak a '60's TV by-phrase) that boldly went where no series had gone before.

Revolution

All in the Family nearly outlasted the decade and rode most of it at the top of the Nielsen ratings. But it didn't start out that way. Producer-writer-creator Norman Lear's comedy had been on the air for scarcely a month and looked unexceptional—like it might have been home in the 1950's, except for the dialogue. What they were saying on the show blew the doors off conventional comedy. As *TV Guide* recognized all those years ago:

> *All in the Family* is a complete breakthrough—one that opens up a whole new world for television and has already made the old world seem so dated that we very much doubt that any new program from here on in will ever be quite the same again.[9]

It wasn't just that for the first time racism, abortion, homosexuality, birth control, and other burning issues of the day were ripe for one-liners. What established a riveting new level of reality in the sitcom format were hilarious, often poignant struggles of four people, Archie (played by Carroll O'Connor); Edith (by Jean Stapleton); Meathead (by Rob Reiner—son of Carl Reiner); and Gloria (by Sally Struthers),

---

8 *New York Times*—"Red Skelton Knockabout Comic & Clown Prince, Dead at 84" September 18, 1997

9 *Fifty Years of Television*, p 18

each grappling with their feelings about one another and the tumultuous world outside the Bunker living room in Queens, New York. The characters were types, certainly—blue-collar bigot vs. intellectual college liberal—but types never before seen on TV. Edith's foggy optimism and Gloria's caught-in-the-middle confusion were vital elements. But it was the firefighting over social issues between Archie and Meathead that stirred the comedy pot—Archie, low on intellectual ammunition but absolutely immovable; and the implacable Meathead refusing to give an inch—that forever altered television and the way it measured creative achievement.[10]

The cast that stirred the comedy pot on CBS's All in the Family, *1971–1979*

The show was based on the British sitcom *'Til Death Us Do Part*, about an irascible working-class Tory and his Socialist son-in-law. Lear altered the British concept to include a blue-collar American family with a right-wing patriarch and his left-wing son-in-law and offered the series to ABC.[11] After filming two pilots, the show was twice rejected, yet a third pilot was shot. This one was picked up by Silverman at CBS for thirteen episodes as a mid-season replacement—and at first blush that must have given him pause to reconsider his decision. *All in the Family* premiered on January 12, 1971 to disappointing ratings.[12] Lear himself admits that if the show hadn't aired mid-season, America would have never seen the fourteenth episode of *All in the Family*. Lear's series, however, had started late and found itself with two weeks in May that were clear of first-run competition from the other two networks that were now into reruns. Lear's series had two original shows left to air and the ratings for both episodes soared above the reruns offered up on NBC and ABC. That first year, also, *All in the Family* took home the Emmy Award for Outstanding Comedy Series. The show did well in summer reruns as word of mouth reached those who hadn't seen the original first run that spring. During the following 1971–'72 season, the series vaulted from out of the Top 50 TV Shows of 1970–'71, past every single series on all three networks to become the top-rated show on television for the next five years.

Critics of the show lambasted Lear for using television as a political soapbox. He was even forced to defend his hit show from his own network's accusations that the series was sending out weekly messages to the rest of the country—messages with which many of the network's sponsors didn't agree. But Lear stood his ground. The only message that could ever be connected to *All in the Family*, he contended, was

10 *Fifty Years of Television*, p 18

11 WGA Writer Speaks Series—"Norman Lear"

12 WGA Writer Speaks Series—"Norman Lear"

Carroll O'Connor (second from left) and Jean Stapleton (second from right), stars of All in the Family. *In the right picture, Mike Evans guest stars as Lionel Jefferson.*

that the show was *real* and that it was this reality in series television that was long overdue.[13] In short, argued Lear, television had given us soulless vanilla for almost two decades and the message in that was very clear. The world is white, protestant, healthy, and upwardly mobile. Virtually every show that aired during the fifties and sixties said so and Norman Lear was about to change all that.

While Dr. Martin Luther King Jr. had quarterbacked the Civil Rights Movement and launched it at television, few would dispute that it was Norman Lear who caught the pass and ran it through the 1970's. Lear followed his hit series *All in the Family* with *Sanford & Son* and *Maude* in September of '72, with *Good Times* in February of '74, *The Jeffersons* a year later. Three of the five shows listed above featured black ensemble casts. Integration into television, if not yet a touchdown, was heading for the goal line. At one point during the '75–'76 season, all five shows above were in TV's Top 10—a feat never accomplished by one show creator before or since. Television audiences bought into black characters and black series and never looked back.

Incestuous Spin-Offs

Lear's shows were incestuous—which is probably one of the nicest compliments that can be afforded a writer. Simply put, the series were all character-driven rather than plot-driven. Take *The Jeffersons.* The series was a spinoff of Lear's masterwork *All in the Family*. George and Louise Jefferson (Sherman Hemsley and Isabel Sanford) were Archie Bunker's next door neighbors in Queens who ascended from their working-class roots on the wings of a successful dry-cleaning business. In leaving Queens for New York's Upper Eastside, the African American family became a fish out of water, not that it ever bothered George. Though their newfound wealth created changes in their lifestyle, one trait always remained true for George—his never-ending mistrust of the white man.[14] George's obstinate demeanor drove

13 *Fifty Years of Television*, p 18

14 WGA Writer Speaks Series—"Norman Lear"

the stories for eleven seasons (1975–'85) and 252 episodes, each one mixing comic poignancy with unbridled arrogance.

Bea Arthur as Maude Findlay stands beside husband Walter (Bill Macy). Co-stars included friend Vivian (Rue McClanahan) and her daughter Carol (Adrienne Barbeau)

Spinning off *All in the Family* three years earlier was *Maude* (1972–'78). Beatrice Arthur, playing the title character, was Edith Bunker's liberal-leaning cousin and proved such a great foil for Archie on *All in the Family* that she received a series of her own. Strong-willed and opinionated, Maude dominated a household that featured husband Walter (played by Bill Macy) and divorced daughter Carol (played by Adrienne Barbeau), and spoke her mind when discussing controversial topics like politics, menopause, and rape.

Maude had an African American maid named Florida Evans (played by Esther Rolle) who, like Maude, was spun off into a series of *her* own called *Good Times*. Rolle's series helped elucidate the struggles of a working-class black family trying to make ends meet on Chicago's south side. Most of the laughs were supplied by Florida's eldest J.J. (played by Jimmie Walker), a hopeless optimist who was always dreaming up schemes to lift the family out of poverty. In looking back on the series, the character played by Walker was very close to the "Kingfish" character Tim Moore played in *Amos 'n' Andy* and reaped some of the same kinds of criticism.[15]

Esther Rolle said yes to the series, in part, because she had long wanted to change the image of the domestic worker. Yet, after reading the pilot script, she declined the offer. Her original character in the pilot script had been developed as a single mother living with three children. Rolle would not be a part of an African American TV series in which the father was absent from the family. Because she insisted, Rolle got a husband in the form of actor John Amos.[16]

The Cast of Good Times (left to right): Florida's younger son Michael (Ralph Carter), daughter Thelma (Bern Nadette Stanis), elder son "J.J." (Jimmie Walker), Florida (Esther Rolle), and husband James (John Amos)

With Norman Lear's *Good Times*, there seemed to be a conscious attempt to replicate *All in the Family*, but in a context relevant to what was going on in black communities across the country. According to Professor

15 Encyclopedia of 20th Century American Television, p 228

16 California Newsreel Production—"Color Adjustment"

Henry Louis Gates, Jr., director of Harvard University's Dubois Institute for African and African American Research: "*Good Times* represented the greatest potential and, in my opinion, the greatest failure. [It had] the greatest potential because it featured an inner-city family that was nuclear … and would talk about real world issues and how a black family dealt with those real world issues like racism and economic discrimination. But what happened? The producers elevated J.J.'s role from one that had been amusing and sometimes sophisticated to that of a buffoon."[17] Says sociologist Herman Gray, commenting on this very point: "His (J.J.'s) humor was tied to a long tradition of minstrel characters whose function on the show was to deflate … a lot of the buildup in the issues that the show [*Good Times*] tried to address. In retrospect, it was a clever use of a character to rob the show of the political bite it might otherwise have had."[18]

That was the rub with television, in general, as the 1970's began. The job of prime time TV, after all, was to entertain, not preach. *The Smothers Brother Comedy Hour* had learned this maxim the hard way. In regard to race, white America has always been uncomfortable in dealing with the victimization of any culture—more so then than now. No series, black or white, wanted to evoke guilt in its audience. "What makes you feel guilty," Norman Lear once said, "makes you feel uncomfortable."[19] And that thought begged a bigger question. Could prime time break the mold of traditional comedy and still be comforting to America?

By the mid-1970's, so-called ghetto sitcoms populated prime time viewing and were attempting to do just that—give its white audience a glimpse of what blacks were faced with in the real world, yet not so much that they turned away from the show. Sociologist Dr. Herman Gray illuminates: "On the one hand, the reality of the black inner-city experience was finally being rendered on television. On the other, however, these programs presented the inner-city ghetto as a place where human beings could actually survive, unscathed—and that was far from the case." The impetus for changing American society that could have come from showing these real world situations as shameful hell-holes was completely missed.[20] Poverty in the "projects" or the slums as portrayed on the set of *Good Times*, *Sanford and Son*, or *What's Happening* stopped short of addressing the offensive conditions that actually existed in real inner-city neighborhoods for fear of offending white America. The alchemy by which television would one day transform racial oppression and guilt into high ratings would not be emerging from the world of comedy any time soon. Rather, it would come from the world of drama, though its long-awaited arrival was still several years away.

---

17 California Newsreel Production—"Color Adjustment"

18 California Newsreel Production—"Color Adjustment"

19 WGA Writer Speaks Series—"Norman Lear"

20 California Newsreel Production—"Color Adjustment"

"Chuckles Bites the Dust"

While Norman Lear was the biggest show in town, in the 1970's, he wasn't the only one. Moving backward scarcely six months, a second CBS jewel of the new decade had already been born. Although it was to eventually become one of television's most beloved sitcoms and garner twenty-nine Emmy Awards—second only in the comedy arena to *Frasier's* 37—*The Mary Tyler Moore Show* didn't exactly start out that way. The series made its debut in 1970 and for the next seven years, like *All in the Family*, surprised critics and audiences alike. Few people thought the series would succeed. Mary Tyler Moore playing Mary Richards was, after all, a career-oriented woman in her 30's who was sensitive, compassionate, and moral. Not exactly a prototype of the in-crowd, me-generation, 1970's-world into which America was moving. Compared to the popular series of the day whose comedy depended on satire for its laughs (*Maude*, *The Bob Newhart Show*, and *All in the Family*), *MTM* (as the series and later her company would come to be known) was sincere and sweetly funny.[21]

Like *All in the Family,* however, the show tackled issues of the day. *MTM* focused on those that related to women and their place in what had traditionally been a "man's world." That was the show's real difference. As a central character on television, Mary Richards was the first never-married, independent career woman on the tube. Other series had featured working women, both on *Our Miss Brooks* (1952–56) that starred Eve Arden as a teacher, and on *The Gale Storm Show* (1956–60) that featured Gale Storm as a cruise director on an ocean liner. These shows, however, were about romance, not work. And *That Girl's* Ann Marie, while independent and unmarried, was a woman in her early 20's who had not yet launched her career. Mary Richards, on the other hand, was 30 and had been working for several years in another city before moving to Minneapolis. Overnight, women across American realized that their life could be more than just a husband hunt.[22]

The series set the benchmark for what could be achieved by women in the workforce by using two *distinct* comedy platforms in the same series. Mary's apartment and office served as those platforms and stood as apt metaphors for the internal dichotomy many women faced in the 1970's.[23]

Career vs. marriage was ripe now for comedic discussion. At home, the adorably single Mary had neighbors who were forever dropping in seeing to it that dating, cooking, and entertaining were sure to end badly. Rhoda Morgenstern (played by Valerie Harper), a 30-something Jewish woman from New York who worked as a window dresser at a Minneapolis department store, was one of those neighbors. So was Mary's well-meaning but self-absorbed landlady Phyllis Lindstrom (played by Cloris Leachman) who, like Rhoda in 1974, went and spun off her own series a year later.

---

21 *Encyclopedia of 20th Century American Television*, p 223

22 *Time*—"17 Shows That Changed TV" September 6, 2006

23 *Fifty Years of Television*, p 20

Mary Tyler Moore (Mary, left) in her Minneapolis apartment with neighbor Valerie Harper (Rhoda, center) on The Mary Tyler Moore Show

Yet, there was also the WJM-TV comedy platform where good-hearted Mary fought to keep her innate niceness from sabotaging her ambition—no easy chore when surrounded by co-workers like Edward Asner's cranky-but-affectionate portrayal of Lou Grant, Mary's boss (another cast member, by the way, to spin off his own show in 1977). There was the sensible yet smoldering news writer Murray Slaughter (played by Gavin MacLeod); and preening fathead anchorman, Ted Baxter (played incredibly well by Ted Knight). Later, actress Betty White came on board as hostess Sue Ann Nivens, WJM's hostess of the "Happy Homemaker Show." Sue Ann was desperate to attract any man she could find, and her exploits usually led to a discussion of other socially relevant issues surrounding men as the inferior of the two species.

In the third season, issues surrounding equal pay for women, pre-marital sex, and homosexuality were woven into the show's comedic plots. In the fourth season, the subject of marital infidelity and divorce were explored with Phyllis and Lou, respectively. In the fifth season, Mary refused to reveal a news source and was jailed for contempt of court. While in prison, she befriended a prostitute who sought Mary's help in a subsequent episode. In the final seasons, Ted dealt with intimate marital problems, infertility, and adoption, while Mary overcame an addiction to sleeping pills. In the fall of 1975, the show explored humor in death in the classic Emmy-winning episode "Chuckles Bites The Dust.[24] The episode went on in 1997 to be rated the number-one syndicated episode in the twentieth century and helped earn the show the second of three Emmy Awards for Outstanding Comedy Series in 1975.

The episode finds that Chuckles, a clown, has been hired as the grand marshal for a circus parade after WJM news anchor Ted Baxter is ordered by Lou Grant, his boss in the newsroom, to turn down the "honor." The next day, as Mary and Murray are watching Ted deliver the live newscast, Lou rushes into the newsroom in shock and tells the staff that Chuckles was killed during the parade. He had dressed as one of his characters, Peter Peanut, and a rogue elephant tried to "shell" him, causing fatal injuries. At the funeral, the jokes continue until the service is about to start, at which time a final scolding by Mary encourages all of the attendees to become properly somber. However, Mary alone begins to laugh uncontrollably during the eulogy as the minister recounts Chuckles' comedy characters and comic routines. She tries to stifle her emotions, but simply cannot contain herself. The minister is led to console Mary, reminding her that laughter was in keeping with Chuckles' life and urges her to laugh, whereupon Mary breaks down and sobs instead.[25]

---

24 *TV Guide & Nick at Night*— "The 100 Greatest TV episodes of all time!" 1997 June

25 Mary Tyler Moore Show: "Chuckles Bites the Dust" teleplay October 25, 1975

Chuckles' Eulogy

"Chuckles the Clown brought pleasure to millions. The characters he created will be remembered by children and adults alike: Peter Peanut, Mr. Fee-Fi-Fo, Billy Banana, and my particular favorite, Aunt Yoo Hoo. And not just for the laughter they provided—there was always some deeper meaning to whatever Chuckles did. Do you remember Mr. Fee-Fi-Fo's little catch phrase? Remember how, when his arch rival Señor Kaboom hit him with a giant cucumber and knocked him down, Mr. Fee-Fi-Fo would always pick himself up, dust himself off and say, 'I hurt my foo-foo'? Life's a lot like that. From time to time we all fall down and hurt our foo-foos. If only we could deal with it as simply and bravely and honestly as Mr. Fee-Fi-Fo. And what did Chuckles ask in return? Not much. In his own words, 'A little song, a little dance, a little seltzer down your pants ...'"

—*MTM* writers

The characters from *The Mary Tyler Moore Show* provided the focus for several successful spin-offs in the 1970's: *Rhoda*, *Phyllis*, and *Lou Grant*. The latter was significant in that it represented the successful continuation and transformation of a character across genre lines. In the new show Asner played Grant as a newspaper editor in a serious, hour-long, issue-oriented drama. MTM Productions developed a reputation, begun in *The Mary Tyler Moore Show*, for creating what became known as "quality television," readily identifiable by its textured, humane, and contemporary themes and characters.[26]

The series was the first from MTM Productions, the company formed by Moore and her then-husband, Grant Tinker. MTM went on to produce an impressive list of landmark sitcoms and dramas in the 1980's including *Newhart*, *The White Shadow*, *Hill Street Blues*, *Remington Steele*, *St. Elsewhere*, and *L.A. Law*, as well as its own series' spinoffs. The show became the anchor of the CBS Saturday night schedule and, along with *All in the Family*, *M*A*S*H*, *The Bob Newhart Show*, and *The Carol Burnett Show*, was part of one of the strongest nights of network programming ever offered.[27]

The Third Crown Jewel

It is one of the unsolved mysteries of American television that the CBS hit series *M*A*S*H**, a tragic-comedy about an unpopular war almost as dire in its effects as Vietnam, should have retained for more than a decade a popularity rating right up there with the one-time event miniseries or a national crisis. Week after week, year after year, from 1972 to 1983, its siren song of "incoming wounded" beckoned 33 million viewers away from teary soaps, drug saga dramas, and the T&A on ABC. "It was, for its time," said *TV Guide*, "an isle of joy in an ocean of junk; an outrageous, irreverent, and meaningful series that took

26 Museum of Broadcast Communications website—*"MTM Show"*

27 Museum of Broadcast Communications website—*"MTM Show"*

Hawkeye (played by Alan Alda, left) and Klinger (portrayed by Jamie Farr, right), stars of M*A*S*H*.

comedy away from the mundane forever." In short order, *M*A*S*H** became the third jewel in the CBS ratings crown within the span of two short years.[28]

When the television series aired in 1972, it was initially thought to be based on the Academy Award–winning Robert Altman movie of 1970 by the same name. It was, however, as much a lift from the 1968 Richard Hooker book, M.A.S.H.: A Tale of Three Doctors, on which Altman's movie was based. The core story to all three "M.A.S.H. mediums" surrounds a Mobile Army Surgical Hospital unit working out of Korea in 1951. Thanks to Altman's success at the box office, *M*A*S*H**, the TV series, finally found a home on the small screen. But there was more to its success than just the movie. First off, the TV show came on board the CBS schedule after 50,000 Americans had already died in Vietnam and at a time when the American people had had their fill of war, especially an undeclared one (a war waged by presidents without Congressional approval). Thus, many fans were ready for an anti-war television series—a black comedy dealing with the insanity of war. More importantly, however, the series began by getting away from the WWII stereotypes where the Nazis were always the bullies, the Japanese always shifty, and our guys always decent and heroic, if ever-so-arrogant.[29]

Instead of a commanding officer who looked like a gray-flecked man of distinction in a whiskey ad, we had first Henry Blake (played by McLean Stevenson), half dolt, half locker-room buddy; and later Sherman Potter (played by *Dragnet* sidekick Harry Morgan), a sentimental, bandy-legged holdover from WWII with enough horse sense to know that parade and discipline are impossible to maintain in conscripts bogged down in a jungle clearing. The colonel's tolerance of Corporal Max Klinger (played by Jamie Farr) and his transvestitism was a shock to early viewers, but provided a constant reminder of how much eccentricity had to be tolerated when commanding a group of often-overworked human beings pushed to the limit of sanity by nothing but boredom and death.[30]

And the CO's weren't the only ones playing cross-type. Ranking subordinates like Margaret "Hot Lips" Houlihan (Loretta Swit), was another startling novelty—a woman major working beside her asinine and un-heroic boyfriend, Maj. Frank Burns. Offsetting these weirdos was a group of commissioned officers led by the series star Alan Alda, who played Capt. Benjamin Franklin Pierce, nicknamed "Hawkeye," a surgeon in the 4077th M.A.S.H. unit who'd been drafted back into military service when his reserve unit

28 *Fifty Years of Television*, p 196
29 *Fifty Years of Television*, p 196
30 *Fifty Years of Television*, pp 196–197

had been called up for active duty at the start of the Korean War. Hawkeye's roommates were just as cavalier as he was. "Trapper" John McIntyre (played by Wayne Rogers) and later Capt. "BJ" Honeycutt (played by Mike Farrell) shared a tent they called the "swamp" (because of their still) with Hawkeye. After Larry Linville (Maj. Burns) left the show, his series replacement, David Ogden Stiers as the Boston-bred surgeon Charles Emerson Winchester III, moved into the swamp with Hawkeye. Many of the more innocent characters in the series were also played across type. Father Mulcahy (played by William Christopher), for example, was no heroic priest in the mold of screen actors Bing Crosby or Pat O'Brien, but a limited, slow-witted man of the cloth. And Gary Burghoff's Cpl. Walter "Radar" O'Reilly, Assistant to the Commandant, turned out to be a befogged child with ESP, unsure even of his own virginity.

Original cast of M*A*S*H* *(clockwise from bottom left): Loretta Swit, Alan Alda, McLean Stevenson, and Wayne Rogers*

Yet it was Hawkeye, the gifted surgeon-prankster, who held the whole family together for its eleven-year run—and did so with one quality that audiences everywhere understood: fundamental decency. That was the bottom line for a unit awash in exhaustion, emergencies, and physical peril. The patient came first—the patient of either side and any color. What's more ,no general, or visiting congressman, or CIA inquisitor was ever allowed to forget it.[31]

As the decade progressed, the series made a significant shift from being primarily a comedy to becoming far more drama-focused. This was partly due to creator Larry Gelbart's departure from the series in 1976 and executive producer Gene Reynolds leaving the show at the end of the following season. This, coupled with the departure of Larry Linville (Maj. Frank Burns) that same year, saw the series lose not only its comedic brain trust, but also its comic foil in less than a season.

Beginning with the sixth season (1977–1978), series' star Alan Alda and new executive producer Burt Metcalfe became the "voice" of *M*A*S*H** and continued in those roles for the remaining six seasons. By year eight, in 1979, the writing staff had been completely overhauled and *M*A*S*H** displayed a different feel—consciously moving between comedy and drama, unlike the seamless integration of years gone by. Yet, even so, many episodes from the later years were praised for their experimentation with the half-hour sitcom format, with episodes like: "Point of View," an episode shown from the point of view of a wounded soldier; "Dreams," which showed the lyrical and eventually disturbing dreams of the 4077 personnel; and "Life Time," an episode that took place in real time.[32]

31 *Fifty Years of Television*, p 197

32 The Complete Book of M*A*S*H*, pp 225–226

In point of fact, many of the storylines that aired throughout the decade were based on actual events and medical developments that materialized during the Korean War. Early 1950's events like McCarthyism, the Dodgers–Giants playoff game in 1951, and the stardom of silver-screen goddess Marilyn Monroe were all incorporated into various episodes. So accurate was their research that when it was discovered that no black American doctors were reported to have ever worked in the Korean War, African American actor Timothy Brown, who had appeared in eight episodes during season one as Captain "Spearchucker" Jones, another surgeon in the 4077th, quietly disappeared from the show.

All in all, the series was remarkable in that it created what in television is a visual rarity—a TV series with a cast of recognizable *human beings*. The audience must have loved it. When the last original episode was aired in 1983, 77% of all the people watching television that evening were said to have been watching the series finale of *M*A*S*H*.[33]

"Jiggle TV"

In early 1974, while still the head of programming at CBS, Fred Silverman ordered the *Maude* spinoff, *Good Times*, in part to cut into the momentum of an ABC show that was being groomed to win Tuesday night. Based on the 1972 blockbuster smash *American Graffiti*, ABC's *Happy Days* had the smell of success written all over it until CBS's *Good Times* threatened to push it off the schedule. So well had Silverman's plan worked at CBS that, by 1975, ABC finally realized it was losing its best prospect (*Happy Days*) for a long-running series and could bear it no longer. The American Broadcasting Company made Fred Silverman an offer (to use the idiom of the day) he couldn't refuse. ABC more than tripled Silverman's CBS salary and named him the new president of ABC Entertainment.[34]

Ironically, Silverman's hiring put him in the awkward position of now having to save *Happy Days*—the very show that *Good Times* had brought to the brink of extinction.[35] Silverman not only succeeded in sending *Happy Days* back to the top of the ratings heap, but he also generated a hit spin-off from that show, *Laverne & Shirley*, that was just as popular as the original.

As Silverman settled in at ABC, he swapped one great producer in Norman Lear for another in Aaron Spelling—such was Silverman's management style. Producers Spelling and Lear couldn't have been further apart as creative contemporaries, but then neither was ABC like CBS. The junior network was third in the annual sweeps and had been there forever—or so it must've seemed in 1970. This was not to say that ABC hadn't birthed a fair share of the highly rated sitcoms that rolled through the sixties—it had: *That Girl, Bewitched, The Courtship of Eddie's Father, The Odd Couple, The Partridge Family, and The Brady*

33 Encyclopedia of 20th Century American Television, p 224

34 *Tube of Plenty*, pp 481– 482

35 Ebony—"Bad Times on the Good Times Set" 1975 September

Bunch, to name a few. On the drama side the network there was *Room 222*, a top-thirty show that received Emmy Awards in its debut year of 1969. And as the decade turned, ABC had the number-one show in 1970, *Marcus Welby, M.D.*, starring Robert Young from *Father Knows Best* fame.

ABC's The Mod Squad *starred Tige Andrews, Peggy Lipton, and Michael Cole. "One Black, One White, One Blonde" went the show's hype line. A cop show for the Counterculture Generation 1968–1973*

By 1973, however, the junior network was again foundering, having only two shows in the top twenty. During the 1974–'75 television season it got worse. *Happy Days*, which had premiered in the sixteenth spot at the end of the '73–'74 season, was out of the top thirty when Silverman arrived in 1975.[36] The ABC target audience that year was 18 to 35 years old—youngest of the three national networks. Advertisers would kill for that demographic if only ABC had the shows to reach them. Silverman felt that what ABC really needed was a "hook" that would pull young male audiences away from the genres they'd grown comfortable watching on the two other networks—a task that was easier said than done. While viewing current ABC projects, however, Silverman glommed onto *The Mod Squad* and must've seen the wave of the future in that show—hip, stylish, and counterculture-friendly. Silverman met with *Mod Squad's* executive producer, Aaron Spelling, and laid out the three-year game plan for ABC.

"Jiggle TV" at its best! Original 1976 cast of Charlie's Angels*: (clockwise from left) Jaclyn Smith, Farrah Fawcett, and Kate Jackson*

The hook Silverman wanted Spelling to use to grab male demographics across the board was as time-honored as a pinup poster from World War II—women. Every series not only had to have one, but have one who would "jiggle" when commanded to do so. In 1976, Spelling complied with Silverman's directive and brought "jiggle TV" to the airwaves with the soon-to-be-smash-hit *Charlie's Angels* (1976–'81). While the all-girl action-series starring Farrah Fawcett, Jaclyn Smith, and Kate Jackson (and later Cheryl Ladd, Shelley Hack, and Tanya Roberts) purported to solve crimes with gun play and stylish action, mostly what this well-endowed, female cast *really* did was "strut their stuff" for the camera, week in and week out, wearing the latest designer threads.

---

36 Entertainmentscene.com –"Top TV Shows-1960s"

Consummate "jiggle attire" for the show included loose-fitting garments that allowed the show's female stars to move in a way in which their breasts or buttocks could be seen to shift or jiggle, as it were, on camera. In processing this concept, one needs to understand that during the latter half of the 1970's, sex and TV ratings became intertwined. A TV quotient was derived to measure a series' "T&A" ("tits and ass").[37] This much-heralded measurement was soon exposed in print and ads as the "jiggle quotient" in television. The more T&A a series offered audiences, the higher its television rating and share tended to be. Aaron Spelling's TV shows delivered strong ratings throughout the 1970's.

Spelling also contributed to the cop genre with hip shows like *The Rookies* and *Starsky and Hutch*, then crossed genres again and delivered hits in the nighttime soap opera genre with *Dynasty* and *Hotel*. Yet, his bread and butter series gravitated to fast-paced action with plenty of sexual heat, in shows like *Vegas*, *The Love Boat*, and *Fantasy Island*. Spelling would make sure that its lead female actors would appear in a bikini, bathing suit, underwear, or naked under a towel in each and every show.[38] The hook Spelling applied worked better than advertised. At one point in the late 1970's and early 1980's, Aaron Spelling was producing over one quarter of ABC's prime time schedule. Spelling had so many shows on ABC that industry insiders sarcastically dubbed ABC "Aaron's Broadcasting Company."[39]

Silverman *green-lit* other popular shows with other successful producers as well. *The Bionic Woman* (a *Six Million Dollar Man* spinoff), *Family*, *Three's Company*, *Eight Is Enough*, *Wonder Woman*, and *Soap*, to name a few. These moves not only brought ABC's long-dormant ratings from third place to first, but also landed Fred Silverman on the cover of *Time* magazine as: "The Man with the Golden Gut" (a reference to his programming genius). However, Silverman was also being criticized for relying heavily on escapist fare and for bringing T&A to the small screen. NBC executive Paul Klein publicly began to criticize ABC's television production and marketing strategy under Silverman. Klein branded ABC's programming as "marshmallow porn," referencing shows like *Charlie's Angels*, *Wonder Woman*, *Three's Company*, *The Bionic Woman*, and *WKRP in Cincinnati* as examples where the sexuality of young women was used to induce audience appeal. Klein felt that the programs' plots were often sexist, full of innuendo and suggestive language, and generally unrealistic in nature.[40] It hardly mattered. The 1975–'76 season turned everything around for ABC, sexist innuendo or not. Whereas the previous season had seen only two ABC shows in the top twenty, the 1975–'76 season at ABC, following Silverman's arrival, saw eleven shows in the top twenty; and by the end of the decade, an even dozen, with the first six top-rated shows belonging to ABC.

Truly, though, it was a show launched at the ABC network in 1978, just after Silverman had been lured away to NBC—the same network that only months before had branded him a pornographer—that best defined what a television network could do with 30 minutes of airtime.

---

37 The Gatekeeper: My Thirty Years as TV Censor, p 74

38 *Variety*—"Dynasty: The Making of a Guilty Pleassure" December 28, 2004

39 Complete Directory To Prime Time Network TV Shows, p 1041–1045

40 Censoring Sex: A Historical Journey Through American Media

The ABC series was called *Taxi*. With a mostly unknown but talented ensemble of actors, and a bevy of writers, producers, and directors who knew their way around a TV set, *Taxi* garnered 18 Emmy Awards in just five years—and on two different networks, no less (ABC, of course; and in its final year on NBC). The blue-collar comedy was hailed for its acting, but then look who they had, arguably one of the best-cast ensembles, comedy or drama, ever assembled: Tony Danza, Jeff Conaway, Danny DeVito, Marilu Henner, Judd Hirsch, Carol Kane, Andy Kaufman, and Christopher Lloyd. It is no wonder that historians refer to *Taxi* as the *tipping point* in American sitcom. What *Taxi* did was take the fun from the escapist sitcoms of the 1960's and meld it perfectly with the relevant comedy of the *All in the Family*–type satires of the 1970's, to give viewers a totally different kind of literate comedy hybrid.[41]

Drama Across the Dial

As much as audiences loved to laugh, there was, for much of the 1970's, a wealth of drama as well. The life and death excitement of crime stories and medical series had been a staple of broadcasting since the early days of radio, but not in any meaningful way. In TV series such as *Dragnet* and *Dr. Kildare*, for example, police officers and doctors were more often symbols of justice and medicine than fully realized characters. In the 1970's, however, those genres became more realistic in two distinct ways. First, they were more violent. Secondly, they portrayed cops and docs as real people, and not iconic caricatures who never received so much as a scratch in the line of duty.

One of the first series in this new breed of cop show was NBC's *Police Story* created by former L.A. policeman Joseph Wambaugh—a series that focused on the psychological toll on the men who faced death and violence every day. While the episodes contained all the dramatic aspects of police work audiences loved to watch—drug busts, pimps, thieves, and killers—the show gleamed relevant in the way it dealt with issues like internal corruption, racism, forced retirement, and work-related stress.[42] Actors Vic Morrow, Ken Olin, Robert Conrad, and Jack Warden all starred in the series at various times.

And *Police Story* wasn't alone. NBC also aired *McMillan & Wife* with Rock Hudson and Susan St. James, *Police Woman* starring Angie Dickinson, and *The Rockford Files* starring James Garner. All three shows were as much about the personal lives of the detectives as they were about the crimes solved on the show. With them on NBC was the powerful acting again of Raymond Burr, who gave viewers a look at the very active life of a handicapped cop-turned-department-consultant, in the eight-year NBC hit series, *Ironside*.

---

41 Hollywood Reporter—"TV Milestones" 2004 September, p 60

42 Encyclopedia of 20th Century American Television, p 282

And then there was NBC's *Columbo,* starring Peter Falk as the bumbling, stumbling detective in the rumpled raincoat by the same name. Lt. Columbo may have played "dumb" with the suspects he was chasing, but in truth he was as crafty as any fox on television. He had to be to find the one loose thread in that week's otherwise perfect murder. When the series first aired in 1971, it was part of NBC's Sunday Night Mystery Wheel alongside *McMillan & Wife* and *McCloud.* This latter offering starred Dennis Weaver (of *Gunsmoke* fame) as U.S. Marshal Sam McCloud—a fish out of water from Taos, New Mexico, using cowboy skills and horseback riding to solve inner-city crimes in New York. Like *The Bold Ones* launched a few years earlier, each of the three series would appear every third week in the NBC Mystery Wheel timeslot.

Apart from the big city, there were two enormously popular CBS dramatic series in the '70's that crossed type—each lasting nine wonderful seasons. Part of their longevity stemmed from the fact that both series were about the struggles of the poor (the first dramas of their kind) and defied TV's long-standing custom of addressing only the concerns of the rich and the middle class.

One was *The Waltons,* a series that chronicled the struggles of a family in Virginia's Blue Ridge Mountains during the Great Depression. The Walton clan was seen through the eyes of high-schooler John-Boy Walton (Richard Thomas), the eldest of seven children raised by John and Olivia Walton (Ralph Waite and Michael Learned). One of the virtues of this popular series was the realistic depiction of the passage of time. During its nine-year run, John-Boy went to college, started a newspaper, sold a novel, and became a war correspondent—pretty much parroting the true-life story of series creator Earl Hamner.[43]

The Waltons, *1972–'83 on CBS. Original cast of Grandma Walton (Ellen Corby) and John "John-Boy" Walton, Jr. (Richard Thomas)*

Running a close second to *The Waltons* as a series that broke with traditional TV drama was NBC's *Little House on the Prairie.* When launched in 1974, *Little House ...* was criticized as a "flatlanders" knockoff of *The Waltons*—that is until surpassing *The Waltons'* ratings in the last few years of the decade. The series starred Michael Landon (Little Joe on the 1960's series *Bonanza*) as the patriarch of a family's hardscrabble life in 1870's Minnesota.[44] An ancillary goal of the series was to help children learn to read and the show sent millions of younger viewers back to the public libraries. There, many feasted on a litany of the Laura Ingalls Wilder books, the inspiration for the series.

43 *Fifty Years of Television*, p 130

44 *Fifty Years of Television*, p 131

NBC's Little House on the Prairie *grazed on high TV ratings for most of the 1970's. Pictured is Michael Landon as Charles Ingalls*

As the decade rolled along, there were softer dramas to be seen, like ABC's *Owen Marshall, Counselor At Law*, starring Arthur Hill; and *Longstreet*, a short-lived but powerful 1971–'72 show featuring actor James Franciscus as a blind detective who used his other four senses to solve crimes. And there was CBS's *Cannon*, a P.I. show starring William Conrad as an unlikely, middle-aged, overweight hero, whose five-year run to open the decade marked him as the first successful P.I. series since *Peter Gunn*, 15 years earlier.

Police Procedurals

In 1972, a new crime genre hit the streets of San Francisco, though it wouldn't prove to be a TV mainstay for another twenty-five years. The genre would come to be called the "police procedural" and first hit the pavement two decades before *CSI* ever swabbed a blood drop. The series was appropriately titled *The Streets of San Francisco* and ran for five seasons on ABC (1972–'77). It starred Academy Award–winner Karl Malden and newcomer Michael Douglas as pragmatic cops who burned shoe leather while investigating evidence surrounding the crime. At the center of the series was veteran cop and widower, Lt. Mike Stone played by Malden, who had more than twenty years of police experience in the street. Stone was partnered with energetic plainclothes detective, Assistant Inspector Steve Keller (Michael Douglas), a 28-year-old college graduate with no experience on the police force. Stone would become a second father to Keller as he learned the rigors and procedures of detective work. Eventually, Keller was promoted to full inspector; and as the series went on, the actor playing him (Michael Douglas) became a star himself.[45]

Michael Douglas (left) follows the evidence on ABC's The Streets of San Francisco *1972–'77*

Following the second episode of the fifth and final season, Douglas left the show when his film career took off after successfully producing the feature film, *One Flew Over the Cuckoo's Nest*, which had won him (as executive producer) the Academy Award for Best Film of 1975. Douglas' character's absence on the TV series was explained by having him take a teaching position at a local college. Lt. Stone went on to partner up with another detective, but the change was not

45 The Streets of San Francisco: A Quinn Martin TV Series, p 43

popular with audiences and the show was canceled at the end of the season because of fallen ratings.[46] Nevertheless, *The Streets of San Francisco* was among the first series to be shot on actual locations, giving the show a realistic canvass for its gripping evidence-based stories.

Ironically, it was the police procedural that got America hooked to another kind of crime drama—the non-fictional kind. One of the most significant stories of the twentieth century began as a two-bit burglary at a Washington hotel called the Watergate and led the TV news every day from June 25, 1973 to August 8, 1974, spilling into prime time television on numerous occasions.

The Watergate Scandal

The Senate investigation into the dishonesty of an American president and his staff was better than fiction, and Watergate Committee Chairman Senator Sam Ervin, Jr. was every bit as good as Columbo when it came to pulling threads and ferreting out truth. Shortly after 1 am on June 17, 1972, a security guard at the Watergate Hotel Complex noticed duct tape covering the latch on several doors in the complex and called the D.C. police. Five men were discovered inside the offices of the Democratic National Committee and arrested on the spot. Two days later it was publicly revealed at the arraignment that one of the burglars was a Republican Party security aide. Former Attorney General John Mitchell, who at the time was the head of President Richard Nixon's re-election campaign, denied any involvement with the Watergate break-in. However, when a cashier's check for $25,000, earmarked for the Nixon re-election campaign, was found in the bank account of one of the Watergate burglars, a conspiracy that would take down a president began to unravel.

By April 30, 1973, the scandal had blown wide open. Nixon asked for the resignation of H.R. Haldeman and John Ehrlichman, two of his most influential aides, both of whom were indicted, convicted, and ultimately sentenced to prison. Nixon then fired White House Counsel John Dean, who went on to testify before the Senate and became the key witness against the President, who still maintained his innocence. Three months earlier, the United States Senate voted 77–0 to approve Senate Resolution 60, establishing a select committee to investigate the Watergate Burglary. Democratic Senator Sam Ervin from North Carolina was named its chairman the following day. The hearings held by the Senate Committee, in which Dean and other former administration officials testified, were broadcast from May 17 to August 7, 1973. The three major networks at the time agreed to take turns covering the hearings live, such that each network maintained coverage of the hearings every third day, starting with ABC on May 17 and ending with NBC on August 7.[47] An estimated 85% of Americans with television sets tuned in to at least one portion of the hearings.[48]

46 Blip TV—John Morrison Interview with Casting Director Anne Brebner 2011 March

47 Museum of Broadcast Communications website—"Watergate"

48 Museum of Broadcast Communications website—"Watergate"

The Watergate saga proved to be one of the most compelling stories in the history of broadcast journalism, and much of it was uncovered by two reporters working for the *Washington Post*. Bob Woodward and Carl Bernstein broke what many historians feel was the story of the twentieth century. The tale involved more than just a sitting president who had obstructed justice, lied to the American people, and manufactured evidence that ruined political lives. It involved the integrity of the American presidency and a true constitutional crisis that bitterly divided the country once again.

On Monday, July 16, 1973, in front of a live, televised audience, the Chief Minority Council Fred Thompson asked White House Assistant Alexander Butterfield if he was *"aware of the installation of any listening devices in the Oval Office of the President*?[49] Butterfield's revelation of the taping system transformed the Watergate investigation yet again. Special Prosecutor Cox immediately subpoenaed the tapes, as did the Senate, but Nixon refused to release them, citing his executive privilege as President of the United States. Moreover, he ordered that Cox drop his subpoena request. When Cox refused, Nixon ordered Attorney General Elliot Richardson to fire him. When Richardson refused him as well, Nixon demanded Richardson's resignation and that of his deputy William Ruckelshaus—actions that met with considerable public criticism.

The issue of access to the tapes ultimately found itself before the Supreme Court. On July 24, 1974, in *United States v. Nixon*, the court ruled unanimously that claims of executive privilege over the subpoenaed tapes were void. They ordered the president to release them to the special prosecutor, which Nixon did a week later—all but one. That one showed up a week later with an 18-minute gap that Nixon's secretary, Rosemary Woods, said she deleted by accident. This same audio tape, dated June 23, 1972 and recorded only a few days after the Watergate break-in, documented the initial stages of the cover-up. Because of the tape's incriminating nature, television covered the story closely. Overnight, the audio tape became known as the White House's "smoking gun."[50] The tape revealed Nixon and Haldeman meeting in the Oval Office and formulating a plan to block investigations by having the CIA falsely claim to the FBI that national security was involved. Prior to the release of this tape, President Nixon had denied political motivations and claimed he had no knowledge prior to March 21, 1973 of any involvement by senior campaign officials. "I'm not a crook," he told four hundred Associated Press managing editors.[51]

The June 23rd tape proved that the President of the United States had, for more than two years, lied to the nation, to his closest aides, and to his own lawyers. When Republican senators approached the President with news that enough votes now existed to remove him from office, Nixon decided to resign. In a nationally televised address from the Oval Office on the evening of August 8, 1974, the President said in part:

---

49 The Boston Globe— "Select Chronology for Donald G. Sanders"

50 Watergate Special Prosecution Force—"Transcript of a Recording of a Meeting between President Nixon and H.R. Haldeman"

51 The American Presidency Project—"Richard Nixon: Question-and-Answer Session at the Annual Convention of the Associated Press Managing Editors Association, Orlando, Florida, 1973"

> ... I have never been a quitter. To leave office before my term is completed is abhorrent to every instinct in my body. But as President, I must put the interest of America first. America needs a full-time President and a full-time Congress, particularly at this time with problems we face at home and abroad. To continue to fight through the months ahead for my personal vindication would almost totally absorb the time and attention of both the President and the Congress in a period when our entire focus should be on the great issues of peace abroad and prosperity without inflation at home. Therefore, I shall resign the Presidency effective at noon tomorrow. Vice President Ford will be sworn in as President at that hour in this office.[52]

In the end, Richard Nixon, the man whose ego had used television to launch and drive his own career, ruin those of others, and vault himself into the White House, found himself on nearly every television in America, exposed for the liar he was and the criminal he was later pardoned for being. And all in front of 50 million TV viewers a day.

Long-Form Television

While the 1970's were a mixture of comedy and drama echoing through a country mired in strife at home and abroad, the long-form drama that arrived on the scene seemed like a cool reprieve. Most were but ninety minutes in length and made exclusively for television. Little first-run movies aired weekly on networks and thus was born still another new television genre—the MOW. That was their handle, these "movies of the week." And the first network to dive into this new movie game was ABC.

By the early 1970's, ABC had formed its first theatrical division, ABC Pictures (later renamed ABC Motion Pictures). It made some moneymaking films in the late '60's and early 1970's like Bob Fosse's *Cabaret*, Woody Allen's *Take the Money and Run*, and Sydney Pollack's *They Shoot Horses, Don't They?* And that got ABC thinking. Why not make movies for the small screen as well as the silver screen. The innovative concept became a reality and was launched under the title: *ABC Movie of the Week*. This series of made-for-TV films aired once a week on Tuesday nights. Three years later, Wednesday nights were added, and by the end of the decade, every network had multiple movie nights on their fall schedule.

One of the first MOW's to reach the small screen occurred in November of 1971. It was a 74-minute film entitled *Duel*, starring TV veteran Dennis Weaver as a terrified motorist stalked on a remote highway by the unseen driver of a mysterious 1955 Peterbilt tanker truck. The truck boasted all of the characteristics of a malevolent beast. The MOW was written by Richard Matheson, based on his own short story, first published in *Playboy Magazine*, and directed by none other than Steven Spielberg. *Duel* was Spielberg's feature-length directing debut (albeit a TV movie), one he'd earned following a well-received turn

52 Public Broadcasting Service—"President Nixon's Resignation Speech"

directing a segment of the anthology television series *Night Gallery*. Initially shown on American television as an *ABC Movie of the Week* installment, *Duel* was eventually released to cinemas in Europe and Australia as a 90-minute feature. The film's success enabled Spielberg to establish himself as a legitimate film director, and due to the distinguished body of work that would subsequently follow him, the MOW *Duel* has claimed a kind of mythic status over the decades that followed.

Two weeks after *Duel aired* there was *Brian's Song* starring feature actors James Caan of *Godfather* fame and Billy Dee Williams of *Lady Sings the Blues*—both of whom had been nominated for Academy Awards. *Brian's Song*, the highly acclaimed winner of five Emmy Awards, a Peabody Award, the DGA Directing Award, the WGA Writing Award, an NAACP Commendation, and a Congressional Citation[53] as one of the truly moving television and screen achievements of its time, was also one of the best-loved movies ever made for television. *Brian's Song* was an *ABC Movie of the Week* in 1971 that recounted the details of the life of Brian Piccolo. The telefilm depicts the moving story of the close friendship between Chicago Bears football teammates Gale Sayers, an African American, and Brian Piccolo, who was white.

Both Piccolo and Sayers were star players for the Chicago Bears, and soon crossed racial lines to become roommates and best friends. When Sayers suffers a mid-season knee injury, it's Piccolo who prods and inspires him to a complete recovery. It's then that fate deals its cruelest blow as Brian Piccolo, just 26, is stricken with malignant cancer, leaving roles reversed. Sayers now plays a pivotal role in Piccolo's heroic fight against the disease, one the young fullback was sadly fated to lose.

The production was such a success on television that it was later shown in theaters as a first-run theatrical movie, but was soon withdrawn due to the fact that most of America had already seen the film on television. That aside, many critics have hailed *Brian's Song* the finest MOW ever made.

Birth of the Miniseries

While the 90-minute MOW was growing in popularity and many times based on factual events, there was a new long-form hybrid in the making that would come to be known as the *miniseries*. The term "miniseries" is used to refer to a single finite story told in more than two and fewer than thirteen separately broadcast episodes (what today would be seen on broadcast television as a half-season).[54] In short, a programming event that wasn't designed as a 22-week-long TV series, but couldn't fit into one night either. It was somewhere in between, epic in scale and based on the best-selling books of the day.

53 Movies Made For Television: "The Tele-feature and the Mini-series 1964–1986," pp 53–54

54 Museum of Broadcast Communications website—"Miniseries"

Until the coming of age of premium cable channels on television in the late 1990's, it was generally agreed that both soap operas and prime time series could not afford to allow their leading characters to develop, since the shows were made with the intention of running indefinitely. The burgeoning cable-series market of today runs contrary to this maxim and it's this contradiction that separates it from broadcast television, a medium that still creates its series like it always has, with characters that remain unchanged and comfortable for us to visit each week. In a miniseries, on the other hand, there is a clearly defined dramatic arc (beginning, middle, and end), as there would be in any conventional play or novel and now in the high-end series developed for premium cable networks as well. Characters can change, mature, or even die as the series proceeds.

In 1970, Leon Uris' best-selling novel QB VII took America by storm. This four-part novel highlights the events leading to a life-shattering libel trial in the United Kingdom. Parts one and two concern the plaintiff Adam Kelno, a doctor pressed into the service of the Nazis after Poland was overrun at the onset of WWII. As head physician in a concentration camp, he has the opportunity to save many prisoners from the gas chambers. Upon returning to private practice after the war, the good doctor is confronted with allegations that he collaborated with the Nazis, performing ghastly medical experiments at their beck and call. Parts three and four deal with the defendant's search to vindicate himself in open court. At first, Kelno is staunchly defended, but as more evidence comes to light in the trial, his checkered past is revealed. *QB VII* became the first miniseries ever produced, when ABC made a gutsy call in April 1974 to launch four 90-minute serials, running them once a week for four consecutive weeks.[55] The production received impressive reviews and surprisingly strong ratings.

These ratings led ABC to try again with an Irwin Shaw novel, Rich Man, Poor Man. Between February 1 and March 15, 1976, *Rich Man, Poor Man* became the superb, 12-hour television adaptation of Irwin Shaw's novel chronicling the widely divergent paths of two brothers over a 20-year span.[56] The compelling story of familial jealousy made for an extraordinarily successful miniseries, garnering a record twenty-three Emmy nominations and winning four. The TV rating for the final episode of *Rich Man* ... was among the five highest ever received up to that time. Off the point but true to history, the miniseries helped launch the mega-career of actor Nick Nolte, whose portrayal of the free-spirited Tom Jordache earned him an Emmy nomination for Outstanding Dramatic Actor.

Attempting to capitalize on ABC's incredible success with both their miniseries, CBS launched one of their own following Silverman's departure—*Helter Skelter*. The 1976 telefilm was based on prosecutor Vincent Bugliosi's 1974 book by the same title and leads the audience through the gruesome Tate–LaBianca murders at the hands of Charles Manson and his "family" of killers. The miniseries aired over two nights as a pair of 90-minute movies made for television.

55 Museum of Broadcast Communications website—"Elton Rule/QB VII"

56 Encyclopedia of 20th Century Television History, pp 296–297

According to the theory put forward by the prosecution, Manson had loved the Beatles' song by the same name and used the term "helter skelter" to describe an anticipated race war Manson was predicting would come. Unlike the ratings numbers for both of the ABC miniseries, those for CBS were low. Industry grumblings suggested that the ratings for *Rich Man, Poor Man* had been a fluke; the show, a one-time wonder. To prove it wasn't, ABC aired their third mini-series in January of 1977—and the face of television was changed yet again.

Back to Our Roots

The miniseries was called *Roots* and was destined to become the most successful and celebrated series of any kind in the 20th century. It was also a big part of the reason the American Broadcasting Company would finish the 1976–1977 season atop the Nielsen ratings, for the first time in its thirty-year history. For eight consecutive nights, America sat riveted as never before by the 12-hour dramatization of author Alex Haley's account of his African ancestry. At the time, *Roots* was the most-watched program ever made for TV, with a finale drawing more than 80 million viewers and 71% of the entire television audience—third highest in the history of television.[57] This staggering statistic went a long way toward answering the question posed earlier in this chapter: Was there a way for television to one day transform racial oppression and "white guilt" into high ratings? The answer, most definitively, was found in *Roots*.

The saga rolls through seven generations of an African American family, beginning in 1750 on the Ghana Coast of Africa. The miniseries depicts the capture of a young African warrior, Kunta Kinte (played by USC drama student LeVar Burton), by white slave traders and his subsequent transportation to America. Spanning nearly 225 years, the epic follows Kinte (slave name "Toby") and his descendants through the tragic story of slavery in the United States and the ultimate triumph of emancipation and opportunity for the Kinte-Haley family.

Roots received thirty-six Emmy Award nominations, winning nine as well as a Golden Globe and a Peabody Award. The cost of the production at the time was the most ever spent on a television show of any kind and ran a whopping $6.6 million (177M USD 2012).[58] The cast was enormous and looked like a virtual who's who of character actors. Edward Asner, Vic Morrow, Lloyd Bridges, and Lorne Green, among others, were complemented by a remarkable gathering of African American actors led by Burton and Amos, and included as well Cicely Tyson, Leslie Uggams, Louis Gossett, Jr., and Ben Vereen as the charismatic Chicken George. Quite literally, it took a nation too often separated by racial differences and bound it back together with the power of storytelling.

---

57 *Fifty Years of Television*, p 137

58 Ottawa Citizen—"New Roots series expected to yield big bucks for ABC" February 20, 1979

Executive producer David Wolper's task wasn't easy. Many early naysayers thought he'd never get the project off the ground. Even Wolper himself admitted that the idea of pitching a story where the whites were the villains and the blacks were the heroes in a market where 90% of the audience was white didn't sound like a very good idea.[59] But Wolper didn't see the project in those terms. He saw it as a story about an underdog overcoming adversity and about the power of family—and so did the rest of the country. Never had so many white Americans watched "anything black" in the history of television. The aftermath of *Roots* found workers in the plants, executives at the water cooler, and students at their lockers talking about the previous night's episode. Dialogues were opening up between blacks and whites outside of television. Clearly, there was something that gripped Americans about this story of a twentieth-century black man going back to Africa to find his roots. Henry Louis Gates, Jr., director of the W.E.B. Dubois Institute for African and African American Research at Harvard University, thought so, too. Said Gates in 1992: "It showed black people being just like every other immigrant group in America."[60]

To that end, *Roots* was an assimilation story made palatable to white America through the Kinte-Haley saga of movement into America. *Roots* was careful not to indict America, rather only specific individuals responsible for the unconscionable grief caused by the institution of slavery. With the airing of *Roots*, black families had finally found a place in mainstream television, less by changing society than by adapting to it. With the airing of *Roots*, prime time had selectively reframed American history by transforming a national disgrace into an epic triumph of the family and the American dream.[61]

By the end of the 1970's, black Americans were firmly planted in leading roles across the tube. And as the decade wound down there came two more. With yet another arrow in his quiver, Norman Lear fired it at NBC in November of 1978. *Diff'rent Strokes*, became another 100-episode hit for Lear. The sitcom about two black boys who come to live with a white millionaire when their mother, his maid, dies on the job was one of comic pathos. Culture clash fueled the comedy but it was child star Gary Coleman's retorts that kept viewers watching.

Then, in the fall of 1979, a black butler *spinning off* the ABC series, *Soap*, arrived to light up the airwaves with the driest humor of them all. The series was called *Benson*. Robert Guillaume played the butler Benson Dubois, an employee of Governor James Gatling (actor James Noble). Gatling was a governor whose heart was in the right place, but whose mind was sometimes missing in action. As it turned out, Governor Gatling was cousin to Jessica Tate (played by actress Katherine Helmond) and Mary Campbell (Cathryn Damon), two sisters on the ABC prime time parody *Soap*, on which the stories on that show were centered.[62] The sarcastic Tate butler (Benson Dubois) was hired away from the Tate family by cousin James Gatling to be the head of household affairs for the scatterbrained governor and his daughter.

59 California Newsreel Production—"Color Adjustment"

60 California Newsreel Production—"Color Adjustment"

61 California Newsreel Production—"Color Adjustment"

62 Museum of Broadcast Communications website—"Benson"

Smarter and more sensible than the people he served, Benson became the show's voice of reason—a trait that took him from butler to budget director in a single season.

With the success of *Roots* and other black series, and with the creative muse of Norman Lear having left its unmistakable imprint on television in the 1970's, TV had finally delivered a positive image of black success. Emancipation of the airwaves had been achieved. Network sponsors around the world had confirmed as much—in dollars and *sense*. Many black shows now did great box office and network executives were thrilled with their bottom lines. Even so, apart from the money, many critics still wondered if black roles on television had truly reached the Promised Land.

Discussion Questions

A. Shape-Shifting

- The 1970's shift in programming from escapist to relevant reflected what attitudes in the youth demographic that were being courted by prime time television?
- The only network television executive to lead all three networks, how did Fred Silverman work his magic from 1970–1981?

B. Revolution

- *All in the Family* erased the line in the sand for what previously tabooed topics for television series?
- When confronted with criticism from his own network, how did Norman Lear respond to his critics?

C. Incestuous Spin-offs?

- What simple truth followed many of the sitcom spinoffs of the 1970's relative to structure? How did this "truth" broaden the TV landscape?

D. Chuckles Bites the Dust

- *The Mary Tyler Moore Show* set the new benchmark for what could be achieved by women in the workforce. How was this accomplished on the show?

E. Third Crown Jewel

- What elements in a sitcom about war can catapult a series like *M*A*S*H** into so many years of syndication?

F. Jiggle TV

- Aaron Spelling was brought to ABC to raise ratings. What was the essential element in his scripts to attract more viewers? Give an example of this slant on series television.

G. Drama Across the Dial

- The life and death excitement of dramatic stories had been a staple of broadcasting since the early days of radio, but until the 1970's, none of it ever resonated with audiences in any meaningful way. What elements were now being injected into episodes to change this pattern?

H. Police Procedurals

- What were the original shows that fit into the "police procedural" genre?

I. The Watergate Scandal

- Where did you learn your "Watergate" facts? What details listed in this chapter had you forgotten or never learned?

J. Long Form Television

- The *Movie of the Week* concept emerged in the early 1970's. In your opinion, does the MOW still have a place in TV viewing?

L. Back to our Roots

- The saga of *Roots* riveted the American audience to their TV's for eight unprecedented nights. Considering the state of race relations in 1977 America, how did this miniseries not only prevail but capture viewer's hearts?

CHAPTER TWELVE

Wide World of Sport

1960–1980

Embryonic Journey

The topic of "symbiosis" can lead to disagreement among scientists. Some believe the word refers to *mutualisms* found only among the animal world—that is to say, relationships between mammals of different species where both species derive a benefit. Others believe these *mutualisms* extend beyond mammals to include *all* life forms throughout the cosmos as well as inanimate objects and ideas. If that be the case—if the world is indeed to be our oyster—the domains of sport and television are two such "cosmic species." Both have been a part of our global landscape for most of the last hundred years (counting radio) and the relationship between these two worlds has certainly been a symbiotic one. The world of sport has helped to grow the business of television, while TV has enabled sporting ventures, world-wide, to become high-end family entertainment. Both "species" have derived enormous benefits from the other that might never have happened had each world not found its symbiotic partner.

In discussing the interface between sports and television, it should be noted that this was not a *chicken-or-egg* situation. Sports came first by as much as 4,000 years. In fact, while radio covered college football games, heavyweight prize fights, and professional baseball in New York as early as 1921, it was 1939 before American television broadcast a sporting event—a college baseball game between the Columbia

World's first televised sporting event, 1936's *Jesse Owens Olympics*. The U.S. quickly jumped on the bandwagon in 1939.

Lions and the Princeton Tigers. NBC covered the game from Baker Field in upper Manhattan, but the coverage was minimal, consisting of a one-camera set-up with a point of view along the third-base line.[1]

Five years later, in 1944, the first network sports *broadcast* also turned up at NBC—*The Gillette Cavalcade of Sports.* The show's premier featured a Featherweight Boxing Championship that matched up pugilists Willie Pep and Chalky White[2]—two fighters who would have long ago been forgotten had they not been the first ones ever to be witnessed boxing on television. It should be noted that the show was created for WWII vets injured in battle and residing in VA hospitals around the country. Few viewers outside these hospitals were likely to have seen the show. At the time, less than 5,000 TV sets had been sold throughout the entire country.

Within four years, however, sports would become a fixture on 1940's prime time television programming, often accounting for one third of the four networks' total evening fare (DuMont was still a network then). But as the 1950's advanced, prime time television's other genres began to mature and develop their own loyal audience, fifty percent of whom were women. Gradually, sports began to disappear from prime time television, settling into a very profitable and successful weekend niche. *The Gillette Cavalcade of Sports*, however, remained on the NBC network for twenty years and was part of NBC's regular Friday night, prime time lineup from 1948 until 1960, showing sports programs that included boxing, wrestling, and roller derby, among others. It was during television's embryonic years that TV's love affair with sports began in earnest.

At the onset of this symbiosis between sports and television, sports helped TV far more than television assisted sports. The reason was obvious—few Americans owned a TV set. In 1948, during the first full year of regularly scheduled network broadcasting, less than 1% of the country owned a television. In contrast to the nearly 300,000,000 American TV sets in existence in 2012, only 190,000 sets were in use in 1948.[3] To put that meager figure in proper perspective, there were sixteen major league baseball teams

1 Museum of Broadcast Communications website—"Sports & Television"

2 Museum of Broadcast Communications website

3 Museum of Broadcast Communications website—"Sports & Television"

in 1948. If each stadium held 45,000 fans and there were eight games on any given day, more fans in the country would have been at the ballgame than owned a television set.[4]

Suffice it to say, during the late 1940's and early 50's, it was the world of sports broadcasting that impacted the world of television. Sporting events during that era actually got fans to become TV set owners and no sport had a larger national following—an audience—than baseball. Thus, putting baseball on TV not only attracted advertising dollars, it actually lured more and more viewers to the medium itself. Televised games became a tool used by the networks to get fans to buy a television instead of a baseball ticket. While the notion that you had to entice people to buy a television set might seem foreign to anyone born in the late twentieth or early twenty-first century, that's oftentimes the way of the world when it comes to new technology. It takes time for the technology to become a common item of ownership. When a technology is new, people must be convinced that they need it. Moreover, in the early days of any new technology, that new item can be very expensive. Such was the case with television, initially.

Over time, of course, the price of TV sets dropped, dramatically, and that fact alone altered the symbiotic relationship between TV and sport. While there had been fewer than 10,000 sets in the country as late as 1945, that figure had soared to around six million in 1950; and by 1960, over sixty million American families had sets.[5] Sports, which had been helping television survive as a business, began to reap its symbiotic rewards as the nation moved from almost no one owning a TV set to almost everyone owning one. Moreover, as the population began moving away from the urban hubs of America (where all the ballparks were) and into suburban tract homes, it became more difficult for families to attend sporting events and easier to watch them on television. Discovering its growing audience, television suddenly found itself needing more sports programming to satisfy this new, heavily male, 18–49 demographic. As the demographic steadily grew, professional sports leagues also began expanding, finally coming to understand their true worth.

This expansion saw more television stations set up shop in cities with sports franchises tied to them. More TV stations and teams in more cities meant more of the country had found a rooting interest in sports. Television ratings rose in proportion to the growing fan base. By the 1970's, women began to encroach on the male-loaded sports niche—on and off the field. Not only were women watching sports on television, but they were also forming teams and leagues of their own. The passage of the National Collegiate Athletic Association's (NCAA) Title Nine, in 1972, finally allowed women "between the lines."

To illuminate the difference between the TV–Sports paradigm of 1950 and that of 1970, one has only to turn to the Los Angeles Rams. The NFL team resided on the west coast in those days and being a forward-thinking football franchise, signed a contract to allow a local TV station in the area to televise six of their eight home games in 1950. The contract specified, however, that any loss of revenue to the

4 Chapman University Lecture (10) – "The Business of Sports on TV," p 2

5 The World Book Encyclopedia—"Television," p 119

Rams—that is to say, a loss of ticket revenue due to lack of attendance—would have to be reimbursed to the Rams by the sponsor of the TV broadcast. The two home games not televised took in an average of $77,000 in ticket sales. The six games that were televised took in only an average of $42,000. Thus, the sponsor had to pay $198,000 in compensation.[6] The contract was not renewed by the local station for the 1951 season. The TV station's sponsor felt that they had simply paid too much.

The network fees paid to sporting leagues are no different from the fees they pay studios to create weekly shows—a "licensing fee." The license fee paid to the Rams that season in L.A. was more of a guarantee than a fee and amounted to less than $200,000. In 1970, just twenty years after the Rams had shrewdly snagged their six-figure "indemnity deal" from a disappointed sponsor, license fees had gone up. That year, the networks paid $50 million to broadcast the National Football League (NFL) games, $2 million for the National Basketball Association (NBA), and $18 million for Major League Baseball (MLB). In 1985, just fifteen years later, those figures had risen to $450 million, $45 million, and $160 million, respectively.[7] Considering the exponential increase in what networks now paid to sports leagues, the local L.A. TV station in 1950 got quite a deal.

These large increases were fueled by growing public interest in professional sports, which was in turn spurred on by more and better TV coverage. To meet the escalating cost-of-doing-business in sports, television upped their advertising rates and sponsors compensated as well by raising the prices of their goods and services. At the end of the day, consumers would pick up the tab for it all, drinking $12 beers at the ballpark and eating $10 hotdogs at the rink or arena. The benefits derived from the sport by the fan simply outweighed all the other negatives. It was truly a symbiotic, win-win situation—television and sports whirling together in a maelstrom of cash.

Even so, it should be noted that the symbiotic relationship between sports and television that had existed in 1948 had, by the end of the century, completely reversed itself. Television in 2000 was now supporting sports. TV's "symbiotic partner" had been seen as cost-effective programming while the medium was growing up. By century's end, however, the world of sports had grown up, too, and what networks were paying to court this world bordered on the obscene.

ESCALATING NETWORK FEES

LEAGUE	1970	1985	2000
NFL	$50M	$450M	$18B (7 YRS)
NBA	$2M	$45M	$4.6B (6 YRS)
MLB	$18M	$160M	LOCAL BY TEAM

6 Chapman University Lecture (10) – "The Business of Sports on TV," pp 2–3

7 Museum of Broadcast Communications website—"Sports & Television"

As the century turned, the networks agreed to pay the NFL $18 billion to broadcast its games for seven years and $4.6 billion for the rights to broadcast NBA games for six years.[8] Major League Baseball teams now owned their own TV stations and broadcast their games locally for fans in the region. These numbers above, being that they are in effect the license fees for these "shows," point to an 800% rise in football revenue over those fifteen years and a whopping 1000% rise in NBA revenue.[9] Television had needed sports early on to grow an audience and the audience it grew now clamored for sports, twenty-four hours a day.

Prime Time Symbiosis

In 1970, the American Broadcasting Company set out to prove that the symbiosis between television and sports could exist in prime time and tried something the other two national networks had already rejected—airing professional football games on prime time television. While CBS and NBC had both paid a bundle to air NFL games on Sunday afternoon, both had passed on the idea of prime time football, feeling they could never capture the "entertainment" audience needed to consistently win that night's prime time TV rating. The high ratings football received from a male-dominated audience on Sunday afternoon was one thing. Transferring that daytime male-oriented audience to the far more lucrative prime time hours when women controlled the nighttime dial would simply never work.

Almost everyone in television in 1970 (or sports, for that matter) considered *Monday Night Football* a foolish venture for even the most desperate of primetime schedules. This contention was more than mere conjecture. CBS had already tried prime time games a half-dozen times between 1966 and 1969, even featuring the mighty Green Bay Packers coached by the legendary Vince Lombardi in two of these games, but the experiment had not translated into successful TV ratings.[10] The games were aired on Friday night, at the same hour that high school football games were played across the country. Low audience ratings weren't CBS' only problem. CBS had inadvertently "messed" with an American institution—high school football—where Friday nights were sacred. The CBS network, realizing the folly of their ways, quickly shied away from the fray.

NBC tried their luck in 1968 with a somewhat different "football experiment" featuring the AFL's Oakland Raiders and the New York Jets; the ratings this time around were better. Truthfully, the "experiment" wasn't really an experiment at all, but a mistake in judgment. As the story goes, the Jets and Raiders put up almost 700 passing yards of offense between them before the game was through. The lead had vacillated back and forth the entire game and with just over a minute left to play, the Jets had kicked a field goal to put themselves on top 32–29.[11]

---

8 Museum of Broadcast Communications website—"Sports & Television"

9 Museum of Broadcast Communications website—"Sports & Television"

10 NFL Record and Fact Book, p 369

11 Stay Tuned, p 143

The game being played in Oakland was a late-afternoon game on the West Coast, but an evening game back East. With the 7 pm "witching hour" for prime time viewing on Sunday night fast approaching in New York, NBC had to make a call. Would they play the scheduled movie that was due to begin any moment, or the nail-biter of a football game already in progress? NBC, knowing that Timex had purchased the entire two-hour advertising block for the network's Sunday night movie, made the call to air the movie.[12] The film for that evening was *Heidi*, a heartwarming if clichéd telefilm about a cute little 10-year-old girl who prances around in the Swiss Alps with her benevolent grandfather. The programming snafu lit up the switchboards at NBC like never before. As syndicated columnist Art Buchwald wrote in his column the next day: "Men who wouldn't get out of their chairs during an earthquake rushed to the phones to shout obscenities." Even famed NBC newscaster David Brinkley chimed in on the following evening's *Huntley-Brinkley Report,* blaming the move on a "faceless button-pusher in the bowels of NBC," then replayed the final frantic minute of the game on the six o'clock news.

The programming change might not have been so bad had the score remained the same, but the Oakland Raiders scored twice in the last minute of the game to win 43–32. The protest calls to NBC were instantaneous and so overwhelming that the switchboard blew twenty-six fuses in over the next hour.[13] The result of what would come to be called "The Heidi Game" was, generally speaking, twofold. NBC dropped out of the prime time football business for the next forty years ... and ABC jumped in.

Roone

It's been said that lots of people have good ideas, but precious few know what to do with them. Roone Pickney Arledge, Jr. was one who *did* know what to do with every innovation that crossed his path, *Monday Night Football* included. But the man who would one day hold the presidencies of both ABC Sports *and* ABC News, concurrently, and create such enduring series as *Nightline, 20/20, ABC World News,* and *Monday Night Football*[14] started out like many college graduates returning from military duty in the 1950's—in the unemployment line. Arledge had worked for the DuMont Television Network before being drafted and returned to find himself out of a job when DuMont went under in 1956. Contacts he made there, however, paid dividends, landing him a job soon after as a stage manager at NBC's New York City affiliate, WRCA. One of Arledge's assignments there was to help produce a children's puppet show hosted by Shari Lewis. In 1958, the program won a New York City Emmy Award.[15]

Arledge used his success to convince his superiors at WRCA to let him film a pilot of a show he called *For Men Only*—the TV version of Hugh Hefner's sophisticated *Playboy* magazine. WRCA weatherman, Pat

12 Stay Tuned, p 141

13 Stay Tuned, p 143

14 Museum of Broadcast Communications website—"Roone Arledge"

15 The Thrill of Victory: The Inside Story of ABC Sports, p 13

Hernon, who had hosted the pilot episode, began showing the kinescope of Arledge's series to people around New York City hoping to sell the show. One of those people was a former ad agency account executive named Edgar Scherick, who was now producing sports shows for fledging ABC. Scherick had sold his Sports Programs, Inc. production company to ABC, who needed counter-programming to offset ratings gains savored by the other two networks, with the proviso that he (Scherick) head up sports production at ABC. Creating programming for ABC Sports, even before it became a formal division of the network, Scherick and ABC programming chief Tom Moore pulled off a good many programming deals involving popular American sporting events around the country. The popularity and variety of the sporting events gave Scherick an idea for a new show, but he'd need some talented help to pull it off.[16]

It was about this time that Scherick screened Arledge's *For Men Only* pilot. Scherick wasn't interested in the pilot per se, but rather the stage manager who'd produced it. Scherick was impressed with the writing-production talent Roone Arledge brought to bear and scheduled a meeting between them. The encounter would become historic. Arledge was immediately taken by Scherick's vision and quickly realized that ABC was the organization he was looking to join. Moreover, the lack of ABC's formal organization offered Arledge the opportunity to claim real power when the network matured, so he signed on with Scherick as an assistant producer[17]—and another symbiotic relationship was formed. Soon after arriving at ABC in 1960, Arledge sent Scherick a memo filled with television production concepts that sports broadcasts have adhered to ever since. Network sporting broadcasts had previously consisted of simple set-ups and focused on the game itself. The genius of Arledge, as revealed in the memo, was not that he offered a different way to broadcast games to sports fans. His genius was to recognize that television wasn't a vehicle for broadcasting games *to* sports fans at all, but rather one for *bringing* the sports fan to the game.[18] The Arledge memo would come to change the paradigm of sports broadcasting in the twentieth century.

In January 1961, Scherick called Arledge into his office and asked him to attend the annual AAU board of governors meeting and cut a deal to broadcast AAU events on ABC. Scherick had a vision for a new sports series and wanted Arledge in on the ground floor. Scherick needed product for this new venture and the weekly AAU track and field events scheduled around the country that spring and summer presented a start-up programming opportunity that the other networks wouldn't have. Arledge returned with a deal for ABC to broadcast all AAU events for an annual fee of $50,000 (3.8M USD 2012).[19] Next, Scherick needed sponsors for the show and tapped into his NCAA college football sponsor list to fill that bill. Scherick and Arledge telephoned their sponsors and strong-armed them into coming on board the new show. Advertise on their show, went the message, or forget about buying commercial time on NCAA college football games that fall. It's ironic that it took this kind of arm-twisting to get sponsors to invest

16 The Thrill of Victory: The Inside Story of ABC Sports, p 22

17 The Thrill of Victory: The Inside Story of ABC Sports, p 24

18 *ESPN Page 2 Online*—"Arledge's World Flowed with Ideas"

19 The Thrill of Victory: The Inside Story of ABC Sports, p 31

in a show that would dominate Saturday afternoons for the next 45 years, but such were the tenuous beginnings of ABC's classic *Wide World of Sports.*

Wide World of Sports suited Scherick's plans to a tee. By exploiting the speed of jet transportation, now commonplace, and flexibility of videotape, Scherick was able to undercut NBC and CBS's advantages in broadcasting live sporting events. In that era, with communications nowhere near as instantaneous and universal as they are today, ABC was able to safely record events on videotape for later broadcast without worrying about an audience finding out the results. During that first year, Arledge, his colleague Chuck Howard, and a talented announcer named Jim McKay (who left CBS for this chance) made up the show on a weekly basis. Arledge had a genius for dramatic story lines that unfolded during the course of a game or event. This together with McKay's honest curiosity and reporter's bluntness gave the show an emotional appeal that attracted viewers who might not otherwise have watched a sporting event.[20]

The events, themselves, were as varied as the locales in which they were performed: cliff diving from Acapulco, ping pong matches from Beijing, rodeo riding in Wyoming, curling in Nova Scotia, and jai alai from Mexico. The goal of the series was to showcase sports from around the globe and the series originally ran for two hours on Sunday afternoons. *Wide World of Sports* would usually feature two or three sports per show, but included types of sports not previously seen on American television—hurling, surfing, logger sports, slow-pitch softball, cricket, demolition derby, Australian rules football, and badminton. In 1974, the show even chose to cover Evel Knievel's failed jump across the Snake River in spectacular fashion.

Daredevil Evel Knievel and his X-2 Skycycle steam-powered Snake River Rocket (not shown here) failed to cross the river when its chute opened early.

For Arledge, *Wide World of Sports* was a showcase that allowed him to demonstrate his ability as an administrator as well as a producer—and as a producer Roone Arledge was almost without peer. Arledge personally produced all ten of the ABC Olympic broadcasts; and it was during those years that Arledge was said to have coined the ABC Sports one-liner: "The thrill of victory and the agony of defeat." The line may have come from Arledge, but part of the pictorial used in association with it actually came from *Wide World of Sports* producer, Dennis Lewin. On March 7, 1970, Lewin was in Lubiana, Yugoslavia, working a figure skating event when he caught the televised crash on *Eurovision* of ski jumper, Vinko Bogataj, at the ski jumping competition in Oberstdorf, West

20 *ESPN Page 2 Online*—"Arledge's World Flowed with Ideas"

Germany.[21] Bogataj catapulted dramatically off the side of the jump, doing multiple somersaults as he plummeted down onto groups of officials, broadcasters, and spectators. Miraculously, no one was seriously hurt—not even Bogataj. The magnificent failure was featured weekly on the *Wide World of Sports* promo at the start of every show, beginning March 21, 1970, the day it first aired on the series, and every week thereafter for the next 28 years under the show's narration: "... and the agony of defeat."

Being the last radio network to emerge on the scene left ABC with fewer resources, less history, and almost no momentum as television emerged in the late 1940's. The only way ABC could ever hope to catch up was through innovation and counter-programming. And that's what Roone Arledge used at ABC Sports to vault the network forward. With *Wide World of Sports*, Arledge gave us first-of-their-kind production innovations—things we take for granted today, but were genuine sparks of genius in 1960. Introducing such techniques as slow motion, freeze frame, instant replay, and split screen,[22] Arledge turned sporting events into dramas. So, too, did his use of the "up close and personal" moments with athletes from around the world—common today, of course, but 50 years ago they were the first of their kind as well. As Arledge promised in his memo to Edgar Scherick, television needed to bring fans to the game; to make them feel like they'd actually been there to see it. Arledge used television to turn athletes into three-dimensional figures and by so doing increased their appeal to audiences around the world. This new and younger sports audience was soon to become part of ABC's prime time demographic. Arledge was growing a loyal fan base and with it, ABC's cachet as a network.

Arledge was also a master at putting the cameras *inside* the sporting events—giving the viewer a sense of what it felt like to actually be *in* the game, rather than just watching it—then took these techniques and applied them to Olympic broadcasts. Cameras were placed inside luges in the winter competitions and underwater during water polo matches in the summer games. Jim McKay's gifted announcing became a household fixture on Sunday afternoons and was used to augment dramatic footage and storylines resulting in a dramatic new style of broadcasting.

Olympic Gold

Nowhere was this dramatic broadcasting style and Arledge's deft touch more apparent than it was at the Munich Olympics in the summer of 1972. ABC Sports had, of course, been to the Olympics before. They had first televised the 1968 Winter Olympics from Grenoble, France, four years earlier to record Alpine skier Jean-Claude Killy's successful run at the "Triple Crown of Alpine Skiing" (Men's Downhill/Slalom/Giant Slalom). As it came to pass, the feat was never to be repeated in the twentieth century and matched only once before, by Austrian skier Toni Sailer in the 1956 Winter Games.

---

21 Stay Tuned, p 127

22 Like It Is, p 105

By the summer of 1968, ABC found itself front and center at the Summer Olympic Games in Mexico City. There, ABC Sports captured Bob Beamon's 29'2½" leap into the *long-jump* history books. It wasn't that the jump set a world record, but by how much it set the record. In a sport that moved forward in quarter-inch increments, Beamon's jump eclipsed the old mark by a whopping 21¾ inches—a feat that would stand for 23 years. To say it was the jump of a lifetime is more than a euphemism, it's true. Bob Beamon never jumped over 27 feet again.[23] The 1968 Summer Games, however, would be marred that year by political protests when black sprinters Tommie Smith and John Carlos raised their arms into the air in racial solidarity, proclaiming "Black Power" from the top of medals podium. Their silent protest for an end to racial and economic discrimination in America lasted all the way through the U.S. National Anthem. Olympic officials were outraged—no one more so than International Olympic Committee (IOC) President, Avery Brundage. Before the night was over, Brundage and the IOC stripped both Smith and Carlos of their gold and bronze medals, respectively, and quickly expelled them from the Summer Games.

Roone Arledge had been a big part of these '68 Summer Olympics and there are those who would argue that he orchestrated most of it. The Arledge-driven television coverage was great to begin with, but after the "political moment" shared by Smith and Carlos on the podium at the Medals Ceremony, the Olympics transcended sport and became compelling entertainment. ABC sportscaster Howard Cosell's "up close and personal" interview with gold medal winner Tommie Smith, after the incident, not only fueled the drama of the moment, but ABC's prime time Nielsen ratings as well.

The Munich Olympics of 1972 opened benignly enough as all eyes were on American swimmer Mark Spitz who would end up doing the impossible—winning seven gold medals in one Olympics. What Mark Spitz accomplished in 1972, in Mexico City, would stand for 36 years and serve as an innocent prelude to the madness that would follow in week two of the Munich Games.

In the wee hours of a Tuesday morning, September 5, 1972, a group of eight Palestinian terrorists belonging to the Black September organization broke into the Olympic Village and took eleven Israeli athletes, coaches, and officials hostage in their apartments. Two of the eleven hostages who resisted were killed in the first moments of the break-in, though the subsequent standoff in the Olympic Village lasted for almost 18 hours.[24]

The politics of racial discrimination in America in 1968 had transcended into the politics of global terrorism abroad four years later. In what some historians still hail as television's finest hour, executive producer Roone Arledge, director Don Ohlmeyer, announcer Jim McKay, and ABC Sports dedicated every available television resource to cover the terrorist take-over of the Israeli compound in the Olympic Village. This deplorable action required unprecedented TV coverage. Though the Israeli compound was immediately cordoned off by German SWAT police, ABC journalists managed to gain access. So determined was Peter

23 The Guardian—"50 stunning Olympic moments No2: Bob Beamon's great leap forward" 2011 November

24 Stay Tuned, p 148

Jennings to stay on the scene that he hid in a bathroom as security cleared his building. Sportscaster Howard Cosell convinced a guard he was a shoe salesman and was somehow allowed entrance. Rookie TV reporter Bill Toomey, who'd won the decathlon in the '68 Games four years earlier, put on his Olympic jogging suit from Mexico City and ran past guards unnoticed.[25]

Late in the evening of September 5th, the terrorists and their hostages were transferred by helicopter to Furstenfeldbruck, a nearby military airport, ostensibly to board a plane bound for an undetermined Arab country. The German authorities planned to ambush the terrorists, but underestimated their numbers and were thus undermanned. During the botched rescue attempt, all of the nine remaining Israeli hostages were killed. Four of them were shot and then incinerated when a Palestinian detonated a grenade inside their chopper. The five remaining hostages in a second helicopter were then machine-gunned by another terrorist. All but three of the Palestinians were killed as well and the survivors were quickly arrested by German police.[26]

Critics around the world lauded ABC's journalistic effort. A network sports division had handled one of the most spectacular cold war stories of the twentieth century as well as any hard news department in the country. Anyone alive at the time remembers veteran announcer, Jim McKay, visibly shaken by the information he'd just received in his earpiece from the ABC control room, announcing ... "Our worst fears have been realized tonight. They're all gone."[27]

On the afternoon of the following day, the Munich Games resumed. Allowing the games to continue was seen as an outrage by many who felt that the IOC and specifically Brundage, its president, had not given the event its proper respect. As Pulitzer Prize–winning sports columnist Jim Murray wrote: "Incredibly, they're going on with it. It's almost like holding a prom dance at Dachau."[28] Suffice it to say, the tragedy of the Munich Games left an indelible tableau in the minds of the millions who watched, reshaping both the world of sports and the world around it for decades to come.

Monday Night Football

As early as 1964, NFL Commissioner Pete Rozelle had envisioned the possibility of playing at least one weekly football game each season during the prime time hours in order that football might garner a greater TV audience. During subsequent negotiations on a television contract that would begin in 1970, Rozelle concentrated on signing a weekly Monday night deal with one of the three major networks. After sensing reluctance from both NBC and CBS to dismantle their highly rated prime time programming

---

25 Stay Tuned, p 149

26 *The Independent*—"Olympics Massacre: Munich – The real story" January 23, 2006

27 Stay Tuned, p 150

28 Stay Tuned, p 151

schedules for what both networks considered to be a risky venture, Rozelle spoke with ABC, a network desperate to break the competition's stranglehold on prime time.

While Rozelle may have conceived of the show and sold it to ABC, Roone Arledge, then president of ABC Sports, knew how to execute it. ABC couldn't just do Sunday afternoon football on Monday night. To do that would be tantamount to proving CBS and NBC right. The show would never find a prime time audience and quickly disappear from the schedule. If ABC's show was to be successful, it would have to stress entertainment over athletics[29] and turn boring, grind-it-out football into a weekly prime time party.

Arledge's concept for the series started in the broadcast booth. He felt he could combine the best elements of sports and entertainment by forming a team that could emulate Rowan & Martin for laughs, Huntley and Brinkley for incisive reporting, and Lucy and Ricky for ridiculous behavior.[30] Thus, Arledge paired Keith Jackson, one of the best play-by-play men in the business, with two very different personalities. One was the urbane, hard-driving editorial voice of sportscaster Howard Cosell. The other, a fun-loving Texan and the former quarterback of the Dallas Cowboys, Don Meredith. Together on Monday night, the two often created *buzz* that carried over to the office water cooler on Tuesday morning. Cosell brought a dynamic personality laced with a journalistic flair and wasn't afraid to take on subjects or offend people—even those around him in the booth. Meredith, on the other hand, knew how to get under Cosell's collar, while at the same time appealing to the average fan. The two played off each other—Cosell in his urbane way and Meredith in his laid back, cornpone way.

In addition to the three-man broadcast booth, ABC outdid its Sunday competitors from a technical standpoint as well. Whereas most Sunday games in the '70's employed four or five cameras, ABC used nine, including sideline cameras and two hand-helds.[31] Yet despite all the innovation and theatrics, early reviews predicted no more than a 24% share of the Monday night prime time audience. They were wrong. *Monday Night Football* garnered a 31% share of the Monday night audience—and this kind of rating in only its first season.[32] That success would continue over the course of the forty-two seasons (and counting), helping establish a phenomenon on Monday nights in the fall of every year. Movie attendance dropped. Bowling leagues shifted their contests to Tuesday nights. Yet still, Roone Arledge was looking to improve the show. Arledge thought he needed one more big name to push the series from good to sensational and supplanted Keith Jackson with Frank Gifford, a former running back with the New York Giants. Gifford had no problem letting Cosell and Meredith become the stars of the show—not when the show's ratings were on the rise.

Monday Night Football first aired on ABC on September 21, 1970, with a game between the New York Jets and the Cleveland Browns. Advertisers were charged $65,000 per minute by ABC during the clash,

29 Stay Tuned, p 145
30 Stay Tuned, p 145
31 Stay Tuned, p 146
32 Stay Tuned, p 147

a cost that proved to be a bargain when the contest found to have collected 35 million viewers, 20% of whom were women. The Browns defeated the Jets, 31–21 in a game that featured a 94-yard kickoff return and an interception of a Joe Namath pass late in the fourth quarter that was returned for the game-clinching touchdown.[33]

Monday Night Football Premieres. Jets QB Joe Willie Namath tosses fourth-quarter interception to Cleveland linebacker Billy Andrews who returned it 25 yards for a touchdown. September 21, 1970

Monday Night Football not only changed the face of prime time television, but also America's Monday night habits. Restaurants and sports bars drew big crowds by hosting Monday Night Football parties. Booing the television screen at the bar every time Howard Cosell's face appeared on it became a popular contest. America either loved Cosell or loved to see him shut down. Cosell's presence initially caused the Ford Motor Company, the show's main sponsor, to ask for his removal. ABC refused and Ford had a change of heart once the show's high ratings were made public. Cosell left the show in 1983 and Meredith, a year later with no appreciable loss of audience. Over the years, star players like Fred Williamson, Alex Karas, Fran Tarkington, O.J. Simpson, Joe Namath, Dan Dierdorf, and Boomer Esiason have helped host the show, as did comedian Dennis Miller. Al Michaels took over for Frank Gifford in 1986 and directed the show's play-by-play announcing for the next twenty years, most of it alongside Hall of Fame football coach, John Madden.[34]

Whatever their attitude about Howard Cosell in the 1970's, viewers tuned in to ABC on Monday nights in huge numbers and not all of them were watching from home. It wasn't unusual for politicians, musicians, and even movie stars to drop by the broadcast booth at the game and chat it up with Cosell, Meredith, and Gifford. Richard Nixon and Ronald Reagan both dropped by to signal their approval. Same, too, with John Lennon and John Wayne. Everyone wanted to be a part of ABC's weekly "party." Rival networks, which had once laughed at the idea of prime time football, now scampered to find effective counterprogramming.[35]

By bringing sports to Monday's prime time lineup, Arledge created a hit show for ABC's schedule for the next thirty years. Considering that the difference between the network who wins the weekly rating "sweeps" and the one who ends up in third place (...or worse) can hinge on a single day, Arledge's gamble played a large part in ABC's rise from obscurity to become the number-one TV network in America. In

33 Namath: A Biography, p 346

34 Stay Tuned, p 147

35 Stay Tuned, p 147

Monday Night Football, Arledge had created a three-hour, top-ten hit show—that is to say an entire night of prime time programming for half of every year through the rest of the 20th century.

No small wonder that Arledge's success at ABC Sports led to his promotion, in 1977, to head their news division at the same time as well. There, he oversaw the development of *20/20* and *Nightline*—two other hugely profitable franchises that finally helped bring ABC up to par with its older rivals. A 1994 article in *Sports Illustrated* ranked the most influential figures in the history of modern sports. In that ranking, they rated Roone Arledge third, behind only Michael Jordan and Muhammad Ali. A 1990 *Life* magazine article on the 100 most influential Americans of the twentieth century also included Roone Arledge in their rarefied air.[36]

Sex in the Age of Tennis

It was billed as the "Battles of the Sexes," and the match was played as much for gender bragging rights as it was for a paycheck. The female gender could not have been better served. The Wimbledon Champion Billie Jean King was, in 1973, a major force in the women's professional sports empowerment movement, and at 29 years of age, she was in her athletic prime as well.[37] Bobby Riggs, her opponent, had likewise won at Wimbledon's Center Court—in 1939, five years before King was born. Seeing that he was as good a hustler as he was a tennis player (Bobby Riggs rose in 1939 to be the number-one player in the world), Riggs was reputed to have played the male chauvinist card, coming out of retirement in 1973, in order to drum up income for himself while championing the sport he loved. Riggs challenged a number of the world's greatest female tennis players to a match, claiming that the female game was inferior to the men's game and that no female player in the world could beat Riggs, even at the age of 55. The first match he corralled was on Mother's Day 1973, with Margaret Court, the Woman's Number One tennis player in the world. Although 25 years older than Court at the time of the match, Riggs was in excellent shape and dispatched her in straight sets.

The press dubbed it the "Mother's Day Massacre."[38] Knowing how firmly committed King was to the women's sports movement, Riggs used the newspaper headline defaming Court to goad outspoken Woman's Liberationist Billie Jean King into a second payday.

ABC won the bidding war to air the event, reportedly paying $750,000 to show the man-versus-woman *singles* match globally to 36 countries. The event was staged at the Houston Astrodome in front of 30,000 fans while 50 million more watched the prime time event on television.[39] The boisterous fans

---

36 Life Magazine—"Life Lists 20th Century's Most Influential Americans" September 1, 1990

37 Stay Tuned, p 152

38 Stay Tuned, p 153

39 Stay Tuned, p 154

in attendance cheered on both players in a circus-like atmosphere resembling that of a heavyweight championship fight. While King demolished Riggs in straight sets, the $200,000 (1.1M USD 2012) that King won was nothing compared to the pride women around the country felt about themselves and about their gender. As a true sporting event, the "Battle of the Sexes" was essentially meaningless. Yet, it did prove how huge and untapped the world of women's tennis truly was and the potential it had to drive prime time ratings.

Round Ball Goes Prime Time

King and Riggs were not the only prime time "event" to use the Houston Astrodome. The University of Houston Cougars played basketball there from time to time as well. On the evening of January 20, 1968, the hometown Cougars were hosts to the undefeated and number-one ranked team in the nation, the UCLA Bruins. From 1964 through 1975, the UCLA Bruins were the dominant NCAA men's basketball program, winning NCAA Division I Basketball Championships in 1964, 1965, and 1967—and then, for good measure, seven more titles in the next eight years. UCLA was the gold standard and as formidable an opponent as you could ask for—and so that's what Houston did. They called the Bruins and asked for the game.

The Houston Cougars were looking to prove their worth as an elite basketball program and couldn't have picked a better game to do it. The Bruins arrived in Houston with a 47-game, two-and-a-half-season winning streak intact and the number-one ranking in college basketball. The Cougars were #2 in the polls and also undefeated—their last loss coming in the previous year's NCAA Basketball Tournament at the hands of none other than UCLA. The Saturday night game was televised nationally via a syndication package through the TVS Television Network, with Dick Enberg announcing. TVS owner Eddie Einhorn paid $27,000 (178,000 USD 2012) for the broadcast rights on TVS and signed up 120 stations, many of which would preempt regularly scheduled prime time network programming to air the game.[40]

Up to that point, only NCAA post-season games had been broadcast nationally, so there was much skepticism regarding whether or not anyone other than the 52,693 fans who had filled the Astrodome would watch it. An oversimplification, perhaps, but with Einhorn having just under half of the affiliate strength of each of the other three broadcast networks, audience numbers were a concern, though they needn't have been. The Saturday night broadcast drew a healthy prime time television audience and the numbers continued to grow throughout the game. The "Game of the Century" lived up to its billing and in the process established college basketball as a viable national television product.

---

40 *Houston Chronicle*—"It's been 20 years since...The Game of the Century" January 20, 1988

As it came to pass, the Houston Cougars pulled off the upset, 71–69, ending the UCLA Bruins' 47-game winning streak. Aside from the seesaw battle and tight score, the game also disproved the myth that a national audience would never watch a regular season college basketball game on prime time television. A year later, NBC became the first major network to broadcast the 1969 NCAA Championship Basketball Game, at a cost of more than $500,000 (3.2M USD 2012). In 2008, the NCAA deal with CBS to televise the *entire* NCAA Basketball Tournament was worth $545 million.[41]

This was what the NBA was looking for in the late 1970's—a TV "hit" like the one college basketball received from the UCLA–Houston game in 1968. Professional basketball had witnessed a lull in popularity that had lasted ten years—since the Lakers–Celtics rivalries of the 1960's. Sports audiences in the '70's shied away from the NBA players and the drug scandals that seemed to follow them. Some speculated at the time that white audiences were turned off by black dominance of the NBA—a league accentuated by the Afro hairstyles of the 1970's.[42]

And then came a storyline right out of a holiday movie—the hit the NBA had been praying for. Earvin "Magic" Johnson and Larry Bird had followed each other from the 1979 NCAA Championship Basketball Game into the pros. Their final college game had set an NCAA TV ratings record and they took those ratings with them into the NBA. Not only were Bird and Johnson the two best players in the league, each played on one of the two most storied franchises in basketball history—franchises that had a heated rivalry if not an outright hatred for the other. If that weren't enough, there was the rivalry between the east and west coasts and between two different styles of basketball that each of those coasts represented: The flash and dazzle of Magic Johnson and the "Showtime" Lakers vs. the blue collar, in-your-face style of basketball common to the Boston Celtics.

Magic Johnson and Larry Bird—one black, one white—turned out to be the perfect casting for a long-time, riveting rivalry. It's no coincidence that the league's TV ratings soared during this time. Bird was a twelve-time NBA All-Star and was named the league's Most Valuable Player (MVP) three times. He played his entire professional career for Boston, winning three NBA Championships. Johnson was selected first overall in the 1979 NBA draft by the Lakers, playing his entire career in L.A. He won a championship and an NBA Finals MVP Award in his rookie season, and then won four more championships with the Lakers during the 1980's. Larry Bird was all business on the court—and for Bird and the Celtics, business was good. Magic Johnson, by contrast, always looked like a wide-eyed kid who'd just found a puppy under the family Christmas tree … a moment before he scored his nightly triple-double (double-digit points/rebounds/assists) on the opposing team. Then, in 1991, after taking a routine physical just before the start of the 1991–'92 NBA season, Johnson learned he'd tested positive for HIV/AIDS. At a press conference held on November 7, 1991, Magic Johnson made a public announcement that he was retiring from

41 *San Antonio Express-News*—"College Basketball: UH & UCLA, under the big top" January 19, 2008

42 From Set Shot to Slam Dunk, p 203

NBA basketball.[43] Nine months later, Larry Bird did the same—but not before he and Magic took home gold medals from the '92 Barcelona Olympics, as a part of America's coveted "Dream Team."

As the 1990's progressed, the hold that Bird and Johnson had on an audience was yet another symbiotic affair. The two handed the ball off to Michael Jordan who in turn passed it to Shaquille O'Neal and then Kobe Bryant and now, it seems, LeBron James. Through it all, the NBA has never looked back and never has it looked more financially solvent. In 1970, the networks paid the NBA $2M for the rights to broadcast a year's worth of games. By 1985, just six years into the Bird–Johnson era, the networks paid $45M to the league—almost 20 times the revenue it generated prior to Magic Johnson and Larry Bird's arrival. By 2002, league revenues from television had grown another 1000%, thanks in part to Michael Jordan ... and a six-year network television package worth $4.5B.[44]

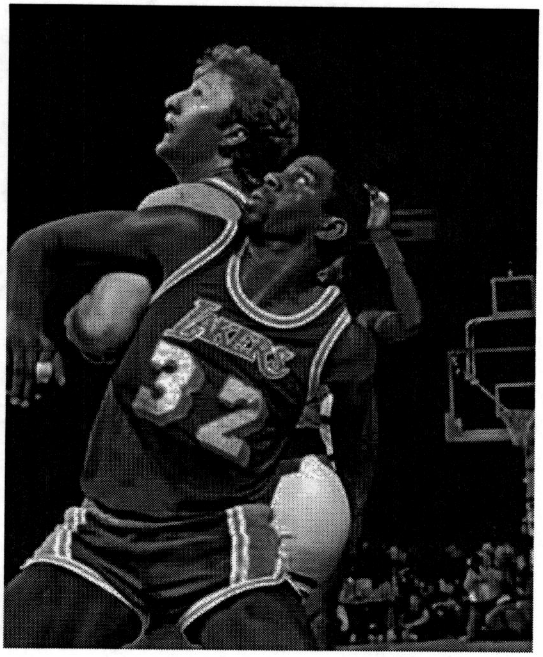

Earvin "Magic" Johnson of the Lakers and Boston's Larry Bird would win eight NBA championships between them and move professional basketball forward into prime time television

By the turn of the twenty-first century, sports and television had melded into one of the most profitable mergers in the annals of business. Why these contests of skill on the court have become so popular with television viewers is up for debate. One line of reasoning says that while viewers still identify with their team and the players on it, most arenas are located in urban areas, miles from the fans they purport to serve. Another explains that sporting events offer real TV heroes and villains to root for, as opposed to the fictional characters portrayed in prime time dramas and comedies. Still others say it's a matter of fans living out a secret desire vicariously through "trained professionals" who are more likely to succeed.

A fourth reason, however, seems the easiest to understand. Simply put, televised sports do what all good prime time programming does—create tension while providing surprise. The New York Mets stealing a World Series victory from the Boston Red Sox in game six of the 1986 matchup, with two out in the tenth-inning and the Mets two runs down comes to mind. Or how about Red Sox catcher Carlton Fisk's dramatic tenth-inning home run in the '75 World Series; or Tiger Woods setting the tournament record at Augusta National, while winning the '97 Masters Golf Tournament on a course he would not have been

---

43 *ESPN*—"Magic Johnson announces he's HIV-positive" November 7, 1991

44 Museum of Broadcast Communications website—"Sports & Television"

allowed to join six years before? Then, too, there's that game in one's lifetime that provided a miracle finish: Doug Flutie's "Hail Mary" pass in the Orange Bowl in '84; Kirk Gibson's walk-off home-run as a Dodger in game one of the '88 World Series; or the 1980 hockey game in Lake Placid, New York, that not only produced a gold medal for Team USA, but also helped change the course of world history at the same time.

Discussion Questions

A. Embryonic Journey

- Describe the symbiotic relationship of early television and the sporting events it aired.

B. Prime Time Symbiosis

- In 1968, "The Heidi Game" discussed in this chapter not only scared off NBC from any weekly football televising but also brought home what attitude about American football that was capitalized on by ABC?

C. Roone

- Who does Roone refer to?
- Name at least three of the producing innovations that helped create the successful ABC "*Wide World of Sports*" in 1961.

D. Olympic Gold

- How did televising the Olympics, and, in particular, the 1972 Munich Games, turn a global sporting event into riveting newsworthy entertainment?

E. Monday Night Football

- Trace the background and rise of ABC's *Monday Night Football* and discuss how this programming changed the face of Monday night viewing.

F. Sex in the Age of Tennis

- What was the true relevance of the well promoted "Battle of the Sexes" tennis match in 1973?

G. Round Ball Goes Prime Time

- What sports highlights that have been caught on camera have remained classics for sports fans?

- Can you imagine the world of television without sports programming? Support your opinion.

CHAPTER THIRTEEN

A Second Golden Age

1980–1990

Prime Time Miracle

It was more than a hockey game. It was us against them—freedom vs. tyranny—and no one in the world gave America a chance of coming out on top. As athletes from around the world gathered in Lake Placid, New York, for the 1980 Winter Olympics, discontented Americans were mired in a winter of their own.[1] The U.S. Embassy in Iran had been overrun by Iranian students three months earlier and 52 Americans were taken hostage. If that weren't insult enough, the Red Army had spoken. The Soviets had invaded Afghanistan the previous December, thumbed their nose at the United Nations' sanctions, and dared America to stop them. American President Jimmy Carter had vowed to retaliate, but when he did, it was to boycott the Summer Olympics that year in Moscow. The pros and cons of the boycott were tossed about the halls of Congress. Some worried that the action could be perceived by the world as a symbolic gesture rather than a strategic act. Most, however, backed the President's action because

1 HBO Sports—"Do You Believe in Miracles?"

of its dramatic visibility to the citizens of the Soviet Union, regardless of whether or not it provoked the desired action on the part of the Red Army.[2]

Truthfully, it might have been an all-time low point for U.S. self-esteem and it shouldn't have been. The very word "America" had, for decades, conjured up images of a cherished land filled with miracles, where anything was possible. The hostage crisis in Iran, however, had trumped that illusion and sapped the nation's morale in the process; and now there were the Soviets to deal with as well. The world was at a crossroads that could have well led the planet's two super-powers into World War III. Thus, as the U.S. hockey team squared off against the Soviet Union on February 22, 1980, in their semi-final medal-round match, the icy battle gave lasting meaning to the term "cold war."[3]

President Jimmy Carter delivers "Crisis of Confidence" speech. June 15, 1979

So extraordinary was the confluence of events that February that it would be hard to imagine it ever happening again. As the decade turned, so had our luck and luster as a nation. Our international cachet had plummeted. No one paid attention to what Americans said anymore. A dark cloud seemed to hover over the country. It began with the shootings at Kent State by National Guard troops in May of 1970 and continued on through America's 1975 defeat in Vietnam. There was the Watergate Scandal and the Three Mile Island disaster involving a nuclear power plant meltdown. Long lines at the gas pump were commonplace as were exorbitant interest rates at the bank. And at the end of the decade, it was a lasting image seen mostly through the grey-black smoke of a burning flag that resonated with Americans and left us feeling helpless. Fifty-two blindfolded American hostages stuck in Iran for 444 days and all of it pointing to just how powerless America had become. U.S. President Jimmy Carter, himself, was seen as an expression of America's self-doubt and lack of self-confidence. This expression was galvanized in 1979, when America's embattled leader told the nation it was in "a crisis of confidence" that threatened its national spirit.

At the end of the 1970's, American amateur ice hockey was suffering from the same malaise as the nation itself. In the 20 years since winning the 1960 Olympic Gold Medal in Rome, American teams had become increasingly unable to compete with the Europeans—especially the Soviet Union, whose players were amateurs in name only. At the time, America's Olympians were *always* amateurs—college kids or recent graduates who, while they still played the game, were not anywhere near the level of the Soviets. There

2 Bilderberg Meeting Report 1980 (text)—"Relations Among the Allies: Communication, Understanding, Leadership April 18–20, 1980

3 HBO Sports—"Do You Believe in Miracles?"

was really no way for the U.S. hockey team to be competitive, so the feeling going into 1980 was "Let's not get embarrassed." That was the goal—to avoid humiliation.

In July of 1979, the best amateur players in the country were invited to Colorado Springs to try out for the 1980 Olympic team. In the course of ten days, all competed in a pressure-packed round robin under the watchful eye of Olympic hockey coach Herb Brooks, the best and most successful college hockey coach in the country. An iconoclast, Brooks not only had his own way of thinking, but he also had a history with the Olympic team. Brooks was the last player to be cut from the 1960 USA Gold Medal team, one day before the Games in Rome began. The event left Brooks with a bit of unfinished business to attend to and he promised to shake American hockey out of its slumber.

First, he had to trim the roster from 80 to 26—not that any of that mattered to the Russians, who neither feared nor respected the U.S. team. These American kids were, after all, merely inexperienced amateurs up against the older, stronger Soviet professionals—a hockey machine that had recently routed the NHL All-Stars 6–0 to win the Challenge Cup.[4] The U.S. team had a formidable "challenge," themselves, and that task was made more difficult by an embarrassing exhibition loss to the Soviets ten days prior to the start of the 1980 Winter Games. On February 9, 1980, at Madison Square Garden in New York, the Soviet national hockey team served notice on Team USA, crushing the U.S. 10–3 before a deflated American crowd. In an ironic twist, Soviet hockey coach Viktor Tikhonov later said that their one-sided victory led his team to underestimate the Americans and ultimately *help* Team USA draft a surprise ending to their Olympic matchup with the Russians in the medal round.[5]

The Americans weren't supposed to make that round; the Soviet Union was. In Olympic group play, however, the Americans surprised many, including the Swedes, who were favored to win their game. Team USA earned a dramatic 2–2 draw with Sweden by scoring with 27 seconds left in the game. Following the tie with Sweden came the 7–3 victory over the Czechs, who had been a favorite for the silver medal. The U.S. team ran off three more wins, beating Norway, Romania, and West Germany to advance to the medal round along with Sweden. In the other group, the Soviets stormed through their opposition, undefeated.

The day before the U.S. v Soviet match, columnist Dave Anderson wrote in the *New York Times*: "Unless the ice melts, or unless the United States team or another team performs a miracle of biblical proportions as did the American squad in 1960, the Russians are expected to easily win the Olympic gold medal for the sixth time in the last seven tournaments." The game was aired live in Canada, but not in the United States. After the Soviets declined a request from ABC to move the game from 5 pm to 8 pm for U.S. television (this would have meant a 4 am start in Moscow for Soviet viewers), ABC decided to broadcast the late-afternoon game on tape-delay during prime time that evening.[6]

---

4 HBO Sports—"Do You Believe in Miracles?"

5 The Boys of Winter, pp 46–48

6 The Boys of Winter, p 45

As they had done in several previous games, the U.S. team fell behind early, but in the waning seconds of the first period, American Mark Johnson sliced between the two defenders, found the loose puck, and scored with one second left in the period. The second period saw the Russians play like the Soviet team of old and pull ahead by the end of the period, 3–2.

What happened next, however, really has no words to describe it save one: "miracle." With the score tied midway through the third period, Mike Eruzione, the American captain, was left undefended as he received a pass from teammate Mark Pavelich and fired a slap shot past the Soviets' reserve goalie who had been screened by a fellow player. The goal gave Team USA a 4–3 lead, its first of the game and one they hung onto for the final ten minutes of the contest. When the horn sounded and the Americans had won the game, 8,500 delirious fans rose from their seats as one. As announcer Al Michaels said, looking back, "That's when sound became feeling."[7]

Fans often forget that the U.S. had to beat Finland in the final game to win the gold medal—and they did, 4–2, coming from behind with three unanswered goals in the final period. When the dust cleared, the Soviets had left New York with a black eye. Late in July, they suffered another when 65 nations failed to attend the Moscow Olympics, protesting the Red Army's unprovoked invasion into Afghanistan.

Celebrating the "Miracle on Ice" after defeating Finland.

While there was no way to have predicted the rapid fall of the Soviet Union, their first misstep into Afghanistan cost them dearly. The Soviet Union had entered the 1980's as one of the world's two super powers and departed the decade as a 70-year-old footnote to history. Gone was their political mantle, their economic system, and the communist way of life. With that loss, so went the Soviet Empire's global identity, then their satellite nations, and ultimately the Berlin Wall. The Afghan War was as unpopular in Russia as the Vietnam War was in America and lasted nearly as long. Fifteen thousand Soviets were killed and another 400,000 incapacitated by battle wounds, disease, or serious illness sustained during their ten-year conflict.[8]

The tragic waste of lives during those ten years wasn't all the Soviets lost. They lost the future. As the 1980's unfolded, America oversaw development of the microchip technology and the birth of the home computer, but in Russia that was not the case. By 1989, the Soviet technology running Mother Russia was estimated to be eight generations behind that of the Unites States. Drained of their political cachet

7 HBO Sports—"Do You Believe in Miracles?"

8 Détente and Confrontation, pp 1017–1018

and mired in a recession stemming from the country's declining oil production, the Soviet Union that the world had known for much of the 20th century was nearing an end.

While many factors played into the demise of the Soviet Union, that first crack in its proverbial armor happened on an ice rink nestled in the Adirondack Mountains in February, 1980. David slew Goliath. Twenty American kids had done the impossible and in doing so became the vehicle for making people excited again about waving the American flag. It was, as announcer Al Michaels called it, a miracle.[9] Embassy press attaché Barry Rosen, one of the 52 American hostages released from fourteen months of Iranian captivity the same day Ronald Reagan took office (January 20, 1981), put it best. "Captivity shows you the depravity of human beings," Rosen said, after viewing the hockey game. "The hockey game showed you the apogee of human achievement."[10]

Reaganomics

The "miracle" at Lake Placid had inspired the nation. Waking up from a decade of dashed expectations, rampant inflation, gas shortages, the hostage crisis, presidential scandals, and a 700% increase in drug use from the 1960's, Americans began embracing the "Happy Face" '80's and elected a movie star to the White House to lead the country. The coronation of Ronald Reagan couldn't have worked out better if it had been scripted, and with the hostages returning from Iranian captivity just minutes following Reagan's inauguration, many felt it had been. Simultaneously covering both events, TV cameras wove together two stories that had nothing to do with the other and created a persona for Ronald Reagan that would fuel two administrations. It was a new age. Politics and television were officially dating.

By the late 1970's, the magazine *Advertising Age* noted that television had already revolutionized politics, turning political slogans into national sales pitches. When candidates for political office went out to speak before crowds, it was often to obtain 30-second commercial spots, all bought on the same basis as ads used to sell tires, vinyl records or fast food. By 1980, American television was already incorporating something into its programming that TV audiences would come to see as the norm—national elections run as merchandising ploys. Fundraising costs had become such a central concern for candidates that many politicians simply turned to television in the hope of getting the biggest bang for their buck.

Emerging as the centerpiece in this union of television and politics, Ronald Reagan appeared to have everything working for him. He had been a radio sportscaster in Des Moines, Iowa, early in his career, and from there went on to become a leading man in Hollywood. Considered to be a liberal at the time, Reagan was voted President of the Screen Actors Guild. Yet, as Reagan transitioned from movies to

9 HBO Sports—"Do You Believe in Miracles?"

10 HBO Sports—"Do You Believe in Miracles?"

Democrat *Ronald Reagan, host of* The G.E. Theater *on the set of his show, circa the 1950's*

television, he became the series host for the *General Electric Theater*, and quickly made friends with the show's more conservative sponsors.

Soon enough, Reagan began to actually represent G.E. on lobbying matters in Washington, enunciating views on various corporate concerns. Government interference in business and the loss of economic freedoms became favorite discussions leading to political maxims that would one day propel him into the White House. That day turned out to be one in January, 1981—the same day 52 American hostages returned home from Iran.[11]

Television saw it all, as President Reagan knew it would, and his presidency seemed to symbolize the dominant role of TV in American life. Ironically, even as Reagan was a big fan of the medium, he was not a fan of the FCC who monitored it. Of special significance to the Reagan Administration was the persistent theme of *deregulation*. Among the agencies to be reduced in power and budget, and thereby limited in what Reagan thought to be potentially destructive interference on commerce, was the Federal Communications Commission—watchdog regulator of the airwaves since the Federal Communications Act of 1934. In fairness to Reagan, he had correctly deduced that the FCC had given the three broadcast networks "favored nation" status for almost half a century and thought that every network should have a shot at the brass ring.

Republican *Ronald Reagan, America's 40th president, being congratulated by outgoing president Jimmy Carter on Inauguration Day*

The three broadcast networks were concerned and rightfully so. Cable players were entering the television mix with a host of new technologies and all of it was threatening to undermine television's status quo. If deregulation and market forces were really to be left to fate, as Reagan hoped, the cable upstarts could do just that—change the business forever. Economic blessings enjoyed by only three television networks for the last 50 years were now to be split by hundreds. Clearly, it was a new ballgame. The coming of cable television was at hand—the very same hand that operated the remote control in living rooms across America.

11 *Tube of Plenty*, pp 483–484

En route to the arrival of cable programming, television in the early 1980's reflected the growing economic prosperity in America. Gas prices were dropping; interest rates, too. We'd given the Soviets a black eye at Lake Placid that sent them reeling from a misstep from which they never recovered. More importantly, we'd gotten our hostages back from Iran alive. The United States was regaining its global prestige while the Soviets were losing theirs, and Americans celebrated by buying everything in sight.

This conspicuous consumption became an offshoot of an economic philosophy known as *Reaganomics*—a kind of "trickle down" economics that became popular during the Reagan Era of the 1980's. Reagan's economic views were a loose amalgam of fiscal libertarianism, supply-side economics, and tax theory propounded by economist William Laffer. Laffer considered the conventional prescription of stimulating the economy by increasing government spending to be potentially wasteful. Instead, he thought taxes should be cut and incentives created to encourage savings and investment.[12] To this view Reagan added an addendum to Laffer's theory stating that economic growth resulting from such a tax policy would generate new revenues. Thus, it was theorized, with fewer taxes levied on the job creators, companies would have more money to create more jobs. Theoretically, those jobs would translate into more discretionary income, which in turn would lead to more spending. More spending pointed to a stronger bottom line for the corporate job creator and lower unemployment.

Yet, while unemployment under Reagan's leadership did drop significantly, 40% of the new jobs created revolved around low-wage, low-skill service jobs with no perks or benefits. This was in sharp contrast to the 1960's. From 1963 to 1973, 40% of all new jobs in the United States were high paying and came with benefits, while only 20% were at the bottom of the scale. From 1979 to 1985, however, the reverse was true as low-paying jobs accounted for 40% of the job growth, with high-paying jobs constituting only 10% of those available.[13] In short, the 1970's economy was restructuring itself. High-wage, high-skill manufacturing jobs were disappearing. The auto industry alone lost 250,000 jobs between 1979 and 1982.[14] Yet, despite the economic inequality between the rich and the poor, 38% of the country was still considered affluent. Society called them Yuppies—*young urban professionals*—and with 30 years of earning potential still ahead of them, television advertisers fought tooth and nail to reach this new demographic.

Who Shot J.R.?

Prime time soap operas proliferated much of the decade, tossing big production dollars, opulent wardrobes, and outlandish characters at audiences that loved what they saw. Dormant since the 1960's, the genre roared back to life like an oil gusher with ratings-winner *Dallas* in 1978. The series' was among the

12 Encyclopedia.com—"Reaganomics"

13 Encyclopedia.com—"Reaganomics"

14 Encyclopedia.com—"Reaganomics"

most popular shows of the 1980's, and its weekly displays of extravagance fit the mood of the yuppie-driven decade. *Dallas* was panned as being predictable with characters that seemed more like caricatures than real people—and *Dallas* reveled in that fact. The show, after all, was a nighttime soap opera, and part of a melodramatic genre that hadn't been seen in prime time since the cancellation of *Peyton Place* a decade earlier.[15] The series told the story of a Texas oil family, and starred Larry Hagman as J.R. Ewing, the ruthless, womanizing head of the Ewing family business. The cast included him and his wife Sue Ellen (played by Linda Gray); his parents, Jock (played by Jim Davis) and Ellie (by Barbara Bel Geddes); his younger brother Bobby (played by Patrick Duffy); and Bobby's wife Pamela (portrayed perfectly by Victoria Principal). All lived on the ranch where they schemed week to week to battle enemies and out-fox rival oil families.

By the end of the second season, *Dallas* had settled into its Friday night time slot and the Nielsen (A.C. Nielsen Company) Top 10, drawing 30 to 40 million devoted viewers every week.[16] As a result of the show's popularity, CBS asked the producers for two additional episodes, which presented a small problem. With the series for *that* season already in the can, the producers had no idea what to do with the extra two hours they'd been given. According to legend, the creative team had one good idea the entire week. They'd shoot J.R. and figure out "who done it" over the summer.[17]

The question "Who shot J.R.?" was debated by fans through the summer and fall of 1980, causing an international buzz. With this season-ending cliffhanger, *Dallas* had finally given prime time a memory. "Until that show," says Dr. Robert Thompson, a professor and founding director of the Center for the Study of Popular Television at Syracuse University, "TV was still operating under the assumption that every episode needed to collectively erase the memory of what every character was previously doing and start fresh again."[18] In short, *Dallas* turned serialization into big business. Networks came to understand that viewers could remember things that happened seven days before and appreciated a continuing storyline.[19] With an estimated global audience of 350 million viewers in 57 countries,[20] *Dallas* was on everyone's mind. The mania in England and France was even greater than it was in America. *Time* and *People* magazines ran cover stories. Odds-makers created betting lines for the characters, as to who might have pulled the trigger. If that weren't enough, suspense heightened further, following an actors' strike delaying the start of the fall television season by two months.

The two-hour episode aired Friday, November 21, 1980. Around the country, restaurants, theaters, and other public places sat near-empty as over 80 million Americans turned in to get the answer. As most every baby boomer will remember, J.R. was shot by Kristin, his vengeful, scheming sister-in-law, with

15 Stay Tuned, p 34
16 Stay Tuned, p 35
17 Stay Tuned, p 36
18 Hollywood Reporter—"TV Milestones" 2004 September, p 60
19 Hollywood Reporter—"TV Milestones" 2004 September, p 60
20 Stay Tuned, p 34

whom he'd had an affair. At the time of its showing, the episode was the highest-rated single episode in TV history, topped only by the CBS series finale of *M*A*S*H* two years later.

Dallas was an innovative and influential program that spawned the hit spin-off *Knots Landing* and a host of soapy imitators like *Falcon Crest, Melrose Place, and Beverly Hills, 90210.* And of course there was ABC's *Dynasty*, a contender to the Ewings and clearly the only soap competition *Dallas* ever faced. *Dynasty* was the series where big oil met big hair and fostered one of the greatest female rivalries on television, pitting faithful TV wife Linda Evans against the back-biting she-devil Joan Collins. The trades branded the series "trash with flash"[21] and in 1985, *Dynasty* used both to out-Nielsen the mighty Ewings for first place in the TV ratings war.

But the opulence didn't end with soaps. Hip dramas like *Miami Vice, Remington Steele*, even *The A-Team* used the era's prosperity to their advantage, creating a kind of cultural phenomenon. While the super hip and cool ... *Vice* and ... *Steele* defined '80's male fashion, the overheated *A-Team* turned macho theatrics into prime-time fun, making a superstar out of Mr. T and his nine gold chains—conspicuous consumption at its very best.[22]

Yet, Mr. T and the *A-Team* aside, *Remington Steele* was about more than conspicuous consumption. The series was birthmother to a new TV genre for NBC—the *dramedy*. Pierce Brosnan starred with Stephanie Zimbalist in a television version of a throw-back to the *Thin Man* feature series of the 1940's. Hip detectives embroiled in edgy drama laced with sexy sarcasm, witty banter, and romantic farce that translated into a gaggle of like-minded shows over the next eight years—*Mickey Spillane's Mike Hammer, Scarecrow & Mrs. King, Crazy Like a Fox*, and *Moonlighting* among them.

Moonlighting starred Cybill Shepherd as Maddie Hayes, a former high-end fashion model who discovered that her business manager had embezzled most of her earnings, and Bruce Willis as David Addison, a brash young private detective.[23] Addison ran the Blue Moon Detective Agency; one of the few holdings left from Maddie's lost funds, and used his charm to talk Maddie into keeping her interest in the agency while coming on board to work alongside him. One must remember with *Moonlighting* that Bruce Willis was hardly a household name at the time—it was Cybill Shepherd, the real-life 1970's model-turned-movie star, whom viewers initially tuned in to see.

---

21 *Fifty Years of Television*, p 145

22 Brought To You In Living Color, p 158

23 *New York Times*—"The Madcap Behind 'Moonlighting'" March 30, 1986

Hill Street Station

In 1978, a desperate NBC lured Fred Silverman away from number-one ABC to help turn their fortunes around like he had the others. NBC had suffered serious defections of several longtime affiliates in markets like Atlanta, Baltimore, Baton Rouge, Charlotte, Indianapolis, Jacksonville, Minneapolis-St. Paul, and San Diego, to name a few. Most were wooed away by ABC, the number-one network during the late 1970's and early 1980's. Had the decade ended for the NBC the way it had begun, however, this defection might not have occurred. After all, the 1970's had started strong for NBC, thanks to hits like *Adam-12*, *Laugh-In*, and *The Dean Martin Show*—but these series did not last. Even with new shows like *Police Woman*, *Quincy, M.E.*, *Sanford and Son*, *Chico and the Man*, and *The Rockford Files*, the network was faltering badly.

In 1974, under new president Herb Schlosser, NBC tried to go after younger viewers with a series of costly movies, miniseries, and specials that not only failed to attract the desirable 18–34 demographic, but alienated older viewers as well.[24] It should be noted that the 18–34 demographic was to the 1970's what the 18–49 demographic is today. That demographic has always been important because of its sheer numbers derived from the baby boom that occurred between 1946 and 1964. In 1974, baby boomers were just reaching their 30th birthday, bringing dominance to the 18–34 demographic. As that population aged, the window on disposable income grew, leaving 21st-century advertisers fighting to reach viewers inside the coveted 18–49 demographic window.

When Schlosser's first season tanked and no series NBC introduced in the fall of 1975 was renewed, the call to Silverman was made. The acquisition of Fred Silverman took a couple of years, but his 1978 hiring was seen as a coup by the brass at NBC. Silverman's three-year tenure at that network, however, proved to be a difficult period marked by few successes. With the notable exceptions of *Diff'rent Strokes*, *Real People*, *The Facts of Life*, and the mini-series *Shogun*, Silverman couldn't buy a hit.[25] Failures accumulated rapidly under his watch—*Hello, Larry* and *Supertrain* among them. In a tortured stroke of irony, many of NBC's shows created by Silverman were beaten regularly in the ratings by shows he himself had green-lighted at both CBS and ABC while running those networks. Worse yet, when U.S. President Jimmy Carter pulled the American team out of the 1980 Summer Olympics in Moscow, NBC was forced to cancel 150 hours of coverage at a cost to the network of $87M, putting the network's future in serious jeopardy. NBC had been counting on $170M in advertising revenues to not only pay for the Olympics but for the 1975–76 fall season as well.[26]

Despite these failures, there were high points in Silverman's tenure at NBC, including the series commitments for *Cheers* and *St. Elsewhere* and the launching of the critically acclaimed television series *Hill Street Blues* in 1981. For better or worse, every cop show since *Dragnet* had played off the typical conventions

24 *Time Magazine*—"Struggling to Leave the Cellar" May 14, 1979

25 *Time Magazine*—"Struggling to Leave the Cellar" May 14, 1979

26 *Time Magazine*—"NBC's Retreat from Moscow" May 19, 1980

of the genre first established by Jack Webb's memorable character, Joe Friday. Cops were good, honest, hard-working guys who had no life apart from the precinct. And then came *Hill Street Blues*. During its six-season run from 1981 to 1987, the show garnered 26 Emmy Awards and 96 nominations, making it the most-honored drama series of its generation.

The genesis of the project resided with NBC president and CEO Fred Silverman, who was looking for a realistic urban police series to win back audience ratings. Silverman commissioned a series from MTM Productions, co-owned by Mary Tyler Moore and her then-husband Grant Tinker, both television icons in their own rights. Tinker, as it turned out, in the summer of 1981, would go on to replace Silverman as NBC president. In 1980, however, while Tinker was still running his avant garde studio, MTM asked Steven Bochco and Michael Kozoll to the Silverman-driven project as series writers. Bochco and Kozoll had worked together as writers on the ill-fated CBS series *Delvecchio*, a lawyer-detective show that was canceled after only a year. The good news was that the two found themselves together again at MTM. What NBC wanted was a cop ensemble piece. Bochco and Kozoll agreed to write and produce it, under two conditions. Bochco and Kozoll would need both total creative control as well as a meeting with the highest levels of NBC to discuss the network's standards versus their own.[27] NBC, by then a distant third in the three-way ratings race, said yes to both requests.

The result of that meeting was the birthing of *Hill Street Blues* (*HSB*), a cop show that would set new rules for almost every aspect of the action-adventure formula. *HSB* stood every genre convention on its ear. Cops were now vulnerable. Police officers made mistakes. Some drank. Most swore. And many times the cops finished second to those who actually perpetrated the crimes. Writers Kozoll and Bochco had circumvented the conventional wisdom of the genre. Told that audiences could track no more than three episodic plot lines in any story, *HSB* incorporated double-digit story lines in every episode, then strung them along for several episodes in a row, and sometimes over an entire season.[28]

While it was the *Dallas* episode "Who Shot JR?" that first gave prime time TV a weekly memory, it wasn't until the airing of *Hill Street Blues* that prime time television provided us with a continuous pipeline of stories that were actually *worth* remembering. Those stories were driven by an ensemble of characters like no cops we'd ever seen before under one precinct roof. Genre wisdom said that viewers would not be able to follow more than five to six weekly regulars, so Bochco and Kozoll integrated 14 characters into every story after its maiden season. To say that the Hill Street Station was staffed by a memorable collection of nonconformists doesn't do the casting justice.[29] There was: Ramrod reactionary Lieutenant Howard Hunter (James Sikking) heading up the SWAT team; Detective Mick Belker (Bruce Weitz) who growled at his collars; and the streetwise, no-nonsense Lieutenant Norman Buntz (Dennis Franz). Running command at the precinct was Captain Frank Furillo (Daniel Travanti), the coolest head at the precinct to be sure, but even he was hounded for alimony by his ex-wife Fay (Barbara Bosson), while sleeping with

27 Museum of Broadcast Communications website—"Steven Bochco"

28 Brought To You In Living Color, pp 152–153

29 Brought To You In Living Color, p 153

the public defender Joyce Davenport (Veronica Hamel). No one who watched the show regularly could forget thesaurus-mouthed Sergeant Phil Esterhaus (Michael Conrad) who presided over the morning briefing and always sent the troops off with "Let's be careful out there."[30]

The "morning briefing" was one of the earmarks of the series. The overlapping conversations, the decrepit settings, the shaky camera work, all of it set the tone of each episode even before the opening credits had run. Esterhaus's briefing at the onset of each show allowed both his precinct cops and the prime time TV audience to review the stories and characters already in play.[31] At roll call each and every week was Officer Andy Renko (Charles Haid); Renko's partner, Officer Bobby Hill (Michael Warren); Lt. Ray Calletano (Rene Enriquez); the pseudo-suave, lounge-lizard Detective J.D. LaRue (Kiel Martin) and his partner, Detective Neal Washington (Taurean Blacque). Rounding out the starring cast was Sgt. Henry Goldblum (Joe Spano); and partners Officers Lucy Bates (Betty Thomas) and Joe Coffey (Ed Marinaro).

The pilot was produced in 1980, but was held back as a mid-season replacement until January, 1981, so as not to get lost among the onslaught of other programs that had debuted that fall. It rolled out of the gate at a crawl and was out of the top 50 shows by the second episode, but the critics wouldn't let it go. They loved it, as did the loyal fan base who continued watching. Yet, for all its critical accolades, the series was never anything close to a hit. Coming in 83rd out of 97 series, *HSB* had the dubious distinction of being the *lowest*-rated TV series in history ever to be renewed for a second season.[32]

But renewed, it was—and the awards just kept coming. Four times in six seasons it won the Emmy for Best TV Drama. It can truthfully be said that while the show never cracked the Nielsen Top 20, *HSB* paved the way for such '90's hits as *NYPD Blue* and *Homicide: Life on the Street* as well as for several NBC shows in the 1980's—one of them a breakthrough medical drama about a rundown Boston hospital, where patients had finally found the nerve to do something on television they'd never done before—they sometimes died.

Elsewhere

In the summer of 1981, Fred Silverman resigned from NBC and Grant Tinker became president of the network. Equally as important, however, was that 31-year-old Brandon Tartikoff became the new NBC programming tsar. When Tartikoff took over, a writers' strike was looming, affiliates were defecting, and the network had but three prime time shows in the top 20: *Little House on the Prairie*, *Diff'rent Strokes*, and *Real People*.[33] Johnny Carson, dean of the late-night airwaves, was reportedly in talks to move his

30 Brought To You In Living Color, p 153
31 Brought To You In Living Color, p 153
32 *Newsday*—"Last Call for the Cop Show That Broke All the Rules" May 10, 1987
33 *My Life in "Toons": From Flatbush to Bedrock in Under a Century*, pp 188–189

landmark late-night talk show to ABC. The entire cast and writers of *Saturday Night Live* had left that late-night sketch-comedy series and their replacements had received some of the show's worst critical notices. While the network claimed moderate successes with *Gimme a Break!*, *Silver Spoons*, *Knight Rider*, and *Remington Steele*, its biggest hit in this period was *The A-Team*, a top-ten show that helped NBC navigate through two more rocky years of programming.[34]

It was no secret that Tartikoff had inherited a schedule full of aging dramas and very few sitcoms. That he showed patience with promising shows like *Hill Street Blues* would bode well for both Tartikoff, personally, and his employer, NBC. *HSB* had rated poorly in its first season, but instead of canceling it, Tartikoff moved the Emmy Award-winning police drama to Thursday night where its ratings improved dramatically. He used the same tactic with *Cheers* and later with *St. Elsewhere*. Tartikoff was able to do this because shows like these attracted the upscale, 18- to 34-year-old viewers (at the time, the demographic most desired by advertisers), allowing NBC to collect the same ad revenue as their higher-rated, mass-audience competition, even though fewer viewers tuned in.[35]

One of these "demographic hits" was *St. Elsewhere*. In 1982, the doctors at Boston's fictitious St. Eligius Hospital took a page out of *HSB* and broke with TV's tradition of depicting the medical profession as a well-scrubbed haven for virtuous miracle workers. Instead of paging Drs. Kildare or Welby, the hour-long drama called on a gritty ensemble cast to portray the rough goings-on in a Boston city hospital disparagingly known as St. Elsewhere—a dumping ground for patients shunned by fancier medical centers. As *St. Elsewhere* had come from the same MTM Production Shop that produced *Hill Street Blues*, it was likened to that groundbreaking cop show for three things: Its lack of a major star (though Denzel Washington certainly went on to become one); its multiple storylines that carried over from week to week; and its roaming camera that picked up snippets of conversation in an intense workplace.[36]

The doctors were stressed out, imperfect professionals, but it was the patients who made the show special. They were different and no longer treated as stoic caricatures resigned to a stereotypic if blissful fate. Rather, patients now appeared as frightened, vulnerable, and traumatized human beings—just like they would in real life. Unlike previous medical series, the patients on *St. Elsewhere* sometimes died. This last fact was credited with the show finishing 86th in the Nielsen's out of 98 shows released along with it in 1982.[37] Yet again, the series (like *HSB*) was miraculously renewed by Tartikoff, breaking *HSB*'s dubious "comeback" record set just a year earlier.

NBC decided not to cancel the series after new audience-composition demographics reports revealed that the show's fans were high-income viewers between 18 and 49 years of age, a fact that was heavily

---

34 Live From New York: An Uncensored History Of *Saturday Night Live*, pp 191–193

35 *Time*—"Coming Up From Nowhere" September 16, 1985

36 *Fifty Years of Television*, p 154

37 *Fifty Years of Television*, p 154

hyped to advertisers.[38] The series stuck around for six terrific seasons even though it rarely cracked the ratings top 40. By 1984, the 18–34 demographic had slid forward from 34 to 49 years of age. Not only were the first of the baby boomers now almost 40, but the last of them were now 18 and many of the affluent ones had tuned into the show.

The personal and professional experiences of the staff and patients at St. Eligius is why viewers came to watch and where the major focus of each week's episode usually lay. Viewers quickly learned that there were no guarantees at St. Eligius, as beloved "regulars" were occasionally—and suddenly—written out of the show. One doctor left when it was discovered that he was a serial rapist. Another when he was diagnosed with terminal cancer. Truly, the IV drip at *St. Elsewhere* in the 1980's ran straight and true to *ER* in the '90's, in terms of character complexity, plot development, and cultural relevance.

Dr. Donald Westphall (Ed Flanders) was St. Eligius's chief of staff and served as the quiet voice of integrity. Other characters on the series included Dr. Mark Craig (William Daniels), an egotistical heart surgeon; Dr. Auschlander (Norman Lloyd), a veteran doctor who was fighting cancer; Dr. Ben Samuels (David Birney), a free-spirited doctor who had slept with just about every female at St. Elsewhere; Dr. Wayne Fiscus (Howie Mandel) who was having an affair with a pathologist at the hospital, Dr. Cathy Martin (Barbara Whinnery). There was the dedicated physician Dr. Jack Morrison (David Morse) who often neglected his young wife who then died, leaving him feeling guilty about that neglect; and Dr. Annie Cavanero (Cynthia Sykes) who often became too emotionally involved with her patients' problems. There was Elliot Axelrod (Stephen Furst from *Animal House* fame), an overweight physician who battled obesity; and African American physician Dr. Phillip Chandler (Denzel Washington) who was always trying to prove his own worth. Rounding out the 15-member ensemble were Nurse Helen Rosenthal (Christina Pickles) and Dr. Victor Ehrlich (Ed Begley, Jr.), a clumsy California surfer-M.D. who crossed swords with just about every other doctor in the place. In the end, the legacy of *St. Elsewhere* cannot be overlooked. The series, while never a ratings winner, nevertheless helped usher in the age of the demographic hit—a Nielsen category now given to a series that's embraced by the *right* demographic audience as opposed to a huge one.[39]

Dramatic Resurrection

The quality of drama, alone, in the 1980's signaled a second Golden Age of Television—a case that could be made by the aforementioned two series alone. Yet, NBC wasn't the only network creating great drama. There were other notable dramas as well, among them CBS's *Cagney & Lacey*. If it had simply come and gone like other series, *Cagney & Lacey* (1982–88) would have still earned a place in TV history as the first buddy cop show that starred two women. But *C&L* was also notable for the very fact that after it came

38 *Fifty Years of Television*, p 154
39 *Hollywood Reporter*—"TV Milestones" 2004 September, p 71

and went, it returned again stronger than ever, thanks to a letter-writing campaign that persuaded CBS to reverse its decision to cancel the show in 1983, just one year into its six-year run. Sharon Gless played Christine Cagney, a fun-loving but ambitious detective. Tyne Daly portrayed Mary Beth Lacey, a more settled wife and mom.[40] The show successfully tried to approximate real life, embracing the personal and professional struggles surrounding two New York City police detectives who happened to be women.

The series broke with traditional television by honoring women's friendships—a radical departure from the myth that women couldn't get along. Before *C&L*, women on TV had tended to be seen either as *tokens* in a man's world, or *rivals* for a man's affections.[41] In the few instances when women were permitted friendships (Lucy-Ethel on *I Love Lucy*), the relationship was often comedic, even catty. Said feminist activist Gloria Steinem about *Cagney & Lacey*:

> I consider '*Cagney & Lacey*' the best show on television. Along with NBC's '*Hill Street Blues,*' '*Cagney & Lacey*' has brought a human resonance to television police work that renders the simple good-guy-bad-guy cop shows of the past hopelessly obsolete. The most authentic touches are found in the wonderfully strong acting of Sharon Gless and Tyne Daly. The characters are so convincing that one can imagine them growing and changing like real people. It's this human accuracy that makes the show attractive to women who normally tend not to care for cop shows. After all, even though few women are police detectives, most women have demanding jobs, whether inside or outside the home. '*Cagney & Lacey*' is one of those rare shows that reflect the reality of women's lives.[42]

As meaningful as *C&L* was to women and CBS alike, NBC was developing a buddy cop show of their own. According to network lore, *Miami Vice* sprang from two words printed on a cocktail napkin—"MTV cops."[43] The napkin belonged to NBC president Brandon Tartikoff and ended up on the desk of Anthony Yerkovich, an award-winning writer from *Hill Street Blues*. With producer-director Michael Mann executive-producing the show, *Miami Vice* became the epitome of *hip* and spent the next five years in the TV-ratings stratosphere. The music used on the show only added to the show's cutting-edge look. The synthesized instrumental music of Jan Hammer set the weekly stage for the countless pop and rock hits fed back to viewers in stereo. Among the bands and artists who contributed their music to the show were Phil Collins, Jackson Browne, Tina Turner, Meat Loaf, ZZ Top, Glenn Frey, Pink Floyd, Bryan Adams, U2, and The Police. With the music driving every pastel-tinged episode, many viewers felt there was nothing cooler than Sonny Crockett (Don Johnson) and Ricardo Tubbs (Phillip Michael Thomas) flying past Miami's art deco hotels in Crockett's Ferrari in hot pursuit of that week's drug dealer du jour.[44]

---

40 *Fifty Years of Television*, p 207

41 *Fifty Years of Television*, p 207

42 *Fifty Years of Television*, p 206

43 *Hollywood Reporter*—"TV Milestones" 2004 September, p 71

44 Brought To You In Living Color, p 158

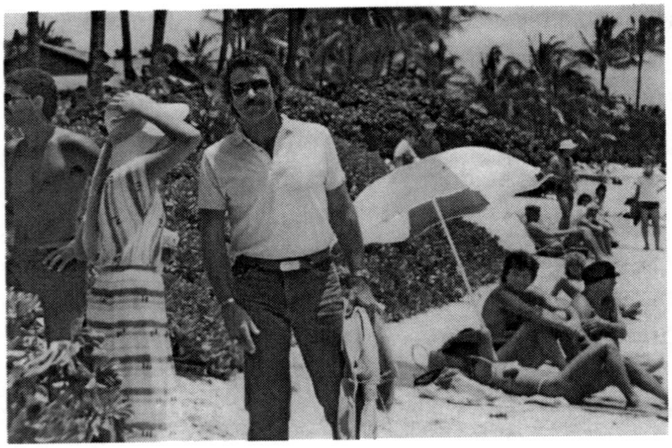

Epitome of '80's Cool. Tom Selleck stars in NBC's *Magnum P.I.*

Actually, there may have been one series that rivaled ... *Vice* for cool; one heartthrob that stood above Sonny Crockett. The detective deserving mention lived in Hawaii and was driving a red Ferrari four years before Crockett got his license. The man who gave Tommy Bahama a line of clothing, women hot flashes, and the Smithsonian his Detroit Tigers baseball cap was Tom Selleck. His character's name was Thomas Magnum and the CBS series was appropriately titled *Magnum, P.I.*

An Emmy Award-winning actor for his starring role in the series, Tom Selleck played the Magnum character to perfection. He was a very different kind of detective. Magnum was a veteran of the Vietnam War who woke up as a Navy SEAL at age 33, only to find out that he'd never been 23.[45] That was the essence of the show. The eight seasons from 1981 to 1989 were the least responsible period in our leading character's life. Magnum owed everyone money and was always tricking his friends into doing him favors. He was living free in someone else's house and driving his host's red Ferrari. And while he always managed to mess up his relationships with women *on* the show, Selleck had no problem attracting women viewers *to* the show; nor retaining male viewers in the process.[46]

In truth, *Magnum P.I.* was the successor to another handsome lone-detective from the 1970's, Jim Rockford. James Garner, who had first come to the attention of the television public as a 1960's star in the camp western *Maverick*, returned to TV in 1974 to star in a new NBC series called *The Rockford Files.* From 1974 to 1980, Gamer played Jim Rockford, a private detective and former convict, who had been imprisoned for a crime he did not commit. Exonerated after a five-year stint, Rockford took on detective work specializing in cases that seemed utterly hopeless. Assisting Rockford with his investigations was his father, a retired trucker played by Noah Beery, Jr. Like *Magnum, P.I., The Rockford Files* dealt with problems of the human condition; and Selleck has even gone so far in past interviews as to give Garner his due[47] for helping to develop the character of Thomas Magnum for the show.

One of the more enduring and less-talked-about attributes of the *Magnum P.I.* television show was how it portrayed Vietnam veterans. In that vein, the series charted new territory when, for the first time on TV, soldiers from the unpopular war were portrayed in a positive light. Much of the enlightenment surrounding these storylines came through the dialogue between Selleck and co-star John Hillerman

45 *Fifty Years of Television*, p 227

46 *Fifty Years of Television*, p 227

47 *Fifty Years of Television*, p 227

playing Jonathan Quayle Higgins III, the former British military officer and caretaker for the mansion Magnum called home. While the two characters continually bickered throughout the series, they also entertained a grudging respect for each other rooted deeply in their shared military backgrounds.[48] It was this shared respect for the military that meandered through rough storylines and helped America in its own small way to finally understand that the *warrior* is not to blame for a bad war. Thomas Magnum helped us see that, accept the truth, and finally understand the soldier's sympathetic plight.

Hopscotch

By 1982, it was becoming more and more apparent that ABC had run out of steam. Its dominance in the late 1970's had carried the network into the early 1980's, but by 1985, seasoned shows like *Benson* and *The Love Boat* had run their courses, while earlier hits under Silverman like *Three's Company* and *Laverne & Shirley* were already gone. NBC was in dire straits, as well, due in part to the many failed programs greenlighted by Silverman during his 1978–81 tenure there. Thus, CBS once more steered clear of basement dweller NBC and hopped over ABC in the early '80's ratings. This was done courtesy of *Magnum, P.I.* and *Dallas,* in particular, and with help from a veteran supporting cast that included *Simon & Simon,* and *Falcon Crest*, and *Dallas* spin-off *Knots Landing* as well as new hits like *Newhart, Kate & Allie, Cagney & Lacey, Scarecrow and Mrs. King*, and *Murder, She Wrote.*

The resurgence, however, was short-lived. CBS had gone deeply into debt as a result of the failed effort by Ted Turner to take control of the network, and the fallout was affecting their prime time schedule. By 1983, CBS president Tom Wyman and the board of directors were determined to oust the network's 81-year-old founder, William Paley, whom they now considered an impediment to the future of CBS—and oust him they did by a unanimous vote.[49] From his official retirement in April of 1983, however, Bill Paley wanted back in. CBS was the cornerstone of Paley's life and in 1985 he tried to reclaim the throne by aligning himself with billionaire Lawrence Tisch, chairman of Loew's Inc. (theater chain) and a minority owner in CBS, who wanted to take over the company. Paley was counting on the liaison with Tisch to take back the chairmanship and with it, control of the board. The move backfired, however, when new majority owner Larry Tisch, after paying $800M for a 24.9% stake in the company, appointed himself chairman of the board and left CBS founder William Paley out of a job, estranged from the company he created and forced into discomfiting retirement.

Like CBS, ABC also saw its ratings dip, though with NBC still floundering in the ratings basement, ABC fared no worse than second place in the Nielsen's through the 1983–84 season.[50] After all, though the dominance ABC experienced in the 1970's had clearly waned by 1984, the network still enjoyed healthy

48 *Hollywood Reporter*—"TV Milestones" 2004 September, p 64

49 Biography Channel—"William Paley: The Eye of CBS"

50 Up the Tube: Prime-Time TV in the Silverman Years, pp 214–216

ratings from shows like *Hotel, Moonlighting, Dynasty, MacGyver,* and *Who's The Boss?*; and from *The Wonder Years, Thirtysomething,* and *China Beach* as the decade wound down.

Somewhere in the middle, however, the network slumped, leaving many critics at the time to tie this decline in viewership to founding ABC chairman Leonard Goldenson's departure in 1986. Like his counterpart, William Paley at CBS, Goldenson had also withdrawn to the sidelines and ABC's ratings and earnings reflected this loss of drive. The momentum that had propelled the network through the 1970's was now offering TV fare that was often less compelling and, thus, short-lived. Comedies like *At Ease, Aloha Paradise,* and *I Married Dora* were forgettable if remembered at all; and ABC dramas like *Eye to Eye, A Fine Romance,* and *Buck James* lasted but a half-dozen episodes each.

Under the circumstances, ABC seemed ripe for a takeover—not that the other networks weren't going through the same metamorphosis at the very same time. That same year (1986) GE was reacquiring RCA for its prize nugget, NBC, at a cost of $6.4B (13.2B USD 2012), while billionaire Larry Tisch was grabbing CBS. What was surprising about the ABC deal was that no one expected the buyer to be a media company barely one tenth the size of ABC.[51] Nevertheless, ABC was acquired by Capital Cities Communications (owner of several of ABC's most critical affiliate stations), in 1986, for $3.5B (7.2B USD 2012) and changed its corporate name to Capital Cities/ABC. Capital Cities chairman Tom Murphy and its president Daniel Burke became chief executive and president of ABC, respectively. Both are credited with streamlining ABC's operations and increasing profitability until their tenure ended, in 1996, when the Walt Disney Company acquired ABC and renamed the broadcasting arm ABC, Inc.

The truth of the matter was that ABC, while profitable, became a perennial third in the ratings game and would find itself waiting an entire generation to reclaim the ratings crown it had held from 1978 through the 1982–83 season—a disappointment that can be traced back to three magic letters: N ... B ... C. In 1984, *The Cosby Show* and *Miami Vice* debuted on the National Broadcasting Company and immediately posted high ratings. *The Cosby Show's* triumphant success led to a renewed interest in sitcoms, while *Family Ties* and *Cheers*, both of which premiered in 1982 to mediocre ratings, saw their viewership increase from having *The Cosby Show* as a Thursday night lead-in.[52] NBC moved out of the cellar that season and firmly into second place. Within a year, the Peacock network would be back in first place by riding other huge hits through the 1985–86 season: *The Golden Girls, L.A. Law, 227,* and *Family Ties*. By the 1988–89 season, NBC was home to an astonishing 18 of the 30 highest-rated programs including *Matlock*, another Andy Griffith-driven, 200-episode series, and won every week in the ratings for 12 consecutive months—an achievement that would not be repeated in the 20th century.[53] What's more, NBC retained the annual broadcast ratings crown for eleven of the next twelve years.

---

51 *Tube of Plenty*, p 510

52 Toasting Cheers: An Episode Guide to the 1982–1993 Comedy Series, p 17

53 Museum of Broadcast Communications website—"National Broadcasting Company"

Promised Land

President Reagan said it was his favorite TV series and even had *his* people call *their* people to try to set up a scene in the show where the former actor could actually appear.[54] The producers of *Family Ties* (1982–89) turned him down. The show didn't need the president. Truthfully, it was the president who needed the show—and the national audience that went with it. A top-20 series for six of its seven years, and the second half of NBC's Thursday night knockout one-two punch, *Family Ties* had found a life of its own.

It came with a new face, and one destined for international fame. Michael J. Fox played the role of conservative teen Alex Keaton who perpetually dismayed his liberal parents with his love of William F. Buckley and "trickle down" economics. Actress Justine Bateman played his shopoholic sister Mallory who, while knowing nothing about the country's political history, could've written a book on fashion. The two of them were enough to make their idealistic parents (Meredith Baxter Birney and Michael Gross) want to reexamine the family tree. Younger sister Jennifer (Tina Yothers) simply wanted to be a kid while baby brother Andrew (Brian Bonsall) learned all about Wilsonian democracy and Keynesian economics from big brother Alex before he ever started teething.

Series creator Gary David Goldberg has admitted that he had originally intended for the show's storylines to emphasize the elder Keatons—one-time flower children struggling to reconcile anti-war politics of their youth with adult realities. In writing those shows, however, it was their son Alex, the unrepentant capitalist, who was stealing every scene. Ironically, it was during the casting process of *Family Ties* that NBC programming head, Brandon Tartikoff, unexcited about the casting of Michael J. Fox, finally relented to the show's creator, Gary David Goldberg, saying: "Go ahead if you insist. But I'm telling you, this is not the kind of face you'll ever see on a lunch box."[55] Years later, after the movie *Back to the Future* cemented Michael Fox's stardom, Fox good-naturedly sent Tartikoff a lunch box with the young superstar's picture on it. Tartikoff kept the lunch box in his office for the rest of his career.

Family Ties launched Michael J. Fox "back to the future" and then on to ABC's *Spin City* and a second hit series that outlasted Fox himself. Back in the mid-'90's, Fox had been diagnosed with Parkinson's disease, which had begun to affect his ability to perform. In January 2000, Michael J. Fox, TV icon and movie star for almost 20 years (and only now in his mid-30's), sadly announced that he was leaving the show. Reflecting back on Fox's career, no '80's TV viewer will forget the clash of values and political opinions that were played for laughs within the safe confines of a family-friendly show. The chasm between the values of Steve and Elyse Keaton and those embraced by their children provided an effective mirror of the ways our nation was changing and questioning itself in the decade of yuppie-dom and the era of conspicuous consumption.[56]

---

54 Brought To You In Living Color, p 156

55 The Last Great Ride, p 131

56 Brought To You In Living Color, p 157

One of the ways we as a nation—and as a television audience—were changing during the decade was in terms of our sheer numbers. Yuppies were getting married. Baby boomers were having kids and producing offspring in numbers America hadn't seen since the months immediately following World War II. Families were in vogue again and television saw one it just couldn't resist.

The Cosby Show was a throwback to the 1950's and in its first year finished number three in the Nielsen ratings—but did those ratings ever blossom. The series became the number-one show in America for five of the funniest years on TV, with a weekly share over 50 (i.e., 50% of American homes watching TV at that hour were watching *The Cosby Show*). In short, all this sitcom did was change the face of television, rocket actor Bill Cosby into superstardom and help alter the perception of African American families forever. What made the show extraordinary for its time was that the Huxtables were upper-middle-class African Americans—a black doctor and a black lawyer with a black daughter at Princeton. As funny and lighthearted as the show was, it also presented an undisguised challenge to widely held assumptions about black families. The Huxtables were everything (educated, stable, professional, and affluent) that bigoted whites (say, Archie Bunker) would think an African American family could never be.[57]

The series starred Bill Cosby as Cliff Huxtable, an OB/GYN, married to Wall Street attorney Clair Huxtable (Phylicia Rashad), with both leads working hard to parent their five children. Eldest daughter Sondra (Sabrina Le Beauf) was married while her college-age sister, Denise (Lisa Bonet) was away at Princeton but home on weekends. Eldest son Theo (Malcolm-Jamal Warner) was always tap-dancing around his teenage transgressions while sharing screen time with younger sisters Vanessa (Tempestt Bledsoe) and Rudy (Keshia Knight Pulliam).

The Cosby Show, like *Hill Street Blues* and *St. Elsewhere* before it, had NBC nervous. After all, hadn't rival ABC just turned it down? How good could the show really be? NBC programming head, Brandon Tartikoff, thought it could be a major hit and persuaded NBC to try six episodes. In September of 1984, the first one was shown and astonished the industry by beating out *Magnum P.I.* with a 43 share in the overnights.[58] Though the NBC slogan "Must-See TV" would be another six years in coming, the Second Golden Age of Television had already arrived.

By the following year, *The Cosby Show* set up the powerhouse Thursday-night lineup for fledgling NBC that included *Family Ties*, *Cheers*, *Night Court*, and *Hill Street Blues*. Twelve months after *Cosby* aired, NBC won back the ratings war, the reins of which it would hold onto for the next dozen years. With its focus on the Huxtable clan, *The Cosby Show* revived family sitcoms while exploring the meaning of family life in all its incarnations. In the groundbreaking first episode, son Theo tells his father he isn't interested in having a career. "Dad," he smiles. "Can't you just accept me and love me 'cause I'm your son?" After a thoughtful pause, Cosby responds: "That's the dumbest thing I've ever heard."[59] As the audience roared, Cosby would

57 Brought To You In Living Color, p 173

58 Brought To You In Living Color, p 172

59 Brought To You In Living Color, p 172

later remember that the show, in that moment, had found its voice—a tough but loving family dynamic that was playful, funny, and real.

As much as NBC's *The Cosby Show* paved the way for a return of the sitcom to prime-time prominence, ABC's *Roseanne* (1988–97) made the dial safe again for a blue-collar TV family. In fact, critics found that cross-over audiences gravitated even more to *Roseanne*, a downscale family, than they had to the Huxtables over at *The Cosby Show*. On the series, actress Roseanne Barr played Roseanne Conner, the down-to-earth, sarcastic wife of beefy building contractor Dan Conner (played by John Goodman). The couple lived in a small home in Lanford, Illinois, with their three children. Eldest daughter, Becky, played by Lecy Goranson (until 1993) and then by Sarah Chalke until the series left the air in 1997; their eleven year-old daughter, Darlene, played by Sara Gilbert; and six-year-old son, D.J., portrayed by Michael Fishman.

"Must-See TV"

The term refers to an advertising slogan used by NBC to brand its prime time blocks of sitcoms during the 1990's and is most often applied to the network's Thursday night lineup. The line-up is what proved the slogan. Thursday nights on NBC in the '80's and '90's featured some of the finest series in the history of television and became a large part of TV's "Second Golden Age" during the 1980's. Some of NBC's Thursday night fare included: *Family Ties, Cheers, The Cosby Show, Night Court, Seinfeld, Wings, Frasier, Friends,* and *Mad About You*. There were the dramas, too: *Hill Street Blues, L.A. Law, St. Elsewhere, ER*, and *West Wing*. All of this programming was born within a 20-year window that NBC refers to, now, in a historical sense, as "Must-See TV." It was NBC's Thursday night programming that led the network to dominate prime time ratings on Thursday nights in the 1980's and 1990's and dominate the annual ratings wars for more than a decade.

Almost from the onset, the series was prone to controversy. *The Cosby Show* was warm and fuzzy, but *Roseanne* was very much down to earth. In *Roseanne* we're met with a family of very average-looking people who are struggling through matters of sex, debt, domestic stability, and other social issues relevant to the day including alcoholism, menstruation, masturbation, obesity, domestic violence, and infidelity.[60] The show was also significant for its portrayal of feminist ideals including a female-dominated household run by a female lead whose likability did not rely on her appearance. Said the star of the show, Roseanne Barr, during its first season: "I'm not Lucy tryin' to hide 20 bucks from Ricky, or June Cleaver glidin' around a dust-proof house in pearl earrings and high heels. I'm a woman who works hard and loves her family. If my kids are alive at the end of the day, I've done my job."[61] Suffice it to say, *Roseanne's* in-your-face honesty touched a nerve with women everywhere. The show, featuring characters who were overweight, underpaid, and trying to make ends meet while raising three kids took

60 *New York Times*—"'Rosanne' and the Risks of Upward Mobility" May 18, 1997

61 *Fifty Years of Television*, p 231

exactly four weeks to leapfrog over everyone but ... *Cosby* for the number-two spot on television and there is where it mostly stayed for the next six years.

Déjà Vu

In March of 1985, the Australian conglomerate News Corporation's $250-million purchase of half of Twentieth Century Fox Holdings, parent company of the 20th Century Fox movie studio, sent a shock-wave through Hollywood. Two months later, News Corporation, owned by billionaire Rupert Murdoch, agreed to pay $2.55B (5.25B USD 2012) to acquire independent television stations in six major U.S. cities from Metromedia, which would, in conjunction with Fox Studios, both produce and distribute programming.[62] The cornerstone for the Fox Broadcasting Company (FBC) had just been laid.

Metromedia had first acquired these stations from the metaphorical ashes of the DuMont Television Network "fire sale," back in 1956, and that fact alone brought a serendipitous synergy to the News Corp. deal. Here was DuMont in the mid-1950's selling its stations to Metromedia because it could no longer compete with the other three networks, and here was Metromedia, 30 years later, relinquishing those same stations to a "new" fourth broadcasting network that would likely vanish faster than DuMont. From the outside looking in, the Fox Broadcasting Company (referred to now as FOX) appeared to be slipping right back into DuMont's 30-year-old shoes. In October 1985, 20th Century Fox made it official by announcing its intentions to form a fourth television broadcast network[63] geared to compete with the three major U.S. TV networks, NBC, CBS, and ABC.

The FBC's first program was a late-night talk show appropriately titled, *The Late Show*, debuting on October 9, 1986, with comedian Joan Rivers hosting. After a strong start, the show quickly descended in the ratings and by early 1987 Rivers had quit the series. Guest hosts filled in, but none were of Rivers' caliber. The network had already decided to cancel the show when the series began a ratings spike with its final guest host, comedian Arsenio Hall. The hope was that Hall would sign on to *The Late Show* full-time, but when he signed a deal in October 1988 with Paramount Television to develop his own syndicated late-night talk show, FOX's *The Late Show* was quickly canceled.[64]

FOX debuted in prime time on April 5, 1987, with the series *Married ... with Children* and *The Tracey Ullman Show*, then added one new show per week over the next three weeks, including *21 Jump Street*, starring the soon-to-be mega-movie star Johnny Depp, to complete its Sunday schedule. Beginning on July 11 that summer, the network rolled out its inaugural Saturday night schedule with the two-hour TV movie premiere of *Werewolf*. As it had done with Sunday night, FOX released several series over the next

---

62 *Boxoffice*—"Fox Buys Into TV Network" November 3, 1986

63 *Boxoffice*—"Fox Buys Into TV Network" November 3, 1986

64 Arsenio Hall, pp 47–48

few weeks that included *The New Adventures of Beans Baxter*, *Karen's Song*, and *Down and Out in Beverly Hills*. While ... *Beans Baxter* had some staying power, the latter two offerings did not. The two series were replaced with *Women in Prison* and *Second Chance* for the 1987–88 fall season—FOX's first fall season launch.

The 1989 TV season saw FOX add its third night of programming—a trend that would continue until the fall of 1993, when all seven nights were finally filled. Unlike the three senior networks, which aired prime time programming from 8 to 11 pm Monday through Saturday and from 7 to 11 pm on Sunday, FOX has traditionally avoided programming the 10 pm hour, leaving that hour to affiliates to program locally—mostly with late-night news. The network did schedule programming in the 10 pm hour on Sunday nights between 1989 and 1992, but never added 10 pm programming on any other night.[65]

This programming strategy was a *first* in national broadcasting and, as it turned out, not the only one. It was in 1989 that FOX first introduced its Saturday night "reality combo" of *Cops* followed by *America's Most Wanted*, both conspiring to be programming staples on FOX for the next two decades. In 1989, another first turned out to be even more enduring—a quirky midseason-replacement series airing in mid-December that no one saw coming: *The Simpsons.* The series was an ultra-hip cartoon laced with biting satire that was laugh-out-loud funny. The show ranked in a three-way tie for 29th place in the 1989 Nielsen ratings, thus making it the *first* FOX series to ever break the top 30.[66]

Dysfunctional Duet

Out of the two dozen series that FOX produced during the 1980's, two of them were directly responsible for the stabilization of FOX during its formative years. Both *Married ... with Children* and the prime-time cartoon classic, *The Simpsons,* helped to keep the network in the trades and on the tongues of television viewers, even if their popularity didn't immediately translate into high ratings.

Created by 33-year-old Matt Groening in the lobby outside television writer-producer-director and show creator James Brooks' office, *The Simpsons'* collaboration that began that afternoon was memorable. Legend has it that Brooks had contacted Groening about creating a series of animated shorts based on Groening's syndicated cartoon strip, "Life in Hell," to be aired during *The Tracey Ullman Show* on FOX. Sitting in the lobby, however, it occurred to Groening that animating these cartoon strips into TV shorts would require him to rescind all publication rights, since the comic strip was based on true-life events in Groening's own life. Groening didn't want to lose those rights, so instead he chose a second approach and formulated his version of a dysfunctional family, fictional though they be, naming them the Simpsons

65 The Fourth Network, pp 21–23

66 *USA Today*—"Nielsen's Top 50 Shows" April 18, 1990

and pitching it to Brooks.[67] The series that may one day own all the records for years of service and episodes produced began as a gaggle of sketches on *The Tracey Ullman Show* in 1987.[68] So well received were the sketches that Groening, Brooks, and the animators at Klasky Csupo subsequently transformed them into a half-hour series for FOX.

The dysfunctional Simpson family lived then (and still does) in the typical, if fictitious, American town of Springfield filled with most of the things contemporary American towns have—malls, prisons, dump sites, a mountain of burning trees, toxic waste, prostitution, pedophiles, and a nuclear power plant. As Homer Simpson might put it: "Everything a growing boy or lesbian could want."[69] The show's satire was as insightful as it was daring and always wickedly funny.

The animated comedy that the network hoped would last five years has lasted almost five times that long. Set to commence with its 24th season on the FOX network in the fall of 2012, the longevity of the series is due in no small part to the connection the series has established with its audience. For 24 years, that connection has been finally honed in the satirical parody of a middle-class American lifestyle as epitomized by Homer, Marge, Bart, Lisa, and Maggie Simpson, a quirky brood to say the least, covering all sides of the human condition. The standard bearer against what all future animated series will be measured is also the longest-running continuous comedy sitcom in TV history. In 2007, *The Simpsons* passed *Ozzie & Harriett*'s incredible sitcom series run of 435 episodes, aired on ABC between 1952 and 1966[70]—a record that had stood for over 40 years. In 2009, the series surpassed even *Gunsmoke* as the longest-running American prime time, scripted television series, though it should be noted that *Gunsmoke* still holds the record for most series episodes at 635.[71] Currently, *The Simpsons* is nearing 530 episodes ... and counting.

Since its debut in 1989, *The Simpsons* has been honored with 27 Emmy Awards, 30 Annie Awards (animation awards), and a Peabody Award (for distinguished or meritorious public service by radio or television station programming). If that weren't enough, *Time* magazine's December 31, 1999 issue dubbed *The Simpsons* the 20th century's best television series. Two weeks later, the Simpson "family" was awarded a star on the Hollywood Walk of Fame. Most extraordinary, perhaps, is that in 2005, Homer's exclamatory catchphrase "D'oh!" was officially adopted into the English language.[72]

As good as *The Simpsons* was for the Fox Broadcasting Company's reputation during those early days, there was one FOX series even more important to the network's growth: *Married... with Children*. The airing of the sitcom in April 1987 was the network's maiden voyage into the prime time TV world and

---

67 British Broadcasting Company—"The Simpsons': America's First Family"

68 British Broadcasting Company—"The Simpsons': America's First Family"

69 Encyclopedia of 20th Century American Television, p 328

70 *Hollywood Reporter*—"TV Milestones" 2004 September, p 27

71 Museum of Broadcast Communications website—*"Gunsmoke"*

72 *BBC News Online*—"It's in the dictionary, d'oh!" June 14, 2001

everyone was holding their breath. FOX executives had high hopes for the show that were quickly dashed by low overnight ratings. Ron Leavitt, the show's co-creator along with Michael G. Moye, had to chuckle. "I remember our head of programming calling up the next day to tell us we were number two in the time slot with the six-n-under crowd," Leavitt reminisced. "And he was serious."[73] While the figures eventually changed for *Married ...* the series never cracked the top ten. It didn't matter. *Married ... with Children* may well have served an even greater purpose as it, along with *The Simpsons,* helped define and stabilize an entirely new broadcast network.

In a way, both series were a reflection of what the Fox Broadcasting Company would ultimately become—counter-programming to what every other network had to offer. In an era ruled by *The Cosby Show* coziness, for example, *Married ...* chronicled the unholy Bundy household: Al Bundy (Ed O'Neill) who played his family like marks; Peg Bundy, Al's ditzy wife (Katey Sagal); Kelly Bundy (Christina Applegate); and Bud Bundy (David Faustino). Branding the Bundys a "family" was stretching it. Their living room, where most of the comedy took place, often proved an uneasy ride laced with rabid backbiting, moronic gloating, and sexual ridicule.[74] The show seemed intent on circumventing the holy grail of episodic television—that every script have at least one character to root for. Gratefully, *Married ... with Children* did not and that was where the series' humor lay for eleven of the funniest years on prime time television.

Law of the West

At the end of the day, television in the 1980's was very much akin to TV in the 1950's. *Roseanne* wasn't that much different in tone than *The Honeymooners. The Simpsons* were a lot like *The Flintstones*—only a whole lot funnier. The Bundys, though brutally sarcastic, shared a distant kinship with the Nelsons—Ozzie, Harriett, David, and Ricky, even though the series were polar opposites. And *The Cosby Show,* though far more sophisticated, wasn't that much different in set-up, structure and gender from Robert Young starring in that 1950's classic, *Father Knows Best.* As with drama, comedy in the '80's had taken a page out of history and resurrected television. And the '80's weren't done yet.

As if NBC in the 1980's needed another landmark drama to punctuate their already impressive resume, *L.A. Law* joined NBC's growing family of superb dramatic series in October of 1986. Created by *HSB* creator-writer-producer Steven Bochco and former Los Angeles D.A. Terry Louise Fisher, who'd produced on *Cagney & Lacey, L.A. Law* was interwoven with courtroom dramas in search of humanity. *L.A. Law* drew viewers into the tangled world of lawyers, deploying the *HSB* and *St. Elsewhere* approach of an ensemble cast and multiple storylines—all of it in the elite firm of McKenzie, Brackman, Chaney & Kuzak.

---

73 *Hollywood Reporter*—"TV Milestones" 2004 September, p 75

74 *Fifty Years of Television*, p 217

Since both *HSB* and *L.A. Law* were created by the same hand, it's not surprising that the two series were structured in much the same way. Senior partner Leland McKenzie (Richard Dysart) spent the opening of every episode trying to corral his boisterous brood of attorneys. Each week, TV audiences sat in on the power struggles at the morning partners' meeting chaired by Douglas Brackman, (Alan Rachins), the firm's tight-fisted managing partner. Chaney, the third name on the office door, was found dead at his desk in Episode One, prompting divorce lawyer Arnie Becker (Corbin Bernsen) to stake his claim to the vacated office before the opening titles appeared.

The private lives and public romances of the firm's lawyers were also prominently featured. First and foremost, there was lecherous Arnie Becker who slept with just about everybody on the show including his much-put-upon secretary, Roxanne (Susan Ruttan).Tax lawyer Stuart Markowitz (Michael Tucker) was married to fellow partner Ann Kelsey (Jill Eikenberry, Tucker's real-life wife). Also stealing pillow time on camera was litigating partner Michael Kuzak (Harry Hamlin) and Assistant D.A. Grace Van Owen (Susan Dey), against whom Kuzak would often find himself pitted against in court.[75]

While the private lives of the attorneys played a prominent part in the show, the series counterbalanced its soap-operatic tendencies by presenting well-crafted legal plots dealing with defective products, Tourette's syndrome, outing homosexuals, discrimination against fat people, and even dwarf tossing. Always breaking new ground, Bochco added another charter to the 1987 line-up—an office boy nearing middle-age named Benny Stulwicz (Larry Drake). Benny was one of the first developmentally challenged characters seen in a recurring role on TV and it won Drake back-to-back Emmys for his extraordinary portrayal. Drake's awards were but a part of the Emmy bonanza harvested by the show. *L.A. Law* raked in 20 nominations its rookie season (one less than *HSB*'s record haul) and 19 in its second. It was named Outstanding Drama Series in its first year on the air, and again for three consecutive seasons beginning with the 1988–89 season.[76]

Although *L.A. Law* always posted respectable Nielsen's, the show never made it into the top 10. As it turned out, a lot of sponsors didn't care. The show's appeal with affluent young professionals cemented its reputation. Yuppies were in and so was *L.A. Law.* Observers ascribe the surge in law school applications in the late 1980's and early '90's to the popularity of the series.[77] A TV bonanza that led to a slew of gritty law shows in the '90's and the birth of a new TV guru. His name was David E. Kelley, a Boston-bred attorney-turned-TV-writer-turned-Emmy-Award-winning show-runner and creator who got *his* start in television at McKenzie-Brackman as well.

75 Brought To You In Living Color, p 166

76 Brought To You In Living Color, p 167

77 Brought To You In Living Color, p 167

The Big Chill

No demographic grouping identified more with the 1980's than the "yuppie" (Young Urban Professional) and the producers of the ABC series *Thirtysomething* (1987–1991) knew that. *Thirtysomething* was influenced by the 1983 cult-classic film and baby-boom wake-up call, "The Big Chill," and the TV show reflected the angst felt by baby boomers and yuppies in the United States during the 1980's.[78] Expectations relating to femininity and masculinity introduced during the era of second-wave feminism (also called the feminist movement or Women's Liberation Movement) were changing. *Thirtysomething* producers Marshall Herskovitz and Edward Zwick saw this change as well and introduced a new kind of hour-long drama. Their series focused on the domestic and professional lives of young urban professionals (yuppies)—a socio-economic category of increasing interest to the television industry in the 1980's. So stylistic were the storyline innovations that critics were led to praise the series. As the *New York Times* chose to say: "*Thirtysomething* is as close to the level of an art form as weekly television ever gets."[79]

During its four-year run, *Thirtysomething* attracted a cult audience of upwardly mobile television viewers who strongly identified with the characters on the show. Even after its cancellation in 1991, *Thirtysomething* continued to influence television programming in everything from the look and sound of certain 1980's TV advertisements to situation comedies about groups of friends who talked all the time[80] and treated each other like family (*Seinfeld*, *Friends*, *Wings*, and even CBS's hour dramedy *Northern Exposure*, to name a few disciples).

F.Y.I.

While no one would ever mistake Rosanne Barr for Mary Tyler Moore, Candice Bergen as Murphy Brown might have given Mary a run for her money. Just as *Roseanne* had recognized the death of the female lead in sitcoms and stepped in to reintroduce her, so too did Diane English in creating *Murphy Brown* for CBS. Set at a Washington D.C. television station studio, this sitcom was about a fictional weekly news magazine show, "F.Y.I.," seen Wednesday nights and in its 12th successful year when *Murphy Brown* first hit the CBS airwaves in November, 1988.[81]

As the veteran star reporter of the fictitious "F.Y.I," series, Murphy Brown was opinionated, independent, sarcastic, and ambitious—determined to retain her place of importance in the male-dominated news-reporting business. She lived life to the fullest, drinking and smoking to excess, which landed Bergen's

78 Museum of Broadcast Communications website—"*Thirtysomething*"
79 Museum of Broadcast Communications website—"*Thirtysomething*"
80 Museum of Broadcast Communications website—"*Thirtysomething*"
81 Encyclopedia of 20th Century American Television, p 247

character in the Betty Ford Clinic where she underwent treatment for her addictions.[82] Murphy, the character, was, in spite of herself, a successful and competent TV reporter and an impressive on-camera presence.

Appearing with Bergen from 1988 through 1998 were the fictitious network's 25-year anchorman Jim Dial (played by Charles Kimbrough); "F.Y.I.'s" investigative reporter Frank Fontana (played by Joe Regalbuto); Corky Sherwood, a former Miss-America-turned-feature-reporter (portrayed by Faith Ford); and "F.Y.I's" neurotic young executive producer, Miles Silverberg (played by Grant Shaud).

During its ten-year run and 247 episodes, *Murphy Brown* dealt with issues like breast cancer and single motherhood—issues that somehow crossed over into the real world when then-Vice President Dan Quayle used Bergen's character as an example of flawed morals after Murphy Brown became an unwed mother. As creator Diane English illuminates: "It felt strange that the Vice President was talking about her (Murphy) as if she were real."[83] If nothing else, the incident demonstrated how much power television truly has to crystallize issues and then draw public attention to them.

Candice Bergen holding her Emmy award for Murphy Brown

In the end, what the series really stood for was friendship—specifically, how friends and family are sometimes intertwined. It was a comedy template that *Thirtysomething* had tried a year before *Murphy Brown* first aired and one that would dominate the greed-is-good '90's, though *Murphy ... and Thirty ...* were hardly the first series in the 1980's to use it.

Last Call

That distinction falls to the first of the blockbuster ensemble comedies, *Cheers*, debuting in 1982. One could argue, of course, that *M*A*S*H* had led the way into the world of ensemble comedy a decade earlier—and technically that was true. But *M*A*S*H* was an issue-oriented comedy surrounding people who came together by chance and directive. *Cheers* was an upbeat, devil-may-care series about long-time *friends* choosing to be together in the same place every week—a bar where everybody knew their name.

82 Encyclopedia of 20th Century American Television, p 247
83 *Hollywood Reporter*—"TV Milestones" 2004 September, p 78

Few television sitcoms have won the affection and loyalty of TV critics and viewers alike that NBC's *Cheers* earned. Like *The Mary Tyler Moore Show* and *Taxi*, *Cheers* relied on a similar mix of quirky personalities brought together inside a common workplace. Unlike the others, however, *Cheers* was staged in a bar—a "workplace" that millions of viewers frequented in real life and would happily return to, week after week. And who could blame them? Cheers—the bar—was a tavern filled with witty dialogue, acerbic putdowns, and comic situations that avoided social issues and preachy innuendo and one that reveled in its disregard for political correctness.[84] When the final line of the series was uttered ("We're closed.") in 1993, the public outcry was unprecedented.[85] Urban myth has it that grown men watching the final episode at bars around the country cried in their beers.

The series' hero and the bar's owner Sam Malone (superbly played by Ted Danson), a former relief pitcher for the Boston Red Sox nicknamed "Mayday" Malone, was a shameless, albeit charming, womanizer, irresistible to everyone but his leading lady Diane Chambers (Shelley Long). The erudite barmaid with a passion for literature had a body Sam couldn't take his eyes off and a mind that gave him a headache. Based on an actual Boston bar (the Bull and Finch Pub), series creators Glen and Les Charles and James Burrows wanted to avoid glorifying drinking so they had made the bar's owner and their leading man a recovering alcoholic. "We wanted to create a Katharine Hepburn-Spencer Tracy type relationship," Burrows told the *New York Times*.[86] Sam and Diane's on-again-off-again romance finally ended with Diane rejecting Sam's marriage proposal during the fourth season and ultimately leaving the show.

During Season Three, Diane had taken a hiatus from Sam as she and her psychiatrist Frasier Crane (Kelsey Grammer) became an item. Frasier was insecure and snooty, himself a case-study in neurosis[87]—and the one character who would go on to own, star in, and produce the most successful prime time spin-off in television history, *Frasier*. There to witness Frasier's unabashed arrogance at this early date were two affable tavern regulars Cliff (John Ratzenberger) and Norm (George Wendt). The know-it-all postman and easy-going accountant traded one-liners and enjoyed the put-downs of career waitress Carla (Rhea Perlman). Tending bar with Sam were Coach (Nicholas Colasanto) and later, following Colasanto's death in 1985, by Woody (played by actor Woody Harrelson). When Shelley Long left the show in 1987, actress Kirstie Alley stepped in as Rebecca and never missed a beat.

During its eleven seasons and 275 shows, the series earned 26 Emmy Awards and 111 nominations, though it hardly started out that way. *Cheers* premiered on September 30, 1982, and like *HSB* and *St Elsewhere* before it, was almost canceled during its first season after its premiere episode finished 74th out of 77 shows.[88] Eventually, *Cheers* became a highly rated prime-time show, earning a top-ten rating during eight of its eleven seasons, including one season at number one.

---

84 Brought To You In Living Color, p 154

85 Encyclopedia of 20th Century American Television, p 62

86 Stay Tuned, p 45

87 Brought To You In Living Color, p 155

88 Stay Tuned, p 46

When "last call" finally came in 1993, *Cheers* was hailed a success by almost everyone on the planet. Its final episode drew a 64 audience share of the evening, second only to the final episode of *M*A*S*H** as the highest-rated weekly TV episode.[89] Not only had *Cheers* introduced the world to a cast of world-class actors, but it had actually advanced the serialization of sitcoms by being the first comedy to perfect the use of the "cliffhanger."[90] No small wonder why *Entertainment Weekly* placed the series #4 on its list of the 100 greatest TV shows of *all time*; and why *TV Guide*'s Top 50 featured it at #18. Cheers to the most critically acclaimed series in the Second Golden Age of Television!

Discussion Questions

A. Prime Time Miracle

- How did the 1980 Winter Olympics hockey semi-finals game between the amateur U.S. team and the well-oiled professionals on the Russian Team become a metaphor for the eventual disillusionment of Russia and kick start pride into the ailing American consciousness?

B. Reaganomics

- Summarize what you know of *Reaganomics* and his "coming of political age" in the fish bowl of 1980's television.

C. Who Shot JR?

- When the *Dallas* series finale of the 1979–80 season posed the question, "Who Shot J. R.?," it became the first serialized TV show in prime time television history. What new assumptions was *Dallas* making about American audiences? Why was this innovative?

D. Hill Street Station

- Certainly not the first police series on television, what new writing mindset set the 1981 *Hill Street Blues* series apart from previous series?

E. Elsewhere

89 Stay Tuned, p 47

90 Brought To You In Living Color, p 155

- When a young Brandon Tartikoff was hired in 1981 as NBC's head of programming, what were the strategies and priorities that put him and his career on the fast track? What new shows reflected these attitudes?

F. Dramatic Resurrection

- The 1982 *Cagney and Lacy series* and the 1980 *Magnum, P. I.* series resonated with audiences for different reasons. Who comprised their audiences and why did they remain faithful to these popular series?

H. Promised Land

- '80's sitcoms *Family Ties, The Cosby Show*, and *Roseanne* all excelled in family dynamics, even though these dynamics were different for each TV family. What did these sitcoms have in common and what were their differences?

I. Déjà vu

- What network in 1986 joined the ranks of prime time broadcasters ABC, NBC and CBS and showed them that outsiders could contend for audience shares during the sacred prime time slots? What were the first shows aired on this new network?

- What audience demographic did it hope to capture?

J. Dysfunctional Duet

- In the late 1980's, both FOX shows *The Simpsons and Married…* with Children served as counter-programming to the TV fare on rival networks. What was their net effect on the Fox Broadcasting Company (FBC) as a whole?

L. The Big Chill

- *Thirtysomething's* four year run from 1987–1991 filled a need for audience demographics synonymous with the show's title. What did the writers end up capturing in this finely crafted TV series?

M. F.Y.I.

- What content of the 1988 *Murphy Brown* series became tossed around in the political arena, as if this were reality TV rather than a sitcom? Do you think being sited in political rhetoric advances the ratings of a program or that some people accept the viewpoints at face value and switch viewing habits?

N. Last Call

- Name the most critically acclaimed sitcom of TV's "Second Golden Age." How did it differ from the most successful sitcom of a decade earlier, *M*A*S*H*?

CHAPTER FOURTEEN

Freedom of Choice

1985–2000

Serendipity

In 1974, Philips Electronics launched a drive to create an optical audio disc with a sound quality superior to that of a vinyl record. Two years earlier, Philips had combined efforts with the Music Corporation of America (MCA) to create and demonstrate laser disc technology, publicly exhibiting the video disc for the first time in 1972. Its first volume-customer was the music business and in October 1982, Billy Joel's Grammy-winning album, "52nd Street," became the first album released on CD. On March 2, 1983, CD players and discs (16 titles from CBS Records) were released in the United States, leaving the March event to be seen, in retrospect, as the "Big Bang" of the digital-audio revolution.[1]

Even as many of us loved music CDs for the songs that drove a generation from puberty to retirement, others saw the technology differently. To the entrepreneurial eye, music CDs weren't about the music

1 *Tube of Plenty*, p 505

at all, but about a new kind of collection medium that doubled as a long-range archive holder. While a compact disc (CD) could record film and television and music in compact form, most of the electronics industry at the time surmised there were other applications for the CD beyond entertainment that needed to be explored. If a single disc could accommodate a rock-n-roll album, why not a book or an encyclopedia, or the data bases in every Fortune 500 company?[2]

Though the CD market would grow exponentially over the next few years, it was another laser-related medium branching off the CD market that quickly blitzed the communications business with a shock wave all its own. It had long been thought that lightwave communication (fiber-optics) might be one day used to carry all communication. In the 1960's, experiments led to an understanding that razor-sharp laser beams, normally traveling in straight lines, could be made to travel through hair-thin glass fibers. Test results on the applications ascribed to fiber-optics suggested that their capacity to transport communication far exceeded that of the coaxial cable. It soon became apparent that a fiber-optic bundle entering the home held more information, took up less space, and cost less to use than the current telephone cable. Moreover, fiber-optics were also able to handle cable television and computer systems in addition to fax machines and telephone chores—and accomplish all of it, simultaneously.[3]

The unbridled growth of American technology in the 1980's ran parallel to the unprecedented number of U.S. corporate mergers, buy-outs, and hostile take-overs as giant companies swallowed up smaller ones. Media companies became prime targets as conglomerates in and out of media, seeking a wider diversification of their corporate portfolios, were becoming increasingly convinced that communications, driven by the new digital technology, was the road to power and profit.[4] Already in Hollywood, Paramount had come under control of Gulf Western; United Artists had been swallowed up by Transamerica; and Columbia Pictures by Coca-Cola, which was later supplanted by Sony. By 1987, in television, Capital Cities had gobbled up ABC, a company ten times larger than itself.[5] Billionaire Larry Tisch had used dollars from real estate to leverage his purchase of CBS. And not to be left out, General Electric had reacquired RCA in order to get its hands on NBC—the media end of the company. In 1989, the takeover by Time, Inc. of the Warner Empire created another international media colossus, Time-Warner.

The struggle among technologies, the hostile takeovers by corporations looking to diversify into media, and the rise of *deregulation* had conspired, serendipitously, to stir the proverbial pot of what would soon become cable TV. It was, however, the Reagan Administration's deregulatory policies that trumped all cards on the 1980's merger-minded table. Not to slight the technology revolution since it, of course, was driving *all* business, but deregulating the prime time airwaves, as Reagan did, meant the ether was now in play for everyone—or so it was predicted.

---

2 *Tube of Plenty*, p 505

3 *Tube of Plenty*, p 506

4 *Tube of Plenty*, p 509

5 *New York Times*—"ABC is being sold for $3.5 billion; 1st network sale" March 19, 1985

For decades, in accordance with the anti-monopoly clauses in its own charter, the FCC had limited the number of stations that could be owned and operated by any one owner. The rule—one that had stood since the Federal Communications Act of 1934—said that any one owner could own seven radio and/or television stations. That was it. Following Reagan's election victory, however, the new President appointed Mark Fowler to head up the FCC. As the new FCC chairman, Fowler shared the President's belief that "market forces" were the solution to most social and political ills in America and proposed to Reagan that the FCC amend the "seven station limitation" rule and up it to twelve. Reagan saw this as a chance to help "deregulate" the entertainment business and leave the market forces to reign supreme. On April 1, 1985, the "12 station rule" became FCC law.[6]

"Market forces" did in fact take over as the Reagan Administration hoped they would, but with freedom in the '80's marketplace came unabashed greed in the 1990's as global conglomerates began to turn a predatorial eye on many of these new broadcast networks. With conglomerates needing to niche-cast in order to reach demographically desirable pockets of their global audience, cable television was almost too good to be true. The media takeover possibilities seemed endless and with the Reagan Administration on their side, every corporate merger, hostile or not, was welcomed as the fait accompli of a healthy economy. In a very real sense, trickle-down economics had trickled up. Wall Street arbitrageurs began to speculate in network stocks.[7] *Change* became the watchword of television as the cable interlopers feverishly stormed in to challenge the supremacy of broadcast TV.

Cable Upstarts

At its core, cable television is a system of providing TV programs to consumers via radio frequency (RF) signals. These signals are then transmitted to television sets through coaxial cables, or through digital light pulses sent through optical fibers (fiber-optics) located in the subscriber's home.[8] While both cable TV and broadcast TV use radio waves to carry their images, they do so from different parts of the same electromagnetic spectrum, operating on different frequencies. The cable box in the subscriber's home serves as the antenna needed to pick up the network's cable signal and the receiving circuit inside that box has been encoded to pick up only those frequencies emanating from the cable television "section" of the electromagnetic spectrum.

Cable television began modestly in the late 1940's as an adjunct for improved reception of outlying areas marooned from available TV stations. Community Access Television (CATV), as cable television was originally called, provided a simple perfunctory service. By plugging a cable into a community antenna perched high atop the nearest hill or mountain, those households willing to pay for it could now find

6 *Tube of Plenty*, p 510

7 *Tube of Plenty*, p 509

8 This Business of Broadcasting, p 10

a grouping of between 12 and 15 programs to watch. For the first 25 years or so, CATV was merely a tool used to amplify what the local TV station closest to the CATV antenna was already providing. While mountains might have blocked the local station's reception, the cable running directly from the big new antenna to the viewer's home was unencumbered and the picture it produced was often clearer than the original network broadcast.

As the 1970's progressed, subscription TV won an added following when cable networks began offering supplementary programming of their own. The programs amounted to little more than a few extra sporting events, movies, or concerts during the year, but it did give viewers a wider choice and that was enough to keep the cable business growing throughout the decade.

By the end of the 1970's, America had over four thousand cable suppliers and 15 million subscribers,[9] yet this seemingly successful cable paradigm was already changing. The cable boom that would flourish throughout the 1980's wasn't so much due to the cable business as much as it was to the satellite-feed business, to which cable companies were now officially "attached." Among the early cable players linked to satellites were networks like the Entertainment and Sports Programming Network (ESPN); the Cable Satellite Public Affairs Network (C-SPAN); Ted Turner's Cable News Network (CNN); the Music Television Network (MTV), a 24-hour Weather Channel; a network dedicated to children's programming called Nickelodeon; Hugh Hefner's soft-porn network, the Playboy Channel; and the most prestigious one of all, Home Box Office (HBO). These new entities were not really cable systems per se, but rather satellite delivery systems tied into existing cable distributors. Under various financial arrangements with satellite owners, cable companies could now draw from global satellite feeds and provide their subscribers with scores of viewing choices rather than the dozen or so they'd been offering before hooking up to their satellite.

A two-tier cable arrangement quickly evolved and remains in place to this day—premium cable and basic cable. As the 1980's were beginning to bloom, HBO, a Time, Inc. subsidiary offering recently released Hollywood films, major sporting events, and stand-up comedy acts, did so without commercial interruption.[10] For the privilege of not having to wade through commercials to view a televised program, subscribers would pay a "premium" fee on top of the cable fee already charged to them. Under this agreement, HBO and other *premium* channels like Showtime, Cinemax, and The Movie Channel rapidly became lucrative profit centers for their respective owners. This was Tier-1 of the two-tier cable system—the premium cable tier. Tier-2 was the basic cable tier and was composed of networks that, in addition to subscription fees, were also funded by advertising. This meant sitting through commercials while watching programs, just like one did when viewing broadcast television. A subscriber's "basic cable" package could include Nickelodeon, ESPN, MTV, C-SPAN, TBS, and CNN and two dozen others, all for one, low Tier-2 price. The cable company could afford to do this, of course, because of the advertising dollars

9 *Tube of Plenty*, p 493

10 *Tube of Plenty*, pp 494–495

that helped to supplement the subscription fees paid to the cable company. Signing up as well for HBO or Showtime, however, would add significantly to the subscriber's monthly bill, though there were many who felt that commercial-free television greatly outweighed the added fees.

Home Box Office

In 1965, cable pioneer Charles Dolan won a franchise to build a cable system in New York City's Lower Manhattan and laid down the first urban underground cable system in the United States. Sterling Manhattan Cable (SMC), as the company was called, was using a network of microwave relay towers to distribute its programming with the help from a CATV system in Wilkes-Barre, Pennsylvania, but Dolan was already thinking bigger. He was predicting that networks would soon be sending their signal by satellite and word of this attracted the attention of some very deep pockets.

Within months, Time-Life, Inc. had purchased 20 percent of SMC. Shortly after Time-Life came aboard, Dolan pitched his idea for an independent, satellite-driven "movie channel" to Time-Life management and persuaded them to back it. Dolan called his movie channel The Green Channel, though it might have been renamed "The *Blue* Channel," since both the channel and the cable company would lose money over the next six years, growing deeper in debt to Time-Life, Inc. On November 8, 1972, The Green Channel became Home Box Office. By March of 1973, Time-Life, Inc. had forced Dolan out, changed the name of SMC to Manhattan Cable Television and taken control of HBO—a network that would, over the next 40 years, come to reach 29 million U.S. subscribers, making it the second-largest premium cable network in America, with programming that is now seen in over 150 countries.

For almost a decade, however, HBO's broadcast day spanned just nine hours (3 pm–midnight), though half of those hours came in touch with prime time. Then, in December 1981, HBO expanded its programming schedule to 24 hours a day—something Cinemax, Showtime, and The Movie Channel had already adopted. For 40 years, HBO's programming has primarily consisted of theatrically released motion pictures, made-for-cable movies, documentaries, boxing matches, stand-up comedy, and concert specials. The first program broadcast on HBO, in 1973, was the feature film, "Sometimes a Great Notion," starring Paul Newman and Henry Fonda. On September 30, 1975, HBO became the first TV network to deliver signals via satellite when it showed the *Thrilla in Manila*—the legendary boxing match between heavyweight fighters Joe Frazier and Muhammad Ali. And in 1983, the network premiered its first made-for-pay-TV movie, *The Terry Fox Story.*

HBO's user base remained rather constant for the next five years, but greatly expanded in 1988 when the Writers Guild of America went on strike.[11] While standard television channels (due to the writers'

---

11 The Online Television Museum: HBO Website

strike) could broadcast only reruns, HBO had original movies, recent feature hits, and sold-out concerts to watch. A year later, they had even more. With subscribers on the upswing and the merger between Time, Inc. (HBO's owner) and the Warner Empire in place, HBO added another element to its programming arsenal by creating original weekly prime time series to help bring more viewers to the network.

One of the new series to come along immediately after the WGA strike was the American horror anthology television series, *Tales from the Crypt*. The show aired on HBO from 1989 to 1996 and was based on the 1950's EC Comics series by the same name.[12] The HBO anthology series found itself in a unique position. That *Tales from the Crypt* was a premium cable series meant that viewers watching the show were *paying* handsomely to see it. In a very real sense, HBO's audience had chosen to pay premium dollars to free itself from the network censorship that all other series airing on broadcast television were subject to. *Tales from the Crypt* took full advantage of the opportunity they'd been given and laced the series with provocative eye candy that included chilling violence, gore, sex, full nudity, and profane language—TV fare that had not appeared on prime time television up to that time. HBO subscribers loved it and begged for more.

HBO delivered. From 1990 through 1997, HBO created and produced a run of successful half-hour adult comedies that included *Dream On*, *Arliss*, and the award-winning *The Larry Sanders Show*, among others. All of the HBO comedies were serialized (having continuous storylines from show to show and season to season) and fast-paced. The humor was character-driven, often X-rated, sexually suggestive, and always uncensored, prompting the network to adopt its new slogan: "It's Not TV. It's HBO." The slogan became a '90's catch phrase that emanated from the subscribers, themselves. "How can they get away with that?" was the question often asked by HBO viewers who'd been raised on network-censored television all of their lives. The answer, "It's not TV, it's HBO," was bawdy and brash and representative of a new kind of in-your-face network that delivered prime time television with cutting-edge style.

These early HBO comedies were beloved by subscribers if not always by the TV critics. *Arliss*, for example, starred Robert Wuhl as Arliss Michaels, the president of a sports agency who has been likened to a Jerry McGuire-type of sports agent, but without a conscience. *Arliss* (rendered in its logo as *Arli$$)* was a sitcom about a sports agent and his group of associates. The series ran on HBO from 1996 to 2002 and served again as an example of how HBO (and all premium networks) differed from traditional networks in the 1990's.

Viewers were paying for the privilege of watching commercial-free television and because so many of those watching HBO were citing *Arliss* as the sole reason they paid for the HBO network, it didn't matter that TV critics disliked the show. *Entertainment Weekly* consistently referred to it as one of the worst shows on television.[13] ESPN.com columnist Bill Simmons repeatedly wrote about how awful the show

---

12 Comic Book Encyclopedia—"*Tales from the Crypt*"

13 *Entertainment Weekly*—"EW's Ken Tucker names 2002's 5 Worst TV Shows"

was, even while his employer (ESPN) was acquiring the rights to air *Arliss* in reruns on ESPN Classic.[14] At the end of the day, the network served the fan base, not the critics, and that fact alone kept the show on the air for a very healthy seven-season run.

The Larry Sanders Show, on the other hand, had both the fan base *and* the critics' hearts and went on to become one of the most acclaimed television comedies of the 1990's. The sitcom aired from August 1992 to May 1998 and starred stand-up comedian Gary Shandling as the vain, neurotic talk show host Larry Sanders. The storylines centered on the running of his TV show and the multitude of people behind the scenes. The series was notable for featuring celebrities playing exaggerated, self-parodying versions of themselves as well as for its character-based humor and the honors bestowed on it.

The show won 24 major awards, including three Primetime Emmy Awards, five CableACE Awards, four American Comedy Awards, and two British Comedy Awards, among a slew of others. The show also received 86 nominations, including 56 Primetime Emmy Awards nominations, five Directors' Guild of America nominations, six Writers' Guild of America nominations, six American Comedy Awards nominations, and three Golden Globe nominations. When it retired from the airwaves in 1998, the series ranked #38 on *TV Guide*'s "50 Greatest TV Shows of All Time."[15]

Yet, for the many golden statuettes *The Larry Sanders Show* earned for its avant garde network, the series that actually kick-started HBO's trek through the 1990's was a show entitled *Dream On*. The adult-themed sitcom about the family life, romantic life, and career of Martin Tupper, a divorced New York City book editor, starred Brian Benben and Wendie Malick. Created by Marta Kauffman and David Crane—the same team who would later create the '90's blockbuster hit *Friends* for NBC—*Dream On* ran for six seasons on HBO between 1990 and 1996.

The show centered on Martin Tupper's (Benben's) life in New York City as he juggled apartment living with his teenage son, a love-hate relationship with his ex-wife, Judith, and the pressures surrounding his job as book editor for a small New York publisher, while forever trying to find happiness in the bedrooms of the women he dated. The series was notable for its frequent use of old movie and TV show clips used to convey Martin's inner life and feelings. The clips gave the show much of its quirky appeal, reminding viewers about the impact of television on their state of mind.[16]

More than that, *Dream On* became the first cable offering to fall into the "friends as family" template—a template used for both comedy and drama that would permeate all network programming in the 1990's. Relationships in the '90's were not as clearly defined as they had once been. How people lived and loved took on a whole new meaning. Gay living was on the rise. Couples of the same gender were raising children. Heterosexual couples were having families outside of wedlock, while baby boomers nearing

---

14 ESPN.com/Archives—Columnist Bill Simmons

15 *Entertainment Weekly*—"EW's Ken Tucker names 2002's 5 Worst TV Shows"

16 *New York Times*—"A Modern Life Lived in 50's and 60's Images" July 10, 1990

middle age were leaving marriages for greener pastures. Divorce in America was on the upswing. Many children were commuting between two different households every month. Against this backdrop, the Tupper family unit in *Dream On* didn't seem that farfetched. In the end, the series played to the fantasies of both men and women and was significant for being one of the first American sitcoms to use uncensored profanity and nudity in almost every show.

Band Identities

The networks called them "cablers," the dirtiest word in commercial television. Broadcasting upstarts who sought to revolutionize television, obliterate the status quo, and change the business forever—or so it was feared. By the mid-1990's, they were well on their way. Cablers were making their own forays into weekly scripted entertainment and viewers were responding. As the number of cable channels continued to grow, cable television proved an irresistible lure offering around-the-clock "prime time" to subscribers, covering almost any niche or domain viewers could ask for. To compete in this brave, new, multi-channel world, the four commercial networks (FOX now included) began to create distinct brand identities (sometimes referred to as *band* identities) attempting to carve out niches of their own. ABC, for example, aspired to be family friendly, while CBS earned a reputation for appealing to older viewers. FOX, of course, gained a foothold in the ratings game by catering specifically to the young (18–24 demographic), leaving NBC seeking loyalty from young urban professionals.

In 1995, as if the programming universe wasn't crowded enough, Time-Warner and Paramount jumped into the pixel fray by launching TV networks of their own. Taking their cues from FOX, both networks geared their prime time offerings down to an even younger audience. The WB (Time-Warner's offering) sought to "out-youth" FOX, going after the coming-of-age audience with teen-skewing series like *Buffy the Vampire Slayer* and *Dawson's Creek*. UPN (from Paramount) looked to attract young males with *Star Trek Voyager* and *WWF Smackdown* and both infant networks reached out to the under-served black audience with sitcoms galore.[17]

"Freedom of Choice" was the mantra the '90's would proudly chant. TV audiences in the final decade of the 20th century were quickly learning that they no longer had to flip to broadcast television to enjoy a sitcom or drama—a lesson no network broadcaster wanted its audience to master. Yet, despite fierce network efforts to hang on to viewers, broadcasters' audience shares continued to shrink. TV watchers were embracing a world where the once-almighty commercial networks were gradually becoming just another choice on the onscreen program guide.

17 *Hollywood Reporter*—"TV Milestones" 2004 September, p 77

The partial cast of the WB's biggest hit, Buffy the Vampire Slayer. *Left to right: Tom Lenk (Andrew), Emma Caulfield (Anya), Alexis Denisof (Wesley), Alyson Hannigan (Willow), Anthony Head (Giles), show creator Joss Whedon, and Michelle Trachtenberg (Dawn).*

Nielsen Ratings

With the competition growing as the 1990's began, Nielsen ratings became even more important. The A.C. Nielsen Company was founded in 1923 to give marketers reliable and objective information on the impact of their marketing and sales programs. Its preeminence in the fields of radio and television audience sampling began with its radio broadcast research in the early 1930's. While there have been other ratings gatherers over the years, The Nielsen Company (as it is now referred to) stands virtually alone as the means by which we measure television audience share and operates in more than 100 countries.[18] Nielsen moved from radio to television in 1950, creating the Nielsen Television Index and using it in just 300 homes its rookie year. By 1953, 700 households were using what Nielsen called the *audiometer*—a device that first linked the tuning dial on a radio, then later the TV channel selector with a moving roll of paper that was in perfect sync with the dial.[19] Currently the Nielsen ratings cover some 5,000 homes, each scientifically chosen with accurate demographics in mind.

To fairly evaluate these demographics in the 1990's, Nielsen equipped each of its households with a "people-meter"—a device designed to store information at one-minute intervals including data pointing to whether a set is off or on, and to which channel it's tuned. The metering device transmits its information to A.C. Nielsen, giving the central office computer a household's entire day's viewing picture in about five seconds.

18 This Business of Broadcasting, p 25
19 This Business of Broadcasting, p 24

In a very real sense, the channel selection knob on each set is monitored by The Nielsen Company. Every 24 hours, Nielsen not only reports on what programs are watched, but for how long they are watched, and by whom. Tracking the minute-by-minute station changes every 24 hours, Nielsen can determine the age, sex, color and ethnicity of every family member tuning into prime time TV on any given night.[20]

For networks, audience measurement, as *share* and *rating*, is essential in proving a series' real worth. The share tells networks if a series should be moved to another slot, if it needs to change focus, or if it should be dropped altogether. Ratings tell networks what they can charge advertisers for commercials. Advertisers agree to pay a certain dollar amount per rating point, so that when a series' ratings drops, so does the amount that the advertiser is willing to pay for their spots.

Family Values

Unfortunately, none of this audience-response technology boded well for ABC, whose television ratings, in the early 1990's, ran a distant third to CBS and ratings-champ NBC. While the ABC network had a firm grip on its "family friendly" brand identity, the programming that sprang from that identity did so in a decade where the "family," in the traditional sense, was changing. It wasn't that ABC got the "family" part wrong; it was an antiquated definition that betrayed them. The nation, in the first social transition to the left since the Vietnam War, found itself defending those who departed the traditional bounds of marriage while looking away from the Disney-like world of "family values" we'd had delivered to our living rooms since Ozzie and Harriet first invited us into their home 40 years before. Ironically, by 1996, The Walt Disney Company would actually acquire Capital Cities/ABC and rename the broadcasting group ABC, Inc.

ABC's relationship with the Disney Company dated back to 1953, when Leonard Goldenson, then ABC's president, pledged Walt Disney the money he needed to complete his new Disneyland theme park. As a bonus on its investment, ABC won first right of refusal on the Walt Disney anthology television series and exercised its right to broadcast *The Wonderful World of Disney.* The series would air on all three networks between 1954 and 1990, when NBC finally canceled its Sunday night version of the show, *The Magical World of Disney*, because of poor ratings. The house that Mickey built would lose some of its luster in the nineties for the same reason the ABC network was losing theirs.

Following the Capital Cities takeover of ABC in 1986, the network seemed to grow into a far more conservative company than it had been at any other time in its history. The innovative broadcaster that had led the way with the miniseries saw its medium fade away right along with its slate of cutting-edge comedies. Jim Janicek, a writer-producer for ABC Entertainment, had been hired to combat the problem.

---

20 This Business of Broadcasting, pp 24–25

Janicek was in charge of promoting Tuesday and Friday night comedies. By 1988, he had already tabbed Tuesdays for ABC as "Terrific Tuesday" and suggested ABC restructure the night to include *Moonlighting*, *Who's The Boss?*, and *Roseanne*.

Balki Bartokomous (Bronson Pinchot) and Larry Appleton (Mark Linn-Baker), starring in Perfect Strangers. *Two years after its arrival, ABC picked the series to kick off its TGIF comedy block that would outlast the 20th century*

The retooled night proved an immediate success for ABC, leaving Janicek to turn his attention to Friday. Janicek decided to create an ABC family-friendly comedy block for Friday nights.[21] With *Webster*, *Benson*, and *Diff'rent Strokes* nearing the end of their Friday night series runs, ABC, at Janicek's direction, inaugurated the 1988–89 season with *Perfect Strangers*, *Full House*, *Mr. Belvedere*, and *Just the Ten of Us*, then branded the Friday night block: "TGIF" (Thank Goodness It's Friday).

The TGIF banner for Friday night was often compared with its Thursday night, NBC counterpart, "Must-See TV." By the following season *Family Matters* (a spinoff of *Perfect Strangers*) and the *Brady Bunch*-inspired *Step by Step* were added to the Friday night TGIF lineup. And in 1993, *Hangin' with Mr. Cooper* and *Boy Meets World* would come to be included under the TGIF banner as well.

Janicek's first attempt to again replicate the success of "Terrific Tuesdays" and "TGI Fridays" came in the fall of 1991 when ABC rolled out a three-hour Wednesday night comedy block, loosely referred to as "The Hump" (as in "over the hump" of the work week).[22] The Hump amassed a series of shows that included *The Wonder Years*, *Growing Pains*, and *Doogie Howser, M.D.* among them. Yet, as successful as these shows may have been, there were just as many forgettable Wednesday night offerings. *Davis Rules*, *Married People*, *Sibs*, *Good & Evil*, and *Anything But Love* were among the ABC Wednesday night fare that was *anything but* stellar. Two of these five series were canceled inside of as many months and a third by the end of its first season. By November of that year, ABC was convinced that The Hump, as a three-hour block of comedy, was not going to work and opened up the 10 o'clock hour to another Steven Bochco production, *Civil Wars*. The sophisticated 1991 legal drama about New York City divorce attorneys felt a lot like *L.A. Law*, but without the staying power, and lasted only two seasons and 36 episodes. As it turned out for Bochco and ABC, things couldn't have worked out better.

---

21 IMDb website—Biography for Jim Janicek

22 Beyond Control: ABC and the Fate of the Networks, p 261

Class of '93

Even before it premiered in September of 1993, controversy swirled around the new Bochco-created drama for ABC, *NYPD Blue*. The series was rumored to push the bounds on nudity and profanity in network television causing 57 of ABC's 225 affiliates to preempt the first episode and boycott the show. Reverend Donald Wildmon and the American Family Association (AFA) referred to the series premiere as "soft porn" and took out full-page ads in major newspapers asking viewers to boycott the show.[23] The boycott worked for half a season, though most of the affiliates defecting were in small-market areas amounting to no more than 15% of the show's potential audience. Midway through Season One, 18 of the 57 defecting affiliates had already returned.[24] By the start of Season Two, the rest would follow. The show's vindication came after 26 Emmy Award nominations and a ratings success that made it the only new series in TV history to make the Nielsen Top 20 in every major adult demographic market. Evidently, those affiliates struggling with conscience finally had a look at the bottom line and decided it wasn't as risqué a series as the rumors foretold.

"Initially, we benefited from a lot of criticism and concern surrounding the series," said Dennis Franz (the show's star) back in 2005, at the end of … *Blue*'s 12-season, 261-episode run. "We got a lot of attention, but when viewers saw it, they realized this was an intelligent police drama that required some thinking."[25] While Franz, Bochco, and other cast members concede that the series stretched the prime time boundaries at the time, what *NYPD Blue* did first, other series have since emulated many times over. From the start, the trademark cinéma vérité shooting style of the show gave it a greater urgency. Like *Hill Street Blues*, Bochco's landmark '80's cop show, *NYPD Blue* presented the frailties and flaws of those who enforced the law right alongside their dedication and heroism. While the series was originally intended as a vehicle for David Caruso (an *HSB* alumnus) starring as Detective John Kelly, it was his partner Dennis Franz, co-starring as veteran Detective Andy Sipowicz, who stole the show. That year Franz won the first of four Emmy Awards for his portrayal of a bitter drunk and patron of prostitutes who, over the life of the series, became a loving husband and father.[26]

Class on the airwaves was not limited to Steven Bochco. Chris Carter's *The X-Files* came along on FOX, in 1993, becoming a mega-hit for the young network, attracting millions of loyal fans. Playing to the conspiracy-theory crowd, FOX's *The X-Files* tapped into a vein of distrust in government disclosure that originated in the 1970's. The show's creator, Chris Carter, whose formative years coincided with the Kennedy assassinations and the Watergate hearings, thought the show hit the airwaves at just the right time. "If it had come ten years later, post-2001," said Carter, "it might've been received differently."[27]

23 *Time*—"The Decency Police" March 20, 2005
24 *Hollywood Reporter*—"TV Milestones" 2004 September, p 84
25 *Hollywood Reporter*—"TV Milestones" 2004 September, p 84
26 *Hollywood Reporter*—"TV Milestones" 2004 September, p 84
27 *Hollywood Reporter*—"TV Milestones" 2004 September, p 81

As it was, the series came along in the greed-is-good '90's, during a bear market, the likes of which America had never seen. The rich were getting richer and middle class mistrusted their government because of it. Viewers skeptical of Wall Street, corporate influence peddling, and Congress, itself, were turning away from traditional mentors and considering alternative explanations.

The immediate success of the FOX sci-fi mystery thriller was unexpected. *The X-Files'* audience received the show's tenuous accounts of alien abductions, demonic possession, and government cover-ups with unabashed enthusiasm, and the series rapidly grew a cult following.[28] *The X-Files* was the biggest hit FOX had up until its premiere in '93 and turned FBC into a major prime-time player in the ratings wars, almost overnight. Truthfully, much of *The X-Files'* success can be attributed to the chemistry between its two stars. Actors David Duchovny and Gillian Anderson, playing F.B.I. agents Fox Mulder and Dana Scully, respectively, quickly made household names out of the show's leading characters. Mulder and Scully were part of a government unit that investigated "X-Files" cases involving unusual phenomena—extraterrestrial abductions, UFO's, genetically altered creatures, telekinetic beings, and cloning.[29] Mulder believed that his own sister had been abducted by aliens as a child and was thus convinced the supernatural existed. Scully, on the other hand, was usually skeptical of the cases they were chasing. Nevertheless, the series took stories and their characters in exciting directions and twisted their endings such that audiences stuck around for each of the series' 200 episodes. The show's by-phrases, "I want to believe" and "The truth is out there," were taken to heart by millions of FOX viewers, every week, for nine successful seasons.

The Class of '93 touched CBS as well. The 1992–93 season had been good to the Tiffany network. Under former CBS programming chief and the network's current president Jeff Sagansky, CBS had broken through NBC's stranglehold on TV ratings and won the year, largely on the strong numbers from new shows, *Hearts Afire* and *Dr. Quinn, Medicine Woman*, along with help from veteran series like *Evening Shade, Designing Women, Murphy Brown, 48 Hours,* and *Murder, She Wrote.* Having perennial favorite *60 Minutes* leading prime time on Sunday night didn't hurt either. That winning season, ten out of the top 20 shows were seen on CBS, including one of the unsung heroes supporting this rare CBS ratings grab, *Northern Exposure.*[30]

Starting out as an eight-episode summer replacement series on CBS in 1990, *Northern Exposure* returned for seven more episodes in spring 1991, until becoming a regular part of the CBS network's schedule in 1991–92. The engaging one-hour dramedy featured picturesque Alaskan scenery, a unique and fiercely independent lifestyle, and a wonderful set of eccentric characters inhabiting the fictitious town of Cicely, Alaska. Over the course of *Northern Exposure*'s five-year run, the series was nominated for over fifty Emmy awards and multiple Golden Globe awards, in addition to the back-to-back Peabody Awards presented to the show's creators, Joshua Brand and John Falsey, in 1991 and 1992.[31]

---

28 *Hollywood Reporter*—"TV Milestones" 2004 September, p 81

29 *The X-Files*—"Travelers" Aired March 29, 1998

30 Encyclopedia of 20th Century American Television, p 260

31 IMDb website—Awards for *Northern Exposure*

The knock on CBS following its 1993–94 ratings slump the following season was that the network's demographics skewed almost ten years older than ABC, NBC, and FOX—and at a time when the culture in America was getting younger. In fact, even in the 1992–93 season in which CBS won the TV ratings crown, NBC made more money. NBC had captured the all-important 18–49 demographic with most of its shows, while many of CBS's shows drew a female audience over 40. While more viewers may have watched CBS during the 1992–93 season, because of the network's aging demographic, advertisers paid fewer dollars to CBS than they did to NBC's lower-rated (but more demographically desirable) shows. In fact, it wasn't until 1993 that CBS had any kind of '90's ratings hit at all in the 18–49 demographic category—a western, of all things, featuring a woman as lead. Thus, it was no secret that when *Dr. Quinn, Medicine Woman"* first made its television debut as a two-hour movie-of-the-week on New Year's Day, 1993, no one thought it would ever work as a weekly series.

Set in the 1860's, *Dr Quinn* ... centered on a single female physician, Dr. Michaela Quinn, played to Golden Globe-winning perfection by veteran actress Jane Seymour. Because of Quinn's father's recent death and the inescapable fact that opportunities for female doctors in 1860's Boston, where she lived, were severely limited, Michaela had migrated west to Colorado Springs in order to open her practice in a rural town. There, she was greeted with hostility by the townspeople who resented the rather obvious fact that the doctor who finally landed in their frontier town was, God forbid, a woman.[32] Critics praised Seymour's acting, the show's look, and the forward-thinking stories, but branded Seymour a fish out of water when it came to the Wild West. Once again, the viewing audience disagreed with the critics' report and began tuning in to the show in droves.

The show's instant popularity prompted CBS to order it picked up for the coming fall season. What the cynics were slow to understand was that America didn't view the show as a western, but as a family show, in perfect keeping with the no-holds-barred world around it. "Dr. Mike" (as Michaela was often referred to by the townsfolk in Colorado Springs) was, after all, a single mom raising three orphaned kids and dating rugged young widower, Byron Sully (played by Joe Lando), to plenty of steamy reviews. Not exactly June and Ward Cleaver, Ozzie and Harriett Nelson, or the Bunkers. Yet Quinn and her untraditional brood *were* a family. A different kind to be sure—one embracing friends instead of relatives.

Dr. Quinn, Medicine Woman was a big hit in the United States, generating 150 episodes and two TV movies and was syndicated globally in over 100 countries following its successful six-season run. The series drew large ratings for CBS, despite the fact that it aired on Saturday nights when networks, pointing to low viewership, rarely previewed new episodes. Moreover, the show captured the all-important male/female 18–49 demographic for its time slot, making it a staple on Saturday nights for CBS for the next four years. *Dr. Quinn...* was best known for its large supporting cast and high-concept storytelling and often used

32 Encyclopedia of 20th Century of American Television, p 92

its semi-historical setting as a vehicle to address issues of gender and race within the community. One episode took on homophobia when the famous poet Walt Whitman came to town.[33]

At the end of Season Five, CBS revealed that the show's demographics had changed. The majority of *Dr. Quinn's...* audience no longer resided in the male/female 18–49 grouping, but now with women over 40 years of age.[34] To combat this marketing problem, CBS ordered the writers to give the show an edgier feel, hoping to draw more men back into the audience mix. That next season, Michaela had a painful miscarriage, dealt with a diphtheria outbreak, and was shot point-blank by a man who resented doctors and developed post-traumatic stress disorder because of it. The edgier stories did what the network had hoped they would, helping the show to garner three million more viewers on average per week than the previous year. Even so, CBS decided to cancel the series before the 1998–99 season—an event that stirred a massive fan uproar, the likes of which hadn't been seen since the campaign to save *Star Trek* in the mid-1960's.[35] While the effort to bring back the series failed, it did prompt CBS to make two *Dr. Quinn ...* television movies that aired over the next three years.

In looking back, the show's success stemmed from the fact that people could relate to the characters who, while living 130 years before them, shared many of the same concerns, sensibilities, and quest for freedom as the eleven million weekly viewers watching the show. The CBS series had taken a page out of the NBC "guide to success," where friends on the show connected with each other as if they were family. It was a template that began with *Cheers* on NBC and one that would drive the Peacock network's programming as the 1990's began.

Dramatic Juggernaut

In the first nine months of the decade, three NBC shows were introduced that would help win the 1990's for the Peacock almost before the decade had begun. Two of them were comedies and the one (*Wings*) that premiered in April of 1990 opened with really bad reviews. The sitcom went on to embarrass all of its detractors, lasting for seven years and 172 episodes, and was a Top 30 show for most of its prime time stay. More important than its longevity, however, was the demographic the show captured. Yuppies with lots of disposable income to spend were tuning in. Like *St. Elsewhere* before it, *Wings* became a "demographic hit" embraced by the *right* audience as opposed to a huge one.

The series centered around brothers Joe and Brian Hackett (played by Tim Daly and Steven Weber) who owned a one-plane airline company on Nantucket Island called Sandpiper Air. The Hackett brothers hung out with a group of cronies between flights and these hilarious souls—friends to be sure—found

33 *Dr. Quinn, Medicine Woman*—"The Body Electric" Aired April 5, 1997

34 *Los Angeles Times*—"Fans, Seymour Rally Against Dr. Quinn's Cancellation" May 27, 1998

35 *Los Angeles Times*—"Fans, Seymour Rally Against Dr. Quinn's Cancellation" May 27, 1998

themselves in a very real way to be family. There was the Hackett brothers' lifelong friend Helen Chappel, played by actress Crystal Bernard, who ran the terminal's lunch counter; an eccentric maintenance man and local philosopher, Lowell Mather, portrayed by Thomas Haden Church; and an airport taxi driver, Antonio Scarpacci, played to Emmy-winning performances by Tony Shalhoub.

Yet, good as this first offering would turn out to be, it was little more than a programming hors d'oeuvre compared to the full-course meal NBC was about to unveil. Five months after *Wings* premiered, NBC struck oil again with two haunting notes that hadn't been heard since the days of *Dragnet*—and with syndicated reruns and spinoffs flooding cable TV, those notes haven't stopped resonating yet. The landmark series was titled *Law & Order* and those two resonating notes were preceded by the familiar refrain:

> In the criminal justice system, the people are represented by two separate yet equally important groups: The police, who investigate crime, and the district attorneys, who prosecute the offenders. These are their stories.[36]

While few viewers are likely to remember the short-lived 1963 drama titled *Arrest and Trial* on ABC, the obscure series, like *Law & Order*, was really two series in one. Half of the 1963 drama was about the police who investigated a crime, while the second half devoted to the lawyers who represented the criminal. A quarter century later, that 1963 series was to become the basis for the most durable dramatic series in the history of television.[37] *Law & Order* (1990–2010) was the brainchild of former *Miami Vice* writer Dick Wolf who adopted his concept to suit the mood of the nation in the 1990's. In the original *A&T* series, the mood of the sixties had been one of compassion and usually found its lawyers defending the wrongfully accused. In 1988, when Wolf was first approached by NBC to do the show, crime was on the rise and politicians were defined by their stance on the death penalty. Wolf made the prosecuting attorneys the lawyer-heroes of the show. *L&O* thus focused on the process of catching and convicting criminals rather than getting them off.

CBS passed on the pilot for that very reason, certain that the show wouldn't track well with female audiences. Given the opportunity to pick up the series, NBC was so intrigued by its story-driven nature they took a flyer—and for a few very lean years probably wished that they hadn't. *L&O* was a slow starter in the ratings, finishing outside the Nielsen Top 30 in its first three seasons. To make matters worse, NBC also sustained revenue losses on the show when advertisers steered clear of episodes about abortion clinic bombings and assisted suicide by AIDS patients.[38] The network's patience was rewarded, however, when repeats of *Law & Order* began airing several times daily on cable network A&E, which NBC was invested in at the time. While '80's TV drama had emphasized character and serialized stories aimed at hooking viewers every week, episodes of *L&O* started and ended in the same hour. These self-contained hours were just right for the generation of channel-surfing viewers, and the added cable exposure helped turn

36 Brought to You In Living Color, p 200
37 Brought to You In Living Color, p 200
38 Brought to You In Living Color, p 201

the show into a 20-year phenomenon churning out 456 hour dramas—second only to *Gunsmoke* in the total number of dramatic episodes aired. "It was nicotine for the eyes," said Dick Wolf, the show's creator and executive producer. "The reason you can watch them as often as people do is because it's a complete hour of television. It doesn't matter if you've been there every night for 14 years or whether you haven't seen an episode in the last six."[39]

While some say *L&O* was so story-driven as to make it actor-proof, it should also be noted that '90's viewers in the network's urban professional demographic didn't see the series as a cop show, but rather as a new kind of "family" series composed of friendships set in a precinct. Whether it was Detective Lennie Briscoe (played by the late Jerry Orbach) and partner, Detective Mike Logan (played by Christopher Noth); or Briscoe and Benjamin Bratt (who played Detective Rey Curtis); or Briscoe and Jesse L. Martin (as Detective Ed Green); all interplayed drolly with their boss, Lieutenant Anita Van Buren (portrayed by S. Epatha Merkerson)—interacting more as family than workmates.

On the legal side of the equation, it was the same thing. Whether it was assistant D.A. Ben Stone (played by Michael Moriarty) mixing it up with boss Adam Schiff (played by Steven Hill); or asst. D.A. Jack McCoy (Sam Waterston) interacting with Schiff and other asst. D.A.s like Claire Kincaid (Jill Hennessy), D.A. Jamie Ross (Carey Lowell), or D.A. Abbie Carmichael (Angie Harmon), the relationships between characters for a full 20 seasons remained the same—partners who interacted like family was the name of the game.

Masters of Their Domain

That game was about to get a lot more lucrative for NBC with the launching of what would become its third ratings success and second blockbuster in almost as many months. This third offering, however, would turn out to be decade-defining—even more than *Cosby* had defined the '80's and *All in the Family*, the 1970's. It was a show about nothing—or so said the critics—and it was routinely funnier than *The Honeymooners* and *I Love Lucy* combined.

The NBC show originally debuted before a test audience, in 1989, under the name *The Seinfeld Chronicles*, but reviews from the audience were so bad that NBC was said to have offered the series to FOX who wanted nothing to do with it. NBC programming head Brandon Tartikoff thought it "too Jewish" and "too New York" for mainstream America,[40] but was intrigued by the characters and the writing nonetheless. Programming executive Rick Ludwin, who'd first suggested giving Jerry Seinfeld a television series, went out on a limb by canceling a Bob Hope television special, then used the money he'd saved on the special to produce four more of *The Seinfeld Chronicles* episodes, instead.[41]

---

39 *Hollywood Reporter*—"TV Milestones" 2004 September, p 80

40 Brought to You In Living Color, p 186

41 Brought to You In Living Color, p 186

Renaming the series *Seinfeld* and adding a woman to its starring lineup, NBC liked what they saw in the four back-up episodes during the fall of 1989 and released the series the following June—right after *Cheers* and *Wings* and just before *Law & Order*. While slow to become a ratings hit, *Seinfeld* did become an immediate cult favorite, relying on its memorable sight gags and catchphrases and the most celebrated TV comedy of its generation to grow its base. When *Cheers* retired in 1993, *Seinfeld* seized their prized Thursday night 9 o'clock time slot and greatly surpassed the ratings even *Cheers* had gotten—and *Cheers* was a Top 5 show. That year, *Seinfeld* won the Emmy Award for Outstanding Comedy Series, beating out its family-oriented, time-slot competitor, *Home Improvement*, on ABC.

Tom's Restaurant was one of the primary New York locations for the comedy Seinfeld

At its core, *Seinfeld* was a show proving that normal life is actually quite peculiar.[42] Like its predecessors *Taxi* and *Cheers*, *Seinfeld* earned the critics' notice for its fine writing and oddball characters, as Jerry and his circle of cronies took absurd sketches to new heights. There was the inimitable Cosmo Kramer (Michael Richards) always lurching around Jerry's apartment like a cross between Baby Huey and Frankenstein's monster; brittle Elaine Benes (Julia Louis-Dreyfus) whose vulnerability stayed well hidden beneath a devil-may-care savoir faire; and hapless worrywart George Costanza (Jason Alexander) who was neurotic enough to make Woody Allen seem positively serene. And then there was stand-up comic Jerry Seinfeld (as himself) playing this kind of bemused ringmaster to his stable of malcontents.[43]

None of the principal characters on the show were related by family or work connections, but remained distinctively close friends throughout the seasons, giving the series a strong sense of community. Unlike other sitcoms, however, no moral lesson was ever passed along to the viewer. In distancing itself from the traditional sitcom morality play, *Seinfeld* broke several conventions of mainstream television. The leading characters, for example (obnoxious charmers, all of them) were thirty-something singles with vague identities and a conscious indifference to morals. Moreover, the boundary between reality and fiction was frequently blurred (Jerry Seinfeld playing himself was the most obvious). And there was also the fact that unlike your average sitcom protagonists, Jerry wasn't particularly nice to the women he dated, nor even to his friends. In one episode, Jerry admits that he would have sold Kramer down the river in a New York minute for a date with the buxom heiress to the O'Henry candy fortune. In another, he steals the last loaf of rye bread from a little old lady.

42 *Fifty Years of Television*, p 236
43 *Fifty Years of Television*, p 236

Perhaps there was something inherently funny about the claustrophobia of New York apartment living. Or maybe it was the unexpected story turns, the chances that each actor took, or the catchphrases that took American discourse by storm: "Yada, yada, yada," "No soup for you," "Master of my domain," and "re-gifting." Or was it the episodes themselves that made *Seinfeld* the funniest comedy ever? There was George defining "shrinkage" after being caught by his girlfriend just out of a cold swimming pool with his pants down; Elaine being dismissed by the Soup Nazi; Jerry, George, and Elaine all but ignored while waiting for a table at a Chinese restaurant; Kramer manning up and driving a Saab past empty on the car's gas gauge; and George calling up Marisa Tomei for a date just hours after hearing that his fiancée had died.

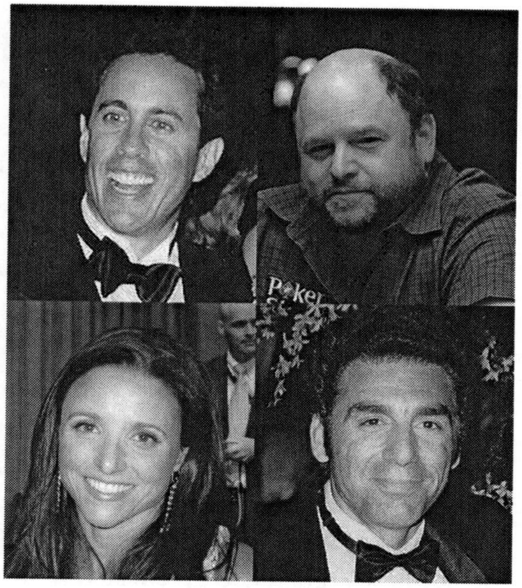

(Counterclockwise from bottom left): Julia Louis-Dreyfus as Elaine Benes; Michael Richards as Cosmo Kramer; Jason Alexander as George Costanza; and Jerry Seinfeld as himself starring in Seinfeld, *arguably the best TV show of the 20th century. Photo by Alan Light.*

It's been said that *Seinfeld* was a comedy about nothing, but in truth it might have been viewed as a series woven around modern manners as they happened to impact the series characters' day-to-day existence. Combining a strong sense of style and deportment with a witty repartee (used in part to mask the characters' insecurities), *Seinfeld* was the first TV series since *Monty Python's Flying Circus* to be widely described as a *postmodern* show. Postmodernism, by definition, is skeptical of explanations that claim to be valid for all groups, cultures, traditions, or races—and so was *Seinfeld*.[44] Postmodernism says that absolute truth is relative to the individual and not the collective—a *Seinfeld* trademark. Unlike most sitcoms, *Seinfeld* also declined to include any moments of pathos in the series where the audience was made to feel sorry for any of the characters—another postmodern trait. Finally, most episodes revolved around the principal characters meddling in the lives of other characters on the show, usually resulting in humiliation, embarrassment, or emotional disaster.

Addressing the *Seinfeld* series in 2011, linguistics professors Elizabeth Magnotta and Alexandra Strohl, from the University of Montana, wrote that the humor on *Seinfeld*—arguably the best of the 20th century—was crafted from what they termed "a violation of expectation." Rather than humor coming from an expected action preceded by a well-engineered set-up, *Seinfeld's* humor came instead from an "unexpected result"—something the audience wouldn't necessarily foresee. Strohl and Magnotta note that for humor to result from this "unexpected response," that response must have an appropriate

44 A Primer on Postmodernism, p 174

emotional climate (setting, characters, prior discourse, and a topic) for it to work.[45] In a very real sense, the humor on *Seinfeld* wasn't about setting up and paying off jokes (as Jerry's "opening monologue" each week might lead one to believe). Rather, it was about setting up and paying off whole scenes, within which the humor would unfold at its own pace. On *Seinfeld*, the laughs at home always seemed more spontaneous than they did for traditional sitcoms, since the viewer wouldn't always know when the next laugh was coming.[46]

In 1998, *TV Guide* wrote about the series that had garnered a combined 83 Emmy and Golden Globe nominations as it was leaving its remarkable eight-year, 180-episode run. Said *TV Guide* writer Jay McInerney: "How original was '*Seinfeld*'? I can only assume they must've kidnapped an NBC executive and held him hostage until they got the green light. How else could the show have ever reached the airwaves?"[47] In the end, the audience was left with nothing but a comic afterglow at the unlikely fates and unseemly follies of four chronically maladjusted Manhattanites.[48] They might've added that the series was the highest-rated show on television, over a full season, with a 53 share that it held for five years in a row. Every week from 1993 through 1998, 53% of the American households watching television on Thursdays at 9 pm, tuned in to watch what *TV Guide*, *Entertainment Weekly*, and *Time* magazine went on to tab as the "Number One TV Show of All Time"—*Seinfeld*.[49]

"Tossed Salads and Scrambled Eggs ..."

Great comedy can take you to the top of the Nielsen's faster than great drama—it's a statistical fact. But great comedy *and* great drama can make you an absolute fortune. So it was with NBC in the 1990's. Most everything they touched turned to gold—and all of it off two initial shows, *Seinfeld* and *L&O*, the cornerstones of Peacockdom from which all riches grew.

Seinfeld's popularity spawned other clones that only added to the NBC money pot. Thinking back, there was *Mad About You*: Like *Seinfeld* BUT Jerry and Elaine are married. *Will & Grace*: Like *Seinfeld* BUT Jerry and Kramer are gay. *Caroline in the City*: Like *Seinfeld* BUT Jerry is Elaine and Elaine is Jerry. And of course there was *Friends*: Like *Seinfeld* BUT with great-looking, 20-something actors. And to think that all of these series were shows about friends who interfaced like family. Same with the cast on *3rd Rock from the Sun*. More so, even, with the eleven-season, 264-episode run of the greatest prime time sitcom spinoff in TV series history, *Frasier*—friends *and* family there, to be sure.

45 27th Northwest Linguists Conference "A linguistic analysis of humor: A look at *Seinfeld*"
46 27th Northwest Linguists Conference "A linguistic analysis of humor: A look at *Seinfeld*"
47 *Fifty Years of Television*, p 237
48 *Fifty Years of Television*, p 235
49 "A Show about Nothing: Seinfeld and the Modern Comedy of Manners" website

When NBC's entertainment chief Warren Littlefield learned in early 1993 that the network was losing *Cheers*, their number-one show, at the end of the season, he went to the writing team of David Angell, Peter Casey, and David Lee and asked them to mine a new show from *Cheers'* rich ensemble of characters.[50] The team felt Frasier Crane was the character with the greatest potential, but Kelsey Grammer, who played him, wanted a different role. Angell, Casey, and Lee pitched a series to NBC where Grammer would play a wealthy, Malcolm Forbes-like, paraplegic publisher with a street-smart, Hispanic live-in nurse.[51] Grammer liked the concept, but NBC didn't. The whole idea behind the spinoff was to capitalize on the enormously popular character Grammer had played on *Cheers*, yet the idea being pitched was completely unrelated.

Eventually, Angel, Casey, and Lee came around to pitching Littlefield *Frasier*—a dysfunctional family comedy that, like *The Mary Tyler Moore Show* before it, incorporated two distinct comedy platforms in the same series. One platform included Frasier's avant garde, skyscraper apartment, while the other encompassed "The Dr. Frasier Crane Show" on talk radio station KACL. At home, Fraser lived the bachelor life alongside his disabled father, Martin Crane (John Mahoney); Daphne Moon (Jane Leeves), his dad's caregiver and secret heartthrob of Frasier's younger brother, Dr. Niles Crane (David Hyde Pierce); and Martin's dog Eddie (played by a Jack Russell terrier named Moose). As a sidebar, Niles, while married and officially living elsewhere, never wanted to be at home with his wife, Maris, a character often harangued on the show though never once seen in eleven seasons. As host of "The Dr. Frasier Crane Show," Frasier played a radio station psychiatrist surrounded by an assortment of lovable neurotics. "Bulldog" Briscoe (Dan Butler), the sports guy at KACL whose show followed Frasier's, was one of them. So was Roz Doyle (Peri Gilpin), Frasier's man-hungry producer, who was forever coddling Frasier's insecurities. Over the duration of the show, Roz became Frasier's close confidante and sometime-adversary and late in the series, if only briefly ... his lover.

When *Frasier* debuted as a spinoff of *Cheers*, in 1993, no one expected it to have a life as long as its esteemed predecessor, but that's exactly what happened. In fact, *Frasier* went beyond *Cheers*, becoming the only comedy series in television history to win the coveted prime time Emmy Award for Outstanding Comedy Series five years in a row.[52] The secret to the show's immediate success might have simply been the fact that *Frasier* gave its audience credit for having a brain. Few sitcoms ever aimed as intellectually high as *Frasier* did in terms of writing, yet the story of Dr. Frasier Crane's migration west from the Boston bar "Cheers" to Seattle was never decisively erudite, either.

At home or at work, Frasier and Niles, successful psychiatrists that they were, could always be counted on for humorous asides born out of their sibling rivalry. Both brothers possessed fine tastes, pursued intellectual interests, and had high opinions of themselves, but were frequently reduced to ten-year-olds when clashing with their down-to-earth, blue-collar father. The series remained consistently superb, in

---

50 Brought To You In Living Color, p 184

51 kenlevine.blogspot.com—"How FRASIER came to be"

52 *Entertainment Weekly*—"The Doctor Is In" September 16, 2002

part because the lead actors on the show all stayed with the series for each of its eleven seasons. Adding Grammer's many appearances as Frasier Crane in *Cheers* to his eleven years as Frasier Crane on *Frasier*, Kelsey Grammer ultimately tied the record for the longest-running character on prime time television, equaling James Arness' twenty years as Marshal Matt Dillon on *Gunsmoke*.[53] Though this record was recently surpassed by the principal cast of *The Simpsons*, Grammer and Arness hold the record in live-action series.

Reoccurring themes on the show played well with the change in cultural mores going on in America in the '90's. Most swirled around the slow erosion of Niles' marriage and the sexual tension between Niles and Daphne Moon, Martin's live-in caregiver. While Niles pined for Daphne, Frasier's search for love continued, as did Martin's search for a new life after retirement. All of this angst frequently drove the Crane brothers to visit Café Nervosa, their favorite upscale java shop, where they discussed their patients' phobias, delving into how *mixed up* most of them were—phobias *and* patients. It was this "mixed up" clientele that inspired the lyrics to the show's signature song heard every week during the closing credits: "I hear the blues a callin', tossed salads and scrambled eggs ..."[54] The whimsical metaphor referenced the distraught callers phoning in to Frasier's daily talk show with their disconnected thoughts. Asked by *TV Guide* as the show was winding down to describe this very complex series in a single sentence, executive-producer Christopher Lloyd said at the time: "It's really [*a series*] about these two guys [Frasier and Niles] who have an idea of this utopian world where people are polished and smart and treat each other well and every week these same two guys get strong evidence to the contrary."[55]

The Struggle for Network Supremacy

In 1993, FOX, the unabashed newcomer, outbid CBS for the rights to air the National Football League, resulting in several CBS affiliates switching to FOX for the 1993–94 season—and beyond. The loss of the NFL, along with an ill-fated effort to court younger viewers, led to a drop in CBS's ratings, sending the Tiffany network's prime time schedule into distress for the last half of the 1990's. Still, CBS was able to produce some hits to help carry the network through the end of the decade—*The Nanny*, *Becker*, *Touched by an Angel*, *Walker, Texas Ranger*, and a true top-fifteen hit for seven of its nine seasons on television, *Everybody Loves Raymond*.

The CBS show came along in the middle of another remarkable series run on rival network ABC, *Home Improvement*. Based on the stand-up comedy of Tim Allen, *Home Improvement* made its debut on ABC on September 17, 1991, and became one of the highest-rated sitcoms of the entire decade.[56] Unlike *Home*

---

53 *The London Independent*—"Kelsey Grammer has heart attack" June 3, 2008

54 kenlevine.blogspot—"The story behind 'Tossed Salad and Scrambled Eggs'" April 9, 2012

55 *Fifty Years of Television*, p 213

56 *Inside The Actor's Studio*—"Tim Allen" Aired May 28, 2006

Improvement, Everybody Loves Raymond seemed to struggle for every rating point it ever got, but finally become a Top 15 show for seven of its nine seasons, after premiering in 1996, in the 8:30 Friday night time slot, in 84th place.[57] *Home Improvement* had none of … *Raymond*'s *early* problems, finishing in the Nielsen Top 10 in each of its eight seasons (1991–99), with half of those seasons in the Nielsen Top 5. In 1994, the series peaked and finished the year as the number-one show on television.[58]

Home Improvement centered on Tim Taylor (Tim Allen), his spouse, Jill (Patricia Richardson), and their three sons (Brad, Randy, and Mark). Each episode included Tim's own home improvement TV show, called "Tool Time"—a show-within-a-show where Tim was joined by mild-mannered assistant, Al Borland (Richard Karn) and "Tool Time" eye-candy, Heidi Keppert (Debbe Dunning). Heidi's primary duty on the show was to introduce Tim and Al at the beginning of every "Tool Time" show with the line: "Does everybody know what time it is?" Humor in the show often revolved around minor injuries Tim sustained while demonstrating the power tools he used on the show. Here was the "Tool Time" host unable to properly use his own tools and this incongruity proved to be humorous. Tim would usually absolve himself of the mistake by using the injury he'd just sustained as an example of what viewers were *not* to do, so that miscue always looked planned.

Everybody Loves Raymond, while conceptually different from its ABC counterpart, was itself driven by a hero in Raymond Barone (Ray Romano) who shared certain characteristics with Tim. While Ray was reluctant to ever take a stand and Tim, a cocky know-it-all, both sitcom leads often failed to take things seriously, making jokes early and often in nearly every situation, no matter how troubling or problematic. On *Home Improvement*, Tim had trouble talking to Jill, his wife, about life issues, while Ray on … *Raymond* had trouble taking responsibility doled out by Debra, his wife, which in turn led to their "life issues" and the couple's comic riffs.

The Taylors lived in suburban Detroit, Michigan, and had a neighbor named Wilson (Earl Hindman) who was often the go-to guy for solving Tim and Jill's problems. Over at the Barone household in Long Island, New York, the show revolved around the life of Italian-American Raymond (Ray) Barone, whose problems were also impacted by "outsiders"—namely his mother, father, and brother who lived across the street. A newspaper sportswriter for *Newsday*, Ray lived with his wife Debra (Patricia Heaton), their daughter Ally, and identical twin sons, Michael and Geoffrey. Raymond's parents, Marie (Doris Roberts) and Frank (Peter Boyle), and brother Robert (Brad Garrett), were clearly the major nemesis to Ray and Debra's relationship and the frequent comic bane of the couple's frustration. Debra was always put off by Marie, Ray's mother—an insulting, controlling, and manipulative (Did we say controlling?) woman who constantly criticized Debra and coddled Ray, clearly favoring him over Robert. This motherly snub in turn led to the older brother's many insecurities. Yet, the heart of both shows lay in its stars' devotion to their respective

57 The Complete Directory to Prime Time Network and Cable TV Shows (1946—Present), p 1694

58 *Entertainment Weekly*—"ABC Hits a Home Run" April 28, 1995

families. It was this familial devotion that won over viewers and raised the bar of both shows above the typical, disposable family comedies of their era.

Hope and Kelley

Comedies weren't the only genres fighting for network supremacy in the mid-1990's. Ten o'clock dramas also clashed in prime time. In 1994, two one-hour medical series came head to head—CBS's *Chicago Hope* and NBC's *ER*. Twenty years earlier, author Michael Crichton had written a screenplay by the same title ("ER") based on his own experiences as a resident physician in a hospital emergency room.[59] The screenplay went nowhere and Crichton moved on with his life. Then, in 1990, he published his best-selling novel Jurassic Park, and three years later began a collaboration with director Steven Spielberg on the film adaptation of the book.[60] Crichton and Spielberg then turned to the *ER* script, but decided to film the story as a two-hour television pilot rather than as a feature film.[61]

Spielberg's company Amblin Entertainment shot the pilot script as virtually unchanged from the original screenplay Crichton had written in 1974. The only substantive changes made by the producers in 1994 were that the Susan Lewis character became a woman and the Peter Benton character became an African American and the running time was shortened by 20 minutes in order for the pilot to air in prime time on network TV. Warren Littlefield, NBC entertainment president at the time, was impressed by the pilot but had concerns about diving back into a TV medical franchise game so soon after *St. Elsewhere*, NBC's "demographically desirable" '80's hospital saga. After Spielberg joined the *ER* project as a producer, however, NBC changed its mind and ordered six more episodes to back up the pilot should the series move forward—and move forward, it did.

ER premiered opposite a Monday night football game on ABC and did surprisingly well. In a move that was hardly coincidental, the two-hour pilot episode of *Chicago Hope*, CBS's new medical franchise series, was broadcast one day *before* NBC's *ER* premiere in a special Sunday time slot—and it too did well, as critics had predicted. After the first week, both Chicago-based hospital dramas were moved to the 10 pm Thursday time slot at their respective networks and went head to head for the remainder of the 1994–95 season. "When we moved it to Thursday it just took off," commented Littlefield on *ER*'s skyrocketing success. This bite by NBC into what CBS perceived as its 10 pm *apple* surprised CBS and the other broadcast networks, too, but most astonished were critics who had not seen this coming. Almost all of them had predicted that David E. Kelley's new medical drama, *Chicago Hope*, would crush the NBC/Amblin-produced competition.[62] It did not. In fact, after the season ended, *Chicago Hope* retreated to Monday

59 Body Trauma TV: The New Hospital Dramas, p 24

60 *Time*—"Television: Angels with Dirty Faces" October 31, 1994

61 *Hollywood Reporter*—"TV Milestones" 2004 September, p 82

62 MSNBC—"ER Closes Door, Leaves Behind Satisfying Legacy" March 24, 2009

nights in search of better ratings, while *ER* held its same time slot for the next 15 years—and *this* was the real surprise. After all, *Chicago Hope* creator-writer-producer and all-around TV wunderkind, David E. Kelley, had just come off four consecutive years of leading two different series on two different networks to back-to-back Outstanding Drama Series Emmys. The CBS hospital show was to be more of the same.

David Kelley had broken into commercial television much like Crichton had. He'd been a Boston lawyer who had turned to writing just as Crichton had been a Harvard M.D. when he found his muse. Kelley received his law degree from the Boston University School of Law where he wrote for the Legal Follies,[63] a sketch comedy group composed of Boston University law students, which still holds annual performances. In 1983, after law school, while working for a Boston law firm, Kelley wrote a screenplay, "From the Hip," a legal thriller, which was optioned in 1986. That same year, Steven Bochco was searching for writers with a law background for his new NBC legal series, *L.A. Law*. After receiving a copy of Kelley's movie script from his own agent, Bochco made Kelley a writer and story-editor on the show. In Kelley's second year on the series, he became executive story-editor and a co-producer. In 1989, as Bochco stepped away from the series, Kelley became the show's executive producer.

During the next two years, Kelley received two Emmy Awards for Outstanding Writing in a Dramatic Series, while *L.A Law* received back-to-back Emmys for Outstanding Drama Series, for both the 1990 and '91 seasons. In 1992, after co-creating *Doogie Howser, M.D.* with Bochco, Kelley formed his own production company, David E Kelley Productions, striking a three-series deal with CBS.[64] Kelley's first creation, *Picket Fences*, focused on the police department in the fictional town of Rome, Wisconsin, and was influenced in no small part by *Northern Exposure*, CBS's quirky 1990 offering.[65] Critically acclaimed as the series was, *Picket Fences* never found a sizable enough audience, though it did go on to win dozens of Emmy nominations and 14 Emmy Awards, including consecutive Outstanding Drama Series statuettes for its first and second seasons on air.[66]

Under pressure from CBS to develop the second of his three commitments, Kelley launched the medical drama *Chicago Hope* starring Mandy Patinkin and Adam Arkin, and plotted its stories through "upscale medicine in a high-tech world run by high-priced doctors."[67] During its six-year run, it won seven Emmys and generally high critical praise, but only middling ratings.[68]

That was not the case for NBC medical drama, *ER*. While *Chicago Hope* broke the Nielsen Top 30 only once in its six years on television, *ER* finished no worse than 8th in any of its first ten years. Moreover, in

63 *New York Times*—"He's a Lawyer. He's a Writer. But Can He Type?" February 7, 1990

64 David E. Kelley: The Man Behind Ally McBeal, p 28

65 David E. Kelley: The Man Behind Ally McBeal, p 27

66 Advanced Primetime Awards Search website

67 *New York Times*—"The Operation Was A Success: 'ER' Lives" October 23, 1999

68 *New York Times*—"Doctor Shows for the High-Tech 90's" September 19, 1994

six of those seasons, it finished in the money, first, second, or third; and in three of its first five seasons on television, *ER* was the number-one show on TV.

Trying to figure why one show succeeds and one doesn't is not always easy. But given that there were so many neutral variables between these two particular shows leaves one curious. Both shows, for example, were set in the same town, Chicago. Both had comparable casts both in numbers and talent. There was real production muscle on both sides as well (Spielberg/Crichton and NBC; David E. Kelley Productions and CBS) and proven success all around. And finally, both shows premiered within 24 hours of each other, ostensibly reaching out to the same audience. Yet, one ends up with mild acclaim and mediocre numbers and one ends up being nominated for 375 industry awards and winning 116 of them, including 22 of the 124 Emmy Awards for which it was nominated.

Until *ER*, TV medical dramas were mostly character studies in hospital settings and that tone had run its course with TV viewers. Perhaps *Chicago Hope* fell victim to some of that viewer blow-back, though the style of the show was certainly contemporary. Or maybe it was the characters on *Chicago Hope* seemed a generation "older" than those on *ER* and thus reached out to the wrong Thursday-night demographic. Or maybe it was simply that *ER* was actually *original* both in its look and in its writing. While the weekly stories were central to the series, creator Michael Crichton felt it just as important for the series to capture the frantic pace, high-pressure look, and the actual equipment and vocabulary of an emergency room.[69]

Gurneys were forever bursting through doors as the camera careened down the halls at breakneck speed. "The reason our show took off," George Clooney (Dr. Doug Ross on *ER*) told *TV Guide* in 1995, "was because it was something you hadn't seen before."[70] Sure, portraits of overworked doctors and nurses were nothing new to television. But no audience this side of a cable documentary ever saw as much blood and guts in an emergency room. As it turned out, it was hard to say which action was more riveting—the operating room or the bedroom romance between Clooney's hard-partying, self-redeeming screw-up of a character, Dr. Doug Ross, and suicidal head nurse Carol Hathaway (played by Julianna Margulies).[71]

Sharing screen time with Clooney and Margulies in the ER at Chicago's Cook County General Hospital was a stable of characters who once again took on the shape of a family—over-worked professionals while on the job... dysfunctional *friends* when off the clock. Dr. Mark Green (played by Anthony Edwards) was chief resident in the emergency room who had serious personal problems at home with a demanding lawyer wife. There was Dr. Susan Lewis (Sherry Springfield), a proper young woman looking for Mr. Right. Dr. Peter Benton (played by Eriq LaSalle) was a demanding African American physician with a serious identity problem. And Dr. John Carter (Noah Wyle), an inept last-year resident with parents who had tried to buy his love with money and failed to see a profit.[72]

69 *Hollywood Reporter*—"TV Milestones" 2004 September, p 86

70 *Fifty Years of Television*, p 193

71 *Fifty Years of Television*, p 193

72 Encyclopedia of 20th Century American Television, p 108

But Amblin Entertainment sure did. So did co-producer Warner Brothers. When it came time in 1998 for NBC to negotiate a new deal with the series' studio, the license fee (what a network agrees to pay to a studio to produce each episode of their show) went from about $2.5M per episode to 13M per episode, making it the most expensive license fee paid to a studio by a network in the 20th century.[73]

Two Mints in One

In 1995, David E. Kelley entered into a five-year deal with 20th Century Fox Television to produce shows for both the ABC and FOX television networks, each agreeing to take two series. If one network passed on a project, the other got first right of refusal. Kelley retained full creative control.[74] *Ally McBeal* on FOX and *The Practice* on ABC were the first two projects to come from this deal.

Premiering as a midseason replacement for 1996–1997, *The Practice* was Kelley's chance to write another courtroom drama, but one focusing this time on the less-glamorous realities of a small law firm. Kelley claimed that he conceived the show as something of a rebuttal to *L.A Law* (for which he'd written) and its romanticized treatment of the American legal system.[75] *The Practice* would be the first of four successful series by Kelley that were set in Boston, and all four shows would draw incredible critical applause. *The Practice* received 15 Emmy Awards in its eight seasons on television and back-to-back Emmy Awards for Outstanding Drama Series in 1998 and '99, as well as a Peabody Award that same year. Even so, low to middling ratings still haunted the show until 1998, when ABC moved it from Saturday night to Sunday, allowing it the opportunity to spend two seasons inside the Nielsen Top 10.

The New York Times described *The Practice* as "the profoundly realistic, unending battle between soul-searching and ambition"[76]—ambition revolving around the law firm of Robert Donnell and Associates (later becoming Donnell, Young, Dole & Frutt) and manifested in the various high-profile criminal and civil cases that often mirrored real-life current events. Conflict between legal ethics and personal morality was a recurring theme on the show and usually played itself out through what the partners in *The Practice* sarcastically called "Plan B." This kind of alternative plan was only used as a last resort, when the firm was losing its case. One of the firm's lawyers would create uncertainty with the jury as to their client's guilt by accusing an innocent "third party" of the crime in open court in order to plant the seed of "reasonable doubt." The series starred Dylan McDermott as Bobby Donnell, the firm's senior partner, a deeply sensitive and compassionate man who continually struggled with his conscience. His partners and associates at the firm included Michael Badalucco as Jimmy Berluti; Lisa Gay Hamilton as Rebecca Washington; Steve Harris as Eugene Young; Camryn Manheim as Ellenor Frutt; Kelli Williams as Lindsay

---

73 Brought To You in Living Color, p 213

74 Switching Channels: Organization and Change in TV Broadcasting, p 26

75 *Variety*—"Kelley acts as judge, jury for series quality" May 3, 2001

76 *New York Times*—"Ally McBeal Teams Up With Less Flitty Lawyers" April 27, 1998

Dole; and Marla Sokoloff as Lucy Hatcher. These partners in the firm had consciences, too, but checked them at the courtroom door when it came to winning cases. Their nemesis usually resided in the district attorney's office where Lara Flynn Boyle (as asst. D.A. Helen Gamble) was there to challenge Donnell and his legal brood.

In 1999, at the Emmy Awards annual Hollywood gala, David E. Kelley and his ensemble of actors from *The Practice* paraded on stage for a second time in as many years to receive the second of their back-to-back Emmys for Outstanding Drama Series ('98 and '99). Yet, on this particular evening, history of a different kind would be made. *Ally McBeal*, a one-hour legal dramedy also created by Kelley, had premiered in 1997 on FOX, and in a well-executed fait accompli, was awarded the Outstanding Comedy Series for 1999 as well. It was the first and only time in the history of the Emmy Awards that one producer had won top honors in both comedy and drama in the same year and the first time a *one-hour* comedy had ever won the award.

As the 1990's wound down, networks owned by TV companies *other* than the three broadcasting giants (CBS, ABC, NBC) finally began producing and airing prime time series fare that surpassed the Big Three. Because HBO and other cable networks were not restricted by Federal Communication Commission codes that kept other broadcast network shows from being as candid as they might have liked about such subjects as sex, homosexuality, drugs, ambitious business practices, and politics, shows airing on the cable networks began to attract a growing audience and gradually began to change America's viewing habits.[77]

Ally McBeal was such a show. The series punctuated the life and loves of an attractive Boston lawyer named Ally McBeal (Calista Flockhart) whose courtroom confidence eroded quickly into an unusual assortment of personal neuroses once Ally was away from her work. In contrast to *The Practice* and its stable of idealistic lawyers, the attorneys at Cage, Fish and McBeal were into their careers solely for the money.[78]

The fictionalized law firm where most of the characters worked was depicted as a highly sexualized environment, symbolized by its unisex restroom. Lawyers and secretaries in the firm routinely dated, flirted with, or had a romantic history with each other, and frequently ran into former or potential romantic interests in the courtroom. Using this kind of story matter, the series was very successful in attracting the 18-to-34-year-old female audience demographic.[79] *New York Times* columnist Maureen Dowd quoted two young, professional women, remarking that they liked shows with female characters like themselves, single and obsessed with sex.[80] For 40-something professionals, women and men alike, talk around the "water cooler" at white-collar job sites across the country often centered on the travails of

77 Encyclopedia of 20th Century American Television, p 13

78 David E. Kelley: The Man Behind Ally McBeal, p 8

79 *New York Times*—"Liberties: She-TV, Me-TV" July 22, 1998

80 *New York Times*—"Liberties: She-TV, Me-TV" July 22, 1998

Ally McBeal. Described by the *New York Times* as a "stylish, sexy, smart and opinionated" trial lawyer, the *Times'* article labeled Ally as an emotional train wreck apart from the office—something young professionals understood.[81]

Despite its success, *Ally McBeal* did receive negative criticism from TV critics and feminists, some of whom found the title character annoying and demeaning to women (specifically professional women).[82] They pointed to her perceived flightiness, lack of demonstrated legal knowledge, short skirts, and extreme emotional instability.[83] Perhaps the most notorious example of the debate sparked by the show was the June 29, 1998 cover story of *Time* magazine, which juxtaposed the television character, Ally McBeal, with three pioneering feminists (Susan B. Anthony, Betty Friedan, and Gloria Steinem) and asked "Is Feminism Dead?" The question went unanswered as the series lasted just five seasons and 112 episodes, leaving the air two years before *The Practice* and for the same reason—low ratings. Both shows had seemingly worn out their welcome with viewers.

With *The Practice*, however, the end of the series was less conventional. In 2003, Bobby Donnell left the firm, fearing he had become the company lawyer he had long resented. In truth, the critically acclaimed television actor who'd been nominated for three Best Dramatic Actor Emmys and won two Golden Globes for the same role had been fired. ABC had agreed to renew the show only if the budget per episode was drastically cut and, thus, the stars of the show were the first items to be jettisoned. As Donnell leaves the show at the end of Season Seven, he names Eugene (Steve Harris) as senior partner. Along with Ellenor (Manheim), Eugene decides to make Jimmy (Badalucco) a full partner and extends an offer to Lindsay (Williams) who leaves instead to start her own practice. All of this radical story departure occurred awkwardly at the end that seventh season. When Season Eight began with nearly half the original cast missing, fans waited for an explanation that never came. Instead, Kelley responded by hiring James Spader for the role of Alan Shore—a character whom the *New York Times* described as "a lecherous, twisted antitrust lawyer with a breezy disregard for ethics."[84] Thus, the final episodes of *The Practice* in the spring of 2004 were more focused on introducing the new characters (Spader included) from Kelley's next Boston-based legal series, *Boston Legal*, that would premiere the following September.

Lose Some, Win Some

By century's end, NBC had dominated the television ratings game for an entire decade and looked poised to carry this momentum into the 21st century. With the lone exception of CBS from the mid-1950's through the mid-1960's, no network had ever dominated like this for so long. It needs to be remembered

81 *New York Times*—"Ally, the Talk Around the Water Cooler" November 23, 1997

82 *Western Journal of Communication* 2005 April, p 168

83 *Time*—"Is Feminism Dead?" June 29, 1998

84 *New York Times*—"Same Old Law Firm, New Snake" September 27, 2003

that back in the 1956–57 season, when CBS's series seized nine of TV's Top Ten rankings, the network had but two competitors, not the one hundred twenty or so stations NBC faced during the last five years of the century. By the 1999–2000 season, NBC had been atop the TV ratings heap for a staggering 12 of the past 13 years, losing only once to CBS in the 1992–93 television year when the Peacock came in second. Everything NBC touched in the nineties seemed to tap into the heartbeat of the cultural change that was racing through the decade. From 1995 through 1999, NBC had three of the Top 5 shows in all six years, and four of the Top 5 in all but two of them. That's why, in 1996, when NBC canceled its TV drama *JAG* (American military acronym for "Judge Advocate General") before it had even completed its first season, critics hardly questioned the move, figuring NBC knew what it was doing. After all, the series had finished 79th in the Nielsen ratings. That fact alone would have silenced all criticism had there actually been any. Given NBC's urban professional demographic (their brand identity), NBC had made the right choice for its audience.

CBS's network demographic, on the other hand, was older-skewing than NBC's (almost ten years older by some estimates) and the rival network picked up the canceled NBC series as a midseason replacement, beginning in January of 1997. CBS's decision to offer *JAG*, a military show, to its older demographic proved to be as insightful as it was profitable. The series played for nine additional seasons and spawned the hit spinoffs *NCIS* and *NCIS: Los Angeles*. Ironically, it was the hipper-looking spinoffs that helped the CBS network begin to grow the younger audience it so ardently desired. Over 220 episodes of the original series were produced during its ten-year run in America (nine of those years on CBS), while the show was also seen in over 100 countries worldwide. *JAG* was so popular with viewers that it actually entered syndication early, in 1999, and in 2012 was still being rebroadcast throughout the country on the USA (cable) Network.

In 1998, Warren Littlefield left NBC and Scott Sassa replaced him as president of the network's entertainment division. Sassa oversaw development of all NBC shows, but seemed to take a special liking to *The West Wing*, *Law & Order: Special Victims Unit*, and *Fear Factor*[85]—NBC's answer to ABC's *Who Wants To Be A Millionaire*? Yet, no sooner had Scott Sassa arrived on the scene that he left NBC after only a year and named Garth Ancier his replacement. Ancier, not yet 45, had already served as president of both the Fox Broadcasting Company and head of programming for the WB (Warner Brothers) network, which he helped launch in 1994. Ancier, it was said, knew great material when he saw it and had single-handedly put *7th Heaven*, *Dawson's Creek*, *Charmed*, *Buffy the Vampire Slayer*, and *The Jamie Foxx Show* on the air while at the WB. Ancier's arrival at NBC proved to be a very good thing, if only for the project that had now been left languishing under three NBC administrations (Littlefield/Sassa/Ancier)—Aaron Sorkin's *The West Wing*. It was Ancier, in 1999, who was responsible for putting Sorkin's show on the air, just before passing off the keys to the NBC castle to *his* successor, Jeff Zucker, in 2000.

---

85 Desperate Networks, p 51

The West Wing first sprang to life following the success of 1995 theatrical film *The American President*, for which Aaron Sorkin wrote the screenplay and in which Martin Sheen played the White House chief of staff. Sorkin had gone *unprepared* to a 1997 "pitch" lunch with producer John Wells, and in a panic to come up with a series idea, Sorkin pitched Wells a political TV drama that centered on the White House senior staff. Unused plot elements from his earlier work, *The American President*, were subsequently employed in the creation of what would become an Emmy-winning success, *The West Wing*.[86] Proving that plotlines involving national security or educational funding could be just as riveting as a good crime story, the series focused on the inner-workings of the White House. "I think there's a misconception that Aaron [Sorkin] was a civic-minded guy who wanted to teach America about government," said Bradley Whitford, who played Josh Lyman, deputy chief of staff, during the show's final season. "The reason the show works is that Aaron wants you to laugh, be entertained and be moved... *while* he is teaching you about your government."[87]

The West Wing gave viewers a behind-the-scenes glimpse into the Oval Office, as seen through the eyes of its eclectic group of frenzied staffers and a devoted First Family. Far from being the jaundiced cynical group of common public perception, the White House staff was passionate, dedicated, and out to do the best they could under trying circumstances. The producers thought of *The West Wing* as a family drama, in the friends-as-family mold. The show's staffers, after all, spent long hours together apart from their real families and with their president, Jed Bartlet (Martin Sheen), who ruled the roost as the undisputed patriarch and moral compass. "After all," says Sorkin, "the show takes place in his house."[88] Other "household" members of the dramatic ensemble included John Spencer (as chief of staff Leo McGarry); Allison Janney (as press secretary C.J. Cregg); Richard Schiff (as communications director Toby Ziegler); Rob Lowe (as deputy communication director Sam Seaborn); Bradley Whitford (as deputy chief of staff Josh Lyman); Janel Moloney (as his assistant, Donna Moss); and Stockard Channing (as First Lady Abigail Bartlet).

"The premise of every [*West Wing*] story began with the belief that people wanted to be challenged," said the show's co-executive producer, Tommy Schlamme. "We wanted viewers to understand the moral complexities of the life that people [in politics] face."[89] Schlamme was a big fan of the series' signature dialogue style filled with snappy, intellectual banter that Sorkin had first perfected on his ill-fated series—the critically acclaimed but seldom watched—*Sports Talk*, a year earlier. This rapid-fire repartee would be spoken on the series as the characters walked from one place to another; and the "walk and talk" became an integral part of *The West Wing*'s signature visual style. While critics often praised the series for its writing, others faulted the show as being unrealistically optimistic and sentimental.[90] A large part of this criticism came from the perceived naiveté of the characters. TV critics openly wondered what cave these morally pure characters climbed out of and how they ever found their way into the White

---

86 *Seattle Post-Intelligencer*—"Aaron Sorkin is a man of many words" March 7, 2000

87 *Hollywood Reporter*—"TV Milestones" 2004 September, p 90

88 Brought To You in Living Color, p 223

89 Brought To You in Living Color, p 223

90 *West Wing Continuity Guide website*—"Overlaps between West Wing and Sports Night Episodes"

House. And yet, that was the point of the exercise—to lift politics out of the gutter it had been stuck in since the scandal-ridden seventies.

The West Wing's success would, in part, be measured in gold statuettes. In its first season, the series garnered nine Emmy Awards, a record for the most won by a series in its first season.[91] In addition, the series received the Emmy Award for Outstanding Drama Series four years in a row (2000–2003), tying *Hill Street Blues*, *L.A. Law*, and *Mad Men* for most awards won in this category.[92] Each of its seven seasons earned a nomination for the award. Garnering 27 Emmys in all, *The West Wing* ranks fourth all-time in the number of Emmy Awards won by a series, behind *Frasier* (37), *The Mary Tyler Moore Show* (29), and *Cheers* (28). That *The West Wing* was a drama, however, makes it the most-honored program ever in that category.[93] Yet, more than the trophies, the series' success reaffirmed the relationship between television and its viewers. In the summer of 2001, a Harvard survey revealed that America's view of politicians had dramatically changed for the better in the three years since the series began—and it cited *The West Wing* as the reason for the shift.[94]

Guns & Roses

Beginning in 1997 with its first one-hour dramatic narrative series *Oz*, HBO started a trend that would become commonplace with premium-cable providers as the century turned—creating original prime-time series, comedies as well as drama. Although *Oz*, a prison drama, received critical acclaim, it was not until 1999 that HBO achieved both Emmy success *and* critical mass (an audience) with the premiere of its second one-hour narrative series, *The Sopranos*. In its six-season run, *The Sopranos* received 111 Emmy nominations, resulting in 21 wins, two of them for Outstanding Drama Series—the first cable series to be so honored. And that was only half of the HBO story that year.

Eleven months earlier, HBO had released its fifth comedy of the decade, *Sex and the City*—and with it, the proverbial "locker room" suddenly became coed. *Sex and the City* (*SATC*) took subscription television by storm. The series featured four comely women whose frank sexual chat turned chic New York City bistros into the female equivalent of a guys' stagger. Considering the times, the series had to be delivered on cable since there was no way characters on a broadcast network could have gotten away with saying and doing the graphic "stuff" routinely showcased in the series. Yet, *SATC* was well crafted. As *TV Guide* reported in 2000, "[HBO] also got a sharply written, seamlessly acted, poignant adult comedy." The series revolved around newspaper columnist and self-titled "sexual anthropologist" Carrie Bradshaw (Sarah Jessica Parker) and her three frisky friends, publicist Samantha (Kim Cattrall), lawyer Miranda (Cynthia

91 Permium.edition.cnn.com—"West Wing sets Emmy record" 2009 September
92 Primetime Emmy Awards—"Database: *The West Wing*"
93 Primetime Emmy Awards—"Database: *The West Wing*"
94 Brought To You in Living Color, p 223

Nixon), and art dealer-turned-museum-volunteer Charlotte (Kristin Davis).[95]

Hello, New York! The sassy star from HBO's Sex and the City *and the show's lead, Sarah Jessica Parker, on set.*

Criticism about the influence the show had on adolescents and the way women and young girls viewed themselves abounded.[96] *Sex and the City*, along with the NBC sitcom *Friends* (a series to be discussed in Chapter 15) were specifically recognized for "glamorizing" sex while conveniently forgetting to mention downsides like pregnancy and STD's that sometimes accompanied it. By 2008, a study published in the *American Journal of Pediatrics* found that females 12–17 who watched "sexually charged" shows were twice as likely to get pregnant as those who did not. Alas, Joan Swirsky, a New York–based journalist and author, wrote in 2003: "Yet another example that feminism is dead is the popularity of *Sex and the City*, the HBO show that features 30- and 40-something women sending out the unmistakable messages to females both younger and older that careers, money, looks and, ostensibly, intelligence are nothing compared to doing *anything* to get a man, including endlessly obsessing about the subject, engaging in loveless or even likeless sexual encounters"[97] until he's nabbed.

Though only Samantha was as promiscuous a series character as the criticism and tabloid hype suggested, the four women certainly upended conventional depictions of relations between the sexes. "The men are playing all the women's roles in this show," Parker told *TV Guide* in 1998. "The women [on the show] are in control."[98] Over the course of its six seasons, *Sex and the City* was nominated for over 50 Emmy Awards, winning seven times, and for 24 Golden Globe Awards, winning eight. In 2007, *Sex and the City* was listed as one of *Time* magazine's "100 Best TV Shows of All Time." A year later, *Entertainment Weekly* put *SATC* on its end-of-the-decade "best-of" list, saying: "A toast to the wonderful wardrobe from *SATC*, which taught us that no flower is too big, no skirt too short and no shoe too expensive."[99] Nor, it seems, were the premium cable fees, as 2.5 million more subscribers signed up for HBO following *SATC*'s first season.

By 1999, the broadcast networks, already bloodied by a 15-year turf war with the cable channels that had cost them 17% of their former market share, were *kneecapped* by a deadly new cable foe: *The Sopranos*. The HBO series, unfettered by network censors capitalized on American's abiding fascination with the Italian

95 *Fifty Years of Television*, p 234

96 Women and Language—"Constructions of Active Womanhood and New Femininities," pp 91–98

97 Newsmax.com—"The Death of Feminism II: 'Sex and the City'" 2003 July

98 *Fifty Years of Television*, p 234

99 *Entertainment Weekly* 2009 December, pp 74–84

Bada Bing! Redefining "family values," the cast and crew of The Sopranos *film the Final Episode on location.*

Mafia by asking the question: What would happen if a shrewd but depressed mobster, struggling to operate a RICO-diminished business while maintaining a healthy suburban lifestyle, suffered an "is-that-all-there-is" midlife crisis?[100] The answer could be found between 1999 and 2007 on one of the most riveting shows to ever grace the airwaves. As sardonic and darkly funny as *The Sopranos* routinely was, it was also brutally honest and at times shockingly gruesome. A serial noir that raised the bar on quality, *The Sopranos* seamlessly mixed sex and violence and mob cuisine with robust amounts of psychotherapy to the gratitude of millions of adoring subscribers.

The story of *The Sopranos* was initially conceived by veteran television writer, producer, and director David Chase as a feature film about "a mobster in therapy, having problems with his mother."[101] After input from his manager, however, Chase decided to adapt it into a television series. In 1995, David Chase signed a development deal with the Brillstein-Grey production company and wrote the pilot script.[102] Drawing heavily from his personal life experience growing up in New Jersey, Chase applied his own family dynamic to his mobsters.[103]

As the series began, Tony Soprano (James Gandolfini) was a capo (Mafia captain) in the New Jersey-based DiMeo crime family, but would be promoted to DiMeo's underboss after Season One. Yet, Tony was also the patriarch of the Soprano family household and had to reconcile family life at home with his Mafia career. Suffering panic attacks because of his duplicitous nature, Tony seeks the help of psychiatrist Jennifer Melfi (Lorraine Bracco) and begins to revisit his relationship with his poisonous mother, Livia (Nancy Marchand), who dies after Season Two before any revelations are made. Shuttling between his meat-market Mafia clubhouse, the Bada Bing Strip Club, and his Jersey Lake home, Tony managed to avoid prison, kill his rivals, deal with his children's school problems, and convince his wife Carmela (Edie Falco) that the affairs he was prone to having meant nothing.[104] While their marriage was constantly challenged by Tony's brazen infidelity, Carmela herself struggled to reconcile the cold reality of Tony's mafia business with the material rewards it brought her.

---

100 *Fifty Years of Television*, p 55

101 *Written By*—"Wiseguys: A conversation with David Chase and Tom Fontana" 2007 May

102 *Vanity Fair*—"An American Family" 2007 April

103 Salon.com—"Chasing TV" 2007 August

104 *Fifty Years of Television*, p 55

Tony's close circle of cronies within the DiMeo crime family included relatives like cousin Christopher Moltisanti (Michael Imperioli), but mostly friends and confidants like his consigliere, Silvio Dante (Steven Van Zandt), and pals Paul "Paulie Walnuts" Gualtieri (Tony Sirico) and Salvatore "Big Pussy" Bonpensiero (Vincent Pastore). All were longtime Mafia soldiers and close allies who had broken into the business working for Tony's father. As the saga unfolds, Tony Soprano finds himself a man burdened with too much responsibility, teetering on the balance beam between mayhem and salvation.

Many critics have asserted that *The Sopranos* is the greatest and most groundbreaking television series of all time. The writing, acting, and directing have often been singled out for praise, while the show has also received considerable attention from critics and journalists for its mature and artistic content, technical merit, music selections, cinematography, and willingness to deal with difficult and controversial subjects.[105]

The New Yorker editor David Remnick called the show "the richest achievement in the history of television."[106] "Perhaps the greatest pop-culture masterpiece of its day," said *Vanity Fair* contributor Peter Biskind.[107] Following its initial airing in 1999, *The New York Times* stated, "[*The Sopranos*] just may be the greatest work of American pop-culture in the last quarter century."[108] And *TV Guide* ranked *The Sopranos* fifth on their list of the "Top 50 TV Shows of All Time,"[109] though it should be noted that no drama finished in front of it, just comedies: *Seinfeld*, *I Love Lucy*, *The Honeymooners*, and *All in the Family*. The fact that a landmark series this good was produced by a network that had only been in the prime time series business for little more than a decade spoke volumes about how far and how fast the cable television business had grown.

Perhaps the strongest accolade came from costar Edie Falco who, in character as Tony's wife Carmela during one of the episodes, says to her husband: "You're like an alien life force among us"[110]—and she was partly right. James Gandolfini, alongside creator David Chase, were indeed "out of this world" in helping to make *The Sopranos* the crowning achievement of 20th century prime time series television that it was.

---

105 *Time*—"The Sopranos – The 100 Best TV Shows of All-TIME" October 2007

106 *The New Yorker*—"Family Guy" 2007 June

107 *Vanity Fair*—"An American Family 2007 April

108 *Stanford* Magazine—"Family Man" 2002 September/October

109 *Fifty Years of Television*, p 254

110 PopMatters—"Part 4: Feasts from the Fringe" 2007 October

Discussion Questions

B. Cable Upstarts

- What was the initial reason for the emergence of cable stations during their first quarter century on the air?
- What is meant by the "two tier" arrangement that helps define cable television?
- What do you feel was the initial reason to pay for premium cable TV when there were already awarding winning series being offered by the broadcast networks?

D. Band Identities

- By the 1990's, broadcasting was slowly being supplanted by niche-casting. Cable channels were branding themselves for marketing purposes and broadcast TV wasn't far behind. What were the broadcast network brands?

E. Nielsen Ratings

- What is the value of the *Nielsen Ratings* to networks?

F. Family Values

- The TV sitcom families of the 1980's differed from those in the 1990's in what respect? How did "family values" in '80's and 90's sitcoms affect TV programming during their respective decade? How would family shows from one decade have fared in the other?

G. Class of '93

- In the 90's, the creators of the 'hot' shows became household names to fervent fans. Who were these men and what shows were introduced under their creative control?

H. Dramatic Juggernaut

- What show was referred to in this chapter as 'cast proof'? What evidence is offered to support this claim?

I. Masters of Their Domain

- *Seinfeld*, sometimes referred to as the sitcom about nothing, garnered critical acclaim and a loyal audience. What was the "nothing" in the show that made it the Number 1 television series of the 20th century?

J. Tossed Salads and Scrambled Eggs

- For a show to produce a spin-off, certain characters seem to take on a life of their own. What was the premise of *Frasier*, where did the lead character by the same name hail from, and what led the series to such a successful run?

K. The Struggle for Network Supremacy

- *Home Improvement* and *Everybody Loves Raymond* were sitcoms that revolved around two families. From what you read, do you think the audience share these comedies commanded drew their audience from the same demographic or from different ones? Explain.

L. Hope and Kelley

- Why do you think changing a program from one night of the week to another can make or break a show? How was this in the case of the 1994 medical series, *ER*?

- Given that *Chicago Hope* and *ER* seemed to share some of the same genes, what speculation was given for the bigger success of *ER*?

M. Two Mints in One

- David E. Kelley's 1996 *The Practice* and 1997 *Ally McBeal* added to Kelley's growing resume of hit shows. What was the premise of each and how were different from the many shows that preceded them?

N. Lose Some, Win Some

- In 1999, *West Wing* put the White House in American households and helped to change Americans' perceptions about politicians and politics. Writer Aaron Sorkin's successful drama was appealing on what levels with viewers?

O. Guns and Roses

- 1998 *saw Sex and the City* on HBO followed the next year by *The Sopranos*. What elements in these premium cable shows separate them from broadcast television? What trends in TV watching did these HBO series start?

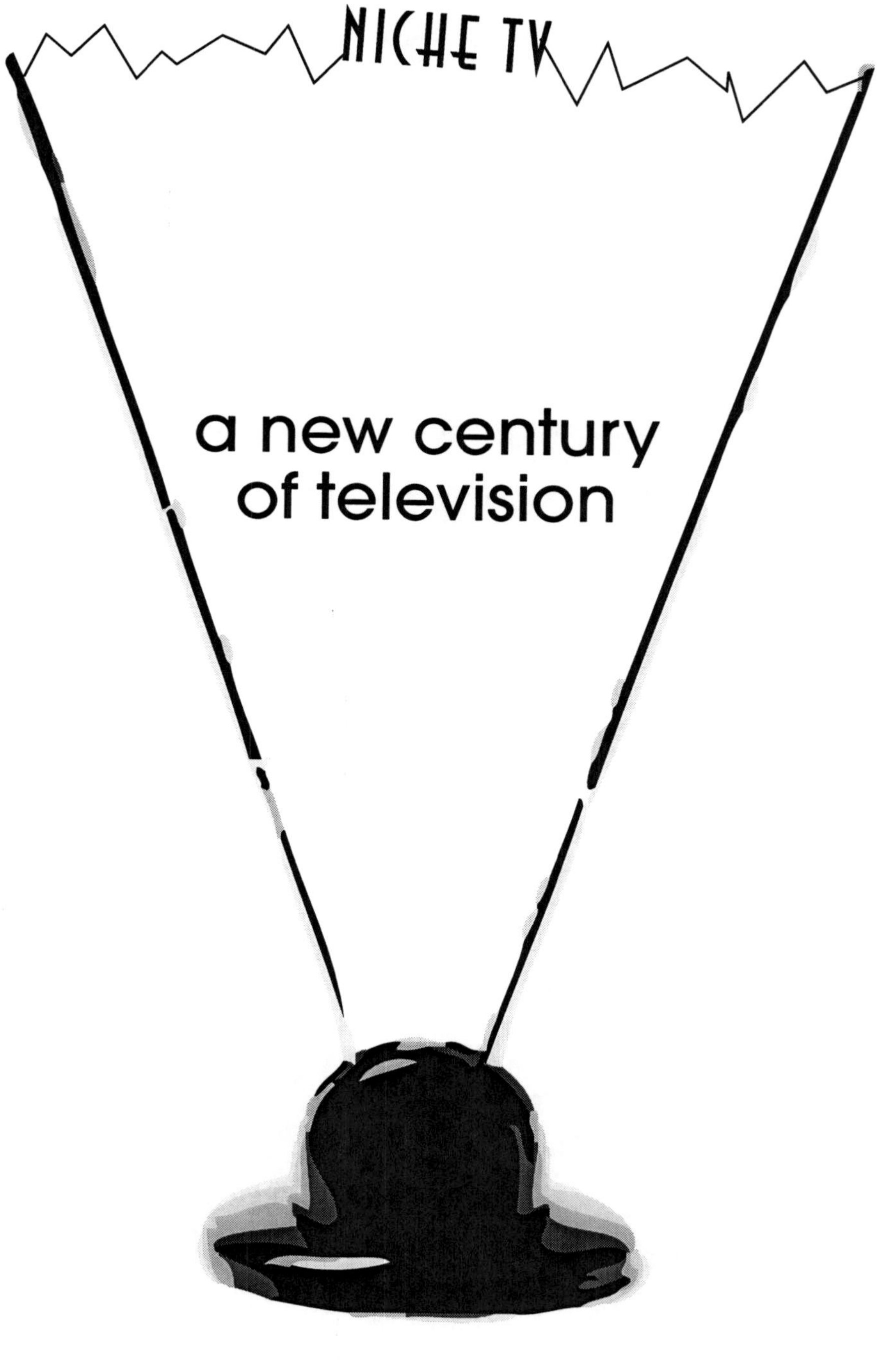
NICHE TV
a new century of television

CHAPTER FIFTEEN

Paradigm Shift

2000–2012

Reality Check

In his much-touted book of 1962, The Structure of Scientific Revolutions, twentieth-century American physicist Thomas Kuhn asserted that *paradigm shifts* occurred in science when changes took place in the basic assumptions—or paradigms—of a ruling theory.[1] Kuhn held that a student outside the sciences, working in the humanities, for example, would rarely, if ever, come across a shift in primal assumptions, because "shifts" in disciplines apart from science rarely varied in any meaningful way. Changes in what was *fashionable* from one era to the next, argued Kuhn, did not constitute a shift in paradigms. Habits, tastes, verbiage, fashion, gender power, and ruling political parties in America changed all the time, but the basic construct of language, or constitutional law, or cotton fabric remained the same.

1 The Structure of Scientific Revolutions, p 139

Moreover, these superficial changes could come and go and come again. Like fads, changes in the humanities or the arts could be revisited. Not so with science. Galileo's discovery that the earth revolved around the sun altered scientific thought and redefined 17th-century Europe's place in the world as well as the solar system. There was no going back. Newton's discovery of gravity altered the accepted notions of 18th-century physics. Two centuries later, Einstein's "Theory of Mass and Energy and Special Relativity" corrected Newton, once again changing the paradigm of physics while redefining man's limitations on Earth.

Unlike physics, the paradigm shifts defining the electronic frontier moved us forward at the speed of sound and light. Heinrich Hertz "jumped" a spark across a gap and the communications industry went airborne. Marconi harnessed Hertzian waves and the wireless emerged. Philo Taylor Farnsworth created the picture tube, and radios could suddenly see.

By the 1960's and continuing through the end of the century, "paradigm shifts" were occurring in business-models *apart* from science, and the term was routinely applied to non-scientific events. University of Sussex linguistics professor R.L. Trask, in his turn-of-the-millennium book, Mind the Gaffe: A Troubleshooter's Guide to English Style and Usage, suggests that the term "paradigm shift" was being overused as the century wound down and its power diminished. Many in science felt that sensationalists in the non-science world were using the phrase as a synonym for seminal change in products, corporations, or ideas where no such change truly existed.[2] Two years earlier, however, in the world of TV programming, that was not the case. Seminal change collided with TV industry muse, head-on—and the paradigm that had guided prime time television programming through its first fifty years inexplicably shifted gears.

By the summer of 1999, Conrad Riggs, a young TV business-affairs executive, had left his network desk job and gone to work for an energetic, if still unproven, British producer named Mark Burnett. Burnett had secured the U.S. rights to a British TV show called *Sole Survivor,* from British television producer Charlie Parsons, who'd come up with the reality-based concept in 1992. For two years, Burnett and Riggs had pitched Parson's concept around Hollywood—a pitch calling for a new kind of prime time television show with enormous potential, and one that no American TV audience had ever seen.[3] Four years earlier, ABC had been offered the project by Burnett, alone, before he'd even secured American rights from Parsons, but alas they had finally passed on the project for the *second* time.[4] Worries over projected revenue and unknown production costs made ABC nervous, and the network had ultimately turned it down. That was the bad news. The good news was that this recent "final pass" by ABC, while taking four long years to come, now left Burnett and Riggs free to visit CBS.

2 Mind the Gaffe!: A Troubleshooter's Guide to English Style and Usage

3 Desperate Networks, p 67

4 Desperate Networks, p 67

That visit took some doing, but on July 27, 1999, Mark Burnett and Conrad Riggs met with a hungry young development executive at CBS named Ghen Maynard and pitched their idea.[5] Maynard was what ad men in the 1950's might have tabbed a junior executive. Yet, even so, Maynard wasn't naïve to what he was about to hear. Riggs had sent over a sample of Burnett's talent "reel" that included a show Burnett had created and produced for The Discovery Channel called *Eco-Challenge*—a documentary-like show where "real people" challenged Mother Nature and often got the worst of it. Maynard thus knew, as the meeting started, that "reality TV" was on the table.

In truth, reality television as a genre was not new. The concept of non-actors reacting honestly to life began on radio with Allen Funt's *Candid Microphone* as early as 1947. Funt was a television writer, producer, director, and TV personality who came up with a winning format that actually outlasted the century. On August 10, 1948, Funt brought his radio concept to prime time television and changed the show's name to *Candid Camera*.[6] The series on television involved concealing cameras and filming ordinary people being confronted with unusual situations. Sometimes "trick" props were used to baffle and frustrate the unwitting participants, who had no idea they were being filmed. When the joke was revealed, victims would blush at the show's catchphrase: "Smile, you're on *Candid Camera*." The format appeared on U.S. TV networks and in syndication aftermarkets in each succeeding decade, and on through the show's final original broadcast on May 5, 2004.

And *Candid Camera* was not alone. Other unscripted shows on the networks during that 1948–49 season included *Talent Scouts* (predecessor to *American Idol* and a top-ten show for the first five years of network TV), and two contestant game shows: *Quizzing the News* and *Break the Bank*. Just as *Candid Camera* had been preceded in radio by *Candid Microphone*, so had these quiz and talent shows first been heard on radio. Radio game shows like *The $64 Question*, and talent contests like *Ted Mack's Original Amateur Hour* had come first.

With the arrival of 1950's, other TV game-participant shows appeared on television. *Beat the Clock* and *Truth or Consequences* were two early "reality" offerings in the genre, both involving non-acting contestants in wacky competitions or hilarious stunts. As it turned out, quiz and game shows were among the most popular *unscripted* prime time television fare of the decade. Top 20 shows of that era included *The $64,000 Question*, *Twenty-One*, *I've Got a Secret*, *The Price Is Right*, and *You Bet Your Life*, hosted by comic icon Groucho Marx. The *fact*-based series *You Asked for It* (1950–1959) was driven by viewer requests (as the series' title implies), and could rightly be seen as the precursor of today's audience participation-driven reality TV shows, where viewers cast votes to help determine the course of each episode.

Late in the 1950's it was learned that several of these game shows had, in fact, been rigged for profit, and that the American TV audience had been duped into thinking otherwise. Not surprisingly, the genre's

---

5 Desperate Networks, p 70

6 Infoplease.com—"Reality TV Takes Hold" 2000 May

popularity declined throughout much of the 1960's. Networks countered the programming loss with violent dramas and escapist humor and a glut of mediocre variety shows. While game shows did return in the 1970's with contestant-driven series like *The Dating Game*, *Jeopardy*, and *The Newlywed Game*, these shows were *not* seen in prime time, but rather as syndicated shows (off-network programming) in the hours leading up to prime time. Still, they featured non-acting people speaking without cue cards, and that template has served them well. All three of these syndicated game shows have spanned more than five decades on television and still continue be shown to this day.[7]

As the 1970's commenced, however, a new kind of prime time reality show was being conjured up by an unlikely prime time network—the Public Broadcasting Service (PBS). From May 30, 1971 through New Year's Eve that year, PBS produced as different a television series as had ever graced the airwaves, documenting the day-to-day moments of an average American family for seven long months.[8] On January 11, 1973, after being edited down from over 300 hours of raw footage, PBS ran the commercial-free series, *An American Family*, as 12 one-hour episodes on Thursday nights at 9:00 pm, grabbing viewers away from commercial programming by the tens of thousands.[9]

In 1973, the Loud Family became An American Family *on PBS. Back (from left): Kevin, Grant, Delilah, and Lance Loud. Front (from left): Michele, Pat, and Bill Loud*

For an hour each week, viewers (whom some critics at the time referred to as "voyeurs") stepped into the Santa Barbara, California, home of Bill and Pat Loud, and over the next twelve weeks watched this average family of seven deteriorate in front their eyes. The groundbreaking program documented the break-up of the Loud family via the separation and subsequent divorce of parents Bill and Pat Loud. Under the unblinking gaze of the documentary cameras, viewers were privy to intimate secrets, bursts of raw emotional anger, and several seminal moments in the series. In Episode Two, viewers watched as Lance Loud, eldest of the five Loud children, revealed to his mother, on a trip the two had taken to New York, that he was gay. Later in episode eight, viewers recoiled when Pat Loud asked her philandering husband Bill to move out of the house.[10]

7 *New York Times*—"Bachelor No. 1 And the Birth of Reality TV" January 26, 2003

8 *Fifty Years of Television*, p 156

9 *Fifty Years of Television*, p 156

10 PBS—*An American Family* Anniversary Edition 2011 July

Popular reaction varied, but many prominent viewers agreed that it was a watershed moment in prime time programming. No less than anthropologist Margaret Mead proclaimed the camera-as-witness series "as new and significant as the invention of drama or the novel."[11] Yet *An American Family* also triggered a rash of sharp criticism. The Louds themselves refuted the documentary as a distorted view of their lives. Said Pat Loud in her 1974 autobiography, Pat Loud: A Woman's Story, "The family felt that [producer Craig] Gilbert and the editors were too eager to include pessimistic scenes," adding that if she had known then what she knew now, she would never have consented to do the show.[12] Some critics balked at her and her husband's naïveté, wondering how an upper-middle class family like the Louds could be hoodwinked into putting themselves in front of the cameras, 24 hours a day—especially when those cameras were being wielded by Oscar-winning documentarians Alan and Susan Raymond.

Following *An American Family's* final episode, one truth was clear. Whatever controversies the series may have had, the show proved that "reality" programming—like a train wreck—holds a gripping fascination all its own.[13] It was this discovery along with the Writers' Guild strike of 1988 that would lead to several unscripted series in the 1990's. FOX came first, in 1989, with *Cops*, a series born out of the WGA strike in an effort to keep their prime time pipeline filled. The show was cheap to produce and required no actors, writers, or expensive set-ups; and it would later lead to a second unscripted FOX series in the '90's, *When Animals Attack*. The MTV reality television series *The Real World* (1992–08) was sandwiched into this mix as well. Later in the decade, there would of course be ABC's contestant-driven *Who Wants to Be a Millionaire*—the #1-rated prime time show for 1999. As the century turned, however, a final reality show would rear its head—this one over at CBS. The series not only ushered in the new century in eye-popping style, but also went on to alter the paradigm of prime time programming across the tube.

The Tribe Has Spoken

The prime time series that Mark Burnett pitched to CBS "junior" executive Ghen Maynard in the summer of 1999 was called *Survivor*, and everything about it sounded wildly unique. The series Burnett was proposing sounded like a cross between *Who Wants to Be a Millionaire* and *Lord of the Flies*.[14] The show would maroon a group of 16 strangers (acting as one or more tribes) in a desolate locale with just the clothes on their backs, a sack of rice, and one luxury item (done away with in subsequent seasons), be it a toothbrush, notebook, or a pair of sunglasses. Each contestant would then provide food, water, fire, and shelter for themselves, while competing in challenges to earn either a reward or immunity from "expulsion" during the next round of contestant-elimination votes. The last two or three survivors, explained Burnett, would face a jury composed of those players already voted off the show. This jury would

11 *Fifty Years of Television*, p 156
12 *Fifty Years of Television*, p 156
13 *Fifty Years of Television*, p 156
14 *Fifty Years of Television*, p 108

Richard Hatch was the first contestant to win the title of "Sole Survivor," and with it the one million dollars.

interrogate the final few "survivors," then vote for the winner of the game. The show's title of "Sole Survivor" would be worth one million dollars in prize money to one worthy champion.

The payoff for Maynard was Burnett's explanation of how the concept could play out as a microcosm of society, complete with leaders, bullies, and ruthless cliques. Maynard had been a social psychology major at Harvard and was immediately enthralled by the dynamics in play.[15] On a tropical island, sixteen half-naked contestants (initially chosen from 16,000 applications, then "whittled down" to 800 videotaped interviews) endured hardship, surmounted challenges, formed allegiances, and struggled to avoid elimination in order to win one million dollars for twelve weeks' work. The show, as Burnett described it, was hip and sexy, and Maynard thought it just the kind of series CBS president and CEO Les Moonves was trying to find in an effort to lower the network's older-skewing demographic. A show that would draw the all-important 18–49 audience to CBS without sending the network's core audience of retirees off to the History Channel.[16]

It took five months, but on 24 November 1999, Mark Burnett, Conrad Riggs, and several of the executives at CBS who were backing the project sat down in Les Moonves' office so their boss could hear the pitch. The green light for the series wasn't immediate—Moonves wanted the show to pay for itself before committing to it. Burnett and Riggs went out and acquired the sponsors necessary to cover the advertising revenue for each of the 13 shows they'd been promised, and on Wednesday night, May 31, 2000, CBS premiered the series. With the May rating sweeps having come and gone, *Survivor* was assured of facing only minimal, if any, original programming. Sensing what CBS was up to, however, ABC announced that they would be airing a "new" episode of *Who Wants to Be a Millionaire* to go head to head with *Survivor* that Wednesday. The fact that … *Millionaire* was the #1 prime time show didn't bode well for CBS and *Survivor*. Some thought the ABC move punitive since CBS had been able to succeed where ABC had twice failed. Moonves shared those beliefs, but Stu Bloomberg, an ABC executive, defended his network's move. "It's a competition, isn't it?" he stated rhetorically. "Obviously we don't want them to get on the air and get traction."[17] But traction is exactly what CBS got.

The following morning's ratings brought cheers from CBS executives, and instantly raised the network's morale. ABC and their popular game show had drawn 17 million viewers to CBS's 15.3 million, that's true, but CBS and *Survivor* had beaten the ABC game show in every category of younger viewers: 18–49, 18–34, and even teens (12–17)—demographics CBS hadn't reached with any numbers in years. The

15 Desperate Networks, p 70
16 Desperate Networks, p 71
17 Desperate Networks, p 84

following Wednesday, ABC tried again to derail *Survivor*, but again their effort was thwarted—especially with the young. This outcome staggered ABC. Here they had just announced that their game show was adding a fourth edition per week to their fall schedule, and now, thanks to *Survivor*, that very game show was looking vulnerable.

For twelve years, now, and twenty-four seasons (spring and fall of each television year through spring 2012), *Survivor* (2000–) has been one of the top 20 most-watched shows for 22 of those 24 seasons, and in the top 10 for it first eleven seasons on television.[18] That first season on the island of Palau Tiga near Borneo (*Survivor*: *Borneo*), contestant Richard Hatch became the show's first millionaire and proved to the world that secret alliances and greed can be a winning combination. Hosting the show since its inception through 2012, Jeff Probst continued to moderate the Tribal Counsel at the end of each show, during which tribe mates vote one of their own out of the tribe and off the show. The first time each player visits Tribal Council, they are asked to take a torch and light it from the fire pit present at every Council. It is understood that fire represents the contestant's life. As long as the contestant has fire, they are still in the game. As the series catchphrase goes: "When your fire's gone so are you."[19]

The meteoric rise of *Survivor* was unexpected. No one could have foretold the fanfare the series received. Two weeks into its 2000 summer run, CBS executives were already touting exotic locales as possible destinations for the following "season," which CBS Chief Leslie Moonves wanted ready by January.[20] The sequels were already starting and would take viewers from the Australian Outback to the Brazilian Highlands (*Survivor: Tocantins*) to the Mayan Ruins (*Survivor: Guatemala*) and on to China, each for 12-week seasons and 13 shows. The series quickly became the leader in American reality television, and the first reality series to realize both high ratings and significant profit. The American public had something to do with that. By season two and for half of the next decade, the *Survivor* series was being watched by upwards of 25 million weekly viewers; and some weeks that count came close to (and at times passed) the 50M mark.[21] Moreover, because the show had tapped into the all-important 18–49 demographic category, advertisers were paying millions of dollars more to CBS for each commercial hour.

By 2005, however, the show's sizzling popularity had begun to wane. Not only was the genre becoming more and more familiar, but the world of reality television had grown exponentially more competitive in the five years since *Survivor's* debut. Worse, word spread that the "reality" on *Survivor* seemed contrived, and that contestants now seemed too affected with their own stardom. Yet, that aside, watching regular folks plot and scheme against one another in an exotic locale was fresh and original. Moreover, the cost of the hour episodes ran, on average, between one-tenth and one-fifth of the cost of conventional hour programming. Ten o'clock dramas were costing networks two to three million dollars in 1999—and a series like NBC's *West Wing*, well over that. *Survivor*'s costs, on the other hand, ran between $500K and

18 *The Atlantic*—"Survivor… 10 Years Later: Why It's Outlasted Its Competition" 2011 February

19 CBS Prime Time TV Series—Survivor (various seasons)

20 Desperate Networks, p 86

21 U.S. Nielsen Ratings—"2000–2001 TV Season" May 2001

$700K per episode—90% less than the cost of *West Wing*. Yet, even at one-tenth the cost, the series was still able to garner more advertising dollars (because of its demographics) than most of the expensive hour dramas. Thus, *Survivor*, even in "decline," was a win-win deal for CBS. While *Survivor* was named the Number One reality series of all time by Entertainment Weekly in 2009,[22] more important to history was the fact that the show became prime time TV's answer to America's guilty pleasure, leading viewers on a descent into voyeurism from which they have never returned.[23]

Early Rumblings

With the success of CBS's *Survivor* in the summer of 2000, reality TV proved itself more than ready for prime time television, and on the verge of global popularity that has only marginally, if ever, been slowed. Since 2000, reality shows in general—and *Survivor* and *American Idol* (the runaway reality ratings hit of the new century's first ten years), in particular—have continually topped the U.S. TV ratings season-average in every year of this century. *Survivor* actually led the TV ratings in 2001, while *American Idol* lorded over the Nielsen ratings for seven consecutive years (2004–11). Moreover, *Survivor* and the *American Idol* series, along with shows like *America's Next Top Model, Dancing with the Stars, Fear Factor, Big Brother*, and *The Apprentice* have all been successfully syndicated in dozens of countries around the world.

NBC saw the "unscripted" writing on the wall as early as 2001, and leaped into the reality series business with two new game shows. The first was imported from Great Britain and titled *The Weakest Link*. The second, *Fear Factor*, was created here in the United States. With *The Weakest Link*, NBC hoped to short-circuit ABC's *Who Wants to Be a Millionaire*, but the NBC series never really caught on, lasting only two seasons. For a time, the sports stunt/dare reality game show *Fear Factor* did rival *Survivor* for the same audience, and did become a hit show during its maiden summer on the air, in 2001. The show built strong ratings for the next couple seasons, but over the final few years, its ratings declined. In 2006, FOX's interactive-singing reality series, *American Idol*, was seen on Tuesday nights, and *Fear Factor*'s ratings descended even further. NBC put its show on hiatus for the remainder of 2006 season before officially canceling *Fear Factor* that May. Even so, over its five-year run, *Fear Factor* became the first network reality show in history to be syndicated, and earned NBC a reported $600 million in advertising revenue while on the air.[24]

What gains NBC might have made on *Fear Factor*, they squandered on shows like *Lost*—a short-lived reality-travel game show similar to ABC's *The Amazing Race*. Yet, NBC wasn't alone in its reality failures. The Peacock network could draw consolation from the fact that ABC and FOX continued to flounder in the reality game as well. Reality shows with low ratings in 2000 and 2001 included ABC's *The Amazing*

---

22 *Entertainment Weekly*—"20 Best Reality Shows Ever" 2009 July

23 *Fifty Years of Television*, p 108

24 *Entertainment Weekly*—"NBC Reviving Fear Factor" June 2, 2011

Race and *The Mole*, while FOX's game shows *Boot Camp* and *Who Wants to Marry a Multi-Millionaire* never really got started. *The Mole* and *Boot Camp* would be canceled in short order and ABC's *The American Race* retooled and renewed for another season (a retooling that rekindled viewer interest and turned the series around). But it was FOX's second entry in the 2000 season, *Who Wants to Marry a Multi-Millionaire* that provided a lesson all networks looking to dive into reality television would have to learn.

That lesson was learned first-hand by Mike Darnell, FBC's impresario of reality TV, in the months immediately preceding *Survivor*'s spectacular run on CBS. Darnell was an "idea-man" with connections to his ultimate boss, News Corp's CEO, Rupert Murdoch. Partly because of that and partly because it was a money-making venture, no one at FOX got in Darnell's way. Thus, in February of 2000, as an answer to ABC's hit game show *Who Wants to Be a Millionaire*, Darnell had come up with a surefire response. Darnell had been to a family wedding earlier the previous year, and while watching the marriage ceremony, he'd come up with an idea for a blockbuster series. Darnell connected the dots and likened the fascination that people have for weddings with the fascination people have with making lots of money—like they did on ABC's *Who Wants to Be a Millionaire*. Both ideas represented facets of the American Dream. Getting rich and getting married seemed to Darnell to be two sides of the same cultural coin.[25] Mike Darnell meant to wed them.

The two-hour program that Darnell would come to propose was outlandish. A virtual beauty pageant of single women would vie to marry an unseen man just to get his money. The politically incorrect FOX Special *Who Wants to Marry a Multi-Millionaire* aired in February 2000 and was a runaway hit in the ratings. Better yet, the ratings for the show escalated at 30-minute intervals for the entire duration of the show, indicating that women were phoning, texting, or I.M.ing other women *during* the show to alert friends who might not have been watching. Its runaway success made Mike Darnell the talk of Hollywood, if not the National Organization for Woman (NOW). Despite the program's high ratings, the series was harshly condemned by liberal and conservative alike. The liberal-leaning NOW branded the show "exploitative," while the conservative-leaning Media Research Center denounced the show as "demeaning."[26]

And that was the good news. The bad news for Mike Darnell and FOX came scarcely a week later, while Rick Rockwell, the show's multi-millionaire, and Darva Conger, his bride, were on their honeymoon. Questions were suddenly raised by the press about just how rich Rockwell really was. FOX stated that Rockwell had $750,000 in liquid assets and a net worth of just more than $2 million.[27] While it appeared Rockwell did have some real estate holdings in San Diego, several of his other claims were called into question. Rockwell claimed, for example, to have given up his career as a comedian in 1990 in order to become a motivational speaker, yet several organizations where he was to have spoken said they had never hired him.[28]

---

25 Desperate Networks, p 92

26 *People*—"TV's Reality check" March 20, 2000

27 *People*—"TV's Reality check" March 20, 2000

28 *New York Times*—"Fox Network Will End 'Multimillionaire' Marriage Specials" February 22, 2000

And then came the "smoking gun." One of Rockwell's former girlfriends had filed a restraining order against him for domestic violence in 1991. The woman alleged that Rockwell assaulted her and stalked her when she tried to break off their engagement.[29] Rockwell swore the incident had been badly exaggerated, but that it had happened at all presented FOX with a public relations nightmare that only got more embarrassing when it was finally discovered that Rick Rockwell wasn't their star's real name. After returning from her honeymoon, nurse Darva Conger quickly expressed regret for taking part in the show and had the marriage annulled. FOX pleaded innocent but it didn't matter. The vetting they had run on Rick Rockwell wasn't as complete as it should have been. The network was now responsible for putting an "innocent" woman contestant together with an alleged woman-beater, using an alias, on prime time television, and nothing FOX said or did could change that. Due to the controversy, FOX not only canceled a scheduled repeat of the episode, but shut down any future installments on the show as well. Though the special was lucrative for FOX and the concept franchiseable, the fallout from women would likely negate any long-term financial gains by the series, and could well find female viewers turning away from the network altogether.[30]

What networks were discovering was that reality television, while cheaper to produce and much of the time wildly original, was also tougher to control. The genre's spontaneity was both the bane and the beauty of every series. While shows could appear fresh and original, there was always the chance in an unscripted series that contestants or stunts could go awry, and the series blow up in the network's face. On the CBS series *Big Brother*, for example, where contestants are housed communally together in Orwellian fashion with cameras watching their every move, claustrophobia has led to real, on-camera fistfights that have resulted in legal entanglements for the network and its producers. Same with contestants on ABC's *The Amazing Race*, as well as the syndicated series *Cheaters*. With unscripted material and non-acting contestants comes less network control, the possibility of marginalizing the life of the series, or even destroying the network's brand.[31]

Rescue Me

While a network's brand was core to its audience and always on the minds of its executives, there came a Tuesday morning in September of 2001 when it ceased to matter at all. Reflecting back on that ill-fated day, network branding was the last thing on the minds of Americans—even the misanthropic network executives normally hip-deep in cut-throat television programming. On this day and for the next several months, Americans pooled sympathies and opened their hearts.

29 *Time*—"An Online Paper Trail" February 27, 2000

30 *Time*—"An Online Paper Trail" February 27, 2000

31 *Newsweek*—"Will Reality TV Survive?" October 10, 2001

Though it's been over a decade since the terrorist attack of 9/11, pop culture still has questions about how to approach the greatest tragedy on U.S. soil since the American Civil War. Should the proper tone be direct, as with Oliver Stone's feature film *World Trade Center*, or Paul Greengrass' *United 93*? Or do we face up to it with denial as Adam Sandler did in the film "Reign Over Me," or with the bristling defiance of Spike Lee's *25th Hour*? Lee's story of Monty Brogan's last 24 hours of freedom before going to prison for dealing drugs is set against the aftermath of 9/11 and serves as much as an urban historical testament to a great city under siege.

Not knowing how to approach the subject of 9/11 has posed a challenge for filmmakers, authors, and artists in general. In the first few weeks following the attack, Hollywood rushed to erase images of the Twin Towers from films like *Zoolander* and *Serendipity*. A decade later, the culture is still reluctant to take on the events of that day. What *is* known is that the attacks resulted in the deaths of 2,996 people, including the 19 hijackers and 2,977 victims.[32] The victims included 246 on the four planes (from which there were no survivors), 2,606 in New York City in the towers and on the ground, and 125 inside the Pentagon.[33]

Time magazine book critic and best-selling author Lev Grossman says that "novelists specialize in making the familiar fresh and new, but even ten years later, the attacks still feel all too painfully fresh." Jeremy Gerard, theater critic for Bloomberg News adds that "We haven't seen a really great, lasting work of art that captures how we felt that day. What we've seen is more journalistic in tenor."[34] ARTNews executive editor Robin Cembalest shares that view: "In general, it's hard to make art on any kind of dramatic historic event. The great artworks on the great tragedies are the exception rather than the rule."[35]

Which is why it was odd to find that of all the art media that have tried to deal with this difficult subject, it was a prime time cable television series that best captured the heartbreaking stories connected to 9/11, as well as the vivid memories of a life-altering event which, for most Americans, will forever be fixed to a specific time and place. *Rescue Me*, created by actor Denis Leary and director Peter Tolan, imparts the story of a firefighter who spent 9/11 at Ground Zero and now has regular conversations with the ghost of his cousin who died trying to rescue office workers at the site. With alcoholism and rage used to cope with his post-9/11 life, FDNY senior firefighter Tommy Gavin (Denis Leary), and his Harlem firehouse carried the stories for seven seasons in the FX cable series *Rescue Me*.

"It's a thoughtful, literate, sophisticated treatment of a guy who already had a lot of major issues," says Robert Thompson, a Syracuse University professor. "September eleven just lit the fuse on those problems."[36] As the series beleaguered protagonist, Leary was electrifying in his role as Gavin, a deeply

---

32 The Online Rocket—"Lost lives remembered during 9/11 ceremony" September 12, 2008

33 CNN Archives—"First video of Pentagon 9/11 attack released" May 17, 2006

34 *New York Post*—"Works of Heart" September 2, 2011

35 *New York Post*—"Works of Heart" September 2, 2011

36 *New York Post*—"Works of Heart" September 2, 2011

Ground Zero "Tribute in Light" by the Municipal Art Society made its debut in 2002 at the 9/11 Memorial in Lower Manhattan

driven first-responder with a combustible personality and personal demons to match, though much of his disdain for social mores was due to the fact that he was a relapsed alcoholic. Through seven groundbreaking seasons, we followed his gripping story, along with those of his crew. Provocative, profane, and unflinchingly honest, the series served as an unforgettable journey of courage, conflict, and ultimate salvation. As the pilot episode commenced, Gavin struggled with the loss of his cousin and best friend, Jimmy Keefe, who frequently visited him in surrealistic visions. Gavin and his wife had already separated and Tommy had moved across the street. Though he was ill-tempered, self-destructive, hypocritical, and often manipulative, most of his actions were well-meaning.

The show was warmly greeted when it premiered in July of 2004, and garnered Denis Leary and Peter Tolan an Emmy nomination for Outstanding Writing in a Drama Series. Tolan also received an Emmy nomination for Outstanding Directing in a Drama Series, while Leary received a second Emmy nomination the following year, this one for Outstanding Lead Actor in a Drama Series. Critics praised the show's willingness to take risks and talk about family depression, alcoholism, homophobia, and the aftermath of the September 11, 2001 attacks.[37]

The debut episode was seen by almost 4.1 million viewers, ranking eighth all-time for series premieres in basic cable; and seasons one and two averaged 2.7 and 2.8 million viewers, respectively—again, solid basic cable numbers.[38] The series' final moments revealed that the show had come full-circle, and recalled the series' very first episode, with Tommy Gavin speaking to the new academy class. This time, however, Gavin does so with more clarity, and a warning for the "probies" not to drown their sorrows with sex, violence, and alcohol. Gavin, if not fully healed, was at least heading in the right direction. After seven tumultuous years on television, our poster boy for PTSD (post-traumatic stress disorder) had become a better person. And Tommy Gavin wasn't alone. In the three years following 9/11, New York had become a better city. The people had rallied, and one of their own, American tycoon Donald Trump, wanted to find a way to show his city off to the rest of world.

37 MSNBC—"Denis Leary plays with fire on 'Rescue Me'" August 3, 2006
38 ZAP2it—"FX Fired Up about 'Rescue Me' Ratings" July 24, 2004

You're Fired!

Going back three years, to the months immediately following the terrorist attack in New York City, the reality TV business seemed to plateau, leading some to speculate that reality television was a temporary fad that had pretty much run its course.[39] Mark Burnett disagreed and created a reality game show for NBC that would rival his early masterwork for CBS, *Survivor*. Hosted by Donald Trump, *The Apprentice* was billed as the "ultimate job interview" in the "ultimate jungle." Trump's extravagant lifestyle, outspoken manner, and role on the NBC reality series is why audiences were tuning in to watch. Love him or hate him, Trump was the driving force behind the first few seasons of the show. Even the show's logo made Donald Trump out to be just another skyscraper on the New York skyline.

The game show originally went like this. Sixteen to eighteen business-oriented people would compete in an elimination-style competition to win a one-year, $250,000 starting contract to run one of Donald Trump's companies. The show's contestants, or "candidates," came from various enterprises, but were typically found to have backgrounds in real estate, accounting, restaurant management, consulting, sales, and marketing. During the first six seasons of the 12-week show, the candidates were divided into teams and housed in a communal penthouse, allowing relationships to fester or grow depending on how the contestants reacted to one another. Each week, teams were assigned a task. One candidate from each team served as the project manager for that task, and the winning team received a reward. The losing team, however, faced "expulsion" at a boardroom meeting following the challenge, where one of its members would be "terminated" from the show. Each show typically ended with Trump delivering the bad news across the boardroom table in a catchphrase that became the euphemism of its day: "You're fired."

As the competition wound down, the final two candidates were assigned different tasks, each supported by teams made up of contestants who'd already been fired. After the tasks were completed, a final boardroom meeting occurred to select a winner. With testimonials from the team members and final chance for the candidates to prove themselves to Trump and the other judges on his tribunal (many times real CEO's), Trump would ultimately turn to one of the two finalists and utter the magic words every job applicant is dying to hear: "You're hired."

The Apprentice turned out to be the breakout rookie hit of the 2003–04 U.S. television season, drawing 20 million fans per episode,[40] and helped NBC at a time when the network's two long-running successful comedies, *Friends* and *Frasier*, were ending their series' runs. *The Apprentice* filled the void on Thursday nights as NBC held on to the tagline "Must-See TV," even though CBS was quickly becoming the most-watched network on Thursday night.

---

39 *Newsweek*—"Will Reality TV Survive?" October 10, 2001

40 U.S. Nielsen Ratings—"Viewership numbers of primetime programs 2003–04" 2004 May

On July 6, 2007, after a serious drop in audience share during seasons five and six (a third of what it was during season one), it was announced that *The Apprentice* had been renewed for a seventh and eighth season, but that the show would be retooled in an effort to revitalize interest in the series.[41] Beginning in January 2008, the show would now be called *The Celebrity Apprentice* and would feature celebrities (rather than unknown candidates) in competition with one another, each playing the game to raise money for various charities.[42] Moreover, the show would be cut back from *two* 12-week seasons a year to *one* 12-week season, commencing in first few months of each new year. British tabloid editor Piers Morgan was declared the first victor of *The Celebrity Apprentice*, while later winners would include Joan Rivers and Arsenio Hall.[43]

Although the series was still one of the most-watched programs on NBC through 2012, in the advertiser-friendly 18–49 age demographic, the franchise's total audience has greatly diminished. That *The Celebrity Apprentice* was renewed for a 13th season[44] is not only a testament to how important the 18–49 demographic is to advertisers, but also serves to punctuate NBC's fall from the pinnacle of TV ratings—a perch from whence it had once dominated prime time television with some of the most memorable TV series ever.

Pop Phenomenon

By the summer of 2002, three of the four biggest broadcast companies had breakout hit TV shows airing on prime time television. CBS had two, *Survivor* and *CSI* (a procedural crime drama that mushroomed into a cash cow for its network)—both launched as the millennium turned. NBC, for all its miscues of late, still had *Friends* and *ER*. Even anguished ABC had found magic that spring with its cheesy, romantic reality hit, *The Bachelor*—a series that seemed more staged than it did "real." It was simply unfair that the Fox Broadcasting Company had nothing even close to a national phenomenon in its programming division, save for the new hour-drama, *24*—a series received well by critics, but boasting only marginal ratings.

FOX needed a breakout hit of its own—the kind of hit, from which prime time nights are won and executive careers are carved—and no one knew that better than FOX entertainment division head Sandy Grushow. A month earlier at the "upfronts," in New York, Grushow faced down the grim task of selling his network's affiliates and advertisers on the first season in eight years at FOX that didn't have *Ally McBeal* or *The X-Files* in the mix.[45] The two greatest hour series in the network's history had finally been sent to

41 Realityworld.com—"Report: NBC to announce renewal of Donald Trump's *The Apprentice*" 2007 July

42 Tvseriesfinale.com—"The Apprentice: Trump Says NBC Wants Him Back" 2007 May

43 NBC.com—"Donald Trump and Mark Burnett Want to Help America Get Back To Work" 2010 March

44 *Deadline Hollywood*—"Full 2010–11 Season Series Rankings"

45 Desperate Networks, p 175

American Idol—The reality series every broadcast network passed up at least once turned out to be the series viewers loved to watch. The highest-rated prime time show on television for the past ten years is still tracking with audiences everywhere!

pasture. Grushow's job was to find a series that could take FOX to the Promised Land—and at a price the network could afford. The challenge presented a dichotomy that when solved would fill the coffers of both FBC and the new show's "unknown" producer Simon Cowell—a British music executive whom the FOX network planned to "lowball" in order to keep the costs down.

A year earlier, Cowell began this odyssey while sitting at a meeting in Los Angeles with executives from a network he'd never heard of before that morning, UPN (United Paramount Network), but seeing that Cowell had never pitched a TV series in America before, all things were more or less equal. Cowell had enormous faith in the idea that he and his partner Simon Fuller (manager of the '90's girl rock band, Spice Girls) had developed. After all, Fuller was the most successful manager of music acts in the U.K. and Cowell was the most successful artist-and-repertoire (A&R) man currently working in Britain. Both knew how to launch new singing artists, and now they had an idea for a show that would allow them to use their talents on camera.[46] If that weren't enough, Cowell and Fuller had just sold this same series in the U.K. This should have raised an eyebrow or two with the UPN execs, but alas, it did not. UPN, unimpressed, felt the pitch was little more than a "talent search" show and dismissed it out of hand. Even as Cowell argued passionately that the show was about discovery and the American Dream, no one at UPN was listening. One executive asked, dismissively, what it was Cowell thought UPN was supposed to do for him. When Cowell pointed out to the executive that it was Cowell who could help UPN, the room went silent and Cowell was shown the door.[47] It wouldn't be the last time that happened.

Cowell's direct, no-nonsense demeanor, though off-putting to some, was to become one of his greatest assets. At this early juncture, however, Cowell and Fuller were unknowns in America and their confidence and passion were often mistaken by network executives for unbridled arrogance. Nevertheless, Cowell and Fuller pitched the project to broadcast networks, to MTV and to other cable networks, always with the same result—"We'll get back to you." U.S. response to the series was in sharp contrast to the way *Pop Idol* (the British version of the show) had been sold in the U.K. The series overseas had taken all of 30

46 Desperate Networks, p 176

47 Desperate Networks, p 177

The face of American Idol, *British record executive and judge Simon Cowell*

seconds to sell, and by the fall of 2001, Cowell and Fuller had *Pop Idol* on the British airwaves.[48]

Alix Hartley, a British-born talent agent with an expertise in music and a strong affiliation with Hollywood's Creative Artists Agency (CAA), had seen *Pop Idol*'s first few episodes on British TV and wanted to help bring the Cowell-Fuller series to American television. At Hartley's urging, CAA lined up with Simon Cowell and Simon Fuller and went back with the project to all the networks that had refused the show the first time around. ABC said no again, in part because "the music gimmick" as a ratings tool had already failed twice in reality formats on two different networks, one of which was their own. In early 2000, ABC had tried out a show titled *Making the Band*, but could never find a demographic beyond prepubescent girls to watch it. The WB (Warner Bros Network) played to that very demographic, but already had its own talent-search project, *Pop Stars*, in the pipeline—a series patterned after the *Pop Idol* template, but for girl bands only. They said no as well. CAA then met with Jeff Gaspin, NBC's head of reality programming, but NBC passed on the project in the room. CAA had called Ghen Maynard at CBS but when the initial phone conversation went south, the project was left with one last legitimate shot, this one at FOX.[49]

The British producers had gotten nowhere with their pitch to FOX, earlier that spring, but Alix Hartley and Simon Fuller, cloaked in the CAA banner, went in to see Mike Darnell just the same. By the time the pitch took place in October 2001, reality television was again undergoing serious scrutiny in the wake of 9/11, and networks were already discussing "comfort television" programming (non-violent and non-offensive TV shows) until America recovered.[50] Mike Darnell was an idea-man of the first order who had managed to keep his job, even after the fiasco surrounding his project at FOX, *Who Wants to Marry a Multi-Millionaire*, a year earlier. But "comfortable" (as in safe) was not normally an adjective used to describe Darnell's programming ideas, nor, for that matter, the *Pop Idol* pitch. If the project was going down in flames, best that it be heard one final time by an executive who was not afraid to take chances. Darnell took the pitch and liked it, but told CAA that they'd have to find advertising for the project before FOX would order it (just like *Survivor* had been ordered to do over at CBS).

By early 2002, two things had happened to help the show's chances. First, CAA visited the Winter Olympics in Salt Lake City where their client, Coca-Cola, had a huge presence. When asked by CAA to come aboard

48 Desperate Networks, p 178
49 Desperate Networks, p 181
50 Desperate Networks, p 182

the *Pop Idol* project, Coke jumped at the chance.[51] The second thing that transpired was that *Pop Idol* in England was the runaway hit show of their 2001–02 fall season—a fact that did not go unnoticed. One of those watching *Pop Idol* in the U.K. was Elizabeth Murdoch, daughter of Rupert Murdoch, CEO of News Corp and owner of the FOX network. It turned out that Liz Murdoch was a fan of the series. When talks between FOX and CAA stalled over advertising dollars and license fees, Liz Murdoch was brought into the conversation by her friends at CAA and asked to go to bat for the American version of the show with her father, which she enthusiastically agreed to do.[52]

Sandy Grushow, head of FOX entertainment, thought the command decision that had come from Rupert Murdoch (Liz's father) to FOX to greenlight the series and up the original order from eight shows to fifteen had put the network in a bad position to conclude a favorable deal with Cowell and Fuller and CAA—and he was right. FOX had to give up ancillary rights to the producers, which, if they'd had the time, they would have won for themselves by grinding down the opposition. With Murdoch's mandate, however, they had no time, and grudgingly conceded backend perks to Cowell and Fuller. To help soften the blow, the network low-balled their face man (Cowell), paying him a paltry $25,000 to produce and "judge" the entire first season of the series, with no option for a second season.[53] Grushow's hopes for the summer series were decidedly modest, and he didn't want to be beholden to an unknown producer when the show fizzled out. While Grushow did feel the summer series would resonate well with teenage girls, he didn't see it gaining a foothold with the all-important 18–49 demographic and thus becoming the hit show FOX desperately needed.[54]

The show was renamed *American Idol: The Search for a Superstar* (shortened after season one to *American Idol*), but even before the show's debut on 11 June 2002, a major flaw in the show's original concept needed to be addressed. The judging wasn't the problem—the selection of Cowell's partners in crime went rather smoothly. FOX brought in Randy Jackson, onetime bass player for the band Journey, who had become a successful record producer for Columbia Records; and Paula Abdul who had solid musical credentials of her own to help judge the talent alongside Cowell. Ryan Seacrest won the host position (though Seacrest did co-host the first season with comedian Brian Dunkleman) with an on-screen enthusiasm that made him an overnight sensation—no worries there, either. The flaw, it turned out, revolved around how to schedule the "weekly vote." In England, *Pop Idol* had no problem with fan participation (voting for their favorite contestant). The U.K. was totally contained in a single time zone. Everyone in the country saw the series at the same hour and voted at the same time. The network news anchors would then announce that week's loser, two hours later, before signing off for the night.

That was problem for the American version of the show. FOX *didn't* have a ten o'clock prime time hour—their nightly news actually started at ten pm, immediately following the show. Thus, there was

51 Desperate Networks, p 184

52 *New York Times*—"How a Hit Almost Failed Its Own Audition" April 30, 2006

53 Desperate Networks, p 194

54 Desperate Networks, p 176

no two-hour voting-block available. Moreover, America had three mainland time zones to worry about (and during Standard Time, Hawaii lies three time zones west of Pacific Time and Alaska, one), meaning that people in the west would be seeing the show three hours after the people living in the east. Keeping to the Murdoch mandate that nothing be altered from the original series meant fans of the show in the west would never get to vote, while fans in the east would have only an hour to cast their own votes. None of that was going to work, and everyone at the meeting knew it. Among those in attendance was series creator Simon Fuller who wondered why the tally couldn't simply be announced the following morning. Again FOX blanched—the network didn't have a morning show, either. Preston Beckman, the scheduler at FOX, who was also at the meeting, threw out the best idea of the evening. "Really," he began, "the only thing I can think of is that we do a second show every week."[55] The series would thus feature a *performance* night and a *results* night and would run back to back on Tuesday and Wednesday nights. The unorthodox programming turned out to be a prime time boon for FOX.

Beckman's solution was implemented and the series was launched. The Tuesday night premiere was the most-watched show on American television that night, drawing nearly ten million viewers, giving FOX the best viewing figure for the 8:30 pm spot in over a year.[56] The Wednesday night edition passed eleven million; and both editions ranked even better among the young viewers, beating all competitors in the coveted 18-to-49 demographic. The audience steadily grew, and by finale night at summer's end, it had grown to more than 40 million viewers watching as Kelly Clarkson won top honors as the first "American Idol."[57] The series had something for everyone. Whether it was auditioning the warblers and the stars, side by side, or engaging viewers with the contestants through nationwide audience voting, or simply the presence of the caustic-tongued judge Simon Cowell giving each episode an edge no talent show (short of *Pop Idol* in Britain) had ever seen, the series grew into a pop phenomenon.[58]

The growth of the show continued to swell, right along with Simon Cowell's salary. That second season saw Cowell's salary grow from $25K per season to $50K per week.[59] The show itself started off better than it left off. With a season premiere of 26.5 million, the season went on to attract almost 22 million viewers per week, and was placed second overall amongst the 18-to-49 age group.[60] The Season Two finale saw Ruben Studdard defeat Clay Aiken on stage, and thereby become the second "American Idol" in America. The show became the highest-rated *American Idol* episode (ever) at 38 million for the final hour.[61] Before the start of the 2004 season, Simon Cowell was signed for three more seasons with a contract that would push his salary north of $8M per year. In hindsight, that seemed only fair. By season three, the show nobody had wanted to buy was now a runaway hit around the world. In the U.S., *American Idol* had

55 Desperate Networks, p 182
56 *BBC News*—"U.S. Pop Idol proves ratings hit" June 14, 2002
57 *New York Times*—"Success of 'American Idol' to Spawn Many Copycats" September 6, 2002
58 *BBC News*—"U.S. starts Pop Idol search" April 29, 2002
59 Desperate Networks, p 1195
60 *New York Times*—"Success of 'American Idol' to Spawn Many Copycats" September 6, 2002
61 Realitytvworld.com—"'American Idol's sixth season finale averages over 30 million viewers" 2007 May

become the top show on television in the 18-to-49 demographic grouping—a position it has held for all subsequent years up to and including Season Ten. Cowell's salary had grown right along with *Idol's* popularity. By the 2004–05 season, Simon Cowell was the number-one reason viewers were tuning in to the show. That year, *American Idol* had become the most-watched series among all viewers on American TV, with an average viewership of 26.8 million. The show reached its peak in season five with numbers averaging 30.6 million.[62]

In season ten, Cowell's last on the show, he'd seen his annual salary rise from eight million to 36 million to $144 million per season. While one hundred forty-four million dollars may seem like a lot of money for five months' work, it's but a fraction of the estimated $900 million (some sources say over a billion) that *American Idol* commands in ad dollars during those same five months.[63] These figures are truly staggering, but well deserved. Discounting its summer debut in 2002, *American Idol*, to date, has never finished out of the Nielsen Top 5; and from season two on, neither the performance day nor the results day has finished lower than third. In 2011, *American Idol* made more history when it became the first show to ever top a single night's Nielsen ratings for seven years in a row.[64]

The series was described by a rival TV executive as "the most impactful show in the history of television."[65] It has also become a recognized springboard for launching the career of many artists as bona fide stars. According to *Billboard* magazine, in its first ten years, "*American Idol* has spawned 345 *Billboard* chart-toppers and a platoon of pop idols, including Kelly Clarkson, Carrie Underwood, Jennifer Hudson, Clay Aiken, Jordin Sparks, and others, while remaining a TV ratings juggernaut."[66] And yet, this wealth of fame and fortune doesn't begin to tell the whole story. What *American Idol* did for the music industry pales in comparison to what it has done for the reality-TV business. The music business had been home to the "rising star" since CBS first gave singer Kate Smith her own radio show, 70 years before. Television, however, had been composed of hour dramas and 30-minute sitcoms and two-hour movies of the week. *American Idol* showed the power of a brand new genre and what it could do to a network's bottom line. The series delivered the American public to a genre that was cheaper to produce, easy to watch, and able to reach all-important youth market, so critical to securing advertising dollars. *American Idol* sold the business of reality television to the American public, and by doing so, opened up a niche market in cable television that now rivals broadcast TV for viewers and prime time advertising dollars, every night of the week.

---

62 Realitytvworld.com—"American Idol's sixth season finale averages of 30 million viewers" 2011 February

63 *New York Post*—"Simon Offered $144M to Stay on Idol" June 30, 2009

64 *USA Today*—"5 reasons American Idol may go on nearly forever--or not" January 17, 2012

65 *New York Times*—"For Fox's Rivals, American Idol Remains a 'Schoolyard Bully" February 20, 2007

66 *Billboard*—"Ten Years of American Idol Chart Dominance: Clarkson, Underwood ..." June 11, 2012

Housewives and Castaways to the Rescue

By the summer of 2003, morale inside the dour halls at ABC had settled into a kind of purgatorial malaise, where mediocrity had become the accepted order of the day. From a programming standpoint, not much was working. *Alias, My Wife and Kids*, and *Ten Simple Rules for Dating My Daughter* were the bright spots, to be sure, but when the latter two shows ran into the meteoric blast of twice-a-week *Idol*, their light was quickly dimmed.[67] ABC took note of FOX's success, and plugged reality into their own schedule, as well, with offerings like *Extreme Makeover, Are You Hot?*, and *I'm a Celebrity, Get Me Out of Here* (another *Survivor* knockoff), but nothing seemed to resonate with its dwindling audience-share. The network even stooped to gratuitous pandering with *The Search for America's Sexiest People*, featuring bodacious babes and chiseled hunks in skimpy swimsuits that left little to the imagination. Sadly, the groveling hadn't worked on any level. ABC's ratings were still lousy, and its sales even worse.[68]

Inside ABC, employees wondered how long it would be before the Disney managers became so uncomfortable with the people running the entertainment division of their "family friendly" network that heads began to roll. Lloyd Braun, chairman of ABC Entertainment, must have wondered himself, even while on vacation that summer in Hawaii. Braun's frustrations had peaked some months earlier when the bean-counters at Disney hamstrung him by undercutting his ability to land *The Apprentice*—the blockbuster hit series that went to NBC, instead. Braun had also watched the brass at Disney run *Who Wants to Be a Millionaire*, the network's only real hit in years, into the ground, airing it three to four times a week and cutting its shelf life in half. ABC had made only eleven pilots during the 2000–01 pilot season—one-third the industry average—and hadn't rebounded from the bloodbath yet.[69] Things might have been rosier had ABC bought *Survivor* or *CSI*, both of which they'd been offered before being picked up at CBS.

Suffice it to say, Lloyd Braun needed his vacation. That evening, Braun and his family ventured down to the hotel's annual clambake, and it was there on the beach that the idea first came to him. Braun had just seen Tom Hanks in the movie *Cast Away* on television the night before, and wondered what it would be like to find himself alone on an island with no chance of ever being rescued. The idea of a television series suddenly swept over him—one that crossed the film *Cast Away* with the hit reality show *Survivor* to create a new world, but one that was absolutely real.[70] Not some supercilious throwback to the groan-some spoof that was *Gilligan's Island*, mind you, but a completely realistic look at a group of plane-crash survivors without a prayer of getting home.

It took time to gather support for the idea, but by the early fall of 2003, Braun and his partner Susan Lyne, president of ABC Entertainment, ordered a script from Spelling Television based on Braun's concept. Jeffrey Lieber was hired to write the teleplay. The initial draft was titled *Nowhere*, but even after the

67 Desperate Networks, p 225
68 Desperate Networks, p 226
69 Desperate Networks, p 198
70 Desperate Networks, p 207

rewrites, the script never measured up to what Braun thought it could be. Thus, in January 2004, Braun contacted J. J. Abrams to write a new pilot script. Abrams, who had created the TV series *Alias* wasn't all that sure he wanted the job—not at first. Abrams finally warmed to the idea on the condition that the series would have a supernatural angle to it and he collaborated with Damon Lindelof to create a series "bible" for a five-season run of the show.[71] Lieber, the original writer, would later, through WGA arbitration, receive a story credit for the *Lost* pilot and a "created by" credit on all subsequent series episodes.[72]

Lost's two-part pilot episode was the most expensive in ABC's history, with cost estimates ranging between ten and fourteen million dollars—three times more than the average production cost of an hour-long pilot in 2004.[73] The series debuted that September, becoming one of the biggest critical and commercial successes of the 2004–05 television season. Yet, before it had even aired, Lloyd Braun, the ABC executive who'd thought it up, was fired by ABC's parent company, Disney. The move, in part, was because of low prime time ratings—that and the fact that Braun and his people had never gotten a successful drama on the air. But mostly, Lloyd Braun was fired because he had greenlighted *Lost*, staking the network's immediate future to a wildly expensive and incredibly risky project.[74] That the risk panned out became the grand irony. Capping its successful first season, *Lost* won the Emmy Award for Outstanding Drama Series for 2005, while J. J. Abrams was awarded an Emmy for his work as director of the pilot episode.[75] If that weren't enough praise, *Lost* swept the guild awards that year, winning the WGA Award for Outstanding Achievement in Writing (Drama); the Producers Guild Award for Best Production; the DGA for Best Direction (Drama); and the SAG Award for Best Ensemble Cast.[76] As the year ended, *Lost* was voted Entertainment Weekly's 2005 Entertainer of the Year; and in 2007, the series was listed as one of *Time* magazine's "100 Best TV Shows of All-*TIME*."[77]

The show's success must have been bittersweet for Braun, even as the irony of it all was continuing to grow. Just prior to his unceremonious dismissal from ABC, in the spring of 2004, Lloyd Braun had put a second project into the development hopper as well—a deliciously wicked dramedy, *Desperate Housewives*. Braun's successor as chairman of ABC Entertainment, Stephen McPherson, landed the position that April, and his timing couldn't have been better. No sooner had he walked through the door than he found he'd inherited a windfall of fortune, the likes of which the American Broadcasting Company hadn't seen in the last quarter century. To his credit, McPherson knew what he had, and focused all of his promotional time and money on *Lost* and *Housewives*,[78] determined to make sure the two shows were seen by as many eyeballs as possible.

---

71 Desperate Networks, p 239

72 *Chicago magazine*—"Cast Away" 2007 August

73 *Honolulu Star-Bulletin*—"New series gives Hawaii 3 TV shows in production" May 17, 2004

74 *London Daily Telegraph*—"The man who discovered Lost – and found himself out of a job" August 14, 2005

75 Emmy.com—"EMMY AWARDS for TV Year 2005"

76 Hollywood Foreign Press Association—"Golden Globe Nominations and Winners (2005)" 2008 February

77 *Time*—"The 100 Best TV Shows of ALL-TIME" September 6, 2007

78 Desperate Networks, p 293

Mark Cherry's pilot script for *Desperate Housewives* was universally beloved, and faced none of the acrimony surrounding the development of *Lost*. McPherson, like Braun, championed ...*Housewives* from the beginning, though truth be known, it was probably ABC president Susan Lyne, a woman, who was its strongest proponent. As a prominent female executive in a male-dominated industry, Lyne knew that with the passing of *Sex and the City*, women missed their "girl shows." The HBO hit had drawn women to it by the millions and the premium cable giant had found nothing since its retirement to replace it—or, for that matter, had anyone else. Women were obviously still hungry for a series that was just about "them," and the Sunday night nine o'clock hour was wide open. Lyne wanted to grab the *Sex and the City* audience by the throat and never let it go.[79]

Desperate Housewives premiered two weeks after *Lost* and drew over 21 million viewers to the show (one million more than *Lost* had), making it the best new TV drama premiere for the year, the highest-rated show of the week, and the best performance by a pilot for ABC since *Spin City* in 1996.[80] The show followed the lives of a group of suburban women (Susan, Lynette, Bree, and Gabrielle), as seen through the eyes of their dead neighbor, Mary Alice Young, who had committed suicide in the very first episode. Mary Alice turns out to be the show's narrator for all eight seasons and the one who introduces our four female leads as they work through domestic struggles and family life, while facing the secrets, crimes, and mysteries hidden behind the doors of their seemingly perfect suburban neighborhood.[81] During the course of the first season, Bree fights to save her marriage; Lynette struggles to cope with her demanding children; Susan fights the block's newcomer, Edie Brit (Nicolette Sheridan), for the affections of a male neighbor; while Gabrielle tries to prevent her husband from discovering the affair she is having with their gardener. And all the while, the core mystery of the season—the unexpected suicide of Mary Alice Young—is slowly but surely revealed.

The series, like *Lost*, was critically well received, and found itself being likened to the popular black comedy film of the day, *American Beauty*. While the show's themes and appeal to female viewers were compared to *Sex and the City*, its mysteries were thought to more resemble those of David Lynch's classic TV series from the 1990's, *Twin Peaks*.[82] And like *Lost*, as well, this series had legs—double entendre not intended. While *Lost* could be *found* on ABC for six suspenseful seasons and 121 episodes, *Desperate Housewives* lasted for eight successful seasons and over 180 episodes.

The two series, premiering within two weeks of each other, received equal credit for turning around ABC's quarter-century of declining fortunes. The fact that both series were capturing over twenty million weekly viewers for the same network (half of whom were part of the 18-to-49 demographic), sent the network's TV ratings skyrocketing to unprecedented levels. The ABC network, under McPherson, followed up on its prosperity with the premieres of *Grey's Anatomy*, a medical show serving as the midseason

---

79 Desperate Networks, p 252

80 *Prime Time Pulse*—"*Housewives* Premier Cleans Up for ABC" April 10, 2004

81 TV.com—"Desperate Housewives Cast & Crew"

82 TeeVee.org—"Fall '04: "*Desperate Housewives*" October 5, 2004

replacement for *Boston Legal*, in early 2005; and in 2006, with the romantic dramedy, *Ugly Betty*—both popular with viewers and critics alike. In June 2005, just a year into his reign, McPherson found what ABC thought it might never unearth—a reality hit all their own. *Dancing with the Stars* became the interactive reality hit of the 2005 summer, and is now completing its sixteenth 12-week season with over 300 episodes in the can.

Housewives with Attitude! The cast from Wisteria Lane included (from left): Dana Delany as Katherine Mayfair; Teri Hatcher as Susan Delfino; Brenda Strong as Mary Alice Young; and Andrea Bowen as Julie Mayer. Eva Longoria, Marcia Cross, and Felicity Huffman (not pictured) also made up the core cast.

As the decade rolled on, however, the luster of ABC's newfound success began to fade—especially in the world of unscripted fare. Though ABC has repeatedly attempted to launch new unscripted summer shows like *Shaq's Big Challenge*, *Fat March*, and *Brat Camp*, nothing has taken hold. One show of note in ABC's attempt to expand its reality TV brand was *The One: Making a Music Star*. The show came in response to five years of utter dominance by *American Idol* over even ABC's most popular shows, and attempted to combine a talent competition with a traditional reality show. It didn't work. *The One* received unanimously negative reviews, pulled some of the lowest ratings in TV history, and was canceled after only two weeks.

In 2010, after recording its lowest weekly rating since its inception in 2004, *Lost* was canceled, as was the overnight sensation, *Ugly Betty*. The series' ratings had hovered at around eight million viewers in its Thursday night time slot, but collapsed dramatically when it was moved to Friday night. ABC tried shifting it again to Wednesday night, but with *Modern Family* and *Cougar Town* already in place, *Ugly Betty* was canceled as well.[83] With ABC's two former hit shows now out of the picture, the network's remaining top two veteran shows *Desperate Housewives* and *Grey's Anatomy* would record their lowest-ever annual rating, in the 2009 TV season—a trademark that continued through their 2010–11 TV season as well.[84]

83 *USA Today*, "*Ugly Betty* cancelled by ABC" January 27, 2010

84 *Deadline Hollywood*—"ABC Will End 'Desperate Housewives' In May 2012" August 5, 2011

Crime Spree

As fast as ABC again appeared to be slipping into a ratings decline, the network still managed to "out-rate" NBC, in 2009, for the third straight year—and by a larger margin than it had the previous year. None of this bothered CBS who held tight to the number-one TV ratings ranking for the eighth time in the last ten years, on the backs of their two monster hits, *Survival*, and the stylish hour-drama that continues to reach 80 million worldwide viewers every week—*CSI: Crime Scene Investigation* (also tabbed *CSI: Las Vegas*).[85]

By the end of November, 2000, the CBS police procedural series *CSI* was the undisputed hit of the new season, piling up Friday-night ratings that no network had seen in years—twenty to twenty-five million domestic viewers each week. Even more impressive, the show was pulling in more young adult viewers than any other show on television across the board.[86] Yet, that this day had come at all was hard to believe. Even as the CBS team met in New York for the *upfronts* the previous May, just hours before the CBS fall schedule was to be announced to the network's affiliates and advertisers, the Anthony Zuiker-created *CSI* series was still no shoe-in to make the 2000 CBS fall schedule.

It had been that kind of journey for the show. For starters, the pilot pitch for *CSI* was the last pitch to be approved for script, that year; and the last script greenlighted for production. CBS even offered their lead William Petersen the starring role in another series. To his credit, Petersen said no. If that weren't enough, Touchstone, the production company producing the series with Jerry Bruckheimer, got word from its bosses at Disney to shut down production after the pilot was shot. No show for CBS was going to be produced by a Disney-owned company. Disney backing out meant that CBS was holding the bag for all of the show's costs. At that moment, most thought CBS network head Les Moonves would simply cut the show from its pilot production schedule and move on without it. Instead, CBS, at Moonves' direction, took the show to a Canadian production company, Alliance-Atlantis,[87] offered them a half-interest in the *CSI* series, and had the show in full production before the middle of June.

CSI: Las Vegas was, at its core, a weekly murder mystery with episodes that were mostly self-contained, just like the ones seen on the *Law & Order* franchises. The show led to the resurgence of a genre (the police procedural) that had gone dark since the days of *The Streets of San Francisco*, a popular ABC show from the 1970's. The *CSI* series was set up to follow Las Vegas crime scene investigators working the nightshift for the Las Vegas Police Department (LVPD) on their cases. William Petersen as CSI Supervisor Gil Grissom, practically became a household word. Marg Helgenberger as Catherine Willows, Grissom's #2; investigators Jorja Fox as Sara Sidle, Gary Dourdan as Warrick Brown, George Eads as Nick Stokes, Eric Szmanda as Greg Sanders; and Paul Guilfoyle as Captain Jim Brass—they were in our homes so much of the week that they almost seemed like family.

---

85 *TV by the Numbers* – "'CSI: Crime Scene Investigation' Is The Most Watched Show In The World" June 14, 2010

86 Desperate Networks, p 133

87 Desperate Networks, p 131

Rather than initiating gunplay, car chases, and the normal run of physical interaction with suspects that audiences were accustomed to in typical crime-dramas, the crime scene investigators in this series used the crime scene's physical evidence to solve their grisly murders, in unusually graphic fashion. The show has inspired a host of other cop-show procedurals—FOX's *Bones*, ABC's *Castle*, and CBS's own additional successes with police procedurals like *Cold Case*, *Without a Trace*, *Criminal Minds*, *NCIS*, *The Mentalist*, and *Person of Interest* as well as *CSI* spinoffs *CSI: Miami* and *CSI: NY*. All three *CSI* franchises mix deduction, gritty subject matter, and character-driven drama into their storylines, using state-of-the-art macro-photography and plenty "snap-zooms" to pull off the unique visual look of the show.[88]

By March 2012, approaching its 13th season, *CSI* had grown an audience over its 12-year run that may never leave the show.[89] During that time *CSI* was recognized as the most popular dramatic series internationally by the Festival de télévision de Monte-Carlo, which has three times awarded it the "International Television Audience Award (Best Television Drama Series)."[90] In 2012, *CSI* was again named the most-watched show in the world for the fifth time in its 12-season run.[91]

That the series has continued to receive unprecedented popularity for over a decade was expected. CBS executives sensed, early on, that this series was going to be a juggernaut—and halfway into the show's first season, CBS went for broke to prove it. Moving *CSI* from Friday to Thursday, CBS decided to pit both *Survivor* and *CSI: Las Vegas* against NBC's "Must-See" Thursday night lineup that included *Friends*, *Will & Grace*, *Just Shoot Me*, and *ER*. During NBC's 20-year, prime time Thursday night reign, other network executives had tried similar moves, without success, in an effort to undo NBC's stranglehold on Thursday night. But this time, as the new century commenced, the opposition's metaphorical hammer was golden. When the dust cleared later that spring, CBS had "stolen" Thursday night away from NBC, and with it the Nielsen ratings crown for most of the next ten years. With Thursday night (America's TV night) now on the CBS side of the ledger, Les Moonves and his network could experiment more freely with the placement of their prime time comedies *Everybody Loves Raymond*, *The King of Queens*, *Mike & Molly*, *Two and a Half Men*, *How I Met Your Mother*, *The New Adventures of Old Christine*, and the biggest comedy to hit the network since ... *Raymond*, *The Big Bang Theory*. With the exception of the 2007–08 television season in which FOX ranked as the top-rated network (due completely to the popularity of *American Idol*), CBS has ended up as the top-rated prime time network in every other TV season since 2000.[92]

---

88 Desperate Networks, p 132

89 *TV by the Numbers*—"CBS Renews 18 Shows" March 14, 2012

90 Monte Carlo Television Festival—"TV Festival 2010: 2010 Awards listing" 2010 June

91 *TV by the Numbers*—"CSI... Is The Most Watched Show In The World" March 14th, 2012

92 TV by the Numbers—"CSI... Is The Most Watched Show In The World" 2010 June

Friendly Persuasion

As the series initially took to the airwaves, the only part of *Friends* that seemed even marginally original was the show's focus on "twentysomethings" who were ambivalent about both their future and the commitment that comes with growing up. Apart from that, however, many critics shrugged at the 1994 *Friends'* debut, thinking it just another *Seinfeld-Cheers* hybrid, born more out of marketing than imagination.[93] Yet the show did have two intangible qualities. First, the writing on the series was first-rate, led by the show's creators, Marta Kauffman and David Crane. Second, the six talented actors hired to bless the series just happened to be insufferably attractive. Looking back on the first true ensemble comedy in television history (a comedy with no one starring presence, save the group as a whole), it's hard to imagine there was ever a time when Jennifer Aniston, Matthew Perry, Courteney Cox, David Schwimmer, Lisa Kudrow, and Matt LeBlanc were six unknown actors on a fall series hoping to get the "back nine" episodes picked up for the spring.[94]

The series that would make stars out of all six cast members began its odyssey in 1993 under the title *Insomnia Café*. The series was pitched by Kauffman and Crane to producer Kevin Bright, who was still the show-runner on their previous creation for HBO, *Dream On*.[95] Together, the three partners pitched a seven-page treatment of the series to NBC. Warren Littlefield, then president of the network, had been looking for a comedy involving young people living together after college and sharing responsibility, but people who interfaced like "surrogate family members."[96] The "friends as family" template had served NBC well since the glory days of *Cheers* in the 1980's, but never before had it actually been written into fabric of a show. The apartment building where the six friends lived felt more like "the family home," where members routinely entered the rooms of their siblings without ever knocking. The characters on *Friends* were constantly using each other's apartment as their own.

The pitch Littlefield heard was about sex, love, relationships, and careers, all coming together at a time in the characters' lives when anything was still possible. NBC liked the pilot script and ordered the pilot episode produced under the working title *Six of One*, primarily to avoid any similarity with *These Friends of Mine*, a sitcom in development at ABC. *That* series starred Ellen DeGeneres and would come to be re-titled *Ellen* before airing on ABC in the spring of 1994.[97] While *Ellen* would last four solid years, birth 109 episodes, and move on into the lucrative world of off-network syndication, her show's historic moment came in 1997. During what has been termed the "Puppy Episode," Ellen (DeGeneres), both as the star of the show and the character she played on it, *came out* as a lesbian on prime time television. The episode garnered media exposure and ignited controversy, prompting ABC to begin each episode with a parental advisory warning.

---

93 *Fifty Years of Television*, p 205

94 *Hollywood Reporter*—"TV Milestones" 2004 September, p 88

95 *New York Times*—"Birth of a TV Show: A Drama All Its Own" March 08, 1994

96 *Baltimore Sun*—"They leave as they began: With a buzz" May 2, 2004

97 *New York Times*—"The Conception and Delivery of a Sitcom; Everyone's a Critic" May 9, 1994

Back at NBC, it had become apparent that the Crane-Kaufman-Bright project had achieved "favored nations" status with the Peacock network, and Littlefield was soon getting calls from agents in town wanting him to cast their clients in the series. NBC's casting director pared down the one thousand actors who had applied for each of the six leading roles to 75, then finally down to six. With starring roles filled, the rewrites on the pilot script completed, and the series' title changed yet again from *Friends Like Us* to *Friends*, the series premiered in NBC's coveted 8:30 pm Thursday night time slot on September 22, 1994, then spent the next ten consecutive years as the lead-in show on the number-one network, during the three most lucrative hours on weekly television. Filmed in front of a live studio audience at Warner Bros. Studios, the series that had opened with 15 million viewers tuning in to watch Episode One, closed up shop ten years later with 51 million viewers watching Episode 236, making it the fourth-most-watched series finale in television history. Moreover, the series finale of *Friends* turned out to be the most-watched episode, thus far, on any network and in any genre, during the first ten years of prime time television in the 21st century.[98]

That NBC had won back the ratings crown they'd lost to CBS the year before was due, in large part, to a revitalized showing by *Friends*, which had drawn 24.5 million viewers a week for 24 weeks to claim most-watched honors, and the number-one series ranking of the year for itself and its network. Jeff Zucker, president of NBC Entertainment since 2000, could hardly contain his satisfaction. His network had thwarted the pesky challenge posed by CBS's *Survivor* and *CSI: Las Vegas* and reclaimed its hold on Thursday night—America's dedicated TV night for the last 20 years. The anchor show that made the NBC schedule work was coming back for a ninth season, though it was costing NBC $7M per episode for the privilege. The license fee NBC paid to Warner Bros. made *Friends* the most expensive show per half hour in television history—a million dollars more than the $13M license fee NBC paid for the hour show, *ER*.[99]

Given the license fee Warner Bros. was being paid to produce *Friends*, it was hard to believe the studio was still producing the series at a deficit—that is until you looked at the salaries being paid to the cast. By the 2002 season, *each* of the six "friends" who had started out making $22,500 per episode were now earning $24M per season—one million dollars to each actor per episode.[100] The leverage the show's talent was able to use to secure their contracts with Warner Bros., and the leverage Warner Bros., in turn, was able to use to corral its license fee from NBC, only went to prove just how impactful *Friends* was to television. Bob Wright, vice-chairman of General Electric and chairman and CEO of NBC Universal, knew this.[101] At the network's top-level budget talks that winter, Wright told Zucker that the NBC network could not afford a collapse of Thursday night—the night NBC had used to rewrite TV economics for a quarter century. Beginning with *Cosby* and *Hill Street Blues*, and a string of other NBC hits that had been discreetly timed to meet the bloated demand from advertisers to buy time on Thursdays for weekend movie sales, NBC had made an absolute fortune with their "Must-See TV" Thursday night fare. Other advertisers, seeing

---

98 Indyposted.com—"Top 10 Most Watched Series Finales" 2010 May

99 Desperate Networks, p 213

100 Desperate Networks, p 214

101 *Forbes*—"Zucker Named NBC CEO" December 15, 2005

what the movie studios were up to, joined in on the Thursday night advertising frenzy and transformed day four of the work week into a night of riches for any network that was able to control it.[102] NBC had been that network since the mid-1980's, and Wright was adamant that they stay that course. Zucker was given his marching orders. He would find a way to keep *Friends* going through the 2003–04 season, even if it cost NBC $10M per half-hour episode to do it. Moreover, he'd use the time between now and then to find a suitable series replacement for 2005. Zucker's task wouldn't be easy. Replacing a show like *Friends* that had been nominated for 63 prime time Emmy Awards, and ranked 21st on *TV Guide*'s "50 Greatest Shows"[103] might simply be impossible to do.

Fall from Grace

As the millennium turned, so, it seemed, had NBC's fortunes. In 2001, CBS chose its hit reality series *Survivor* to anchor its Thursday night line-up. CBS's success was seen as a chink in the NBC armor and an unspoken suggestion that NBC's Thursday-night dominance could be broken. When *CSI: Las Vegas* joined *Survivor*, the unspoken suggestion became a fact. Though *Friends* fought back in 2002 to stave off the inevitable for another couple of years, with its retirement in 2004 and that of *Frasier* as well, NBC was left with several moderately rated shows and few true hits. By then, even its major sports offerings had been reduced to the Olympics, PGA Tour golf, and a floundering Notre Dame football program that no longer seemed relevant. NBC's ratings fell to fourth place. CBS now had the catbird seat at the top of the crow's nest, followed by a resurgent ABC, and FOX, which would eventually come to be the most-watched network for the 2007–08 season—the only time that has happened in its first 25 years of business. While the latter half of the 2000 decade saw smaller audience shares across the network spectrum, NBC was the network hardest hit.

In December 2005, NBC began its first week-long prime time game show event, *Deal or No Deal*, and were surprised with high ratings. The show returned in March 2006 on a multi-weekly basis and became one of only two bright spots that year, alongside the NBC sitcom *My Name Is Earl*. The 2005–06 season was one of the worst for NBC in the last three decades, with only the one fall series, *...Earl*, sticking around for a second season. That same year, NBC aired its fourth spinoff from the *Law & Order* franchise, this one titled *L&O: Trial By Jury*, in an effort to help ease the network's descent, but this new franchise offering didn't take. The other three franchise staples still helped NBC's ten o'clock hour, three nights a week, with each show in 2005 still drawing more than eleven million viewers. The 2006–07 season was a mixed bag for NBC, with the series drama *Heroes* becoming a surprise hit on Monday nights, while the highly touted *Studio 60 on the Sunset Strip*, from acclaimed creator-writer-producer Aaron Sorkin, lost a third of its premiere-night viewers by week six, and was soon canceled. On a more positive note, *Sunday*

102 Desperate Networks, p 215

103 *Fifty Years of Television*, p 254

Night Football had returned to NBC after eight years; *Deal or No Deal* stayed strong; and two of NBC's comedies, *The Office* and *30 Rock*, passed the Emmy Award for Outstanding Comedy Series, back and forth, four years running.[104] In 2008, *30 Rock* received 17 Emmy nominations, breaking the record for the most nominations for a comedy series in a single season, previously held by *The Larry Sanders Show* in 1996, with 16 nominations.[105]

In 2007, Jeff Zucker succeeded Bob Wright as president and CEO of NBC Universal, while Ben Silverman replaced Kevin Riley as president of NBC Entertainment. Yet despite the shuffling of network executives, nothing really changed at NBC. No new prime time hits emerged in the 2008–2009 season, even though NBC did have the good fortune to have both the Super Bowl and the Beijing Olympic Games in which to promote their new offerings. The venues didn't help. NBC simply had nothing worth promoting. *Heroes* and *Deal or No Deal* both collapsed in the ratings and were soon canceled. In 2009, Jeff Gaspin replaced Ben Silverman as president of NBC Entertainment—and things went from bad to worse. Even the *L&O* franchise was now looking vulnerable. By 2009, two of its staples had lost three to four million weekly viewers and *L&O: Criminal Intent*, a whopping 6.5 million viewers per week, leading NBC to cancel two of the franchises by 2011, leaving only *L&O: SVU* still in production at the end of 2012.

Jeff Zucker admitted in a press interview in 2009 that many at NBC no longer believed that the network could find its way back to number one in prime time.[106] As if to punctuate that sentiment, NBC had burrowed into a very distant fourth place, barely able to edge out the CW, the network successor to the WB-UPN merger in 2006. So low had the network sunk that occasionally NBC would find itself beaten in the weekly ratings by programming on some of the more popular cable channels. Something radical needed to happen at NBC to pull it from the doldrums, and Jeff Zucker had a novel, if ill-advised, idea.

Late Night Goes Prime Time

When Conan O'Brien replaced Jay Leno as host of *The Tonight Show* in 2009, the network gave Leno a new talk show, appropriately titled *The Jay Leno Show*, committing to air it every weeknight at 10:00 pm ET/PT (9:00 pm CT/MT), as an inexpensive comedic alternative to the procedural dramas and other one-hour fare that typically aired during that time slot.[107] In doing so, NBC became the first U.S. broadcast network in decades, if ever, to broadcast the same show every weekday during prime time hours. Its executives called the decision to effectively launch five new ten o'clock shows at once "a transformational moment in the history of broadcasting."[108] Conversely, industry critics promptly denigrated NBC for abandoning

---

104 Academy of Television Arts & Sciences—The 60th Primetime Emmy Awards 2008 July

105 *Los Angeles Times*—"30 Rock breaks comedy record at Emmy nominations" July 23, 2008

106 *Media Daily News*—"Zucker weighs In On Leno, NBC's Future" March 18, 2009

107 *Variety*—"NBC unveils primetime plans" May 4, 2009

108 *New York Times*—"NBC Builds Anticipation for 10 pm" August 4, 2009

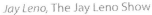

Jay Leno, The Jay Leno Show

Jeff Zucker, CEO NBC-Universal

Conan O'Brien, The Tonight Show

the network's *own* storied history of airing quality dramas at that hour. The unanimous consensus of industry insiders was that the move would hurt NBC by undermining a reputation built on successful scripted shows.[109] And the critics were right.

NBC had breached the most sacred of industry covenants: "If it ain't broke, don't fix it." *The Tonight Show* had become an annual $200M annuity for NBC, and Jeff Zucker was threatening to lose it all to "cost-cutting" measures normally saved for Saturday morning kids' shows, if even then. The producer who had come from daytime TV (Zucker had been the executive producer of the NBC morning show *Today* for eight years until hitching his future to prime time in 2000) was effectively applying a worn-out band-aid (five nights of continuous *Leno*) to a victim who'd been flattened by a train (NBC's ratings decline). Zucker didn't see it that way—not at first.

Way back on September 27, 2004, at the 50th anniversary of *The Tonight Show*'s debut, the transition Zucker was hoping for seemed perfect. At that gala, NBC announced that Jay Leno would be succeeded by Conan O'Brien in 2009.[110] Leno had set the date as his retirement year, and O'Brien's ascension onto the late-night throne was expected. Moreover, it was no secret that O'Brien had been approached by other networks, including ABC and FOX, offering to move him to an earlier time slot. Not wanting to lose O'Brien to an archrival, NBC had promised O'Brien Leno's spot. Jay Leno would host his final episode of *The Tonight Show* on Friday, May 29, 2009, while O'Brien would take over hosting duties commencing the following Monday, on June 1, 2009.[111] NBC, then afraid of losing Leno to another network after he'd

109 *Time*—"Jay Leno Is the Future of TV. Seriously" September 3, 2009
110 *New York Time*—"Conan O'Brien to Succeed Jay Leno in 2009" September 27, 2004
111 *USA Today*—"Leno's last Tonight guest is Conan O'Brien" May 14, 2009

retired, offered Leno a new nightly prime time series, *The Jay Leno Show*, which debuted in September 2009.[112]

Everything played out like clockwork in the first month following Leno's departure from late-night television, as it did as well for the first episode of *The Jay Leno Show*. *Leno* had earned great first-week national rating estimates, averaging 17.7 million viewers per show, an 11 Nielsen rating and an 18 market share.[113] Everything looked just fabulous ... until the second week of the show. Up against stiff competition from fall premieres on other networks (cable stations now included), Leno's audience fell to six million viewers and continued downward, settling in at around five million.[114] While these ratings looked bad compared to the competition, NBC was quick to argue that because *The Leno Show* was so much cheaper to produce than the scripted fare on the other networks, *Leno*'s numbers were still well within NBC's expectations.

What NBC failed even then to grasp was that *The Jay Leno Show* was no longer a late-night series, but a prime time series. As a 10 pm show, it had a responsibility as a "lead-in" for the local newscasts that fell to NBC's affiliated stations immediately following Leno's show. The "local news" was, in turn, a "lead-in" for *The Tonight Show* airing right after the late-night news. And *those* numbers—*The Tonight Show's* numbers—were falling right along with *Leno*'s. That said, it would be wrong-headed to think that Leno alone was pulling down the very show he'd carried on his back for the past twenty years. After all, while *The Tonight Show with Conan O'Brien* saw strong ratings during its premiere week in early June, it was already leaking viewers by the start of July—two months before *The Jay Leno Show* ever aired. The ratings slide of overall viewers was such that from August 13–19, 2009, Letterman's repeats were beating O'Brien's new episodes.[115] By early September, before *The Jay Leno Show* premiered, *The Tonight Show* had already lost the overall viewer ratings for eight consecutive weeks.

Two months after the premiere of *The Jay Leno Show*, ratings for *The Tonight Show* were down "roughly two million viewers a night, year-to-year" from when Leno hosted the program, and it was clear to all that the "NBC experiment" had been a colossal failure. Jeff Zucker's cost-cutting chess move had blown up in the network's face.[116] Not only had NBC failed to provide *The Tonight Show*—a 55-year NBC institution that had, by itself, brought in close to 15B dollars worth of advertising over its lifetime—it had also failed to understand the viewership loyal to each of its two talents. Conan O'Brien drew a younger audience—college-age viewers who tended to stay up for shows like *Late Night with Jimmy Fallon* and *The Late Late Show with Craig Ferguson*. *The Tonight Show* audience was 15 years older, on average, and tended to retire before either of these after-midnight shows were aired. The appeal of Conan O'Brien spoke to generation X, but it was, and still is, baby boomers who watched *The Tonight Show*. Now, with Leno on at ten o'clock, and a strange new face (Conan O'Brien's) on at 11:30 pm in place of Leno, viewers began tuning into

---

112 Broadcasting Cable—"Jay Leno Taking Over 10 PM On NBC" December 8, 2008

113 ZAP2it—"TV ratings: The Jay Leno Show debuts to 17 million-plus" September 15, 2009

114 *Daily Finance*—"Why NBC's not sweating Leno's falling ratings" September 25, 2009

115 *Broadcasting & Cable*—"Late-Night Ratings: Letterman Repeats Top Conan Originals" August 13, 2009

116 MSNBC —"Is Leno's 10 pm experiment nearing an end?" 2009 November

David Letterman on CBS—a second choice, perhaps, but a face the demographic tuning in could still relate to. Leno's fan base would return to late night if he did, but was still hooked on network dramas at ten o'clock—a learned behavior that television had been teaching its audience for over sixty years.

Leno's low ratings resulted in a domino effect on ratings for *The Tonight Show* and *Late Night with Jimmy Fallon*, which had also seen lower ratings than CBS's *The Late Late Show with Craig Ferguson* every week since September.[117] It was reported in the *Los Angeles Times* that the ratings for many high-rated local news broadcasts over various NBC affiliates had fallen sharply. Local affiliates blamed *The Jay Leno Show* for its poor lead-in, and were posturing to leave the Peacock and defect to other networks.[118]

It was obvious to all that if O'Brien continued hosting at 11:30, it would mark the first year in *Tonight Show* history that series would have actually lost money, not to mention affiliates.[119] Thus, in January 2010, NBC announced the canceling of *The Jay Leno Show*, citing complaints from many disgruntled affiliates, whose local newscasts significantly dropped in the ratings as a result of the change.[120] *The Jay Leno Show*—the same show that had just failed at ten o'clock—would return to the 11:35 pm–12:05 am time slot, and *The Tonight Show* would roll back 30 minutes along with it, with Conan O'Brien hosting, and there would be the peace. This, however, caused considerable backlash, as O'Brien had not been given any choice or prior notification of the move. Furthermore, his contract guaranteed him a minimum of three years as host of a show beginning at 11:30. O'Brien refused to be a part of Zucker's chess moves, leading to a "host and time slot controversy" that garnered O'Brien tremendous public and professional support. With Jeff Zucker and NBC hit with a backlash of public outcry, Leno would end up returning as host of *The Tonight Show* effective March 1, 2010, while O'Brien accepted a multi-million dollar buyout from NBC, and went on to host a new show, *Conan*, on the TBS cable network starting in November 2010.

While Jeff Zucker announced on September 24, 2010 that he would step down as CEO of NBC Universal once Comcast's purchase of NBC was completed, it hardly seemed enough. In response to a public controversy over the network's reported rescheduling of late-night hosts, Meg James and Matea Gold of the *Los Angeles Times* declared that Zucker's tenure had led to "a spectacular fall by the country's premiere television network" and dubbed the intra-network feud and subsequent public relations fallout "one of the biggest debacles in television history."[121] Under Zucker, NBC had fallen from being the number-one-rated network in America to the lowest-rated of the four broadcast networks.

Days later, *New York Times* columnist Maureen Dowd wrote that in Hollywood there had been a single topic of discussion: "How does Jeff Zucker keep rising and rising while the fortunes of NBC keep falling and falling?" She explained that Zucker "is a master at managing up with bosses and calculating

---

117 *New York* Magazine—"Will Somebody Please Save NBC?" November 8, 2009
118 *Los Angeles Times*—"Jay Leno's new time slot wreaks havoc for NBC affiliates" October 19, 2009
119 *Chicago Tribune*—"Conan destructive to Tonight Show and media unfair, Leno tells Oprah" January 28, 2010
120 *USA Today*—"NBC to give Leno 30-minute show at old time slot" January 10, 2010
121 *Los Angeles Times*—"How Zucker's Leno quick fix got NBC into a quagmire" January 10, 2010

cost-per-hour benefits, but ... he could not program the network to save his life." Dowd also reported that an unnamed "honcho at another network" stated that Zucker was a case study in the most destructive media executive ever to exist. "You'd have to tell me who else has taken a once-great broadcasting network and literally destroyed it."[122]

Cable Niche—Prime Time Anytime

For most of the 1990's, both premium and basic cable networks performed two services for their customers during prime time hours, providing them with sports and movies in no particular order. HBO was the first network to provide prime time series with *Tales From The Crypt* in the late 1980's, and continued with their provocative offerings through the end of the decade. In July 2001, HBO launched HBO-on-Demand, the first premium subscription video-on-demand enhancement in the United States.[123] HBO was getting into the prime time series business, but realized even as the century turned, that premium cable viewers didn't always have the time to watch shows during the hours of 8 and 11 pm. To help them out, HBO offered its customers a value-added option, and now allowed them to select series episodes that had aired earlier and replay them hours (or even days) later.

The timing of HBO's video-on-demand enhancement was serendipitous. During the first few years of the decade, the series produced and broadcast for prime time by the premium cable companies were among the most-watched shows on cable television, and among the most critically acclaimed on any network, broadcast or cable. Following *Sex and the City* and *The Sopranos*, HBO gave us *The Wire* in 2002, and although it did not surpass *The Sopranos* ratings-wise, it came close to amassing the same kind of critical praise.

Other prime time series dispensed by HBO during the new century's first decade accounted for some of the most successful series on television. Comedies like *Curb Your Enthusiasm* (2000–present), *Flight of the Concords* (2007–09), *Bored to Death*, and *Hung* (both airing from 2009–11). While some had short shelf lives, all four comedies were stamped with critic approval. Moreover, like the network's dramas, the comedies also had of cutting-edge themes. *Curb Your Enthusiasm* asserts the Jewish identity of its characters in ways that no other show has. By incorporating episodes that deal directly with Jewish identity and tradition, the show offers a commentary on what it means to be a Jew in modern American society.[124] *Hung* tackled the secret life of an unhappy, financially strapped high school history teacher and athletic coach in suburban Detroit, who attempts to maintain a "normal" life while going into business as a male

122 *New York Times*—"The Biggest Loser" January 12, 2010

123 *Tribune Business News*—"Cable Subscribers Need Not Order Expanded Packages to Get Premium Channels" December 1, 2002

124 You should see yourself: Jewish identity in postmodern American culture, pp 279–285

prostitute. *Entourage* (2004–11) was really a dramedy that tackled recurring themes centering on the strength of male camaraderie and its importance over work.

Yet, as good as the comedies were, HBO's dramas were often better. Preceding *The Wire* in 2001 was *Six Feet Under* (2001–05), a show about a family-run mortuary that focused on human mortality and the lives of those who deal with it on a daily basis. *Deadwood*, in 2004, was an HBO western set in 1870's South Dakota, before and after the area's annexation by the Dakota Territory. The series charts the town of Deadwood and its growth from camp to town, incorporating rugged themes ranging from female servitude to the birthing of communities to western capitalism. The series featured a large ensemble cast; and many historical figures appeared as characters on the show, including Wild Bill Hickok, Calamity Jane, and Wyatt Earp. Two years later, the HBO drama, *Big Love*, took on the Mormon Church inside a fictional drama about a fundamentalist Mormon family that practiced polygamy as a way of life.

These shows, all of them, were series of substance and mostly unlike anything being produced on broadcast television. In 2010, HBO struck oil again with the premiere of *Boardwalk Empire*, a period drama focusing on Enoch "Nucky" Thompson (Steve Buscemi), a quasi-political figure and full-time gangster who rose to prominence in Atlantic City, New Jersey, during the prohibition era of the 1920's.[125] Ten months after its premiere, *Boardwalk Empire* was nominated for 18 Emmy Awards, including Outstanding Drama Series, Outstanding Lead Actor in a Drama Series (Steve Buscemi), and Outstanding Supporting Actress in a Drama Series (Kelly Macdonald).[126] The new series was also tabbed for Best Writing in a Drama Series, then went on to win the Golden Globe for Best Dramatic Series of the 2010–11 season.

Since 2010, HBO has continued to look for series diversity, producing *Game of Thrones*, a medieval fantasy; *True Blood*, a vampire saga; and *The Newsroom*, a new Aaron Sorkin project that looks at how the nightly news is spun and disseminated in America. Yet, as varied and topical as these shows are, they rather pale beside HBO's production of *Rome*, in 2005. The series was set in Rome, 2,200 years ago, and featured a sprawling ensemble cast of characters, many of whom were based on real figures from historical records. The lead protagonists were two unlikely soldiers, Lucius Vorenus (Kevin McKidd) and Titus Pullo (Ray Stevenson), who found their lives intertwined with key historical events. *Rome* was a ratings success for HBO from the beginning and was honored with numerous awards and nominations in its two-season run.

Watching *Rome* was like watching a theatrical feature every week on television, not unlike one of the network's newer offerings, *Game of Thrones*. The money allocated to *Rome* was substantial. HBO and the British Broadcasting Corporation (BBC) agreed to co-produce the series, committing a US$100–110 million (£62.7 million) budget to the production of twelve 1-hour episodes, with HBO contributing $85 million, and the BBC contributing $15 million.[127] The BBC contributed £800,000 to every episode

125 FlicksNews.net—"Boardwalk Empire Promos" June 13, 2010

126 *Inside TV* (EW.com)—"Emmy nominations 2011: Boardwalk Empire scores" July 14, 2011

127 *BBC News*—"Small screen hits and misses" December 14, 2005

of *Rome* in its first season.[128] *Rome* is the largest co-produced series with the American film market in the BBC's history. *Rome* also marked the first series on which HBO and the BBC worked together as co-producers. Moreover, the industry awards assigned to *Rome* during its two seasons had feature film written all over them. Capping its successful first season, in 2006, *Rome* won four Emmy Awards out of eight nominations. Michael Apted, a feature director with 25 films to his credit, won the Directors Guild of America (DGA) Award for his work on *Rome* in that category. The series itself was nominated for a WGA writing award and a Golden Globe Award for Outstanding Television Series (Drama). *Rome* won a Visual Effects Society (VES) award in the category of Outstanding Visual Effects. Additionally, Rome was nominated for a Cinema Audio Society Award (CAS) for Outstanding Achievement in Sound Mixing.[129]

In short, the series was being produced and distributed as a feature film and had the price tag to prove it. And therein lay the problem. The series was simply too expensive to produce for television. To that point, HBO chairman Chris Albrecht announced in a July 2006 that season two of *Rome* would be its last. Albrecht cited the fact that the series (called "notoriously expensive" by *Broadcasting & Cable*) had been developed under a two-year partnership contract with the BBC, and that it would have been difficult for the BBC to extend their end of the contract due to the series' costs.[130] Many industry insiders suspected that HBO no longer want to spend there either, and thus the mesmerizing show that should have lasted at least five years, lasted two.

In the early 2000's, right there alongside HBO, was the other premium cable giant, Showtime. The CBS Corporation-owned network (originally a Viacom subsidiary until 2005) joined HBO in launching several additional multiplex channels that included Showtime Showcase, Showtime Beyond, and Showtime Extreme. Soon after, Showtime followed HBO's lead and created an on-demand feature so that their series wouldn't be missed. Though the early part of the decade saw more marginal productions like Showtime's animated comedy *Queer Duck* (2002–04); a live-action comedy, *Rude Awakening* (1998–2001); and a one-hour drama, *Queer as Folk* (2000–05), by 2005, that all changed with the airing of its newest half-hour dramedy *Weeds*. The unconventional series ran for eight nail-biting seasons, 102 half-hour episodes, and garnered numerous industry accolades and awards.

Weeds, as it turned out, was inspired by crime dramas like *The Shield* and *The Sopranos*—two successful dramatic series using an "antihero" as protagonist.[131] And so *Weeds* would have one, too. Leading actress Mary-Louise Parker played that role. As a single mother, Nancy Botwin (Parker) lived in Agrestic, California (a fictionalized suburb of Los Angeles) with her two children Silas and Shane (15 and 10, respectively). The pilot opens a few weeks after the untimely death of Nancy's husband, who succumbed to a heart attack while jogging with their younger son. Nancy begins selling marijuana to maintain her upper-middle-class lifestyle originally provided by her deceased husband's structural engineering salary. The series

---

128 *BBC News*—"BBC backs its explicit Rome epic" October 17, 2005

129 *HBO.com*—"Rome News" December 17, 2005

130 ZAP2it—"Two and Out for Rome" July 12, 2006

131 *New York Times*—"Television Review: Mom Brakes for Drug Deals" August 5, 2005

follows the events in Nancy's life as she gets drawn into the criminal system, develops a client base, starts a front to hide her selling, creates her own strain of weed, constantly relocates her family, and tries to stay out of jail long enough to protect her children, Silas (Hunter Parrish) and Shane (Alexander Gould). And to think (come the award ceremonies) the series has always been considered a comedy. Featured in the ensemble cast are Nancy's slipshod brother-in-law Andy Botwin (Justin Kirk); foolish acquaintance Doug Wilson (Kevin Nealon); and her narcissistically vulgar neighbor Celia Hodes (Elizabeth Perkins), a manic PTA mother who left the series after the fifth season.

The show debuted to an immediate fan base, earning the network's highest ratings ever for a series premiere. The notoriety that surrounded *Weeds* seemed to help lure other like-minded and "twisted" series to the Showtime banner. Some of them included: *Dead Like Me* (the show's hero becomes the Grim Reaper); *Californication* (a novelist plagued by personal demons blames his longtime writer's block on hedonism); *Nurse Jackie (*an emergency room nurse struggles to hide her drug addiction); *Shameless* (single father of six tries to keep his dysfunctional family together); *The Big C* (a woman dying of cancer tries to reclaim her own life); and *United States of Tara* (a suburban housewife and mother copes with dissociative identity disorder and her multiple personalities). Yet all of these Showtime series and their wildly inventive themes stand at the feet of one of the most bizarre series premise in the history of television, and one of the most satisfying—*Dexter*.

The series, which debuted on Showtime in October 2006, will commence with its eighth and final mesmerizing season, in June 2013. The series centers on Dexter Morgan (Michael C. Hall), a blood-spatter analyst for the fictitious Miami Metro Police Department. Orphaned at the age of three due to the murder of his mother, Dexter is adopted by Miami police officer Harry Morgan (James Remar) and his wife. After discovering that young Dexter has been killing neighborhood pets for several years, Harry tells Dexter that he believes the need to kill "got into him" at too early an age. Harry believes Dexter's need to kill will only grow stronger. To keep Dexter from killing innocent people, Harry begins teaching Dexter "The Code": Dexter's victims must be killers themselves who have murdered someone without justifiable cause and are likely to do so again. Dexter must also always be sure that his target is guilty, and thus, frequently goes to extreme lengths to get undeniable proof of his victim's guilt before putting the killer through a soul-searching execution.

Working beside Dexter at Miami Metro are the show's supporting cast: actress Jennifer Carpenter plays Debra, Dexter's adoptive sister and co-worker (and later his boss); Lauren Velez as Lieutenant (later Captain) Maria LaGuerta, Dexter's supervisor; David Zavas as Detective Sergeant Angel Batista; and C.S. Lee as lab tech Vince Masuka. Erik King portrayed the troubled Sergeant James Doakes for the first two seasons until running into Dexter, himself. Desmond Harrington joined the cast in season three as Detective Joe Quinn, following Doakes' brutal (series) death.

Although reception to individual seasons has varied, *Dexter* has been nominated for nineteen Emmy awards spread out among several categories. *Dexter* was nominated for Outstanding Drama Series four times in a row, from 2008 to 2011, and the show's star, Michael C. Hall, had been nominated as Outstanding Lead Actor in a Drama Series four times in a row, from 2008 to 2011. *Dexter* has also received over a dozen Creative Arts Emmy Awards, while being nominated as well for seven Golden Globes (winning two); fourteen Satellite Awards (winning seven); eighteen Saturn Awards as the top science-fiction work of the year (winning five); eight Screen Actors Guild Awards (winning one); and five Writers Guild Awards as well.

While the critics have mostly loved the series, the Parents Television Council (PTC) has not, and publicly protested the decision to broadcast reruns of *Dexter* over the public airwaves,[132] citing that "the series compels viewers to empathize with a serial killer, to root for him to prevail, to hope he doesn't get discovered."[133] The PTC called on the public to demand local affiliates preempt *Dexter*, and warned advertisers the PTC would take action against any that sponsored the show.[134] Following the PTC's press release, CBS (parent company to Showtime) added parental advisory notices to its broadcast promotions, and ultimately rated *Dexter* TV-14 for broadcast television.

Basic Excellence

On September 30, 2002, the basic cable network AMC changed its format from a classic movie channel (films made before 1950) to a more eclectic movie channel, airing films from all eras, with the majority of the new inventory coming from the 1950's through the 1980's, including colorized movies, now, as well.[135] Up until 2002, AMC had provided uncut and uncolored films without commercial interruption, something no other basic cable channel could afford to do. At the time, AMC's revenue stream came from the cable providers who were anxious to offer the AMC "classic" movie fare to their subscribers. Though AMC's decision in 1998 to gradually begin putting ads between nightly screenings of their movies came as a surprise to AMC viewers, audience defection was minimal. Viewers still felt unencumbered watching their movies so long as the commercials were being placed *between* the films and not in them.[136] By 2002, however, that was no longer the case. More ads were necessary to pay for the cost of the "upgraded" movie inventory, and AMC was forced to sandwich ads into the middle of films like every other basic cable network. Kate McEnroe, then president of AMC Networks, cited lack of cable-operator subsidies as the reason for the additional advertising, but her reasoning fell on deaf ears as the network's viewership began to defect.[137]

---

132 *Advertising Age*—"Parents Television Council Denounces CBS' Dexter Plan" December 5, 2007

133 *The Independent*—"Dexter the serial killer loses his mojo" December 31, 2008

134 *Time*—"Dexter, Decency and DVR's" January 30, 2008

135 *Variety*—"AMC Unveils More Contemporary Slate… " May 13, 2002

136 *Multichannel News*—"AMC on sponsorships: Roll 'em!" 1997 March

137 *Variety*—"AMC Unveils More Contemporary Slate… " May 13, 2002

The cast and crew of Breaking Bad *at PaleyFest 2010: creator Vince Gilligan, R.J. Mitte (Walt Jr.), Aaron Paul (Jesse Pinkman), Anna Gunn (Skyler White), Bryan Cranston (Walter White), Dean Norris (Hank), and producer Mark Johnson*

After watching its audience gradually decline over the next five years, AMC took a page out of the premium cable networks' playbook and decided to develop prime time series of their own to win back their viewers. The AMC network catchphrase "Story Matters" was borne out by two of the finest series to hit the airwaves during the last decade. Both basic cable series would collectively come to be nominated seven times for the Outstanding Prime Time Drama Series Emmy Award, in one five-year stretch, lifting the network's stature and cachet immeasurably. AMC's unexpected success lured back not only their network's defecting base, but several million new viewers as well.

Both series were just as fresh and original as those finding life on the *premium* cable stations, and even more critically acclaimed. *Mad Men* (2007 to present), the first of the two series to air, took on Madison Avenue's advertising world in New York City in the 1950's and '60's, and made viewers believe they'd been transported back in time. *Breaking Bad* (2008–2013), the second series, aired six months later, training its cameras on a struggling high school chemistry teacher who had been diagnosed with advanced lung cancer at the beginning of the series. Actor Brian Cranston plays Walter White, a middle-aged high school chemistry teacher who turns to a life of crime, producing and selling methamphetamine with a former student, Jesse Pinkman (Aaron Paul), in the hope of securing his family's financial future before he dies.

Breaking Bad has received widespread critical acclaim, particularly for its writing, cinematography, directing, and acting, and has already been nominated three times for the Outstanding Dramatic Series in its five-year run. The series has won six Emmy Awards—including three consecutive Emmy wins as Outstanding Lead Actor in a Drama Series for its star Brian Cranston, and one Emmy win for Aaron Paul in the Outstanding Supporting Actor category.[138] Cranston's interaction with his series wife Skyler (Anna Gunn) is uncomfortable from the beginning and only gets worse. Pregnant with their second child prior to her husband's diagnosis, Skyler becomes increasingly suspicious of Walter after he begins behaving oddly and in unfamiliar ways. The series is rounded out nicely with a bevy of "bad guys" with whom

138 *Los Angeles Times*—"Mad Men and Bryan Cranston three-peat at Emmys" August 29, 2010

Walter must interface and eventually kill to save his own life, his partner's life, and ultimately the lives of his family.

Ross Douthat of *The New York Times* compared *Breaking Bad* to *The Sopranos*, stating that both series are "morality plays," in which Walter White and Tony Soprano "represent mirror-image takes on the problem of evil, damnation and free will." Douthat goes on to say that while Walter is a man who "deliberately abandons the light for the darkness," Tony, on the other hand, is "someone born and raised in darkness" who turns down "opportunity after opportunity to claw his way upward to the light."[139] It is this dynamic that has led some critics to label *Breaking Bad* as the greatest television drama of all time.

Of course, those working on the other AMC series, *Mad Men*, would be well within their right to disagree. Moreover, they would have good reason. The period piece about Madison Avenue advertising executives in the 1950's and '60's was immediately lauded by critics, winning 15 Emmy awards in just five seasons—four of them won in a row for Outstanding Drama Series (2008–11).[140]

The *Mad Men* series was initially set in the 1950's and '60's at the fictional Sterling/Cooper advertising agency on New York's Madison Avenue, and later at the newly created firm, Sterling/Cooper/Draper/Pryce. The focal point of the series is Don Draper (Jon Hamm), the agency's creative director, and one of the agency's marquee names. Plotlines revolve around the business of ad agencies as well as the personal lives of the characters therein. Stories regularly depict the changing moods and social mores of America in the 1950's and '60's, while hinting of far more radical changes in the decade still to come. Highlighted in the storylines are cigarette smoking, daytime drinking, sexism, feminism, adultery, homophobia, and racism.[141] Themes of alienation, social mobility, and ruthlessness underpin the tone of the show. To that point, MSNBC noted that the series "mostly remains disconnected from the outside world [of today], so that the politics and cultural trends of the time ('60's) are illustrated through people and their lives, not through broad sweeping arguments."[142]

Mad Men (series still airing) has been the subject of much gender-based discussion. The show presents a subculture in which men, many of whom are engaged or married, frequently enter into sexual relationships with other women. Critics have observed that most of the main characters have strayed outside of their marriages.[143] ABC News noted that "as the show's time frame progressed into the 1960's, series creator Matthew Weiner didn't hold back in depicting a world of liquor-stocked offices, boozy lunches and alcohol-soaked dinners." One incident in the second season finds advertising executive Freddy Rumsen losing his job after urinating on himself. Don, his wife Betty (January Jones), the firm's director of account services Herman "Duck" Phillips (Mark Moses), and the firm's co-founder Roger Sterling (John

---

139 *New York Times*—"Good and Evil on Cable" July 28, 2011

140 TVGuide.com—"Kristin Chenoweth, Jon Cryer Win First Emmys" September 20, 2009

141 *New York Times*—"Smoking, Drinking, Cheating and Selling" July 19, 2007

142 MSNBC—"*Mad Men* characters soften difficult themes" August 12, 2009

143 *Entertainment Weekly*—"Mad Men Explained: A – Adultery" October 17, 2010

Slattery) were singled out by television reporters for their excessive drinking. Today, our culture rebukes that kind of behavior, but in the 1960's, bad behavior resulting from heavy drinking could be considered "macho, even romantic, rather than as a compulsive disease with dire consequences."[144] One reviewer called the fourth season a "sobering tale of drunken excess" as Hamm's character struggled with his addiction to alcohol.[145]

Yet, though the series more often than not illuminates the seedier side of human condition, its depiction of a time gone by is so pure and the show's stylized look so captivating, that the lure to turn away from the trouble on the screen runs contrary to our voyeuristic nature. The rating numbers at AMC bear this out. The *Mad Men* premiere in July 2007 rated higher than any other AMC original series to date (900,000 viewers)—and that was just the beginning.[146] The show's second season premiere more than doubled the first season's, while the finale for season two also rated significantly higher than the finale for season one, up over 20% to 1.75 million viewers. So good was this second finale that when rebroadcast at a later time that same evening, another 1.2 million people watched the show.[147]

The third-season premiere of *Mad Men* aired in August 2009, grabbing 2.8 million views on its first run. The fourth-season premiere was falling into a wonderful pattern for the AMC network, with the pilot once again becoming the most-watched episode in AMC history. The fifth-season premiere, "A Little Kiss," topped even that to become the most-watched episode of *Mad Men* to date, receiving 3.5 million viewers and 1.6 million viewers in the 18–49 demographic. Before the fifth season, *Mad Men* had never achieved above a 1.0 in the 18–49 demographic, and now they were almost doubling any number that went before. Charlie Collier, AMC's president, continues to praise the show at every turn, remarking:

> For each of the five *Mad Men* seasons Matthew Weiner and his team have crafted a beautifully told story, and each season a larger audience has responded; a rare accomplishment. We couldn't be more proud of this program, the brilliant writers, cast and crew, and the entire team on each side of the camera.[148]

Mad Men has been credited with setting off a wave of renewed interest in the fashion and culture of the early 1960's. According to *The Guardian* in 2008, the show was responsible for a revival in men's suits, especially suits resembling those of that time period, with higher waistbands and shorter jackets, as well as "everything from tortoise shell glasses to fedoras."[149] According to the website BabyCenter, the show led to the name "Betty"—the name of Don Draper's first wife—soaring in popularity for baby girls in the United States in 2010.

---

144 *ABC News*—"Television's Booze Hounds" September 13, 2010

145 *The New Republic*—"Mad Men Waldorf Stories Review" August 30, 2010

146 *Hollywood Reporter*—"AMC *Mad* about rating for series bow" July 20, 2007

147 *Broadcasting & Cable*— "Mad Men Season Finale Draws 1.75 Mil Viewers" October 27, 2008

148 TV by the Numbers—"Season Five Premiere Is Most Watched Episode of *Mad Men* ever" March 26 2012

149 *The Guardian*—"How *Mad Men* became a style guide" August 1, 2008

The trend here is well afoot. American TV watchers, in meaningful numbers, are tuning into cable series and vesting themselves in those shows for the long haul. The fact that these cable dramas are actually influencing our life choices apart from the TV-watching, itself, is a staggering indication of how far TV culture has drifted away from commercial television, and how quickly viewers have made the move. No longer are audiences sitting down to watch a network for the evening. Audiences, today, are grabbing their TV-watching in bite-sized chunks, selecting shows—not channels—to watch. With the quality of the scripted prime time cable series only getting better, the migration from commercial TV is well underway. The strangle hold that broadcast television once had on its industry is officially over. As the century turned, the "big four" broadcast networks (CBS/ABC/FOX/NBC) had lost 17% of their viewing audience to cable television, down from percentages in the mid-90's where the broadcast networks had been hovering at since the earliest days of television. Today, twelve years later, as we enter the second decade of the 21st century, the "big four" own less than 50% of the TV market, down almost 30% since 2000.[150] The unfortunate trend for advertisers and their symbiotic broadcast networks is hard to mistake. Network-owned conglomerates have countered the trends by buying up cable networks to help recoup losses in audience share given up by their broadcast arm, but advertisers are still feeling their way along.

Prime Time Goes Digital

If cable television and reality programming have shown us anything in the last 10 years, it's that the TV paradigm is changing, leading us right into the brave new world of the Internet, streaming video, and other innovative technologies that are re-shaping television even as this book goes to press.

Television has clearly come a long way, both creatively and as a business, since the days of Milton Berle and the ten-inch black-and-white screen. Each time a new technology blooms inside the industry, the medium seems to evolve. Before the coaxial cable came to be, the networks aired live shows in the Eastern and Central zones, then shot kinescopes off the monitors for west coast viewing days later.

The invention of video tape in the late 1950's meant shows could be performed live while simultaneously being recorded on tape. Demands for larger TV screens echoed through manufacturing centers. Color soon became the rule for TV owners rather than the exception. People were no longer thrilled just to receive any image in their home, they wanted those images bigger and of better quality. With production costs rising, networks reacted by trimming the number of original episodes they ordered for each series. In the early days, 39 shows was standard issue for every season, with thirteen of those episodes repeated during the summer. That number shrank to 36, then to 32, 26, and now 22, which presently

150 Television in the Multichannel Age: A Brief History of Cable Television

stands as the norm for those series airing on broadcast television.[151] On cable television, where series air on a year-round basis, the normal series order is currently at twelve or thirteen episodes per year.

Remote controls have also changed television, both creatively and as a business. Viewers could now channel surf from the comfort of their homes, making it easier than ever to change stations. Producers and networks needed to devise better ways to keep the audience from switching channels and tuning out commercials. Main titles began to disappear, or, at the very least, they became shorter and more simplified. Where the end credits once ran on screen by themselves, we now find them compressed to the side of the screen and augmented with outtakes from upcoming shows.

When affordable VHS recorders hit the market in the early 1980's, people began "time-shifting," recording shows "now" for more convenient viewing "later." The VHS recorder gave viewers the ability to fast-forward through commercials. DVDs came next, and with them came the opportunity to simply *rent* an entire TV season and view it over the weekend. Great for producers receiving DVD revenue, but bad for network profitability and advertisers. Consumers were becoming harder to reach.

While many in the TV industry saw each of these innovations as a threat to the status quo of the day, most conceded that television had always managed to adapt to the technology and it would do so again. That being said, the networks and their traditional business model (one that now in fuses "reality" into the new industry paradigm) are staring down the barrel at the two most formidable challenges they have ever faced—DVRs and the Internet.

The invention and inclusion of the digital video recorder (DVR) into our lives has made the scheduling of TV shows at specific times and on specific nights more and more irrelevant. Yet, the issue at hand is not one of convenience, but one of money. DVRs, as it turns out, also make it easier than ever to skip commercials—the life blood of the revenue stream that has fueled the broadcast industry for over sixty years. And therein lies the first of the two aforementioned challenges. Advertisers must find a better way to reach consumers using DVRs; and networks, whose revenue streams depend on advertising dollars, need to help them.

Added to the challenge that advertisers and networks face in reaching people with DVRs, there is also the problem of reaching people who now watch their series television on the Internet. As more and more viewers continue to migrate to the World Wide Web to view their prime time favorites, networks and advertisers will need to follow these defectors and lure them back to the fold with an Internet product that the Internet viewers' "outside the box" thinking now requires. Once that's accomplished, networks will need to find a way to get advertisers to pay for it. Just as the television programming model adapted to unscripted (reality) television at the turn of the century, so it now seems that the TV paradigm is changing yet again.

---

151 WGA Writer Speaks Series—"Norman Lear"

By 2010, it was readily apparent that both broadcast and cable networks were moving to the Internet, as were independent writer-producers. Short-form Internet TV series were now being developed apart from networks by film students, independent producers, and any person in the world with a smart phone. These Internet series were called *webisodes*—episodes of a television series designed for distribution over the Internet. The key word is *series.* A webisode (or web-episode) is defined as an individual installment of an ongoing premise with recurring characters. It can be a big-budget, intricately filmed science-fiction extravaganza with dazzling special effects like the internet series, *Sanctuary*, with an estimated, first-season, 13 episode-cost of $21M—arguably the most ambitious film project to date designed for direct release over the Internet.[152] Or it can be as low-tech and cheap to make as a static webcam shot from your front porch

In truth, short-form episodic film series have been around since before the days of television, some originating as early as the silent movie era. Charlie Chaplin, Harold Lloyd, and Buster Keaton all created popular webisode series shot on film, and exhibited them in theaters alongside the newsreel and the feature presentation.[153] For years, the equipment and film-processing necessary to create even a two-minute film was so expensive that only professionals could afford to make these shorts. However, with the advent of lightweight and relatively affordable personal camcorders in the mid-'80's, that all changed. It suddenly became possible for millions of people to shoot their own videos, though the avenue to post-production and distribution still remained unavailable to those outside the media power elite.

The digital and Internet revolution of the 1990's changed all this. Suddenly, you didn't need a $100,000 flatbed machine to edit your film. Digital technology meant your average home computer could handle the task. Camcorders were cheaper than ever, required no more technical expertise than a flashlight does, and yet were increasingly capable of producing a quality video image. Working in synergy with all of this, high-speed broadband connections were developed, making inexpensive web dissemination possible. For millions of amateur video enthusiasts, film distribution was now just a mouse-click away.

Still, there was one small problem left to solve for amateur video makers dying to show the world their wares: How would the audience know where to find their video on the Internet? Enter YouTube. Founded by Steve Chen, Chad Hurley, and Jawed Karim, three former employees of the Silicon Valley firm PayPal, the website had a simple but powerful concept.[154] Users could post and view any type of video, professional or amateur, on this one-stop shopping site. It was like one giant short-video multiplex, and anyone in the world could hop from theater to theater for free, without ever leaving the comfort of their own laptop.

---

152 *Burnaby Now*—"Made-on-Burnaby show gets Beedie's backing" October 8, 2008

153 Chapman University Lecture (14) – "Brave New World...," p 8

154 *USA Today*—"Video websites pop up, invite postings" November 21, 2005

The first YouTube video was posted on April 23, 2005. By November, the site had 200,000 viewers watching 2 million short videos per day,[155] even though the site was still in its experimental stages. December 15, 2005 marked YouTube's official debut. Within a month, users were watching an astonishing 25 million videos per day. By July 2006, that number topped 100 million, with 65,000 new videos being uploaded daily.[156]

The public hunger to consume short videos was not lost on the professional world. If millions of eyeballs were leaving broadcast television in favor of video viewing on the Internet, then Hollywood and the networks wanted in. Global media giant Sony Pictures Entertainment jumped in early, creating a site called Grouper (later changing its site name to Crackle), a multi-platform video entertainment network and studio that distributed the hottest emerging talent on the Web. Traditional broadcast networks like ABC, CBS, and NBC weren't far behind. Broadcast networks, while at first cursing Internet video as the enemy, quickly realized it was here to stay, and that they needed to be part of it if they wanted to survive, let alone thrive. Networks made full episodes of their shows available online, and soon discovered that rather than losing their overall audience, Internet versions of their series actually expanded their reach.

For advertisers, who had long relied on television to provide the precious eyeballs *they* needed to survive, the new Internet video culture presented a variety of problems. Not only were fewer people watching traditional network television, but those who did were now armed with TiVo and other devices that let them skip the commercials entirely. TiVo, for the record, uses a DVR to provide an on-screen guide of scheduled broadcast programming, allowing the user to record every new episode of a series, and "wish-list" their searches to find and record shows. The technology matches the viewer's interests by title, actor, director, category, or keyword.[157] Advertisers quickly realized they needed to retool their thinking. Rather than merely placing the same old ads in this new entertainment arena, advertisers seized the opportunity to create and produce new short-form content of their own that married their sales message with entertainment. Consumer giant Unilever promoted its new spray bottle version of I Can't Believe It's Not Butter through a series of webisodes titled *Sprays of Her Life*. The webisodes were clever soap opera parodies pushing the slogan: "Romance. Passion. Deception. Vegetables. Watch things heat up when the refrigerator lights go down!"

In the old network television advertising paradigm, advertisers looked for shows whose audience overlapped a portion of the advertisers' target consumer group, and then bought 30-second spots on the show, hoping the audience would stick around long enough to receive their message. But in this new, short-form Internet video world, advertisers can actually design their entertainment to appeal to their consumers and embed their message seamlessly into the entertainment itself.

---

155 YouTube—"Me at the zoo" Aired April 23, 2005

156 *USA Today*—"You Tube serves up 100 million videos a day online" July 16, 2006

157 *Virgin Media*—"Virgin Media Selects TiVo For Next Generation TV Platform" November 24, 2009

For independent producers, the Internet allows them to create the kind of content they themselves would want to watch, and then seek out an audience with similar tastes. Initial advertising hopes sought to reach two million regular viewers per network series. While this number would be considered dismal on broadcast television, it would be a phenomenon of enormous size on the Internet. And with the social media now "sharing" every byte of molecular media, the growth of an initial episode (and its embedded advertising) could go viral (exponentially larger) overnight.

Creative people in a variety of artistic pursuits are discovering the enormous power of the Internet to provide what might be called "exposure opportunity." The Groundlings, a legendary Los Angeles improvisational theater troupe that helped launch the likes of Lisa Kudrow, Will Ferrell, and the late Phil Hartman has spent decades performing in their 99-seat theater. However, after shooting the spoof "David Blaine Street Magic" in the alley behind their building, in 2006,[158] and then posting it on YouTube, the video racked up 18 million plays. That, in a nutshell, defines the true, overwhelming, tsunami-like power of the Internet. If the Groundlings performed that same sketch in their theater to sold-out audiences every night of the year, it would take just short of 182,000 performances and over 6,000 years to reach an audience of 18 million.[159] On the Internet, with no additional performances required, the identical distribution scenario took less than a month.

Discussion Questions

A. Reality Check

- *An American Family*, a 1973 PBS documentary, became a ratings hit and revealed what about the taste of American TV audiences?

B. The Tribe Has Spoken

- 2000 ushered in a new CBS reality series, *Survivor*. An instant success, how was this show a game changer for network television?

C. Early Rumblings

- Trace the rise and fall of the 2000 special, *Who Wants to Marry a Multi-millionaire*? What were the lessons learned here for networks?

---

158 YouTube—"David Blaine Street Magic," Aired October 12, 2006

159 *LA Times Entertainment*—"Like magic, Groundlings turn viral" June 22, 2008

D. Rescue Me

- How would you, as a television executive, respond to the 9/11 terrorist attack on U.S. soil in a way that was respectful, entertaining and lucrative? Would you avoid the subject altogether? Explain.

E. You're Fired!

- Donald Trump, ax wielding entrepreneur of NBC's *The Apprentice*, carried this show for audiences. Which demographics audience has kept this reality series about the New York robber baron that fired people from his projects on a weekly basis on TV for so many seasons?

F. Pop Phenomenon

- The success of *American Idol* belies the rocky road this series took to be on TV. What were the speed bumps that obstructed the path of this UK spinoff?

G. Housewives and Castaways to the Rescue

- ABC was floundering for a sustainable hit when it aired what two programs in 2004? What was the gist of each show?

H. Crime Spree

- *CSI* was, at heart, a murder mystery. However, this CBS 2000 runaway hit challenged previous detective yarns in what ways?

I. Friendly Persuasion

- A hit from the start, *Friends* owed its success to what components in its ten year history with NBC?

K. Late Night Goes Prime Time

- What factors led up the 2010 decision by NBC to cancel *The Jay Leno Show*, a move that created public outcry on Conan O'Brien's behalf?

L. Cable Niche-Primetime Anytime

- What did HBO's *On-Demand* do in 2001 to launch a new way of watching television?

- Perhaps the finest of HBO's original programming, what ultimately sidelined the 2005 series *Rome* after only two seasons?

- The new millennium's first decade ushered in an onslaught of new and creative premium cable shows. Rising to the top of that ratings heap was *Dexter*, a cop show as critically well received as it was popular. What set this series apart from the many other offerings?

M. Basic Excellence

- A basic cable network, AMC soon joined the original programming trend with its first series smash, *Mad Men*, in 2007. How did *Mad Men* affect consumer trends in its first four seasons?

- With premium and basic cable networks contributing programming that is weaning away viewers from commercial television in growing numbers, what does the future hold for broadcast television?

N. Prime Time Goes Digital

- What are the major technological advances that have enhanced television viewing since the 1950's?

- 'Going viral' is altering the way independent filmmakers do business. What phase of their business has been most impacted? Has the Internet been a friend or foe? Explain.

- How are advertisers marketing products in productions that are made for the internet and bypass the traditional television experience?

Appendix 1

Afterword

Three More for the Road

Soon after the preliminary draft of the book was competed, my sister called to tell me that I'd snubbed two of her pet shows, and failed to even mention the best comedy on TV. *The Carol Burnett Show* was her favorite series growing up, as it was for baby boomers everywhere. That particular variety/sketch comedy television show debuted in 1967 and was stocked with a bevy of talent who could all have had contracts on *SNL*. Carol Burnett, Harvey Korman, Vicki Lawrence, Lyle Wagooner, and Tim Conway would have given Tina Fey, Will Ferrell, Molly Shannon, Dan Aykroyd, and Billy Crystal a run for our laughter. The eleven-season CBS hit ran for 278 episodes and came in 16th on TV Guide's "50 Greatest TV Shows."[1] So yes—my sister had a point. So did my brother with *Mork & Mindy*, and my aunt with *The Brady Bunch* and *The Golden Girls*. A cinematographer friend from college who shot most of the *Seinfeld* episodes wondered how in the world I'd forgotten to mention *The Bob Newhart Show*—both of them. Students from San Diego State University who helped vet the book were appalled that I'd neglected to print a single word about the British TV series, *Dr. Who*, which ran on the BBC from 1963 to 1989, and again on BBC America since 2005. I reminded them that the series in the book were U.S. productions that aired during prime time hours here in the states, though I don't think the disclaimer did much to mollify them.

---

1 *Fifty Years of Television*, p. 254

A colleague from my days making films for the U.S. Navy after college called to tell me I'd eliminated *Wild Wild West*, entirely, and hardly mentioned *Hawaii Five-0* (the first one premiering back in 1968), and wondered how I could still look myself in the mirror. A fraternity brother I trusted to read the book phoned to ask why *WKRP in Cincinnati* and *Baywatch* got virtually no mention at all. And my 97-year-old step-mother, who still climbs three flights of stairs to her assisted-living apartment and reads her own menu at the IHOP, wondered if she'd missed the "chapter" on *Matlock* and *Murder, She Wrote*, and asked where she could find them. My daughters loved *The Wonder Years*; my brother-in-law, *The Nanny*; my cousin, *Family Guy* and *South Park*; and my dad loved *Superman*—the 1952 syndicated version starring George Reeves as the "man of steel," costumed in a Banlon bodysuit that had more wrinkles than Reeves.

There was *Arrested Development*, *Deadwood*, *The Shield*, *The Wire*, *Big Love*, and my personal favorite, *MacGyver*; along with shows still running—*The Big C*, *Californication*, *It's Always Sunny in Philadelphia*, *Sons of Anarchy*, and *The Good Wife*—all excluded from mention, not because they weren't memorable series—they were ... and are. The dilemma posed is that these are but two dozen prime time series out of over 7,000. While the textbook does survey and scrutinize 65 years of prime time television, it is not a cover to cover, floor to ceiling almanac of its shows. Nonetheless, there are three series that still need mentioning, not only for their longevity and lifetime audience draw, but also for their impact on American culture apart from television.

STAR TREK

In 1964, creator-writer-producer Gene Roddenberry pitched the original *Star Trek* TV series to Desilu Studios as a "*Wagon Train* to the stars."[2] *Wagon Train* was a top-rated western of its day and revolved around people on a journey of discovery. That in a nutshell is what Roddenberry presented NBC—a western in space. Though the network rejected the show's first pilot, NBC executives were so impressed with the concept that they made the unusual decision to commission a second: "Where No Man Has Gone Before." The first regular episode of *Star Trek* (also referred to as *Star Trek: The Original Series*) aired on NBC, Thursday, September 8, 1966. While the show initially enjoyed high ratings, the average rating of the show by the end of its first season dropped to 52nd (out of 94 programs).[3]

Unhappy with the show's ratings, NBC threatened to cancel the series during its second season, but backed off when the show's fan base conducted an unprecedented letter-writing campaign, petitioning the network to keep the show on the air.[4] NBC renewed the show, but moved it from Thursday to Friday, and substantially reduced its budget. In protest Roddenberry resigned from his role as producer and

2 *Star Trek*—Series Bible, First Draft, March 11, 1964

3 *Broadcasting*—"The numbers game, part one," September 19, 1966

4 *Inside Star Trek: The Real Story*, pp 381–382

reduced his direct involvement in the process of molding the series. Despite a renewed letter-writing campaign by an energetic fan base, NBC canceled the series in 1969—or so it was thought.

After *Star Trek*'s cancellation, Desilu (who was now owned by Paramount following its acquisition of Desilu in 1967) sold the series' syndication rights to help recoup the original series' production losses. Reruns began in the fall of 1969 and by the late 1970's the series aired in over 150 domestic and 60 international markets. This resurgence of viewership emerging from the show's "aftermarket" helped *Star Trek* develop a cult following even greater than its popularity during the original run.[5] The series' newfound success led to rumors of reviving the franchise.

Filmation Productions along with Paramount Television did just that, producing the first post-original series show, *Star Trek: The Animated Series*. The show ran on NBC for 22 half-hour episodes over two seasons on Saturday mornings from 1973 to 1974. In 1975, in response to the franchise's newfound popularity, Roddenberry had begun developing a new series, *Star Trek: Phase II*, for Paramount Television, when parent company Paramount Studios stepped in to redirect the project. On the heels of the success generated by the science fiction movies *Star Wars* and *Close Encounters of the Third Kind*, Paramount made the decision to turn Roddenberry's TV pilot episode of *Phase II* into the feature film, *Star Trek: The Motion Picture*. The film opened in North America in 1979 and earned enough at the box office for Paramount to create a sequel.

The success of the critically acclaimed sequel, *Star Trek II: The Wrath of Khan*, reversed the fortunes of the franchise. Paramount went on to produce six *Star Trek* feature films between 1979 and 1999, as the franchise's popularity continued to grow. In response to the popularity of *Star Trek*'s feature films, the franchise returned to television with *Star Trek: The Next Generation* (*TNG*) in 1987. By 1993, *TNG* was the highest-rated syndicated series, and spun off a 1993 sequel titled *Star Trek: Deep Space Nine*. In 1995, Paramount Television became the United Paramount Network (UPN) and launched its fourth *Star Trek* series, *Star Trek: Voyager*, which lasted until 2001, and became the flagship of the new network's prime time lineup. In 2001, as *Voyager* was departing the galaxy, UPN released its fifth and final series of the franchise, *Star Trek: Enterprise*, which ran until May of 2005.

Star Trek and its spin-offs have achieved global popularity, but the show's cultural impact goes far beyond its longevity and multi-billion-dollar profitability. The franchise has gone on to inspire designers of technologies that include hand-held mobile phones and GPS mapping apps, and it brought the notion of teleportation to popular attention with its depiction of "matter–energy transport." In 1976, NASA named its prototype space shuttle Enterprise, after the series' fictional starship.[6] And of course, *Star Trek* conventions have become popular with "trekkies" (younger fans) everywhere.

---

5 *Milwaukee Journal*—"Cult Fans, Reruns Give '*Star Trek*' an Out of This World Popularity" July 3, 1972

6 National Aeronautics and Space Association—"Shuttle Orbiter Enterprise (OV-101)"

Yet, beyond *Star Trek*'s technical innovations, one of its greatest and most significant contributions to television history hails directly from its multicultural, multiracial cast. While common in television shows from the 1970's onward, this melding of cultures was considered controversial and daring in 1966. The *Enterprise* crew included a Japanese helmsman, a Russian navigator, a black female communications officer, a Vulcan first officer, an Irish propulsion officer, and an American captain and medical officer—and there was scarcely a TV viewer alive at the time who didn't know them all by name: William Shatner as Captain James T. Kirk; Leonard Nimoy as Vulcan first officer Spock; DeForest Kelley as medical officer Dr. Leonard "Bones" McCoy; James Doohan as propulsion officer Montgomery "Scotty" Scott; Nichelle Nichols as communications officer Uhura; George Takei as helmsman Sulu; and Walter Koenig as navigator Chekov. In reviewing the longevity of the 45-year franchise, one is mindful of the Vulcan catchphrase Spock was fond of repeating, "... live long and prosper."

SATURDAY NIGHT LIVE (SNL)

From 1965 until the fall of 1975, NBC ran *The Best of Carson* reruns of *The Tonight Show* (then in its 11th year), airing them on the weekends, at the discretion of the local affiliates. *The Tonight Show Starring Johnny Carson* was the gold standard of late-night programming, and by 1974, Carson was beginning to understand that. Not yet half way through his 30-year career, Carson announced that he wanted the weekend shows pulled and saved so that they could be aired during weekdays, allowing him more time off.[7] NBC president Herbert Schlosser approached his vice president of late-night programming Dick Ebersol and asked him for a show to fill the Saturday night time slot. At the suggestion of Paramount Pictures executive Barry Diller, Schlosser and Ebersol then approached Lorne Michaels, who had been a writer on *Laugh-In* and come to Diller's attention. By the following year (1975), Michaels had assembled a talented cast including Dan Aykroyd, John Belushi, Chevy Chase, Jane Curtin, Garrett Morris, Laraine Newman, Michael O'Donoghue, and Gilda Radner.

Launched on October 11, 1975 as a live broadcast from New York's Rockefeller Center, *Saturday Night Live* rose from the wasteland of network television time slots to become a pop culture phenomenon, causing a seismic shift in the landscape of television comedy-variety, the likes of which had not been seen since Sid Caesar's *Your Show of Shows* went on the air a quarter-century before. Millions of Americans left the bars early on Saturday night to get home in time to watch that week's guest host shout those immortal words, "Live from New York, it's Saturday night!" To that point, it should be noted that the show's original title was *NBC's Saturday Night*. At the time of the show's premier, Howard Cosell had a sports show on the air called *Saturday Night Live with Howard Cosell*. When Cosell's show was canceled in 1976, NBC purchased the rights to the show's title and officially adopted it on March 26, 1977.[8]

---

7 NBC.com—"About the Show, *SNL* Beginnings"

8 NBC.com—*Saturday Night Live* (History)

Before *SNL* hit the air in 1975, the very notion of a comedy-variety show serving a late-night audience seemed wrongheaded to be sure; and as a show needed to attract young people on Saturday night, it seemed patently absurd. The good news was that because NBC's gamble was predicted to fail, the network had really nothing to lose. Research had shown that people wouldn't be home on Saturday nights, so any ratings number that even came close to the Johnny Carson reruns would be welcome. As Lorne Michaels (just 30 when he created the show) admitted back in 2002: "In the beginning, there was this sort of intoxicating freedom. We were doing the show for ourselves, and the fact that we were making it up as we went along was thrilling."[9] This sense of freedom was experienced by not only the performers, but by a disbelieving audience as well. Television in the mid-1970s wasn't that far removed from its censorious roots, and here was a gang of smart, funny comedians with rock and roll sensibilities making thinly disguised references to sex, drugs, and unholy acts.[10]

"The traditional variety show needed to be redefined," Michaels declared—and he certainly did that.[11] Broadcasting from Studio 8H at 30 Rockefeller Plaza, *SNL* has aired 732 late-night episodes since its debut, and began its 38th season on September 15, 2012.[12] While the show has been declared dead many times over the years, it has always managed to reinvent itself. An amazing roster of comedic genius and the characters that genius has spawned has continually risen to the occasion. From Bill Murray's lounge singer, to Eddie Murphy's Gumby, to Mike Myers' and Dana Carvey's suburban basement rockers Wayne and Garth, to John Belushi and Dan Aykroyd's Blues Brothers, to Tina Fey's "Sarah Palin," the series' "star reel" is truly one of a kind.

Fittingly, the show has been well honored for its efforts. Since debuting in 1975, *SNL* has received 36 Prime Time Emmy Awards, two Peabody Awards, and four WGA Awards.[13] In 2009, it received a total of 13 Emmy nominations for a lifetime total of 126, breaking the record for the most award-nominated show in Emmy history, previously set with 124 by the medical drama *ER*.[14] By August 2012, *SNL* had received a record total of 156 Emmy nominations.

The centerpiece of every show has been the "Weekend Update"—a "sketch concept" that followed Lorne Michaels from his days as a writer on *Laugh-In*, where the show's hosts Dan Rowan and Dick Martin spoofed newsmakers in their weekly segment, "*Laugh-In* Looks at the News—Past, Present & Future." Using their own *SNL* "Weekend Update" desk to pitch their political parodies, The Not Ready for Prime Time Players (*SNL* cast) seems to have had a definite effect on at least two elections. In what has been

9 *Made You Laugh*, p. 61
10 *Fifty Years of Television*, p. 31
11 *Fifty Years of Television*, p. 3
12 *Stay Tuned*, p. 30
13 Primetime Emmy Award Database
14 *TV Week* website—"With 13 Additional Emmy Nominations, *SNL* Breaks Record as Most Nominated Show in History"

dubbed "The SNL Effect," voters reported being influenced by the show's parodies in the voting booth. According to pollster Mike Dabadie, the so-called "effect" was observed during the 2008 presidential campaign. Two-thirds of voters who responded to the poll said they had seen a broadcast of politically charged content on *SNL*.[15] And in 1976, President Gerald Ford claimed that comedian Chevy Chase's imitation of Ford during his presidential reelection campaign helped lead to his defeat.[16]

Over the years, *SNL* has been shown in prime time on several occasions, but none was more memorable than the show's 25th Anniversary Special in 2000. Following the broadcast, the *New York Times* said, "*SNL* is still the most pervasive influence on the art of comedy in the history of contemporary television culture."[17] Over the years, it has been lauded as a revolutionary force in comedy and criticized as a comic boot camp.[18] But for the 129 comics who stepped onto that stage and the millions of viewers who have tuned in over the years, the series has come to symbolize some of the most innovative humor ever to grace American television.

60 MINUTES

Tick-Tick-Tick-Tick-Tick-Tick ... For decades, that sound has signaled the Sunday night cadence in households across America, as viewers settled in to watch a show that has "turned investigative journalism into dramatic entertainment"—so said *TV Guide* in 2002.[19] And the tradition continues. The program may be titled *60 Minutes*, but its captivating stories have kept Americans glued to the series for almost half a century, leaving one to wonder if the show can go on forever (like *Today* and *The Tonight Show* have).

Created by Don Hewitt, the series was delivered as the forerunner of a new TV genre—the reporter-centered investigation. Using this unique journalistic style, the reporter, not the story, became the star—and stars they all were. Harry Reasoner, Mike Wallace, Charles Kuralt, Walter Cronkite, Roger Mudd, Eric Sevareid, and Morley Safer (who in 2012 still co-hosted the show) were there at the beginning, helping to create an anomaly in television—a provocative, thought-provoking hour of non-fiction that action-oriented-thrill-a-minute-channel-surfing TV viewers couldn't get enough of.

When the show first aired in 1968, it seemed an unlikely candidate to become an American institution, let alone a staggering network profit center and the inspiration for a host of imitators—NBC's *Dateline NBC*; ABC's *20-20*; and CBS's own *48 Hours* and *60 Minutes II*.[20] Initially, *60 Minutes* debuted as a bi-weekly

---

15 *SmartBrief*—"The *SNL* Effect: *SNL* Political Skits Make Real Impact on Voters"

16 *Fifty Years of Television*, p. 32

17 *New York University Alumni Magazine*—"Live From New York, It's ..." Spring 2008

18 *Made You Laugh*, p. 64

19 *Fifty Years of Television*, p. 39

20 *Fifty Years of Television*, p. 39

show hosted by Harry Reasoner and Mike Wallace, airing on alternating Tuesday nights at 10 pm. In the show's first edition, Reasoner describes the series as a "kind of a magazine for television," featuring stories of national importance, but woven around people either involved with, or in conflict with, those issues. Each story was—and still is—limited to thirteen minutes of airtime.

When Reasoner left CBS in 1970 to co-anchor ABC's evening newscast (he would return to *60 Minutes* in '78), Morley Safer joined the team, and took on Reasoner's duties of reporting less-aggressive stories. Safer was softer than Reasoner, and even more of a contrast to the urbane but uncompromising Wallace who (when he chose to) took to his interviews with an unrelenting gusto. Both Wallace, with his hard-hitting reports, and Safer, with his, attracted a growing audience, particularly during the waning days of the Vietnam War and those surrounding the Watergate scandal. While other networks covered these events as well, no major-network news show could touch the in-depth investigative reporting carried out by *60 Minutes*. When the FCC implemented the Prime Time Access Rule in 1975, networks were ordered to lengthen prime time on Sunday by an hour for family viewing. CBS gave *60 Minutes* that extra hour and the show has remained in that same time slot for the past 37 years.

For most of the 1970s, *60 Minutes* included within its weekly broadcast a segment called "Point/Counterpoint," in which a liberal and a conservative commentator debated a particular issue. This segment usually ran at the end of the show, and originally featured James J. Kilpatrick representing the conservative side and Nicholas von Hoffman for the liberal. When von Hoffman departed in 1974, Shana Alexander took over Hoffman's place. The "Point/Counterpoint" segment was an innovation that caught the public imagination as a live version of competing editorials. Public awareness of the segment peaked when the segment was lampooned by the NBC comedy series *SNL*. The *SNL* parody featured Jane Curtin and Dan Aykroyd as fervent debaters, with Aykroyd playing the conservative debater who would typically begin his faux debate each week on *SNL* with the words: "Jane, you ignorant slut."

By 1976, *60 Minutes* had become the top-rated show on Sunday nights in the U.S. By 1979, it had achieved the number-one Nielsen rating for all television programs—a feat previously unheard of for a news broadcast in prime time.[21] Part of this success was due to the arrival of Andy Rooney to the show. In 1978, "Point/Counterpoint" was replaced by a new "Andy Rooney" segment that ran until Rooney's death in 2011. Each *60 Minute* episode usually ended with Rooney mixing brutal sarcasm with humorous commentary to expound on topics of varying import, ranging from international politics to his personal philosophy on everyday life.[22]

But while Andy Rooney gave us a feel-good minute at the end of every episode, Wallace and Safer and the many journalists (Dan Rather, Ed Bradley, Morton Dean, Charles Osgood, Charlie Rose, Forrest Sawyer, Connie Chung, Paula Zahn, Bryant Gumbel, Katie Couric, Steve Kroft, Lesley Stahl, Bob Simon, and Scott

---

21 *USA Today*—"Nielsen's Top 50 Shows" November 5, 1978

22 *60 Minutes: 25 Years of Television's Finest Hour* Santa Monica, p 17

Pelley among them), who followed in their very large footprints, gave viewers something of national or regional import to ponder. From Dan Rather's trek into Afghanistan during the Soviet invasion that came to predict the fall of the Soviet Union ten years later; to Ed Bradley's March 2000 death row interview with convicted Oklahoma City bomber, Timothy McVeigh, leading to a federal policy prohibiting face-to-face interviews with death row inmates;[23] to the1989 airing of a report claiming that the use of the chemical daminozide on apples presented an unacceptably high health risk to consumers. Apple sales dropped when the Environmental Protection Agency (EPA), because of the *60 Minute* report, banned its use on U.S. food crops. These stories and hundreds more have helped alter federal policy, derail hazardous commerce, and expose fraudulent behavior and world health risks for nearly half a century.

"One of the great joys," said *TV Guide* in 1984, "is watching the correspondents discover the story at the same time that we do"[24]—a series paradigm that has worked for almost fifty years. As of September 26, 2011, *60 Minutes* had won a total of 95 Emmy Awards, a record unsurpassed by any prime time show on any network. The show currently holds the record for the longest continuously running program of any genre scheduled during American network prime time, and was rated #6 on *TV Guide*'s 50 Greatest Shows of All Time.[25]

---

23 CBS News—"McVeigh Vents on 60 Minutes" March 13, 2000

24 *Fifty Years of Television*, p. 39

25 *Fifty Years of Television*, p. 254

Appendix 2

"The Upfronts"
A History of Television Class Project

OVERVIEW

By nature and design, university survey courses gravitate toward larger enrollments, with some classes having as many as 500 students in a single section. Most of these survey classes, however, lie somewhere within the 50–200 student range and meet in smart-rooms where visual stimuli are well supported by technology. While the technology allows each student-group presentation to be disseminated to the rest of the class, organization at the instructor level is a must for overseeing all group projects through each of their steps to fruition.

Because of the larger enrollments, survey courses often give but an overview of a curriculum's subject matter. The voluminous nature of the subject usually requires the instructor to isolate various events within that subject's purview, and use those events as bullet points for each week's lectures. Television history, as a curriculum for study, illuminates the point. While there are no existing records (only approximations) of how many television shows are produced each year in the United States, at the close of 2010, there were 4,728 television broadcast stations—including local and educational stations—in the United States, many of them filling 24 hours of airtime a day. This being the case, the number of TV programs created in the U.S. each year could number in the tens of thousands. Even if this number was reduced to include only prime time shows on broadcast television in the 20th century, the number of shows that would need to be discussed in a 16-week course would approach four thousand—an impossible chore, to be sure.

The "Upfronts Project" cuts into that formidability by helping instructors to disseminate information that might otherwise be missed. Student-groups (between 6 and 35 groups, depending on the size of the class) explore TV shows on their own and report their findings back to the class. In a sense, instructors can lead students to teach themselves, thus creating a far more robust classroom setting in the process. Each group takes a network's TV season between 1953 and 2005, and reprograms it with shows mined from another decade. Each group then pitches their "new fall season" in an 8-minute overview using PowerPoint or Prezi presentations, just like the broadcast networks do every spring with their affiliates at the "upfronts" in New York. Shows and details that professors could never hope to cover are covered for them by their students.

THE UPFRONTS PROJECT

Setting up:

Students will need an electronic copy of A Guide to TV by *TV Guide*. A call to the book's publisher, Barnes & Noble, by the university's textbook procurement folks should net them a master copy. The website **crazyabouttv.com** works too.

If using their e-book, students will download the files that bring them to the section titled "Primetime and Saturday Morning Program Grids—1953–2005" (maybe four fifths of the way through your CD to Folder 10/11).

If using the website, **crazyabouttv.com**, click on any series listed for details about that show.

Each student is part of a group of 6 to 7 "student executives" who will collectively design all support material for their pitch presentation. Depending on class size, anywhere from 6 to 35 groups will be needed. The assigned groups can be coordinated through your university's Blackboard system. Email addresses are attached to each student-group so that communication between group members and leaders and the instructor is painless.

Group leaders (chosen by the instructor) draw for their Fall Season their Network and the Decade from which they will mine their shows. [Note: Having students draw on the day of the midterm just before the test begins virtually ensures that you'll have every group leader in class that day.]

THE DRAW

What's to be included on the paper each student-group receives:

1956–1957	1987–1988	2004–2005
NBC	ABC	CBS
70's	60's	80's

- Each group is assigned a "fall season" ('55–'56/'87–'88/'01–'02), which it will be tasked to re-program.
- Each group is assigned a "network" (NBC/CBS/ABC). [Note: FOX, the CW, and all cable networks are missing. They weren't around for much of the 20th century and thus to keep the playing field level, it helps to use the "big three" only.]
- Each group is assigned a "decade" ('90's/'50's/'80's) from which they can mine their shows. [Note: Each fall season will *differ* from the decade ascribed to it.]

Students are welcome to mine shows from FOX/UPN/WB/CW when searching in decades where these networks appear. Cable series can only be mined after 2000. Each group thus has ten years and at least three networks full of programs at its disposal to fill but one TV network's season. The object of the project from here on out is simple.

THE OBJECTIVE

What the student-groups are attempting to do:

Using programs procured from one decade, each group will create a New Fall Line-Up for a network's season in another decade. This doesn't mean that students have to match western with western, drama with drama, or comedy with comedy. If it happens to work out that way, fine—and much of the time it might. What's important is that the student-groups match the shows in terms of "demographic tone." Gritty westerns are a lot like gritty crime shows. Yet *Bonanza* (a western) was really a family drama—more like *The Waltons* than *Deadwood*. Variety hours in one decade might easily pass for dramedies in another. Reality shows, like sports shows, could well capture the same target audience. Relative to tone, *Law &*

Order in the 1990s wasn't much different from the *Playhouse 90* anthology series of the 1950's. Audiences might watch both for the very same reasons.

THE PROCESS

What the student-groups are expected to do:

By the class immediately following "the draw," each group will have used either their *TV Guide* e-book, or Googled "United States Television Network Schedule" for the year in question, in order to create a hard copy of their fall season for their instructor to review. Every prime time show on the schedule must be in its place *precisely as it was* during their chosen year. [Note: By parsing out project duties like this—that is to say having certain elements due on certain dates—student-groups tend not to fall behind.]

Turning to the group's decade from which it will draw new shows, students can uncover information about shows by reviewing either the e-book or the **CrazyAboutTV** website. Every prime time series ever aired is in the book and on the website. The series choices belong to the students—ones their group will defend in its pitch during weeks 14 and 15 (15 only if class size is under 100). Between the midterm and the pitch, students will put together projects a week at a time, beginning with the draw.

Working on the project over the next month, each group is given time during class to prepare for their pitch presentation. On week 13 or 14 (depending on class size), student-groups deliver a "reloaded" fall season grid like their original grid, save that this time it will be filled with "replacement shows" from their assigned decade. Again, student-groups are given time in class to work out final details of the following week's pitch presentation, which will involve PowerPoint or Prezi visuals.

The night (or nights—again depending on class size) of the pitch, student-groups, dressed in business attire, have eight (8) minutes to pitch their network's "new season" to their peers (who serve as affiliates) in an upfronts setting. Presentations may incorporate various bits of analysis including Nielsen ratings, demographics, and how their series fit into the socio-political history of the time. A rubric used to grade the group's performance includes: Logic/History/Design/Clarity/Delivery/Eye Contact/Time. All students in the group receive the same grade.

Appendix 3

Chronology

TV's Journey—Lab to Living Room to Web

1844 • Samuel F.B. Morse sends first electric telegraph message over telegraph lines at 16,000 miles per second.

1874 • Thomas Alva Edison sells Western Union the rights to his Quadruplex Telegraph system for $10,000.

1876 • Alexander Graham Bell demonstrates use of the telephone.

1884 • German engineering student Paul Nipkow discovers television's scanning system and patents world's first mechanical television system called the Nipkow Disc.

1887 • Physicist Heinrich Hertz demonstrates the existence of electromagnetic waves.

1895 • Guglielmo Marconi sends wireless signals around his block, ringing doorbells.

1896 • Supreme Court decision in *Plessy v. Ferguson* promotes "separate but equal" clause leading to rigid segregation in America.

1897 • Marconi Wireless Company formed in Great Britain.
• German scientist Karl Braun invents the cathode ray tube.

1899 • Marconi visits U.S., demonstrates wireless technology for U.S. army and navy, and establishes American Marconi in Massachusetts.

1901 • Marconi sends first long-distance wireless message from Cornwall, England to St. Johns, Newfoundland, 2,100 miles away.
• Canadian Aubrey Fessenden achieves limited success with experiments in wireless voice transmission.

1906 • Inventor Lee de Forest develops the Audion tube for voice transmission with amplified sound.
• Inventor of television, Philo Taylor Farnsworth, born August 19, 1906.
• Fessenden broadcasts Christmas Eve music program and *Bible* reading to ships at sea.

1907 • The word "television" first used in *Scientific American*.

1908 • De Forest uses Audion tube to broadcast from Eiffel Tower.

1912 • News of *Titanic* disaster reaches U.S. via American Marconi operator David Sarnoff.
• Federal Radio Act of 1912 passed. Broadcasting licenses now required by law.

1914 • World War I commences. Civilian wireless transmissions suspended.

1916 • Office Manager David Sarnoff drafts the "radio box memo" urging American Marconi to market "radio music boxes."

1918 • World War I ends. U.S. Navy pushes for government monopoly over wireless transmission.

1919 • Congress settles for "private monopoly" of wireless broadcast—and the Radio Corporation of America (RCA) is born.
• GE and AT&T enter cross-licensing agreement with RCA to absorb American Marconi, taking over its assets.
• Samuel Paley opens the Congress Cigar Company in Philadelphia.

1920 • Westinghouse launches first radio station in America, KDKA, Election Day, 1920.

1921 • Westinghouse and United Fruit join AT&T and GE in RCA's cross-licensing pact.
• Sarnoff pitches RCA "radio music box" idea. 500,000 radios are sold just 12 months.

1922 • Philo Farnsworth draws first sketch of a television picture tube on the blackboard of his high school chemistry class.
• AT&T introduces toll broadcasting (i.e., radio commercials) creating new revenue stream.

1923 • Federal Trade Commission (FTC) begins investigation into allegations of RCA's radio monopoly.
• Sarnoff makes friends of former foes and RCA richer than ever with licensing-fee idea.
• A.C. Nielsen Company founded to give marketers reliable and objective information.

1924 • RCA begins private arbitration with AT&T in secrecy. AT&T leaves the broadcasting business forever.
• RCA inherits AT&T's flagship station and 19 others. The acquisition becomes the cornerstone of the National Broadcasting Company.

1925 • Inventor Charles Jenkins, mechanical television's biggest proponent, demonstrates the synchronized transmission of images and sound.
• Russian inventor, Vladimir Zworykin, applies for second electronic television system patent that is granted in 1928.

1926 • Farnsworth enters "50-50" TV partnership with George Everson and Leslie Gorrell.
• Farnsworth's share cut from 50% to 20% as Crocker Bank partners up with Farnsworth.
• RCA officially launches the NBC network on November 15, 1926.
• Scottish inventor John Baird produces first live moving image with his electromechanical television system.
• Congress Cigar Company goes public. Stock offering makes William S. Paley a millionaire at 25.
• Government defeat in *U.S. v. Zenith* leads to period of "airwave piracy."
• Another Zworykin TV camera experimental demonstration blows up at Westinghouse.

1927 • Farnsworth applies for all-electronic television system patent, January 7, 1927. Patent is granted in 1930.
• RCA divides NBC into two networks: NBC Red and NBC Blue.
• Mechanical TV strikes first blow. Jenkins broadcasts crude 48-line transmission of Secretary of Commerce, Herbert Hoover, from Washington D.C. to NY (221 mi).
• Baird bests Jenkins, sending mechanical TV image from Glasgow to London (438 mi).
• Farnsworth transmits first image (a straight line) with his new electronic TV system.
• Radio Act of 1927 passed by Congress. Federal Radio Commission formed to handle broadcast licenses.
• "The Jazz Singer" debuts—and the film business is ripe for sound.
• Bill Paley invests $500,000 in United Independent Broadcasters, allowing them to merge with the Columbia Phonographic Broadcasting System.

1928
- Farnsworth's TV demonstration fails before Hollywood crowd.
- Farnsworth demonstrates electronic television system for press, September 3, 1928.
- British Parliament selects Farnsworth's all-electronic television system over Baird's electro-mechanical system following side-by-side demonstrations in London.
- Joe Kennedy and David Sarnoff merge FBO into RKO leading RCA to manufacture sound systems for talking pictures.
- Paley becomes majority share-holder in and president of CPBS, changing the company name to the Columbia Broadcasting System (CBS).

1929
- RCA merges with the Victor Talking Machines Company—RCA-Victor is born.
- Stock market crashes in late October.
- *Amos 'n' Andy* becomes national radio series on the NBC network.
- Paramount buys 49% of CBS.
- Getting nowhere at Westinghouse, Zworykin pitches "electronic television" to Sarnoff and RCA, and is eventually hired.

1930
- David Sarnoff becomes president of RCA.
- U.S. Justice Department launches anti-trust suit against RCA and patent allies.

1931
- Farnsworth turns down RCA offer of $100,000 for Farnsworth's company.
- Farnsworth turns to Philco to help produce electronic television system.

1932
- RCA buys out patent partners, unifies the company under one flag.
- NBC becomes wholly owned subsidiary of the "new" RCA.

1933
- Independent inventor Edwin Armstrong discovers a way to eliminate static from radio broad casts and FM radio is hatched.
- NBC drives a wedge between Philco and Farnsworth resulting in the dissolution of their partnership.

1934
- Communication Act passed. Federal Communication Commission (FCC) replaces FRC.
- Farnsworth files suit against Zworykin and RCA over patent infringement.

1935
- Patent Court is unequivocal in upholding Farnsworth's electronic television claim and the "priority of invention" is awarded to Farnsworth.
- Journalist Edward R. Murrow joins the CBS network.

1936
- NBC conducts first experimental TV broadcast using the call letters, W2XBS.
- 1936 Olympics serves as the world's first televised sporting event.

1937 • NBC mobile TV unit active throughout New York City.
• Murrow dispatched to London to cover the Nazi advance through Europe.

1938 • Orson Welles broadcasts H.G. Wells' "War of the Worlds" on his radio show *Mercury Theater on the Air.*
• CBS airs the *CBS World News Roundup*. Longest-running program in broadcast history, the radio show, at 75, has never left the air.
• The House Un-American Activities Committee (HUAC) created by Congress.

1939 • RCA loses patent appeal and is forced to license Farnsworth's patents.
• Farnsworth Television & Radio Corporation approved by SEC.
• At New York World's Fair, Sarnoff declares himself "Father of Television" at RCA Exhibit.
• RCA pays Farnsworth $1,000,000 over 10 years for patent violations.
• First American broadcast of sporting event covers Princeton–Columbia baseball game.

1940 • NBC broadcasts first dramatic TV series, *The Streets of New York*, to a measly 2,500 TV set owners in all of New York City.
• Murrow describes the Nazi blitzkrieg over London.
• B-film actress Lucille Ball marries Cuban band leader Desi Arnaz.

1941 • CBS begins field tests with color television.
• America enters WW II.

1942 • CBS primed to produce mechanical color television sets, when the manufacturing of receivers for civilian use is suddenly halted by the War Department.

1943 • U.S. Supreme Court orders NBC to sell one of its two networks.
• NBC sells its Blue network to Life Savers candy magnate Edward J. Noble for $8M.

1944 • "D-Day Landing" is broadcast live via wireless transmitters manned by G.I.'s.

1945 • Noble's Blue Network Company, Inc. officially changes its name to the American Broadcasting Company.
• WW II ends. Middle class emerges in America.

1946 • NBC teams up with Gillette to broadcast prize fights from Madison Square Garden to veterans in hospitals just home from the war.

1947 • NBC partners with the DuMont Television Network to broadcast the World Series.
• Paley persuades *Amos 'n Andy* creators Charles Correll and Freeman Gosden to leave NBC for CBS.

- First of the anthology series *The Kraft Television Theater* airs on NBC.
- President Harry S. Truman signs into law the Federal Employees Loyalty Program.
- Lunatic used car salesman Earl "Madman" Muntz jumps from the car biz into the TV-selling biz and lowers the price of the American television set by as much as 70%.
- HUAC hearings on Hollywood commence.
- *Counterattack*, a weekly anti-Communist newsletter, surfaces in New York's business district.
- "The Hollywood Ten" blacklisted.

1948
- FCC creates Joint Technical Advisory Committee (JTAC) to study color television demonstrations from all networks.
- Supreme Court forces producer-distributors to divest themselves of their exhibition arms, in *U.S. v. Paramount et al.*
- NBC launches "Mr. Television," Milton Berle, as permanent host of *The Texaco Star Theater*.
- Moving from radio to television, *Candid Microphone* segues to *Candid Camera* and becomes one of TV's first reality shows.
- Community Access Television (CATV) first reaches homes in rural America.
- Lucille Ball stars with Richard Denning in the CBS radio hit, *My Favorite Husband*.
- FCC orders a freeze on television broadcast licenses that lasts four years.

1949
- NBC introduces its electronic color television system for the JTAC.
- JTAC selects the CBS mechanical television system over Sarnoff's objections.
- "Dum De Dum Dum" becomes NBC's calling card in the iconic police drama *Dragnet*.
- Syndicated columnist Ed Sullivan hosts CBS's *Toast of the Town* for the next 21 years.
- First of the prime time westerns, *The Lone Ranger* hits the TV trail on ABC.

1950
- FCC formally licenses CBS electro-mechanical color television system and declares it the standard for America television.
- Senator Joseph McCarthy promotes Red Scare tactics by giving "Wheeling Speech" to West Virginia's Republican Women's Club.
- Dancer Paul Draper's appearance on *Toast of the Town* attacked in the press.
- Korean War begins.
- *Counterattack* publishes the "Red Channels" report on Communists in America.
- CBS initiates a loyalty oath for all employees.
- Comedian Sid Caesar's *Your Show of Shows* premiers on NBC.
- Art Baker hosts *You Asked for It*—"oddities" provide reality programming for small screen.
- TV icon Jackie Gleason first appears on DuMont's *The Colgate Comedy Hour*, perfecting his sketch-comedy with a bit he calls "The Honeymooners."
- AC Nielsen moves from radio to TV with the Nielsen Television Index created to measure and rate TV audience share.
- Robert Tarlton develops first commercial cable television system in the United States.

1951 • CBS airs first color television broadcast (electro-mechanical)—a variety show, *Premier*.
• CBS's color television production suspended by the DOD due to Korean War.
• Murrow given Paley's blessing to commence with a CBS documentary series, *See It Now*.
• *Amos 'n' Andy* moves to television. Ernestine Wade reprises her radio role as "Sapphire Stevens" on TV, becoming the first black woman to star in a prime time series.
• Actor Philip Loeb from *The Goldbergs*, accused of being a communist, loses his TV job.
• Lucille Ball and real-life husband Desi Arnaz take Lucy's CBS radio show to television under the title *I Love Lucy*. Both take salary cuts in exchange for series aftermarket.

1952 • Brainchild of NBC VP Sylvester "Pat" Weaver, Jr., *The Today Show* is launched.
• Vice President Richard M. Nixon saves his career with "Checkers Speech."
• The Korean War ends.
• *The Adventures of Ozzie & Harriet* airs first of its 435 episodes—a sitcom record that stands for 42 years.
• Lucy's pregnancy forces series to shut down. Episodes from Season 1 are replayed to cover Lucy's downtime—and the "rerun" is born.

1953 • CBS gives up on mechanical color-TV system.
• RCA awarded license for an electronic-color television system that reigns through the remainder of the 20th century.
• Senator McCarthy wins a second term.
• 700 "Nielsen Families" hook up to the *audiometer*, connecting national audience to Nielsen tallies.

1954 • First national electronic color broadcast occurs New Year's Day, 1954, with the Tournament of Roses Parade.
• NBC's *The Tonight Show* premiers with host Steve Allen—and a 2nd Pat Weaver "institution" is born.
• Army–McCarthy Hearings conclude with McCarthy having accused the military, State Department, and the White House of sympathizing with Communists.
• Supreme Court decision *Brown v. Board* overturns *Plessy v. Ferguson*, allowing for integrated public schools.
• "Thunder on Sycamore Street" airs on Westinghouse Studio One, stoking racial fears.
• *Wonderful World of Disney* premiers on ABC.
• Demagogue Joe McCarthy undone by Murrow's anti-McCarthy exposé on *See It Now*.
• Senate votes to censure Joe McCarthy, December 2, 1954.

1955 • Blacklisted and out of work, actor Philip Loeb O.D.'s on sleeping pills in NY hotel.
• *The Honeymooners* becomes a 30-minute sitcom on CBS.
• CBS cancels *See It Now*'s weekly series when sponsors leave the show in deference to

McCarthy. The show, however, continues as a "series of special reports."
- Legendary actor John Wayne introduces *Gunsmoke* to America—a drama series that would run for 635 episodes—most in the annals of American television.
- The DuMont Television Network goes under, discontinuing its prime time programming.
- Rosa Parks refuses to give up her seat on a Alabama bus—and the Civil Rights Movement is born.
- Montgomery Bus Boycott led by local minister Martin Luther King, Jr.

1956
- The quiz show *Twenty-One* is launched on NBC.
- *Playhouse 90*, paragon of the anthology series, debuts on CBS.
- Metromedia acquires DuMont in what is tantamount to a fire sale.
- Videotape developed, replacing the kinescope.
- *The Nat King Cole Show* debuts on NBC—the first African-American to lead in a series since *Amos 'n' Andy*. Cole's series was canceled after only a year.

1957
- Senator Joe McCarthy dies of cancer at 49.
- Racial hatred rears its ugly head when nine black students enroll in Little Rock Central High School.
- Charles Van Doren, *Twenty-One's* big winner, turns out to be a big loser when it's discovered that *Twenty-One* gave Van Doren and others answers ahead of time.
- World's first artificial satellite, Sputnik 1, launched into earth orbit by Soviet Union.
- Desilu sells back *I Love Lucy* aftermarket to CBS for 4 million dollars.

1958
- Quiz Show Scandal breaks—network licenses in jeopardy.
- Paley cancels *See It Now* "for good." Murrow ends 23-year relationship with CBS.

1959
- Rod Serling creates *The Twilight Zone* for CBS to avoid sponsor censorship.
- Nixon–Khrushchev "Kitchen Debate" in Moscow.
- Khrushchev travels to U.S. to better American perceptions of the Soviet people.
- Cowboys dominate television as 7 of the 10 top-rated shows are Westerns.
- Popular series, *The Untouchables*, is condemned by many for its use of violence.
- Clint Eastwood garners fame as a supporting cast member in the TV series *Rawhide*.
- Quiz show scandals alter TV advertising paradigm. Magazine concept replaces single series sponsor. Advertising time now sold in 15-, 30-, and 60-second blocks.

1960
- American U-2 spy plane pilot Francis Gary Powers is shot down over Russia.
- Richard Nixon and John F. Kennedy meet center stage in The Great Debates—first of their kind to be televised.
- Kennedy elected President by the narrowest popular vote in U.S. history.

• ABC sports-producer Edger Scherick and new ABC-hire Roone Arledge create *Wide World of Sports*.

1961 • Connecticut Senator Tom Dodd and his sub-committee studies television violence.
• FCC Chairman Newton Minow addresses the National Association of Broadcasters.
• *The Dick Van Dyke Show* premiers, showcasing luminous newcomer Mary Tyler Moore.

1962 • Television is invited to watch as Lt. Col John Glenn becomes the first American astronaut to orbit Earth.
• President Kennedy pledges to put a man on the moon by the end of the decade.
• First U.S. communication satellite, Telstar 1, provides live transatlantic television feed.
• Communications Satellite Act calling for the privatization of Telstar is signed into law.
• Escapist sitcoms flourish on television.
• Johnny Carson takes over *The Tonight Show* from host Jack Parr … who replaced Ernie Kovacs … who replaced Steve Allen. Carson's reign lasts 30 years.
• Cuban Missile Crisis brings televised ultimatum to prime time.

1963 • Hughes Aircraft Corporation develops synchronous satellite system, solving line-of-sight problems.
• Dr. Martin Luther King, Jr. gives his "I Have a Dream" speech to 200,000 people at the Washington Monument—and millions more on television.
• President Kennedy assassinated in Dallas, Texas.
• Millions watch on television as Jack Ruby guns down accused assassin Lee Harvey Oswald during Oswald's transfer to federal prison.
• President Lyndon B. Johnson takes the Oath of Office on Air Force One.

1964 • Freedom Riders Schwerner, Goodman, and Chaney are murdered in Mississippi by the Ku Klux Klan.
• Escalation of the Vietnam War begins with the Gulf of Tonkin Resolution.

1965 • NBC launches color TV with prime time fall schedule and its signature series, *Bonanza*.
• Bill Cosby stars with Robert Culp in the first integrated series on television, *I Spy*.
• Charles Dolan starts the Sterling Manhattan Cable company (SMC) in NYC with help from a CATV system in Pennsylvania.
• Time-Life, Inc. purchases 20% of SMC.

1966 • ABC's *That Girl* becomes the first socially conscious comedy, letting women know they don't need to sacrifice a career for marriage.
• Gulf+Western diversifies, buying fledgling Paramount Pictures to get leg up in

communications business.
- NBC's *Star Trek* debuts, launching a 40-year saga to a place no series had gone before.

1967
- *The Fugitive* scores big with finale as 72% of America tunes in to watch—most to that point in Nielsen ratings history.
- Desilu Studios sold to Gulf+Western for $67M.
- Gulf+Western changes name to Paramount Television.

1968
- College basketball becomes prime time entertainment when #1 UCLA and #2 University of Houston hook up in "Game of the Century."
- CBS anchorman Walter Cronkite hosts "Viet Nam Special Report" during prime time. Cronkite tells America it's losing the war.
- Johnson announces on television that he will not seek a second term as president.
- Reverend Martin Luther King, Jr. is assassinated in Memphis.
- Robert Kennedy is assassinated in Los Angeles 15 minutes after winning the California presidential primary.
- Dianne Carroll stars in *Julia*—the first black woman to lead a prime time series in 15 years.
- *Laugh-In* revamps the "garden variety" variety show with relevant humor.
- Democratic National Convention in Chicago ends in what a dozen reports would later call a "police riot."
- Richard M. Nixon rises from the political ashes to win the U.S. presidency.
- "The Heidi Game" stirs up prime time controversy as NBC switches from football to holiday family movie with no warning.
- Television covers the space race as U.S. astronauts orbit the moon for the first time.
- U.S. sprinters Tommy Smith and John Carlos are stripped of medals for bringing political protest to Mexico City Olympics.
- *Tick-tick-tick-tick-tick*—CBS launches *60 Minutes* and an unlikely institution is born.

1969
- PBS launches hit series for children called *Sesame Street*.
- *The Smothers Brothers Comedy Hour* is "censored" off the air.
- U.S. astronauts Armstrong and Aldrin become first to land on the moon.

1970
- Nixon orders secret and illegal bombing of Cambodia.
- Four Kent University students gunned down by Ohio National Guard after campus protests led to ROTC bombing.
- *The Mary Tyler Moore Show* debuts on CBS with duel "platform"—home and office. The series showed that women could have both.
- *Monday Night Football* premiers on ABC.
- Philips develops the first home videocassette format (**V**ideo **H**ome **S**ystem).
- Fated adversaries 'til the end: Farnsworth dies in March, Sarnoff in December.

1971 • CBS series *All in the Family* premiers to disappointing ratings but soon becomes #1 show on television.
• CBS programming chief Fred Silverman begins systematic elimination of the network's popular "country-oriented shows" in a move that became known as the "rural purge."
• Ban on cigarette advertising on television goes into effect.
• Steven Spielberg's TV movie "Duel" is among the first made directly for television.
• MOW *Brian's Song* goes on to win 5 Emmys, a Peabody, DGA & WGA awards, and NAACP citation.

1972 • Comedian George Carlin arrested while performing his "Seven Dirty Words You Can't Say on TV" comedy act in Milwaukee.
• Watergate break-in at Democratic National Headquarters dismissed by Republican White House as a "third-rate burglary."
• *M*A*S*H* becomes CBS's third comedy blockbuster in less than two years.
• Passage of NCAA's "Title Nine" finally allows women "between the lines."
• Palestinian terrorists attack Munich Olympics, killing 11 Israeli athletes and coaches.
• Time-Life's Green Channel on SMC changes its name to Home Box Office.

1973 • *An American Family* debuts on PBS, giving audiences a voyeuristic look into the lives, loves, and fears of a Santa Barbara (CA) family.
• *Miller v. California* becomes the applicable test for "obscenity law" in America.
• Watergate Hearings give PBS record ratings.
• 18-minute gap on one of the Watergate tapes becomes "smoking gun" that trips up Nixon, pointing to a White House cover-up.
• Billy Jean King defeats Bobby Riggs in a tennis match dubbed "The Battle of the Sexes."
• With *Streets of San Francisco*, a new genre is born—the police procedural.

1974 • Richard Nixon becomes first American president to resign from office.
• ABC makes gutsy call turning Leon Uris' best-selling novel *QB VII* into TV's first mini-series.
• Federal Election Campaign Act (FECA) requires political campaigns to report names, addresses, and occupations of donors of $200 or more.

1975 • Silverman jumps the CBS ship for ABC.
• After 11 years, the world watches as the Vietnam War come to an inglorious end on prime time television.
• HBO first to use satellite feed to deliver Muhammad Ali–Joe Frasier heavyweight championship bout dubbed the "Thrilla in Manila."
• *Saturday Night Live* (*SNL*) premiers on NBC, turning low-rated TV hour into cash cow.

1976
- Silverman's "Jiggle TV" helps make ABC a ratings topper.
- America celebrates 200th birthday.
- Philips initiates first public demonstration of its optical digital audio disc—and the compact disk is born.

1977
- ABC's mini-series *Roots* airs in January, depicting one family's saga through 225 years of slavery in America, breaks TV audience ratings records.
- ABC becomes #1 network under Silverman.
- Out-of-work media salesman Bill Rasmussen launches first 24/7 sports network, calling it the Entertainment Sports Programming Network (ESPN).

1978
- NBC hires Silverman away from ABC.

1979
- NCAA Finals match-up between Michigan State's Magic Johnson and Indiana State's Larry Bird helps college basketball set NCAA TV ratings record.
- American Embassy in Iran overrun by students. 52 American hostages taken captive.
- *Sports Center* debuts on ESPN.

1980
- The Soviets invade Afghanistan.
- Team USA's defeat of the Soviet Union at the Lake Placid Winter Olympics previews a changing world order.
- Ted Turner creates CNN—first 24-hour news service. "We won't go off the air until the world ends," quipped Turner on the day he opened. To this day, the network has never been off the air.
- America boycotts the Moscow Summer Olympics.
- NBC forced to cancel 150 hours of programming due to U.S. Olympic Boycott.
- *Magnum P.I.* charts new territory when it comes to acceptance of Vietnam vets.
- Former actor Ronald Reagan is elected president.
- Ratings record-setting *Dallas'* episode, "Who Shot JR," airs in November on CBS.

1981
- Iranian hostages released as President Ronald Reagan takes the oath of office.
- Fred Silverman leaves NBC to Grant Tinker and new programming head Brandon Tartikoff.
- *Hill Street Blues* is launched on NBC and alters the fabric of episodic paradigm.
- Cable Channel HBO expands programming schedule to 24 hours a day.

1982
- NBC's *St. Elsewhere* ushers in the era of the "demographic hit"—a Nielsen category embraced by the "right" demographic audience as opposed to a large one.
- With 60.2 Nielsen rating and 77 share, *M*A*S*H** finale stands alone as the most-watched prime time TV episode in the 20th century—125 million viewers.
- *Family Ties* becomes Reagan's favorite series and launches career of Michael J. Fox.

- Reagan Administration fosters "Reaganomics" (trickle-down economics) and begins era of federal deregulation.
- First of the blockbuster ensemble comedies, *Cheers* debuts in last place and is nearly canceled.
- Billy Joel's Grammy-winning album "52nd Street" is first to be released on CD.

1983
- CBS's *Cagney & Lacey*, canceled one year into its six-year run, is renewed because of letter writing campaign. Women were well served by this drama series.
- NBC's *Remington Steele* becomes point-series for a new TV genre—the dramedy.
- First made-for-pay-TV movie, *The Terry Fox Story*, airs on HBO.

1984
- *The Cosby Show* rockets Bill Cosby to super-stardom while helping alter the perception of the African-American family on television.
- Inspired by a cocktail napkin bearing two words ("MTV cops"), *Miami Vice* debuts on NBC—and network ratings soar.
- Disney shareholders bring in Michael Eisner and former Warner Brothers chief Frank Wells to strengthen the company.

1985
- Paley ousted at CBS when Loews Theater chain owner, Larry Tisch, buys controlling interest in the network.
- News Corp buys Metromedia TV stations in order to start 4th broadcast network.

1986
- Capital Cities Corporation acquires ABC.
- GE takes over RCA, paying $6.4B for prize nugget NBC and selling off the rest.
- Bob Wright appointed president and CEO of NBC Universal Group.
- *The Late Show* with Joan Rivers premiers on FOX—and a 4th broadcast network is born.
- What he did for cops with *HSB*, Steven Bochco does for lawyers in creating *LA Law*.

1987
- Cutting-edge comedy *Married . . . with Children* becomes first prime time series for FOX.

1988
- *Roseanne* debuts on ABC and makes the dial safe again for blue-collar families.

1989
- FOX's award-winning animated comedy *The Simpsons* premiers and becomes the network's first top-30 show.
- Time, Inc. acquires Warner Bros—and media colossus Time-Warner is formed.
- "TGIF," a family-friendly prime time television programming block, is launched on ABC.
- *The Seinfeld Chronicles* debuts to horrible numbers. NBC tries selling it to FOX who wants nothing to do with it.
- Based on the EC Comic series by the same name, HBO's *Tales from the Crypt* becomes cable TV's first weekly scripted series produced for prime time viewing.

1990 • *Seinfeld Chronicles* changes its name to *Seinfeld*, adds a woman to the cast, goes on to become the first-ever series (comedy or drama) to rate highest over a full season.
• Children's Television Act creates "safe harbor" for adult series between 10 pm and 6 am.
• *Law & Order* premiers on NBC. Series franchise would become the most durable in TV history and was considered by many industry executives to be actor-proof.

1991 • *Home Improvement* becomes top-rated show and one of the very few successes enjoyed by ABC during the entire decade.
• David Letterman vies with Jay Leno to host *The Tonight Show* after Carson's retirement.
• Big shoes to fill for Warren Littlefield who takes over NBC for Tartikoff, off to Paramount.
• Lakers basketball star Ervin "Magic" Johnson announces that he has tested positive for HIV/AIDS and retires from professional basketball.

1992 • *The Larry Sanders Show* garners 24 major awards and 53 Emmy nominations serving notice that "It's not TV. It's HBO."
• Johnny Carson retires from *The Tonight Show*.

1993 • CBS MOW *Dr. Quinn, Medicine Woman* becomes network's surprise series of the year.
• NBC, wanting greater viewership on Thursday nights, creates the "Must See TV" slogan to brand its comedy block.
• Writers Marta Kauffman and David Crane pitch *Insomnia Café* to producer Kevin Bright. Bright changes the title to *Six of One* and pitches it to NBC, which then develops the series under the working title *Friends Like Us*.
• *The X-Files* debut on FOX gives the network its first blockbuster hit.
• ABC launches *NYPD Blue*, a controversial (and award-winning) Bochco cop show that pushed the bounds of nudity on broadcast TV. Series became the only show to make Nielsen Top 20 in every demographic category during its inaugural season.
• *Frasier* debuts on NBC—goes on to be the greatest comedy spinoff in the annals of TV.

1994 • *E.R.* vs. *Chicago Hope*: Medical shows debuting hours apart vie for programming dominance in the 90's.
• *Friends Like Us* shortens its title to *Friends* and debuts in the coveted 8:30 Thursday night time slot, where it remains for the next ten seasons.

1995 • Time-Warner jumps into pixel fray debuting its own network, the WB.
• Paramount follows Time-Warner lead and launches UPN as the sixth American broadcast network.
• DVDs (Dissociated Vertical Deviation disks) invented by Philips for increased storage capacity over compact discs.
• Les Moonves becomes president of CBS Entertainment.

- First prime time game show in America to be staged away from a studio set, *Eco-Challenge* premiers on The Discovery Channel.
- CAA founder Michael Ovitz brought in by Disney's Eisner after Katzenberg resigns.

1996
- *Everybody Loves Raymond* proves a bright spot for CBS and the first series developed under Les Moonves' reign to lower the network's "geriatric-skewing" demographic
- Telecommunications Act calls for V-Chip to help parents block shows from their children.

1997
- HBO's *Oz*, a prison drama, becomes the premium cable network's first one-hour drama.
- Ellen DeGeneres' historic moment arrives during an episode of *Ellen*, where DeGeneres, both in character and as herself, comes out as a lesbian on prime time television.
- Industry alliance develops TV Ratings Key and mandates its use for every show on TV.

1998
- Warren Littlefield leaves NBC leaving a revolving door of short-lived presidents.
- With the debut of *Sex and the City*, HBO's fifth comedy release of the decade, the proverbial locker room in America became coed.

1999
- Writer-producer David E. Kelley pulls off TV first, winning Emmys for both Outstanding Drama (*The Practice*) and Outstanding Comedy (*Ally McBeal*) in same year.
- Writer/director Aaron Sorkin morphs "An American President" into *West Wing* for NBC.
- While *Oz* won critical acclaim for HBO, it isn't until the debut of *The Sopranos* that the network has a drama that earns Emmy success as well as critical mass (an audience).
- British producer Mark Burnett secures the U.S. rights to a British TV show called *Sole Survivor* and pitches his idea to American with little initial success.
- The DVR (Digital Video Recorder) is invented to allow consumers to record on hard-disk-based digital video recorders making "time shifting" more convenient.
- *Law & Order* spinoff *Law & Order: Special Victims Unit* (*SVU*) debuts. Dramatic powerhouse like its parent show, the series entered its 14th season in 2012.

2000
- Michael J. Fox leaves ABC's *Spin City*, announcing he has Parkinson's Disease.
- *Survivor* premiers on CBS and knocks ABC's *Who Wants to Be a Millionaire?* from the Nielsen #1 spot in just two weeks.
- Richard Hatch becomes *Survivor*'s first million-dollar winner.
- Answer to the question: *Who Wants to Marry a Multi-Millionaire?* turns out to be no one when runaway ratings are topped by "runaway bride," as groom turns out to be a fraud.
- Jeff Zucker takes the reins as new NBC president.
- CBS's police procedural drama *CSI: Crime Scene Investigation* (also known as *CSI: Las Vegas*) is the undisputed hit of the season.
- Robert Iger comes aboard as president of Disney.

2001
- 2,977 people die when Osama bin Laden and his terrorist network al-Qaeda attack New York's World Trade Center.
- British record guru Simon Cowell pitches new talent show around town with no success.
- HBO launches HBO-on-Demand—the first subscription video-on-demand service in U.S.
- *Law & Order: Criminal Intent* debuts. Show lasts ten seasons—part of a franchise that is now in its 23rd consecutive season on prime time television.

2002
- FOX, needing a breakout hit, finds one in *American Idol: Search for a Superstar* (name shortened after Season 1 to *American Idol*). Series breaks all Nielsen ratings records including the one that counted most: seven straight seasons as #1 show on TV.
- Basic cable network AMC changes programming format, leading to more commercials.
- CSI spinoff *CSI: Miami* debuts—and runs ten seasons.

2004
- *The Apprentice* debuts as the ultimate job interview. Contestants are curtly dismissed each week by billionaire Donald Trump with his national catchphrase: "You're fired."
- HBO's *The Sopranos* becomes first cable show to win the Emmy for Outstanding Drama Series—the first of two such awards to go with 20 other Emmys and 111 nominations.
- *Rescue Me* draws huge cable audience, weaves its 7-season tale of the 9/11 attacks.
- Braun fired for greenlighting *Lost*—the most expensive series pilot in ABC history.
- *Lost* debuts on ABC, becomes both the critical and commercial success of the season, then wins the season's Emmy for Outstanding Drama Series.
- NBC announces Conan O'Brien will replace Jay Leno in 2009 after Leno retires.
- *Desperate Housewives* follows *Lost* with the same critical and commercial success, leading ABC's charge from outhouse to penthouse.
- Third CSI spinoff, *CSI: New York*, premiers on CBS and pushes the franchise forward.

2005
- JJ Abrams wins the trifecta, honored for his work on *Lost* with Emmys for writing, directing, and producing.
- ABC finds reality gold of their own in *Dancing with the Stars*.
- Les Moonves becomes president and CEO of CBS Corporation.
- *Weeds* debuts to an immediate fan base and earns premium cable network Showtime its highest-rated series premier ever.
- UPN's 17-year *Star Trek* franchise comes to an end.
- First YouTube video posted in April. By November 200,000 viewers watching 2M shorts.
- Disney's Iger succeeds Eisner as president and CEO of The Walt Disney Company.

2006
- *Dexter*'s debut on Showtime is protested by Parents Television Council (PTC) because of its gruesome content. Series centers on Dexter Morgan, a blood-spatter analyst for the Miami Metro P.D., who moonlights as a serial killer.

• Viacom and CBS Corporation split. CBS takes over "Viacom" name on NYSE.
• CBS-owned UPN melds with the WB to form new broadcast network, the CW.

2007 • Zucker succeeds Bob Wright as CEO of NBC Universal Group.
• AMC gets into the prime time series game with *Mad Men* to combat shrinking audience.

2008 • NBC's *30 Rock* accepts 17 Emmy nominations, breaking previous comedy series record.
• *Breaking Bad* premiers 6 months after *Mad Men*—and AMC network is suddenly hot.
• Wall Street crashes. Banks bailed out by U.S. government.
• Barack Obama becomes the first African-American elected President in U.S. history.

2009 • Zucker tells press that many at NBC no longer believe the network can bounce back.
• Conan O'Brien replaces Jay Leno as *The Tonight Show* host—and ratings plummet.
• Late Night moves to Prime Time when *The Jay Leno Show* fills NBC's 10 pm hour.

2010 • Leno returns as host of *The Tonight Show*. O'Brien sues NBC.
• Zucker announces he's stepping down at NBC Universal following Comcast purchase.
• Brian Cranston becomes 3-peat winner for Best Actor in a Drama Series, *Breaking Bad*.
• A $4.3M webisode, "Sanctuary," is posted on Internet.

2011 • Comcast purchases 51% of NBC Universal as GE throttles back.
• AMC's *Mad Men* wins fourth consecutive Emmy for Outstanding Drama Series.

2012 • *Law & Order: SVU* airs the 990th original episode in the *Law & Order* franchise.

Appendix 4

American Reality Genres

(Shows listed chronologically, minimum 6 episodes)

Documentary

In this genre, camera crews follow the daily interactions of people in ordinary places, or follow people in a specific profession.

An American Family (1973) • PBS
The Real World (1992) • MTV
Road Rules (1995) • MTV
Airline (2003) • A&E
Bug Juice (1998) • DISNEY
True Life (1998) • MTV
Making of the Band (2000) • MTV/ABC
Scariest Places on Earth (2000) • FOX FAMILY
Project Greenlight (2001) • HBO
Sorority Life (2002) • MTV
American Chopper (2003) • DISCOVERY
Fraternity Life (2003) • MTV
The Restaurant (2003) • NBC
Starting Over (2003) • SYNDICATED
American Casino (2004) • DISCOVERY
American Hot Rod (2004) • DISCOVERY
Amish in the City (2004) • UPN
Bands Reunited (2004) • VH1
The Casino (2004) • FOX
The First 48 (2004) • A&E
College Hill (2004) • BET
Family Plots (2004) • A&E
Laguna Beach: The Real Orange County (2004) • MTV
Dog Whisperer (2004) • NATIONAL GEOGRAPHIC

Deadliest Catch (2005) • DISCOVERY
Miami Ink (2005) • TLC
Who's Your Daddy (2005) • FOX
8th & Ocean (2006) • MTV
Bonds on Bonds (2006) • ESPN
King of Cars (2006) • A&E
Deadline (2007) • ITV2
Ice Road Truckers (2007) • HISTORY
Kate Plus 8 (2007) • TLC
Ax Men (2008) • HISTORY
BBQ Pitmasters (2009) • TLC
The Colony (2009) • DISCOVERY
Pawn Stars (2009) • HISTORY
Teen Mom (2009) • MTV
Toddlers & Tiaras (2009) • TLC
American Pickers (2010) • HISTORY/LIFETIME
The Generations Project (2010) • BYU CHANNEL
Throttle Junkies (2010) • SYNDICATED
Oddities (2010) • DISCOVERY
Sister Wives (2010) • TLC
American Restoration (2010) • HISTORY
Auction Hunters (2010) • SPIKE
Hardcore Pawn (2010) • TRUTV
Storage Wars (2010) • A&E
Swamp People (2010) • HISTORY
Dance Moms (2011) • LIFETIME
Here Comes Honey Boo Boo (2012) • TLC
Bikini Barbershop (2012) • AXS TV

Dating

Couples or singles in this genre are brought together in dating or romantic situations.

The Dating Game (1965) • ABC
The Newlywed Game (1966) • ABC
He Said She Said (1969) • SYNDICATED
Love Connection (1983) • SYNDICATED
Blind Date (1999) • SYNDICATED
Who Wants to Marry a Millionaire? (2000) • FOX
Fifth Wheel (2001) • SYNDICATED
Dismissed (2001) • MTV
Temptation Island (2001) • FOX
The Bachelor (2002) • ABC
EX-treme Dating (2002) • FOX REALITY
Meet My Folks (2002) • NBC
Average Joe (2003) • NBC
The Bachelorette (2003) • ABC
For Love or Money (2003) • NBC
Joe Millionaire (2003) • FOX
Married by America (2003) • FOX
Boy Meets Boy (2003) • BRAVO
Who Wants to Marry My Dad? (2003) • NBC
Room Raiders (2004) • MTV
My Big Fat Obnoxious Fiancé (2004) • FOX
Playing It Straight (2004) • FOX
Date My Mom (2004) • FOX
Parental Control (2005) • MTV
Next (2005) • MTV
Flavor of Love (2006) • VH1
I Love New York (2007) • VH1
Age of Love (2007) • NBC
The Pick Up Artist (2007) • VH1
A Shot at Love with Tila Tequila (2007) • MTV
Rock of Love with Bret Michaels (2007) • VH1
When Spicy Meets Sweet (2008) • MTV
Real Chance of Love (2008) • VH1
Momma's Boys (2008) • NBC
For the Love of Ray J (2009) • VH1
More to Love (2009) • FOX
Seducing Cindy (2010) • FOX

Hidden Camera

Perhaps the oldest reality-show genre, its popularity began in radio and became a part of television's early lore.

Candid Camera (1948) • ABC
TV's Bloopers & Practical Jokes (1984) • NBC
Totally Hidden Video (1989) • FOX
Cheaters (2000) • SYNDICATED
Spy TV (2001) • NBC
The Jamie Kennedy Experiment (2002) • WB
Oblivious (2002) • TNN/SPIKE TV
Girls Behaving Badly (2002) • OXYGEN
Punk'd (2003) • MTV
Scare Tactics (2003) • SYFY
Boiling Points (2004) • MTV
Hi-Jinks (2005) • NICK AT NITE

Game Shows

Largest and most successful of the reality genres, this one features contestants who compete for prizes. Some compete on stage. Others (more recently) compete while living together in close quarters.

(on set—ratings leaders by year)

Cash and Carry (1946) • DUMONT
Breaking the Bank (1948) • ABC
Quizzing the News (1948) • ABC
What's My Line? (1950) • CBS
Beat the Clock (1950) • CBS
Truth or Consequences (1950) • CBS
You Bet Your Life (1950) • NBC
I've Got A Secret (1952) • CBS
Name That Tune (1952) • NBC
Masquerade Party (1952) • NBC
The $64,000 Question (1955) • CBS
Queen for a Day (1956) • NBC
Who Do You Trust? (1956) • CBS
The Price is Right (1956) • NBC
Tic-Tac-Dough (1956) • NBC
Twenty One (1956) • CBS
To Tell the Truth (1956) • CBS
Concentration (1958) • NBC
GE College Bowl (1959) • CBS
Password (1961) • CBS
The Match Game (1962) • NBC
Let's Make a Deal (1963) • NBC
Jeopardy (1964) • NBC
Hollywood Squares (1966) • NBC
The Joker's Wild (1973) • CBS
The $10,000 Pyramid (1973) • CBS
Card Sharks (1973) • NBC
Wheel of Fortune (1975) • NBC
Family Feud (1976) • ABC
Win, Lose or Draw (1987) • NBC
American Gladiators (1989) • SYNDICATED
Who Wants to Be a Millionaire? (US) (1999) • ABC
Weakest Link (US) (2001) • NBC
Deal or No Deal (2006) • TROS

(in close quarters—ratings leaders by year)

Eco-Challenge (1995) • DISCOVERY
Big Brother (1997) • CBS
The Challenge (1998) • MTV
Survivor (2000) • CBS
The Mole (US) (2001) • ABC/FOX REALITY
The Amazing Race (US) (2001) • CBS
Cannonball Run 2001 (2001) • USA
Fear Factor (2001) • NBC
Boot Camp (2001) • FOX
Murder in Small Town X (2001) • FOX
Lost (2001) • NBC
Beg, Borrow & Deal (2002) • ESPN
Under One Roof (2002) • UPN
Dog Eat Dog (2002) • NBC
Endurance (2002) • NBC
I'm a Celebrity ... Get Me Out of Here! (US) (2003) • ABC
Paradise Hotel (2003) • FOX
The Apprentice (2004) • NBC

The Benefactor (2004) • ABC
Forever Eden (2004) • FOX
Mad Mad House (2004) • SYFY
Beauty and the Geek (2005) • WB
Solitary (2006) • FOX REALITY
Treasure Hunters (2006) • NBC
Unan1mous (2006) • FOX
Pirate Master (2007) • CBS
I Love Money (2008) • VH1
Wipeout (2008) • ABC
I Survived a Japanese Game Show (2008) • ABC
13: Fear is Real (2009) • CW
Great American Road Trip (2009) • NBC

Talent Searches

Similar to the game-show genre in that there are eliminations and a final winner, this genre centers on contestants competing a specific skill or talent, rather than a random challenge.

The Original Amateur Hour (1948) • DUMONT
Arthur Godfrey's Talent Scouts (1948) • CBS
The Gong Show (1976) • NBC
Star Search (1983) • SYNDICATED
Band on the Run (2001) • VH1
American Idol (2002) • FOX
WWF Tough Enough (2001) • MTV
America's Next Top Model (2003) • UPN
Last Comic Standing (2003) • NBC
Nashville Star (2003) • USA
Surf Girls (2003) • MTV
The Assistant (2004) • MTV
Dream Job (2004) • ESPN
Next Action Star (2004) • NBC
The Rebel Billionaire: Branson's Quest for the Best (2004) • FOX
Project Runway (2004) • BRAVO
The Contender (2005) • NBC
Hell's Kitchen (2005) • FOX
Dancing with the Stars (US) (2005) • ABC
Rock Star: INXS (2005) • CBS
The Next Food Network Star (2005) • FOOD NETWORK
So You Think You Can Dance (2005) • FOX
The Ultimate Fighter (2005) • SPIKE
Skating with Celebrities (2006) • FOX
America's Got Talent (2006) • NBC
Top Chef (2006) • BRAVO
American Inventor (2006) • ABC
Who Wants to be a Superhero (2006) • SYFY
The One: Making a Music Star (2006) • ABC
Rock Star: Supernova (2006) • CBS
Knight School (2006) • ESPN
Grease: You're the One That I Want (2007) • NBC
Ego Trip's (magazine) The (White) Rapper Show (2007) • VH1
The Next Iron Chef (2007) • FOOD NETWORK
On the Lot (2007) • FOX
Top Design (2007) • BRAVO
Phenomenon (2007) • NBC
Pussycat Dolls Present: The Search for the Next Doll (2007) • CW
America's Most Smartest Model (2007) • VH1
America's Best Dance Crew (2008) • MTV
Stylista (2008) • CW
Ego Trip's Miss Rap Supreme (2008) • VH1
I Know My Kid's a Star (2008) • VH1
Scream Queens (2008) • VH1
Redemption Song (2008) • FUSE TV
The Glee Project (2011) • OXYGEN
The Voice (2011) • NBC
The X Factor (2011) • FOX
Face Off (2011) • SYFY

Science/Animal World

This genre documents scientific analysis or exploration firsthand.

When Animals Attack (1996) • FOX
The Crocodile Hunter (1997) • DISCOVERY
Mythbusters (2003) • DISCOVERY
Human Wrecking Balls (2008) • G4
Doing Da Vinci (2009) • DISCOVERY

Paranormal

Shows place participants into frightening situations that ostensibly involve supernatural or paranormal activity.

The Scariest Place on Earth (2000) • ABC FAMILY
Fear (2001) • MTV
Celebrity Paranormal Project (2006) • VH1
Paranormal State (2007) • A&E
Ghost Hunters (2008) • SYFY
Finding Big Foot (2011) • ANIMAL PLANET

Law Enforcement

In this genre, camera crews follow cops and bounty hunters in the pursuit of criminals.

Cops (1989) • FOX
Rescue 911 (1989) • CBS
Real Stories of the Highway Patrol (1993) • SYNDICATED
LAPD: Life on the Beat (1995) • SYNDICATED
World's Wildest Police Videos (1998) • FOX
Dog the Bounty Hunter (2003) • A&E
The Academy (2007) • FOX REALITY
Inside American Jail (2007) • SPIKE
DEA (2008) • SPIKE
Steven Seagal: Lawman (2009) • A&E

Stunts

These series featured people performing stunts and reenactments of allegedly paranormal events.

Ripley's Believe It or Not! (1949) • NBC
You Asked For It (1950) • DUMONT
Real People (1979) • NBC
That's Incredible (1980) • ABC

Court Room

Showing actual cases with the actual parties involved is the reality trend. Parties submit lawsuits to the show via their website, telephone, or through studio research.

People's Court (1981) • SYNDICATED
Judge Judy (1996) • SYNDICATED
Judge Mathis (1999) • SYNDICATED
Judge Joe Brown (1998) • CBS
Judge Mills Lane (1998) • SYNDICATED
Judge Hatchett (2000) • SYNDICATED
Judge Alex (2005) • SYNDICATED

Makeover

This increasingly popular genre features ordinary people having home or lifestyle makeovers with the assistance of professionals.

This Old House (1979) • PBS
A Makeover Story (2000) • TLC
Trading Spaces (2000) • TLC/DISCOVERY
Made (2002) • MTV
While You Were Out (2002) • TLC
Extreme Makeover (2002) • ABC
Monster Garage (2002) • DISCOVERY

What Not To Wear (2003) • TLC
Clean House (2003) • STYLE
Clean Sweep (2003) • TLC
Monster House (2003) • DISCOVERY
Queer Eye for the Straight Guy (2003) • BRAVO
Knock First (2003) • ABC FAMILY
Extreme Makeover: Home Edition (2003) • ABC
Pimp My Ride (2004) • MTV
Designed to Sell (2004) • HGTV
The Swan (2004) • FOX
Overhaulin' (2004) • TLC
Dr. 90210 (2004) • E!
Queer Eye for the Straight Girl (2005) • BRAVO

Lifestyle Change

In this genre, ordinary people experience an extraordinary change in themselves, their environments, or their occupations.

Faking It (US) (2003) • TLC/DISCOVERY
The Biggest Loser (2004) • NBC
He's a Lady (2004) • TBS
Nanny 911 (2004) • FOX
Trading Spouses (2004) • FOX
Wife Swap (2004) • ABC
Supernanny (2005) • STYLE
30 Days (2005) • FX
Intervention (2005) • A&E
Shalom in the Home (2005) • TLC
Survival of the Richest (2005) • WB
Bad Girls Club (2006) • OXYGEN
Fat March (2007) • ABC
Charm School (2007) • VH1
From G's to Gents (2008) • MTV
Tool Academy (2009) • VH1
Hoarders (2009) • A&E

Historical Re-Creation

This genre takes modern-day contestants and drops them into the lifestyle of historical people or places.

1900 House (1999) • PBS
Colonial House (2004) • PBS
MTV's The 70s House (2005) • MTV
Kid Nation (2007) • CBS

Voyeuristic

This genre, launched most successfully of late by the music and arts channels, follows a camera crew into the lives of celebrities or celebrity wannabes.

This Is Your Life (1952) • NBC
The Anna Nicole Show (2002) • E!
The Osbournes (2002) • MTV
The Surreal Life (2003) • WB
Newlyweds: Nick and Jessica (2003) • MTV
Rich Girls (2003) • MTV
The Simple Life (2003) • FOX
'Til Death Do Us Part: Carmen and Dave (2004) • MTV
The Ashlee Simpson Show (2004) • MTV
Blow Out (2004) • BRAVO
Gastineau Girls (2004) • E!
Growing Up Gotti (2004) • A&E
I Married a Princess (2005) • LIFETIME
Meet the Barkers (2005) • MTV
Filthy Rich: Cattle Drive (2005) • E!
Being Bobby Brown (2005) • BRAVO
The Princes of Malibu (2005) • FOX
Hogan Knows Best (2005) • VH1
Run's House (2005) • MTV
Tommy Lee Goes to College (2005) • NBC
The Girl Next Door (2005) • E!

Kathy Griffin: My Life on the D-List (2005) • BRAVO
House of Carters (2006) • E!
The Hills (2006) • MTV
The Real Housewives of Orange County (2006) • BRAVO
Gene Simmons Family Jewels (2006) • A&E
Rob & Big (2006) • MTV
Number 1 Single (2006) • E!
Life of Ryan (2007) • MTV
Keeping Up with the Kardashians (2007) • E!
Kimora: Life in the Fab Lane (2007) • STYLE
Flipping Out (2007) • BRAVO
Snoop Dogg's Father Hood (2007) • E!
The Real Housewives of New York (2008) • BRAVO
The Real Housewives of Atlanta (2008) • BRAVO
The City (2008) • MTV
The Real Housewives of New Jersey (2009) • BRAVO
Jersey Shore (2009) • MTV
The Real Housewives of Beverly Hills (2010) • BRAVO
Son of a Gun (2011) • MTV
The Real Housewives of Miami (2011) • BRAVO

Appendix 5

7 Words You Can Never Say on Television

(On Broadcast Television, Anyway)

While broadcast standards may differ throughout the world, most of the words on George Carlin's original list (below) remain taboo on American broadcast television. Truth be told, Lenny Bruce, the edgy comic whose heyday included the 1950's, said them all first. Bruce was arrested in 1966 for saying the words in alphabetical order, beginning with "ass" and "balls," which are no longer on that list. Carlin, like Bruce, was arrested for "disturbing the peace" when he performed a track off his 1972 album, "Class Clown," at a concert in Milwaukee that same year. The album track was titled: "Seven Words You Can Never Say on Television"—a monologue in which Carlin not only identified these words, but also expressed amazement that these particular words would bother anyone at all.

Those original seven words are:

Shit
Piss
Fuck
Cunt
Cocksucker
Motherfucker
Tits

Bibliography

Weiss, Werner. "The Birth of the 'E' Ticket at Disneyland," Yesterland.com, July 9, 2009. (http://www.yesterland.com/eticket.html). Retrieved: 2011-10-28.

Berra, Yogi; Kaplan, Dave. When You Come to a Fork in the Road, Take It! New York: Hyperion Books, 2001. Reviewed: *Publishers Weekly*, May 21, 2001. (http://www.publishersweekly.com/978-0-7868-6775-2). Retrieved: 2011-10-15.

Miller, Kenneth, et al. The LIFE Millennium. New York: LIFE Books, 1998.

Nash, Bruce. "Modern Marvels: Television—Window to the World." The History Channel, 1999.

Walsh, Bryan. "The Electrifying Edison," *Time*, July 5, 2010.

Hughes, D. E. *"Research in Wireless Telegraphy," The Electrician*, 1899.

Barnouw, Erik. Tube of Plenty: Evolution of American Television, 2nd ed. New York: Oxford University Press, 1990.

Marconi, Guglielmo. "Wireless Telegraphic Communication: Nobel Lecture, 11 December 1909." Nobel Lectures Amsterdam: Elsevier Publishing Company, 1967.

"Guglielmo Marconi," Encyclopedia Britannica. Chicago: Encyclopedia Britannica, Inc., 1993.

"Auto Interests Buy de Forest Radio Co.," *New York Times*, April 6, 1923.

Aldridge, Rebecca. The Sinking of the Titanic. New York: Infobase Publishing, 2008.

Slotten, Hugh Richard. Radio and Television Regulation: Broadcast Technology in the United States 1920–1960. Maryland: JHU Press, 2000.

Hendricks, Gordon. The Edison Motion Picture Myth. Berkeley: University of California Press, 1961.

"David Sarnoff—U.S. Media Executive." Museum of Broadcast Communications website. (http://www.museum.tv/eotvsection.php?entrycode=sarnoffdavi). Retrieved: 2012-02-13.

Schwartz, Evan I. The Last Lone Inventor. New York: Harper Collins Publishers, 2002.

Farnsworth, Elma G. Distant Vision: Romance and Discovery of an Invisible Frontier. Salt Lake City, Utah: Pemberly Kent Publishers, Inc., 1990.

"The Sketch." The Philo T. Farnsworth Archives website. (http://www.cmgww.com/historic/farnsworth/index.html). Retrieved: 2012-01-14.

"Philo Taylor Farnsworth (1906–1971)." The Virtual Museum of the City of San Francisco. (http://www.sfmuseum.org/hist10/philo.html). Retrieved: 2012-01-31.

"The Nipkow disk." Users.swing.be. (http://users.swing.be/philippe.jadin/nipkowdisk.htm). Retrieved: 2012-02-21.

Abramson, Albert. The History of Television, 1880 to 1941. No. Carolina: McFarland & Co., 1987.

Kamm, Antony and Baird, Malcolm. John Logie Baird: A Life. Edinburgh: NMS Publishing, 2002.

"Announcing the National Broadcasting company, Inc.," United States Early Radio History, 1926. (http://earlyradiohistory.us/1926nbc.htm). Retrieved: 2012-01-09.

Swift, Thomas P. "Red and Blue Networks of NBC To Be Split; WJZ May Be Sold," *New York Times*, January 9, 1942.

Schatzkin, Paul. The Boy Who Invented Television. Maryland: Teamcom Books, 2002.

Documentary Film: "Birth of TV at World's Fair." You Tube—Retro Clip, 1939. (www.youtube.com/watch?v=U4hPX_PLC-o). Retrieved: 2012-02-04.

"Biography of Philo Taylor Farnsworth," University of Utah Marriott Library Special Collections. (http://content.lib.utah.edu/cdm/ref/collection/UU_EAD/id/2160). Retrieved: 2012-03-05.

Documentary Film: "William Paley: The Eye of CBS." The Biography Channel, 2002.

Cooper, Patricia Ann. Once a Cigar Maker. Champaign, IL: Univ. of Illinois Press, 1987.

Barnouw, Erik. A Tower in Babel: A History of Broadcasting in the United States to 1933. New York: Oxford University Press, 1966.

McLeod, Elizabeth. Amos 'n' Andy—In Person. No. Carolina: McFarland & Co., 1999.

"Amos 'n' Andy To Start New Radio Series." *The Pittsburgh Press*, July 28, 1929.

Goodman, Mark. "The Radio Act of 1927 as a Product of Progressivism ." Mississippi State University. (http://www.scripps.ohiou.edu/mediahistory/mhmjour2-2.htm). Retrieved: 2012-03-17.

Simmons, Steven J. Fairness Doctrine and the Media. University of California Press, 1978.

Murray, Michael. Encyclopedia of Television News. Phoenix: Greenwood Publishing Group, 1998.

Halberstam, David. The Powers That Be. New York: Alfred A. Knopf, 1979.

Bergreen, Laurence. Look Now, Pay Later: The Rise of Network Broadcasting. New York: Doubleday and Co., 1980.

"Approves Buying of Blue Network," *New York Times*, October 13, 1943.

"Radio Listeners in Panic, Taking War Drama as Fact," *New York Times*, October 31, 1938.

Brinkley, Alan. The Unfinished Nation. "Chapter 23—The Great Depression." New York: McGraw-Hill Publishing, 2010.

Barnouw, Erik. The Golden Web: A History of Broadcasting in the United States, 1933–1953. New York: Oxford University Press, 1968.

Brown, Ross. "The Business of Sports on TV," Chapman University FTV 240 Lectures (Lecture 10 of 14), 2007.

Goldenson, Leonard H., Wolf, Marvin J. Beating the Odds. New York: Macmillan, 1991.

Lomartire, Paul. "Have I got news for you about Molly," *The Palm Beach Post*, June 18, 1994.

"TV Milestones—Shows that have gone the distance …," *Hollywood Reporter*, September 2004.

"Actor Is Dropped From Video Cast," *New York Times*, January 8, 1952.

"Blacklisting." Museum of Broadcast Communication website. (http://www.museum.tv/eotvsection.php?entrycode=blacklisting). Retrieved: 2012-04-09.

"Philip Loeb Dead; Prominent Actor; Body Found in Midtown Hotel; Overdose of Sleeping Pills "Apparent Cause," *New York Times*, September 2, 1955.

"Television in the United States." Encyclopedia Britannica Online. (http://www.britannica.com/EBchecked/topic/1513870/). Retrieved: 2012-04-12.

Caesar, Sid and Friedfeld, Eddy. Caesar's Hours: My Life in Comedy, with Love and Laughter. New York: PublicAffairs, 2005.

McCrohan, Donna. The Honeymooners' Companion—The Kramdens and the Nortons Revisited. New York: Workman Publishing, 1978.

Lackman, Ron. The Encyclopedia of 20th Century American Television. New York: Checkmark Books, 2003.

Hyatt, Wesley. A Critical History of Television's The Red Skelton Show, 1951–1971. North Carolina: McFarland & Co., 2004.

DuBrow, Rick. "TV in Review," *The News-Dispatch*, February 20, 1970.

Caute, David. The Great Fear: The Anti-Communist Purge Under Truman and Eisenhower. New York: Simon & Schuster, 1978.

Griffith, Robert. The Politics of Fear: Joseph R. McCarthy and the Senate. Massachusetts: University of Massachusetts Press, 1970.

Transcript: "A Report on Senator Joseph R. McCarthy," *See it Now*. CBS-TV, March 9, 1954. (http://www.lib.berkeley.edu/MRC/murrowmccarthy.html). Retrieved: 2012-03-31.

Morgan, Ted. Reds: McCarthyism in Twentieth-Century America. New York: Random House, 2004.

Boddy, William. Fifties Television: The Industry and Its Critics. Champaign, IL: University of Illinois Press, 1992.

Laswell, Mark. TV Guide: Fifty Years of Television. New York: Crown Publishing Group, 2002.

Van Doren, Charles. "All the Answers: The quiz-show scandals—and the aftermath," *The New Yorker*, July 28, 2008. (http://www.newyorker.com/reporting/2008/07/28/080728fa_fact_vandoren). Retrieved: 2012-04-01.

Lloyd, Norman. Recounted in a *Public Radio* interview on KUSC's "The Evening Program with Jim Svejda," June 22, 2012.

"Special Collector's Issue: 100 Greatest Episodes of All Time," TV Guide, June 28, 1997.

Documentary Film: "Rod Serling: Submitted For Your Approval." American Masters, 1995.

Documentary Film: Riggs, Martin. "Color Adjustment." Public Broadcasting Service, 1992.

Coleman, Robin R. Means. African American Viewers and the Black Situation Comedy: Situating Racial Humor (Studies in African American History and Culture). New York: Routledge, 1998.

Rains, Craig. "Little Rock Central High 40th Anniversary" website, 1997. (http://www.centralhigh57.org/1957-58.htm). Retrieved: 2012-04-06.

Warren, Earl, Chief Justice of the United States Supreme Court. "Brown v. Topeka Board of Education 347 U.S. 483," 1954.

Chafe, William H. The Unfinished Journey Since WWII. North Carolina: Oxford University Press, 2002.

Burns, Stewart. Daybreak of Freedom: The Montgomery Bus Boycott. North Carolina: UNC, 1997.

Edmerson, Estelle. A Descriptive Study of the American Negro in United States Professional Radio, 1922–1955. Los Angeles: University of California Los Angeles, 1955.

Shulman, Arthur; Youman, Roger. How Sweet It Was. Television: A Pictorial Commentary. New York: Bonanza Books, a division of Crown Publishers, 1966.

"Little Rock Nine," Civil Rights Movement—Veteran's Section website, 1957. (http://www.crmvet.org/tim/timhis57.htm#1957lrsd). Retrieved: 2012-04-15.

Reitan, Ed. "RCA-NBC Firsts in Color Television, a Chronological List of Significant Firsts by the Radio Corporation of America and the National Broadcasting Company in Color Television," RCA Press Release, March 27, 1955.

Poynton, Charles A. Digital Video and HDTV: Algorithms and Interfaces. Massachusetts: Morgan Kaufmann, 2003.

"New Television System Transmits Images in Full Color," *Popular Science*, December 1940.

"CBS Demonstrates Full Color Television," *Wall Street Journal*, September 5, 1940.

"Washington Chosen for First Color Showing; From Ages 4 to 90, Audience Amazed," *The Washington Post*, January 13, 1950.

"RCA to Test Color TV System On Three Shows Daily Beginning Today," *The Wall Street Journal*, July 9, 1951.

"Westerns: The Six-Gun Galahad," *Time*, March 30, 1959.

Screen Source presents: 20 Most Popular TV Shows Each Year in the 1950's website. (http://www.amug.org/~scrnsrc/top_tv_shows_50s.html). Retrieved: 2012-04-19.

Smith, Cecil. "Gunsmoke," *Los Angeles Times*, September 1975. (http://www.answers.com/topic/gunsmoke-tv-series). Retrieved: 2012-04-23.

"Television," The World Book Encyclopedia. Chicago, Illinois : World Book, 2003.

Bonanza. Episode One/Scene one, 1959.

Dragnet. Episode One / Overture, 1951.

Sanders, Coyne Steven; Gilbert, Tom. Desilu: The Story of Lucille Ball and Desi Arnaz. New York: William Morrow & Company, 1993.

Brown, Ross. "Late Night and Daytime," Chapman University FTV 240 Lectures (Lecture 6 of 14), 2007.

Pocock, Chris. The U-2 Spyplane; Toward the Unknown. Atglen, Pennsylvania: Schiffer Military History, 2000. (https://www.cia.gov/library/center-for-the-study-of-intelligence/csi-publications/csi-studies/studies/vol46no2/article06.html). Retrieved: 2012-04-29.

Bochin, Hal. Richard Nixon: Rhetorical Strategist. Connecticut: Greenwood Publishing Group, 1990.

Garner, Joe. Stay Tuned: Television's Unforgettable Moments. Kansas City: Andrews McMeel Publishing, 2002.

Safire, William. "The Cold War's Hot Kitchen," *New York Times*, July 24, 2009.

"Moscow Debate Stirs U.S Public", *New York Times*, July 27, 1959.

Morton, Bruce. "Kennedy-Nixon debate changed politics for good," CNN Politics. September 26, 2005. (http://articles.cnn.com/2005-09-26/politics/kennedy.nixon_1_kennedy-nixon-debate-cbs-executive-makeup?s=PM:POLITICS). Retrieved: 2012-04-27.

Webley, Kayla. "How the Nixon-Kennedy Debate Changed the World," *Time*, September 23, 2010. (http://www.time.com/time/nation/article/0,8599,2021078,00.html). Retrieved: 2012-05-01.

Brioux, Bill. "50 Years Later: the Kennedy-Nixon Debates," TV feeds my family website, September 30, 2010. (http://tvfeedsmyfamily.blogspot.com/2010_09_01_archive.html). Retrieved: 2012-03-31.

Schefter, James. The Race: The uncensored story of how America beat Russia to the Moon. New York: Doubleday, 1999.

Kennedy, John F. "Special Message to the Congress on Urgent National Needs," *Historical Resources*, John F. Kennedy Presidential Library and Museum website, May 25, 1961. (JFK/Urgent+National+Needs+Page+4.htm). Retrieved 2012-05-01.

National Aeronautics & Space Administration. Gemini Program. Venice, CA: Revell, Inc., 1965.

Talese, Gay. "Frank Sinatra Has a Cold," *Esquire*, April 1966.

Rogers, David. The Beverly Hillbillies (3-act stage play adapted from the TV Pilot). 1968.

Weiner, Ed, et al. The TV Guide TV Book: 40 Years of the All-Time Greatest Television Facts, Fads, Hits, and History. New York: Harper Collins, 1992.

Documentary Film: "The Writer Speaks—Norman Lear." WGA Series, 1998.

"Cosby to Exit WB in August To Join Own Record Firm," *Billboard*, June 1, 1968.

King, Martin L. " I Have a Dream " Speech. *U.S. Constitution* Online, August 28, 1963. (http://www.usconstitution.net/dream.html). Retrieved: 2012-04-02.

Cagin, Seth; Dray, Philip. We Are Not Afraid. New York: Avalon Publishing Group, 1988.

"The Best of Laugh-In." PBS Programming website. (http://www.pbs.org/about/news/archive/2011/pbs-laugh-in/). Retrieved: 2012-05-06.

Robinson, Marc. Brought To You in Living Color. New York: John Wiley & Sons, Inc., 2002.

Karnow, Stanley. Vietnam: A History. New York: Viking Press, 1991.

"Vietnam War." Swarthmore College Peace Collection.

Karnow, Stanley. Vietnam: A History (ed. 1983). New York: Penguin Books, 1983.

Documentary Film: "The Last to Leave." Pat Clark Productions, 2011.

"Vietnam War Facts." Sgt Hack's Vietnam Military Collection website. (http://www.uswings.com/vietnamfacts.asp). Retrieved: 2012-03-31.

Aitken, Jonathan. Nixon: A Life. Washington, D.C.: Regnery Publishing, 1996.

"Censorship." Museum of Broadcast Communications website. (http://www.museum.tv/eotvsection.php?entrycode=censorship). Retrieved: 2012-04-29.

Linder, Doug. "Filthy Words by George Carlin" website. (http://law2.umkc.edu/faculty/projects/ftrials/conlaw/filthywords.html). Retrieved: 2012-05-06.

Supreme Court Decision: "Miller v. California" 413 U.S. 15 (1973), Justia.com—US Supreme Court Center. (http://supreme.justia.com/cases/federal/us/413/15/case.html). Retrieved: 2012-05-03.

"Communications Act of 1934—Public Law No. 416." 73d Congress, June 19, 1934. (http://www.criminalgovernment.com/docs/61StatL101/ComAct34.html). Retrieved: 2012-05-03.

Erenkrantz, Justin R. "George Carlin's Seven Dirty Words" website. George Carlin Script. Performed at the Summerland Festival, Milwaukee, 1972. (http://www.erenkrantz.com/Humor/SevenDirtyWords.shtml). Retrieved: 2012-05-10.

Samaha, Adam M. "The Story of FCC v. Pacifica Foundation (and Its Second Life)." Chicago: The Law School of the University of Chicago, 2010. (http://www.law.uchicago.edu/files/file/314-as-story.pdf). Retrieved: 2012-05-11.

Supreme Court Decision: "Federal Communications Commission v. Pacifica Foundation, 438 U.S. 726 (1978)." United States Reports, volume 438.

Mifflin, Lawrie. "U.S. Mandates Educational TV for Children." *New York Times*, August 9, 1996.

Bianculli, David. Dangerously Funny: The Uncensored Story of the Smothers Brothers Comedy Hour. New York: Touchstone, 2009.

Silverman, David. You Can't Air That: Four Cases of Controversy and Censorship in American Television Programming. New York: Syracuse University Press, 2007.

Documentary Film: "Smothered: The Censorship Struggles of the Smothers Brothers Comedy Hour." Time-Warner, 2002.

Barbera, Joseph. My Life in "Toons": From Flatbush to Bedrock in Under a Century. Atlanta, GA: Turner Publishing, 1994.

Smith, Cecil. "Jim Nabors finished with Gomer," *The Blade* , January 31, 1969.

Harkins, Anthony. Hillbilly: A Cultural History of an American Icon. New York: Oxford University Press, 2005.

Severio, Richard. "Red Skelton, Knockabout Comic and Clown Prince of the Airwaves, Is Dead at 84," *New York Times* Online, September 18, 1997. (http://www.nytimes.com/1997/09/18/arts/red-skelton-knockabout-comic-and-clown-prince-of-the-airwaves-is-dead-at-84.html?src=pm). Retrieved 2012-05-07.

Poniewozik, James. "17 Shows That Changed TV," *Time* Online, September 6, 2006. (http://www.time.com/time/magazine/article/0,9171,1659718-1,00.html). Retrieved 2012-05-09.

"The 100 Greatest TV episodes of all time!" website. Staff of *TV Guide* & *Nick at Night*, June 25, 1997.

Lloyd, David. The Mary Tyler Moore Show: "Chuckles Bites the Dust" teleplay. October 25, 1975.

Kalter, Suzy. The Complete Book of M*A*S*H*. New York: Abradale Press, Harry M. Abrahams, Inc., 1984.

"Bad Times on the *Good Times* Set," *Ebony*, September 1975

"Top TV Shows–1960s," Entertainmentscene.com. (http://www.entertainmentscene.com/top_tv_shows_60s.html). Retrieved: 2011-12-29.

Schneider, Alfred R.; Pullen, Kaye. The Gatekeeper: My Thirty Years as TV Censor. Syracuse University Press, 2001.

"Dynasty: The Making of a Guilty Pleasure," *Variety*, December 28, 2004. (http://www.variety.com/review/VE1117925790). Retrieved: 2012-05-19.

Brook, Tim; Marsh, Earle. The Complete Directory To Prime Time Network TV Shows. New York: Ballantine Books, 1992.

Semonche, John E. Censoring Sex: A Historical Journey Through American Media. Maryland: Rowman & Littlefield, 2007.

Rosen, James. The Streets of San Francisco: A Quinn Martin TV Series. Philadelphia: Autumn Road Company, 2011.

TV Series: *Aspect Ratio*. John Morrison Interview with Casting Director Anne Brebner. Blip TV, 2011 March. (http://blip.tv/aspect-ratio-cfi/aspect-ratio-march-2011-4983970). Retrieved: 2012-03-15.

Garay, Ronald. "Watergate." The Museum of Broadcast Communications website. (http://www.museum.tv/eotvsection.php?entrycode=watergate). Retrieved 2012-05-20.

Kranish, Michael. "Select Chronology for Donald G. Sanders," *The Boston Globe*, July 4, 2007.

"Transcript of a Recording of a Meeting between the President and H.R. Haldeman in the Oval Office on June 23, 1972 from 10:04 to 11:39 am," Watergate Special Prosecution Force (PDF). (http://www.nixonlibrary.gov/forresearchers/find/tapes/watergate/wspf/741-002.pdf). Retrieved 2012-05-21.

"Richard Nixon: Question-and-Answer Session at the Annual Convention of the Associated Press Managing Editors Association, Orlando, Florida," The American Presidency Project, November 11, 1973. (http://www.presidency.ucsb.edu/mediaplay.php?id=4046&admin=37). Retrieved: 2012-05-21.

"President Nixon's Resignation Speech." Public Broadcasting Service, August 8, 1974. (http://www.pbs.org/newshour/character/links/nixon_speech.html). Retrieved 2012-04-30.

Marill, Alvin H. Movies Made For Television: The Tele-feature and the Mini-series, 1964–1986. New York: Baseline/New York Zoetrope, 1987.

Cunningham, Stuart. "Miniseries." Museum of Broadcast Communications website. (http://www.museum.tv/eotvsection.php?entrycode=miniseries). Retrieved: 2012-05-24.

"Elton Rule/*QB VII*." Museum of Broadcast Communications website. (http://www.museum.tv/eotvsection.php?entrycode=ruleelton). Retrieved: 2012-05-24.

"New Roots series expected to yield big bucks for ABC," *Ottawa Citizen* Online, February 20, 1979. (http://news.google.com/newspapers?id=t0MzAAAAIBAJ&sjid=Vu4FAAAAIBAJ&dq=cost%20abc%20%246%20million%20and%20ran%2012%20hours&pg=5309%2C265933). Retrieved: 2012-05-28.

"*Benson*." Museum of Broadcast Communications website. (http://www.archives.museum.tv/eotvsection.php?entrycode=benson). Retrieved: 2012-05-28.

"Sports and Television." Museum of Broadcast Communications website. (http://www.museum.tv/eotvsection.php?entrycode=sportsandte). Retrieved 2012-03-25.

NFL 2001 Record and Fact Book. New York: Workman Publishing Co, 2001.

"Roone Arledge." Museum of Broadcast Communications website. (http://www.museum.tv/eotvsection.php?entrycode=arledgeroon). Retrieved: 2012-03-29.

Sugar, Bert Randolph. The Thrill of Victory: The Inside Story of ABC Sports. New York: Hawthorne, 1978.

Wiley, Ralph. "Arledge's World Flowed with Ideas." *ESPN Page 2* Online. (http://espn.go.com/page2/s/wiley/021209.html). Retrieved: 2012-03-18.

Cosell, Howard. Like It Is. Chicago: Playboy Press, 1974.

Bagchi, Rob. "50 stunning Olympic moments No2: Bob Beamon's great leap forward," *The Guardian*, November 23, 2011.

Reeve, Simon. "Olympics Massacre: Munich – The real story," *The Independent*, January 23, 2006. (http://www.independent.co.uk/news/world/europe/olympics-massacre-munich--the-real-story-524011.html). Retrieved: 2012-03-26.

Kreigel, Mark. Namath: A Biography. New York: Viking, 2004.

"Life Lists 20th Century's Most Influential Americans," *Life* Magazine, September 1, 1990.

Wizig, Jerry. "It's been 20 years since they've played The Game of the Century," *Houston Chronicle*, January 20, 1988.

Carter, Al. "College Basketball: UH and UCLA, under the big top," *San Antonio Express-News*, January 19, 2008.

Salzberg, Charles. From Set Shot to Slam Dunk. New York: McGraw-Hill, 1998.

Weinberg, Rick. "Magic Johnson announces he's HIV-positive," ESPN.com., November 7, 1991. (http://sports.espn.go.com/espn/espn25/story?page=moments/7). Retrieved: 2012-03-31.

"Relations Among the Allies: Communication, Understanding, Leadership," Bilderberg Meeting Report, in Aachen, German (text), April 18–20,1980.

(http://wikileaks.org/wiki/Bilderberg_meeting_report_Aachen%2C_1980/Text#Afghanistan). Retrieved: 2012-04-02.

Documentary Film: "Miracle on Ice." HBO Sports, 2001.

Coffey, Wayne. The Boys of Winter. New York: Crown Publishers, 2005.

Garthoff, Raymond L. Détente and Confrontation. Washington D.C.: The Brookings Institute, 1994.

Horowitz, Joy. "The Madcap Behind 'Moonlighting,'" *New York Times*, March 30, 1986. (http://www.davidandmaddie.com/chemistry-nytimes86.htm). Retrieved 2012-06-01.

"Struggling to Leave the Cellar," *Time*, May 14, 1979. (http://www.time.com/time/magazine/article/0,9171,916805,00.html). Retrieved: 2012-05-24.

"NBC's Retreat from Moscow," *Time*, May 19, 1980. (http://www.time.com/time/magazine/article/0,9171,924130-1,00.html). Retrieved: 2012-04-05.

Fetherston, Drew. "Last Call for the Cop Show That Broke All the Rules," *Newsday*, May 10, 1987.

Corliss, Richard. "Coming Up From Nowhere," *Time*, September 16, 1985. (http://www.time.com/time/magazine/article/0,9171,959821-5,00.html). Retrieved: 2012-06.01.

Shales, Tom; Miller, James A. Live From New York: An Uncensored History Of Saturday Night Live. New York: Back Bay Books, 2003.

Bedell, Sally. Up the Tube: Prime-Time TV in the Silverman Years. New York: Viking Press, 1981.

Bjorklund, Dennis. Toasting Cheers: An Episode Guide to the 1982–1993 Comedy Series. North Carolina: McFarland & Company, Inc., 1997.

"National Broadcasting Company." Museum of Broadcast Communications website. (http://www.museum.tv/eotvsection.php?entrycode=nationalbroa). Retrieved: 2012-05-29.

Tartikoff, Brandon. The Last Great Ride. New York: Hyperion Books, 1992.

James, Caryn. "'Rosanne' and the Risks of Upward Mobility," *New York Times* Online, May 18, 1997.

"Fox Buys Into TV Network; Makes 390 Features Available," *Boxoffice*, November 3, 1986.

King, Norman. Arsenio Hall. New York: William Morrow & Co., 1993.

Kimmel, Daniel M. The Fourth Network. Chicago: Ivan R. Dee, Publisher, 2004.

"Nielsen's Top 50 Shows," *USA Today*, April 18, 1990.

Documentary Film: "The Simpsons': America's First Family." BBC (DVD). UK: 20th Century Fox, 2000.
"*Gunsmoke*." Museum of Broadcast Communications website. (http://www.museum.tv/eotvsection.php?entrycode=gunsmoke). Retrieved: 2012-06-06.
"It's in the dictionary, d'oh!." *BBC News* Online, June 14, 2001. (http://news.bbc.co.uk/2/hi/entertainment/1387335.stm). Retrieved: 2011-12-14.
"Thirtysomething." Museum of Broadcast Communications website. (http://www.museum.tv/eotvsection.php?entrycode=thirtysomethi). Retrieved: 2012-06-02.
Mogel, Leonard. This Business of Broadcasting. New York: Billboard Books, 2004.
Kleinfield, N.R. "ABC is being sold for $3.5 billion; 1st network sale," *New York Times*, March 19, 1985.
The Online Television Museum: HBO website. (http://www2.tv-ark.org.uk/International/usa/hbo.html). Retrieved: 2012-06-10.
Goulart, Ron. Comic Book Encyclopedia. New York: Harper Entertainment, 2004.
"EW's Ken Tucker names 2002's 5 Worst TV Shows," *Entertainment Weekly*, January 23, 2003.
Columnist Bill Simmons on "Arliss," ESPN.com/Archives, 2002.
O'Connor, John J. "A Modern Life Lived in 50's and 60's Images," *New York Times*, July 10, 1990. (http://www.nytimes.com/1990/07/10/arts/review-television-a-modern-life-lived-in-50-s-and-60-s-images.html). Retrieved: 2012-06-11.
"Biography for Jim Janicek," IMDb website. (http://www.imdb.com/name/nm1371018/bio). Retrieved: 2012-06-09.
Williams, Huntington. Beyond Control: ABC and the fate of the Networks. New York: Atheneum, 1989.
Poniewozik, James. "The Decency Police," *Time*, March 20, 2005.
Shiban, John; and Spotnitz, Frank. "Travelers" (Episode 15/Season 5). *The X-Files*. Aired March 29, 1998.
"Awards for *Northern Exposure*," IMDb website. (http://www.imdb.com/title/tt0098878/awards). Retrieved: 2012-06-09.
"The Body Electric" (Episode 21/Season 5). *Dr. Quinn, Medicine Woman*. Aired April 5, 1997.
Lowry, Brian. "Fans, Seymour Rally Against Dr. Quinn's Cancellation," *Los Angeles Times*, May 27, 1998. (http://articles.latimes.com/1998/may/27/entertainment/ca-53673). Retrieved: 2012-06-04.
Magnotta, Elizabeth and Alexandra Strohl. "A linguistic analysis of humor: A look at *Seinfeld*," Working Papers of the Linguistics Circle, Vol. 21, No. 1, 27th Northwest Linguists Conference, University of Victoria, 2011. (http://journals.uvic.ca/index.php/WPLC/article/view/5944). Retrieved: 2012-06-15.
Pierson, David P. "A Show about Nothing: Seinfeld and the Modern Comedy of Manners" website. (http://year11englishspace.wikispaces.com/file/view/SITCOM2.pdf). Retrieved: 2012-06-10.
Grenz, Stanley J. A Primer on Postmodernism. Michigan: William B. Eerdmans Publishing Co., February 1996.
Casey, Peter. "How FRASIER came to be," kenlevine.blogspot.com. (http://kenlevine.blogspot.com/2006/12/how-frasier-came-to-be.html). Retrieved: 2012-06-12.
O'Connor, Mickey. "The Doctor Is In," *Entertainment Weekly* Online, September 16, 2002. (http://www.ew.com/ew/article/0,,351305,00.html). Retrieved: 2012-06-13.
Gorman, Steve. "Kelsey Grammer has heart attack." *The Independent* (London), June 3, 2008.

Levine, Ken. "The story behind 'Tossed Salad and Scrambled Eggs,'" kenlevine.blogspot.com, April 9, 2012. (http://kenlevine.blogspot.com/2012/04/story-behind-tossed-salad-and-scrambled.html). Retrieved: 2012-06-13.

"Tim Allen" (Episode 15/Season 12). *Inside The Actor's Studio*. Aired May 28, 2006.

Brooks, Tim; Marsh, Earle. The Complete Directory to Prime Time Network and Cable TV Shows (1946–Present) (9th *Ed*). New York: Ballantine Books, 2007.

"ABC Hits a Home Run," *Entertainment Weekly*, April 28, 1995. (http://www.ew.com/ew/article/0,,297031,00.html). Retrieved: 2012-06-14.

Jacobs, Jason. Body Trauma TV: The New Hospital Dramas (illustrated ed.). U.K.: British Film Institute, 2003.

Richard, Zoglin; Smilgis, Martha. "Television: Angels with Dirty Faces," *Time*, October 31, 1994. (http://www.time.com/time/magazine/article/0,9171,981691-2,00.htm). Retrieved: 2012-06-14.

Young, Susan C. "*ER* closes door, leaves behind satisfying legacy," MSNBC, March 24, 2009. (http://today.msnbc.msn.com/id/29843242#.UJQo49fkL7E). Retrieved: 2012-06-13.

Carter, Bill. "He's a Lawyer. He's a Writer. But Can He Type?," *New York Times*, February 7, 1990.

Levine, Josh. David E. Kelley: The Man Behind Ally McBeal. Toronto: E C W Press, 1999.

Advanced Primetime Awards Search website. (http://www.emmys.com/award_history_search?person=david+e.+kelley&program=&start_year=1949&end_year=2010&network=All&web_category=All&winner=All). Retrieved: 2012-06-17.

O'Connor, John J. "The Operation Was a Success: 'ER' Lives," *New York Times*, October 23, 1999. (http://www.nytimes.com/1994/10/23/arts/television-view-the-operation-was-a-success-er-lives.html). Retrieved: 2012-06-10.

O'Connor, John J. "Doctor Shows for the High-Tech 90's," *New York Times*, September 19, 1994. (http://www.nytimes.com/1994/10/23/arts/television-view-the-operation-was-a-success-er-lives.html). Retrieved: 2012-06-10.

Caves, Richard E. Switching Channels: Organization and Change in TV Broadcasting. Massachusetts: Harvard University, 2005.

Levine, Stuart. "Kelly acts as judge, jury for series quality," *Variety*, May 3, 2001. (http://www.variety.com/article/VR1117798567?refCatId=1048). Retrieved: 2012-06-13.

James, Caryn. "Ally McBeal Teams Up With Less Flitty Lawyers," *New York Times*, April 27, 1998. (http://www.nytimes.com/1998/04/27/arts/television-review-ally-mcbeal-teams-up-with-less-flitty-lawyers.html). Retrieved: 2012-06-14.

Dowd, Maureen. "Liberties; She-TV, Me-TV," *New York Times*, July 22, 1998. (http://www.nytimes.com/1998/07/22/opinion/liberties-she-tv-me-tv.html). Retrieved: 2012-06-18.

Kimberly, Stevens. "NOTICED: Ally, the Talk Around the Water Cooler," *New York Times*, November 23, 1997. (http://www.nytimes.com/1997/11/23/style/noticed-ally-the-talk-around-the-water-cooler.html). Retrieved: 2012-06-18.

Hammers, Michelle L. "Cautionary Tales of Liberation and Female Professionalism: The Case *Against Ally McBeal*," *Western Journal of Communication*, April 2005.

"Is Feminism Dead?" (Interview: Phullis Chesler and *Time Magazine*, June 25, 1998). Reprinted: *Time*, June 29, 1998 (http://www.phyllis-chesler.com/663/is-feminism-dead). Retrieved: 2012-06-15.

Stanley, Allesendra. "Same Old Law Firm, New Snake," *New York Times*, September 27, 2003. (http://www.nytimes.com/2003/09/27/arts/television-review-same-old-law-firm-new-snake.html). Retrieved: 2012-06-17.

"It's Production for Littlefield," *New York Daily News*, October 27, 1998. (http://articles.nydailynews.com/1998-10-27/entertainment/18084019_1_warren-littlefield-nbc-west-coast-peacock-network). Retrieved: 2012-06-24.

Carter, Bill. Desperate Networks. New York: Broadway Books, 2006.

Levesque, John. "Aaron Sorkin is a man of many words," *Seattle Post-Intelligencer*, March 7, 2000. (http://web.archive.org/web/20101019144914/http://www.seattlepi.com/tv/sork07.shtml). Retrieved: 2012-06-20.

"Overlaps between *West Wing* and *Sports Night* Episodes." *West Wing* Continuity Guide website. (http://west-wing.bewarne.com/overlaps/sports_episodes.html). Retrieved: 2012-06-17.

"*West Wing* sets Emmy record," Premium.edition.cnn.com, September 11, 2000. (http://edition.cnn.com/2000/SHOWBIZ/TV/09/10/emmys.05/). Retrieved: 2012-06-23.

"Database: The West Wing." Prime Time Emmy Awards. (http://www.emmys.com/award_history_search?person=&program=West+Wing&start_year=1949&end_year=2010&network=All&web_category=All&winner=All). Retrieved: 2012-06-26).

Baxter, Judith. "Constructions of Active Womanhood and New Femininities: From a Feminist Linguistic Perspective, is 'Sex and the City' a Modernist or a Post-Modernist TV Text Full Text?," *Women & Language*, 2009.

Swirsky, Joan. "The Death of Feminism II: *'Sex and the City',*" Newsmax.com, July 24, 2003. (http://archive.newsmax.com/archives/articles/2003/7/23/131352.shtml). Retrieved: 2012-06-23.

Geier, Thom; et. al. "The 100 Greatest Movies, TV Shows, Albums, Books, Characters, Scenes, Episodes, Songs, Dresses, Music Videos, and Trends that Entertained Us over the Past 10 Years," *Entertainment Weekly*, December 11, 2009.

Lee, Mark. "Wiseguys: A conversation between David Chase and Tom Fontana," *Written By* (WGA monthly magazine), May 2007. (http://www.wga.org/writtenby/writtenbysub.aspx?id=2354). Retrieved: 2012-06-26.

Biskind, Peter. "An American Family," *Vanity Fair*, April 2007. (http://www.vanityfair.com/culture/features/2007/04/sopranos200704?currentPage=1). Retrieved: 2012-06-20.

Dougherty, Robin. "Chasing TV," Salon.com, August 21, 2007. (http://web.archive.org/web/20070821035655/http://www.salon.com/ent/int/1999/01/20int.html). Retrieved: 2012-06-28.

Poniewozik, James. "The Sopranos—The 100 Best TV Shows of All-TIME," *Time*, October 2007. (http://web.archive.org/web/20100208232027/http://features.metacritic.com/features/2010/best-tv-of-2009-and-the-decade/). Retrieved: 2012-06-29.

Remnick, David. "Family Guy," *The New Yorker*, June 2007. (http://www.newyorker.com/talk/comment/2007/06/04/070604taco_talk_remnick). Retrieved: 2012-06-29.

Oxfeld, Jesse. "Family Man," *Stanford Magazine*, September/October 2002. (http://alumni.stanford.edu/get/page/magazine/article/?article_id=37319). Retrieved: 2012-06-27.

Kuhn, Thomas S. The Structure of Scientific Revolutions. 3rd ed. Chicago, IL: University of Chicago Press, 1996.

Trask, R.L. Mind the Gaffe!: A Troubleshooter's Guide to English Style and Usage. New York: HarperCollins Publishers, 2006.

Rowan, Beth. "Reality TV Takes Hold," Infoplease.com, July 21, 2000. (http://www.infoplease.com/spot/realitytv1.html). Retrieved: 2012-06-27.

James, Caryn. "Bachelor No. 1 And the Birth of Reality TV," *New York Times*, January 26, 2003. (http://www.nytimes.com/2003/01/26/movies/television-radio-bachelor-no-1-and-the-birth-of-reality-tv.html). Retrieved: 2012-06-23.

"America's First Reality TV Show," *Neatorama*, June 25, 2007. (http://www.neatorama.com/2007/06/25/americas-first-reality-tv-show/). Retrieved: 2012-07-01.

"Survivor ... 10 Years Later: Why It's Outlasted Its Competition," *The Atlantic*, February 16, 2011. (http://www.theatlantic.com/entertainment/archive/2011/02/survivor-10-years-later-why-its-outlasted-its-competitors/71247/). Retrieved: 2012-06-25.

Survivor, CBS Prime Time TV Series (various seasons), May 2000-present.Ma

"20 Best Reality-TV Shows Ever," EW.com, July 7, 2011. (http://www.ew.com/ew/gallery/0,,20308599,00.html). Retrieved: 2012-06-29.

"2000–2001 TV Season," U.S. Nielsen Ratings, May 2001.

"NBC Reviving *Fear Factor*," *Entertainment Weekly*, June 2, 2011. (http://insidetv.ew.com/2011/06/02/nbc-reviving-fear-factor/). Retrieved: 2012-07-01.

Smith, Kyle. "TV's Reality Check," *People*, March 20, 2000. (http://www.people.com/people/archive/article/0,,20130638,00.html). Retrieved: 2012-07-01.

Carter, Bill. "Fox Network Will End 'Multimillionaire' Marriage Specials," *New York Times*, February 22, 2000. (http://www.nytimes.com/2000/02/22/business/fox-network-will-end-multimillionaire-marriage-specials.html). Retrieved: 2012-06-30.

Labi, Nadya . "An Online Paper Trail," *Time*, February 27, 2000. (http://www.time.com/time/magazine/article/0,9171,39942,00.html?iid=chix-sphere). Retrieved: 2012-06-30.

Smith, Kyle. "Works of Heart," *New York Post*, September 2, 2011. (http://www.nypost.com/p/entertainment/movies/works_of_heart_j1UuXJJHxGL8A5lO6ahBwL). Retrieved: 2012-07-02.

"Will Reality TV Survive?," *Newsweek*, October 10, 2001. (http://www.thedailybeast.com/newsweek/2001/10/10/will-reality-tv-survive.html). Retrieved: 2012-07-01.

"Lost lives remembered during 9/11 ceremony. *The Online Rocket*, September 12, 2008. (http://www.theonlinerocket.com/news/lost-lives-remembered-during-9-11-ceremony-1.2333384#.UJdxdNfkL7E). Retrieved: 2012-07-01.

"First video of Pentagon 9/11 attack released," *CNN*.com. Aired May 17, 2006. (http://edition.cnn.com/2006/US/05/16/pentagon.video/index.html). Retrieved: 2012-07-04.

"Denis Leary plays with fire on 'Rescue Me,'" *msnbc.com*, August 3, 2006. (http://today.msnbc.msn.com/id/14173614#.UJd2UdfkL7E). Retrieved: 2012-07-05.

"FX Fired Up about 'Rescue Me' Ratings," ZAP2it.com (KTLA 5 Morning News) website, July 24, 2004. (http://www.highbeam.com/doc/1G1-119758022.html). Retrieved: 2012-07-04.

"Viewership numbers of primetime programs during the 2003-04 television season," U.S. Nielsen Ratings, May 2004.

Rocchio, Christopher; Rogers, Steve. "Report: NBC to announce renewal of Donald Trump's *The Apprentice*," *Realityworld.com*, July 6, 2007. (http://www.realitytvworld.com/news/report-nbc-announce-renewal-of-donald-trump-the-apprentice-5462.php). Retrieved: 2102-06-27.

"*The Apprentice*: Trump Says NBC Wants Him Back," TVseriesfinale.com, May 31, 2007. (http://tvseriesfinale.com/tv-show/the-apprentice-trump-says-nbc-wants-him-back/). Retrieved: 2012-06-29.

"NBC, Donald Trump and Mark Burnett Want to Help America Get Back To Work," *NBC Entertainment News* Online, May 17, 2010. (http://www.nbc.com/news/2010/03/17/nbc-donald-trump-and-mark-burnett-want-to-help-america-get-back-to-work-with-new-version-of-popular/). Retrieved: 2012-06-29.

Andreeva, Nellie. "Full 2010-11 Season Series Rankings," *Deadline Hollywood*, May 27, 2011. (http://www.deadline.com/2011/05/full-2010-11-season-series-rankers/). Retrieved: 2012-06-30.

Carter, Bill. "How a Hit Almost Failed Its Own Audition," *New York Times*, April 30, 2006. (http://www.nytimes.com/2006/04/30/business/yourmoney/30idol.html?_r=0). Retrieved: 2012-07-05.

"US *Pop Idol* proves ratings hit," BBC News, June 14, 2002. (http://news.bbc.co.uk/2/hi/entertainment/2044410.stm). Retrieved: 2012-07-01.

Carter, Bill; Elliott, Stuart. "Success of 'American Idol' To Spawn Many Copycats," *The New York Times*, September 6, 2002. (http://www.nytimes.com/2002/09/06/business/the-media-business-advertising-success-of-american-idol-to-spawn-many-copycats.html). Retrieved: 2012-07-06.

"US starts *Pop Idol* search," *BBC News*, April 29, 2002. (http://news.bbc.co.uk/2/hi/entertainment/1957221.stm). Retrieved: 2012-07-02.

Rocchio, Christopher; Rogers, Steve. " '*American Idol*'s sixth season finale averages over 30 million viewers," Realitytvworld.com, May 24, 2007. (http://www.realitytvworld.com/news/american-idol-sixth-season-finale-averages-over-30-million-viewers-5225.php). Retrieved: 2012-07-06.

"Simon Offered $144M to Stay on Idol," *New York Post*, June 30, 2009. (http://www.nypost.com/p/entertainment/tv/item_28wsGrag0ZcsHePqZN3HWM). Retrieved: 2012-07-07.

Keveney, Bill. "5 reasons *American Idol* may go on nearly forever—or not, USA Today, January 17, 2012. (http://usatoday30.usatoday.com/life/television/news/story/2012-01-14/American-Idol-endurance/52625742/1). Retrieved: 2012-07-05.

Carter, Bill. "For Fox's Rivals, *American Idol* Remains a 'Schoolyard Bully'," *New York Times*, February 20, 2007. (http://www.nytimes.com/2007/02/20/arts/television/20idol.html?pagewanted=all). Retrieved: 2012-07-05.

Bronson, Fred. "Ten Years of *American Idol* Chart Dominance: Clarkson, Underwood," *Billboard* Online, June 11, 2012. (http://www.billboard.biz/bbbiz/industry/record-labels/ten-years-of-american-idol-chart-dominance-1007290752.story#XBg7x0WVrUFuvZjW.99). Retrieved: 2012-07-07.

Bernstein, David. "'Cast Away'," *Chicago Magazine*, August 2007. (www.chicagomag.com/Chicago-Magazine/August-2007/Cast-Away/index.php?cp=2&si=1#artanc). Retrieved: 2012-07-10.

Ryan, Tim. "New series gives Hawaii 3 TV shows in production," *Honolulu Star-Bulletin*, May 17, 2004. (http://archives.starbulletin.com/2004/05/17/news/story7.html). Retrieved: 2012-07-06.

Craig, Olga. "The man who discovered Lost—and found himself out of a job," *The Daily Telegraph* (London), August 14, 2005. (http://www.telegraph.co.uk/news/worldnews/northamerica/usa/1496199/The-man-who-discovered-Lost-and-found-himself-out-of-a-job.html). Retrieved: 2012-07-10.

"EMMY AWARDS for *Lost* for TV Year 2005," Emmy.com. (http://www.emmys.com/shows/lost). Retrieved: 2012-07-11.

"Golden Globe Awards for *Lost* TV Year 2006," Hollywood Foreign Press Association (http://www.goldenglobes.org/browse/?param=/film/26051). Retrieved: 2012-07-11.

Poniewozik, James "The 100 Best TV Shows of All-TIME," *Time*, September 6, 2007. (http://entertainment.time.com/2007/09/06/the-100-best-tv-shows-of-all-time/slide/lost-2/). Retrieved: 2012-07-11.

Jaffer, Murtz. "'Housewives' Premiere Cleans Up for ABC," *Prime Time Pulse*, April 10, 2004. (http://insidepulse.com/2004/10/04/21768/). Retrieved: 2012-07-12.

"Desperate Housewives Cast & Crew," TV.com. (http://www.tv.com/people/brenda-strong/). Retrieved: 2012-07-09.

Schmeiser, Lisa. "Fall '04: "*Desperate Housewives*," TeeVee.org, October 5, 2004. (http://www.teevee.org/2004/10/fall-04-desperate-housewives.html). Retrieved: 2012-07-09.

Oldenburg, Ann. "'Ugly Betty' Canceled By ABC," *USA Today*, January 27, 2010. (http://content.usatoday.com/communities/entertainment/post/2010/01/ugly-betty-canceled-by-abc-/1#.UJh-7dfkL7E). Retrieved: 2012-07-11.

Finke, Nikki; Andreeva, Nellie. "ABC Will End 'Desperate Housewives' In May 2012 After 8th Season," *Deadline Hollywood*, Friday August 5, 2011. (http://www.deadline.com/2011/08/exclusive-abc-will-end-desperate-housewives-in-may-2012-after-8th-season/). Retrieved: 2012-07-13.

Bibel, Sara. "CSI: Crime Scene Investigation' Is The Most Watched Show In The World," *TV by the Numbers*. March 14th, 2012. (http://tvbythenumbers.zap2it.com/2012/06/14/csi-crime-scene-investigation-is-the-most-watched-show-in-the-world-2/138212/). Retrieved: 2012-07-15.

Gorman, Bill. "CBS Renews 18 Shows," *TV by the Numbers*, March 14, 2012. (http://tvbythenumbers.zap2it.com/2012/03/14/cbs-renews-18-shows-the-good-wife-blue-bloods-2-broke-girls-the-mentalist-mike-molly-many-more/124487/). Retrieved: 2012-07-15.

Kolbert, Elizabeth. "Birth of a TV Show: A Drama All Its Own," *New York Times*, March 08, 1994. (http://www.nytimes.com/1994/03/08/arts/birth-of-a-tv-show-a-drama-all-its-own.html?pagewanted=all&src=pm). Retrieved: 2012-07-15.

Jicha, Tom. "They leave as they began: With a buzz," *The Baltimore Sun*, May 2, 2004. (http://www.baltimoresun.com/topic/bal-friends-buzz0502,0,495484.story). Retrieved: 2012-07-13.

Kolbert, Elizabeth. "The Conception and Delivery of a Sitcom; Everyone's a Critic," *New York Times*, May 9, 1994. (http://www.nytimes.com/1994/05/09/arts/the-conception-and-delivery-of-a-sitcom-everyone-s-a-critic.html). Retrieved: 2012-07-17.

Boyer, Allison. "Top 10 Most Watched Series Finales," Indyposted.com, May 6, 2010. (http://www.indyposted.com/21133/top-10-most-watched-series-finales/). Retrieved: 2012-07-12.

Levine, Greg. "Zucker Named NBC CEO," December 15, 2005. (http://www.forbes.com/2005/12/15/nbc-zucker-cbs-cx_gl_1215autofacescan14.html). Retrieved: 2012-07-14.

"The 60th Primetime Emmy Awards/Past Winners," Academy of Television Arts & Sciences, July 2008. (http://www.emmys.tv/awards/primetime-emmy-awards/2008/nominationswinners-0). Retrieved: 2012-07-18.

O'Neil, Tom. "30 Rock breaks comedy record at Emmy nominations," *Los Angeles Times*, July 23, 2008. (http://goldderby.latimes.com/awards_goldderby/2008/07/30-rock-and-joh.html). Retrieved: 2012-07-13.

Goetzl, David. "Zucker Weighs In On Leno, NBC's Future," *Media Daily News*, March 18, 2009. (http://www.mediapost.com/publications/article/102392/). Retrieved: 2012-07-20.

Schneider, Michael. "NBC unveils primetime plans," *Variety*, May 4, 2009. (http://www.variety.com/article/VR1118003149?refCatId=14). Retrieved: 2012-07-15.

Stelter, Brian. "NBC Builds Anticipation for 10 pm," *New York Times*, August 4, 2009. (http://www.nytimes.com/2009/08/05/business/media/05adco.html). Retrieved: 2012-07-13.

Poniewozik, James. "Jay Leno Is the Future of TV. Seriously," *Time*, September 3, 2009. (http://www.time.com/time/magazine/article/0,9171,1920300,00.html). Retrieved: 2012-07-15.

Carter, Bill. "Conan O'Brien to Succeed Jay Leno in 2009," *New York Times*, September 27, 2004. (http://www.nytimes.com/2004/09/27/business/media/28CND-NBC.html?_r=0). Retrieved: 2012-07-15.

"Leno's last Tonight guest is Conan O'Brien," *USA Today*, May 14, 2009. (http://usatoday30.usatoday.com/life/television/news/2009-05-14-leno-conan_N.htm). Retrieved: 2012-07-14.

Grossman, Ben. "Jay Leno Taking Over 10 P.M. On NBC," *Broadcasting & Cable*, December 8, 2008. (http://www.broadcastingcable.com/article/160535-Jay_Leno_Taking_Over_10_P_M_On_NBC.php). Retrieved: 2012-07-14.

Porter, Rick. "TV ratings: *The Jay Leno Show* debuts to 17 million-plus," ZAP2it.com, September 15, 2009. (http://blog.zap2it.com/frominsidethebox/2009/09/tv-ratings-the-jay-leno-show-debuts-to-17-million-plus.html). Retrieved: 2012-07-15.

Bercovici, Jeff. "Why NBC's not sweating Leno's falling ratings," *Daily Finance*, September 25, 2009. (http://www.dailyfinance.com/2009/09/25/why-nbcs-not-sweating-lenos-falling-ratings/). Retrieved: 2012-07-17.

Weprin, Alex. "Late-Night Ratings: Letterman Repeats Top Conan Originals," *Broadcasting & Cable*, August 13, 2009. (http://www.broadcastingcable.com/article/327538-Late_Night_Ratings_Letterman_Repeats_Top_Conan_Originals.php). Retrieved: 2012-07-17.

Brioux, Bill. "Is Leno's 10 p.m. experiment nearing an end?," msnbc.com, November 9, 2009. (http://today.msnbc.msn.com/id/33808107/ns/today-entertainment/t/lenos-pm-experiment-nearing-end/#.UJkrvdfkL7E). Retrieved: 2012-07-16.

Harris, Mark. "Will Somebody Please Save NBC?," *New York Magazine*, November 8, 2009. (http://nymag.com/news/media/61857/). Retrieved: 2012-07-19.

Flint, Joe. "Jay Leno's new time slot wreaks havoc for NBC affiliates," *Los Angeles Times*, October 19, 2009. (http://articles.latimes.com/2009/oct/19/business/fi-ct-nbc-affils19). Retrieved: 2012-07-20.

"Conan destructive to Tonight Show and media unfair, Leno tells Oprah, Chicago Tribune, January 28, 2010. (http://featuresblogs.chicagotribune.com/entertainment_tv/2010/01/affiliates-executives-screwed-up-tonight-show-leno-tells-oprah.html). Retrieved: 2012-07-19.

Levin, Gary. "NBC to give Leno 30-minute show at old time slot," *USA Today*, January 10, 2010. (http://usatoday30.usatoday.com/life/television/news/2010-01-10-leno10_N.htm). Retrieved: 2012-07-21.

James, Meg and Gold, Matea. "How Zucker's Leno quick fix got NBC into a quagmire," *Los Angeles Times*, January 9, 2010. (http://articles.latimes.com/2010/jan/09/business/la-fi-ct-zucker9-2010jan09). Retrieved: 2012-07-21.

Dowd, Maureen. "The Biggest Loser," *New York Times*, January 12, 2010. (http://www.nytimes.com/2010/01/13/opinion/13dowd.html). Retrieved: 2012-07-22.

Fain, Travis. "Cable Subscribers Need Not Order Expanded Packages to Get Premium Channels," *Tribune Business News*, December 1, 2002. (http://www.highbeam.com/doc/1G1-94845278.html). Retrieved: 2012-07-28.

Brook, Vincent. You should see yourself: Jewish identity in postmodern American culture. New Brunswick, N.J.: Rutgers University Press, 2006.

"'Boardwalk Empire' Promos," FlicksNews.net, June 13, 2010. (http://www.flicksnews.net/2010/06/boardwalk-empire-promos.html). Retrieved: 2012-07-25.

Gay, Verne. "Emmy nominations 2011: Boardwalk Empire scores," Inside TV. EW.com, July 14, 2011. (http://www.newsday.com/entertainment/tv/tv-zone-1.811968/emmy-nominations-boardwalk-empire-scores-1.3024684). Retrieved: 2012-07-26.

Boycott, Rosie. "Small screen hits and misses," *BBC News*, December 14, 2005. (http://news.bbc.co.uk/2/hi/programmes/newsnight/review/4526564.stm). Retrieved: 2012-07-25.

"BBC backs its explicit Rome epic," *BBC News*, October 17, 2005. (http://news.bbc.co.uk/2/hi/entertainment/4350600.stm). Retrieved: 2012-07-29.

"'Rome' News," HBO.com, December 17, 2005.
(http://web.archive.org/web/20051217174922/www.hbo.com/rome/news/). Retrieved: 2012-07-28.

"Two and Out for *Rome*," ZAP2it.com, July 12, 2006. (http://www.zap2it.com/tv/news/zap-romeendingafter-season2,0,5831913.story?coll=zap-news-headlines). Retrieved: 2012-07-29.

Stanley, Alessandra. "Television Review—Mom Brakes for Drug Deals," *New York Times*, August 5, 2005. (http://www.nytimes.com/2005/08/05/arts/television/05tvwk.html). Retrieved: 2012-07-30.

Hibberd, James. "Parents Television Council Denounces CBS's *Dexter* Plan," *Advertising Age*, December 5, 2007. (http://adage.com/article/james-hibberd-rated/parents-television-council-denounces-cbs-s-dexter-plan/122424/). Retrieved: 2012-07-29.

"*Dexter*: the serial killer loses his mojo," *The Independent* (London), December 31, 2008. (http://www.independent.co.uk/arts-entertainment/tv/features/dexter-the-serial-killer-loses-his-mojo-1217792.html). Retrieved: 2012-07-30.

Poniewozik, James. "*Dexter*, Decency and DVRs," *Time*, January 30, 2008. (http://entertainment.time.com/2008/01/30/dexter_decency_and_dvrs/). Retrieved: July 30, 2012.

Dempsey, John. "AMC Unveils More Contemporary Slate, Extra Ads," *Variety*, May 13, 2002. (http://www.welcometosilentmovies.com/news/newsarchive/amc.htm). Retrieved: 2012-07-31.

Forkan, Jim. "AMC on sponsorships: 'roll 'em!'," *Multichannel News/HighBeam Research*, March 24, 1997. (http://www.highbeam.com/doc/1G1-19429076.html). Retrieved: 2012-07-31.

"*Mad Men* and Bryan Cranston three-peat at Emmys," *Los Angeles Times*, August 29, 2010. (http://goldderby.latimes.com/awards_goldderby/2010/08/mad-men-and-bryan-cranston-repeat-at-emmys-while-kyra-sedgwick-finally-wins.html). Retrieved: 2012-08-01.

Douthat, Ross. "Good and Evil on Cable," *New York Times*, July 28, 2011. (http://douthat.blogs.nytimes.com/2011/07/28/good-and-evil-on-cable/). Retrieved: 2012-08-03.

Eng , Joyce. "Kristin Chenoweth, Jon Cryer Win First Emmys," TVGuide.com, September 20, 2009. (http://www.tvguide.com/News/Kristin-Chenoweth-Jon-1009931.aspx). Retrieved: 2012-08-04.

Stanley, Alessandra. "Smoking, Drinking, Cheating and Selling," *New York Times*, July 19, 2007. (http://www.nytimes.com/2007/07/19/arts/television/19stan.html). Retrieved: 2012-08-04.

Denhart, Andy. "'Mad Men' characters soften difficult themes," msnbc.com, August 12, 2009. (http://today.msnbc.msn.com/id/32362041/ns/today-entertainment/t/mad-men-characters-soften-difficult-themes/#.Tzr0j_nhdcc). Retrieved: 2012-08-05.

Schwartz, Missy. "*Mad Men* Explained: A—Adultery," *Entertainment Weekly* Online, October 17, 2010. (http://www.ew.com/ew/gallery/0,,20395708_20412953_20829425,00.html). Retrieved: 2012-08-05.

Carr, Coeli. "Television's Booze Hounds," *ABC News*, September 13, 2010. (http://abcnews.go.com/Entertainment/televisions-treatment-alcohol-mad-men-rescue-pretty-picture/story?id=11574532#.UJliLtfkL7H). Retrieved: 2012-08-05.

Zoller, Matt. "'Mad Men' Waldorf Stories Review," *The New Republic*, August 30, 2010. (http://www.tnr.com/article/books-and-arts/77279/mad-men-review-%E2%80%98waldorf-stories%E2%80%99#). Retrieved: 2012-08-08.

Guthrie, Marisa. "Mad Men Season Finale Draws 1.75 Mil Viewers," *Broadcasting & Cable*, October 27, 2008. (http://www.broadcastingcable.com/article/116056-_Mad_Men_Season_Finale_Draws_1_75_Mil_Viewers.php). Retrieved: 2012-08-10.

Nordyke, Kimberly. "AMC 'Mad' about ratings for series bow," *Reuters/Hollywood Reporter*, July 20, 2007. (http://www.reuters.com/article/2007/07/21/television-madmen-dc-idUSN2023729420070721). Retrieved: 2012-08-06.

Kondolojy, Amanda. "Season Five Premiere Is Most Watched Episode of 'Mad Men' ever," *TV by the Numbers*, March 26th, 2012. (http://tvbythenumbers.zap2it.com/2012/03/26/season-five-premiere-is-most-watched-mad-men-episode-ever/126048/). Retrieved: 2012-08-09.

Allister, Graeme. "How *Mad Men* became a style guide," *The Guardian*, August 1, 2008. (http://www.guardian.co.uk/culture/tvandradioblog/2008/aug/01/youdonthavetowatchmadmen). Retrieved: 2012-08-11.

Mullen, Megan. Television in the Multichannel Age: A Brief History of Cable Television. Malden, MA: Blackwell, 2008.

Price, Nic. "Made-in-Burnaby show gets Beedie's backing," *Burnaby Now* (Canada.com), October 8, 2008.

Brown, Ross. "Brave New World: How The Internet, Streaming Video, And Other New Technologies Are Shaping Television," Chapman University FTV 240 Lectures (Lecture 14 of 14), 2007.

Graham, Jefferson. "Video websites pop up, invite postings," *USA Today*, November 21, 2005. (http://usatoday30.usatoday.com/tech/news/techinnovations/2005-11-21-video-websites_x.htm). Retrieved: 2012-08-13.

Short Film: Lapitsky, Yakov. "Me at the zoo." YouTube. Aired April 23, 2005. (http://www.youtube.com/watch?v=jNQXAC9IVRw). Retrieved: 2012-08-13.

"You Tube serves up 100 million videos a day online," *USA Today*, July 16, 2006. (http://usatoday30.usatoday.com/tech/news/2006-07-16-youtube-views_x.htm). Retrieved: 2012-08-12.

"Virgin Media Selects Tivo For Next Generation TV Platform," *Virgin Media*, November 24, 2009.

"David Blaine Street Magic." You Tube. Aired October 12, 2006. (http://www.youtube.com/watch?v=AYxu_MQSTTY). Retrieved: 2012-08-23.

"Like magic, Groundlings turn viral," *LA Times Entertainment*, June 22, 2008. (http://articles.latimes.com/2008/jun/22/entertainment/ca-groundlings22). Retrieved: 2102-08-26.

Roddenberry, Gene. "Star Trek is," Series Bible, First Draft, March 11, 1964. (http://web.archive.org/web/20060924140423/http://www.ex-astris-scientia.org/misc/40_years/trek_pitch.pdf). Retrieved: 2012-09-02

"The numbers game, part one," *Broadcasting*, September 19, 1966.

Solow, Herbert; and Justman, Robert H. Inside Star Trek: The Real Story. New York: Pocket Books, 1996.

"Cult Fans, Reruns Give 'Star Trek' an Out of This World Popularity," Milwaukee Journal, July 3, 1972. (http://news.google.com/newspapers?id=rx0eAAAAIBAJ&sjid=gX4EAAAAIBAJ&dq=star-trek%20syndication%20|%20rerun&pg=6303%2C2206524). Retrieved 2012:09-03.

Dumoulin, Jim. "Shuttle Orbiter Enterprise (OV-101)," National Aeronautics and Space Association, March 18, 1994. (http://science.ksc.nasa.gov/shuttle/resources/orbiters/enterprise.html). Retrieved 2012-09-05.

NBC.com(http://www.nbc.com/saturday-night-live/about/history.shtml). Retrieved 2012-09-01

Garner, Joe. Made You Laugh. Kansas City: Andrews McMeel Publishing, 2004.

TV Week (http://www.tvweek.com/blogs/tvbizwire/2010/07/with-13-additional-emmy-nomina.php)

Fitzpatrick, John. " The SNL Effect: 'Saturday Night Live' Political Skits Make real Impact on Voters," SmartBrief, November 5, 2008. (http://www.smartbrief.com/news/aaaa/industryPR-detail.jsp?id=2AA143C0-2194-457F-8464-34E5CC68D101). Retrieved: 2012-09-10.

Hollander, Jason. "Live From New York, It's …", New York University Alumni Magazine, Spring 2008. (http://www.nyu.edu/alumni.magazine/issue10/10_culture_snl.html). Retrieved: 2012-09-05.

"*60 Minutes*." Museum of Broadcast Communications website.

Coffey, Frank. 60 Minutes: 25 Years of Television's Finest Hour .Santa Monica, CA: General Publishing Group, Inc., 1993.

Madsen, Axel. 60 Minutes: The Power and the Politics of America's Most Popular TV News Show. New York: Dodd, Mead and Company, 1984.

Credits

Figure 1.1 Guglielmo Marconi, 1901. Copyright in the Public Domain.

Figure 1.5 De Dorest Audion. Source: http://upload.wikimedia.org/wikipedia/commons/1/14/Triode_tube_1906.jpg. Cleared via GNU Free Documentation License.

Figure 2.2 David Sarnoff. Copyright in the Public Domain.

Figure 3.1 Farnsworth Sketch. Source: http://philotfarnsworth.com/actual_sketch.htm. Copyright © by Farnsworth Archives.

Figure 3.2 Cathode Ray Tube. Source: http://en.wikipedia.org/wiki/File:Cathode_ray_Tube.PNG. Cleared via Creative Commons Attribution-Share Alike 3.0 Unported license.

Figure 3.5 Pickford and Fairbanks. Copyright in the Public Domain.

Figure 3.6 U.S. Secretary of Commerce, Hoover. Copyright in the Public Domain.

Figure 3.7 First Live moving image. John Logie Baird, 1926.

Figure 3.11 Beloved Logo (original art that inspired logo). Copyright in the Public Domain.

Figure 4.2 Vladimir Zworykin. Copyright in the Public Domain.

Figure 5.1, Figure 5.6 William S. Paley. Copyright in the Public Domain.

Figure 5.2 Black Tuesday. Source: http://www.gettyimages.com/detail/news-photo/the-front-page-of-the-brooklyn-daily-eagle-newspaper-with-news-photo/78075346. Copyright © by Getty Images. Reprinted with permission.

Figure 5.3 Fibber Mcgee. Copyright in the Public Domain.

Figure 5.5 Wholesome Kate Smith. Copyright in the Public Domain.

Figure 6.1 Orson Welles. Library of Congress, Prints & Photographs Division, Carl Van Vechten Collection, Reproduction number, LC-USZ62-119765. Copyright in the Public Domain.

Figure 6.3 Edward R. Murrow. Copyright in the Public Domain.

Figure 6.5 NBC/VJ day. Copyright in the Public Domain.

Figure 6.7 Jackie Robinson. Copyright in the Public Domain.

Figure 6.8 Gracie Allen & George Burns. Copyright in the Public Domain.

Figure 6.9 Jack Benny. Copyright in the Public Domain.

Figure 6.10 Lucille Ball. Copyright in the Public Domain.

Figure 7.1 Publication: Red Channels. Copyright in the Public Domain.

Figure 7.2 Gertrude Berg. Copyright in the Public Domain.

Figure 7.3 Jimmy Durante. Copyright in the Public Domain.

Figure 7.4 Bud Abbott and Lou Costello. Copyright in the Public Domain.

Figure 7.5 Sid Caeser. Copyright in the Public Domain.

Figure 7.6 Joyce Randolph - Honeymooners. Copyright in the Public Domain.

Figure 7.7 Red Skeleton. Copyright in the Public Domain.

Figure 7.8 Ed Sullivan. Copyright in the Public Domain.

Figure 7.9 The Beatles. Source: http://commons.wikimedia.org/wiki/File:The_Beatles_%28with_Jimmy_Nicol%29_1964_001.png. Cleared via Creative Commons Attribution-Share Alike 3.0 Netherlands license.

Figure 7.10 Joseph McCarthy. Copyright in the Public Domain.

Figure 7.11 Ozzie and Hariet. Copyright in the Public Domain.

Figure 7.12 Groucho Marx. Copyright in the Public Domain.

Figure 7.14 Lawyer Vivienee and Charles Van Doren. Copyright in the Public Domain.

Figure 7.19 Alfred Hitcock

Figure 7.20 Twilight Zone. Copyright in the Public Domain.

Figure 8.3 Rev. Martin Luther King, Jr. Copyright in the Public Domain.

Figure 8.4 Nat King Cole. Copyright in the Public Domain.

Figure 8.5 Little Rock 9. Copyright in the Public Domain.

Figure 8.6 Little Rock 9. Copyright in the Public Domain.

Figure 8.10 The Lone Ranger. Copyright in the Public Domain.

Figure 8.11 Gunsmoke cast. Copyright in the Public Domain.

Figure 8.12 Bonanza. Copyright in the Public Domain.

Figure 8.13 Jack Webb. Copyright in the Public Domain.

Figure 8.14 I Love Lucy. Copyright in the Public Domain.

Figure 8.15 Lucy "spoons her way..." Copyright in the Public Domain.

Figure 8.16 Ethel and Lucy. Copyright in the Public Domain.

Figure 9.2 Nikita Khrushchev. Copyright in the Public Domain.

Figure 9.3 Nixon and Khrushchev. Copyright in the Public Domain.

Figure 9.4 Kennedy and Nixon. Copyright in the Public Domain.

Figure 9.6 John Glenn - Freedom 7. Copyright in the Public Domain.

Figure 9.7 Kennedy - "Moon Speech". Copyright in the Public Domain.

Figure 9.8 Telstar 1. Copyright in the Public Domain.

Figure 9.9 The Untouchables. Copyright in the Public Domain.

Figure 9.10 Dick Van Dyke. Copyright in the Public Domain.

Figure 9.11 The Beverly Hillbillies. Copyright in the Public Domain.

Figure 9.12 Hogans Heroes. Copyright in the Public Domain.

Figure 9.13 Gilligan's Island.

Figure 9.14 Soviet R-12 Missiles. Copyright in the Public Domain.

Figure 9.15 Navy Lockheed P-2H. Copyright in the Public Domain.

Figure 9.16 Kennedy Ultimatum. Copyright in the Public Domain.

Figure 10.1 Perry Mason. Copyright in the Public Domain.

Figure 10.2 David Janssen. Copyright in the Public Domain.

Figure 10.3 I Spy. Source: http://www.gettyimages.com/Account/MediaBin/LightboxDetail.aspx?Id=27270353&MediaBinUserId=7928592. Copyright © by Getty Images. Reprinted with permission.

Figure 10.4 Diahann Carroll. Copyright in the Public Domain.

Figure 10.5 MLK speech. Copyright in the Public Domain.

Figure 10.6 MLK speech. Copyright in the Public Domain.

Figure 10.7 Freedom Marchers. Copyright in the Public Domain.

Figure 10.8 JFk and First lady. Copyright in the Public Domain.

Figure 10.9 LBJ taking oath. Copyright in the Public Domain.

Figure 10.10 Jack Ruby. Copyright in the Public Domain.

Figure 10.11 America Mourns. Copyright in the Public Domain.

Figure 10.12 Marlo Thomas. Copyright in the Public Domain.

Figure 10.13 Laugh-in. Copyright in the Public Domain.

Figure 10.15 Eisenhower and Dulles. Copyright in the Public Domain.

Figure 10.17 Military Attack N. Vietnam. Copyright in the Public Domain.

Figure 10.18 U.S. paratroopers. Copyright in the Public Domain.

Figure 10.19 U.S. paratroopers. Copyright in the Public Domain.

Figure 10.20 Cronkite. Copyright in the Public Domain.

Figure 10.21 Anti-war rally. Copyright in the Public Domain.

Figure 10.24 moon walk. Copyright in the Public Domain.

Figure 10.26 Smothers Brothers. Copyright in the Public Domain.

Figure 11.2 All in the Family. Copyright in the Public Domain.

Figure 11.3 All in the Family. Copyright in the Public Domain.

Figure 11.4 All in the Family. Copyright in the Public Domain.

Figure 11.5 Bea Arthur. Copyright in the Public Domain.

Figure 11.6 Good times. Copyright in the Public Domain.

Figure 11.7 Mary Tyler Moore. Copyright in the Public Domain.

Figure 11.10 MASH. Copyright in the Public Domain.

Figure 11.12 MASH cast. Copyright in the Public Domain.

Figure 11.13 Mod Squad. Copyright in the Public Domain.

Figure 11.14 Charlie's Angels. Copyright in the Public Domain.

Figure 11.16 The Waltons. Copyright in the Public Domain.

Figure 11.17 Little House on the Prairie. Copyright in the Public Domain.

Figure 11.18 Streets of San Francisco. Copyright in the Public Domain.

Figure 12.1 Jesse Owens. Copyright in the Public Domain.

Figure 12.5 Evel Knievel. Source: http://artsbeat.blogs.nytimes.com/2007/12/03/evel-knievel-on-kierkegaard/ Copyright © by Associated Press. Reprinted with permission.

Figure 12.12 Joe Namath. Copyright in the Public Domain.

Figure 12.15 Larry Bird. Source: http://commons.wikimedia.org/wiki/File:Magic_Bird_Lipofsky.jpg. Cleared via Creative Commons Attribution 3.0 Unported license.

Figure 13.1 Jimmy Carter. Copyright in the Public Domain.

Figure 13.3 Celebrating the "Miracle on Ice". Source: http://photos.newhavenregister.com/2012/02/24/photos-the-miracle-on-ice-the-1980-us-olympic-hockey-gold-medal/26452/. Copyright © by Associated Press. Reprinted with permission.

Figure 13.4 Demo Ronald Reagan GE theater. Copyright in the Public Domain.

Figure 13.5 Repub Ronal Reagan. Copyright in the Public Domain.

Figure 13.13 Magnum PI. Source: http://www.flickr.com/photos/82895272@N00/235662921. Cleared via Creative Commons Attribution 2.0 Generic license.

Figure 13.23 Murphy Brown. Source: http://commons.wikimedia.org/wiki/File:Candice_Bergen_at_the_41st_Emmy_Awards.jpg. Cleared via Creative Commons Attribution 2.0 Generic license.

Figure 14.3 Buffy the Vampire. Source: http://commons.wikimedia.org/wiki/File:Buffy_The_Vampire_Slayer_cast.jpg. Cleared via Creative Commons Attribution 2.0 Generic license.

Figure 14.5 Perfect Strangers. Source: http://commons.wikimedia.org/wiki/File:Bronson_Pinchot_and_Mark_Linn-Baker_at_the_39th_Emmy_Awards.jpg. Cleared via Creative Commons Attribution 2.0 Generic license.

Figure 14.11 Seinfeld. Source: http://commons.wikimedia.org/wiki/File:Tom%27s_Restaurant,_Seinfeld.jpg. Cleared via Creative Commons Attribution 2.0 Generic license.

Figure 14.13 Seinfeld (3). Source: http://commons.wikimedia.org/wiki/File:Seinfeld_actors_montage.jpg. Cleared via Creative Commons Attribution-Share Alike 3.0 Unported license.

Figure 14.22 Sex and the City Source: http://commons.wikimedia.org/wiki/File:Sarah_Jessica_Parker_on_the_set_of_%22Sex_and_the_City_II%22.jpg. Cleared via Creative Commons Attribution 2.0 Generic license.

Figure 14.23 Sopranos. Source: http://commons.wikimedia.org/wiki/File:Sopranos-ontheset.jpg. Cleared via Creative Commons Attribution-Share Alike 2.0 Generic license.

Figure 15.1 An American Family. Copyright in the Public Domain.

Figure 15.3 Survivor. Source: http://commons.wikimedia.org/wiki/File:Richard_Hatch.jpeg. Cleared via Creative Commons Attribution-Share Alike 3.0 Unported license.

Figure 15.5 Tribute in Light. Copyright in the Public Domain.

Figure 15.8 American Idol. Source: http://commons.wikimedia.org/wiki/File:American_Idol_Experience_stage.png. Cleared via Creative Commons Attribution-Share Alike 3.0 Unported license. Attribution: RadioFan.

Figure 15.9 American Idol Judges. Source: http://commons.wikimedia.org/wiki/File:Simon_Cowell_in_December_2011.jpg. Cleared via Creative Commons Attribution-Share Alike 2.0 Generic license.

Figure 15.11 Desperate Housewives. Source: http://commons.wikimedia.org/wiki/File:Desperate_Housewives_at_2008_

GLAAD_Awards.jpg. Cleared via Creative Commons Attribution-Share Alike 2.0 Generic license.

Figure 15.17 Jay Leno. Copyright in the Public Domain.

Figure 15.18 Jeff Zucker. Source: http://commons.wikimedia.org/wiki/File:Jeff_Zucker,_CEO_of_NBC_Universal.jpg. Cleared via Creative Commons Attribution 2.0 Generic license.

Figure 15.19 Conan O'Brien. Copyright in the Public Domain.

Figure 15.25 Breaking Bad. Source: http://commons.wikimedia.org/wiki/File:PaleyFest_2010_-_Breaking_Bad.jpg. Cleared via Creative Commons Attribution 2.0 Generic license.

Index

Numbers

A

B

D

H

I

J

K

L

M

Q

R

S

T

U

V

W

X

Y

Z

CPSIA information can be obtained at www.ICGtesting.com
Printed in the USA
LVOW09s0223070915
453092LV00007B/277/P

9 781626 61208